Curriculum Development in the Postmodern Era

This landmark text was one of the first to introduce and analyze contemporary concepts of curriculum that emerged from the Reconceptualization of curriculum studies in the 1970s and 1980s. The field continues to evolve in dynamic and important ways. This new edition brings readers up to date on the major research themes (postmodernism, ecological, hermeneutics, aesthetics and arts-based research, race, class, gender, sexuality, and classroom practices) within the historical development of the field from the 1950s to the present. Like the previous editions, it is unique in providing a comprehensive overview in a relatively short and highly accessible text. Provocative and powerful narratives (both biography and autoethnography) throughout invite readers to engage the complex theories in a personal conversation. School-based examples allow readers to make connections to schools and society, teacher education, and professional development of teachers. *Curriculum Development in the Postmodern Era* ultimately serves as a challenge to renew and reform schools and society in the spirit of the democratic and interdisciplinary vision of the Reconceptualization of curriculum studies.

The Companion Website (www.routledge.com/cw/slattery)—new for this edition—includes an annotated glossary, video clips, invited narratives on theology and aesthetics, an annotated film list, images of art installations, photos, and links to additional resources.

Patrick Slattery is Professor of Curriculum Development and Philosophy of Education and Regents Scholar in the Academy for Educator Development at Texas A&M University in College Station. He holds a joint appointment in the Departments of Teaching, Learning & Culture and Educational Administration & Human Resource Development. He is a lecturer in the summer leadership academy of Massachusetts College of Liberal Arts, and co-director of the Texas A&M Governor's School in Arts and Humanities for Urban Leadership for high achieving high school seniors.

Curriculum Development in the Postmodern Era

Teaching and Learning in an Age of Accountability

Third Edition

PATRICK SLATTERY

Routledge
Taylor & Francis Group

NEW YORK AND LONDON

KH

Grateful acknowledgement is made to the following for permission to reprint material
Excerpt from "Choruses from The Rock" in *Collected Poems 1909–1962* by T. S. Eliot, copyright © 1964, 1963 by T. S. Eliot, reprinted by permission of the publisher.
Excerpt from "Little Gidding" in *Four Quartets*, copyright © 1943 by T. S. Eliot and renewed 1971 by Esme Valerie Eliot, reprinted by permission of Harcourt Brace & Company.
Excerpts from *A Lesson Before Dying*, copyright © 1993 by Ernest J. Gaines, reprinted by permission of Alfred A. Knopf.8.1 on pages 175–177 is taken from figure 8.2 in Donald Oliver and Kathleen W. Gershman, *Education, Modernity, and Fractured Meaning: Toward a Process Theory of Teaching and Learning* (Albany: State University of New York Press, 1989).
Table 9.1 on page 237 is taken from figure 7-3 in William H. Schubert, *Curriculum: Perspective, Paradigm, and Possibility* (New York: Macmillan, 1986).

Third edition published 2013
by Routledge
711 Third Avenue, New York, NY 10017

Simultaneously published in the UK
by Routledge
2 Park Square, Milton Park, Abingdon, Oxon OX14 4RN

Routledge is an imprint of the Taylor & Francis Group, an informa business

© 2013 Taylor & Francis

The right of Patrick Slattery to be identified as author of this work has been asserted by him in accordance with sections 77 and 78 of the Copyright, Designs and Patents Act 1988.

First edition published by Peter Lang 1995
Second edition published by Routledge 2006

Library of Congress Cataloging in Publication Data
Slattery, Patrick, 1953–
Curriculum development in the postmodern era: teaching and learning in an age of accountability/Patrick Slattery.—3rd ed.
p. cm.
1. Curriculum planning. 2. Curriculum change. 3. Education—Curricula—Philosophy. 4. Postmodernism. I. Title.
LB2806.15.S63 2012
375'.001—dc23
2012003791

ISBN13: 978-0-415-80854-5 (hbk)
ISBN13: 978-0-415-80856-9 (pbk)
ISBN13: 978-0-203-13955-4 (ebk)

Typeset in Sabon and Neue Helvetica by Book Now Ltd, London

SFI Certified Sourcing
www.sfiprogram.org
SFI-00453

Printed and bound in the United States of America
by Edwards Brothers, Inc.

4/15/13

The fundamental human quest is the search for
meaning and the basic capacity for this
search is experienced in the hermeneutic process, the
process of interpretation of the text (whether artifact,
natural world, or human action). This is the search
(or research) for greater understanding that
motivates and satisfies us. ... The act of theorizing is
an act of faith, a religious act. ... It is an expression
of the humanistic vision in life.

James B. Macdonald (1988, pp. 105, 110)

Contents

PREFACE TO THE THIRD EDITION   ix

Introduction   1

PART I   Curriculum Development as a Field of Study   **15**

1. Introduction to Curriculum Development, Reconceptualization,
   and Postmodernity   17
2. Historical Perspectives on Curriculum as a Field of Study   37
3. The Reconceptualization of Curriculum Studies   61
4. Postmodern Schooling, Curriculum, and the Theological Text   75

**PART II   Complicated Conversations in Contemporary
Curriculum Development**   **117**

5. The Hermeneutic Circle and the Interpretive Process   119
6. Gender, Sexuality, Race, and Ethnicity in a Multicultural and
   Diverse Milieu   149
7. Postmodern Philosophies in Curriculum Studies   195
8. Curriculum for Interdependence and Ecological Sustainability   207
9. Utopian Visions, Democracy, and the Egalitarian Ideal   229
10. Aesthetic Inquiry, Arts-Based Research, and the Proleptic Moment   243

PART III   Curriculum Development in the Postmodern Era   **267**

11. Time and Complexity   269
12. A Vision of Curriculum in the Postmodern Era   281

GLOSSARY   295
REFERENCES   313
SUBJECT INDEX   337
NAME INDEX   341

Preface to the Third Edition

This book is meant to serve as a guide to the contemporary and reconceptualized field of curriculum and instruction for university students, school district supervisors, curriculum specialists, classroom teachers, pre-service teacher education students, and others interested in understanding curriculum development as it relates to emerging postmodern education paradigms. It could serve as a primary or supplemental text in curriculum development courses, social foundations of education courses, or philosophy of education seminars. As the book proceeds, terms such as curriculum theory, accountability, postmodernism, hermeneutics, pragmatism, aesthetics, chaos theory, poststructuralism, eco-feminism, environmental racism, and critical theory will be discussed in the context of the contemporary educational milieu. However, these terms defy self-evident definitions. Readers may have to reevaluate preconceived notions of the meaning of curriculum development and postmodern education and allow new and sometimes evocative understandings to emerge. This may require a commitment to community discourse and public pedagogy that is missing from most educational literature. At the end of the book is a short annotated glossary to help readers begin the process of investigating complex and unfamiliar terms. A longer annotated glossary can be found on the companion web page at Routledge. I encourage readers to review the short glossary, and perhaps investigate the more robust glossary on the web page, before reading the text. A review of the glossary will provide an important overview of the context of curriculum development in the postmodern era that will make the book much more accessible to students.

Brief Overview

I hope that the process of reading this book about curriculum and postmodernism, two concepts that are very significant in my own personal and scholarly growth, will challenge, affirm, refresh, and sometimes even jolt those who explore its ideas. I often tell my students that, if my seminars are successful, we should all leave class with concerns, doubts, and questions rather than clarity and certainty. This disequilibrium and complexity, I contend, provide an opportunity for further clarification and exploration, which in turn will lead to the emergence of a deep ecology of the schooling process.

This book is divided into three sections. Part I explores curriculum development as a field of study and situates curriculum and instruction in a postmodern context. Particular emphasis is placed on the reconceptualization of curriculum studies that occurred in the 1970s and 1980s and continues to influence elementary and secondary schools and graduate classrooms. Additionally, historical and theological conceptions of curriculum will be introduced. Part II explores many of the issues associated with contemporary curriculum discourses in areas such as hermeneutics, race, gender, sexuality, culture, philosophy, politics, democracy, ecology, aesthetics, autobiography, and cosmology. Because of the complexity of the research in these areas, the purpose of the chapters here is to introduce the themes, provide examples, and point the reader to areas of possible further study. In this sense, part II is designed to appeal to curriculum specialists, teachers, professors, and beginning students who are interested in an overview of curriculum theory or a short supplementary introductory text. Part III presents a proposal for rethinking curriculum development for the postmodern era and the multiple levels of understanding of the issues presented in part II.

Taken as a whole, this book challenges professors, students, and curriculum specialists to transcend traditional approaches to curriculum development and incorporate various contemporary discourses into our reflection and action. However, I acknowledge the contribution of traditional curriculum development in this text in order to remind us that, as we study postmodernism, we carry the past and project the future for each issue explored.

Changes in this third edition are a comprehensive glossary with robust analysis of the complex topics in the text, additional attention to accountability movements in schools, more international references to highlight a global context, several additional narratives and autobiographical reflections, and an invitation to readers to engage the theories in a personal conversation on a new companion web page that includes video clips, suggested films, images of art work, comments by leading scholars in the curriculum field, and links to additional resources.

Finally, I cite Professor James B. Macdonald, now deceased, at the beginning of this book. His writing has been a rich source of reflection for me. In this sense, he has also been a mentor, for his words continue to inspire. He reminds us that what is required in education is a profound faith that there is meaning to our lives. As educators we ultimately must affirm visions of that meaningful life for ourselves, our students, and our planet. The hermeneutic process of discovering this meaning inspired Macdonald. We, too, must believe that our work has the potential for redemptive consequences and a cosmological vision of hope, justice, and compassion.

Personal Philosophical Roots and Aims of This Book

I wrote this third edition of *Curriculum Development in the Postmodern Era* in late 2011 during a time of global economic and political turmoil as evidenced by the following:

revolts and political change in Egypt, Tunisia, and the Middle East; economic protests in Greece, Italy, Britain, and the US; student protests in Chile; the rise of the Occupy Wall Street movement and the continuation of the Tea Party movement in the US; violence and drug wars in Mexico and Colombia; repression and government crackdowns in Iran and Syria; concerns about access to energy, health care, jobs, and education for millions of people; conflicts over diminishment of collective bargaining and workers' rights; intensifying ecological deterioration; and environmental catastrophes in the Gulf of Mexico and Japan. Political, environmental, and economic crises are severe. Simultaneously, we are experiencing turmoil in education: reconfiguration of educational delivery models; expressions of distrust of teachers in the media and government; economic disparity that limits access to education for the middle class and working poor; budget cuts to schools, universities, and grant programs; furloughs and layoffs; and an increased emphasis on accountability and testing in schools. The impact on curriculum development is dramatic. This is most succinctly documented by Peter Taubman in his award-winning book *Teaching by Numbers: Deconstructing the Discourse of Standards and Accountability in Education*. Taubman (2009) writes about his book:

> I want to suggest that teaching, teacher education, and education have increasingly been abstracted and recorded as numbers such as test scores, numerical data, and dollar amounts. These numbers give the impression that what happens in classrooms—extraordinarily complex, psychically tumultuous, and potentially both ecstatic and maddening places of teaching—is best understood as objective, transparent, and measurable. I want to bring into focus the widespread belief that all children can learn as long as their teachers follow directions. ... I want to suggest connections among the marketplace, various educational theories and practices purporting to be objective or scientific, and the aspirations of teachers for security, control, status, and meaning. (p. 2)

Throughout this third edition I will connect global political crises to educational accountability issues, and I will contend that economic, social, cultural, and ecological issues are the substance of curriculum studies. Like Taubman, I believe that the rhetoric of measurable data, compliant teachers, and market-driven ideologies distort and undermine teaching and learning. Additionally, economic, ecological, and social issues are too often ignored or minimized. Who benefits and who loses from the standards and accountability movements? Diane Ravitch, a historian of education and former Assistant Secretary of Education in the US, offers this summary of the impact of the accountability philosophy on teaching and learning:

> I have been thinking recently about how 12 consecutive years of multiple-choice, standardized tests affects children's brains. I wonder what it does to them when they are repeatedly asked to address a question that can be answered by checking one of four boxes. Of course, they know that two of the answers will be very wrong, and then they can guess between the remaining two. But what happens to their ability to think when they are never asked to consider the validity of the question. What if the question is not the right

question? Is there a different way to elicit a better response? What if there are two right answers? Does this format over time teach students to think inside the box, quite literally? Does it punish divergent thinking? Does it squash creativity and originality? (Ravitch, 2011, pp. 111–112)

The important questions raised by Taubman and Ravitch, as well as their masterful deconstruction of the current educational climate, are examples of the postmodern discourses that will be addressed in this text. Each chapter will provide a unique analysis of one dimension of the current issues driving curriculum discourses today.

Critics of previous editions of this book have argued that, without a solid foundation in the basics of STEM (science, technology, engineering, mathematics), reading, cultural literacy, and civics in PK–16 education, students will not have the skills and dispositions to contribute to technological and economic development. Critics demand that teachers must inculcate the basic standards of the academic disciplines and students must demonstrate mastery of data on tests. Addressing local and global issues, critics argue, should happen only after the completion of schooling by mature adults who have a solid grasp of basic information.

My response to the critics is that our modern accountability methods of an education for technological and economic development—a goal that needs to be deconstructed and examined more closely for its impact on the environment, cultural commons, and workers—have actually contributed to the current crises both locally and globally. Modern approaches to curriculum development advocated by corporations, businesses, and governments that I critique in this book have ironically thwarted their goal of technological and economic development. I will argue that *No Child Left Behind* and *Race to the Top*—recent US accountability programs—create a climate where the very problems that these programs purport to ameliorate are actually exacerbated.

My second response to critics is that the philosophy of curriculum development presented here will generate enthusiasm for learning by engagement with important global issues of our time and investment in significant community problems affecting the lives of teachers and students. I believe that learning rooted in community concerns and global issues in all disciplines—STEM, ecology, health, culture, literacy, government, arts, philosophy, and economics—will engender creativity, curiosity, and commitment in PK–16 students and teachers. For those concerned with test scores, my philosophy of curriculum development will also produce measurable success beyond any accountability program. I present examples of my philosophy throughout the book.

Finally, I argue with accountability advocates that we do not have to choose between rigorous lessons in the disciplines and engagement with social, cultural, environmental, and political issues of our time. This is a false choice. Throughout the book I will reference the philosophy of Alfred North Whitehead (1929), who advocated for romance, precision, and generalization in schooling. I might use the words passion, analysis, and imagination also. Others might prefer the terms experience, understanding, and integration. What words resonate with you? No matter what language we use to describe curriculum development in the postmodern era, my reply to critics in this book is that we must deconstruct dualisms and bifurcations that deaden the educational experience and perpetuate the crises we face in the world today.

A more whimsical response to my critics can be seen in a discussion I had about "back to the basics" with parents in my school community when I was a high school principal. Many parents would argue vociferously at school board meetings in favor of the traditional "3 R's of reading, 'riting and 'rithmatic," or the "4 R's," since they often added religion to the list. In meetings I would agree with the angry parents that the curriculum of the school should focus on the traditional basics, but I would argue that we must go back further in time, to the foundation of education and democracy in ancient Greece, to discover what the real basic subjects in the curriculum should be. Like our Greek ancestors, "back to the basics" would then consist of five subjects: geometry, astronomy, philosophy, physical education, and music. And, since music was the most important subject in the traditional Greek curriculum, I argued that we should expand our program to include two hours of music every day for all students. Parents looked at me with confusion but also a degree of respect. My reasoning was logical, and they perceived that I was on their side. But they were not sure what to do with this startling information. This was my postmodern playful deconstruction of the modern "back to the basics" rhetoric, but it was also a very serious rhetorical move to challenge the "back to the basics" argument by extending the logic historically. My argument for a new understanding of the language of "back to the basics" helped many people to reevaluate simplistic notions such as the "4 R's." While my goal was to diffuse tension over debates about the school curriculum, I was—and continue to be—an advocate of music and arts as central to education, as you will see in chapter 10. I also believe that we might improve schooling with more philosophy, physical education, geometry, and astronomy in the curriculum as well.

Perhaps a robust understanding and deep commitment to the arts in the curriculum is the unifying theme of this book. I will not argue for the arts as a privileged activity of elites. Nor will I argue for the arts as simply entertainment or decoration. Rather, the arts become a means for understanding and addressing the serious social, political, and economic issues referenced above. An essay about a new museum in Arkansas by Roberta Smith in the *New York Times* succinctly summarizes my position:

> The [elements of the Crystal Bridges Museum] convey the belief that art, like music and literature, is not a recreational luxury or the purview of the rich. Rather, it is an essential tool for living to which everyone must have access, because it helps awaken and direct the individual talent whose development is essential to society, especially a democratic one. Art, after all, is one of the places where the pursuit of happiness gains focus and purpose and starts expanding outward, to aid and abet that thing called the greater good. (Smith, 2011, p. 1)

The field of curriculum theory, especially with the emphasis on the arts, ecology, and social justice, is the foundation of my research and writing. Curriculum theory is defined by William Pinar as "the interdisciplinary study of educational phenomenon" (Pinar, 2004a, p. x). This is a dramatic time to analyze the interdisciplinary connections among economics, ecology, social upheaval, accountability, and curriculum. In this third edition, I have made these interdisciplinary connections more explicit, and I have extended the discussions of the impact of economic policy and environmental issues on education. In light of the significant impact of accountability and high-stakes testing on curriculum development, I have added updated material on the impact of scientific management and bureaucratic intrusion in the classroom. I have also analyzed the charter school movement and other emerging configurations of curriculum delivery in chapter 2. The most important addition to the third edition is an extensive annotated glossary. I encourage students to read the brief glossary at the end of the book and then go to the companion web page to read a comprehensive analysis of terms used in the text. This is not a traditional modern glossary with definitions; rather, it is an orientation discussion for the text. I have taught curriculum courses from 2009 to 2012 using this new glossary in several universities in Texas, Massachusetts, New York, and California, and internationally in Canada, Chile, and South Africa, and students in various contexts have reported that an initial reading enhanced and clarified the concepts and language in the text.

This third edition includes several additional autobiographical narratives that extend the understanding of curriculum development. As you will discover in the text, autobiography, autoethnography, and narrative analysis figure prominently. In fact, the autobiographical method of *currere* (see glossary and chapter 3) is fundamental to contemporary curriculum theory and the philosophy of curriculum development. As you will experience here, curriculum development in our current international context requires locating individuals in the complexity of the challenges of the postmodern era. I begin with an autobiographical introduction that foregrounds my philosophy of curriculum development.

I began my teaching career in 1975 as a naive and exuberant 21-year-old senior at the College of Santa Fe in New Mexico. The college office of student teaching assigned me to Saint Michael High School to teach two periods of sophomore geometry and one class of theology. This experience not only launched my new career but also initiated an exciting life journey into the world of schooling and curriculum. Thirty-seven years later, as I write this preface to the third edition of *Curriculum Development in the Postmodern Era*, I am still a committed and enthusiastic teacher and educational researcher at Texas A&M University in College Station and lecturer at the summer leadership academy at the Massachusetts College of Liberal Arts in North Adams. I also enjoy presenting invited lectures at various campuses internationally, including most recently Universidad Alberto Hurtado, la Universidad Jesuita de Chile, and York University in Toronto, Canada. In my early career I had the great fortune to teach and to learn from many diverse students in six different high schools in Arizona, New Mexico, and Louisiana. I held secondary certification in mathematics and English, but I also occasionally taught computer science (which was my first undergraduate major at LSU in 1971) and theology (which was my first graduate degree from Saint Mary's College of California in 1980).

There were times in my early career as a teacher when I became very frustrated working in schools. The complex bureaucratic structure, lack of resources, overcrowded classrooms, stacks of assignments to grade, multiple class preparations with few preparation periods, insubordinate students, burned-out colleagues, inadequate facilities, and inane curriculum materials drove me crazy. But I never quit. Why? I was energized by the academic and extracurricular activities in the schools and my friend-ships with colleagues. Throughout my years of secondary school teaching, I sustained a strong passion for literature, theology, mathematics, and the arts. Mentoring students provided a sense of mission and purpose in my life. The school was my community, and the faculty and students were my extended family. I found tremendous satisfaction in my extracurricular assignments as a coach, moderator, and chaperone. I loved counseling, coaching, and conversations with students, so I refused to quit when times got tough. I do not think I even realized the gross injustice of the paltry salary and limited benefits I received. While salary and benefits in the US have improved somewhat throughout my career, the financial crisis and recession threatens to eviscerate whatever improvements in benefits, working conditions, collective bargaining, and salaries that have occurred. Teachers are often blamed or sometimes vilified for perceived educational shortcomings even by political leaders who claim to support quality schooling. I will address the implications of this serious situation throughout this third edition.

Instead of changing careers when overwhelmed by frustration in schools and criti-cisms in society, I decided to return to college for a master's degree in educational leadership. I thought I could fix the problems I had observed in schools. I received certification as a K–12 administrator and served as a principal in two schools over the next seven years. I found that the principalship was even more frustrating than class-room teaching, especially since I was only thirty years old and still a novice at under-standing complex school systems. I was often caught between competing interests on the faculty and the demands of the school board. Limited resources prevented imple-mentation of curriculum and instruction plans. I felt trapped in the conflicting politics of parent organizations, athletic boards, district bureaucracies, and faculty contracts. I made plenty of mistakes! But I also found a great deal of satisfaction working with faculty and parents on important projects to educate students and transform the com-munity. One of my schools even received national recognition, and in 1985 we were invited to an awards ceremony with President Ronald Reagan and Secretary of Education William Bennett at the White House Rose Garden.

I experience life as an adventure in learning. My philosophy of curriculum develop-ment in this text is committed to lifelong learning for students, teachers, and, indeed, all citizens. For educators, our philosophy of education and our openness to new ideas dramatically impact our teaching and learning. How would you describe your philosophy, interests, and passions? Here are a few of mine: reading southern novels and postmodern philosophy texts; listening to live music; traveling to historic and cultural sites; watching SEC college football and NHL hockey; attending provocative film festivals; viewing contemporary art installations and exhibits at museums; march-ing in protest rallies to end the death penalty; working for environmental justice, gay rights, and living wage initiatives; playing chess with my son Josh and friends at grungy coffee houses; cooking gumbo for my family; doing yoga; attending the Austin City Limits music festival, music performances at Tanglewood, Massachusetts, by the Cleveland Orchestra at Severance Hall, and the New Orleans Jazz and Heritage Festival; creating provocative art installations; playing disc golf; talking about architecture and education with my partner Michael, my mom, stepfather, and daughters;

relaxing and playing with my grandchildren; researching educational issues for lectures and papers; working out at the gym; attending Broadway musicals and plays; and meeting friends and engaging in interesting and provocative conversations. I also love Mardi Gras in my hometown of New Orleans.

Every year on September 9th I give myself a "birthday present." I consider the things that I have not yet done in my life, and I look for a way to serve those in need. I combine my quest for new adventures with my commitment to serve the community. One year I learned to scuba dive and studied the ecology of the oceans; another year I read all of the works of Herman Melville and traveled to sites related to the novel *Moby Dick*. In September, 2010, I decided to train for the Livestrong Austin Marathon and Half Marathon. I joined TeamFX—a running team that supports the Austin Children's Shelter. As I crossed the finish line in front of the Texas state capitol on February 20, 2011, I was filled with raw emotion. Not only had I run in the Austin half marathon for the first time in my life, I had raised awareness and money for abused children in the process. In 2012, I will run my first full marathon. In this text you will discover my commitment to lifelong learning, interdisciplinary curriculum, teaching for social justice, and adventures of the mind and body. I will challenge you to create your own lifelong learning plan of educational, spiritual, athletic, and creative adventures. I believe that we must take control of our learning and move beyond the rhetoric of accountability, test scores, and failure in education that dominates politics and the media. You will find many examples of my challenge in this third edition.

With this philosophy of curriculum development and lifelong learning, it was only natural that I returned to college for a doctoral degree at age 32. I was living in Phoenix at the time, and I began a program in philosophy and theology at Arizona State University. A job transfer to Louisiana prevented me from completing the degree, but I continued my studies at LSU in Baton Rouge. Practical considerations led me to pursue the PhD in educational administration rather than philosophy, but, with the arrival of Dr. William Pinar at LSU in 1985 as chair of the department of curriculum and instruction, I decided to change my degree program to the doctorate in curriculum studies. My life and career changed forever.

I met Bill Pinar while registering for classes at a branch campus of LSU in the middle of the rice fields and crawfish ponds of Eunice, Louisiana, in the fall of 1985. Really! I had never heard of Bill Pinar, and I did not even know that he was the new chair of curriculum and instruction at LSU and a famous curriculum theorist. While waiting for materials to arrive at the registration table (in the days before computer registration), Bill and I engaged in a lively discussion about theology, art, psychology, and literature. Bill had studied feminist theology and Black theology at the Colgate Rochester Divinity School; I had studied liberation theology and eschatology in California. Bill had written a paper on Jackson Pollock's painting *The White Cockatoo*; I had experienced an epiphany in the Metropolitan Museum of Art in New York City while viewing Pollock's painting *Autumn Rhythm*. Bill had done extensive research in Jungian psychology; I was attending weekly Jungian dream analysis and reading books about Jung's notion of the shadow. Bill began his career as a high school English teacher and had a particular affinity for Virginia Wolfe; I taught American literature in high schools and had a strong affinity for William Faulkner. We passionately discussed our interpretation of themes in Wolfe's *A Room of One's Own* and *To the Lighthouse* and Faulkner's *The Bear* and *The Sound and the Fury*. We also talked about other authors who had inspired us: Marcel Proust, Zora Neal Hurston, Walt Whitman, Toni Morrison, and Oscar Wilde. Bill shared his anticipation and apprehension about being an anti-racist White male moving to the south from his native Ohio and adopted New York; I explained my positionality as a progressive southern White male from a prominent conservative Catholic family in Louisiana. We both pondered the complex implications that racism, religion, geography, and gender had on our lives.

I barely noticed the long wait for the registration materials to arrive, and in fact I was very disappointed when our conversation had to end. Meeting this new professor named William Pinar was magical and inspiring. Little did I know at the time that this had been my first lesson in curriculum development in the postmodern era.

I did not meet Bill Pinar again until the next semester. I was the principal of a school in Crowley, Louisiana, about an hour west of Baton Rouge on Interstate 10, and Bill was busy starting his new leadership position at LSU. However, his final question at the end of our conversation haunted me for the next six months. I had mentioned to him that I was a doctoral student in educational administration working on a study comparing test scores in two Louisiana school districts. I was investigating the size of district staffing in relation to standardized test scores. Would a larger leadership staff in the central office help to improve test scores, or would site-based spending on testing materials be a more efficient expenditure of scarce resources? To be honest, it was a pretty boring study, and my heart was not in the project. But I wanted to complete the dissertation in educational administration so that I could one day become a superintendent and make more money. In 1985 I had three babies under the age of three!

At his invitation, I met Bill Pinar for lunch the next semester at the stately LSU Faculty Club, where he asked me again how I planned to incorporate Jungian psychology, eschatological theology, southern literature, and abstract expressionist painting into my dissertation research. I was really dumbfounded. I had no idea what he meant. I had not been introduced to any alternative forms of research besides quantitative methodologies. What did these things have to do with data analysis, statistics, and quantitative measures? Bill began to explain his work in autobiography, qualitative methodologies, and reconceptualized understandings of curriculum and instruction. I was amazed by these interesting ideas. Why had no one ever told me about this? Why did I assume, as I had been taught in my education courses, that curriculum development was simply setting goals, writing behavioral objectives, implementing lesson plans, and evaluating test results? Why did I assume that curriculum was simply the lesson plans, textbooks, curriculum maps, teacher guides, interdisciplinary units, chapter tests, student handouts, course objectives, group projects, manipulatives and ancillaries, and scope and sequence charts provided by my school district and the publishing companies? Why did I allow myself to believe my English teachers in high school and college who insisted that good writing was always done in the objective third person and never contaminated with the autobiographical subjectivity of the author? Why was I never exposed to the connections between music and mathematics, the arts and sciences? Why did I assume that test scores were the most appropriate measure of successful teaching and learning? Why did I assume that curriculum happened only in cinder-block school rooms when students were silent and compliant? Why did I assume that quantitative research was the only valid and reliable form of inquiry? Why? Why? Why? I kept asking myself. I felt betrayed by my profession and embarrassed at my naiveté.

Over the next three years at LSU I began to answer these questions as I studied curriculum theory and became immersed in the literature of the reconceptualization of curriculum studies with professors William Doll, Cameron McCarthy, Rosalyn Charlesworth, Jacques Dagnault, Diana Pounder, Tony Whitson, Spencer Maxcy, Leslie Roman, and, of course, William Pinar.

The first edition of this text in 1995 was my first book; the second edition was published in 2006. It has been adopted steadily for sixteen years by college professors and translated into three languages. I wrote the first edition in the early 1990s after I had completed my dissertation, titled *Toward an Eschatological Curriculum Theory* (Slattery, 1989). People often tell me that *Curriculum Development in the Postmodern Era*, more than anything else I have written, dramatically impacted their pedagogy and research. Students and scholars have sent me private e-mail messages and written public journal reviews that praise it as engaging, evocative, and even life changing. Many people particularly appreciate my discussions of hermeneutics, ecology, theology, proleptic eschatology, anti-racist education, autobiography, and philosophy of education.

I have also received many challenges to improve this text. In 2009 I traveled to South Africa to lecture at the University of South Africa in Pretoria. The professors who had adopted the book for their classes reported that many of the concepts and language were inaccessible. They assumed that the cultural context for some important concepts prevented students in South Africa from understanding the meaning of the contemporary curriculum discourses. I had heard the same critique from students in the US. As a result of my conversation with faculty and students at UNISA and elsewhere, I developed a comprehensive glossary to be used before reading the book. I was amazed and pleased by the positive response to the glossary; clearly, it provided access and insight for students. At the end of the volume is a brief overview, and the entire glossary can be found on the companion web page. I urge you to read the entire version before beginning this text and to refer back to it as needed while reading the chapters. Students have consistently reported that reading the glossary before tackling the book helped them to understand and appreciate *Curriculum Development in the Postmodern Era*.

National accountability measures in the US like *No Child Left Behind* in 2002 and *Race to the Top* in 2009 have dramatically altered the educational and political landscape. Cultural studies programs in education have emerged as important new fields of study related to curriculum development. International political and educational landscapes have been dramatically realigned following September 11, 2001. The need to understand curriculum in relation to theology, race and ethnicity, multicultural studies, global economy and trade, ecology, gender and sexualities, and socio-political realignment has been magnified. Curriculum issues have exploded in controversy: evolution and intelligent design theories in biology texts; gender issues; academic freedom; the place of religion and prayer in schools; separation of church and state; gay, lesbian, bisexual, and transgender topics in the classroom and library; testing and accountability measures in schools and classrooms; bullying and violence on campuses; and funding for public education and vouchers for private schools.

I believe that curriculum and instruction are the very heart and soul of schooling. Elliot Eisner, professor of education and art at Stanford, writes: "Clearly, there are few issues that are more central to the experience that students have in schools than the content of the curriculum and the ways in which it is mediated" (1993, p. 38). While this may seem to be an obvious understatement to some, it is, nonetheless, more complicated and controversial than initially apparent.

Consider this analogy. I suspect that there would be little disagreement among physicians, nurses, medical school personnel, and patients that the primary function of the contemporary health-care professions is healing and wellness. Insurance, hospital construction, computerization, and record documentation, although important and often cumbersome, should be peripheral to the primary purpose of healing in the medical field and allied services. As current debates about the reform of the health-care industry unfold in the United States and comparisons with international health-care delivery methods are discussed in the media, we are beginning to recognize the barriers and limitations that restrict our ability to focus on the healing and wellness of individuals. This problem is not just financial but also related to a philosophy of healing.

The education profession has borrowed much terminology from the medical profession (despite the fact that the analogy is problematic). We "test" and "diagnose" students in order to apply appropriate "treatments." Students who are "deficient" are sent to a "lab" for prescriptive remediation. The lab staff performs further tests to ascertain more accurately the extent of the deficiency. If the treatment in the lab works, students are declared "well," and further visits to the lab occur only for relapses. Blurring the boundary between medicine and education, there is even a market for performance-enhancing drugs for physical and academic stamina, not to mention the explosion of drugs like Ritalin and Adderall to address student attention, behavior, and performance. Teachers participate in "clinical" supervision programs to evaluate instruction. Some educators have proposed a form of "triage" through alternative schooling, tracking, tech-prep schools, or promotion exams, while others resist triage in favor of "holistic" approaches (Books, 1992). Eisner (1993) calls curriculum and teaching the "systole and diastole" of schooling when he writes that curriculum and teaching, like the heart, reside within a "body," the school. Eisner continues:

> The school's structure and its function influence the way in which systolic and diastolic operations occur. In turn, the school inhabits an environment and, like the body itself, is not immune to the quality of that environment. ... The educational health of the classroom is intimately related to the school in which it is nested and the health of the school to the environment within which it resides. (1993, p. 38)

Like the medical profession, the education profession has struggled to remain focused on its primary purpose of learning and instruction for students. Donald Schon (1983, 1987, 1991), in several popular books, has challenged all professions to examine their purpose and function in society. In particular, he has encouraged professionals to overcome the debilitating effects of bureaucracy, disconnectedness, and inertia by becoming "reflective practitioners" who promote learning from, in, and through experience. In this book I will support Schon's call for reflection and action in the professions. Specifically, I believe that educators must focus on a renewed understanding of curriculum and instruction in the postmodern global society that emerged in the 1990s.

My thirty-six years of experience in education at various levels of instruction, from elementary classrooms, to high school administration, and to graduate school seminars in several different states, leads me to believe that a robust understanding of the reconceptualized vision of curriculum development in our profession, like wellness, lifetime exercise, organic foods, mental health, and natural healing in the health-care field, must move to the forefront of our thinking and action.

This is not to imply that gallant efforts have not been made to improve curriculum development, design, implementation, and evaluation. The field of educational administration expends much energy promoting administrators as "instructional leaders" and "curriculum innovators." The field of educational psychology has worked for decades evaluating the validity, reliability, and effectiveness of tests, textbooks, and teaching methods. The field of curriculum studies has taught methods courses to several generations of teachers. However, all these efforts, no matter how important or how noble they may have been, must now be reevaluated for four reasons: first, schooling faces many debilitating structural conflicts; second, a postmodern worldview has emerged; third, a reconceptualization in the field of curriculum and instruction has occurred; and, fourth, the international political context is volatile and dangerous, and education must address the economic, ecological, social, health, and theological issues that threaten our survival. Rather than panic over these events, I embrace our contemporary social and educational milieu and look for renewal in the midst of the turmoil and violence.

Professor Dwayne Huebner of Yale University is one prominent scholar who discusses the nature of public discourse surrounding teaching and learning in the university. In his essay titled *Educational Activity and Prophetic Criticism* (Huebner, 1991), he contends that "education happens because human beings participate in the transcendent" (cited in Huebner 1999, p. 396). With Huebner, I believe that education is a prophetic enterprise that seeks justice; curriculum is a public discourse that seeks transformation; and teaching is a moral activity that seeks compassion and understanding. Teaching is not simply a technical enterprise; rather, it is a creative process of "healing, re-integration, re-membering, and re-collection" (Huebner, 1991, p. 1). Education happens when we are confronted by the other and an image of what we are not, and yet remain committed to what we can become. Huebner writes, "Confrontation with the other brings us under question and enables us to shed the idolatrous self into which we have poured ourselves and which now contains us" (1999, p. 397).

I am inspired by Huebner, and I believe that curriculum and teaching are first and foremost a cosmological enterprise directed toward understanding the universe. This was the classical conception of university teaching from the Middle Ages through the Renaissance, a notion that has lost favor among technicists, empiricists, and vocationalists in the modern era. In my philosophy, curriculum and pedagogy must not simply be directed toward preparing students for a career, although career advancement is one of our important but secondary concerns. In other words, teaching in schools and universities is not a preparation for a future life, but it must be, as Dewey wrote in *Experience and Education*, an experience of life itself (Dewey, 1938).

In our contemporary global community, educators must speak with prophetic criticism and engage in public discourse. Dewey took a similar position in his book *A Common Faith* (Dewey, 1934a). In this text he expressed growing dissatisfaction with hypocrisy, scandal, and ineptitude in organized religions. Dewey's concept of the "religious" is dynamic—an outgrowth of his distaste for the static view of the world held by many members of religious denominations that the sacred is somehow separated from the profane. Dewey (1934a) writes, "The actual religious quality in the experience described is the effect produced, the better adjustment in life and its condition, not in the manner and cause of its production" (p. 34). I understand him to mean *social consequences of value* when he explains that the ideal, through imagination and faith, conquers selfishness and produces a better world. I believe that the curriculum and experiences that must be promoted by educators are those which produce a better adjustment to life experiences, create social consequences of value, and foster social and personal transformation for students and society. Thus, to reiterate my philosophy, education is a prophetic and transformative enterprise.

University professors and K–12 teachers must write and teach with a critical prophetic voice. I would like to offer the life and work of four people who have significantly influenced my philosophy of teaching as examples of such a posture. The first, Dorothy Day, was inspired in her youth to actively work for justice in American society after reading Upton Sinclair's (1906) novel *The Jungle*. At the age of twenty she was arrested in front of the White House with a group of 41 women protesting women's exclusion from the electorate. The women began a hunger strike in prison and were later freed. Day is known today as the co-founder, with Peter Maurin, of the Catholic Worker movement in 1933. Their organization established a network of hospitality houses for the poor which continue in operation to this day. Dorothy Day often argued that the class structure in the United States is of our making, and by our consent we must do what we can to change it. Likewise, I argue that the "savage inequalities in educational opportunity" (Kozol, 1991, 2005) and the "invisibility of marginalized children in the society and its schools" (Books, 1998)—an invisibility that shocked the conscience of citizens following the Hurricane Katrina disaster in 2005—not only within the United States but also globally, compel us to radically alter our priorities. In response to the question "What knowledge is most worthwhile?" Patrick Diamond includes the following information in his editorial introduction to an issue of the important Canadian journal *Curriculum Inquiry*:

> There are approximately 100 million children throughout the world who identify the street as their home, while there are almost 90 million children between the ages of 11 and 15 who are forced into regularly contributing to the international workforce. Ten million children under the age of 17 systematically exchange sex for money; millions of others, having been orphaned by the AIDS epidemic and displaced as victims of war, have turned to the streets for

survival. The existence of street children is not limited to the developing world, as the North American experience with homelessness attests. (1999, p. 261)

Along with Diamond, Books, and Kozol, I believe that my work as a university professor is a form of social work directed toward uplifting the lives of students and those whom they will serve in society. My philosophical training in liberation theology and my study of inspiring activists like Dorothy Day, Oscar Romero, Rosa Parks, Martin Luther King, Jr., Gustavo Gutiérrez, Thich Nhat Hanh, Abraham Joshua Heshel, and Mahatma Gandhi, along with my study of the critical theories of Paulo Freire, W. E. B. Dubois, Antonio Gramsci, and Jürgen Habermas, among many others, convinced me that teaching must be directed toward social change, community empowerment, and the liberation of the mind, body, and spirit of individual human beings. This entire book will reflect my commitment to advancing a just, compassionate, and ecologically sustainable global community.

The second example is the Vietnamese Buddhist monk and peace activist Thich Nhat Hanh. During the war in Vietnam, he worked tirelessly for reconciliation between North and South Vietnam. His lifelong efforts to generate peace moved Martin Luther King, Jr., to nominate him in 1967 for the Nobel Peace Prize. Thich Nhat Hanh has been living since the age of forty in exile in France, where he leads people of diverse nationalities, races, religions, and sexes in a process of mindfulness—taking care in the present moment, being profoundly aware and appreciative of life. He was banned by both the non-communist and the communist governments of Vietnam for his role in undermining the violence he saw affecting his people. He championed a movement known as *engaged Buddhism*, which intertwined traditional meditative practices with active nonviolent civil disobedience. He also set up relief organizations to rebuild destroyed villages, instituted the School of Youth for Social Service, and urged world leaders to use nonviolence as a tool. Although his struggle for cooperation meant he had to relinquish a homeland, it won him accolades around the world. Thich Nhat Hanh's reflections on mindfulness are very much like the postmodern proposals I will present throughout this book. The following are seven of his fourteen precepts that inspire my thinking about education, curriculum, and the postmodern world:

- Do not be idolatrous about or bound to any doctrine, theory, or ideology, even Buddhist ones. All systems of thought are guiding means; they are not absolute truth.
- Do not think that the knowledge you presently possess is changeless, absolute truth. Avoid being narrow-minded and bound to present views. Learn and practice non-attachment from views in order to be open to receive others' viewpoints. Truth is found in life and not merely in conceptual knowledge. Be ready to learn throughout our entire life and to observe reality in yourself and in the world at all times.
- Do not force others, including children, by any means whatsoever, to adopt your views, whether by authority, threat, money, propaganda, or even education. However, through compassionate dialogue, help others renounce fanaticism and narrowness.
- Do not avoid contact with suffering or close your eyes before suffering. Do not lose awareness of the existence of suffering in the life of the world. Find ways to be with those who are suffering by all means, including personal contact and visits, images,

sound. By such means, awaken yourself and others to the reality of suffering in the world.

- Do not maintain anger or hatred. As soon as anger and hatred arise, practice the meditation on compassion in order to deeply understand the persons who have caused anger and hatred. Learn to look at other beings with the eyes of compassion.
- Do not lose yourself in dispersion and in your surroundings. Learn to practice breathing in order to regain composure of body and mind, to practice mindfulness, and to develop concentration and understanding.
- Do not live with a vocation that is harmful to humans and nature. Do not invest in companies that deprive others of their chance to life. Select a vocation which helps realize your ideal compassion.

The third example of a prophetic person who has inspired my thinking is David Orr, chair of environmental studies at Oberlin College. I know David through collaboration on projects for curriculum and ecology with Professor Chet Bowers of Oregon and membership in the Greening of Higher Education at Claremont Graduate School with Professor David Purpel of the University of North Carolina, Greensboro. David Orr not only advocates for environmental sustainability, but he also directs projects for sustainability on college campuses—such as the construction of a prototype green building for Oberlin College in Ohio. David's work was featured in the *Chronicle of Higher Education* (2000, January 14). His process for building community consensus and financial support, his attention to curriculum and teaching in every phase of the planning, and his orchestration of the building process as a pedagogical event in the community all combined to so impress the American Institute of Architects that he received national recognition for innovative and imaginative design solutions. David Orr reminds me that teaching and curriculum work must be environmental work. In our teaching, curriculum development, and research we must use every opportunity to connect students to the universe, especially the life-sustaining dimensions of the global community on our very beautiful yet fragile planet.

The fourth example is Dietrich Bonhoeffer, who was born in 1906 in Germany and studied theology at Tübingen before being offered a parish post in Berlin in 1933. He refused the appointment because "non-Aryans" were denied consideration, and the following year he was a founding member of the *Confessing Church*, a leading center of the Protestant resistance. In 1938 he was expelled from Germany and came to the United States to lecture, but he returned to Europe and became a member of the *Abwehr* military intelligence to gain support for resistance. In 1940 he worked with Operation 7 to support smuggling Jews out of Germany. Bonhoeffer was forbidden to publish, teach, or preach, yet he continued to work with the resistance. He had many influential relatives who urged him to be silent; he also had many opportunities to sit out the war in peace while lecturing in America. But Bonhoeffer choose the path of critical prophetic resistance. When it was discovered that he participated in the March 13, 1943, failed assassination plot against Hitler, an involvement that he anguished over and discussed in his book *The Cost of Discipleship* (1966), Bonhoeffer was jailed and eventually sent to Buchenwald. He was court-martialed and hanged on April 9, 1945, at Flossenburg, one week before the Allies liberated the camp. Bonhoeffer wrote before his death, "No one can think of freedom as a substance or as something indi-vidualistic. Freedom is simply something that happens to me through the other. Being free means 'being free for the other'" (1997, p. 45). Bonhoeffer reminds me throughout his writings that freedom can be achieved not through what fancies the mind, but through what is braved in the bold deeds of justice. This is accomplished not through ideas of soaring flight, but through action. And, as if speaking directly to educators, Bonhoeffer offers this additional challenge:

> We have been silent witnesses of evil deeds: we have been drenched by many storms; we have learnt the arts of equivocation and pretense; experience has made us suspicious of others and kept us from being truthful and open; intoler-able conflicts have worn us down and made us cynical. Are we still of any use? What we shall need is not geniuses or cynics or misanthropes of clever tacticians, but plain, honest, straightforward people. Will our inward power of resistance be strong enough, and our honesty with ourselves remorseless enough, for us to find our way back to simplicity and straightforwardness? (1942, p. 56)

Bonhoeffer answered yes with his life and continues to inspire those of us who believe that teaching and curriculum development is the work of critical prophetic resistance. In the text *The Cost of Moral Leadership: The Spirituality of Dietrich Bonhoeffer*, the authors Geoffrey B. Kelly and F. Burton Nelson (2003) contend that, in good times, religious leaders think that they have reinvented the church. In bad times they seek wisdom from those who have gone before them. No wonder, then, that many now ask what Bonhoeffer would have made of our world. When the path to peace seems so uncertain and the relationship between faith and the United States' role in global economic, political, and military campaigns has become so complicated and tragic, we might learn something from Bonhoeffer, the German pastor and theologian who led the resistance to his country's imperialism and militarism.

Dietrich Bonhoeffer is a model for those of us who seek to engage in public moral leadership for social reform and school renewal. As Huebner insisted in his challenge to the universities, a technical curriculum is not enough; we must surpass the technical foundations of teaching and learning in education. In order for voices of resistance and justice to be effective, we must avoid safe research, hypocritical curriculum scholarship, and mundane technical classroom lectures that allude to empowerment while hiding behind the very corporate structures and political regimes that we deconstruct and condemn. Silencing the voices of critical prophetic resistance in our classrooms—whether out of fear, or for financial gain, or for political leverage—diminishes the credibility of educators and makes us no better than the organized religions con-demned by Dewey in 1934 for their hypocrisy, scandal, and ineptitude.

In the spirit of Huebner, Dewey, Freire, Day, Nhat Hanh, Orr, and Bonhoeffer, I believe that curriculum development in the postmodern era must foreground critical and prophetic public discourse for individual transformation and social renewal. Teachers and their students must work collaboratively as partners in the cause of jus-tice and ecological sustainability. I believe that educators must advance a renewed public discourse for justice with their students—a discourse that can direct our classrooms and curriculum toward social work, environmental work, critical prophetic resistance, and, ultimately, social consequences of value. This is my philosophy of curriculum development and teaching that guides the ideas presented in this book.

What are some of the ways that I implement this curriculum philosophy in my classrooms? I begin all of my classes with a reflection on a work of art that consciously foregrounds an issue of social justice related to the central theme of the course. The work of art may be a film, novel, short story, painting, sculpture, statue, or collection of poetry. However, the purpose of the experience is to evoke—in the postmodern sense of eliciting a visceral response of disequilibrium—an immediate and emotional connection to the theme of the course syllabus. For example, in my undergraduate teacher education course on social foundations of education, I begin the class with the novel and film *A Lesson Before Dying*, by Ernest Gaines (1993). This novel is set on a rural Louisiana plantation of the 1940s. The two central characters are Grant Wiggins, an African-American teacher educated in California who returns to his home on the plantation to teach the young children, and Jefferson, a teenage school dropout accused of a murder he did not commit. Jefferson is condemned to die in the electric chair in thirty days, and Grant is reluctantly persuaded by Jefferson's godmother to visit the boy in jail and teach him to read and to walk like a man before his execution. The story explores the relationship between a teacher and a student and the complexities of social issues like slavery, racism, capital punishment, inadequate educational opportunities for the rural poor, religion and education, and a host of other important topics. This novel and film elicit powerful discussions with my students, and they also prepare us for field experiences with children living in poverty in rural and urban schools later in the semester.

One field experience I organize each semester is a trip to Austin to visit several urban campuses. Each student spends half of the day at an upper-class White campus and the other half at a economically poor campus with students of color. At the end of the day I take the group to a restaurant in the warehouse district of Austin for a meal and discussion with the principals and several teachers from the schools we visited. During the dinner discussion the students can explore the discrepancies of race and class that they noticed during the day. At the next class session following this field experience we discuss the chapters from the textbook on the economics of education, and I show the film *Children in America's Schools*, featuring Jonathan Kozol, which documents the plight of schools in high poverty communities. Having had first-hand experience of the economic disparities, my students are much better prepared to explore the complexities of economics and education in our class discussions. In my undergraduate classes I constantly connect art, literature, films, field experiences, and classroom discussions to issues of justice, economics, compassion, and ecological sustainability. I hope to inspire my pre-service teacher education students to address social and economic issues in their own context.

I use the same teaching philosophy in my graduate courses. When I teach philosophy of education, I always include a visit to an art museum in the course syllabus. The Contemporary Museum of Art and the Museum of Fine Arts in Houston are two of my favorites. I spend an entire day with my students, slowly walking through the museums, and we pause to consider the possible philosophical lessons inspired by certain works of art. While I note the parallel between the history of particular philosophical movements and schools of art, the primary purpose of the field experience is to evoke a visceral response to various works of art and allow the graduate students to express their aesthetic understanding. Once they become comfortable philosophizing in an aesthetic context, I challenge them to apply this methodology in a historical context. Sometimes this will involve watching a film such as *Vukovar*, a dramatic and disturbing narrative about the 1992 Bosnian War, *American History X*, a riveting film about high school gangs, violence, and racism, or *Twilight Los Angeles*, a provocative film by Anna Deveare Smith about the aftermath of the 1992 riots in Los Angeles following the Rodney King verdict.

A particularly interesting field experience with graduate students is a walking tour of the statues on the University of Texas campus following our reading of chapters from two books by James Loewen (1995, 2000): *Lies My Teacher Told Me* and *Lies Across America*. We stop in front of the statues of the confederate generals and White slave owners on the South Mall. We talk about why these statues may have been erected in the first place, considering the historical and political climate of the time. We ponder why Woodrow Wilson and Jefferson Davis receive places of honor facing the state capitol, and then we consider Loewen's critique of these two men in our course readings. Then we walk over to the recently installed statue of Martin Luther King, Jr., on the East Mall and discuss the decades-long struggle to have it erected. A dramatic moment on the walking tour occurs when I point out the surveillance cameras in the trees. The students are visibly shocked. I ask them why George Washington has statues of White male confederates surrounding him on the South Mall (without surveillance cameras) but Martin Luther King, Jr., stands alone on the East Mall under constant threat of vandalism. The arts help us to understand the insidious and intractable racism that is embedded in US society.

In short, the world is my classroom, and the arts are my vehicle for exploring the terrain. My goal is to challenge students to connect the subject matter of the curriculum to the lived-world experiences of their surrounding community. I ultimately hope to inspire them to become prophetic voices for justice in schools and society. I reiterate my belief that education is a prophetic enterprise seeking justice, that curriculum is a public discourse seeking transformation, and that teaching is a moral activity demanding compassion and understanding. Teaching is not simply a technical human enterprise of information transmission, cultural assimilation, or career development; rather, as Dwayne Huebner points out, it is a creative process of healing, re-integration, re-membering, and re-collection.

On the companion web page you will find photographs of Piazza d'Italia in New Orleans taken by Professor Anne E. Pautz, a colleague at Louisiana State University. These images appeared on the cover of the second edition of the text. Piazza d'Italia was designed by Charles E. Moore with assistance from architect James Sterling. Completed in 1968, it is a stunning example of the eclecticism, irony, and playfulness of postmodern architecture. Can you spot some of the interesting juxtapositions in this photograph? One example would be the Roman numerals on the electric clock in a building frame over a cobble stone walkway that is reminiscent of the ruins of the Roman Forum. Ironically, the premodern facade is supported by modern materials made of fiberglass and steel. Notice that the keystone in the arch is missing! I remember walking through the Piazza d'Italia with friends after high school dances at the nearby Rivergate Center. As a young man working downtown, I would sometimes sit on the benches for lunch and enjoy the ambiance of the city. While the piazza stands in stark contrast to the linear and functional modern skyscrapers of downtown New Orleans in the upper left-hand corner of the photograph, it is also intimately integrated into the modern milieu of the financial district on Poydras Street. In the 1990s, Piazza d'Italia fell into disrepair. Located near the site of one of the largest land-based casino in the nation, it was spared by Hurricane Katrina, but its future was uncertain. In 2010 it was restored to its original glory, and I recommend visiting Piazza d'Italia if you are ever in New Orleans. I placed these images on the cover of the first and second editions of my book to visually represent an example of postmodern architecture and to invite the reader into a space of reflection on curriculum development in the postmodern era. I invite you to take a metaphorical journey into the piazza with me. Additionally, I use this image to indicate the autobiographical and aesthetic nature of this text. I believe that curriculum development is best understood through the lens of narrative and the arts. On the cover of the third edition I have used an image of my own oil on canvas artwork. Additional images of my artwork can be found on the companion web page. These paintings are examples of my abstract expressionism that will be discussed in detail in chapter 10. You will also find images of my art installations in chapters 4 and 10. Art and aesthetics are at the heart of postmodern curriculum development.

Many people have helped me to think deeply about the issues I discuss in this third edition. I thank all of my teachers and colleagues who have shared their wisdom. I have grown because of you. I thank my students, who have taught me to be humble, inquisitive, and patient. You have helped me to expand my inquiry and deconstruct my sedimented perceptors. I thank my doctoral students for your excellent scholarship. You have kept my thinking fresh and my research robust and animated. I thank my parents, children, and grandchildren for teaching me the joy of love, intimacy, and growth in my life. I thank all of my dear friends for sharing meals, wine, and laughter. You help me to relax and enjoy the process of living at peace in a complex postmodern world. I especially thank Michael for your support and encouragement. You have helped me to experience much joy in life, and I dedicate this book to you.

Patrick Slattery
Austin, Texas
January, 2012

Introduction

In a fascinating book titled *The Dancing Healers*, medical doctor Carl Hammerschlag writes about his encounter with the dancing circle of Native American spirituality. Hammerschlag recalls that, as a young medical intern from New York City, he was assigned to the Santa Fe, New Mexico, Indian Hospital, where he encountered Santiago Rosetta, a Pueblo priest and clan chief. Hammerschlag (1988) writes: "Santiago tried to teach me that if you are going to dance, you have to move. You can't watch the dance; you can't listen to it or look at it. You have to do it to know it. He told me that he could teach me his steps, but I would have to hear my own music" (p. 10).

Hammerschlag was attempting to treat Santiago's illness when they encountered each other. Santiago wanted to see the White doctor's healing dance before he would allow him to touch his body and treat the illness. Hammerschlag recalls in his book that, in order to pacify the elderly gentleman, he lightheartedly performed a little Irish jig near Santiago's bed. But, as he looked into Santiago's eyes, the naive young doctor realized that he had missed the point. Santiago was trying to explain that everything is interrelated: body, mind, and spirit. Dancing is essential in the healing process. Over time Hammerschlag came to understand the wholeness suggested by native spirituality and mystical traditions. He saw how this philosophy contradicted the modern experience of fragmentation and isolation, and he came to understand the spiritual bankruptcy of contemporary medical and social models rooted in domination, control, isolation, and conquest.

Kevin Costner (1990) explores alternatives to this social model in his film *Dances With Wolves*, in which he portrays an American cavalryman stationed alone at the farthest outpost on the northern frontier. When the cavalryman encounters a nomadic Sioux tribe early in the film, he epitomizes the modern metaphor: isolated, independent, and insecure. He attempts to order the environment to maximize control over the unpredictable forces of the frontier, but he is saved from certain death only when he lets go of the security of his fortress and dances before the fire with a wolf. This lone cavalryman experiences a conversion and transformation as he gradually becomes united in spirit with the Sioux. The soldier learns from the Sioux what Hammerschlag learned from the Pueblo—the healing dance of native spirituality. In this book I argue that curriculum development in the postmodern era must be attentive to this healing dance, the spiral of creation, and a yearning for wisdom embedded in the interrelationship of body, mind, and spirit. Educators must recognize and embrace the healing curriculum dance and celebrate the mystical, multicultural, interdisciplinary, social, ecological, and holistic dimensions of the school curriculum (Slattery, 1992b). The dancing circle depends on this eclectic interrelationship in order for learning, healing, and growth to flourish.

I begin this book with Hammerschlag's narrative because Santiago's advice is exactly what I tell my students at the beginning of my classes. I advise my students that I can teach them my philosophy, but they will have to listen to their own voice and take action in their own unique ways. As an author and teacher, I emulate Santiago when he said, "I can teach you my steps, but you will have to hear your own music." In this book I will present my understanding of curriculum development, postmodernism, and other cultural and social issues. I will show you my steps, but you will have to hear your own music and create your own curriculum dance.

This book is purposely titled *Curriculum Development in the Postmodern Era* and not *Postmodern Curriculum Development* or *Postmodern Methods of Curriculum and Instruction*. But I will not present a plan or method of curriculum development. Each reader will have to create a curriculum development philosophy and plan of implementation individually. In this book I will present a vision and understanding of curriculum development that has emerged in our contemporary historical period, which many call the *postmodern era*. The book seeks to explore and understand curriculum development in the challenging, complicated, and complex contemporary world of the 21st century. Postmodernism has been called a worldview, an historical epoch, an attitude, and an eclectic aesthetic sensibility. Critics have called postmodernism relativism gone amok, nihilistic, meaningless linguistic jargon, destructive of Western values—and worse. While these critiques have some validity, I have found that postmodern discourses have been very helpful in my thinking about curriculum development. Let's explore postmodern ideas together in this text and then decide if you also find deeper understanding about curriculum and pedagogy in postmodern philosophy.

Many students, colleagues, and reviewers have suggested that I begin this third edition with an overview of postmodernism and a reflection on other complex terminology that will be encountered in the book. In the spirit of William Pinar's call for *complicated conversations* in the curriculum field in his important work *What is Curriculum Theory?* (2004a, 2011), I introduce a robust commentary on some of the central ideas in this book: postmodernism, deconstruction, hegemony, hermeneutics, identity politics, ecology, and aesthetics. Hopefully, you have already read the glossary at the end of the text. I begin with a lengthy discussion of deconstruction and postmodernism.

Deconstruction, a school of philosophy that originated in France in the 1960s, has had an enormous impact on literary criticism and social analysis. In many ways it upends the Western metaphysical tradition. One of the chief proponents of deconstruction is Jacques Derrida, who wrote:

> I was quite explicit about the fact that nothing of what I said had a destructive meaning. ... The word deconstruction has nothing to do with destruction. That is

to say, it is simply a question of (and this is a necessity of criticism in the classical sense of the word) being alert to the implications, to the historical sedimentation of the language we use—and that is not destruction. (1972, p. 271)

Others who are associated with this movement (although some might contest the labels applied to them) are Michel Foucault, Julia Kristeva, Jacques Lacan, Gilles Deleuze, Félix Guattari, Fredric Jameson, Jean Baudrillard, Mark C. Taylor, Richard Rorty, Douglas Kellner, Paul de Man, and Jean-François Lyotard. These philosophers often echo Derrida, who continually points out the difference between *being* and its representation in reason by recourse to the term différence, which connotes both *difference* and to defer. Deconstruction represents a complex response to a variety of theoretical and philosophical movements of the 20th century, most notably Husserlian phenomenology, Saussurean and French structuralism, and Freudian psychoanalysis.

Students and scholars may use deconstruction with any text (i.e., a written artifact, musical composition, dramatic performance, art installation, visual culture, technology and media, fiction, nonfiction, history, textbooks, or film). Here are some ways that deconstruction might be applied:

- *Problematize*: To make the text problematic on multiple levels by exposing internal contradictions, omissions, exclusions, ambiguities, and injustices.
- *Question*: To raise concerns and questions that cause the reader/viewer/listener to reevaluate the premise of the text.
- *Interrupt*: To reveal the sedimented perceptors—deeply held prejudices and their unconscious roots—and force the reader/viewer/listener to pause and reconsider these assumptions.
- *Contextualize*: To critically evaluate and analyze arguments from the perspective of race, class, gender, sexuality, religion, culture, ability, language, age, ethnicity, geography, psychology, and nationality in order to understand and appreciate the complex forces that shape and influence a text.
- *Challenge*: To demand a reevaluation of hidden and overt assumptions and purposeful exclusions in the representation of the text in light of status quo sociopolitical, cultural, and economic arrangement.
- *Historicize*: To locate the text in historical, cultural, etymological, and theological contexts.
- *Expose*: To delineate asymmetries of power relations and the impact of these dynamics on individuals, cultures, societies, the environment, and human and non-human life.
- *Engage*: To foreground the aesthetic representations of the text in order to release the imagination and envision alternate possibilities/readings of the sub-texts/unconscious responses of the author(s) and reader(s).
- *Trouble*: To create intellectual and emotional dissonance and discomfort for the purpose of encouraging further investigation and social action.
- *Evoke*: To elicit emotional and intellectual reactions that cause the reader/viewer/listener to ponder, think, and act for positive social consequences and individual growth.

An excellent essay on deconstruction was written by Professor Mark C. Taylor following the death of Jacques Derrida in 2004. Professor Taylor, an important postmodern philosopher and theologian, argues that, along with Ludwig Wittgenstein and Martin Heidegger, Derrida was one of the three most important philosophers of the 20th century. Philosophers, theologians, educators, literary critics, psychologists, historians, artists, legal scholars, and architects have all found in his writings insights that have led to a revival of the arts and humanities during the past four decades. Taylor contends that Derrida was also deeply misunderstood:

> To people addicted to sound bites and overnight polls, Mr. Derrida's work seems hopelessly obscure. It is undeniable that they cannot be easily summarized or reduced to one-liners. The obscurity of his writing, however, does not conceal a code that can be cracked, but reflects the density and complexity characteristic of all great works of philosophy, literature and art. Like good French wine, his works age well. The more one lingers with them, the more they reveal about our world and ourselves. ... Mr. Derrida's name is most closely associated with the often cited but rarely understood term "deconstruction." Initially formulated to define a strategy for interpreting sophisticated written and visual works, deconstruction has entered everyday language. When responsibly understood, the implications of deconstruction are quite different from the misleading cliches often used to describe a process of dismantling or taking things apart. The guiding insight of deconstruction is that every structure—be it literary, psychological, social, economic, political or religious—that organizes our experiences is constituted and maintained through acts of exclusion. In the process of creating something, something else inevitable gets left out. These exclusive structures can become repressive—and that repression comes with consequences. In a manner reminiscent of Freud, Mr. Derrida insists that what is repressed does not disappear but always returns to unsettle every construction, no matter how secure it seems. As an Algerian Jew writing in France during the postwar years in the wake of totalitarianism on the right (fascism) as well as the left (Stalinism), Mr. Derrida understood all too well the dangers of beliefs and ideologies that divide the world into diametrical opposites: left or right, red or blue, good or evil, for us or against us. He showed how these repressive structures which grew directly out of the Western intellectual and cultural tradition threatened to return with devastating consequences. By struggling to overcome patterns that exclude the differences that make life worth living, he developed a vision that is consistently ethical. (Taylor, 2004, p. A-28)

This is the same conclusion reached by postmodern ethicist Zygmunt Bauman (1993) in his *Postmodern Ethics*. Solidarity with "the other" is the radical postmodern position to overcome nihilism and diametrical thinking. The Jewish existentialist Martin Buber (1965) established a framework for this position in his book *I and Thou*. This is an important concept that helps to explicate the postmodern philosophy—a concept that is foundational here. One of my primary purposes in writing this book is to expose, investigate, and deconstruct opposing binaries and diametrically opposed opposites— or what I will call bifurcations and dualisms. I agree with Derrida and Taylor that dualistic thinking is very dangerous. Dualism is the outgrowth of philosophical traditions that need to be challenged. The attempts to divide the world into "us" versus "them" pervade our society. In schooling, for example, we constantly divide kids into upper and lower groups, gifted and remedial, athletics and academics, or compliant and behaviorally disordered students. Bifurcation by categories based on race, learning styles, intelligences, social class, gender, sexual orientation, or religion unnecessarily and illogically divides human beings and inflicts tremendous pain and suffering on all of us.

Unfortunately, supporters of Derrida on the left and critics on the right have misunderstood this vision. Many people appropriated his analyses as well as his emphasis on the importance of preserving differences and respecting others to forge an identity politics that divides the world between the very oppositions it was his mission to undo: Black and White, men and women, gay and straight, Christian and Muslim, etc. Betraying Derrida's insights by creating a culture of political correctness, his self-styled supporters fueled the culture wars that have been raging for more than three decades and continue to frame political debate. These debates are most familiar to educators who encounter curriculum conflicts regularly.

Critics contend that Derrida was a pernicious nihilist who threatened the very foundation of Western society and culture. By insisting that truth and absolute value cannot be known with certainty, his detractors argue, he undercut the very possibility of moral judgment. To follow Derrida, they maintain, is to start down the slippery slope of skepticism and relativism that inevitably leaves us powerless to act. Taylor explains:

> This is an important criticism that requires a careful response. Like Kant, Kierkegaard and Nietzsche, Mr. Derrida does argue that transparent truth and absolute values elude our grasp. This does not mean, however, that we must forsake the cognitive categories and moral principles without which we cannot live: equity and justice, generosity and friendship. Rather, it is necessary to recognize the unavoidable limitations and inherent contradictions in the ideas and norms that guide our actions, and do so in a way that keeps them open to constant questioning and continual revision. There can be no ethical action without ethical reflection. During the last decade of his life, Mr. Derrida became preoccupied with religion and it is this area that his contribution might well be most significant for our time. He understood that religion is impossible without uncertainty. Whether conceived of as Yahweh, as the father of Jesus Christ, or as Allah, God can never be fully known or adequately represented by imperfect human beings. (2004, p. A-28)

Following from this argument by Derrida and Taylor, I will argue in chapters 4 and 5 that the study of theology, eschatology, and hermeneutics is essential, and it is perhaps the most urgent element of study in K–12 and university curriculum. Religious zealots and extremists—whether Christian, Jewish, Muslim, Hindu, or others—have set the world on a trajectory of bifurcation, conflict, and destruction. An excellent book, titled *When Religion Becomes Evil*, by Charles Kimball (2002), professor and chair of the department of religion at Wake Forest University and an ordained Baptist minister, exposes this problem with clarity and precision. Former US president Jimmy Carter (2006), also a Protestant Christian, succinctly addresses the political crisis provoked by religious fundamentalism in his volume *Our Endangered Values: America's Moral Crisis*. Jim Wallis (2005), minister, editor of the journal *Sojourners*, and political observer with access to US politicians, presents a similar analysis in *God's Politics*, in which he contends that the political right is "wrong" and the political left "does not get it" on religion. Writers such as Richard Dawkins (2006) and Christopher Hitchens (2007) contribute to deconstructing the conflicts and contradictions in religions from the perspective of atheists. Many academics, religious leaders, and politicians share a heightened sense of concern that I will explicate in this book.

We live at a time when major conflicts are shaped by people who claim to know, for certain, that a deity is on their side. Derrida reminded us that religion does not always give clear meaning and certainty. To the contrary, the great religious traditions call certainty and secularity into question. As we will see in chapter 4, religious belief that is not tempered by doubt and questioning poses a moral danger. Taylor concludes:

> Fortunately, he also taught us that the alternative to blind belief is not simply unbelief but a *different* kind of belief—one that embraces uncertainty and enables us to respect others whom we do not understand. In a complex world, wisdom is knowing what we don't know so that we can keep the future open. (2004, p. A-28)

Derrida's philosophy of deconstruction leads us naturally into an investigation of postmodernism. What is postmodernism? Postmodernism eludes definition. As we saw above, critics claim that it leads to relativism and nihilism. Postmodernism, for some, is too pessimistic and hopeless. Others find strength in the critical deconstruction of oppressive metanarratives and unjust socio-political and economic arrangement. Some revel in the eclecticism and ecumenism that frees individuals from the shackles of ethical or theological indoctrination. However, even enthusiasts of postmodernism, such as Richard Rorty (1997), have challenged the usefulness of the term.

Postmodernism is often playful. However, postmodern play is directed to a very serious purpose. The following words might help to describe postmodernism even though definitions are elusive and contested.

- *Eclectic*: Many styles, multiplicity, and interdisciplinary practices are encouraged. The parts and whole interact in a profound and dynamic harmony even in apparent disorder or dysfunction. Bifurcations are rejected in favor of a holistic philosophy. Inclusion of marginalized and silenced voices—particularly from racial, gendered, sexual, socio-economic, linguistic, religious, and cultural perspectives, including voices of persons of various ages, abilities, languages, and locations—is demanded. Eclecticism is best understood in the architectural roots of postmodernism in the 1950s. See, for example, *What is Post-Modernism?* by Charles Jencks (1986).
- *(Dis)equilibrium*: While uncertainty is not comfortable, a citizen-based democracy is built on participation, which is the very expression of permanent discomfort. Modern, corporate, and rational systems depend on the citizens' desire for inner comfort and predictability. Postmodern (dis)equilibrium is the acceptance of permanent

psychic discomfort as the best understanding of consciousness. This (dis)equilibrium and (dis)comfort can inspire social change and political action. Ambiguity and complexity are not destabilizing; they are generative. An excellent resource for understanding this phenomenon is Simone de Beauvoir's (1949) book *The Ethics of Ambiguity* (see also Slattery & Morris, 1999).

■ *Environmental*: Postmodernism is interactive with many environments. It is a cosmology that unites inside and outside, nature and the body, human and non-human, etc., in a concern for a physically and psychically nurturing milieu that challenges degradation and promotes sustainability. One resource mentioned in the preface is the work of David Orr, chair of environmental science at Oberlin College. See, for example, Orr's *The Nature of Design: Ecology, Culture, and Human Intention* (2002).

■ *Evocative*: Postmodernism presents multiple views without silencing investigation of dangerous and difficult issues. It encourages a multiplicity of historical interpretations and an exploration of the political and the unconscious. This is sometimes called an acceptance of "essential tension" in interpretation.

■ *Energetic*: Like Einstein's concentrations of energy, we are constantly changing and shifting. We do not stand on solid ground but on shifting sands. Thus, ambiguity, uncertainty, and complexity best describe the world. New perspectives constantly emerge and deconstruct the status quo that leads to the surging chaos of the unexpressed. See, for example, William Doll, *A Post-Modern Perspective on Curriculum* (1993), and Sherri Reynolds, "Patterns that Connect: A Recursive Epistemology" (2004b).

■ *Aesthetic*: Through art, architecture, music, drama, literature, dance, and various artifacts of traditional culture, popular culture, resistant culture, and indigenous culture we come to new "landscapes of learning" that "release the imagination" (Greene, 1995) and move us to equity and social justice.

■ *Eschatological*: Every present is conditioned by the past and every present is pregnant with future possibilities. The "already" and the "not yet" create a world of possibilities (Bloch, 1970) and hope (Moltmann, 1967). The past, present, and future are dynamically interconnected rather than segmented on a linear time line. "There is no such thing as was because the past is" (Faulkner, [1950] 1965). Time is proleptic. See, for example, *Ethics and the Foundations of Education: Teaching Convictions in a Postmodern World* (Slattery & Rapp, 2003).

■ *Engaging*: The individual participant shapes the outcome of the project or study. In the spirit of Heisenberg's Uncertainty Principle, the observer determines the actual state of the experiment. As one increases the accuracy of one element of a measurable quantity, a decrease in the certainty with which we can measure the other quantities emerges. We participate in the (re-)creation of works of art. Like Maxine Greene (1978, 1995, 2001), postmodernists believe that the arts are brought to life when human beings engage them imaginatively.

■ *Existential*: Postmodernism seeks situated/contextual learning grounded in existence prior to essence. To overcome malaise is to be awake and alive in the spirit of Henry David Thoreau and John Dewey. We are, in effect, totally free and totally responsible.

■ *Expressive*: Visual forms are analogous to affective responses that evoke feelings. Responsiveness leads to the process of transformation. We must create opportunities for expressive encounters. See, for example, Janet Miller, *Creating Spaces and Finding Voices* (1990).

- *Evolving*: A continual process of dialogue and interaction between apparent opposites rather than static bifurcations. Deconstruction leads to a continual process of examining the assumptions on which we ground our interpretations. See, for example, James Henderson and Kathleen Kesson, *Curriculum Wisdom: Educational Decisions in Democratic Societies* (2004).
- *Experimental*: Process philosophy helps us to understand how to engage with an open system cosmology (Whitehead, 1929, [1929] 1978). This fosters a willingness to try new styles and different approaches. Influences from sensory and unconscious experiences lead to new imaginative realities. Multiple forms of representation are encouraged and supported. Alternate forms of assessment and evaluation are explored. Willingness to risk and improvise is encouraged.
- *Anti-entropy*: An open systems cosmology rather than a closed systems cosmology promotes an interaction across boundaries. Border crossings overcome the debilitating effect of closed systems. Post-formal approaches are generative and overcome entropy.
- *Entertaining*: Postmodernism is playful, ironic, kaleidoscopic, self-critical, and sensitive to the subtleties of difference. It catches you off guard so that you can engage the ironic, celebrate the ambiguous, and investigate the absurd. Postmodernism uses metaphor and irony to express a prophetic vision and evoke community action. This is often reflected in public pedagogy (see glossary) and best explicated by Sandlin, O'Malley, and Burdick, in "Mapping the Complexities of Public Pedagogy Scholarship: 1894–2010" (2011).

These are some of the words and phrases that describe a postmodern attitude and a postmodern understanding of deconstruction. While not exhaustive or comprehensive, such ideas will shape my discussion of curriculum development throughout the book.

Graduate courses such as elementary and secondary curriculum development, curriculum supervision, curriculum evaluation, and curriculum planning are often required as part of advanced degree programs in university departments of curriculum and instruction. Traditionally, a synoptic (comprehensive) textbook with an emphasis on quantitative research methodologies and practical application of curriculum goals, objectives, lesson plans, scope and sequence guides, and evaluation instruments has been used by professors to provide an overview of the areas of policy, planning and design, implementation, and supervision of the school curriculum. Most synoptic textbooks in the past have been consistent with the dominant philosophical approach to curriculum development called the Tylerian Rationale, after Ralph Tyler's influential book *Basic Principles of Curriculum and Instruction* (1949), which has dominated the curriculum field since its publication. In fact, Tyler's handbook itself has often been used as a supplementary reading by professors committed to the rationale, and in the past 75 years it has almost taken on the stature of an icon in the field of curriculum studies. Thus, several generations of graduate students, teachers, supervisors, administrators, and curriculum specialists have been influenced by the Tylerian Rationale and sometimes have been led to believe that this is the only viable conception of curriculum development available for schooling and teachers. While acknowledging the historical contribution of Tyler to curriculum development in the modern era, contemporary curriculum discourses challenge the assumption that his approach should be the basis or the focus of all curriculum studies. In fact, postmodern philosophies challenge and often replace the traditional model of curriculum development itself.

Since the reconceptualization of the curriculum field in the 1970s and 1980s, Tyler's handbook is often used by those who teach historical, political, or theoretical education courses to critique the impact of the rationale paradigm on the curriculum field and classroom practice (Pinar, 1999). In the 1990s major battles were waged over the meaning, purpose, and function of curriculum in the universities, in school districts, among parent groups, in churches, and in political organizations (Wraga, 1999). Various constituencies, some of them local groups concerned about particular programs or books used in their district schools and others committed to national or international paradigm changes in educational philosophies, have brought curricular concerns to the forefront of national debates in the new millennium. In 1988 William Pinar described the reconceptualization of the curriculum studies field this way:

> The field of curriculum has undergone an enormous change—a reconceptualization if you will—during the past twenty years. From a field concerned with the development and management of curriculum it has evolved into a field more concerned with scholarly understanding of several dimensions of curriculum. These dimensions include issues of development and management; however, these are explored through political, gendered, phenomenological, and other means. (1988a, p. v)

This reconceptualized field has resulted in much discussion on the university level, and now it has begun to filter into museum education, school districts, and elementary and secondary classrooms as well. In fact, current curriculum scholars are beginning to write about a "post-reconceptualization" in the field (Malewski, 2009).

This book is not only intended to present a reconceptualized and postmodern perspective on curriculum development, it also seeks to bridge many gaps that currently divide various stakeholders in the curricular debates: traditionalists who cling firmly to the Tylerian Rationale and others who insist on a new understanding of curriculum; university professors of curriculum and school district personnel in elementary and secondary schools; modernists and postmodernists; curriculum planners and critical theorists; curriculum specialists and lay observers of curriculum practices; educational administrators and political special interest groups; and especially teachers and students. There is a definite need for all these stakeholders to consider carefully the historical and contemporary curriculum discourses that can inform and sometimes mediate the contentious debates that currently exist in the United States and other nations concerning curriculum development. Those involved with schooling today, including parents, teachers, students, school board members, professors of education, university graduate students, politicians, and school administrators, are all intimately familiar with the volatility of curricular debates. While many outstanding textbooks have been published which present summaries of curriculum research in order to clarify the various contemporary perspectives on curriculum (e.g., Schubert, 1986; Jackson, 1992; Sears & Marshall, 1990; Pinar, Reynolds, Slattery, & Taubman, 1995;

Edgerton, 1996; Marsh & Willis, 1999; Pinar, 2003, 2004a, 2004b; Kridel, 2010), these books and the themes they discuss are not always accessible to many teachers, curriculum specialists in school districts, and beginning graduate students.

Before commenting on the approach that this book will take to address the curricular debates described above, it is necessary to mention the various synoptic textbooks that have influenced the curriculum field. Without a sense of this historical perspective it will be difficult to understand why a book on curriculum development and postmodern education is even necessary. However, it is hoped that this volume will introduce elements of contemporary curriculum research in such a way that curriculum discourses will become accessible to many more of the stakeholders in the field today, especially those who are involved in the daily struggle to implement curriculum theories in schools as well as graduate students who will one day be the specialists responsible for such implementation in the universities and in classrooms.

Popular synoptic textbooks of the traditional curriculum field include the following texts that have dominated since their first editions appeared between 1954 (T. Galen Saylor) and 1982 (Peter F. Oliva): Ronald C. Doll's (1996) *Curriculum Improvement: Decision Making and Process*; J. D. McNeil's (1990) *Curriculum: A Comprehensive Introduction*; Peter F. Oliva's (2001) *Developing the Curriculum*; T. Galen Saylor, W. M. Alexander, and J. Lewis' (1981) *Curriculum Planning for Better Teaching and Learning*; Daniel Tanner and Laurel Tanner's (2007) *Curriculum Development: Theory into Practice*; J. Wiles and J. C. Bondi's (2002) *Curriculum Development: A Guide to Practice*; Allan C. Ornstein, Linda S. Behar-Horenstein, and Edward F. Pajak's (2003) *Contemporary Issues in Curriculum*; Allan C. Ornstein, Edward F. Pajak, and Stacey B. Ornstein's (2010) *Contemporary Issues in Curriculum*; and R. S. Zais' (1976) *Curriculum: Principles and Foundations*. These texts provide an approach to curriculum development that is compatible with the philosophy of those who are interested in curriculum policy making, the construction of model curriculum practices in schools, and curriculum evaluation as the central focus of their research. Synoptic texts have a long history in the curriculum field dating back to the publication in 1935 of Hollis L. Caswell and Doak S. Campbell's *Curriculum Development*, which established the tradition of synoptic texts in the American curriculum field. Caswell was a pioneer of statewide programs of curriculum development in the 1930s. Perhaps the most comprehensive work in the history of curriculum texts has been done by Craig Kridel, professor at the University of South Carolina and curator of the Museum of Education in Columbia. Kridel published the *Books of the Century Catalogue* (2000), which highlighted 100 of the most influential education texts of the 20th century, and the *Encyclopedia of Curriculum Studies* (2010), which mapped the field. Browsing through the abstracts of the 100 texts and the encyclopedia provides scholars and graduate students with a perspective on the depth and diversity of educational scholarship in the curriculum field. William Pinar (2004a) argues that the era of the traditional synoptic text must shift from an obsession with school-based policy and evaluation to a broader concern to understand the complicated conversations of curriculum in the context of schools, society, and autobiography. I strongly agree. I will spell out this position in detail in chapter 13, where I explain how the curriculum text of the postmodern era does have a direct and important impact on schools and classrooms—albeit in a very different way than the traditional synoptic text. In short, there is not a "theory and practice" split in the synoptic texts of the reconceptualization—in spite of attempts by some critics who continue to claim that the bifurcation of theory and practice is the goal of postmodern and reconceptualized curriculum studies. The opposite is actually the case.

Since the reconceptualization of the field of curriculum and instruction in the 1970s (Jackson, 1992; Pinar et al., 1995) and the proliferation of curriculum literature in the 1990s (Janet Miller, 1990, 2005; Slattery & Rapp, 2003), there has been a virtual explosion of new theoretical constructs that have moved the field beyond both the traditional Tylerian Rationale and the scope of behavioral curriculum planning and classroom practices in the traditional synoptic texts. Textbooks like this one now address issues of race, gender, sexuality, politics, critical pragmatism, phenomenology, poststructuralism, aesthetics, ecology, deconstructionism, social theory, autobiography, ethnography, hermeneutics, literary theory, theology, internationalization, and, of course, postmodernism. Additionally, all the traditional structural disciplines of the curriculum field have been reconceptualized. This is exemplified by the following: *educational evaluation* is seen by Elliot Eisner (1997, 2001) as "expressive," "imaginative," "metaphorical," and "connoisseurship" rather than as objective and scientific; *supervision of instruction* is described by Edward Pajak (1989) as "theatrical and image constructive," by Carl Glickman (1992) as "shared and empowering," and by Nelson Haggerson and Andrea Bowman (1992) as "interpretive inquiry" rather than as "bureaucratic, inspectional, and clinical," as in the traditional supervision models; *policy making* is viewed by Elmore and Sykes (1992) as "less deterministic" and by Reba Page (1990) as "a complex appreciation of relations among school, individual experience, and public life," rather than exclusively as a "rational process of instrumental intervention and analyzable negotiation guiding educational practice" (Wise, 1979); *curriculum theory* is described by William Doll (1993) as "a postmodern process of richness, recursion, relations, and rigor," by William Pinar (2003; 2004a) as a "complicated conversation," and by Erik Malewski and his colleagues (2009) as an "intergenerational conversation" rather than as "concrete elements of a program of instruction" (Tyler, 1949); *curriculum planning and design* is seen as "culturally responsive" (Gay, 2000), "interdisciplinary" (Sizer, 1984), and "opening up possibilities that enable learning rather than as management of expected outcomes" (Carson, 1987); and, finally, educational research itself has expanded to include qualitative, narrative, arts-based, and other alternative forms for representation (Tierney & Lincoln, 1997; Denzin & Lincoln, 2005).

Despite the dramatic changes (some claim a paradigm shift) in the curriculum field, a critical dilemma has developed within the reconceptualized field of curriculum and instruction itself. In the 1970s and early 1980s, curriculum scholars who were writing specifically about race, gender, ethics, politics, autobiography, and phenomenology were relatively small in number. Their voices were usually excluded from mainstream discourses, professional journals, and curriculum textbooks and were virtually non-existent in the curriculum development programs of elementary and secondary education. These scholars remained united in their opposition to the Tylerian Rationale and other quantitative and behavioral approaches to curriculum studies (see, for example,

Giroux, Penna, & Pinar, 1981). By the 1980s this coalition broke down as each group began to claim that their mode of analysis was either superior or normative for the reconceptualized field. Marxist and feminist analyses initially gained ascendancy by 1980 and 1985, respectively. In the 1990s postmodern discourses dominated, but they soon were joined by international, political, queer, postcolonial, poststructural, and aesthetic discourses. A rise of interest in curriculum and pedagogy and an effort to think about the reconceptualization of curriculum in relation to schools and classrooms emerged with the founding of the Curriculum and Pedagogy Conference in 2000 and the *Journal of Curriculum and Pedagogy* in 2004 (Henderson & Slattery, 2004, 2005).

Thus, professors committed to political analysis use texts in the political genre, for example, Bowles and Gintis (1976), Apple (1982, 1985, 2000, 2004), Giroux (1981, 1988, 1992, 2005), Aronowitz (1992), Freire (1970, 1985, 2001), Freire and Macedo (1987), Stanley (1992), McLaren (1997, 1998, 2005), Willis (1977), Wexler (1992), and Kozol (1975, 1991, 2005), and those committed to feminist gender analysis use texts in the feminist genre, for example, Ellsworth (1997, 2005), Lather (1989, 1991), Grumet (1988a, 1988b, 1988c), Noddings (1984, 1989, 1992, 1995), Miller (1987, 1990, 2005), Edgerton (1996), Brady (1995), and Pagano (1990). Those whose work is rooted in phenomenology often reference Aoki (1985, 1988, 1992), Aoki, Franks, and Jacknicke (1987), Greene (1978, 1995, 2001), van Manen (1982, 1984, 1986, 1988, 1990, 1993), Husserl (1964), Merleau-Ponty (1962), Carson (1987, 1992), Jardine (1992), and Pinar and Reynolds (1992). Process philosophers of education cite Whitehead (1929, 1933), Dewey (1899, 1938, 1985), Bergson (1946), James (1958), Griffin (1988a, 1988b), Griffin, Cobb, Ford, Gunter, and Ochs (1993), W. Doll (1993), and Huebner (1975). Scholars who focus on race and curriculum often reference West (1988, 1990, 2001), Gay (1994, 2000), Fine, Weis, Powell, and Wong (1997); Fine and Weis (2003), Nieto (2004), McCarthy (1990, 1993), Castenell and Pinar (1993), and Watkins (1993, 2001). This scenario is repeated in each of the areas of specialization of the field. An excellent website that was established in 2005 by professor Edmund Short (http://www.edcollege.ucf.edu/esdepart/cirs/main.cfm) can help students and scholars navigate this curriculum literature.

In this milieu, very few scholars have written comprehensive synoptic textbooks that attempt to bridge the gap between the various sectors of the field, much less one that attempts to expose practitioners in the schools to the growing body of scholarship that could support efforts to reconceptualize teaching and learning. However, there are some excellent texts that discuss both the traditional and the reconceptualized field with practical and theoretical scholarship included. These authors have provided penetrating analysis for over three decades: Elliot Eisner (1991, 1997, 2001); William Pinar (1975, 1988a, 1994, 1994, 2003, 2004a); and Henry Giroux (1988, 1991, 1992, 1993, 2005). One of the early synoptic textbooks in the field that includes scholarship from the reconceptualization was William Schubert's (1986) *Curriculum: Perspective, Paradigm, Possibility*. The comprehensive scope of this book has made it an excellent resource for graduate students and curriculum specialists who wish to understand curriculum from various historical perspectives.

Ten other publications particularly influenced the field in the 1990s and expanded the work begun in Schubert's 1986 textbook: Philip Jackson's (1992) edited *Handbook of Research on Curriculum*; William F. Pinar et al.'s (1995) *Understanding Curriculum: An Introduction to the Study of Historical and Contemporary Curriculum Discourses*; Patti Lather's (1991) *Getting Smart: Feminist Research and Pedagogy With/in the Postmodern*; Geneva Gay's (1994) *At the Essence of Learning: Multicultural Education*; James T. Sears and J. Dan Marshall's (1990) edited *Teaching and Thinking about Curriculum: Critical Inquiry*; Madeleine Grumet's (1988b) *Bitter Milk: Women and Teaching*; William B. Stanley's (1992) *Curriculum for Utopia: Social Reconstructionism and Critical Pedagogy in the Postmodern Era*; Janet Miller's (1990) *Creating Spaces and Finding Voices*; and James Henderson and Richard D. Hawthorne's (1995) *Transformative Curriculum Leadership*. Obviously this is only a sample of the research published in the 1990s, but students of curriculum development should be aware that extensive scholarship shaped the field at that time and established many research contexts that continue to thrive today.

How can this third edition of *Curriculum Development in the Postmodern Era* expand on this excellent literature and help to create a dialogue between the traditional and reconceptualized curriculum field, particularly in elementary and secondary schools? Many teachers and scholars are interested in exploring the reconceptualized field, but they often feel compelled to conform to traditional practices in the schools, especially in light of the Bush administration's *No Child Left Behind* (2002) and the Obama administration's *Race to the Top* (2009) legislation and other standardized accountability movements globally. This book provides concise and accessible material on the history of curriculum development, the various dimensions of understanding curriculum development, and the major sectors of the reconceptualized field, each with specific examples applicable to elementary and secondary schools in our postmodern society that will help to make such exploration possible.

The intended audience for the book is international and includes professors in large research universities as well as educators in smaller liberal arts colleges, teachers and curriculum specialists in public elementary and secondary schools, and private school educators who have been exposed to some of the possible applications of postmodern philosophy and the reconceptualization of curriculum studies. While not universally accepted, and in some school districts quite controversial, curricular philosophies such as integrated language arts, interdisciplinary studies, curricular immersion, authentic assessment, peer coaching, team teaching, autobiographical and narrative portfolios, mentorship, critical thinking, aesthetic evaluation, community thematic learning, and nongraded primary schools offer an entry into many of the ideas presented in this text. Educators who have incorporated these philosophies into their pedagogy or who would like to explore similar curricular themes desperately need support to situate these proposals within a wider theoretical framework. The opposition to change and innovation in schools is pervasive, and many curriculum leaders abandon their efforts to reconceptualize teaching and learning for lack of support. Additionally, the misapplication of many philosophies and innovations exacerbates public suspicion of some programs. John Dewey (1938) wrote one of his later books, *Experience and Education*, in part to disassociate himself from the misinterpretation of his educational philosophy by some in the progressive education movement in the 1930s. While the curriculum field of today has many philosophical connections to the progressive education movement, curriculum theorists are aware of the excesses and abuses that led to the repudiation of progressive ideas by 1957 with the launch of the Soviet Sputnik satellite and the conservative political reaction of those like Admiral Hyman Rickover. Curricular programs in the 1950s—for example, the "new math" developed by Max Beberman—exemplified the political and social reaction not only to progressive philosophies but also to the Cold War politics of the time. The same phenomenon is occurring in the new millennium with resistance to postmodernism and liberal arts education.

However, postmodern philosophies and the reconceptualized curriculum field can provide the necessary grounding for reflection, renewal, and innovation to move beyond both progressive and conservative curriculum development models of the past, and this book provides access to these postmodern curriculum theories. However, lest we repeat the same misapplication that John Dewey warned against, we should be aware that a variety of understandings and interpretations exists.

The attempt to make such a vast body of research and writing accessible in a short introductory text without being encyclopedic and superficial is a challenge. Even the references to many authors and texts in this introduction may seem overwhelming to those unfamiliar with the literature. My hope is to provide some markers and references that may point the way toward further reading for beginning students and outline some of the influences on my thinking in order to orient the reader to this text. Additionally, the need to balance direct citations, reflective commentary, references, autobiographical experiences, and practical examples in such a text is crucial. I recognize that this volume cannot be inclusive or comprehensive, and I therefore encourage readers to explore the curriculum literature in more depth. However, I hope that this book will uniquely contribute to a richer and more robust understanding of curriculum development and, as Pinar has challenged us, to a complicated conversation about race, class, gender, sexuality, theology, democracy, ecology, aesthetics, accountability, and pedagogy in the global community. I also hope that my colleagues in the fields of curriculum and instruction and foundations of education will enjoy reading my perspective, for we all recognize the importance of each contribution to the tapestry that has become curriculum development in the postmodern era.

Part I
Curriculum Development as a Field of Study

One
Introduction to Curriculum Development, Reconceptualization, and Postmodernity

There has been a virtual explosion of the use of the word *postmodern* for several decades: deconstructive postmodernism, constructive postmodernism, eliminative postmodernism, cultural postmodernism, postmodern art, postmodern society, postmodern theology, postmodern architecture, and so on. Some scholars, for example Zygmunt Bauman (2000, 2003), have even created hybrid phrases such as *liquid modernity* to express a more fluid understanding. Postmodernism can be understood from at least eleven different perspectives, all of which will be explored further throughout this book:

1. an emerging historical period that transcends the modern industrial and technological age;
2. a contemporary aesthetic style in art and architecture that is eclectic, kaleidoscopic, ironic, and allegorical;
3. a social criticism of unified systems of economic and political organization such as liberalism and communism;
4. a philosophical movement that seeks to expose the internal contradictions of metanarratives by deconstructing modern notions of truth, language, knowledge, and power;
5. a cultural analysis that critiques the negative impact of modern technology on the human psyche and the environment while promoting the construction of a holistic and ecologically sustainable global community;
6. a radical eclecticism (*not* compromise or consensus) and double-voiced discourse that accepts and criticizes at the same time because the past and the future are both honored and subverted, embraced and limited, constructed and deconstructed;

7. a movement that attempts to go beyond the materialist philosophy of modernity;
8. an acknowledgment and celebration of otherness, particularly from racial, gendered, queer, linguistic, and ethnic perspectives;
9. a momentous historical period marked by a revolutionary paradigm change that transcends the basic assumptions, patterns of operation, and cosmology of the previous modern age;
10. an ecological and ecumenical worldview beyond the modern obsession with dominance and control; or, finally,
11. a post-structural movement toward de-centering where there is an absence of anything at the center or any overriding embedded truth at the core, thus necessitating a concentration on the margins and a shift in emphasis to the borders.

Critics often maintain that the term "postmodern" is irrelevant because its meaning is elusive and contradictory, and thus it can be defined in multiple ways to suit the needs of any author. While this is certainly a legitimate critique, the philosophy of modernity espoused by such critics often remains mired in Cartesian binary and dualistic thinking, scientific positivism, and structural explanations of reality. Thus, postmodern eclecticism, inclusiveness, and irony frustrate critics and leads them to conclude that postmodernism is relativism that leads to nihilism. However, one thing is abundantly clear: there is a burgeoning belief in scientific, philosophical, political, artistic, literary, and educational circles that, no matter what name we assign to the current social and cultural condition, a radically new global conception of life on the planet and existence in the cosmos is underway. Charles Jencks (1992) describes this worldview:

> Post-modernism has become more than a social condition and cultural movement, it has become a world view. But its exact nature is strongly contested and this has helped widen the debate to a world audience. The argument has crystallised into two philosophies—what I and many others call Neo- and Post-Modernism—both of which share the notion that the modern world is coming to an end, and that something new must replace it. They differ over whether the previous world view should be taken to an extreme and made radical, or synthesised with other approaches at a higher level …. Not a few people are now suspicious of [this] attendant confusion, or bored with the fashion of the term. Yet I cannot think of an adequate substitute for summarising the possibilities of our condition. (p. 10)

Jencks continues by reminding us that the modem period—from about the 1450s to the 1950s, and from the Renaissance when the West became ascendant to the point where it was incorporated within a larger global culture—is on the wane and must be replaced. Whether the postmodern shift is attached to the date 1875, 1914, 1945, or 1960 (each of these dates has its defenders), Jencks insists that a period "out of the Modern" needs to be defined. He continues: "The forces of the modern movement—modernisation, the condition of modernity, and cultural Modernism—have not ended. Indeed, they are often the goals of the Second and Third Worlds …. But the uncontested dominance of the modern world view has definitely ended" (1992, p. 11). We are witnessing this most dramatically in China and India today. Revolutions in the Middle East in 2011 inspire the awakening of an "Arab Spring." Movements like "Occupy Wall Street" and other international "occupy" groups, as well as the "Tea Party" on the right in the US, indicate frustrations with status quo government and the economic arrangements of the modern era. Whether critics like it or not, society has become a global plurality of competing subcultures and movements where no one ideology and *episteme* (understanding of knowledge) dominates. There is no cultural consensus, and—cultural literacy programs notwithstanding—there is no curriculum development consensus either. Even if the fragmentation of culture and education into many sub-cultures has been exaggerated, the shift to a postmodern worldview is evident.

This postmodern shift involves rethinking some very sacred beliefs and structures that have been firmly entrenched in human consciousness for at least the past 500 years. This is not unlike the trauma that was caused in the 16th century by the discoveries of Copernicus and Galileo. Many astronomers were silenced, imprisoned, or excommunicated because their theories challenged the premodern worldview of the religious and political leaders of European society. (Interestingly, it was not until October 31, 1992—350 years after Galileo's death—that Pope John Paul II gave an address on behalf of the Catholic Church in which he admitted that errors had been made by the theological advisors in the case of Galileo. He declared the case closed, but he did not admit that the Church was wrong to convict Galileo on a charge of heresy because of his belief that the Earth revolves round the sun!) Postmodern social, aesthetic, religious, and scientific visionaries have sometimes met the same fate. For this reason, postmodern thinkers will turn to Thomas Kuhn (1970), in his text *The Structure of Scientific Revolutions*, to support the belief that the global community is entering into a radically new understanding of politics, art, science, theology, economics, psychology, culture, and education. Along with Kuhn, postmodern writers call this change a paradigm shift, because humanity is moving towards a new zone of cognition with an expanded concept of the self-in-relation.

There have been at least two previous paradigm shifts in human history: first, the move from isolated nomadic communities of hunters and gatherers to feudal societies with city-states and agrarian support systems and, second, the move from tribal and feudal societies to a capitalist industrial-based economy relying on scientific technology, unlimited resource consumption, social progress, unrestrained economic growth, and rational thought. The first is called the premodern period or the Neolithic revolution, and is dated from about 1000 BCE (before the common era) to 1450 CE (common era). The second is called the modern period or the Industrial Revolution, and is dated from about 1450 CE to 1960 CE. The Neolithic period is characterized by a slow-changing and reversible concept of time rooted in mythology and an aristocratic culture with integrated artistic styles. The industrial period is characterized by a linear concept of time, called the arrow of time, with a bourgeois mass culture of dominant styles. The postmodern paradigm shift is characterized by fast-changing and cyclical concepts of time, with sundry cultures and many genres of expression, and is sometimes called the global information revolution.

Of course, there have been many movements in the past 500 years that have sought to challenge the dominance of the modern concept of culture, time, and economics.

The Romantics and the Luddites of the 19th century are perhaps typical. However, these movements sought to return to a previous premodern existence. The contemporary postmodern worldview is different because it is more than an anti-modern movement; postmodernism seeks to transcend the ravages of modernity with a radically new concept of society, culture, language, and power. Economic disparities and lack of access to health care, jobs, and basic services figure prominently in discussions of the ravages of modernity and the logic of economic policies. Likewise, postmodern educators are committed to a new concept of curriculum development that will complement the social and cultural milieu of this new era in human history.

While there are many concepts of postmodernism, and thus much confusion about its meaning, there are some common characteristics. David Ray Griffin explains:

> The rapidity with which the term postmodern has become widespread in our time suggests that the antimodern sentiment is more extensive and intense than before, and also that it includes the sense that modernity can be successfully overcome only by going beyond it, not by attempting to return to a premodern form of existence. Insofar as a common element is found in the various ways in which the term is used, *postmodernism* refers to a diffuse sentiment rather than to any set of common doctrines—the sentiment that humanity can and must go beyond the modern. (Griffin et al., 1993, pp. vii–viii)

Humanity must transcend modernity, according to the Center for a Postmodern World (1990), in ways that include the following features: a post-anthropocentric view of living in harmony with nature rather than a separateness from nature that leads to control and exploitation; a post-competitive sense of relationships as cooperative rather than as coercive and individualistic; a post-militaristic belief that conflict can be resolved by the development of the art of peaceful negotiation; a post-patriarchal vision of society in which the age-old religious, social, political, and economic subordination of women will be replaced by a social order based equally on the "feminine" and the "masculine"; a post-Eurocentric view that the values and practices of the European tradition will no longer be assumed to be superior to those of other traditions, or forcibly imposed upon others, combined with a respect for the wisdom embedded in all cultures; a post-scientistic belief that, while the natural sciences possess one important method of scientific investigation, there are also moral, religious, and aesthetic intuitions that contain important truths that must be given a central role in the development of worldviews and public policy; a post-disciplinary concept of research and scholarship with an ecologically interdependent view of the cosmos rather than the mechanistic perspective of a modern engineer controlling the universe; and, finally, a post-nationalistic view in which the individualism of nationalism is transcended and replaced by a planetary consciousness that is concerned first and foremost about the welfare of the earth. In short, the world is an organism rather than a machine, the earth is a home rather than a resource to exploit or a possession to horde, and persons are interdependent and not isolated and independent. This introduction to some of the concepts of postmodernism reveals not only the scope of the issues involved in this movement but also the dramatic paradigmatic shift in thinking that must accompany postmodern consciousness. Therefore, the intensity of resistance to postmodernism should not be surprising.

This description of postmodernism has immense implications for education, particularly the way that curriculum is understood in the new millennium. For this reason, I have selected postmodernism as the theoretical construct from which to explore contemporary curriculum development in this book. Curriculum scholars and teachers have much to gain from engaging in the postmodern dialogue, and they also have much to lose by ignoring postmodern philosophy. This does not mean that we should uncritically accept all projects associated with this philosophy. In fact, postmodernism itself must be deconstructed and problematized. Even an early enthusiast of postmodernism, Richard Rorty, has become a skeptic of the term in an editorial titled "Lofty Ideas That May Be Losing Altitude" (Rorty, 1997). Engaging the conversation does not mean embracing all proposals or all practices. The goal is deeper understanding and fresh new possibilities. This first chapter begins with an exploration of postmodernism in order to frame the discussion of the various approaches to contemporary curriculum development in part II.

The postmodern worldview allows educators to envision an alternative way out of the turmoil of contemporary schooling that too often is characterized by excessive testing and accountability models, violence, bureaucratic gridlock, curricular stagnation, depersonalized evaluation, political conflict, economic crisis, decaying infrastructure, emotional fatigue, and demoralization. This is not to imply that every teacher and every school is paralyzed by such problems. There are many outstanding teachers, programs, and curricular innovations. There are even some exciting and innovative postmodern practices in schools, albeit with resistance from those entrenched in modernity or resistant to change. However, the evidence of crisis is discussed on both the political left and right. The solutions proposed may be dramatically different, but the recognition of the problems faced by educators and schools is well documented. Of course, the struggles are sometimes embellished and distorted for political power or economic gain. Some seek to eliminate public education in favor of vouchers, charter schools, and private education. Thus, their embellishment of school crisis must be understood in the context of efforts to dismantle public education. The positive impact of public and private education cannot be overlooked. The historical contributions to both US and global society by well-educated citizens is impressive. The number of Pulitzer Prize winners, Nobel Laureates, inventors, and scholars produced by US schools and universities is the envy of the world. Quality education has lifted the fortunes of many countries internationally. Emerging democracies and economies globally understand the importance of education as an engine not only for prosperity but, more important, for stability and equality. Thus, the notion of crisis in education needs to be taken seriously but also investigated critically for its political manipulation.

The current moment in US education has been described as a "nightmare" (Pinar, 2004a). Characteristics of this nightmare include the lack of public and democratic conversation about education, education's standardization, and the deprofessionalization of teachers. In the US this is reflected in the report *A Nation at Risk* (1983) and the *Goals 2000: Educate America* Act (1994) and continuing with the *No Child Left Behind* Act (2002) and *Race to the Top* (2009). The deprofessionalization of educators is, of course, a complex phenomenon. Some use teacher turnover rates, attrition rates, stagnant wages, and assaults on teachers to bolster the claim that the profession is in crisis. While the demoralization of teachers may be used as one indicator of the problems we face, the notion of crisis in education is more complex. Perhaps the best book to read on this topic is *The Manufactured Crisis*, by David C. Berliner and Bruce J. Biddle (1995). These authors believe, as do many scholars and researchers, that the characteristic that most impedes school reform and educational equity is the huge and growing rate of poverty. Like Jonathan Kozol (1991, 2005) before them, Berliner and Biddle call for equalization of funding across school districts. Perhaps for the first time on a nationwide basis, US citizens recognized the cruel impact of economic disparity and racism in US society as they were horrified by the images on television of the aftermath of Hurricane Katrina. Schools, of course, mirror social inequities even though the rhetoric of education as the great leveling force attempts to persuade us otherwise.

The same phenomenon is evident internationally. In Chile, for example, there were major nationwide student protests and boycotts in 2006 and 2011. High school students were to some degree successful in calling attention to funding inequities and in their demands to change curriculum policies. An excellent film, titled *Machuca*, about the Chilean educational context during the time of President Salvador Allende's socialist government, just before the 1973 *coup d'état* by General Augusto Pinochet, dramatically investigates the connections between education, poverty, power, and privilege. This 2004 film tells the story of two friends, one of whom, Pedro Machuca, lives in poverty and is integrated into the elite school of his friend Gonzalo Infante. The social integration project is headed by the director of the school, Father McEnroe. The film is dedicated to Father Gerardo Whelan, who from 1969 to 1973 was the director of Colegio Saint George, the private English-language school in Santiago that the film's director attended as a boy. It shows the perspective of Gonzalo Infante, a privileged boy who catches a glimpse of the world of the lower class through Machuca, at a moment when the lower classes are politically mobilized, demanding more rights, and forcing fundamental change. The priest in the film is motivated by the liberation theology movement in South America, a topic that I will discuss in more detail in chapter 4. The educational protests in Chile in 2006 and 2011 can be seen as a continuing struggle for equality and social change. Protests for economic and educational equity are fermenting globally today (O'Malley, 2009).

Postmodern philosophy provides an option for understanding the current protests and debates in education and society. While it is certainly not the only theoretical framework being explored by contemporary social scientists and educational researchers, it is one that is pervasive in the scholarly literature and the one that makes the most sense to me. Additionally, I am convinced that postmodernism offers the best theoretical paradigm for exploring curriculum development. This is especially true when time is viewed as a cyclical process where the past and future inform and enrich the present rather than as a linear arrow where events can be isolated, analyzed, and objectified. I will explore this topic further in chapter 4 when I discuss eschatology. From this perspective, we cannot simply rely on the improvement of past curricular methods in order to solve the complex schooling problems of the new millennium. We must have a more integrated view of time and history. In chapters 2 and 3 an historical analysis of curriculum development will be explored as a prelude to the postmodern reflections in part II. But we are ahead of our discussion. Let us return to our investigation of the relationship between postmodernism and curriculum.

Novelist Walker Percy's classic essay titled "The Delta Factor," from his book *The Message in the Bottle*, is an excellent place to continue our exploration of curriculum and postmodernism. Percy (1954) writes the following:

> What does a man [*sic*] do when he finds himself living after an age has ended and he can no longer understand himself because the theories of man of the former age no longer work and the theories of the new age are not yet known, for not even the name of the new age is known, and so everything is upside down, people feeling bad when they should feel good, good when they should feel bad? What a man does is start afresh as if he were newly come into a new world, which in fact it is; start with what he knows for sure, look at the birds and beasts, and like a visitor from Mars newly landed on earth notice what is different about man. (p. 7)

Postmodern theory in education begins by recognizing, along with Percy, that the teaching profession, elementary and secondary schools, pre-service teacher training programs, and institutions of higher education are all "upside down." The world of schooling is in transition, and people are "feeling bad" about the condition of education. If there is any hope of understanding the confusion and malaise that grip not only society but also our schools, it will be found in the emerging discourses and practices in the curriculum field to be introduced in this book.

Walker Percy was not the only writer in the 1950s to challenge some of the underlying assumptions of modernity. The sense of a paradigm shift in the modern age has its roots prior to contemporary educational and literary criticism in the fields of architecture, art, and philosophy. An excellent introduction can be found in three important books by Charles Jencks (1986, 1992, 2002): *What is Post-Modernism?*, *The Post-Modern Reader*, and *The New Paradigm in Architecture*. (Note that some authors omit a hyphen in postmodern to emphasize the end of modernity; others use the hyphen to emphasize the continuity from the modern to the post-modern or the doubly coded irony of the post-modern movement. In literary criticism the hyphen is omitted to indicate a deconstructive intent. However, the hyphen may represent a variety of symbolic, ironic, and/or playful intentions.) Jencks reviews the historical development of postmodernism, and he dates the beginning of the concept to the Spanish writer Federico de Onis. Additionally, Arnold Toynbee (1947), in his *A Study of History*, established postmodernism as an encompassing category describing a new historical cycle that, he contended, started in 1875 with the end of Western dominance, the decline of individualism, capitalism, and Christianity, and the growing influence of non-Western cultures. Jencks (1986) writes that Toynbee "referred to a pluralism and world culture" (p. 8) in a positive tone but still remained skeptical of the "global village" concept. This skepticism remained with postmodern thinking well into the 1960s. Jencks describes what happened next:

Ihab Hassan became by the mid 1970s the self-proclaimed spokesman for the Postmodern (the term is conventionally elided in literary criticism) and he tied this label to the ideas of experimentalism in the arts and ultra-technology in architecture ... in short, those trends which I, and others, would later characterize as Late Modern. In literature and then in philosophy, because of the writings of Jean-François Lyotard ... and a tendency to elide Deconstruction with the Post-Modern, the term has often kept its association with what Hassan calls "discontinuity, indeterminacy, immanence." Mark C. Taylor's (1984) *ERRING: A Postmodern A/Theology* is characteristic of this genre which springs from Derrida and Deconstruction. There is also a tendency among philosophers to discuss all Post-Positivist thinkers together as Post-Modern whether or not they have anything more in common than a rejection of Modern Logical Positivism. Thus, there are two quite different meanings to the term and a general confusion which is not confined to the public. (1986, pp. 8–9)

While Jencks acknowledges the confusion experienced by the general public as well as academic scholars, he continues to explore his question "What is post-modernism?" It is a question, he believes, that can be answered only by recognizing that postmodernism is in continual growth and movement, and thus no firm definitions are possible—at least until it stops moving. This may be frustrating to educators who want to understand the implications of postmodernism for curriculum development. However, as I often remind graduate students and school district personnel, we have been conditioned to believe that our goals, objectives, lesson plans, and educational outcomes must all be *measurable* and *behaviorally observable* in order to be valid. In my career, I have met very few teachers who actually believe this philosophy of education. However, even the majority who do not ascribe to this educational ideology—rooted in scientific management and the Tylerian Rationale—have allowed themselves to be conditioned to behave as though they do. Postmodernism challenges educators to explore a worldview that envisions schooling through a different lens of indeterminacy, aesthetics, autobiography, intuition, eclecticism, and mystery. In this sense, a concrete definition of postmodern education with universal goals, behavioral objectives, and predetermined outcomes is an oxymoron. As you continue to read about curriculum development it will be less frustrating if you keep this thought in mind.

In postmodernism's infancy in the 1960s in art and culture, postmodernists were radical and critical: pop artists and architects who argued against elitism, urban destruction, bureaucracy, and simplified language. By the 1970s, as these traditions strengthened and evolved, the movement became more conservative and academic. Jencks (1986) describes one of the inevitable results: "Many protagonists of the 1960s, such as Andy Warhol, lost their critical function altogether as they were assimilated into the art market or commercial practice" (p. 9).

In the 1980s and early 1990s postmodernism continued to evolve and began to be accepted by professors, academics, and society at large. Thus, postmodernism ran the risk of becoming part of the modern establishment. Jencks (1986) concludes: "[Postmodernism] became as much part of the establishment as its parent, Modernism, and rival brother, Late-Modernism, and in literary criticism it shifted closer in meaning to the architectural and art traditions" (p. 9).

While the evolution of the term "postmodern" in art, architecture, literary criticism, and philosophy is a fascinating phenomenon, our concern here is primarily with contemporary implications of postmodernism for curriculum development. At the beginning of the new millennium, postmodernism is an integral dimension of many political, social, and educational analyses that have a direct impact on schooling. If we are truly at the end of the modern era, the systems of meaning that have supported curriculum development as a field of study for the past 150 years must all come under rigorous scrutiny. A similar reevaluation is occurring in politics that can be instructive for educators, perhaps even essential if the global community is going to appropriately confront violence, terrorism, corporate dominance, ecological degradation, and imperialist urges for empire. Dana Rapp and I (Slattery & Rapp, 2003) attempt to link the failures in Iraq by George W. Bush and his political architects of this tragic war with a failed vision that could not understand or accept alternative possibilities. Postmodern philosophies provide alternative ways of thinking and imagining that may help humanity move beyond the failure of war and terrorism (Carroll, 2004; Chopra, 2005).

Vaclav Havel (1992), former president of the Czech Republic, explains: "The end of Communism is, first and foremost, a message to the human race [that] a major era in human history [has come] to an end. It has brought an end not just to the 19th and 20th centuries, but to the modern age as a whole" (p. E15). Havel explains further that the modern era has been dominated by the belief that the world is a wholly knowable system governed by a finite number of universal laws that humans can comprehend by rigorous analysis and rationally direct for the personal benefit of men and women. The modern era, from the Renaissance to the Enlightenment to socialism, from positivism to scientism, from the Industrial Revolution to the information revolution, has been characterized by rational, structural thinking. Communism, for Havel, was the perverse extreme of this trend because it attempted to organize all of life according to a single model and to subject people to central planning and control regardless of whether this was life affirming. (The parallel to modern curriculum development in *No Child Left Behind* and other accountability models is unmistakable!) Havel (1992) concludes:

> The fall of Communism can be regarded as a sign that modern thought—based on the premise that the world is objectively knowable, and that knowledge so obtained can be absolutely generated—has come to a final crisis .... It is a signal that the era of arrogant, absolutist reason is drawing to a close ... and that we have to see the pluralism of the world, and not bind it by seeking common denominators or reducing everything to a single common equation .... Sooner or later, politics will be faced with the task of finding a new, postmodern face. (p. E15)

The postmodern political clarion call of Vaclav Havel, the banished poet and playwright turned president, is also reflected in the transformation in the Middle East in 2011 in what is known as the Arab Spring. These political upheavals of the past twenty years also beckon educators in the field of curriculum theory to envision a new worldview to complement the postmodern changes evident in the world. Thus, understanding curriculum in light of the fall of communism, the Arab Spring, and other contemporary social and political events is not irrelevant, it is essential. Political studies have become central to curriculum studies in the postmodern era. Postmodern curriculum development recognizes the necessity of incorporating a new consciousness that transcends modern categories in metaphysics, epistemology, and axiology. A reconceptualization of this classical philosophical trinity must emerge that understands existence, knowledge, and ethics in the context of postmodern political, cultural, and social upheaval. Perhaps the end of communism and the beginning of an Arab Spring in the political realm may foretell an end to curriculum development as we have known it for so many decades. The end of the modern era is not simply a vague theoretical construct; it is a challenge to all fields of study—indeed the entire global community—to reconceptualize their understanding of the deepest meaning of life in contemporary society. This is the challenge of the post-modern era for educators and curriculum specialists today.

While there are many outstanding texts available that explore the postmodern challenge to reconceptualize curriculum development, the beginning student of postmodernism should be careful to identify an author's ideological perspective as described at the beginning of this chapter (i.e., historical, aesthetic, political, philosophical, theological, cultural, or a combination of two or more of these emphases). Understanding an author's ideological orientation can prevent a single concept of curriculum from becoming a new positivistic rationale, behavioral goal, or ultramodern master narrative. Postmodernism promotes eclecticism rather than any comprehensive systems of explanation and universal laws.

A book that has influenced many scholars for the past twenty years is William E. Doll, Jr.'s *A Post-Modern Perspective on Curriculum*, in which he presents a post-modern paradigm shift in the understanding of curriculum development. He investigates an open systems cosmology and proposes an educational matrix intended to rival the closed system of 17th-century notions of a stable universe. Doll contends that the stable universe became the philosophical foundation of modernity as well as the scientific principle on which the American curriculum, epitomized in Tyler's Rationale and Taylor's scientific management, was developed. His postmodern educational vision flows from his analysis and "reinterpretation" (1993, p. 13) of Jean Piaget and living systems, Ilya Prigogine and chaotic order, Bruner and the cognitive revolution, and John Dewey and Alfred North Whitehead and process thought. He juxtaposes Dewey and Whitehead from the perspective of poststructuralism and hermeneutics in order to negotiate passages "between Whiteheadian process thought and deconstructive post-structural thought" (p. xiii). Doll's educational matrix describes a process of curriculum experience rooted in "richness, recursion, relations, and rigor" (p. 174) whose order is dependent upon disequilibrium, indeterminacy, lived experience, and chaos rather than a rigid structuralism. This is the major distinction between his postmodern curriculum and other poststructural, feminist, political, and deconstructionist postmodernisms that we will investigate in more detail in chapters 6, 7, and 9.

Central to Doll's postmodern perspective on curriculum is his belief that, just as it led society into the modern age, physics—particularly as evidenced in chaos theory—will lead society out of modernity and into postmodernism. However, the humanities will also join science in the postmodern process. A literal centerpiece of Doll's book is a color plate illustrating the Lorenz attractor, originally used to show unpredictability in long-term weather patterns. This geometric construct of a chaotic process brings into sharp focus the author's view that "self-organization becomes the pivotal focus around which open systems work" (1993, p. 98). In postmodern education the curriculum itself may derive whatever form and substance it will ultimately possess from the referred-to *crossing over* points on attractors. Curriculum must not be forced to these central positions lest we lose the necessary meanderings inherent in the process. The modernist might contend that the postmodern is taking a circuitous route when the shortest distance between two points is the straight line. In postmodernism, this seemingly divergent path is simply one of many acceptable routes where even minuscule changes that are brought about in an open-ended process "will grow into major transformations over time" (p. 98). In the research of contemporary curriculum theorists working within such a context, one comes to feel that the free-form processive dance of postmodernism is indeed preferable to the lock-step linear model of modernity.

While Doll attempts to forge a path between the constructive and deconstructive postmodern theories, others are adamant in their commitment to one or the other of these two perspectives. Patti Lather (1991), in her important and widely cited text *Getting Smart: Feminist Research and Pedagogy With/in the Postmodern*, is perhaps typical of curriculum theorists who support deconstruction, a postmodern philosophy that explores the contradictions within modern paradigms and symbols (especially language) for the purpose of exposing the injustices that emerge from the modern relationship between power and language. Lather contends that society is in the midst of a shift away from the concept of an objective, knowable, factual world "out there" toward a concept of constructed worlds where knowledge is contested and partial. Lather agrees with Michel Foucault (1972a, 1980), who wrote that knowledge is an "effect of power" (cited in Lather, 1991, p. 86) and shaped by the interplay of language, power, and meaning. Lather uses feminist research in the postmodern tradition to promote self-understanding and self-determination so that an emancipatory concept of language and power will emerge in education. Her book exposes the difficulty of building a liberatory curriculum within existing institutions for those who are involved in unequal power relations, especially women.

An example of Lather's deconstructive approach to postmodernism is found in her critique of modernity. She writes:

> To position oneself in the twilight of modernity is to foreground the underside of its faith in rationality, science, and the human will to change and master: Auschwitz, Hiroshima, My Lai, Three Mile Island, Chernobyl. It is not that the dreams of modernity are unworthy; it is what they render absent and their conflictual and confusing outcomes that underscore the limits of reason and the obsolescence of modernist categories and institutions. Not only positivisms,

but also existentialisms, phenomenologies, critical theories: all seem exhausted, rife with subject-object dualisms ... the lust for certainty .... All seem no longer capable of giving meaning and direction to current conditions. The exhaustion of the paradigms of modernity creates an affective space where we feel that we cannot continue as we are. The modernist project of control through knowledge has imploded, collapsed inward, as the boundaries between ideology and science disintegrate. (1991, p. 88)

The deconstruction of modernity and its system of power, language, and meaning becomes the starting point for Lather in her attempt to build an empowering approach to the generation of knowledge for both researchers and classroom teachers. She envisions a democratized process of inquiry characterized by negotiation, collaboration, and reciprocity where knowledge is constructed from self-understanding. In this sense, curriculum development in the postmodern era begins with the deconstruction of master narratives that impose knowledge through unequal power relations where students must be subordinate and submissive to teachers, and then moves to the emancipation of both teachers and students who have been disempowered by this structure. Thus, Lather's understanding of postmodernism emphasizes the political and philosophical perspective. Many feminists have followed her lead over the past twenty years.

In contrast to Lather's political and deconstructive emphasis, David Ray Griffin and his colleagues (1993) promote a constructive postmodernism in *Founders of Constructive Postmodern Philosophy*. For Griffin and his co-authors, the postmodernism of political and feminist writers who have been inspired by Martin Heidegger, Jacques Derrida, and Michel Foucault is really an anti-worldview because it deconstructs and eliminates the elements necessary for a worldview, such as God, self, purpose, meaning, and truth as correspondence. Griffin admits that the ethical concerns of deconstructionists to forestall totalitarian systems and unequal power relations are laudable. However, he joins the critics of some postmodern theories and sees the potential result of deconstruction as relativism and nihilism. Griffin even charges that deconstructionism can be called ultramodernism because its eliminations result from carrying modern premises to their logical conclusion. (Of course, Lather and other feminist researchers with political and deconstructionist emphasis would argue that Griffin is an ultramodernist because he attempts to reconstruct a worldview that includes modernist categories such as *Truth* and *God*.)

Griffin seeks to overcome the modern worldview not by eliminating the possibility of worldviews, but by constructing a postmodern worldview through a revision of modern premises and traditional concepts. He writes,

This constructive or revisionary postmodernism involves a new unity of scientific [in contrast to scientism], ethical, aesthetic, and religious intuitions. It rejects not science as such but only that scientism in which the data of the modern natural sciences are also allowed to contribute to the construction of our worldview. (Griffin et al., 1993, p. viii)

In this respect, postmodernism is seen as a constructive social paradigm. It seeks to integrate the best features of premodern rural, agrarian societies (such as spirituality, cosmology, family/tribal community values) with the best features of the modern urban, technological societies (such as advances in preventative health care, global communication, and transportation) in order to construct a more balanced and ecologically sustainable global community. Constructive postmodernism recognizes that the world community cannot return to a premodern existence and that the negative features of the modern world (such as destruction of the ecosphere, spiritual bankruptcy, terrorism, greed, war, and the depletion of resources) threaten to destroy civilization.

There are many debates about the meaning of postmodernism in educational research that expand on the distinctions made by Lather and Griffin above. Further insights can be found by contrasting the writing of Henry A. Giroux and Chet A. Bowers. Three important books by Giroux examine the cultural dimensions of postmodern theory: *Postmodernism, Feminism, and Cultural Politics: Redrawing Educational Boundaries* (1991); *Border Crossings: Cultural Workers and the Politics of Education* (1992); and *Against the New Authoritarianism: Politics After Abu Ghraib* (2005). Chet A. Bowers takes a different approach in which he emphasizes ecological issues and eco-justice: *Elements of a Post-Liberal Theory of Education* (1987); *Education, Cultural Myths, and the Ecological Crisis* (1993); and *Educating for Eco-Justice and Community* (2001). Both of these prominent professors have written texts that propose distinct variations on the postmodern curriculum dialogue, thus reinforcing the contention that there is no unified conception of the postmodern. Giroux employs the poststructural term *border crossings* to emphasize the importance of political solidarity between critical theory, feminist thought, multiculturalism, and anti-racist theory. Giroux exposes the porous nature of the modern boundaries that have attempted to compartmentalize knowledge and colonize cultures. In curriculum theory, crossing the border necessitates a commitment to postmodern democratic reform where subject-area disciplinary boundaries are traversed. Border crossings allow educators to reject modern academic privilege in favor of honest intellectual exchanges committed to justice and liberation. Giroux's inclusive political theory affirms the democratic, eclectic, and empowerment dimensions of postmodern thought. His most recent work exposes the horrific results of authoritarianism and militarism in the US, the UK, and other nations in a climate of violence, war, corporate economic dominance, dislocation and exploitation of workers, environmental racism, and terrorism. We see these issues at the forefront of international protests and policy debates today.

Like Giroux, Chet Bowers promotes interconnectedness across boundaries. Bowers (1993) writes: "Classroom activities [must] foster a sense of connectedness across generations and between human and other members of the biotic community. Both are required as part of a change in consciousness if we are to achieve genuine sustainability" (p. 7). However, Bowers frames the postmodern educational discussions around ecological concerns rather than political solutions. He questions whether the political process will be effective in getting people to move beyond the modernist paradigm. In his recent writings, Bowers accuses critical theorists of contributing to globalization and industrial degradation of the planet by using a neo-Marxist analysis rooted in revolution. He explains his position in "How Peter McLaren and Donna Houston and Other 'Green' Marxists Contribute to the Globalization of the West's Industrial Culture" (2005). Houston and McLaren (2005) respond to Bowers:

> At the end of the day ... we may have found some common ground with Bowers if not for his insistence on boiling everything down to a linguistic struggle over whether the word *transform* or the word *conserve* is the most appropriate political term. After all, although we take his point that the word *transform* is not always applicable to all possible discussions about education or the environment, surely Bowers must also acknowledge that neither is the word *conserve* .... Collective community projects that are concerned with conserving, reclaiming, restoring, and revitalizing degraded ecological commons often constructed their labor as transformative politics. (p. 204)

The ongoing debates between Bowers and Houston and McLaren are just one example of the intense investigations into issues such as ecology, politics, and justice as they relate to education. Vibrant discussions are an important part of the curriculum field, and often these discussions lead us to fresh insights and robust educational proposals. Sometimes, however, the debates degenerate into personality or territorial clashes. Students of curriculum development should read and study these debates and judge for themselves the ways in which curriculum studies can appropriately address the challenging issues confronting humanity in the postmodern era. The exciting prospect, for me, is that these discussions and debates are taking place in the journals and classrooms in the curriculum field. It is an important time to study curriculum development and curriculum theory.

Another debate that is worth examining is the ongoing struggle to delineate the purpose of curriculum studies by William Pinar, William Wraga, and James Henderson. In a series of articles in *Educational Researcher*, these scholars debated the connection between curriculum theory and school practice. For decades there have been discussions about the assumed theory and practice split in education. I believe that it is a false dichotomy to assume that theory and practice do not inform each other. In fact, postmodern theory has become a vehicle to help me understand the rich and dynamic relationship between theory and practice. Scholarship informs my teaching and writing, and my teaching and writing are the substance of my scholarship. I experience them as a seamless and mutually supportive web of experiences. However, others may not see it this way.

Wraga (1999) contends that many contemporary curriculum professors "were confidently absorbed in their theoretical pursuits while far removed from the constituents they fancied serving. Their work became academic in a narrow sense" (p. 5). As the curriculum field was reconceptualized in the 1980s and 1990s, Wraga contends that curriculum studies sought to distance theory far from practice in the following ways: the characterization of the *reconceptualization* of the curriculum field as a shift from a focus on curriculum development to a focus on heightened curriculum understanding; a repudiation of the traditional field and its alliance with a commitment to practitioners; and the acceptance of non-school phenomena as the subject of inquiry. Wraga (1999) concludes, "In the Reconceptualized curriculum theory one is unencumbered from contemplating school problems" (p. 5).

I listen to Wraga's critique carefully, but it does not resonate with me. I have three children who have attended public schools and public universities. I have two grand-children and many nieces, nephews, and neighbors, and, like the professors I work with, I am very concerned about their health, education, and welfare. My workshops and guest lectures in public and private schools are well received. The reconceptualization of curriculum studies intuitively makes sense to teachers and administrators. They are energized and appreciative. In fact, I believe that the scholarship of the reconceptual-ization of curriculum studies—which this book documents and advances—from the 1970s to the present—more so than the politically, culturally, and theologically detached technical/rational schooling programs of the traditional approaches to curriculum development in the middle of the 20th century and the accountability models today—actually provides greater support to teachers and school curriculum for my children, grandchildren, neighbors, and fellow citizens. As you read this book and explore topics from a postmodern and reconceptualized perspective, see if you agree. You be the judge.

William Pinar (1999) responded directly to Wraga's critique by pointing out the gendered, political, and economic dimensions of our pedagogical aspirations in the democratic process, and he writes:

> In abbreviated form, here are the facts: Schools are no longer under the juris-diction (it was probably always more professional than legal) of curriculum theorists. Multiple stakeholders (not the least among them the textbook pub-lishers) have created something that may look like curriculum consensus but it is more like curriculum gridlock. Genuine (not just rhetorical) reforms—let alone revolutions, such as suggested by the Progressive Educational Association's *Eight Year Study*—are certainly unlikely to be led by university-based curricu-lum scholars and researchers. This is not to say that we in the university have lost interest in teachers or in schools or that we have been seduced by subjects more interesting and exciting (although some students of cultural studies might say that). The simple—if for some, unassimilable—truth is that our influence has decreased over the past 30 years. (p. 14)

My approach to this debate is to remind my students—as I reminded you in the introduction of this book—that I can teach you my philosophy, but you will have to listen to your own voice and implement your own curriculum program. In fact, I believe that any author, professor, or program that offers students an uncritical master plan for curriculum development is merely offering a recipe for disaster. But over and over again we allow ourselves to be deceived by promises of school reform and edu-cational excellence. Below is an example of how one of my students took up this challenge. This example, I believe, will help to illustrate the postmodern and reconcep-tualized emphasis on autobiography and context in curriculum studies.

A graduate student in one of my classes who studied the concepts of reconceptualized curriculum appreciated this perspective, but she could not imagine implementing them in her fourth grade classroom. Her principal demanded daily lesson plans with specific outcomes outlined in the district curriculum guide. The district administered national and state accountability tests in math, reading, science, and language arts. The teacher's tenure depended on how well her students performed on these tests, and her pay scale followed a merit system that rewarded compliance with the prescribed program. She resented the environment the system created, but she saw no realistic chance to deviate. Additionally, her students' behavior was so disruptive and their participation so sporadic that she doubted they would accept a contextual and experiential curriculum. In short, she considered postmodern curriculum philosophy too idealistic and impractical. But for her final course project she explored the possibilities. Since the district did not test the social studies curriculum, and since most teachers skipped the 30-minute social studies block to spend more time on the *important* subjects that would be tested, she decided to experiment with her relatively safe social studies curriculum. For her course project, she videotaped her lessons for a two-week unit on deserts.

Instead of writing lesson plans that followed the textbook script with specific objectives and evaluation requirements, she introduced the lesson with this simple statement: "Today we begin our next unit in social studies. Our topic is deserts." Disinterested and distracted faces could be seen in the video. A few students prepared to take notes. Most sat silently waiting for instructions. Then she dropped her bombshell: "I do not know very much about deserts. I have never been to a desert. We are going to have to figure out how to learn about deserts together." Immediately, one student raised his hand. "I went to a desert in California last summer." He described his trip enthusiastically, but he struggled to remember the name of the desert. Another student suggested that they look at a map and find its name. The class moved to the map. Another student pointed to Africa and said that her father once went hunting on a safari. "What's a safari?" another student asked. The class consulted to the dictionary to find the answer. Over the next few days, the students decided to divide themselves into groups to investigate deserts. One group selected animals of the deserts. They made a small-scale model of a desert and a safari. Another group made maps of the various deserts of the world. Other groups investigated plant life, human habitation, and survival. One group staged a play set in a desert.

This teacher reported to her curriculum development class that she had never seen such enthusiasm for a unit of study in her career. Students who formerly presented severe behavior problems emerged as group leaders. Another group of students went to the library every day at recess to find more information about their topic. The teacher became convinced of the power of the postmodern ideas and reconceptualized curriculum when she completed this experimental project. The maps and models of deserts were displayed in the corridor and caught the attention of other teachers. She began to look for ways to resist the steady dose of the accountability approach to curriculum and instruction in the future. Is this an example of postmodern curriculum or the reconceptualization of curriculum studies? Maybe. Does her experiment represent a postmodern shift or just good pedagogy? Or both? I do not know. However, it was one teacher's attempt at implementing the philosophy she had studied in her graduate class on curriculum development in the postmodern era. She began to shift her view of curriculum as she deconstructed modern accountability methods in her school district. This is certainly a concrete example of connecting theory and practice in a seamless web of inquiry.

One book that my graduate students have found to be most instructive in the post-modern debates is Donald Oliver and Kathleen Gershman's *Education, Modernity, and Fractured Meaning: Toward a Process Theory of Teaching and Learning* (1989). Oliver and Gershman present a process vision of postmodern curriculum as ontological knowing: "We distinguish between two kinds of knowing: technical knowing and ontological knowing. Technical knowing refers to adaptive, publicly transferable information and skills; ontological knowing refers to a more diffuse apprehension of reality, in the nature of liturgical or artistic engagement" (1989, p. 3). They emphasize the common belief of many researchers that, in order for ontological knowing to become part of the curriculum, postmodern metaphors must evolve to challenge and transform the machine metaphor of modernity. Ontological knowing requires metaphors of "organic life and transcendent dance" (p. 3), so that we can come to know with our whole bodies as we move from imagination and intention to critical self-definition, to satisfaction, and finally to perishing and new being. Oliver and Gershman's book contains elements of Lather's self-understanding, Griffin's process philosophy, Giroux's border crossings, and Bowers' ecological sustainability. However, their approach to curriculum development moves beyond the distinction between constructive and deconstructive postmodernism to an ontological and cosmological process curriculum that may offer a possible reconciliation of various antagonistic factions in curriculum studies in the postmodern era.

And finally, before we get too comfortable trying to locate ourselves in the curriculum studies debates of the past thirty years, it is important to listen to the critics who remind us that, historically, it is most often (but not exclusively) White males who lead the debates. As bell hooks (2005) succinctly cautions: "Postmodern theory that is not seeking to simply appropriate the experience of 'otherness' in order to enhance its discourse or to be radically chic should not separate the 'politics of difference' from the politics of racism." We must deconstruct race and gender privilege in the academy and in society. Elizabeth Ellsworth did this in a dramatic way when she published a groundbreaking and widely cited article in the *Harvard Educational Review* titled "Why Doesn't This Feel Empowering? Working through the repressive myths of critical pedagogy" (1989). Ellsworth reflects on her own role as a White middle-class woman and professor engaged with a diverse group of students developing an anti-racist philosophy. In her article she critiques the utopian, rationalist, and sexist assumptions of critical theory being undertaken mostly by White males. She concludes her article with this important comment from one of her graduate students:

> If you can talk to me in ways that show you understand that your knowledge of me, the world, and "the Right thing to do" will always be partial, interested, and potentially oppressive to others, and if I can do the same, then we can work together on shaping and reshaping alliances for constructing circumstances in which students of difference can thrive. (1989, p. 324)

Certainly there are many educators and scholars who identify as a feminist, critical theorist, curriculum theorist, anti-racist theorist, queer theorist, poststructuralist, or postmodernist who are committed to building alliances for justice and constructing circumstances in which diverse human beings can thrive. However, hooks and Ellsworth both remind us of the deeply entrenched and sedimented structures that work against such alliances. I agree that we must foreground racism, sexism, hetero-sexism, classism, ableism, and other structural barriers in society and in our own thinking that reduce our rhetoric about "empowerment" or "critical reflection" to hollow and vacuous concepts. In other words, we must deconstruct our own complicity in oppression and recognize that our knowledge is partial and evolving. We must open up new curriculum spaces.

One of the leading contemporary curriculum scholars who is working in this vein is Lisa J. Cary, formerly at the University of Texas at Austin, and now working at Murdoch University in her native Australia. Her book *Curriculum Spaces: Discourse, Postmodern Theory and Educational Research* is an attempt to understand how exclusion works. It addresses the ways in which some bodies, actions, beliefs, and experiences are legitimized as normal and acceptable, while others are abnormal, deviant, and unacceptable. Cary writes:

> The study of curriculum issues ... calls for an understanding at all times that curriculum is more than a text book, more than a classroom, and more than teachers and students. It is all of the social influences, populist crises, military campaigns, and historical moments that shape our lives—when we are in school and in our lives beyond the classroom. Historically, moves and counter-moves to define curriculum have occurred within highly contested terrain. The position taken in this book is a move to study curriculum as a discursively produced historically, socially, politically and economically inscribed epistemological space. Therefore, I put forward this approach as one way to understand how we know what we know. It is an epistemological approach to study the knowing subject and researcher positionality. This book presents a three pronged approach—bringing together curriculum theory, educational research theory and exemplars of research projects. (2006, pp. xi–xii)

One method that I use to address the issues of difference and diversity raised by Ellsworth and Cary involves community field experiences. I recall a course in multicultural education that I taught at Ashland University several years ago at their university center in Cleveland. At the first class session, I met with the students in a typical classroom on a community college campus. There were twelve graduate students with an equal mix of men and women, White students and students of color, and rural and urban teachers. As we got to know each other, students began to share their diverse religions, ethnicities, and sexual orientations. It was truly a multicultural group.

At the first class session, and before we introduced ourselves, I asked the students to name locations in the greater Cleveland area that they were afraid to visit or where they would be uncomfortable. Several suburban White teachers said that they never go to University Circle in central Cleveland. I asked why. They mentioned the race riots in 1969 (over thirty years in the past) and the news reports of poverty and crime (read "Black" people). They did not mention the world-class art museums or the Cleveland Orchestra. One African-American woman said that she never goes to Little Italy at Murray Hill. I asked why. She began to cry as she told the story of her brother's murder in this Italian neighborhood twenty years previously. She did not mention the excellent restaurants or art galleries. Other students mentioned the mosque in Parma, gay bars downtown, and so forth. I wrote each response on the board. It did not take long to identify twenty "dangerous" or "uncomfortable" places in Cleveland.

My next statement unsettled the students. I told them that we would not be meeting in the university classroom for the rest of the semester. Rather, we would discuss the books and readings each week while we visited the twenty dangerous places listed on the board. I offered one escape clause. I said that anyone in the class could veto any of the locations if they found it too difficult. There were a few initial vetoes on the first night, but, as the semester proceeded, we ended up going to all twenty locations. The White women insisted on bringing their husbands along to University Circle, and the African-American woman who lost her brother insisted on bringing her husband to Little Italy. We welcomed the spouses into our class. Amazing things happened on each field experience—too many to enumerate.

However, here are a few highlights. The White students pleaded with the African-American students to trust them and enjoy our class meeting at an Italian restaurant. However, they were shocked and appalled by the lack of service and rude comments directed at our multicultural group in the all-White restaurant. The gay and lesbian students promised the heterosexual students that they would be comfortable for our class meeting in the gay bar. The heterosexual students were shocked by the relaxed and friendly atmosphere and the number of straight people they met in the gay bar (especially the straight women who hang out in gay bars to avoid being "hit on" by men in the straight bars). They also had their stereotypes about promiscuity and nudity shattered. One closeted gay student decided to come out to the class. Our visit to the mosque in the Cleveland suburb of Parma remains significant in my memory. Shortly after our very informative tour and warm welcome by the imam, this mosque was the first one attacked by a young White man, who rammed his car into the front doors after the terrorist attack in 2001.

I agree with Lisa Cary that we must investigate new curriculum spaces or, as she writes, research that helps us to understand how we know what we know. This is an epistemological question as well as a curriculum question. In my classes we always read challenging texts and write scholarly papers. We engage in lively discussions on the themes for the course. But we do all of this in diverse spaces so that the curriculum materials and syllabus themes intersect with the local community, social and political issues, and multicultural experiences. These curriculum experiences are not arranged simply for entertainment or novelty. Rather, they are purposely designed to elicit epistemological reflection on the meaning of texts and ideas that emerge in the course. Epistemological experiences can be created in any course in any discipline. Topics and themes will be unique to each class, and appropriate experiences will be created to connect to the subject matter of the class in ways that lead to growth. Some teachers might use the excuse of time, money, transportation, university or school district rules, legal liability, or availability of resources to avoid this approach to curriculum spaces. But there is no legitimate excuse. Outdoor spaces on the campus, invited speakers, documentary films, or autobiographical reflection are all capable of contributing to curriculum spaces. Elizabeth Ellsworth (2005) investigates how this process functions in museums and the media in her book *Places of Learning: Media, Architecture, Pedagogy*. In their recent books, Ellsworth and Cary provide fresh new scholarship to help us understand the epistemological places and spaces of curriculum.

In my 35 years of teaching, I have never allowed institutional obstacles to prevent me from creating aesthetic experiences and epistemological curriculum spaces that advance robust understandings for justice, compassion, and ecological sustainability in connection to the course themes. Curriculum development in the postmodern era demands that we find a way around the hegemonic forces and institutional obstacles that limit our knowledge, reinforce our prejudices, and disconnect us from the global community. Lisa Cary (2006) offers this important conclusion:

> This is a call for the study of how we are normalized, how we are embedded within total institutions and how we engage in and negotiate the production of legitimate knowledge. This embeddedness excludes certain ways of being and erases the bodies of those students, teachers, parents, custodians and others who are considered deviant, or outside the norm. Pregnant teens, dropouts, children of color, gay and lesbian teachers and students, female juvenile offenders, charter schools, and alien academics. But it is also important to reveal the discourses themselves and how this knowing impacts the lives and possibilities of being for those we "know." (p. 3)

While there are many other perspectives and several important books that could be investigated in this introduction to the concept of postmodernism and curriculum development, it is not necessary to be comprehensive at this time. Postmodernism will frame our discussion of curriculum development throughout this book, and each of the perspectives introduced here will be included in further discussions in part II. Hopefully, this introduction to the complex philosophical discussions on postmodernism will provide a framework within which to evaluate a robust vision of curriculum development for the postmodern era. Postmodernism is an emerging concept that elicits much debate in political, religious, social, literary, artistic, and educational circles. Although the evolution of its meaning may be an obstacle for some readers, I believe that the possibility of a renewed understanding of curriculum development that will have a positive impact on scholars, teachers, and students will make the effort to explore these emerging concepts worthwhile.

two
Historical Perspectives on Curriculum as a Field of Study

Chapter 1 introduced the concept of historical interpretation from two different perspectives: a progressive series of distinctly separate and chronological events on a linear time line or a processive experience of interrelated occasions with the past and future embedded in the existential present reality. The first perspective is committed to the objective analysis and categorization of discrete parcels of information. These events become quantifiable objects of study. In this case, history attempts to logically explain events according to a grand narrative of human progress through the centuries. On the other hand, the second perspective is committed to ongoing reinterpretation, the primacy of subjective experience, the indissolubility of meaning and context, the importance of social context in the construction of knowledge, and the interdependence of events within time and place. In short, history can be understood either as events separated by time and space or as the integral interrelationship of events unified with(in) time and space. Scholars who embrace logical positivism and analytic philosophy are generally committed to the first perspective. Either these philosophies tend to ignore historical analysis because of the subjectivity inherent in the interconnectedness of contextual realities, or they objectify and segment history in order to control reality so that all events will conform within the paradigm of modernity.

Curriculum scholars in the postmodern era will challenge the assumption that historical interpretation must be directed toward the validation of the knowledge and values of the dominant culture or modern paradigm. Postmodernism celebrates the eclectic, innovative, revisionist, ironic, and subjective dimensions of historical interpretation. This does not mean, as critics claim, that we have come to the end of history. Rather we have come to the end of a unified and singular interpretation of history with a master narrative composed and imposed by the dominant power brokers on Wall Street, in corporations, media, sports, political parties, religions, and the military. When a singular historical view dominates and the cultural context is controlled by such elites, this results in hegemony. Hegemony is described by Peter McLaren (1998) succinctly:

> Hegemony refers to the maintenance of domination not by sheer exercise of force, but primarily through consensual social practices, social forms, and social structures produced in specific sites such as the church, the state, the school, the mass media, the political system, and the family. By social practices, I refer to what people say or do. Social forms refer to the principles that provide and give legitimacy to specific social practices .... Hegemony is the struggle in which the powerful win the consent of those who are oppressed, with the oppressed unknowingly participating in their own oppression .... Hegemony is not a process of active domination as much as an active structuring of the culture and experiences of the subordinate class by the dominant class .... It is an image in which the values and beliefs of the dominant class appear so correct that to reject them would be unnatural, a violation of common sense. (pp. 173–175).

Hegemony in this sense is indoctrination and manipulation, and it can affect classrooms when a teacher does not encourage or allow students to question the prevailing values, attitudes, historical interpretations, and social practices in a sustained and critical manner. It happens when educators either ignore or participate in taunts against religious and ethnic minority students, gay and lesbian students, or other marginalized students. Hegemony insures that minority and marginalized persons remain silent and silenced by coercion and domination. Abuse, embezzlement, and fraud go unchecked. Hegemony operates to organize all school experiences around one activity, for example football in many schools. I played football as a kid, and I am an avid LSU fan. I go to games in Tiger Stadium and enjoy watching college football on TV, but I also recognize the destructive consequences when hegemonic structures dominate. The rape and abuse of children in the football locker room and the cover-up at Penn State University in 2011 is but one of many tragedies related to football that occur in hegemonic contexts. At Penn State, the power of institutional protection and the hegemony of the football program allowed the abuse of children to be ignored and minimized for years. Let's consider football as an example of the condition of hegemony in schools, not because football is the most egregious, but because it serves as a familiar example that educators understand.

When class schedules, bulletin boards, announcements, dress codes, dances, homecomings, rewards, praise, and social standing all revolve around one activity like football, and school leaders do not provide alternate and equitable activities for those who do not participate in the football rituals, then hegemony has the effect of socializing students and organizing the curriculum around football. One horrific result is the way that young people regulate their bodies in order to conform, please, and perform. Consider the following examples: athletes who use performance-enhancing drugs (sometimes with the support and encouragement of coaches who value winning over health and safety); young women who, in an attempt to gain popularity or impress a football player, starve their bodies and become anorexic. As a high school principal,

I discovered that young women were pressured to give their bodies for sex to football players in order, they believed, to gain votes for homecoming queen or some other favor. Young men and women regularly forsake interests in preferred clubs and activities in order to conform to school norms, social pressure, or parental pressure. Football is perceived as a vehicle for acceptance or popularity. This is a curriculum issue, and educators must be aware of the ways in which they contribute to this problem and learn how to break the cycles of drug abuse, eating disorders, sexual abuse, emotional disorders, bullying, and dysfunctional social conformity that result from hegemonic structures.

Football, of course, provides a typical example, but it is certainly not the only one. In order to help students understand this phenomenon, I show two films about high school football: *Remember the Titans* and *Friday Night Lights*. The first film is a positive example of how a coach breaks the barriers of racism that prevent Black and White football players from working together. The second film is a tragic example of how coaches, parents, and administrators in a Texas community obsessed by football abuse students in order to win games. Both of these excellent films demonstrate the impact of hegemony in high schools. Additionally, the book *Friday Night Lights: A Town, a Team, and a Dream* (Bissinger, 1991) is an excellent ethnography for qualitative researchers and graduate students to study. After viewing these films, I show two more important films from the Media Education Foundation of Northampton, Massachusetts: *Killing us Softly* with Jean Kilbourne (Jhally, 1999), a film which addresses gender representations in advertising and how these images contribute to eating disorders and the degradation of women; *Wrestling With Manhood: Boys, Bullying, & Battering* (Jhally, 2003), a film which addresses gender representations in professional wrestling, video games, and other cultural artifacts and how these images contribute to the pervasive bullying, battering, and dysfunctional behavior by young males in schools and society. It is, after all, young men who are committing the vast majority of rapes and school shootings. These films remind us that there are important social and cultural phenomena—many of them destructive—produced by gender socialization and cultural hegemony.

Let me reiterate. I am not claiming that football, advertising, and professional wrestling are the direct cause of bullying, school shootings, anorexia, date rape, violence, and child abuse. I am not even trying to make the case that all sports and media are destructive. My children played hockey and soccer, my brother Kevin and I played baseball, and organized sports were incredibly important in our adolescent development and schooling experiences. Coaches and team sports can have a very positive influence on the lives of students. I am contending that the hegemonic dominance of certain cultural activities and rituals contribute to a climate that can foster such abuse and dysfunction. I do not propose the end of football and wrestling or the banning of advertising. Rather, I propose a postmodern deconstruction of all texts (as explained in the introduction of this book) and the affirmation of an eclectic array of alternatives in schools and classrooms so that the negative impact of hegemony can be overcome.

Listen to the story of one young man recounting his experiences with bullying, sexuality, and football in middle school. Andy Thorson is now a doctoral student at Texas A&M University. His personal experiences are most instructive for educators.

I grew up in an industrial city in southeast Texas whose blue-collar population relied heavily on the oil refineries and chemical plants for employment. The men in my family have worked in the industry since the 1920s, but I was the first man to break this tradition. This did not surprise my family since I had always been viewed as different. I began to notice difference between myself and other males in the fifth grade when I was picked on for being too sensitive. I was not as physically imposing or tough as other young boys. The teasing began small. I was called "cry baby" and pushed around by bigger boys. The taunting intensified when I entered junior high and joined the band. I was the only boy to play the clarinet. Students said that I played a "gay" instrument, even though I was totally unaware that musical instruments possessed a sexual orientation. In seventh grade I joined the football team because I thought it would make me more popular and the teasing would end. Nothing could have been further from the truth. Since I was not physically imposing or aggressive, I was pushed around and tackled very easily on the field. One incident stands out that typifies my experiences on and off the football field.

One day in the seventh grade, after dressing out in my football pads, some other players started to call me a "fag" and said I was a "queer." They warned the other boys not to stand close to me because I might try to kiss them—or worse. It was at this moment that I felt most alone; even my best friend moved away from me. After enduring this treatment in the locker room, I was relieved when the coaches finally arrived and directed us to the field. On the way out, one of my teammates, with the implicit approval of the coaches, taunted me in front of the team with the words, "Hang your helmets on your tail pad, Thorson is walking behind you." A majority of the team members then hung their helmets off their tailbone pads. The coaches were aware that I was being teased and tormented, but gave the usual junior high response to "toughen up" and "stop being so sensitive, you're a football player." It was the typical "boys will be boys" mentality.

I was taught that enduring this teasing would make me mentally and physically tough. This did not prove to be true at that point in my life. If anything, it led me deeper into a depression that had begun to emerge in the fifth grade. I took all the teasing very hard. The other boys made me feel out of place because I fell outside of what they saw as "normal" in regards to the disposition and temperament of a boy. All of this was exacerbated by the fact I grew up in a conservative Christian home where I was always told that it was a sin to be homosexual and that homosexuals went to hell. Hearing this multiple times, especially from my mother, made me feel that something was wrong with me since people obviously thought I was homosexual. It was not until after my sophomore year of high school that I finally became comfortable in my own skin and decided I did not care what others thought of me. I was who I was, and if they did not like it then to hell with them. I believe that ending my quest to be accepted as a stereotypical "masculine" male football player made me a stronger and more confident person. Now I could began to question more and more the things I was taught at home and school.

This questioning attitude and my refusal to accept the social scripts I was given as a child led me to pursue a career as a teacher. Today I work against heteronormativity and gender conformity in my school and look for ways to protect all kids from bullying and harassment. After my junior year in high school, I became comfortable with myself and stopped attempting to live up to others' expectations. I went on to college and graduate school continuing to question everything I had been taught my entire life. Today I am married to a wonderful woman, and we have a beautiful daughter. While others may label me as simply heterosexual, I am much more complex than it appears. I would consider myself within the spectrum that falls under the broad category of queer, which is an umbrella term for anything outside the heteronormative mainstream. I do not fit the heteronormative mold of gender roles and neither does my wife. People still joke that I am the "woman" in the relationship because I am sensitive, loving, and like to share my feelings. Also, while I may not be sexually attracted to men, I do appreciate beauty in men and seek to have close, intimate relationships with my male friends. (Thorson, 2011)

Andy's life narrative is instructive on many levels. He assumed that the coaches would protect him from bullying and taunting. However, the pervasiveness of the hegemonic notions of masculinity, sexuality, and football that led to the behavior by classmates was also deeply ingrained in the psyche of the coaches who participated in the abuse. Teachers, coaches, and principals often perpetuate abuse either overtly (as in the case of the Penn State coach) or by silent complicity. The coaches minimized Andy's torment by saying "boys will be boys" and ignoring the problem. Andy assumed that playing football would change the dynamics in his school, but he was wrong. We also see in Andy's narrative the total lack of understanding of gender and sexuality in the school context. Like many children, Andy was resilient and capable of making personal adjustments in his life. He found himself depressed and alone—without support from his best friend, his coaches, and even his mother, but he found a way to question authorities and make internal adjustments. Despite anti-bullying programs in some schools and "It Gets Better" campaigns to give hope to gay teens and those perceived to be gay, and support from compassionate counselors, parents, and teachers in some schools, this is not enough to prevent the tragedy of youth suicide. Educators must read Andy's narrative and fully understand the complexity of hegemonic forces at work in schools and society. We will discuss this topic in more detail in chapter 6.

In my career, I have seen too many abusive parents and coaches demanding that their children and students play a particular sport or participate in a particular activity preferred by the adult when the student is adamantly opposed and clearly disinterested. I have also seen too many students quit an activity and forsake a natural talent because classmates or teachers denigrate the student's interests with negative taunting such as "the clarinet is a gay instrument" in Andy's narrative above. I particularly remember a situation when I was a high school principal involving a father and his four talented sons. He lamented that his youngest son in seventh grade did not want to play football. His older sons had all been captains and stars on our high school team. Two received scholarships to play college ball. The youngest son was a very talented artist, and he wanted to take drawing classes and painting lessons after school. He refused to play football. The father asked my opinion, and I advised him to give his son art lessons and encourage him to pursue his interests and talents. The father was frustrated by my response, and he told me: "No son of mine is going to grow up to be a faggot. He will play football like his older brothers. There will be no art for my son!" I worry about this kid, his father, and all children who are similarly abused by parents and teachers. This story also reminds us of another dimension of hegemony that is evident in Andy's narrative—heterosexism and homophobia. The father's four sons may or may not have been gay, but playing football or taking art lessons had nothing to do with their sexual orientation. There are heterosexual artists and gay football players in our schools and society.

Curriculum development in the postmodern era deconstructs prejudice and hegemony by challenging the dominance of logical positivism to the study of history and the construction of time as simply a linear sequence of events. Postmodern curriculum encourages the eclectic interests and talents of students, autobiographical reflection, narrative inquiry, multiple interpretations, and contextual understanding. Knowledge is understood as reflecting human interests, values, and actions that are socially constructed and directed toward emancipation and human agency (Habermas, 1970) and not conformity to hegemonic master narratives as in the examples discussed above. Herbert Kliebard (1992b) explains:

> We often make half-conscious decisions as to what knowledge is most appropriate to include in the curriculum then afterwards devise the plausible-sounding reasons for so doing. Those half-conscious decisions are tied in many instances to such matters as social class allegiances and to self-interest generally. As such, curriculum history is not so much involved with traditional epistemological questions as with questions closely associated with sociology of knowledge. History of curriculum is, in other words, critically concerned with what is *taken* to be knowledge in certain times and places rather than what is ultimately true or valid. ... A fundamental question imbedded in the history of curriculum, then, is not simply one of who went to school and who did not, but the way in which the social machinery may be constructed to differentiate access to certain forms of knowledge. [This is] significant not just in a pedagogical sense but in terms of status attainment and social relations, if not social justice. (p. 158)

In effect, the curriculum will seek to understand history contextually rather than delineate a coherent and singular explanation of selective events and artifacts. Just as the curriculum is affected by social conditions and values, so too can the curriculum help to reshape or preserve those conditions and values. The relationship between society and the curriculum is reciprocal. This chapter will introduce the historical dimension of curriculum development from this perspective, which contains many elements of postmodern theory.

Integral to postmodernism is the critique of reason, totality, universal principles, and metanarratives—grand explanations that seek to explain all of reality from a singular perspective. As Charles Jencks posited in chapter 1, this critique is clearly articulated in the work of Jean-François Lyotard. In the text *The Postmodern Condition*, Lyotard (1984) challenges Enlightenment notions of totality and argues that postmodernism is inseparable from an incredulity toward metanarratives. What are these metanarratives? For Lyotard, they are unified historical narratives and overarching philosophies of history. Examples would be the Enlightenment concept of the gradual but steady progress of reason and freedom, Georg Wilhelm Friedrich Hegel's dialectic of spirit coming to know itself, and Karl Marx's drama of the forward march of human productivity and class conflict resulting in proletarian revolution. The postmodern era will reject these and other modern metanarratives because their moral and epistemological theories propose that knowledge, truth, and justice exist independent of contingent, historical practices. In short, Lyotard critiques metanarratives because they privilege one historical analysis without acknowledging their own contextuality and the validity of other discourses. Therefore, metanarratives do not problematize their own legitimacy, and thus attempt to logically order history according to the preconceived modern notions of totality as reflected in patriarchical, technological, colonial, anthropocentric, rationalistic, militaristic, and Eurocentric paradigms. These modern paradigms deny the historical and social construction of their own first principles. As a result, Lyotard concludes, modern metanarratives ignore particularity, contingency, irony, and difference. Henry Giroux (1993) summarizes Lyotard's postmodern perspective succinctly:

> Lyotard argues that appeals to reason and consensus, when inserted within grand narratives that unify history, emancipation and knowledge, deny their own implications in the production of knowledge and power. More emphatically, Lyotard claims that within such narratives are elements of mastery and control in which "we can hear the muttering of the desire for a return of terror, for the realization of the fantasy to seize reality." Against metanarratives, which totalize historical experience by reducing its diversity to a one-dimensional, all-encompassing logic, Lyotard posits a discourse of multiple horizons, the play of language games, and the terrain of micropolitics. (p. 52)

Postmodern curriculum discourses understand history as contextual, multidimensional, ironic, proleptic, contingent, evolving, and autobiographical. Because modern notions of logic are actually ahistorical, the postmodern curriculum effectively resuscitates an authentic historicity. Educators in the postmodern era will no longer be able to simply "teach" history as facts to be memorized. Because the autobiographical, local, and particular are essential in order to understand history, teachers will now have to listen to students and their life stories—encouraging football, art, or other student interests. As feminist scholars insist, history is not simply "his story"—that is, the victory narratives of Anglo-Saxon European Protestant heterosexual male warriors. Rather, "her story" is also integral to history. Especially, history is understood as a recursive contextual experience or, from Lyotard's perspective, "difference, contingency, and particularity." History is also the mystery of autobiography, "my story." We listen to multiple stories, elevate no story as the final narrative, and carefully deconstruct all stories, especially our own.

While this introduction to curriculum history may initially seem difficult and controversial for those beginning the journey toward understanding postmodern curriculum discourses, the challenge for curriculum scholars today is to examine critically their own story in the context of the history of curriculum development. If the reconceptualized curriculum challenges students to *enter* history rather than simply *observe* history from a distance, then teachers must begin historical studies (in any discipline and not simply social studies) by entering this process themselves. This participatory view of history is what Jonathan Kozol has proposed for classrooms. Kozol argues against schooling that is not transformative and that does not participate in history. He writes:

> School teaches history in the same way that it teaches syntax, grammar, and word-preference: in terms that guarantee our prior exile from its passion and its transformation. It lifts up children from the present, denies them powerful access to the future, and robs them of all ethical repossession of the past. History is, as the sarcastic student says, an X-rated film. The trouble is that everyone we know, love, touch, hold, dream to be, or ever might become, has first to be told: I cannot enter. (1975, p. 83)

History, therefore, from the postmodern perspective, must not be seen as a series of events to be memorized but rather as an opportunity to inform the present and provide access to the future. Kozol challenges curricularists to adopt a transformative pedagogy in order to recover a participative mode in history education.

Another contrast between the modern and postmodern view of the function of the social studies curriculum in schools is portrayed in a popular classroom poster entitled "Occupations to Which Interest in History May Lead." The poster lists the occupations of archaeologist, curator, writer, critic, archivist, anthropologist, librarian, or teacher. It is interesting that nowhere on this type of list will there be words to suggest the possible goal of being one who enters history. In contrast, the reconceptualized curriculum challenges both teachers and students to enter into the historical process as participants rather than as observers. Let's explore further to see what this might look like.

Schools are inundated with textbooks and curriculum materials that promote *critical thinking*. Examining these materials carefully reveals that many programs establish boundaries around thinking in which the parameters of knowledge are limited by specific interpretations of human history and culture. Ironically, these curriculum materials are anything but critical exercises because they contain predetermined answers, narrow methodologies, and/or political agendas designed to assimilate students into the hegemonic socio-cultural worldview. However, some educators encourage freedom of interpretation from an autobiographical, postcolonial, and existential perspective. The conflict centers on the question of whether language and social studies teachers, for example, should encourage or even allow subjective interpretation of literature and history, or whether critical thinking should be directed toward a range of legitimate interpretations established by scholarly authorities. Curriculum historians in this milieu insist that authoritative metanarratives cannot present politically, theologically, racially, gendered, and culturally neutral perspectives. History, like knowledge, is constructed in social and cultural contexts. Curriculum development in the postmodern era includes a more eclectic and subjective understanding of hermeneutic interpretation and critical thinking—a topic we will explore in chapter 4. This postmodern approach will be denounced as heresy by those committed to the modernist paradigm. For example, Civitas (Bahmueller, 1991), a typical national framework for civics curriculum in the US, cautions:

> Citizenship training, if it means anything at all, means teaching students to think critically, listen with discernment, and communicate with power and precision. If students learn to listen, read, speak, and write more carefully, they will not only be civically empowered, but also they will know how to distinguish between the authentic and the fraudulent in human discourse .... Civic education for a new century also must provide students with a core of basic knowledge about social issues and institutions, to allow them to put their understanding of democracy into perspective. (p. xvi)

Whose perspective? Which discourses are authentic and which are fraudulent? Civitas, like other conservative organizations that call for cultural literacy, core knowledge, and facts-based curriculum, is concerned with teaching basic information so that students will make decisions that advance status quo political arrangements and will be socialized into a corporate and patriotic political structure. The use of school curriculum to advance a political agenda is evident globally in curriculum materials as the Chinese, Japanese, German, Pakistan, and US authorities (among many others) direct and limit the information to which students under their control are exposed. This is not critical thinking, it is propaganda! How does this political use of curriculum and history impact the lives of citizens? I review this question in more depth on the companion website by considering the story of a controversy about the US history textbook *The American People: Creating a Nation and a Society* (Nash, 2004) in the Hudson, Ohio, public school district.

An informative exercise would be to compare and contrast two articles about social studies standards in American education and the nature of history textbooks. In order to understand the various positions in this debate, read the culturally conservative position in Lynn V. Cheney's (1994) "The End of History" in the *Wall Street Journal* and the politically progressive response by Robert Cohen (1996) in *Social Education*. The political debates about *The American People* in Hudson, Ohio, are a reflection of intense national debates about hermeneutics and history textbooks. There is much at stake in these debates, and ethical responses to global events today are shaped in many respects by the way we approach historical interpretation in schools, classrooms, curricular materials, and textbooks. Having reflected on these specific examples of hermeneutic interpretation in the first part of this chapter, we will now examine specific applications of the interpretive process that will help to contextualize these narratives and others on the web page.

Let us return to the critique of critical thinking. The assumption in the debates above is that students left to their own interpretation or subjective analysis without assistance and authoritative guidance and reason will be unable to participate effectively or appropriately. This is happening in science curriculum, health education, libraries, literature, technology, and many other fields in addition to social studies. The modern approach to science and history contends that knowledge builds on itself through progressive stages. Thus, students must know an objective past before attempting to apply critical thinking in the present. This perspective involves applying the truth of past scientific discoveries and historical analysis in order to build new knowledge.

Curriculum development in the postmodern era will challenge this concept of time and linear progression. Albert Einstein provides a case in point. Einstein had many difficulties as a young man with formal schooling. His vision of the physical universe in his theory of relativity initiated a search for a unified foundation of physics beyond the modern worldview of Newtonian physics. Einstein's theories called into question traditional understandings of time and space, and, by extrapolation, the concept of context-free knowledge accumulation outside time and space, that dominated scholarship in the 19th century. The postmodern rejection of chronophonism, a modern notion that time is chronological and linear, was thus initiated. Was it important for Einstein to challenge classical physics, which dominated formal schooling of his time? I would answer in the affirmative and contend that the conception of curriculum and chronology that pervade modern schooling actually inhibits the creative genius of the Einsteins in our schools today.

Richard Rorty (1979) has effectively demolished the analytic and formal thinking exemplified in the linear approach to history by logical positivism and by the systematic philosophy of Locke, Descartes, Kant, Russell, and Husserl in his book *Philosophy and the Mirror of Nature*. Logical positivists have ignored historical interpretation and relegated the study of history to linear events that may be used to explain and support the modern progress of philosophic thought. Rorty argues that the investigation of correspondences between language or thought and the natural world, as well as theories of representation in philosophy, must be abandoned. His philosophy is utilized by many curriculum scholars to support the belief that the analytic thinking of modernity must be reevaluated so that more emphasis is placed on critical historicity and hermeneutic interpretation in education.

Students often complain about the boredom they experience in schooling, especially history classes. If there is one discipline in the school curriculum that exemplifies Rorty's exposure of the failure of the modern behavioristic and analytic approach to education, it is certainly history classes. History is too often studied as a series of events on a linear time line to be memorized and evaluated in the context of artificially contrived epochs of socio-political or cultural development—and, unfortunately, usually measured by wars and giving a one-sided impression of the nature of human conflict. The linear model divides time into the past, present, and future, and as a result removes any autobiographical connection to the historical events being discussed in textbooks or classroom lectures. In short, history has been decontextualized by the modern curriculum, and as a result, ironically, an ahistorical and anti-historical attitude has emerged in the modern school.

In desperation, teachers address this problem by echoing George Santayana's warning that those who do not remember the past are doomed to repeat it. Frustrated students ignore these pleas from their equally frustrated teachers. And then, to compound the problem, national reports condemn educators because students cannot place the American Civil War in the 19th century or identify the president responsible for the New Deal. Typical is conservative critic Chester Finn's complaint, in *We Must Take Charge: Our Schools and Our Future*, that students are unable to demonstrate competency in subject matter areas. Finn (1991) writes: "Today we want evidence of learning, not just of teaching. We look at outcomes. Unsatisfactory results were what led the Excellence Commission to exclaim that we were threatened by a 'rising tide of mediocrity'" (p. 3). The conservative response has been an unrelenting series of reform proposals, from *A Nation at Risk* in 1983, to *No Child Left Behind* in 2002, to *Race to the Top* in 2009, that call for an increase in accountability tests, standardized evaluation, scientific management, and measured outcomes in education.

Proponents argue that the accountability standards increase student knowledge, opportunity, and educational advancement. Most important, they contend, teachers and administrators can no longer ignore poor, minority, or special needs students because the school is held responsible for measured outcomes for all students in each racial category. Critics contend that the accountability movement is really designed to ensure that American students can demonstrate testing skills and information recall determined by the reformers to be essential for cultural literacy, the socialization of students, and the hegemonic reproduction of the dominant values of American society. The tests will reproduce the same stratified outcomes that have always existed in American society. Proponents believe that accountability will give every child an equal opportunity. On the other hand, accountability tests and measures are seen by critics as instruments that deprofessionalize teaching and destroy the possibility of curricular innovation and student creativity. Ironically, the critics of accountability testing contend, more kids are left behind in the job market and college admissions. (For a summary of the data on these critiques and many informative links, see http://www. susanohanian.org/).

Two of the best collections of essays that investigate accountability and justice issues from several perspectives are *Educational Equity and Accountability: Paradigms, Policies, and Politics*, by Linda Skrla and James Scheurich (2004), and *Leadership for Social Justice: Making Revolutions in Education*, by Catherine Marshall and Maricela Oliva (2006). These two volumes demonstrate the common ground of all scholars: we must address the inequalities and injustices that plague our schools and society. The methods of addressing equity and justice are hotly debated. I agree with Linda Skrla and James Scheurich (2004), who investigated the impact on teaching and pedagogy of the accountability and testing movement, and found that the curriculum is negatively impacted by *No Child Left Behind*. They argue that we must treat the *causes of failure in schools*—chronic under-funding of schools for minority and low-income students; unjust and outdated taxing structures in states; fewer certified teachers, fewer experienced teachers, and higher teacher turnover rates in schools serving limited English-speaking students and poor and minority students; lack of adequate English as a second language (ESL) and bilingual programs for the huge and growing immigrant and non-English speaking population; lack of equitable curriculum resources, counselors, and computers that are urgently needed if students are to have any hope of succeeding on standardized tests and gaining entrance to college; segregated cities and gated communities that remain unaware and unconcerned about the needs of the poor and minority population; dilapidated and unsafe school facilities; lack of attention to the debilitating health conditions among the children in low socio-economic school districts; the devastating impact of poor nutrition and inadequate health care on the ability of poor kids to learn and succeed in school; lack of jobs, living wages, and child care for working parents; dramatically high drop-out rates that are actually exacerbated by school policies and low expectations by administrators and teachers; inadequate facilities that could not possibly house the school drop-out and street children even if they were encouraged to come to school; and outdated textbooks and meaningless curriculum materials that engender boredom—and not just the *symptoms of school failure*—low test scores on state and national accountability tests, high illiteracy rates, and high drop-out rates (Valencia, Valenzuela, Sloan, & Foley, 2004). Echoing this research, Jonathan Kozol calls the conditions of our schools and communities "savage inequalities" and "the shame of the nation" (Kozol, 1991, 2005).

When investigating the accountability measures we must look carefully at factors other than test scores and graduation rates and examine the issues mentioned above. A more just accountability system would present the public with an "opportunities to learn" index that factored in health and nutrition programs, per student funding, qualifications and experience of teachers, and school climate and safety. We must be attentive to drop-out rates, demoralization of teachers, narrowing of the curriculum to adjust to tests, and deprofessionalization of teaching. The negative impact may outweigh the benefits of attention to all children. Additionally, when school districts are under intense pressure to raise test scores, limited resources are directed to students who are "on the bubble" rather than those who are high-achieving talented students or special-need remedial students with less likelihood of passing the test. Potentially more students will be left behind or encouraged to drop out of school. Supporters of the *No Child Left Behind* and *Race to the Top* agendas see the world through very different lenses. Students of curriculum development need to read texts like the two above and deconstruct the accountability proposals carefully. While we certainly must provide an equitable education for all children, we must make sure that we do not create a system that disenfranchises students, deprofessionalizes teachers, makes school leaders automatons, ignores hegemony, and advances a lifeless and rote curriculum in classrooms.

A recent study of the East St. Louis school district highlights these issues. East St. Louis came to our collective awareness in Jonathan Kozol's (1991) *Savage Inequalities* and again in the state oversight committee in 1994. A follow-up study by O'Malley, Roseboro, Donyell, and Hunt (2012) investigated the school district and concluded:

> This instrumental case study reviews the 1994–2004 period of state financial oversight in East St. Louis, Illinois School District 189, with a secondary review of the initial years of *NCLB* implementation. Although the oversight panel's fiscal management did generate financial stability, case findings indicate that its accountability processes did not result in sustained improvements in student achievement indicators despite anticipated links between the two in

the panel's reporting. Furthermore, the oversight process operated as a hierarchical structure without identification of cultural implications. Attention to culture and subsidiarity are indicated for future state–district partnerships oriented toward urban educational reform. (p. 117)

Numerous studies in recent years also document the same phenomenon and should cause educators to deconstruct the assumptions of accountability and state management processes. I argue here that the cultural and social issues cannot be ignored or minimized.

Teachers often agree that their students do not know the factual information required for progressing through the school system and passing standardized tests, but they throw up their hands in desperation, blaming disinterested parents, boring textbooks, overcrowded classrooms, drugs, self-esteem programs, television, poor preparation and ineffective previous teachers, or any other convenient target. However, these teachers continue to use the same methods of teaching and evaluation that have dominated curriculum development for over one hundred years. This, of course, provides ammunition for the accountability reformers. There certainly was no idyllic period of curriculum innovation and creative pedagogy in all schools. Is the problem that educators have not perfected the modern methods? Or is the problem that the modern methods and strategies are no longer appropriate in a postmodern era? The latter possibility is the focus of contemporary curriculum discourses.

Consider the example of the public school system in New Orleans following the floods of 2005. The total collapse of the public school system provided the opportunity for accountability reformers to envision a new charter school system based on merit pay for teachers aligned to student test scores, student graduation rates, and other performance measures. The focus was on firing teachers and eliminating unions. In the years since Hurricane Katrina, new schools in New Orleans have been created in this vision that are being touted as examples of success. It is important to note that, before and after Katrina, New Orleans had a large and highly regarded non-public school system that enrolled up to 30% of the school-age children of the city. Most of these are well-respected Catholic schools. I am a graduate of two of them—Holy Name of Jesus Elementary and De La Salle High School, on St. Charles Avenue in the wealthy uptown district that did not flood in Katrina. I received a first-rate education that has provided me with many benefits throughout my life. Most of the Catholic schools in my youth were all White, but a few of the most recognized Catholic schools in the country were all Black—St. Augustine High for boys, Xavier High for girls, and Xavier University. As an adult, I now recognize that the large enrollment in private and non-public schools by mostly White and mostly middle- and upper-class students (Black and White) discouraged tuition-paying voters from financially supporting public education for the predominantly poor and working-class families of New Orleans. Add to this phenomenon the history of Congo Square and the birth of jazz, slave auctions on the Mississippi, and structural racism in my hometown—including the *Plessy* v. *Ferguson* segregation Supreme Court case of 1896 and the integration of the public schools in New Orleans by the African-American student Ruby Bridges at Frantz Elementary for Whites in 1960—and it becomes obvious that school accountability is not simply a matter of curriculum reform and rigorous standards. Social and cultural factors are always deeply connected to schooling policies and practices. Perhaps economic inequality, inadequate health care, dangerous living conditions, and community prejudice are far more significant factors driving poor educational outcomes.

Recent national reports have praised New Orleans for improving the curriculum and student outcomes with rigorous standards in the new charter schools. However, consider the response to a *New York Times* editorial commending New Orleans by Rodney Watson, a former state administrator and respected school leader. Watson offers this detailed insider analysis in which he reminds us of the complexity of school reform and accountability.

> As a former Assistant Superintendent of Education in Louisiana, the first State Accountability Director, and the point person assigned to recruit and staff the first eighteen schools opened in New Orleans under the Recovery School District after Hurricane Katrina, I would like to comment on the article published in the New York Times recently entitled "Lessons From New Orleans." The article presents a very positive picture of the Recovery School District (RSD), specifically citing Charter Schools as the impetus for improved student achievement. As we look toward second-generation accountability in the US, we must carefully examine specific aspects of our current accountability systems (student achievement data, drop-out, attendance) and include new measures of evaluation (quality teachers, finances, student services, social services) in order to provide for more valid, reliable, and accurate evaluation. I support the operation of a few Charters within a public school setting. Private operators can provide for a healthy and competitive environment that supports creative and innovative educational practices. However, the larger question is this: are Charter Schools *an option* or *the solution* as we open them on a large scale within a district? Only an accurate examination of what exactly is occurring within the RSD can determine if Charters and accountability should serve as a national incubator for school improvement. In order to determine Charter effectiveness, the public should look at individual school growth and performance. We must know how long each school has been in operation, the stability of the student population within each school, and the institutions and licensure programs for educators. We need to know teacher retention rates, appropriate and effective use of state and federal dollars, and programs for meeting individual student academic and social needs.
>
> While the current data support modest to major growth on student test scores since Hurricane Katrina, the results vary dramatically from school to school. Some Charter Schools are abysmal academic failures mired in financial embezzlement. In order to obtain a clear picture of how success has been gauged, it is important to examine all of the data for each school independently to determine how well the Charter Schools are actually performing compared to other public schools. Louisiana has moved to a new performance-based system using letter grades: A, B, C, D, F. These letter grades are based on minimal overall

school performance score in addition to its growth factors. Despite the growth that is praised by the *New York Times*, recently published data indicated that the majority of RSD schools had letter grades of D and F. In terms of comparing RSD schools to schools operated under the New Orleans Parish School Board prior to Katrina, it is important to note that student mobility is a major problem when making comparisons. Generally speaking, most school districts nationwide can track students within a school, district, and state, regardless of mobility. However, because there are so many models of school governance within New Orleans (RSD-run schools, RSD Charters, Orleans Parish Schools, Orleans Parish Charters, Catholic Schools, Private Schools, Home Schools), there is no system in place to track students if they leave or enter a new school. This issue is compounded because the RSD is a district of choice, meaning that parents can enroll a child in any school within the district that is not identified for failure. Because of open enrollment, mobility, and the lack of an effective data-coordinating system, tracking student movement is virtually impossible. Some parents will not cooperate with data collection for a variety of personal and legal reasons. This tracking of students and Charter School cohorts is essential as the state examines value-added measures for schools and teachers. Only with the correct data can Louisiana link student performance to teachers within a school and to the institutions and licensure programs that trained these professionals within the state. (Mobility of teachers who were trained out-of-state is impossible and thus skews the data.)

Higher education has adopted accountability standards with interventions for programs that operate within the schools. As we examine Charter School effectiveness, teacher retention within schools should be given consideration in order to create stable learning environments for students and valid judgments regarding school accountability. In other words, we must ask the following question. In high- or low-performing Charter Schools, how stable is that school score over time based on the retention of teachers? This measure should be given the strongest consideration as the state examines value-added systems that could be affected by cohorts of students and teachers. In terms of funding, the *New York Times* argues that most of the Charters are operating with the same level of funding as the regular public schools within the district. However, in most public schools the majority of state funding goes to maintaining salaries and benefits for staff. This leaves very little operating funds for innovations and support services. Federal dollars (NCLB/IDEA) supplement these services, but how effectively are the dollars being spent and what kind of accountability and audit findings have been released relative to Charter Schools? Most funding is allocated to local districts, rather than schools. The state has a fiscal audit rating system for districts. How could this system be applied to Charters that indicate they are operating within the same budget confines as regular public schools and make expenditures according to state and federal statute/guidelines? This kind of accountability for Charters creates a type of transparency that would enhance second-generation accountability systems.

Finally, looking at how Charters provide the gamut of support services for children, from FAPE (Free and Appropriate Public Education), to special education students, to providing for health, safety, transportation and food services for children, could be an important measure of how effectively these schools are operating. Unlike conventional schools within a district, a central office with infrastructure for providing these services is in place to support public schools. These centralized services provide for additional resources, personnel, and institutional knowledge that support individual schools. Many of the Charters in New Orleans do not have that kind of support and contract these services at a high cost to private vendors without fiscal accountability safeguards. Examining how these factors are implemented and monitored could be a key element to second-generation accountability. As we continue to examine Charter Schools, and more particularly New Orleans as a model Charter School system within the United States, how can we reexamine our current accountability systems to incorporate elements that provide for more transparency and greater accuracy of judgments? Once we have examined these elements of operation we might effectively answer the question: Are Charter Schools good options or solutions for operating low-performing schools in the US? At this juncture, we simply do not have the data to support any firm conclusion. (Watson, 2011)

Watson provides a clear, rational, and timely deconstruction of the rush to accountability and charter schools in the US. Obviously, the history of American education, specifically curriculum development in schools and the emergence of alternative delivery models like charter schools, cannot be reviewed comprehensively in this short chapter. Educators in the postmodern era must be alert to the rhetoric and research on curriculum reform and school accountability. Examine some perspectives on the companion website for this text.

The preceding discussion would obviate the very effort to present a definitive chronology of curriculum development in a linear sequence. However, many excellent books have been published that review the history of American curriculum with sensitivity to a postmodern perspective and the kind of questions raised by Rodney Watson: Herbert Kliebard's (1986) *The Struggle for the American Curriculum: 1893–1958*; Kliebard's (1992a) *Forging the American Curriculum: Essays in Curriculum History and Theory*; Joel Spring's (2004) *The American School: 1642–2004*; George Willis, William Schubert, Robert Bullough, Craig Kridel, and John Holton's (1993) *The American Curriculum: A Documentary History*; and Barry Franklin's (1986) *Building the American Community: The School Curriculum and the Search for Social Control*. These five books provide an insightful introduction to the study of curriculum history and theory for those interested in a more detailed analyses.

Herbert Kliebard reports: "When I was a graduate student there was no such thing as curriculum history as an identified area of scholarship. Of course, elements of what we now think of as curriculum history were commonly incorporated into the general history of education, but no one was identified as a curriculum historian" (1992a, p. xi). Although the field of curriculum history is relatively young, there are already many research methodologies evolving in the field: narrative inquiry, hermeneutics, autobiography, ethnography, revisionist analysis, and primary source exploration. William Schubert (1986) writes that the predominant research methodologies include the following: "surveys of thought, surveys of practice, analyses of movements, case studies, revisionist critiques, and biographies" (p. 88). Schubert provides an example of the postmodern critique of traditional historical methodologies:

> In the early 1970s, a number of books offered a challenge to standard histories of education, the early paragon of which is Cubberley's *Public Education in the United States* (1934) and *The History of Education* (1920). These new histories came to be known as *revisionists*, and they argue that it is a myth that schools will integrate the poor, oppressed, and racially and ethnically diverse. They point out that far from building the traditional "American Dream" of democratic participation, schools effectuate social control in the service of a corporate state. Against this powerful force, they argue that educational change has been illusory. (1986, p. 91)

Schubert introduces not only the variety of methodologies utilized to study the history of curriculum but also one of the postmodern concerns with the traditional approaches to historical analysis. Revisionist historical methodologies will critique and deconstruct master narratives that have not only been repeated for generations but that also form the basis of the curriculum that perpetuates the modern ideology and reproduces its inequities.

An example from the social studies curriculum that exemplifies this problem is reported by historian Carl Brasseaux. Brasseaux explains:

> Malcolm Muggeridge, in a short essay entitled *The Eyewitness Fallacy*, shows that even so-called authoritative eyewitness documents are subject to all sorts of errors, primarily errors of perception. To give you just one example, one of the best known diaries to come out of the Civil War Era was the one written by Mary Chesnut. Her husband was a member of Jefferson Davis' staff. It has been proven fairly recently that she rewrote the diary several decades after the Civil War ... and this, research has shown in the last few decades, was a fairly commonplace event among people who were very influential, people who were shaping the course of history. It's fairly commonplace for writers of diaries to go back and rewrite them purposely to cast themselves in a good light, and the people they disliked in an even worse light. (Cited in Konikoff, 1993, p. 15)

Brasseaux demonstrates the problems associated with the modern reliance on metanarratives in historical analysis. The list of absolute uncontestable facts is actually very limited, and eventually all accounts and artifacts are influenced by subjective memory. Therefore, postmodern historical analysis will not only deconstruct traditional historical methodologies, it will also validate and encourage autobiographical and revisionist approaches. This must also be the focus of our study of curriculum history itself.

Additionally, developments in literary criticism, philosophy, anthropology, and curriculum theory have led historians to rethink how they read and examine sources. Historians Page Putnam Miller and David Thelen (1993) contend that some scholars "no longer confidently read 'texts' from the past as guides to what actually happened" (p. B3). They argue that most historians no longer maintain that the views of the past constructed today, or even documents created contemporaneously with past events, are final statements. Miller and Thelen continue: "We see them as products that reflect the political and personal dynamics and needs of those who created them. The analysis of the context of sources has become as significant as their content" (p. B3). In curriculum studies, likewise, understanding the context of curriculum development models now rivals the content of guides, plans, and models for the focus of study. Postmodernism takes this a step further and incorporates the concept of *différance* as a structuring principle that suggests definition rests not on the source itself but in its positive and negative references to other texts. Meaning changes over time and "ultimately the attribution of meaning is postponed and deferred forever" (Derrida, [1972] 1981, p. 40).

As we discuss historical analysis, it is important to remember that the boundaries between fields and disciplines are fading in postmodern scholarship. While new historical research methodologies will be important elements of the postmodern curriculum, especially in social studies, they are not limited to the field of curriculum history. Curriculum and instruction, like so many other fields, have become interdisciplinary, inclusive, eclectic, and kaleidoscopic. As an example of the postmodern application of these methodologies, I will relate a personal narrative to frame a further discussion of historical curriculum development perspectives.

As a child I often visited my grandmother's home in Shreveport, Louisiana. There was an unusual tradition in the family that had been passed down to each new generation. The children would gather around to listen to stories about the Civil War while my grandmother would rub the side of her head and say "The damn Yankees shot Aunt Dora!" The story was told with passion, and even though I did not understand all the implications of the Civil War, I still grew up hating the elusive but evil "damn Yankees" who shot my aunt.

Dora Navra was the eight-year-old daughter of my great-great-great-great-grandparents Abraham Navra and Ellen Kinney, who settled in Vicksburg, Mississippi, in the 1840s. During the siege of Vicksburg in the summer of 1863 Dora was hit in the head by shrapnel from a cannon fired by Union soldiers as she rushed into town from a cave on the outskirts of the city. Dora had been sent to look for the local doctor to assist in the care of her infant brother, who was ill. Dora survived; Samuel died. And, ever since that fateful day, members of my family have been remembering the hardship caused by the federal soldiers who surrounded Vicksburg in 1863 and inflicted such misery on the citizens.

I do not remember studying the Civil War in any detail in elementary school, high school, or college, even though my transcripts indicate that I have credit for several courses in American history. Not once do I remember studying anything about the siege of Vicksburg, and unfortunately no teacher ever encouraged me to share my family tradition. In fact, I am not sure that I ever made any connection between my unusual family tradition and the study of American history. Even as a college graduate I could not have placed the date of the siege of Vicksburg on a time line, named the generals, or analyzed the reasons for the strategic importance of this event in American history, despite the fact that I took honors history courses in high school and graduated summa cum laude from a traditional liberal arts college. What went wrong? Even though I successfully completed a traditional core curriculum and apparently memorized all the assigned facts about the Civil War, I did not retain this information beyond my exams. We must remember that retention, application, and critical analysis are not a concern of most testing programs. What does it mean if information is quickly forgotten? What learning styles and cultural contexts are at an advantage in the test-taking process? What are the sociological, economic, racial, linguistic, and physiological factors to which we must be attentive? How much time is being spent reflecting on these difficult questions?

It was several years after my undergraduate education, when I took up the hobby of genealogical studies, that I finally made the connection between my family history in Vicksburg and American history. Why did my social studies education and family traditions never intersect during my 24 years of formal schooling? This is a more interesting question than inquiring about my test scores in high school and college.

I am convinced that my ignorance of Civil War history specifically, and American history generally, despite the fact that I memorized the information presented in my classes and passed my American history tests in school with distinction, is the result of two things: I have a strong ability to memorize information and test well, but without long-term retention; and I was never encouraged or directed to make connections between the past and the present, between my relatives who were shot by Union soldiers in the 1860s and my life as a student studying the Civil War in the 1960s.

Traditionally, curriculum development has been concerned with Ralph Tyler's four basic questions in his syllabus for Education 360 at the University of Chicago and published in 1949. These four questions have so dominated the study of curriculum for the past 45 years that they have, in effect, become a curriculum metanarrative called the Tylerian Rationale. Tyler (1949) asks the following four questions:

1. What educational purposes should the school seek to attain?
2. How can learning experiences be selected which are likely to be useful in attaining these objectives?
3. How can learning experiences be organized for effective instruction?
4. How can the effectiveness of learning experiences be evaluated? (pp. v–vi)

Ever since Tyler categorized these four principles of the curriculum, most school districts and educators—whether consciously or unconsciously—have aligned their thinking about schooling experiences with this rationale. Tyler's questions have been codified as the goals and objectives, lesson plans, scope and sequence guides, and mastery of learning evaluations. His influence on the history of curriculum development in American education cannot be underemphasized. In fact, this methodology is at the heart of much of the accountability and testing philosophy today.

Ralph Tyler was also involved in an important curriculum study from 1933 to 1941 that provides further insights about curriculum development. The "Eight-Year Study" followed the progress of students from across the US through their eight-year secondary and college education. The study compared students from secondary schools that implemented individual-centered experimental curriculum with students in schools with a more traditional curriculum. The study concluded that the students in the experimental schools did slightly better in academic studies in college, but were much also much better off in their personal lives. Colin Marsh and George Willis (1999) describe the impact of this study:

> The Eight-Year Study collected data about all phases of students' lives, thus suggesting that curricula were concerned with far more than teaching students factual information. In demonstrating the worth of individual-centered curricula, it also demonstrated the viability of one of the hallmarks of progressive education: Dewey's notion that the curriculum is the experience of the individual .... It investigated the experienced curriculum, not just the planned curriculum or the enacted curriculum, and in this way it was ahead of its time. (p. 269)

Despite the results of the "Eight-Year Study," it did not abandon one assumption that it shared with the scientific testing and measurement movement of the time: that the curriculum could be evaluated in terms of its effect. The dominance of testing, accountability, and measurement continues to be the focus of most national curriculum models. The reconceptualization of curriculum does not share this enthusiasm. Tyler's contribution to the evaluation to curriculum in the early and mid-20th century is significant, but today most curriculum theorists do not share his focus on objectives and evaluation. George Willis (1998) suggests that Tyler's study also ran contrary to Dewey by treating generalized results as more important than the immediate and specific qualities of students' experiences. He writes:

> In creating new techniques for collecting information about developmental growth, the study also seemed to suggest that desirable experiencing could be inferred directly from evidence of growth and that all useful evidence could be somehow discerned objectively, without painstakingly shifting the divergent— and perhaps equally valuable—perspectives of different participants for their own insights. In so embodying a less than full notion of experiencing and a utilitarian means–end rationale implicit in the search for objective results, the Eight-Year Study was thereby also consistent with the technical approach to curriculum evaluation. (1998, p. 346)

Reconceptualized curriculum studies challenge the utilitarian means–end traditional curriculum development model of Ralph Tyler. For example, curriculum development in the postmodern era would encourage qualitative studies to investigate student experiences from a phenomenological, aesthetic, cultural, racial, gendered, and autobiographical perspective. Today we investigate narratives that will not only enhance the study of history and all subjects, but also develop student-centered connections for long-term memory and individual enhancement. One book that provides theoretical support for this postmodern position is *Making Connections: Teaching and the Human Brain* (1991), by Renate Nummela Caine and Geoffrey Caine, and published by the Association for Supervision and Curriculum Development. Donna Jean Carter, ASCD president in 1991, makes the following important comment in her introduction to the book:

> Intuitively, I have known for some time now that many capable youngsters are either so bored with their education or so stressed out by their experiences, that optimum learning cannot take place. I have also seen many students "flower" in a learning environment that builds on their current knowledge base and personal experiences. The authors not only explain why this is so but also show how a reconceptualization of teaching, based on knowledge of brain functioning, can enhance student learning. ... Teachers must become facilitators of learning, and they must expect students to go beyond the surface knowledge frequently achieved through rote memorization and unconnected content. By integrating the curriculum, we can assist students in their search for deeper meaning and thus enhance the brain's quest for patterning. The implications of this seminal work for teaching, testing, and remediation are far reaching. Repeated practice on isolated skills becomes inappropriate as an option for acquiring knowledge. It becomes obvious that skills and content must be presented in a context that is familiar to the learner. This contextual approach also supports authentic modes of assessment. (Cited in Caine & Caine, 1991, p. v)

Carter's introduction to the central theme of Caine and Caine's book helps to explain the problem with my formal history education described above. My study of the Civil War never created an atmosphere where I could make connections to my personal historical context. Caine and Caine challenge another strongly held belief of educators that teaching can be separated into cognitive, affective, and psychomotor domains of learning. Such artificial categorization may be helpful in designing research projects, but it can actually distort our understanding of learning. Caine and Caine contend that the brain does not separate emotions from cognition, either anatomically or perceptually. Cognitive theorists, too, are exploring the concept of the intuitive and nonrational dimension of learning, contending that learning is not a logical progressive sequence. This research supports postmodern understandings of curriculum as multidimensional, autobiographical, kaleidoscopic, and ironic.

During the 19th century an influential movement called faculty psychology (or mental discipline) emerged as the result of the findings of many scholarly reports, including *The Yale Report on the Defense of the Classics* in 1828. *The Yale Report* expressed two key concepts in faculty psychology: discipline and furniture. The aim of the curriculum was to expand the powers of the mind and store it with knowledge. This philosophy of curriculum sought to arrange the information that the memory gathers like furniture in a room. Additionally, it proposed that the muscles of the brain should be exercised routinely like those of other body parts. The faculty psychology movement, therefore, contended that the brain is a muscle in need of rote memorization exercises and mental drills in order to enhance the functioning of the mind, which could then accumulate more information, rearrange the data, and expand the knowledge base.

Caine and Caine (1991) establish the foundation for the postmodern arguments against faculty psychology in their book:

> A physiological model of memory also calls into question the notion that learning must take place through rote memorization. In addition, by understanding properties of our spatial memory system, educators can understand that teaching behavioral objectives ignores other functions of the brain and other aspects of memory and learning. Indeed, we have come to the conclusion that educators, by being too specific about facts to be remembered and outcomes to be produced, may prohibit students' genuine understanding and transfer of learning. (p. vii)

Caine and Caine's work demonstrates that learning and teaching involve multifaceted human beings in complex interactions. The curriculum in the postmodern era will acknowledge this complexity and move beyond narrow definitions and practices. Thus, Caine and Caine provide support for the postmodern curriculum that embraces complexity, tolerance of ambiguity, acceptance of uncertainty, and authentic, situated assessment. Evaluation becomes contextualized for individual teaching environments. The contemporary curriculum will reject formal, standardized evaluation instruments designed for universal application. These dimensions of curriculum and evaluation were not included in the classical curriculum in my formal schooling in the 1950s and 1960s. This inhibited me from making the connection between the rote memorization of facts about the Civil War and my personal family context in relation to the siege of Vicksburg.

The first time I brought my three children to Vicksburg, I retold the family history and visited all the historical landmarks, as well as our family grave sites. We made tomb rubbings and explored the public library to make copies of microfilm newspaper articles about our ancestors. We even took a picture with our three children rubbing their "injured" heads at the grave of Aunt Dora. Everywhere we went in Vicksburg we thought about Aunt Dora and her family. We explored the history of the siege of Vicksburg from the perspective of our family, including a visit to the location of the old Navra home. In short, we experienced history autobiographically in our family context. The children wanted to buy books and read about the battle as we toured every museum in town.

The climax of the Vicksburg trip occurred while we were visiting the old courthouse museum, an elegant Greek revival antebellum stone building that houses many of the artifacts of the Civil War era in Vicksburg. We had never visited the museum before. As we moved from room to room, my nine-year-old daughter Katie ran ahead. Suddenly, we heard her scream in the next room, and we rushed to her side. Katie was standing in awe before a glass case. She could not contain her excitement. Katie had discovered a display of mannequins with clothing of the citizens of Vicksburg from the 1800s. She proudly shouted out the inscription on the case for the entire museum to hear: "This dress was a gift to Ellen Kinney Navra on her wedding day. The shawl was worn by her daughter, Dora Navra." History came alive before my daughter's eyes, and as she gazed at the shawl the echo of five generations of stories about the Civil

War reverberated in her ears. The siege of Vicksburg became her story, never to be forgotten because it was now indelibly imprinted in her psyche. Katie shared this story with her fourth-grade classmates, who were fascinated about the Civil War and wanted to visit Vicksburg. Now Katie and I share this family story in Aunt Dora's rocking chair with her children and my grandchildren Kaiser and Genevieve.

The history of curriculum development in the postmodern era must also be recounted and understood from this autobiographical perspective, as I have done throughout this chapter, and not simply be treated as a utilitarian means–end evaluation for accountability. Our accountability must be to human persons and not tests and measures. The content of the events in the history of curriculum development are meaningless outside the autobiographical context of individual educators engaged in the exploration and excavation of the meaning of the events and the people, both famous/infamous and anonymous, who have been part of this history. Therefore, chapter 3 will continue our discussion of the historical dimension of curriculum development incorporating an autobiographical methodology.

three
The Reconceptualization of Curriculum Studies

Chapter 2 proposed that postmodern curriculum scholars should critically examine the history of curriculum development in the context of their own autobiography and life narratives in order to advance an experiential and participatory perspective in education. This concept of autobiographical historical contextualization, which I discussed in the preface, is rooted in my own experience as a graduate student in curriculum theory at LSU in the 1980s, when I studied postmodernism and was exposed to autobiographical, ethnographic, and phenomenological methodologies. Graduate students and faculty traveled together to the *Journal of Curriculum Theorizing* (now *JCT: An Interdisciplinary Journal of Curriculum Studies*) Bergamo Conference, held every October at the Bergamo Center in Dayton, Ohio. This conference can be traced back to the University of Rochester conference in 1973, which signaled that the reconceptualization of American curriculum studies was underway. It is important to note that a diverse group of scholars attended this conference, and that they were united only in their opposition to the managerial and prescriptive nature of curriculum studies that were aligned with Frederick Taylor's scientific management and Ralph Tyler's principles of curriculum and instruction. Thus, it is a misnomer to call these professors "the reconceptualists." There was no ideological or thematic unity among the participants.

The 1973 curriculum conference followed from a previous tradition. Janet Miller (2005) contends that Professor Paul Khlor, at a conference at the Ohio State University in 1967 titled "Curriculum Theory Frontiers," was the inspiration for the reconceptualization as well as one of the most significant figures in the curriculum field. Khlor helped to organize this conference to honor the 20th anniversary of a 1947 conference held at the University of Chicago, titled "Toward Improved Curriculum Theory," that involved Hollis Caswell, Virgil Herrick, and Ralph Tyler as participants.

Indeed, curriculum theory has been around for a long time, and new ways of thinking were fermenting in many circles before the 1973 Rochester conference.

Publication of *JCT* began in 1978, with William Pinar and Janet Miller serving as editor and managing editor, respectively. Other editors since 1990 have been Jo Anne Pagano of Colgate University; William Reynolds of Oklahoma State University, and now at Georgia Southern University; Brent Davis and Dennis Sumara of York University in Toronto and now at the University of Alberta, Patrick Slattery of Texas A&M University; David G. Smith of the University of Alberta; Marla Morris of Georgia Southern; and now Adam Howard of Colby College. The 1978 conference was held at the Rochester Institute of Technology and chaired by Professor Ronald Padgham, then from 1979 to 1982 moved to the Airlie Conference Center in Virginia. With the support of the University of Dayton, the conference found a home at the Bergamo Center in Dayton in 1983. As a result of the significant influence of Canadian scholars, it was held in Alberta at the Banff Conference Center in 1994.

In 1995 the *JCT* curriculum conference moved to the Highlander Folk School in Monteagle, Tennessee. Founded by Myles Horton, Highlander played important roles in many major political movements, including the southern labor movements of the 1930s, the civil rights movement of the 1940s to 1960s, and the Appalachian people's movements of the 1970s and 1980s. Highlander is also the place where Martin Luther King, Jr., Rosa Parks, and other nonviolent civil rights activists met for training and retreat. This history made Highlander a natural setting for a reconceptualized curriculum conference, with its emphasis on critical theory, social activism, arts-based research, feminism, queer theory, and critical race theory. The state of Tennessee attempted to close Highlander Folk School in the turbulent and racist climate of the 1960s, when the school—just like all activist organizations and prophetic leaders like Martin Luther King, Jr., at that time—was accused of being a haven for communists. With national indignation and the support of some professors at nearby University of the South, Highlander continued to operate and today still serves as a conference and training site. Rosa Parks' death in November, 2005, was a milestone occasion to remind people that she was not simply a tired woman who refused to give up her seat on a bus. She trained at Highlander and worked as organizer for the NAACP. Rosa Parks—the only woman ever to lie in state in the US Capitol rotunda—and the work of the Highlander Folk School in Tennessee are excellent exemplars for curriculum development in the postmodern era.

In the milieu established by *JCT* and its annual conference, the reconceptualization became for me and my colleagues a dynamic experience of exploring emerging concepts of curriculum with a wide array of international educators rather than a remote event that occurred in the 1970s to be studied in a textbook. For those interested in a more detailed analysis of these events, an excellent review of the reconceptualization can be found in chapter 4 of William Pinar et al.'s (1995) *Understanding Curriculum* and chapter 1 of Janet Miller's (2005) *Sounds of Silence Breaking*.

By 1999 the curriculum field had become more diffuse, and other conferences and journals expanded the vision of the reconceptualization and became a new locus for understanding and exploring curriculum. The most prominent are the Curriculum and Pedagogy Conference (C&P), launched in Austin, Texas, in 2000; the International

Association for the Advancement of Curriculum Studies (IAACS) and its US affiliate the American Association for the Advancement of Curriculum Studies (AAACS), launched at LSU in 2001; and the American Association for Teaching and Curriculum (AATC), founded in 1993 by professors John Laska, O. L. Davis, and colleagues at the University of Texas. Davis also edited the Association for Supervision and Curriculum Development's (ASCD) *Journal of Curriculum and Supervision*. AAACS, C&P, and AATC all meet annually. C&P publishes annual proceedings and the *Journal of Curriculum and Pedagogy*, formerly edited by James G. Henderson and Patrick Slattery, and now edited by B. Stephen Carpenter and Stephanie Springgay. AAACS, founded by William Pinar—who moved to the University of British Columbia in 2005—and chaired formerly by Janet Miller of Teachers College at Columbia University and Patrick Slattery of Texas A&M University, and now by Peter Appelbaum of Arcadia University, publishes the *Journal of AAACS* under the editorship of Alan Block of the University of Wisconsin. The curriculum field is dynamic and prolific. And now the next generation of curriculum scholars, organized by Professor Erik Malewski of Purdue University, has initiated a new gathering for post-reconceptualization scholarship in 2006. At this writing, the scholarship of the curriculum field is truly diverse and engaging.

As a beginning doctoral student in 1985, I was unfamiliar with many of the scholars and theories associated with the reconceptualization. Readers of this book may also be encountering this history for the first time. In fact, before entering the program at LSU, I had never heard the word "reconceptualization" used in a curriculum context. I had worked as a high school English and mathematics teacher and as an elementary and secondary principal prior to beginning my doctoral work. I was a member of the Association for Supervision and Curriculum Development and the National Association of Secondary School Principals. Since the mid-1970s I had attended the annual conventions of many national organizations, occasionally presented formal papers, and faithfully read the publications *Educational Leadership*, *Education Week*, *NASSP Bulletin*, and *Momentum*. As a principal I also subscribed to several other journals, including *Kappan* (the journal of Phi Delta Kappa), *ASCD Update*, and *Principal*. None of these conferences or publications included reconceptualized or postmodern curriculum development material.

My involvement in state and national professional associations focused on practical concerns about classroom management, effective schools, testing, and staff development, as well as classroom programs that might efficiently raise test scores and improve instruction so that our campus could become recognized by programs such as Schools of Excellence and National Blue Ribbon Schools. There was seldom any reflection on the theoretical underpinnings, sociological impact, race and gender bias, international connections, or political implications of such programs. Despite my dissatisfaction with many aspects of school bureaucracy in the1980s, I was unaware of the theoretical challenges to the dominant concept of curriculum development that were emerging in the universities. Even while studying for a master's degree in school administration in the early 1980s at Arizona State University, I was never challenged to question Frederick Taylor's scientific management or Ralph Tyler's curriculum rationale, both of which I had learned in my undergraduate teacher training program in New Mexico, and the subsequent application of this philosophy in the schools where I taught in the 1970s. Dare I say that my experiences forty years ago are still being repeated in 2012 as I write this third edition? It seems that our pre-service teacher education and administrator training programs have a long way to go to inform educators about these curriculum developments!

During my tenure as an administrator in several different schools, I was constantly bombarded with innovative reforms, new technology, district programs, and pre-packaged curricular materials—often called "teach proof" to indicate that teachers could not deviate from the lessons—designed to solve all my educational problems. I intuitively realized that these reform proposals would not ameliorate the local or the national schooling crises of the time. However, out of fear of change, ignorance of alternatives, or sheer determination to make the reforms work, I seldom strayed very far from the Taylor and Tylerian model. In the process, I was "Hunterized" (Madeline Hunter's *Master Learning* and *Mastery Teaching*) and "Canterized" (Lee Canter's *Assertive Discipline*). Later I "Bloomed" (Allan Bloom's *Cultural Literacy*), and then I was "Bushed" (The first president George Bush's *America 2000*). I learned how to build an effective school, an essential school, a drug-free school, a James Madison School (William Bennett, 1987, 1988), and a Paedeia School (Mortimer Adler's *The Paedeia Proposal*, 1982). One company even wined and dined me until I agreed to start a Renaissance School. I was required to take 4Mat training, Osiris training, and time management training. I learned to manage by objectives (MBO) and develop an outcomes-based curriculum (OBE). The proliferation of similar strategies continues today, but the names have changed to *No Child Left Behind*, *Race to the Top*, scientifically based research, curriculum mapping, accountability, growth scale value, Annual Yearly Progress, and so forth.

All my efforts finally paid dividends in 1986, when I reached what I thought at the time was the pinnacle of educational achievement: Excellence in Education. William Bennett, then secretary of education under President Reagan, was about to publish a new book titled *First Lessons*, a prescription for improving the elementary school curriculum. In conjunction with the publication, the Department of Education initiated an elementary school competition, similar to an already popular high school program that began in 1983, entitled *Excellence in Education*. Two hundred American elementary schools that exemplified the highest caliber curriculum and instruction would win the award and be invited to a reception at the White House with President Reagan and Secretary Bennett.

I was the principal of a rural elementary school at the time the new competition was announced, and the staff, teachers, and school board were all thrilled to participate. On July 4, 1986, when the winners of the competition were announced, I was vacationing in Orlando, Florida, with my family. I was reading *USA Today* in the hotel restaurant and discovered the article listing "America's Best Elementary Schools" state by state. I was jubilant to see my school on the list, convinced that it was indeed the best!

When I returned home from vacation, I discovered that there was tremendous pride in the local community. This award brought state and national media coverage as well as affirmation for parent volunteers, dedicated teachers, and especially the children. However, during the next school year, bitterness and jealousy surfaced among a few educators and parents from other schools. An award designed to promote excellence also had the effect of generating distrust and friction. Later, I began to question the value of comparing schools in national competitions. Although I did not realize it at the time, this question helped to prepare me to understand one of the central premises of postmodern thinking: the importance of cooperative and collaborative models to replace rampant and destructive competitiveness. Additionally, in the years since receiving William Bennett's excellence award, I have had the opportunity to teach, administer, and observe on many more campuses. I have discovered some truly remarkable schools that have never been recognized. I have also served as principal or evaluator at other schools that have received national or state recognition even though there existed extreme divisiveness and malaise in the school community at the time. My experience with this program has allowed me to evaluate critically the shortcomings of competitive curriculum models and see the wisdom of postmodern alternatives. Schools and classrooms are very fluid and complex, and accountability test scores rarely capture an accurate or complete perspective.

For example, principals often complain that the use of test scores to evaluate instruction is illogical because the attrition rate in the school is so high that they are not testing the students whom they taught. I have worked in school districts where the attrition rate—students enrolled in September but who drop out, transfer, become ill, die, or move before the end of the school year—exceeds 50%. While many districts with a stable population base may only have a 10% attrition rate, some urban and high poverty districts approach 90% attrition. I even worked in a high poverty district in the 1990s with a 110% turnover rate. This means that, by the time spring testing arrived, the entire original enrollment of the school population had turned over, and an additional 10% of the new students who had enrolled during the fall and early spring had also left the school. You might recall that Rodney Watson in chapter 2 called attention to this problem in New Orleans. Can we really logically hold the teachers and administrators accountable for the test scores of those students whom they did not teach? Additionally, these high poverty schools do not even have the curriculum materials and facilities that will allow them to compete (Kozol, 1991, 2005; O'Malley, Roseboro, Donyell, & Hunt, 2012). Following hurricanes Katrina and Rita in Louisiana, school districts in Texas and neighboring states appealed to the national government to exempt them from counting the displaced students who had moved to their school districts from the *NCLB* accountability requirements. Attrition and displacement is the norm in many school districts, and it is not something that just happens after a natural disaster. Again, let me reiterate, schools and classrooms are very fluid and complex, and accountability measures rarely capture an accurate or meaningful perspective of school performance, climate, or success.

The one thing that traditional curriculum development programs and *No Child Left Behind* reforms have in common is a commitment to organized goals, measurable objectives, accountability procedures, and mastery evaluation to achieve a specified educational outcome. While the focus of the proposals may be different, the curricular philosophy undergirding the methodologies remains committed to the modern paradigm. The reconceptualization opened up to me robust investigation of curriculum development theories and programs that challenged the traditional educational models, and it has provided a postmodern alternative to the reforms and programs that dominate educational practice today.

One of the central features of the reconceptualization is attentiveness to autobiographical and phenomenological experience. This is described by William Pinar and Madeleine Grumet in the classic text *Toward a Poor Curriculum*, where the authors outline some of the early thinking about a change of focus in curriculum studies. Pinar and Grumet (1976) challenged the field to focus on internal experiences rather than external objectives. The writing of existentialists Simone de Beauvior, Jean-Paul Sartre, Friedrich Nietzsche, Martin Buber, and Søren Kierkegaard, as well as the psychoanalytic work of Sigmund Freud, Carl Jung, and Jacques Lacan, is integral to their curriculum theory. The imaginative literature of stream-of-consciousness authors such as James Joyce, Marcel Proust, Virginia Woolf, and William Faulkner and the expressionist painting of artists like Jackson Pollock, Lee Krasner, and Franz Klein also had a major influence on Pinar and Grumet. It is important to note the authors' intention in using the fields of philosophy, psychology, literature, and art to inform a reconceptualized curriculum theory:

> The sort of inquiry I want shares the focus of these fields but not their methods of looking. We cannot solely rely on the imagination, however artful its expression, or reports of psychological problems or philosophic accounts of experience. Some synthesis of these methods needs to be formulated to give us a uniquely educational method of inquiry, one that will allow us to give truthful, public and usable form to our inner observations. It is this search for a method I am on now. (Pinar and Grumet, 1976, p. 5)

Pinar (1994) published a retrospective collection of essays that trace this search, titled *Autobiography, Politics, and Sexuality: Essays in Curriculum Theory, 1972–1992*, and a stunning summary of the reconceptualization in *What is Curriculum Theory?* in 2004 and 2011. The method that he describes is committed to an etymological understanding of curriculum as *currere*. The problem with traditional curriculum development, according to Pinar, is that the meaning of curriculum has been misinterpreted. *Currere* is derived from a Latin infinitive verbal phrase that means "to run the racecourse." Curriculum is a verb, an activity, or, for Pinar, an inward journey. The modern curriculum development rationale has truncated the etymological meaning and reduced curriculum to a noun, the racecourse itself. Thus, generations of educators have been schooled to believe that the curriculum is a tangible object—the lesson plans we implement or the course guides we follow—rather than the process of running the racecourse. Of course, critics must be reminded that verbal phrases also contain a noun—the racecourse itself. The shift in focus to the active process of learning has never denied that texts, materials, lessons, tests, and classrooms are important; they are simply not the substance of curriculum or the purpose of education. This apparently simple concept has been responsible for a profound shift in the understanding of curriculum development. As curriculum development in the postmodern era is studied in the 21st century, the reconceptualization of the 1970s will remain an important historical phenomenon that informs schooling praxis. Understanding curriculum, from the perspective of the reconceptualization, must take precedence over traditional curriculum development and program planning. William Schubert (1986) summarizes this position clearly:

> One of the most recent positions to emerge on the curriculum horizon is to emphasize the verb form of curriculum, namely, *currere*. Instead of taking its interpretation from the race course etymology of curriculum, *currere* refers to the running of the race and emphasizes the individual's own capacity to reconceptualize his or her autobiography. The individual seeks meaning amid the swirl of present events, moves historically into his or her own past to recover and reconstitute origins, and imagines and creates possible directions of his or her own future. Based on the sharing of autobiographical accounts with others who strive for similar understanding, the curriculum becomes a reconceiving of one's perspective on life. It also becomes a social process whereby individuals come to greater understanding of themselves, others, and the world through mutual reconceptualization. The curriculum is the interpretation of lived experiences. (p. 33)

Schubert's summary leads us back to Pinar's concept of *currere*, where the method is described in four stages of autobiographical reflection: regressive, progressive, analytical, synthetical. (Synthetical refers to the notion of synthesis and not artificial fabrication.) Pinar and Grumet (1976) write:

> It is therefore temporal and conceptual in nature, and it aims for the cultivation of a developmental point of view that is transtemporal and transconceptual. From another perspective, the method is the self-conscious conceptualization of the temporal, and from another, it is the viewing of what is conceptualized through time. So it is that we hope to explore the complex relation between the temporal and the conceptual. (p. 51)

The first step is the regressive moment where one returns to the past as it impinges on the present. The present is veiled because the past is manifested in who we are and what we do in the existential now. Pinar proposes that we enter the past, live in it, observe ourselves functioning in the past, but not succumb to it. Since the focus of the method is educational experience, special attention should be given to schooling, books, teachers, and other pedagogical experiences and artifacts. We regress to the past, but always with an eye toward a return to the present and to the next step, the progressive moment. The word "progressive" derives from the Latin *progredior*, "to step forward." Here we look, in the language of Jean-Paul Sartre and Ernst Bloch, at what is not yet present. We imagine a future, envision possibilities, and discern where our meditative images may appear to be leading us. The next step, the analytical moment, describes the biographic present, exclusive of the past and future but inclusive of responses to both. Pinar and Grumet (1976) write: "Bracketing what is, what was, and what can be, one is loosened from it, potentially more free of it, and hence more free to freely choose the present" (p. 60). This bracketing allows one to juxtapose the past, present, and future and evaluate the complexity of their multidimensional interrelations. After the analytical moment, a synthetical moment puts the three steps together to help inform the present. The authors conclude:

> The Self is available to itself in physical form. The intellect, residing in the physical form, is part of the Self. Thus, the Self is not a concept the intellect has of itself. The intellect is thus an appendage of the Self, a medium, like the body, through which the Self, the world are accessible to themselves. No longer am I completely identified with my mind. My mind is identified as a part of me. (Descartes' "I think, therefore I am" is thus corrected.) Mind in its place, I conceptualize the present situation. I am placed together. Synthesis. (1976, p. 61)

Pinar's method of *currere* challenges educators to begin with the individual experience and then make broader connections. This parallels our discussion of historical analysis in chapter 2. Curriculum development in the postmodern era is attentive both to the interconnectedness of all experiences and to the importance of the autobiographical perspective. Pinar (1994) concludes that autobiographical studies are

> windows which permit us to see again that which we loved before, and in so doing, see more clearly what and whom we love in the present. The regressive phase of *currere* asks us to speak again in the lost language of cranes, to see again what was outside our windows, and to become married—that is, in unison—with ourselves and with those around us, by renewing our vows to those who are past, exchanging vows with those who are present, and dancing our way until the morning dawns. (p. 267)

Reconceptualized curriculum theory understands time and history as proleptic—that is, as the confluence of past, present, and future in the synthetical moment. In this sense, the reconceptualization is an integral part of the emerging postmodern curriculum. However, as we will see throughout part II, there are various other postmodern perspectives that inform curriculum development.

The importance of the autobiographical process proposed by Pinar and Grumet, as well as other postmodern perspectives such as critical theory, feminist theory, critical race theory, and queer theory, is not central to the work of all curriculum theorists. One example is found in the work of Peter Hlebowitsh (1993), entitled *Radical Curriculum Theory Revisited*. I will cite from Hlebowitsh's summary critique of the reconceptualization at length for two reasons: first, he clearly reflects the philosophical position of those who challenge postmodernism, and, second, he provides an example for readers of the critiques of the reconceptualization of the curriculum field:

> In recent years, the curriculum field has been faced with a new radical commentary that has touted itself as contributing to a reconceptualization of the field's basic tenets. Many of the criticisms offered by these radical elements have been inspired by a critical theory of education that seeks to slay all common

sense or conventional outlooks. The call for a reconceptualization derives from the belief that curriculum study has historically been associated with an atheoretical management agenda that compresses the school experience into low level group procedures. There is indeed a facet of curriculum thought that could be characterized in such a manner; there is also a distinctive legacy of behavioristic manipulation, generated by this tradition, that continues to prevail in the schools. However, the formal study of curriculum theory and development cannot be reasonably reduced to the laws of efficiency and control that drive business/management strategy. It strains credulity to posit the entire development of the curriculum field in such a manner when the growth of the field paralleled the growth of the progressive movement in education. The voice of the formidable progressive forces, which included individuals such as Dewey, Counts, Rugg, and Bode, was not unheard in or merely incidental to the curriculum field. Unfortunately, when curriculum history is drawn with a straight ideological line, distortion results and central figures in the field undergo an unjustified revision. While Jesse Newlon, for instance, could be said to have brought the idea of curriculum to the field of administration, he was not, as has been alleged, driven by the desire to put everything under control of an administratively controlled directorate. In stark contrast, Newlon actually worked to alleviate the central managerial demands of the school by calling for the release of the classroom teacher's intelligence and creativity and by advocating experimentation in the fashioning of learning experiences. (1993, p. 19)

We can see, in Hlebowitsh, that postmodern curriculum theories, critical theories, and theories associated with the reconceptualization agree on one point: curriculum philosophers, scholars, and leaders such as John Dewey, Jesse Newlon, George Counts, Boyd Bode, Harold Rugg, Franklin Bobbitt, David Snedden, W. W. Charters, G. Stanley Hall, Charles W. Eliot, and William Heard Kilpatrick are important figures in the study of the history of the curriculum field. In fact, all of the texts recommended for the study of curriculum history in chapter 2 include an analysis of the impact of these towering figures. However, much discussion continues to surround the meaning, impact, and intention of the theories of these and other educators. Neither Hlebowitsh nor critical scholars have an absolute, final interpretation of these curriculum theories. In fact, as we saw in chapter 1, various people in the curriculum field vigorously debate the meaning of critical theory, cultural theory, feminist theory, and other strands of thought. As mentioned in the introduction, John Dewey himself sought, in *Experience and Education*, to clarify misapplication of his philosophy by some in the Progressive Education movement. Thus, while I appreciate and agree with Hlebowitsh's concern for recognizing the complexity of curriculum history, I do not experience the contemporary curriculum field either as ahistorical or as rewriting a new metanarrative. When scholars deconstruct and I critique scientific management, the Tylerian Rationale, and behaviorist and competitive models of curriculum accountability, none of us is ascribing a singular or unified application of these theories to all historical practices or even to all contemporary scholars. In fact, as we noted in the introduction and chapter 1, critics are not unified and often challenge each other. They seek the "complicated conversation" proposed by Pinar (2004a).

Another debate surrounds the beginning of curriculum and instruction as a specialized field of study. Should curriculum as a field of study be dated from 1918 and the publication of Franklin Bobbitt's *The Curriculum*? Bobbitt argued for the reform of existing curricula after what were then contemporary scientific notions of organization and measurement. However, his book in a sense crystallized theories that had been developing for many years. The scientific movement in education was responding to the dominance of faculty psychology. Charles Eliot was perhaps most visible in developing a rationale for utilizing faculty psychology in the curriculum. This rationale was expressed succinctly in two reports: by the Committee of Ten on Secondary School Studies (1893) and the Committee of Fifteen on Elementary Education (1895). Should the birth of the field be located with the publication of these statements?

Another possibility is to date the beginning of curriculum development as a field of study with the 1923 Denver curriculum revision project and Jesse Newlon, discussed above by Hlebowitsh. Herbert Kliebard (1986) also describes the Denver project:

> The Denver, Colorado, project was initiated in 1922 with an appropriation of $31,500 from the school board for curriculum revision. Elimination of waste seems to have been one of the main considerations. Superintendent Jesse Newlon's recommendation to the school board ... pointed out that, in view of the size of the school budget in Denver, if it turned out that as little as "10 percent of teacher's time is spent on non-essential and misplaced materials in courses of study," that would represent an "annual waste to the Denver taxpayers of $315,000." ... The most lasting legacy of the Denver program was the emphasis given to active teacher participation in curriculum reform. (p. 212)

Was the Denver project initiated by Newlon designed to eliminate waste, empower teachers, foster creativity and experimentation, or centralize administrative bureaucracy? Debates about its purpose and Newlon's intentions continue today, with some scholars arguing that curriculum development as a field began in Denver.

Another date that is proposed for the beginning of the field is 1828, with the publication of *The Yale Report on Defense of the Classics*, which rationalized the classical curriculum with an emphasis on Greek and Latin as school subjects and memorization and recitation as instructional methods. Variations of both faculty psychology and classical curriculum are discernible in the curriculum debates today. Pinar et al. (1995) date the beginning of the field to *The Yale Report*.

What can be seen in the preceding discussion of the debates about dating the beginning of curriculum development as a field of study and the meaning of the events surrounding the history of curriculum studies in microcosm is the dilemma of the modern paradigm. Interpretations depend on the context and perspective of the individual author. Does this mean that historical studies are now irrelevant in the postmodern era? Should we simply focus on the present and future? Obviously not! Contemporary curriculum scholars do not ignore historical analysis. Indeed, Pinar's method begins with the regressive moment. Proleptic eschatology, as we will see in chapter 4, requires an historical experience. However, curriculum development in the postmodern era will insist that the meaning of events cannot be separated from their context, just as the knower cannot be separated from the known, and that all interpreting and bracketing of events must be directed toward a synthetical, integrated understanding.

Despite the critiques from both the left and the right, the curriculum must include some form of autobiographical analysis in order to appropriately address the important questions of curriculum history. The eclectic, ironic, and artistic elements of postmodernism require such a dimension, and the reconceptualization has provided curriculum studies with the challenge to explore curriculum history and the self from this postmodern perspective.

By the 1980s, the movement to reconceptualize the curriculum field had lost the cohesive bonds that maintained the coalition during the first years of struggle and enthusiasm. Opposition to the dominance of the traditional field was no longer a powerful enough force for coalition, as the movement had succeeded in delegitimating the dominance of the ahistorical, atheoretical field that often existed before 1970. With the continued resistance of Marxist scholars to a multiperspectival conception of reconceptualization, with the emergence of autobiographical studies and arts-based autoethnography, with the expansion of existential and phenomenological scholarship, with the burgeoning of feminist theory, queer theory, multicultural theory, cultural studies, and anti-racist theory, and the appearance of postmodernism, the original reconceptualist movement can be said to have disappeared. The success of the reconceptualization brought on its demise (Pinar, 1988a; Pinar et al., 1995). The resurgence of many new and energetic conferences and journals noted above, and even a *post-reconceptualization* movement among young scholars in 2006 at Purdue University, indicate that the reconceptualization of curriculum studies has accomplished groundbreaking significance and contributed a lasting impact to curriculum development.

William Pinar describes the transformation of the reconceptualization:

> It is clear that the American curriculum field was reconceptualized swiftly and rather completely. Replacing the nearly exclusive preoccupation with curriculum development and design were scholarly efforts to understand curriculum. These efforts can be characterized now by the framing of their interest to understand curriculum, i.e., understanding curriculum as a political text, as phenomenological text, as autobiographical text, and the other major sectors of scholarship. (Pinar et al., 1995, p. 231)

The reconceptualization has established a challenge for curriculum specialists, classroom teachers, university professors, and educational administrators to reenvision their pedagogical role, and the autobiographical method provides access to the postmodern visions of curriculum development that are emerging today.

Typical of the emerging autobiographical studies in the curriculum field in the 1990s was Robert J. Graham's (1991) comprehensive and insightful book *Reading and Writing the Self: Autobiography in Education and the Curriculum*. Graham examines the place and use of autobiography in the curriculum from the perspective of literary theory, Deweyan philosophy, and the reconceptualization. He also cautiously examines both the advantages and the pitfalls of the use of autobiography in education throughout the book. Ultimately, though, he concludes: "Although itself not a principle or a theory, autobiography permits access to valid sources of information that facilitate the recovery and inspection of ideas of great relevance to education and to the field of curriculum in particular" (1991, p. 16). Graham contends that, while autobiography provides access to important sources for reclaiming hidden or forgotten aspects of the individual's past, these sources have been "prevented from germinating owing to the constraints imposed by timetables and other institutional practices that mitigate against the use [of autobiography]" (p. 13). The book emphasizes the productive use of autobiography by feminist theorists and ethnic minorities for reclaiming collective voices and redeeming a lost sense of historical consciousness. Thus, Graham concludes by contending, "It behooves all of us who are involved in whatever aspect of public education to begin to consider the extent of our own knowledge and attitudes toward autobiography and its potential as well" (p. 156).

Another important development in autobiography in curriculum studies is found in arts-based research. Perhaps typical is the work of Stephanie Springgay, former chair of the Arts-Based Educational Research SIG of AERA and co-editor of the *Journal of Curriculum and Pedagogy*. Springgay studied at the University of British Columbia—one of the leading sites for arts-based research—under the leadership of professor Rita Irwin. She maintains that the role of contemporary artworks is no longer to form imaginary or utopian realities, but rather to create ways of living and autobiographical models of action. Art, for Springgay, becomes a moment to be lived through, opening up unlimited conversations. Art uses the autobiographical context to create an experience of encounters, intersubjectivities, and the collective elaboration of meaning. Writing about her arts-based dissertation titled *Inside the Visible: Youth Understandings of Body Knowledge through Touch*, Springgay (2004) concludes:

> Inside the Visible disrupts signification in the field of vision and visual culture, research methodologies, and curriculum and pedagogy, informed by an epistemological inquiry grounded difference through touch. It advocates an intercorporeal relationality, a way of knowing and being with, in, and through the body in the world. It is redolent with sensuous knowledge, full of ecstasy and excess. It speaks a language of images and words, smells and textures, sights and sounds. It remains open. It cultivates breath. (p. 15).

The physicality of Springgay's artwork can also be experienced in her language, as she describes the focus on touch, smell, and sensuality in her curriculum theorizing. This is the immediacy of autobiography that the new arts-based curriculum researchers are bringing to the field.

Returning to my autobiographical reflections from the beginning of this chapter, I can now understand the influence of the traditional curriculum methodologies, as well as various reform proposals, on my career as a teacher and principal. I can also place my own teacher training program in the context of the historical events that shaped the philosophy of my undergraduate education program. It further convicts me to carefully examine the content and methods of the pre-service teacher education classes that I teach at Texas A&M today.

My first pre-service teacher education course as an undergraduate student at the College of Santa Fe in New Mexico was entitled "Education Psychology." The ambiance of the city of Santa Fe and the mystique of the Sangre de Christo Mountains created a wonderfully liberating atmosphere for my studies, but this stood in stark contrast to the physical atmosphere of my education class. At the initial meeting for this course, thirty students crowded into a traditional classroom with metal desks facing a black-board. The walls were bare, and florescent fixtures filled the room with light. There were no windows. It was as though the outside world had been shut out. The professor wrote the following statement on the board: "There is no such thing as motivation." The students dutifully copied these words in their notebooks. The professor turned to the class and paused for comments. No one dared to say a word. Finally, I could not resist the urge to speak. Presuming that the professor had written this obviously incorrect statement on the board in order to elicit a reaction, I began to challenge the premise that there was no such thing as motivation. I was quickly chastised. The professor had been a student of Skinnerian behaviorism at the University of Minnesota. This statement became the basis of our semester study of lesson plans and behavioral objectives, as well as the cognitive, psychomotor, and affective domains of learning. To my dismay, even the affective domain was restricted to observable and measurable lessons such as this one example: "The student will demonstrate appreciation of Igor Stravinsky by listening attentively to a recording of *The Rite of Spring* and by identify-ing this music in the soundtrack of the classic Walt Disney cartoon *Fantasia* on a unit test." There was no room for intuition, ambiguity, emotion, intrinsic motivation, complexity, and uncertainty in the curriculum of my undergraduate training.

I remember meeting with the professor to discuss my concerns about behavioral objectives. I did not feel comfortable with the learning theories and objective lesson plans presented in the course, but over the years I continued to receive a steady dose of this approach to teacher training by all of my professors and school administrators. The accountability measures of *No Child Left Behind* and *Race to the Top* that are strangling and suffocating teachers today are based on the same dreadful philosophy that dominated my pre-service teacher education in 1973. However, by the time I started my student teaching I had perfected the methods. I was like the kindergarten student in Harry Chapin's song "Flowers are Red," in which the child uses all the colors of the rainbow to paint flowers. The teacher repeatedly scolds the child and insists that flowers are only red and green. After several punishments, the child finally agrees with the teacher and begins to paint flowers as instructed. The next year the child moves to another school, where the new teacher encourages students to use all their crayons to color flowers. The teacher notices that this new student uses only red and green for coloring. The teacher approaches the child, who adamantly insists that flowers are only red and green. Chapin ends his touching ballad with an uplifting refrain about all the colors of the rainbow, implying that, in time, the teacher was able to gently invite this child to reinvestigate the aesthetic spirit. I deeply fear the loss of creativity, imagination, aesthetic sensibilities, environmental connections, autobio-graphical sensibilities, spiritual awareness, emotional maturity, heightened consciousness, and educational passion in our teachers, students, and citizens. I truly believe that the health and safety of the planet and its citizens are at stake. My commitment to curriculum development in the postmodern era is more than an academic exercise; I believe that the challenges of the reconceptualization offer an opportunity to reevaluate what is most important in schools and society and reinvigorate our learning experiences. The next several chapters will begin to outline some of my thinking in this direction.

Reflecting on my teacher training program is important for me today, as I now teach foundation courses to undergraduate students preparing to become teachers. I constantly recall my own experiences as I select textbooks, structure the learning experiences, show films, invite guest speakers, visit community centers and schools, and encourage prophetic practices. Additionally, Pinar's autobiographical method has provided the support for moving from a scientifically based accountability model and structures in the spirit of the Tylerian Rationale to a postmodern pedagogy. One of the tangible changes in my teaching style affected by the reconceptualization is that I now always structure my classroom in a seminar circle and provide opportunities for the students to share their personal insights and autobiographical perspectives. I also spend several class sessions off campus and in local contexts. I use lots of challenging and provocative documentary films. The students' concerns about their needs and expectations are valued and honored. Additionally, I expose my students to autobiographical methods and assign reflective essays, electronic portfolios documenting field experiences, and online WebCT conversations in small groups.

Curriculum development in the postmodern era will see the emergence of more media, arts and visual culture, cultural studies, reflective journals, public pedagogy, portfolios, place-based learning, and autobiographical methodologies. The reconceptualization in curriculum studies has reminded educators that we can no longer remain ahistorical, detached, impersonal, and "behaviorly objective." In the process of exploring meaning and knowledge, we can no longer separate the context of historical events from the autobiographical experiences of teachers and students. The reconceptualization of curriculum studies has successfully reconnected the past, present, and future in a synthetical and proleptic moment, reuniting body, psyche, and spirit in ways that have enhanced curriculum development in the postmodern era.

four
Postmodern Schooling, Curriculum, and the Theological Text

This chapter investigates religion, spirituality, and culture and the ways that these important dimensions of human life and society inform and are informed by curriculum studies. I frame this chapter around the umbrella concept of theology—the scholarly study of religion and spirituality. The rituals and dogmas of religion inspire faith and morality for many people. Mosques, synagogues, sweat lodges, churches, temples, sacred mountains, ashrams, and cathedrals have been uplifting places of spiritual reflection, personal renewal, and prayerful worship for individuals and communities throughout human history. However, many people have also been repulsed by the financial excesses, brutal inquisitions, hate rhetoric, sex abuse, blatant hypocrisy, terrorist bombings, and violent crusades carried out in the name of religion by religious leaders, prophets, and followers. Religion can alienate and inspire. In either case, it is a powerful cultural phenomenon that must be examined carefully. In fact, many global conflagrations are rooted in religious conflict and theological misunderstandings, and this must be examined by scholars and teachers who desire to ameliorate tensions and advance justice. This is the theological task of chapter 4. It is a scholarly project open to students of any religious or spiritual persuasion. Nothing here should be interpreted as proselytizing, evangelizing, or advancing any religion or spirituality.

There are many people whose religious identity is a cultural imperative and not necessarily an act of faith or spirituality: agnostic Catholics, atheist Jews, separatist Hindu Tamils, political Israeli Zionists, ethnic Christians, social Muslims, militant fundamentalists, or secular Buddhists. Some people are eclectic and ecumenical—they embrace the best practices of many world religions. The Vietnamese Buddhist theologian Thich Nhat Hanh (1995), author of *Living Buddha, Living Christ*, is a good example. Others have no interest in dogmatic or ritualistic religion, but prefer to seek wisdom, insight, enlightenment, and spiritual experience outside of the context of formal religion. No matter how religion and spirituality are understood, they are powerful forces in the lives of individuals—including teachers and students in schools. For many people, religion and spirituality require a personal commitment to a deity, many deities, or possibly a cosmic force such as harmony or justice. Religion may also involve adherence to certain scriptures, rituals, values, clothing, initiation rites, and community worship. For many others, however, religion means only participation in cultural holidays, family rituals, public ceremonies marking the beginning or ending of life, or preparing and eating specific ethnic foods. Religion as cultural heritage, in this case, does not include faith, prayer, and beliefs. I seek to understand curriculum as theological text by exploring religion, spirituality, and culture in all of these complex manifestations and to examine their implications for schools and classrooms.

I have been a student of theology for my entire adult life. My first graduate degree was from a Roman Catholic institution that taught liberation theology, social activism, proleptic eschatology, and progressive ecumenical dialogue. I have practiced yoga and discovered heightened understandings of inner peace. I even spent a year of my life in a novitiate that led to one of the most profound experiences in my life: the monastic silence of the Benedictine order at Christ in the Desert Monastery in Abiquiu, New Mexico. I also studied theology at a large state university with an emphasis on Gnosticism and world religions. My professors were conservative Jews, liberal Protestants, Catholic nuns, agnostic linguists, Gnostic feminists, biblical historians, Greek and Hebrew hermeneutic scholars, and leaders of Latin American liberation theology. I was fortunate to study with many inspiring theologians and listen to their scholarly lectures: Hans Kung, Raymond Brown, Elaine Pagels, Gustavo Gutiérrez, Charles Curran, Mary Minella, Gabriel Moran, and Geoff Kelly.

I present my autobiographical background in order to foreground my context for theology and spirituality. However, it is also important to note that I am an adamant advocate of a democratic vision of the separation of religion from government and church from state. I agree with former US president Jimmy Carter (2006), in his book *Our Endangered Values: America's Moral Crisis*, that the confluence of government and religion by fundamentalists of various religious traditions and ideologies is one of the most dangerous developments in the world today. Democracy and theocracy are incompatible. Rigid ideological denominational proselytizing is anathema to my thinking. I also agree with Protestant evangelical pastor Jim Wallis (2005), in his important book *God's Politics: A New Vision for Faith and Politics in America*, that attempting to ignore or suppress the religious, spiritual, and theological dimensions of cultures and individuals is equally dangerous and destructive. I am on a search for a way to balance these aspirations—separating religion and government while at the same time embracing the spiritual and the theological. Some may contend that this is an impossible quest. Others, such as Richard Dawkins (2006) in *The God Delusion* and Christopher Hitchens (2007) in *God Is Not Great: How Religion Poisons Everything*, do not find a redeeming quality in religion, but rather conflict, contradictions, and conflagration at every turn. Bertrand Russell established a philosophical basis for atheism in his 1927 lecture *Why I am not a Christian*. No matter what your personal beliefs, it is important to understand all of these perspectives.

There has always been an urge in the dominant US culture to assimilate children and immigrants into mainstream society—except, of course, when powerful elites and their allies are insisting that the borders be closed to keep "aliens" out of the country. Each new generation seems to forget their own immigrant heritage. From the fear of Irish and Italian "papists" (Roman Catholics) in the mid-19th century to the fear of "illegal" Mexican workers and "terrorist" Muslims today, the dominant majority—often White, male, heterosexual, militant, and Protestant Christian—has attempted to regulate and assimilate people who are culturally different. Fear and hatred of people who are different—as well as economic greed and exploitation—have led to the brutalization of immigrants, migrant laborers, aboriginal and First Nations people, enslaved servants, and other indentured workers by the dominant and hegemonic powers. This denigration includes what can be called a *cultural bomb* intended to eradicate minority religion, language, and culture either by assimilation or by annihilation.

Schools have been one of the primary sites for socialization, regulation, intimidation, and indoctrination. The curriculum is often used as a cultural bomb to eradicate beliefs. This is documented, for example, in William Watkins' (2001) book *The White Architects of Black Education*. Of course, this can be contrasted with other conflicting and ironic tendencies in the US character. Wealthy corporations, business leaders, financial elites, and even middle-class homeowners in the US hire poor and incredibly hard-working Asian, Latin American, and Eastern European immigrants and migrants for construction and menial labor. The elites also eschew integrated public schools for their own children, thus avoiding exposure to the race or class of the "other" people. The same people who vocally oppose "illegal" immigration benefit tremendously from less costly migrant labor. In a shocking display of hypocrisy, some critics secretly secure immigrant laborers to care for their lawns, children, and mansions and refuse to pay living wages, social security, or health benefits.

In contrast to the assimilation, segregation, and exploitation of poor and minority people and the brutal annihilation of native people and people of color—a savage history that continues today, as evidenced by the inadequate response to Hurricane Katrina in 2005—there is also a long tradition of progressive education, activist schools, sanctuary churches, hospitality houses for battered women and the homeless, labor movements, government safety nets, education unions, and liberal arts curriculum which counter exploitation and poverty. Compassion and care for the poor, suffering, mentally ill, and displaced population is inspiring in these contexts. These competing ideologies and practices—exploitation versus hospitality, isolationism versus engagement, assimilation versus emancipation, economic individualism versus community responsibility, conservative privatization versus progressive public policy—exist side by side in American history. George W. Bush, for example, campaigned in 2000 on a platform of *compassionate conservatism*—the privatization of services for the poor and the distribution of money to religious institutions to care for the hungry, addicted, disabled, and homeless. Hillary Clinton (1996), representing a democratic point of view, wrote a book titled *It Takes a Village*, in which she advocates for building a community of families, churches, educators, medical professionals, and government to work together to care for the needs of all people. These political differences, coupled with intractable racism, sexism, heterosexism, xenophobia, and other prejudices, make the current climate for discussing issues of justice and compassion volatile. Thus, the story of theology and curriculum in schools and society in this chapter is necessarily a very complex and complicated conversation.

We could begin our study of religion and schooling in the US with the Olde Deluder Satan Act of 1647 in the Massachusetts Bay colony that mandated Bible reading in the schools, or the distinctions between the philosophies of Thomas Jefferson and Benjamin Franklin on the role of education and faith in a democracy, or Jane Addams' educational and social vision for women and children at the Hull House in Chicago, which she founded in 1889, or the competing political and educational proposals of Booker T. Washington and W. E. B. Dubois in relation to education for African Americans in the early 20th century. All have interesting and compelling theological connections. However, I prefer to begin in 1840 with the creation of the first public schools in the US, which were called *common schools*. The seeds of the current debates about religion and education can be found in the curricular debates in the 1840s between Horace Mann, the first state superintendent of education in Massachusetts, and Orestes Brownson, Catholic publisher of the *Boston Quarterly Review*. These debates can be instructive for students from any nation: the historical details will be different, but the cultural conflicts are similar.

Immigration to the US was at a peak in the 1840s, particularly because Irish Catholics were fleeing abject poverty and famine. Horace Mann proposed his idea of common schools, which would include a common political creed and a common morality based on what he called "nonsectarian" religion, in order to teach these newly arrived immigrants. His ultimate purpose was to assimilate the masses, particularly immigrants, so that a common Christian democracy could be established. Mann (1848) explains his position: "In this age of the world, it seems to me that no student of history, or observer of mankind, can be hostile to the precepts and the doctrines of the Christian religion, or opposed to any institutions which expound and exemplify them" (p. 102).

The common school movement prevailed in the US, and public education began in earnest in the 1840s. Of course, as Joel Spring (1993) documents, the common school was never common to all children, since many were denied an education. The Catholic minority population vehemently opposed Mann and proposed instead publicly funded sectarian schools—an approach still in effect in Canada today, albeit with complexities and problems of its own, such as the treatment of First Nations indigenous people in boarding schools and the exclusion of some religious schools from approved government programs. Orestes Brownson argued with the minority that nonsectarian Christianity, as put into practice in the common schools, was really nondenominational Protestantism, with readings from the King James Bible and Protestant rituals. Brownson ([1839] 1971) explains: "Education, then, must be religious and political. Neither religion nor politics can be excluded. Indeed, all education that is worth anything is either religious or political and fits us for discharging our duties either as simple human beings or as members of society" (p. 280). Brownson established the argument that the exclusion of religion and politics from the curriculum would make education worthless, but the inclusion would make education offensive to the minority. He continued:

[Mann's] board assures us Christianity shall be insisted on so far, and only so far, as it is common to all sects. This, if it means anything, means nothing at all. All who attempt to proceed on the principle here laid down will find their Christianity ending in nothingness. Much may be taught in general, but nothing in particular. No sect will be satisfied; all sects will be dissatisfied. (pp. 280–281)

Despite Brownson's logic and a vocal Catholic protest, Horace Mann's common schools became the norm, and the majority set out to create a common history, religion, language, and politics in the curriculum of US schools. The Catholic minority reacted by establishing a parochial school system that expanded dramatically from the 1840s to the 1960s, reaching a peak of over 12,000 schools and 7 million students in 1965.

The Catholic school system began to experience a decline in the 1960s and then a leveling off by the 1990s. Some would attribute this phenomenon to four factors: first, Catholics, like many other immigrant communities, over time moved into mainstream American culture and gained wealth and power; second, John F. Kennedy was elected the first Catholic president in 1960; third, the Supreme Court ruled against Protestant prayers and Bible readings in the public schools in *Engle* v. *Vitale* in 1962 and *School District of Abington Township* v. *Schempp* in 1963, thus making the schools less threatening to Catholics and other religious minorities; and, fourth, Vatican Council II in Rome in the early 1960s opened Catholicism to new relationships with the modern world. It is interesting to note that, in 1962, Protestants, who once condemned Catholics as unpatriotic for establishing separatist schools, began steadily to open their own parochial schools. Protestant Christian schools began to flourish during the time when Catholic schools were in decline. Today parochial and private schools of all religious perspectives and philosophies, including Jewish, Muslim, Montessori, Waldorf, and many other charter schools and private schools with a nonsectarian curriculum, account for about 15% of the school population in the US. While much has been written about this phenomenon (see, for example, O'Gorman, 1987; Coleman & Hoffer, 1987; Beutow, 1988; Haynes, 1990; Nord, 1995; Lugg, 2004; Lugg & Tabbaa-Rida, 2006), my interest here is in the relationship between religious schools—of any denomination or creed—and postmodern and reconceptualized curriculum studies. As we proceed, remember that religion is a significant factor and often the hidden script behind many school curriculum controversies—from assimilation in the common schools, to evangelization through prayer and Bible readings in the public schools before 1962, to censored literary books on sex education or gay and lesbian issues since 1990, to intelligent design proposals for the science curriculum in 2005. We ignore religion and theology in our curriculum conversations at great peril. In fact, some argue that we must take religion seriously across the curriculum in order to develop a national conversation and consensus (Nord & Haynes, 1998).

For example, in the US elections on November 8, 2005, intelligent design—an alternative to the theory of evolution based on belief in an intelligent deity—won the approval of the Kansas Board of Education. In the same election, in Dover, Pennsylvania, all eight school board members who had voted to implement intelligent design in the school district were turned out of office. While those who promote intelligent design in the science curriculum as either an adjunct or an alternative to natural selection or Darwinian evolution are not in the majority, they certainly cause conflict in a number of school districts.

What should teachers do about religious creationism and intelligent design in the school curriculum? All educators will have to address this question even if only a few parents or religious leaders challenge the science texts in the school or if the district votes to include intelligent design in the curriculum. You might be surprised to know that I advocate the inclusion of intelligent design in the school curriculum—albeit in a cultural studies, political science, theology, or mythology class. In fact, I propose that we need to include all creation stories in literature and theology classes, among them Native American Turtle Island myths; Middle Eastern creation narratives; the Chinese god Pan Gu, whose body parts formed the mountains and landscape, and the goddess Nu Wa, who wove the broken sky together; The Hindu goddess Saraswathi; the two different stories of creation in the Book of Genesis; Hindu reincarnation theology; Vodun spirits; indigenous spiritualism; and Christian intelligent design mythology. We should also provide cultural analysis of these creation myths from several literary perspectives, embracing the insights of believers, nonbelievers, pantheists, agnostics, Gnostics, and atheists. But we should not incorporate creation narratives in the science curriculum for the same reasons outlined by Brownson above.

It is interesting to note that there are no longer challenges to the Copernican revolution or Newtonian mechanics in the physics curriculum. There is not a clamoring for the "flat earth" society to be given rebuttal space in geography books. Challenges to the laws of gravity by the "floating bodies" theory do not garner support for including resurrection, assumption, or reincarnation of bodies into heaven or nirvana in science texts. Why does the Darwinian revolution and evolution spark such conflict? Why have some scientific theories become firmly accepted in society while others are challenged? Of course, not all religions, including the Roman Catholic Church, believe that evolution is incompatible with faith or with the two Genesis narratives of creation. Faith and science inform each other but are not mutually exclusive. For those who are tired of the tone of the current debates about science and religion and want to investigate deeper theological understandings, I recommend reading process philosophy—for example, Alfred North Whitehead—and process theology—for example, Pierre Teilhard de Chardin. Teilhard de Chardin was a 20th-century mystic priest and palaeontologist—both a scientist and a Christian. He used evolutionary thought to describe the "Cosmic Christ," and he also described the evolutionary growth of the human species intellectually and spiritually. Process thinkers emphasize becoming over being, arguing that humans can advance beyond the turmoil and dysfunction of our present condition. Science is not to be feared by people of faith, but embraced for the possibilities it offers—but also deconstructed when it is used for evil. Tenzin Gyatso (2005), the 14th Dali Lama, recently wrote: "If science proves some beliefs of Buddhism wrong, then Buddhism will have to change." Postmodern theology can help us to grow intellectually and mature spiritually.

Another pertinent example from the November, 2005, election in the US is instructive. The Tampa Bay, Florida, school board previously had heard arguments from

Muslim families to include one holiday at the end of Ramadan on the school calendar in addition to the Christian holidays for Good Friday and Easter Monday and the Jewish holiday for Yom Kippur. The board voted to exclude all religious holidays rather than arguing about which holidays to schedule. This met with outrage in the community. As reported on the CBS Evening News on November 9, 2005, board members in Tampa received threats and angry e-mail messages condemning all Muslims as terrorists and un-American. There were calls for Muslims to leave the country. The board responded to this community pressure by reinstating the Christian and Jewish holidays, but not instituting the Muslim holiday. Should school districts include all local religions on the holiday calendar? Can young women wear headscarfs, veils, or jewelry with religions symbols to school? Should the school cafeteria offer choices for the religious dietary requirements of students? Perhaps not all accommodations will be possible, but the spirit of our efforts must be to accommodate the needs of all students whenever possible—not only in religion, but also physical, dietary, and academic needs. Hospitality, inclusiveness, and graciousness must be our guiding ethic. Unfortunately, exclusion and intolerance is pervasive in our schools, and this intolerance and ignorance will continue to plague us. It is an obstacle that prevents the US and other countries from moving forward as a democracy. Additionally, as I have stated above, democracy and theocracy are incompatible. So how do we appropriately include theology and cultural diversity in the curriculum without establishing religion in the public sphere? Many contend that it is very difficult to embrace religious diversity while still keeping church and state separate—an impossible quest, according to some—so it is best to leave all discussion of religion and spirituality to religious communities and families. I agree that prayer and worship are very personal matters and that proselytizing in the public sphere is destructive. However, we must find an appropriate way to teach theology, textual hermeneutics, cultural diversity, and critical analysis without crossing the line of separation between religion and government.

When I present my arguments for a theological curriculum that is not theocratic by referencing the Taliban and Al Qaeda, most of my students in the US strongly agree with me. After 9/11, Americans became aware of the dangers of theocracy in Afghanistan and Pakistan— even though we were already vaguely concerned about the consequences of militant theocracy in Iran following the US hostage crisis and the Islamic Revolution in 1979. In 2001 we learned that Osama bin Laden had used madrasa Islamic schools to indoctrinate young boys into a militant interpretation of the Koran that distorts jihad as a violent war against the West, using suicide bombing as a vehicle for young men to reach paradise, with its attendant virgins. Such a religious curriculum is abhorrent. But when I ask my students to critique the ways that curriculum in Western schools can also be manipulated to create a political ideology based on militant interpretations of the Christian Bible, they vehemently protest. Many of my students are not sophisticated enough to deconstruct and problematize the ways in which religion in the US undermines democracy and contributes to environmental degradation, hate crimes, sexism, and corporate greed that inflict immense suffering on millions of people globally. There are numerous examples of "home-grown terrorism" rooted in religious extremism, such as the Oklahoma City bombing.

I observe that many people are spiritually immature and religiously illiterate. Some are living in fear of a vengeful god, a demanding parent, or a cult-like pastor. Some have seldom moved out of their psychological comfort zones and physical insular communities to engage people of diverse beliefs, cultures, and perspectives. Others have been indoctrinated by family, spouses, or pastors into destructive behaviors and materialistic lifestyles. Many believers and nonbelievers are very sincere, but they have never been taught or embraced philosophical investigation, critical evaluation, spiritual meditation, and historical analysis, which are the hallmarks of a theological curriculum in the postmodern era—in contrast to indoctrination and blind obedience to a militant theocracy.

Perhaps one of the most helpful approaches to curriculum to address this problem is that of R. Michael Fisher. You will find an extensive discussion of his work and links to his Center for Spiritual Inquiry and Integral Education on the companion website for this book. Fisher (2011) writes:

> My research interest, and invitation to potential collaborators, is to keep asking how postmodern and integral philosophy, theory, and thinking can combine, synergize, and produce one of the most potent "tools" for undermining the current growing culture of fear [see "Fear Matrix" on the companion website] and building a truly nonviolent world. I have a vision the combination of these two is "hot" and "ripe" but it is so hard to get to, the conflict and differences intense, and yet, holding an integral perspective on this conflict, I sense small breakthroughs.

Much has been said about the place of religion and spirituality in the public schools and ways to advance Fisher's integral philosophy. For a variety of views, see, for example, the special issue of *Educational Leadership* in 1999 and the special issue of the *Journal of Curriculum and Pedagogy* in 2005, in which Nel Noddings writes:

> There are people who believe that prayer and other observances should be allowed in our public schools, others who believe that school is not the place for any discussion of religion, and still others who believe that a sensitive examination of religion is essential to any form of genuine education. I locate myself in the latter group .... More than 2000 years ago, Socrates argued that one's life should be examined if it is to be worth living. This examination—a continuous round of reflection, analysis, and discussion—should certainly include religious, existential, and moral questions. As we know, some Athenians found Socrates dangerous, and he was condemned for impiety and corrupting Athenian youth. Today, more than 2000 years later, we still have not found a way to include intelligent discussion of religious matters in our public schools. Young people who are fortunate enough to attend the finest liberal arts colleges benefit from such discussion, but almost all others never have that experience, despite evidence that they long for it and seek answers to religious and spiritual questions. (2005, p. 15)

Noddings provides a cogent and thoughtful analysis of the complex debates over religion and education. However, there are several important theological issues that we must explore before we can move to Nodding's "sensitive examination of religion" and Fisher's "undermining the culture of fear" in the school curriculum. The first topic explores the legal issues surrounding religion and curriculum in the US.

In *Lemon v. Kurtzman* in 1971, the US Supreme Court ruled that government law or practice in relation to religion was constitutional if it met all three of the following tests: 1) the government act that bears on religion must reflect a secular purpose; 2) it may neither advocate nor inhibit religion as its primary effect; and 3) it must avoid excessive government entanglement with religion. In short, teaching about religion in a non-coercive manner that does not advance or inhibit religious beliefs is constitutionally protected. Entangling the school administration or the curriculum in religious faith would be unconstitutional. Obviously, it is very difficult to distinguish between secular and religious purposes—a topic we will discuss in more detail in chapter 5. In 1999 the Supreme Court, in *Santa Fe Independent School District* v. *Doe*, ruled against student-led prayers at football games. Reminiscent of the common school debates, the plaintiffs were a Mormon family and a Catholic family who objected to the Protestant-led prayers. While the Lemon case provides a framework for teachers and administrators to follow when including religion in the school curriculum, not all citizens obey Supreme Court rulings. Governor Rick Perry of Texas went to a public school in Palestine, Texas, after the ruling and participated in a Christian prayer in defiance of the Supreme Court. I am reminded of another southern governor in the 1960s, named George Wallace, who defied the Supreme Court's 1954 *Brown* v. *Board of Education* decision by standing on the steps of the state capitol in Montgomery at his inauguration and vehemently shouting: "Segregation yesterday, segregation today, segregation forever."

How should we respond to such defiance? How should we react when the *Lemon v. Kurtzman* ruling is clearly being violated? My preferred method is to use what some call "guerrilla public pedagogy" (Brady, 2006). In the spirit of peaceful nonviolent resistance of the civil rights movement and in the method of the women's performing arts group called the Guerrilla Girls who create a public theatre spectacle to call attention to social justice issues, I publicly deconstruct issues of religion and education. Because of my theology degree and seminary training, I have often been called upon to lead prayers. Sometimes I accept the offer if it is being held at a private family home or at a church worship service. In these cases, I respectfully conform to the customs of the setting. However, in a public space where sectarian prayers are clearly beyond the law, I will decline and caution the group, though sometimes I use public pedagogy to deconstruct religious intolerance and help to advance education.

In one example at Texas A&M, I was participating in a literary seminar for new faculty and local teachers that was held every Saturday in the fall semester. After the morning seminar lecture, a formal banquet was held for the participants. I was a new professor at Texas A&M, a flagship public institution. I was surprised on the first Saturday when the director of the program led a Protestant Christian invocation before the meal and concluded by asking all to pray "in Jesus' name." The majority of

Baptists and evangelicals in attendance were visibly comfortable with the prayer and responded "Amen" or "Thank you, Jesus." But there were several Jews, Hindus, atheists, Muslims, and agnostics in attendance at the banquet who were very uncomfortable, and they were neither invited to pray differently nor empowered to object. The next week I was asked to lead the invocation. The context demanded that I say something, so I accepted the offer. I began by telling the gathering that, in my religious tradition, Mary, the Mother of God, is the intercessor of our prayers to Jesus, and that I had learned to pray to Mary when sitting on the lap of my recently deceased grandmother. I then recited a litany of Marian titles, such as "Queen of the Universe," followed by the prayer "Hail Holy Queen, mother of mercy, our life, our sweetness and our hope," which I fondly remember saying as a child with my mama. The Protestants in the audience were visible aghast because my prayer to Mary was heresy to them. The conference leader said nothing to me, but there were no more invocations in the future. My Catholic prayer was sincere, but out of context. The Protestants became the minority and they did not like it; my public pedagogy was a curriculum lesson about the Lemon test of the Supreme Court. I believe that such public tactics are sometimes the best way to expose and deconstruct the injustices of hegemony and religious intolerance in society.

We must also be concerned with appropriate ways of studying religious, existential, and moral questions in the schools, as Noddings suggested above. I argue that, in order to fully appreciate and understand art, music, literature, history, science, and social studies, the school curriculum must find a way for students to legally and appropriately study religious imagery, mythology, allusions, metaphors from sacred texts, philosophies of science, church patronage for the arts, political theocracies, ethical debates, historical empires, and a host of other related topics and to do so in the spirit of the Supreme Court ruling in *Lemon v. Kurtzman*.

We must study, too, the ongoing tragedy of colonization, racism, and empire and its connection to religious intolerance and hegemony: Native American spirituality and aboriginal religions worldwide were practically obliterated by ruthless missionaries, politicians, investors, and evangelists (see, for example, the film *The Mission*, the PBS documentary *How the West Was Lost*, and the book *American Holocaust* by David Stannard, 1992); genocide has killed millions in Rwanda, Congo, Sudan, and other African nations following imperialist domination in the 18th and 19th centuries (see, for example, the film *Hotel Rwanda* and the book *King Leopold's Ghost: A Story of Greed, Terror, and Heroism in Colonial Africa* by Adam Hochschild, 1999); African Americans and other minorities were tortured, genitally mutilated, and lynched by ruthless White mobs who wrapped themselves in religious values and patriotism (see, for example, the film about Billie Holiday titled *Strange Fruit*, the photography collection *Without Sanctuary* by James Allen, Hilton Als, John Lewis, and Leon Litwack, 2000, and the book *The Gender of Racial Politics and Violence in America* by William Pinar, 2001); and Hitler executed 11 million people in his attempt to annihilate the Jews as well as other minorities such as homosexuals, the Roma, and the handicapped (see, for example, the films *Europa, Europa, Schildler's List, Nasty Girl,* and *Bent*). These horrific acts do not happen out of context. It is instructive to read Daniel Goldhagen's (1996) book *Hitler's Willing Executioners: Ordinary Germans and the Holocaust*, in which he uncovers evidence that participation in the Holocaust and support for Hitler was widespread in Germany.

Persecution and genocide are not unrelated to small acts of ignorance and intolerance in our schools, classrooms, and communities. We are all "willing executioners" when we ignore injustice and when we allow prejudice to go unchecked. I recall the story of an observant Jewish friend who was forced to clean blackboards every afternoon from October to December in his public elementary school while the majority Christian teachers and students rehearsed for the Christmas pageant in the auditorium. He reported to me that his family did not celebrate Christmas, and he grew up thinking that his religion was deficient because he was the only Jew in his school and he had to wash the blackboards while the other children sang and performed. I have taught school leaders about the Catholic Councils of Baltimore in the 1840s that we discussed above. The Catholic bishops decided to start their own school system rather than to subject the Catholic minority children to the Protestant prayers and proselytization in Horace Mann's common schools. Persons of minority religions have suffered greatly in American schooling and society, and fear of the impossibility of legitimate neutrality causes many people to insist that we remove all vestiges of religion from public schools and government institutions. Persons from majority religions are often ignorant about the ways that religion can coerce, marginalize, and intimidate minorities. Minority rights form a core principal of democracy, but one that is often trampled upon by the power and arrogance of the majority. Minority rights must be protected for the sake of all citizens because, if for no other reason, the majority will one day be the minority.

Our next topic is eschatology. Some think of eschatology as the theology of the "end times" of the earth; others think of it as the theology of hope for the future. In either case, eschatology is, perhaps, the most urgent dimension of theology and culture that must be carefully analyzed in the postmodern era. Violence, ecological destruction, and political conflicts are often related to understandings of eschatology. There are at least three possible approaches to eschatology: realized eschatology, futuristic eschatology, and proleptic eschatology. Let's explore these three philosophies.

The notion of prior experience as a legitimate source of knowledge construction in schools and classrooms allows us to think about education as a life process rather than as fixed information or a static set of procedures. Consider this question: "How can individuals remain committed and hopeful in the midst of the personal and global challenges we face today?" Without a sense of determination, dedication, or hope, it seems to me, all other questions are moot. Some religious theologies of hope defer the consummation of life and all gratification to a distant time or place after death. This is called futuristic eschatology. On the other hand, materialistic conceptions of hope seek resolution of conflict or gratification of the body, mind, or spirit in the present context. This is called realized eschatology. I believe that both of these philosophies contribute to the problems of malaise, terror, anger, and anxiety that plague society and lead to self-destruction and violence. This may take the form of suicide—with guns, drugs, or some other form of anaesthetization—or murder—either instantly with a lethal weapon or slowly with verbal or psychological abuse. Relentless assaults on human persons degrade us all and strip the human community of justice and hope.

If hope is delayed until after death, as some believe, then we live in fear, resignation, or the paralysis of delayed expectations and constant anticipation. We are more likely to become intolerant and vengeful and less likely to take action for justice and peace. Consider Ijaz Kahn Hussein, a college-trained Pakistani pharmacist who joined the holy war in Afghanistan in 2001 with 43 other men—41 of whom were killed. He concludes, "We went to the jihad filled with joy, and I would go again tomorrow. If Allah had chosen me to die, I would have been in paradise, eating honey and water-melons and grapes, and resting with beautiful virgins, just as it is promised in the Koran. Instead my fate was to remain amid the unhappiness here on earth" (Burns, 2002, p. 1). (Note that most Muslims consider jihad a spiritual process of purification, and not, as Hussein said, a violent war.) A similar conclusion is reached by many other religious people who say things like "I am *in* the world but not *of* the world" and dis-dain anyone who does not accept their theology of a delayed parousia (happiness). They shun—and occasionally kill—the "evil and unsaved" people who espouse different beliefs or lifestyles. They assume that the world is evil and that only in a life after death will there be peace and happiness.

It is important that we pause at this point to remember that Timothy McVeigh and his accomplices who bombed the federal building in Oklahoma City in 1995, killing 168 innocent people, did not represent Christianity just because they were baptized Christians and members of churches. Their violent acts on the second anniversary of the fires and deaths at the Branch Davidian Christian compound in Waco, Texas, are not representative of all Christians or Christian faith. The violence of the Tamil Tigers in Sri Lanka does not represent all Hindus or the Hindu faith. Likewise, the terrorist bombings on September 11, 2001, in the US and the continuing suicide bombings in Iraq and Israel do not represent Islam or all Muslims. I believe that it is appropriate to vigorously investigate the participation and financial support of violence by religious leaders—Christian, Hindu, Jewish, and Muslim—to uncover evil acts perpetrated in the name of religion, just as Daniel Goldhagen did in the case of Germany. There are pockets of widespread support for violence and extremism within many world religions—and US Christians, British Muslims, and Israeli Jews are not exempt. But to categorize all Muslims as terrorists, all Christians as fanatics, or all Jews as Zionists is not only inaccurate but also damaging to the process of reconciling our differences and moving forward to ecumenical understanding in the postmodern era.

In the US it is especially important for all students to study Islam and hold dialogue with Muslims in order not only to understand this religion in the midst of our difficult political climate of hysteria, stereotypes, and vengeance, but especially to enhance our own spirituality. I have created a space on the companion website to read statements from all world religions, spiritualities, and philosophies. This is an interactive space, and I encourage readers to spend some time reading entries and consider entering their own autobiographical statement.

Returning to our discussion of eschatology, I sometimes hear preachers and teachers advocate for the advancement of "the end times" in order to fulfill their interpretations of religious scriptures. This, too, is a futuristic eschatology. We are all familiar with religious rhetoric claiming that earthquakes, tsunamis, hurricanes, and illness are a part of a divine plan to end the world—spoken, ironically, with divine omniscience by a fallible human being—or divine retribution for perceived transgressions—again, ironically, spoken by an often less than innocent human being. I found it humorous—in a tragic sense—when preachers claimed in 2005 that Hurricane Katrina was sent by God to wipe out the sinful city of New Orleans—the sort of claim I have heard after every natural disaster. Ironically, the French Quarter, casino, strip clubs, and downtown music halls in my hometown of New Orleans were spared serious damage, but many military bases along the Gulf coast were heavily damaged. Are the military bases where the sin is most prevalent? The middle-class and poor families, many of whom were religious, lost their families, churches, and homes. Who was the *god* of these preachers targeting? In another classic example, some preachers claim that their god hates homosexuals and therefore sent HIV and AIDS upon them. I assume that their god must love lesbian women the most, since lesbians have the lowest incidence of HIV infection. The absurdity of such religious claims about illness and disasters must be vigorously deconstructed. Theological ignorance allows a fearful citizenry to accept illogical and unjust practices in the name of religion.

If I could only recommend three theology books on the topic of "religion and evil" to help address this question, I would suggest *Women and Evil* by Nel Noddings (1989), *When Bad Things Happen to Good People* by Rabbi Harold Kushner ([1981] 2001), and *God and Human Anguish* by theologian S. Paul Schilling (1977). These authors remind us that we must stop blaming God or deities for natural or social evil. "Unbounded love," they say, and not omnipotent retribution and destruction, is the powerful force of their creator. This is one of the imperatives of a postmodern theological curriculum. Postmodern theologians contend that it is not "God's will" for people to suffer; they also argue that it is simply superstitious to believe that a deity grants wishes or orchestrates senseless suffering. We must overcome the damaging and immature theology that conceives of faith as fear of punishment from a vengeful deity.

Additionally, if eschatological hope is realized in the present and found only in immediate self-gratification in this moment on Earth, we also are likely to succumb to greed, consumption, lust, or violence. In both scenarios, we are less likely to work for social improvement and the needs of others because we are so culturally isolated and self-absorbed. There is another alternative to these two conditions of futuristic hope and realized hope: proleptic hope. Proleptic eschatology offers a way to access the strength and determination to act for justice even in the midst of personal tragedies like disease, addiction, or suicide or the turmoil of global events like the 9/11 attacks, terrorism, mass starvation, genocide, the war in Iraq, or rampant sexual abuse of children. Proleptic eschatology can give us optimism of the will and provide a context to advance what John Dewey (1934b) called social consequences and values in order to counteract the malaise and despair resulting from such personal and global tragedy. The nature of evil is one of the most perplexing and challenging theological issues we face.

The word "proleptic" may be unfamiliar to many readers. Literary scholars and English teachers will recognize this word as describing the moment in a short story or novel when the reader becomes fully cognizant of past, present, and future events all in one instant. It is the moment when all of the events of the narrative coalesce. Christian theologians have also used the term to describe the fullness of time—past, present, and future—in the person of Jesus Christ. I like to think of a proleptic event as any experience that transcends linear segmentation of time and nurtures holistic understanding. Have you ever had an experience where time stood still—not in the sense of being completely out of touch with reality, but rather a moment of clarity or understanding about your whole life: what you have done, where you are now, and what you will be in the future? As we noted in chapter 1, William Pinar and Madeleine Grumet (1976) call this a synthetical moment. Some compare this notion to synchronicity in Jungian psychology, the Passover experience of the Judaism, the Eucharist for Catholics and Episcopalians, reincarnation for Hindus, or moments of profound insight and aesthetic awareness for artists. The proleptic experience is difficult to describe because our language is imbedded with dualistic notions of time (e.g., day and night, before and after, past and present, awake and asleep, beginning and end). We may have to suspend our modern notions of clocks, bells, calendars, and schedules and enter a holistic *dreamtime* state like the Aboriginal people of Australia in order to fully comprehend the meaning of the word "proleptic." In dreamtime there is no distinction between what happens while we are awake and what happens while we are asleep. Our night dreams are as real as our waking fantasies, and both are as real as the events of our day-to-day lives. Have you ever taken a nap in the afternoon and awakened only to be unsure about the time of day? In this suspended state you often cannot even distinguish the dream of a deep sleep from the present surroundings of your bedroom or couch. This experience is reminiscent of Dorothy in *The Wizard of Oz* as she awakes at home in Kansas at the end of the film and tries to explain to her family that they really were with her in Oz.

The proleptic experience has been described by many authors, theologians, and scholars in a variety of ways. The Jewish theologian Abraham Joshua Heschel describes the Jews as a people in whom the past endures, in whom the present is inconceivable without moments gone by. The Exodus, he pronounces, lasted a moment, a moment enduring forever. For Heschel, what happened once upon a time happens all the time. The author William Faulkner is famous for capturing the spirit of the South in the United States, and he writes that there is no such thing as the past because the past is still present. Anyone who has grown up in the South knows this experience to be accurate. Memories of the Civil War are not distant history; they are alive. The philosopher Alfred North Whitehead believes that the present holds within itself the complete sum of existence, backwards and forwards, that whole amplitude of time which is eternity. In other words, all of eternity is experienced in each present moment. The Lutheran theologian Jürgen Moltmann reflects on proleptic time in a similar way when he contends that the true present is nothing else but the eternity that is immanent in time. The believer, for Moltmann as well as for Buddhist monks such as Thich Nhat Hanh (1995), is the one who is entirely present in each moment. This is a difficult challenge for modern citizens whose lives are compartmentalized and scheduled to the minute.

James Gleick (1999) describes modern technological gadgetry that is designed to save us time (e.g., cell phones, beepers, computers, e-mail) and the ways in which these devices actually complicate our lives rather than saving us precious seconds. It was originally believed that electronic mail would save time so that we would not have to file, sort, and respond to paper memos. However, e-mail has actually doubled our workload for at least three reasons: the proliferation of e-mail messages that require time to sort out good mail from junk mail; the need to make duplicate paper copies of e-mail messages in order to file and save important communication and documents; and the intrusion of e-mail messages 24 hours a day into our lives. Some workers and some ordinary citizens never get any "down time" from their technology connections. Being constantly "wired" and "on call" takes an exacting toll psychologically, even as technology has reduced cumbersome communication and improved organization in other ways. Engaging the notion of proleptic time does not require a rejection of modern technology. But it does force us to consider the psychological impact of technology on the way we live. There are various and sundry moral dilemmas that have been created by the modern technological world that demand a reevaluation of ethical systems for a postmodern age.

Gleick points out that linear notions of time force us to think in terms of the 1,140 minutes available every day, so we rush to make every second count. Directory assistance is automated, and in some cities, in order to save a nanosecond, the voice now says "What listing?" rather than the old "What listing, please?" How often do you get frustrated by listening to a long answering-machine message? "Door dwell" refers to the time it takes the elevator door to close once you have boarded, and typically lasts for 2 to 4 seconds. Gleick asks his readers if they still reach for the door-close button on elevators anyway. Would you still reach for the button even if you knew that most building managers disable the door-close buttons out of fear of trapped limbs and ensuing lawsuits? What would happen if we lived by the philosophy of Swami Vivekananda, who contends that time, space, and causation are like the glass through which the absolute is seen and that in the absolute there is neither time, nor space, nor causation. So what is time anyway?

The philosopher Friedrich Nietzsche writes about time as "eternal recurrence" and argues that to impose upon becoming the character of being is the supreme will to power. That everything recurs is the closest approximation for Nietzsche of a world of becoming to a world of being. Thus, our lives must be experienced as a journey and a process of becoming and not a search for a static destination. John Dewey applies this concept of becoming to education and concludes that the ideal of using the present simply to get ready for the future contradicts itself. Hence the central problem of an education based on experience is to select the kind of present experiences that live fruitfully and creatively in subsequent experiences. In other words, our task is to experience the future in each present moment rather than simply getting ready for a non-existent future. When students ask teachers why they need to study algebra, for example, and the teacher replies "Because you will need it in the future," then the teacher is reinforcing futuristic eschatology and missing an opportunity to reflect on proleptic time. If we cannot find a way to make algebra relevant and interesting in the present moment, than students are more inclined to feel alienated from mathematics. Additionally, for the vast majority of students there is not some distant future where they will need algebra. Teachers have been perpetuating this big lie in education throughout the modern era. We must find a way to create meaningful connections in each present moment rather than imposing a rationale for delaying meaning and purpose. This is the proleptic task; it is also the urgent ethical mandate of contemporary living.

One of the most irritating comments that I often hear spoken at graduations, bar mitzvahs, confirmations, and other ceremonies of rites of passage is: "You are the future of the church ... the future of the community ... the future of the country." It should not be surprising that many young people refuse to engage in the social, cultural, religious, and political life of the community or work for justice. The language of adults tells them to delay their participation until the future when they are adults themselves. But we need the insights and energy of our young people now. It should also come as no surprise, then, that most students are bored in classrooms and that many drop out of school when subject matter is not meaningfully connected to current events, life experiences, and personal autobiographies. High school drop-out rates before graduation exceed 50% of the students in a many districts, and hover around 25% nationally (Newman, 1997). Unless students are self-starters with personal ambition or curiosity, teachers provide no meaning or purpose for learning when they tell them to study algebra, not because it is interesting or applicable at the present moment, but because they may need it for classes or work in the future—a problematic claim, since this is seldom true. It is dangerous and counterproductive to separate the future from the present, maybe even unethical and educational malpractice.

Alfred Posamentier, professor of mathematics and dean of the School of Education at the City College of New York, would agree. He contends:

> [We must] make math intrinsically interesting to children. We should not have to sell mathematics by pointing to its usefulness in other subject areas [or future occupations], which, of course, is real. Love for math will not come about by trying to convince a child that it happens to be a handy tool for later in life; it grows when a good teacher can draw out a child's curiosity about numbers and mathematical principles at work. The very high percentage of adults who are unashamed to say that they are bad with math is a good indication of how maligned the subject is and how very little we were taught in school about the enchantment of numbers. (2002, p. A25)

This enchantment is an essential element of proleptic eschatology that can release imagination and create meaningful curriculum.

The author Virginia Woolf, in her 1937 novel *The Years*, explained the proleptic experience this way: "There must be another life, here and now, she repeated. This is too short, too broken. We know nothing, even about ourselves. We're only just beginning, she thought, to understand, here and there. She held her hand hallowed; she felt that she wanted to enclose the present and future, until it shone, whole, bright, and deep with understanding" (cited in Pinar, 1988a, p. 151). This, ultimately, is one of the purposes of education: to enfold within each present moment the past, the present, and the future so that our lives will be illuminated with deep understanding.

There is a growing recognition that the educational community cannot address the hopelessness, poverty, gender and sexuality bias, dislocation and exploitation of workers, environmental racism, corporate scandal, violence, and ecological devastation that plague the entire global community and contribute to the decay of the social milieu of schools simply by reacting to the symptoms. Traditional curriculum development models that focus exclusively on improving test scores, rewriting curriculum guides, expanding technology laboratories, upgrading standards, revising textbooks, and perfecting evaluation procedures ignore the ethical, ecological, sociological, and economic crises that threaten society (Slattery & Rapp, 2003). At the other extreme, theoretical discourses that simply analyze the latest political or philosophical jargon without reference to the schooling context also overlook the malaise, anguish, and fear that grip modern cultures. Curriculum scholar David Purpel (1989, 2005) contends that the moral and spiritual crises in society must be at the forefront of curriculum studies, and postmodern schooling must attend to these important issues.

The emerging constructive postmodern vision of schooling in the contemporary global community includes an eclectic and ecumenical integration of spirituality and theology into the very fabric of education. This vision of the centrality of spirituality and theology for postmodern schooling is still evolving. The proponents of the two predominant views of religion and schooling have reached an impasse. One segment of society promotes the total elimination of religion in the curriculum in an effort to protect the rights of minority religious views and freedom of religious expression. This perspective, which I will call the modern ideology, has resulted in the gradual removal of religion from the public schools.

On the opposite side of the debate are members of some religious denominations who insist that schooling must include specific prayers, scripture study, and religious formation. They contend that the "secular humanism" of the public schools is a godless religion in itself, and schooling must return to the traditional Judeo-Christian values and practices upon which *they believe* the United States was founded and upon which American schools were modeled before the 1960s. Proponents of this perspective, which I will call the premodern ideology, have fought against the separation of religion and government with numerous legal challenges of curricular practices, textbook adoptions, and school funding formulas. The intense debate between those who hold either the modern or the premodern ideology has reached a stalemate, with both sides ardently opposing the efforts of the other to control the future relationship between religion and schooling in American society. Additionally, some of those frustrated by this debate have opted out of the public school system by choosing parochial, private, or home schooling. The effort by some curriculum scholars to uncover a postmodern alternative to this impasse begins with the identification of several major trends concerning religion and education in the postmodern literature of the past decade.

Some scholars promote a postmodern theology that is a new spirituality based on an "imaginative, yet secular, response to nature herself" (Fuller, 1985, p. xiii). Other postmodern writers propose "a shared symbolic order of the kind that a religion provides, but without the religion" (Jencks, 1986, p. 43). Hans Kung (1988) does not share the sacred/secular distinction of Fuller and Jencks, but rather he seeks to "help religion to perform a new critical and liberating function of both the individual and society ... in a time of transition from modernity to 'postmodernity'" (p. xv). This epochal transition, for Kung, is a movement toward a new global understanding of various denominations where religion and education, along with art and politics, will be central to understanding the intellectual character of our time. He contends that "the intellectual crisis of our time is decisively *co-determined* by the *religious* crisis, and that without diagnosing and solving the religious crisis, no diagnosis and solution of the intellectual situation of our age can be successful" (p. 6). Religion and education, from this perspective, are thus inseparable.

Harvey Cox (1984), in *Religion in the Secular City: Toward a Postmodern Theology*, shares the view that postmodern education is inextricably linked to religion in the secular society. However, unlike Kung, Cox attributes appeals to "the burgeoning intellectual life of modern times" (p. 177) as the project of modern theology, even from such diverse voices as Friedrich Schleiermacher, Karl Barth, Jacques Maritain, and Paul Tillich. "These disparate modern theologians were all preoccupied with one underlying question—how to make the Christian message credible to what they understood as the modern ... educated, skeptical ... mind" (pp. 176–177). Thus, for Cox, the challenge of postmodern theologians and educators is not to adapt religion to the modern world but rather to forge a conversation with those marginalized by modernity. Theological dialogue with the despised, the poor, and the culturally dominated sectors of society in order to give credence to global religious pluralism and popular piety is the foundation of his postmodern proposal. Through such a dialogue we come to realize that the marginalized evangelize the mainstream power-brokers in society. The poor ground the elites in the present and reveal the mystery of spiritual transformation.

Harvey Cox's proposal flows out of the tradition of "problem-posing" pedagogy established in Latin America by the Brazilian educator Paulo Freire (1970), who viewed the problems of education as inseparable from political, social, and economic problems. Peasants were encouraged to examine critically their life situations and take the initiative to transform social structures that denied them meaningful civic participation. Freire's "Conscientizing as a Way of Liberating" (1971) is considered one of the important philosophical foundations of liberation theology. Liberation theology has utilized Freire's pedagogy to establish *communautés de base* (base communities) that unite religious reflection with social action as a form of praxis that can inspire lasting change in the Latin American community. Theology and education are truly inseparable in this curriculum development model.

Moving in a very different direction than Paulo Freire, Harvey Cox, and Hans Kung, theologian Mark C. Taylor (1984), whom we introduced in the preface, proposes a "postmodern a/theology" as a rebuttal to humanist atheists who fail to realize that the "Death of God is at the same time the death of the self" (p. 20). Taylor's solution is the deconstruction of modern philosophical movements that reject transcendence. David Ray Griffin (1988b) challenges Taylor's theology, and by extrapolation the spirituality of Jencks and Fuller, on the basis that his postmodern theology is eliminative; that is, Taylor eliminates worldviews of God, self, truth, and purpose in the spirit of the deconstructionism of Jacques Derrida. Griffin proposes instead a revisionary theological postmodernism with a reenchantment of the cosmos and a better intuition of its "Holy Center" (p. 52). While acknowledging the contributions of many postmodern scholars, Griffin's constructive and revisionary postmodern theology, especially his work at the Center for Process Studies in California, informs much of the discussion of religion in postmodern schooling today.

Despite the postmodern theological proposals reviewed above, modern educational reforms continue to be committed to scientific and technical methodologies with an emphasis on measurable outcomes (e.g., *America 2000* in 1991 and *No Child Left Behind* in 2003). However, postmodern educators recognize that the crises that plague schools in the 21st century will not be resolved by the exclusive use of any of the modern reform proposals thrust upon education in the past century, often by those committed to the continuation of modernity in government, business, industry, and the military (Kliebard, 1986; Shea, Kahane, & Sola, 1989; Pinar et al., 1995, Pinar, 2004a). The contributions of spirituality, theology, and religion are now beginning to be incorporated into new postmodern revisions.

In contrast to the ideology of the current reform proposals for education, other alternatives are being offered that challenge dominant cultural values and practices of modernity such as the emphasis on consumption over sustainable resource use, competition over cooperation, and bureaucracy over authentic human interaction. For example, the Global Alliance for Transforming Education (GATE), in "Education 2000: A Holistic Perspective" (1991), contends that these dominant cultural values and practices have been destructive to the health of the ecosystem as well as to optimal human development in education. "Education 2000" states: "[Our] purpose is to proclaim an alternative vision of education, one which is a life affirming and democratic response to the challenges of the 1990s and beyond. We value diversity and encourage a wide variety of methods, applications, and practices" (Global Alliance, 1991, p. 1). Unfortunately, many political leaders and even many religious leaders have hampered the creation of such a revisionary view of postmodern schooling. Some scholars contend that, despite the seemingly insurmountable obstacles to this project, a reverent and egalitarian postmodern education will certainly emerge once authentic attention is given to the spiritual and theological issues of the human heart (Moore, 1989).

The incorporation of spirituality, theology, and religious education into postmodern visions of schooling is not universally and uncritically accepted. This is evidenced by the protracted debates over the place of religion in American society outlined at the beginning of this chapter. This debate perpetuates the modern notion of religion as a quantifiable event that can be compartmentalized and separated from other life experiences. The suppression of spirituality, theology, and religious education in modern public and private schools can be attributed to the following: the intense theological divisiveness between religious faiths (Marty, 1984); the public display of hypocritical and sometimes illegal behavior by many prominent denominational leaders; the long history of tolerance of racism, sexism, militarism, and colonialism in the churches (Ruether, 1983a; Pinar, 1988b); the tradition of privatization of matters spiritual in Western societies, especially the United States (Cox, 1984; Whitson, 1991); the apparently irresolvable conflicts over moral issues in the modern technological society (Arons, 1983; Chazan, 1985; Maguire & Fargnoli, 1991; Purpel, 2005; Kesson, 2005); the international politicization of religion with calls for "holy wars" and condemnations of "evil empires" (Wald, 1987; Toffler, 1990; Kimball, 2002; Wallis, 2005); the rise of religious fundamentalism and its impact on education (Provenzo, 1990; Wallis,

2005); transcultural and transnational global evangelization and proselytization by sects and cults, as well as traditional denominations (Glock & Bellah, 1976; Stark & Brainbridge, 1985; Lugg, 2004); scientific empiricism and reductionism that denigrates religion as superstitious and enshrines materialistic atheism in the Newtonian world-view (Cobb, 1988); and the consistent rejection and brutal humiliation of prophetic voices in the churches in both premodern and modern societies (Dewey, 1934a; Bonhoeffer, 1966, 1971). In this milieu there has been a systematic attempt to rid education of all vestiges of religious sensibilities and ensure that "religious intuitions are weeded out from among the intellectually respectable candidates for philosophical articulation" (Rorty, 1982, p. xxxviii), despite the fact that theology was once considered the queen of the sciences, with prominent stature in the university curriculum in the premodern Middle Ages.

The litany of factors that have contributed to the decline of theology in the public school curriculum and university programs of study in the modem era has also had a significant impact on religious education in parochial schools. It is not unusual for religion and spirituality to be compartmentalized and institutionalized as simply one among many courses to be studied. Furthermore, there is a conspicuous absence of theology in the educational discourses of avowed secular scholars. This is attributed by some to the fact that religious conflicts are viewed as irresolvable parochial matters, and thus irrelevant to postmodern schooling (Arons, 1983). Postmodern scholars have not yet discovered a way out of the modern dilemma of religion and schooling chronicled above, and thus have often excluded spirituality and theology from their curriculum proposals. This chapter is on a quest to address this problem.

Of course, there are notable exceptions to this trend. David Ray Griffin (1988a) has called for public life to reflect religious values in his postmodern proposals. David Purpel (1989, 2005) has challenged teachers to become prophets who orient the educational process toward a vision of ultimate meaning and "infuse education with the sacred" (1989, p. 105). John I. Goodlad, Roger Soder, and Kenneth A. Sirotnik (1990) have proposed that the educational community include a vision of morality and values in teacher education programs. Curricularist David G. Smith (1988) has cautioned that education must tell us not simply what we are but, most significantly, what we hope to become. Smith writes that "attention to the eidetic quality of our life together is an attempt to bring into the center of our research conversation everything that we are, as a way of reconciling in the present moment our ends with our beginnings" (p. 435). Philip Phenix (1975), a prominent figure in the reconceptualization literature of the 1970s, has pointed out the significance for schooling of the "lure of transcendence toward wholeness" (p. 333). William Doll (1993) has written that the postmodern curriculum is imbued with a cosmological character that leads to a personal and spiritual transformation.

Among other voices of exception is theologian Gabriel Moran (1981), who has indicated that there is no discernible field that can accurately be called religious education, despite the fact that "religious education is one of the most universal, most urgent, and most practical questions confronting our society today" (p. 9). Denise Larder Carmody (1991) has called for an alliance among feminism, religion, and education, because "there will be no optimal alliance unless feminists, people of faith, and educators can agree that religion is the substance of the good life and that feminism and education are privileged ways of expressing religion" (p. 117). Mary Elizabeth Moore, Dwayne Huebner, Donald Oliver, Douglas Sloan, and Nelson Haggerson all have consistently promoted spirituality, process philosophy, and ethics in their educational research. Despite the voices of these and other scholars who share a vision of spirituality and morality for the postmodern era, theology has emerged only recently as an important dimension of the postmodern curriculum field.

Those educators committed to a postmodern vision of schooling understand well the insight of Alfred North Whitehead (1929), in *Aims of Education*, when he insisted, "The essence of education is that it be religious" (p. 14). Religious education for Whitehead included duty and reverence: the duty to be involved in human community and global concerns and a profound reverence for the cosmos. Whitehead explains: "And the foundation of reverence is this perception, that the present holds within itself the complete sum of existence, backwards and forwards, that whole amplitude of time which is eternity" (p. 14). Scientific discoveries by physicists viewing graphics transmitted from the Hubble telescope reveal images from the very seconds after the Big Bang. Using these images, scientists are beginning to explore the mysteries of creation and eternity. It is fascinating that theoretical physicists in quest of a unified theory are therefore compelled to address theological questions in the face of the new data (Hawking, 1988). The new discoveries have caused astrophysicist George Smoot to exclaim, "If you're religious, it's like looking at God" (cited in Lemonick, 1992, p. 62). Modern science has come full circle since the 18th-century rejection, by Pierre Simon Laplace and others, of religion as a hindrance to the development of modern scientific progress to a realization that religious questions are at the very heart of science (Griffin, 1988a, 1988b).

Having reviewed the landscape that spirituality and theology must traverse in the complex postmodern curriculum dialogue, we are now ready to explore the concept of curriculum as theological text and the struggle of schools to break free from the shackles of modernity. Schooling must resist fundamentalist calls to retreat to premodern religious practices while still preserving ancient religious traditions in the social context of contemporary spirituality and theology. This is a monumental task. And thus, for those who agree with Whitehead that the essence of education is that it must be religious, the lessons from contemporary curriculum discourses offer valuable insights for all those committed to postmodern curriculum development.

Throughout the first half of this chapter the terms "theology," "spirituality," and "religion" have been used interchangeably. However, it is important to note that these words have a unique and evolving etymological history. Volumes have been written over the centuries to explain the precise nuanced meaning of each one. Crusades, inquisitions, witch burnings, and excommunications have all been initiated as a result of theological disagreements involving the interpretation of these words and their codification in sacred books. While religion has traditionally been associated with denominational practices and beliefs, theology is sometimes considered a more systematic and rational study of faith and the holy (i.e., God, transcendence, dogmas, and sacred texts) as related to patterns of meaning that prevail in a historical period or culture (Cox, 1984). Spirituality is associated with the realm of personal faith and supernatural revelation. Following Alfred North Whitehead, religious education in contemporary curriculum discourses is viewed as a process that includes duty, reverence, and personal participation as a form of praxis in exploring cosmology, the mystery of eternity, and transcendence. Postmodern curriculum promotes the exploration of this mystery of eternity and the return of theology to its authentic place as queen of the sciences, not in the premodern sense of an authoritarian monarch to be feared or in the modern sense of an antique barren goddess to be displayed in a museum, but rather as the postmodern benevolent and nurturing Sophia, goddess of eternal wisdom.

T. S. Eliot succinctly critiques the effects of modernity on the churches, society, and schooling in his poem "Choruses from the Rock." He warns that the scientific knowledge and information technology of modernity brings us nearer to death but no nearer to God. Some scholars contend that a postmodern model of curriculum as theological text is our only way out of the stalemate described above. It is also the only way out of this endless cycle of ignorance described by Eliot (1971):

> The endless cycle of idea and action,
>
> Endless invention, endless experiment,
>
> Brings knowledge of motion, but not of stillness;
>
> Knowledge of speech, but not of silence;
>
> Knowledge of words, and ignorance of the Word.
>
> All our knowledge brings us nearer to our ignorance,
>
> All our ignorance brings us nearer to death,
>
> But nearness to death no nearer to God.
>
> Where is the Life we have lost in living?
>
> Where is the wisdom we have lost in knowledge?
>
> Where is the knowledge we have lost in information?
>
> The cycles of Heaven in twenty centuries
>
> Bring us farther from God and nearer to the Dust. (p. 96)

T. S. Eliot's vision of centuries of knowledge and information technology bringing us farther from God and nearer to destruction serves as a profound metaphor for the challenge of postmodern curriculum development. The desolation of modernity and the impotence of its obsession with information in schooling impel us to reconceptualize school curriculum in order to recover the wisdom that is lost in information transmission.

In the postmodern reflections on the school curriculum as theological text, the words "curriculum," "theology," and "text" are understood phenomenologically (emphasizing subjective consciousness and its intentional objects in their pure essences) rather than ontologically (emphasizing concrete natural objects studied in the abstract). The understanding of curriculum that is proposed is not restricted to the modern program of studies in the schools of the last century as codified in textbooks, guides, scope and sequences, and behavioral lesson plans.

Rather, the verb form of curriculum, *currere*, which refers to the running of the race rather than the race course itself, is primary. This process view of curriculum as *currere*, as we saw in chapter 3, emphasizes the individual's own capacity to reconceptualize his or her autobiography, recognize connections with other people, recover and reconstitute the past, imagine and create possibilities for the future, and come to a greater personal and communal awareness. Donald Oliver and Kathleen Gershman (1989) point out that this awareness grounds our knowledge in being, not in methods or techniques. From this postmodern perspective, the curriculum as *currere* is an interpretation of lived experiences rather than a static course of studies to be completed. Likewise, theology is not restricted to the study of objective creeds, codes, and canons. Instead, it is an autobiographical process, a cosmological dialogue, and a search for personal and universal harmony. This concept of theology is rooted in the tradition of Anselm of Canterbury (12th century CE), who insisted that theology was *fides quaerens intellectum* (faith seeking understanding), and the 20th-century theologian Jürgen Moltmann, who situated the believer between the "already" and the "not yet" in an unfolding history with God "ahead" rather than "above." This view of theology avoids a premodern authoritarian confessionalism (e.g., Karl Barth) and a modern subjective decisionism (e.g., Bernard Lonergan). It also responds to the concerns of John Dewey (1934a), who contended that the churches had lost their prophetic voice and were impotent to address the need for social justice.

Finally, the word "text" in the curriculum as understood as theological text is now viewed from a process perspective. Modern schooling has enshrined the written word as an historical artifact to be memorized, comprehended, and regurgitated on a standardized test. In contrast to this dominant view, postmodernity views the text as a phenomenological encounter between word and reader. Reading the text is more closely associated with the Latin *ruminare* (to ruminate and think things over). Like the ruminants (cattle, sheep, and so on) who regurgitate their food from a special compartment of their stomachs to chew the cud in order to aid digestion, readers of a text in school store experiences of the world and use them for personal reflection at leisure. Madeleine Grumet (1988a) has explored this process view of reading the text. She writes: "Meaning is something we make out of what we find when we look at texts. It is not the text. [Unfortunately,] the myth of the meaningful text still flourishes in the classroom" (p. 465). The reconceptualization has challenged educators to wrest meaning from the grips of behavioral knowledge and return it to artistic expression so that students will have something to do with texts in schools. This view of the text brings purpose to the reading process by providing a foundation for personal praxis and intentionality. "It also provides another stage where the possible worlds that the text points to can be identified and experienced as good places for grazing" (Grumet, 1988a, p. 471).

What we see here is a postmodern process view of curriculum as theological text. Each word is reconceptualized by exploring its etymological root in order to reconstitute a fuller meaning. Curriculum, theology, and text are primarily verbs, not merely nouns! They imply movement: running, seeking, and ruminating. Thus, the revisionary postmodern view of religious education is based on phenomenological understandings, and it is identified by the curriculum as theological text.

We can now return to the poem "Choruses from the Rock," where T. S. Eliot laments: "Knowledge of words, and ignorance of the Word. ... Where is the wisdom we have lost in knowledge?" The curriculum as theological text seeks to uncover the wisdom that has been lost in our preoccupation with discrete parcels of knowledge that are measured on standardized tests in modern schools. The challenge of postmodern schooling is to recover a fuller meaning of wisdom. This journey often begins with an exploration of the importance of Sophia, or wisdom.

Wisdom literature abounds—for example, in Jewish Kabbalah, the mystic poetry of Rumi, the way of *Tao Te Ching*, the wisdom of Sufism, Gnostic mysticism, Roman and Orthodox Catholic deuterocanonical scriptures, and the Protestant Apocrypha. The books of Wisdom and Ecclesiasticus, for example, teach that "before all other things wisdom was created, [and] shrewd understanding is everlasting" (*Jerusalem Bible*, 1966, p. 902). In Sufism, the Prophet Muhammad defined wisdom as follows: "Do what you should do when you should do it. Refuse to do what you should not do. And when it is not clear, wait until you are sure" (Fadiman & Frager, 1997, p. 79). Wisdom—or Sophia in Hellenistic Judaism and Gnostic mythology—is the power that bridges the gap between divinity and humanity. In Ecclesiasticus (1: 4) she is described as "First of all created things." In the Wisdom of Solomon, Sophia is likened to the deity, and among feminist theologians like Rosemary Radford Ruether (1983b) she is the modern image of deity abandoned when the masculine imagery of father was canonized by the churches. According to Solomon (7: 25–28), "Sophia is a breath of the power of God, pure emanation of the glory of the Almighty. ... Although alone, she can do all, herself unchanging, she makes all things new" (*Jerusalem Bible*, 1966, p. 884).

As a visual artist, I attempt to understand this concept of bridging the gap between divinity and humanity in some of my work. Take a look at an image of a piece I call *The Hypostatic Union* and, after pondering the image, read my artist statement, in which I use traditional theology to reconceptualize the notion of proleptic eschatology and phenomenological spirituality (see Figure 4.1).

The Hypostatic Union is a vertical assemblage of mirrors and driftwood mounted on a varnished plywood base. The title of this piece is derived from Catholic theology. The term "hypostatic" is used to refer to the union of divine and human natures in the one person, or *hypostasis*, of Jesus Christ—represented by the twisted piece of driftwood. It is classically expressed in the dogmatic definition of the Council of Chalcedon (451 CE), which taught that Christ exists in two "natures," each of which retains it own characteristics. The council also asserted that each nature comes together in one "person" (*hypostasis* in Greek). Literally, this piece has three circular mirrors, 12 inches in diameter, representing the Holy Trinity of Father, Son, and Holy Spirit in Christian theology. The driftwood is an abstraction of the crucified and resurrected Jesus Christ. Together these abstracted symbols recall the Trinity, Crucifixion, and Resurrection, which are represented on all Catholic altars. However, the three mirrors in this abstract representation also allow viewers to interrupt and problematize the traditional notions of the Christian Trinity and the hypostatic union. Where does the

FIGURE 4.1

union of the human and divine occur: above, beyond, within, between, among? The viewer now becomes a part of the hypostatic union in the reflections of the mirrors, uniting the human and divine in multiple combinations. From various angles the viewer can see herself or himself—as well as other gallery visitors and artwork—reflected in the mirrors of the abstracted religious symbols. The hypostatic union then becomes open to fresh interpretations as the space between divine nature and human nature is reconceptualized. The imagined viewer can now see herself or himself as a hypostatic union reflected in the mirrors—although fragmented into multiple post-modern selves by the six vertical panels of mirrors. This insight gives agency to those who have been indoctrinated in the old catechism of a single Christian interpretation of hypostatic union—a theology which often repressed and sometimes deformed their human passions and divine natures. There are references to many other world religions in the piece as well.

In Gnostic mysticism, wisdom is also divine emanation, sometimes appearing as the bride of the Logos (Christ). In the *Apocryphon of John* (II, 1:5) from the Nag Hammadi documents of Egypt (Robinson, 1977), we read about Sophia. "She became the womb for everything, for she is prior to them all, the Mother–Father, the first man, the Holy Spirit, the thrice-male, the thrice powerful, the thrice-named androgynous one, and the eternal aeon" (p. 101). *The Teachings of Silvanus* (VII, 4: 89, 5; 87, 5; 87, 15) (Robinson, 1977) cautions:

> Wisdom summons you in her goodness, come to me all of you ... that you may receive a gift of understanding which is good and excellent .... What else is evil death except ignorance? ... Do not flee from the education and the teaching, but when you are taught, accept it with joy. ... Do not lose my teaching, and do not acquire ignorance, lest you lead your people astray. (pp. 348–349)

Curriculum development in the postmodern era also involves attention to the wisdom embedded in Native American spirituality, for it is in the very sacred land of the native people that American education now finds its home. "If we sell you our land, you must keep it apart and sacred as a place where even whites can go to taste the wind," concluded Duwamish Chief Seattle in a speech given in 1854 at an assembly of tribes preparing to sign treaties with Whites who had conquered their land. Chief Seattle began his famous oration this way:

> The Great Chief in Washington sends word that he wishes to buy our land. But how can you buy or sell the sky, the warmth of the land? The idea is strange to us. ... Every part of this earth is sacred to my people. Every shining pine needle, every sandy shore, every mist in the dark woods, every clearing and humming insect is holy in the memory and experience of my people. The sap which courses through the trees carries the memories of the red man. ... We are part of the earth and it is part of us. The perfumed flowers are our sisters; the deer, the horse, the great eagle, these are our brothers. ... So we will consider your offer to buy our land. But it will not be easy. For this land is sacred to us. (Cited in Armstrong, 1971, pp. 77–79)

In this speech, which is essential reading in its entirety for all postmodern thinkers, Chief Seattle also reflects on God and religion. He contrasts the religion of the White Man's God written on tablets of stone with the Red Man's Great Spirit. He says, "Our religion is the traditions of our ancestors—the dreams of our old men, given them in solemn hours of the night by the Great Spirit; and the visions of our sachems; and it is written in the hearts of our people" (cited in Armstrong, 1971, p. 78). These dreams and visions are never forgotten by the native peoples, and even their dead never forget the world that gave them being. For when the last Native American perishes, and the memories of their tribes have become a myth, Chief Seattle believes that "these shores will swarm with the invisible dead of my tribe, and when your children's children think themselves alone in the field, the store, the shop, upon the highway, or in the silence of the pathless woods, they will not be alone. ... They will throng with the returning hosts that once filled and still love this beautiful land. The White Man will never be alone" (p. 79). The mystery of eternity is clear for Chief Seattle, and the postmodern curriculum seeks to remember what is with us and envision the process of becoming.

The wisdom of Chief Seattle is representative of many global traditions of indigenous people and religious mystics. For example, in his oft-repeated cosmological prayer, Francis of Assisi honored "brother sun and sister moon." The intimate relationship between wisdom, eternity, ecology, and memory is clearly a dimension of postmodern curriculum development that scholars seek to recover and nurture.

I recall a memorable experience participating in a sweat lodge at the First Nations center in Winnipeg, Manitoba, with several of my graduate students. We were met by the leader, who warmly welcomed us, gave us a tour of the property, and then invited to enter the changing hut to remove our clothing and jewelry. The women put on light flowing gowns and the men wore loose gym shorts. After an opening ceremony with tobacco leaves and hot "grandfather" stones at the entrance to the sweat lodge, we crawled through the small entrance to begin the ceremony. We sat on the cool, dank earth in a circle around the white-hot rocks with the canvas roof close to our heads. As the layers of heavy canvas were closed over the opening by an assistant on the outside of the sweat lodge, we found ourselves enveloped in total darkness in a confined space. Our First Nation guide taught us that the sweat lodge was like the womb of mother earth, and we were on a journey of healing and rebirth.

He began the ceremony by pouring a cup of cool water over the stones, and hot steam immediately filled the small lodge. He then gently pounded a drum, intoned ancient chants, and taught indigenous lessons that had been passed down for generations. We were mesmerized, and we started to sweat. We were encouraged to move closer to the ground as the heat intensified. The searing heat was like nothing I had experienced in my life—not even in a sauna. After about 30 minutes I found myself prostrate on the ground, rubbing shoulders with sweaty students on either side of me. We were told in advance that the door would be opened if anyone needed to leave, and I was worried that I might not last the entire two hours—despite the fact that a water break outside of the lodge occurred every 30 minutes.

As I became more desperate in the heat and sweat, something miraculous happened. I bent forward and put my nose into the ground and discovered that I could inhale cool air out of the earth and refresh the inside of my body. Suddenly I was able to endure the searing heat on my skin. My breathing slowed, and I entered a prayerful meditative state—listening to our leader chant and recite lessons with one ear and dwelling on my own rebirth with the other. I wrote the following reflection in my journal the next day. "The sweat lodge will linger in my memory forever. I felt connected to the Earth in ways that I never have before. It was as though I was breathing through an umbilical cord and the sustenance of life was mother earth. The cool air from the ground was sucked up through my nostrils and refreshed my burning body. What an incredible spiritual and ecological lesson!" The sweat lodge experience provided me with wisdom and insights about myself in relation to the earth.

What has become of the wisdom described in these mystical theologies, native voices, and ancient ceremonies? Where in our educational journey do we encounter Sophia? Where is the theology of wisdom in our curriculum? Reflecting on these and other probing questions, contemporary writers are beginning to propose that curriculum must become theological text: a place to encounter Sophia and ruminate on the sacred. Postmodern schooling is seen as a self-immersion in myth, mysticism, cosmology, eternity, and the holy center of life.

In the quest for information and knowledge, the wisdom of the sages of human history has too often been scorned and silenced. Information technology has replaced the encounter in schooling with the metaphysical, the eschatological, the soteriological, and the mystical. Like a disrespectful child or impudent criminal placed in solitary confinement, the theological text has been banished from theoretical discourse and from schools. The warning of postmodern theology that the death of God is also the death of the self can also be applied to modern schooling as an admonition that ignorance of curriculum as theological text is educational suicide. Curriculum development in the postmodern era will understand that the theological curriculum is the self in dialogue with eternal communal wisdom. The absence of this dialogue in modern schooling is a form of nihilism to be resisted.

The words of truth, beauty, sacred, and goodness in the religious myths and ways of enlightenment have been expressed for centuries by indigenous cultures, in philosophical discourses, and by mystery religions in the very breath of their spoken words. This is reflected in the *Tao Te Ching* of Lao Tzu (Needleman, 1989):

> The highest good is like water.
>
> Water gives life to the ten thousand things
>
> and does not strive.
>
> It flows in places rejected and so is like the Tao.
>
> In dwelling, be close to the land.
>
> In meditation, go deep into the heart.
>
> In dealing with others, be gentle and kind.
>
> In speech, be true.
>
> In ruling, be just.
>
> In daily life, be competent.
>
> In action, be aware of the time and the season.
>
> No fight: No blame. (p. 10)

The word of life is also expressed in the Hebrew anthropomorphism *ruach*, or breath. The Johannine Christology (1: 14) expresses the presence of the deity: "The word was made flesh ... full of grace and truth" (*Jerusalem Bible*, 1966, p. 114). The prophecy in 2 Nephi (Ch 29, 2) of the *Book of Mormon* (1961) explains the role of the word: "I will remember your seed, and that the words of your seed should proceed out of my mouth unto your seed; and my word shall *hiss forth* unto the ends of the earth for a standard unto my people" (p. 100, emphasis added). The theological understanding of breath and word is also found in the centrality of breathing in Zen Buddhism and the awareness of *prana in* yoga. In *The Way of Zen* Alan Watts (1957) writes:

> Because Zen does not involve an ultimate dualism between the controller and the controlled, the mind and the body, the spiritual and the material, there is always a certain "physiological" aspect to its techniques. ... Great importance is attached to the way of breathing. Not only is breathing one of the two fundamental rhythms of the body; it is also the process in which control and spontaneity, voluntary and involuntary action, find their most obvious identity. Long before the origins of the Zen school, both Indian Yoga and Chinese Taoism practiced "watching the breath" with a view toward letting it (not forcing it) become as slow and silent as possible. ... Grasping air with the lungs goes hand in hand with grasping at life. (pp. 197–198)

The spoken words about the source of life—this grasping at life—were evident in the oral tradition of religious communities long before the canon of the written text was promulgated. Sophia and Gaia, Yahweh and the Christ, El Shadai and Zeus, spirit, wind, and water: these were living and spoken texts long before they became written texts. The religious, spiritual, and mystical experiences of human culture have been textualized in the canons of faith and codes of moral behavior. Tragically, modern religious texts have concretized the hiss, the *ruach*, and the *prana*. This process led to an educational approach in premodern societies that enshrined the theological text as the curriculum. Premodern cultures and tribal communities zealously guarded their denominational creeds, canons, and rituals. The young were initiated into the tribal religious practices. The theological text, which was the formal code of religion whether written on scrolls or passed down through oral tradition, was the primary curriculum for schooling and cultural initiation.

Challenges to the official text resulted in schisms, reformations, and excommunications throughout the ages. New theological texts were promulgated as the primary curriculum for the splinter community. This premodern perspective of the theological text as the curriculum provided security and continuity for ancient societies. This same security makes a return to premodern structures appealing in the 20th century for those who believe that the only way out of the dilemma of modernity is to retreat to a form of schooling that imposes denominational religion and dominant cultural values through the school curriculum. From this premodern perspective, religious education becomes indoctrination and initiation.

Of course, since the 18th century the modern world has increasingly ignored this phenomenon and found its security and salvation in scientific positivism and technology rather than traditional religious values. The Enlightenment created a new educational paradigm that understood curriculum as a technological text. This paradigm was as much a proposal to advance society into enlightened thinking as it was a reaction against the authoritarian theology of the Middle Ages. Science replaced religion as the voice of authority on the mysteries of the universe. The ecological, emotional, and sociological dilemmas brought on by the Enlightenment project and the science of modernity require that we not return to another form of premodern authoritarian theology, but rather that we create a revisionary curriculum for the postmodern era that includes theology. The preceding discussion can be summarized in the three modes of analysis in the following matrix (see Table 4.1).

While not exhaustive, the matrix attempts to delineate some of the major distinctions between premodernity, modernity, and postmodernity in issues related to curriculum, theology, and education. Postmodernity seeks to respond to the worldviews of premodernity and modernity, as outlined above. In particular, the concept of predetermined texts as the core curriculum has met with intense debate in the educational community since the publication of E. D. Hirsch's (1987) *Cultural Literacy* and William Bennett's (1987, 1988) two James Madison School volumes. The current debates over reform proposals in education, which we examined in the first three chapters, are similar to the reaction to the dependence on inflexible official texts in some religious sects. For example, the Gnostic *Testimony of Truth* (IX 3: 29, 6–25) begins with a bitter polemic against the scribes of the law who have perverted the light of truth. The *Testimony of Truth* is a homiletic that contends that undefilement belongs to those of the light:

> I will speak to those who know to hear not with the ears of the body but with the ears of the mind. For many have sought after the truth and have not been able to find it; because there has taken hold of them the old leaven of the Pharisees and the scribes of the Law. (Robinson, 1977, pp. 406–407)

In Christian Scriptures, Jesus also condemns the scribes and pharisees who have become bound by the written code and are unable to be self-reflective. He speaks seven woes in Matthew's Gospel (23: 29–34):

> Alas for you, scribes and pharisees, you hypocrites! You who build the sepulchers of the prophets and decorate the tombs of holy men, saying, "we would never have joined in shedding the blood of prophets, had we lived in our fathers' day." So! Your own evidence tells against you! ... Serpents, brood of vipers, how can you escape being condemned to hell? That is why I am sending you prophets and teachers. (*Jerusalem Bible*, 1966, p. 36)

It is significant to note here that prophets and teachers are sent to challenge the hypocrisy of the pharisees, who, like teachers of the law in modern schooling, have abandoned a vision of the spirit infusing education. Teachers in postmodern schools have the opportunity to be prophets and create a fresh new vision of curriculum as theological text.

Theology as Curriculum Text	Curriculum as Technological Text	Curriculum as Theological Text
Premodern	Modern	Postmodern
Denominational	Secular	Ecumenical
Transcendent	Anthropocentric	Anthropomorphic
Autocratic	Individualistic	Communitarian
Mythological	Technological	Ecological
Dependent	Independent	Interdependent
Past Tradition	Present Reality	Proleptic Hope
Metanarrative	Cartesian Dualism	Integrated/Eclectic
Dogmatic	Scientific	Spiritual
Fundamentalism	Positivism	Process Philosophy
"God is above"	"God is dead"	"God is ahead"
Faith in the Canon	Faith in Humanity	Faith Seeking Wisdom
Literacy/Reading as Comprehension	Literacy/Reading as Decoding	Literacy/Reading as Ruminating
Cultural Literacy	Functional Literacy	Critical Literacy
Natural Law	Behavioral Goals	Currere

TABLE 4.1 Premodern, Modern, and Postmodern Theologies

As premodern theological texts concretized their vision, the path to wisdom and holiness was narrowed. In the *Koran* this is clearly articulated in the opening words:

> In the name of Allah, the Beneficent, the Merciful. All praise is due to Allah, the Lord of the worlds. ... Thee do we serve, and thee do we beseech for help. Keep us on the right path. The path of those upon whom thou hast bestowed favors. Not the path of those upon whom thy wrath is brought down, nor of those who go astray. (*Qur'an*, 1990, p. 1)

Additionally, in some traditions not one word of the text may be altered, as seen in the Revelation of John (22: 18–20) in Christian scripture: "I warn everyone who hears the words of the prophecy of this book: If anyone adds anything to them, God will add to him the plagues described in this book. And if anyone takes away words from this book of prophecy, God will take away the tree of life in the holy city described in this book" (*Jerusalem Bible*, 1966, p. 339). These two examples create an image that condemns to darkness and death those outside the text. The text becomes truth incarnate, and thus the curriculum of initiation for future generations. We will examine in detail the complexity of scriptural interpretation of both religious and non-religious texts from laws and handbooks to bibles and dogmas in a moment. Let us pause to examine the context for scriptural analysis.

I often tell my students that there is no such thing as *the* bible—in the sense that there are many religious texts that are considered holy and inspired such as the Koran, King James Bible, Book of Mormon, Bhagavad Gita, mysticism of Rumi, Hindu scriptures, Catholic Jerusalem Bible, and many other scriptures considered *the* bible in different cultures. And even the "Christian" Bible is not uniform in canon or interpretation. The Protestant Bible has 66 books, the Roman Catholic Bible has 72 books, and the

Orthodox Bible has more books in the various traditions. There is no universal bible and no universal master narrative to interpret the various translations. So where does this leave us? Do we reject all scriptures and bibles as contradictory and irrelevant? Do we fight to the death to prove that our preferred bible is the one, true word of God? Or do we embrace postmodern diversity and let go of the need for certainty, consensus, and uniformity? This is a part of our quest in this chapter for understanding curriculum as theological text.

Perhaps the most important book on this topic is *Beyond Belief: The Secret Gospel of Thomas* by Elaine Pagels (2005). In this book, Pagels explains how Christianity began, and she traces the development of its earliest texts, including the secret Gospel of Thomas, which was rediscovered in Egypt in 1945. The texts are called the Nag Hammadi scriptures, named after the city in Egypt where they were discovered. Most Christian denominations either suppress this information or discourage members from reading this material, because its very existence challenges their authority and their biblical interpretations. I introduce Pagel's book to my students by first requiring them to do some research on the history of the canon (official books) of the Christian scriptures. They are often amazed by what they find in a simple Internet search. There were many gospels in the early church in addition to Mark, Matthew, Luke, and John—such as gospels of James, Peter, Philip, Mary, and Thomas. There were competing factions in early Christianity that advocated for some of these books and condemned others. Who decided which books were inspirational and which were to be rejected? Why was John's gospel included in the canon and not the more logical choice of the Gospel of Thomas? John, of course, is very different from the others and quite mysterious, while Thomas is more like the synoptic texts Matthew, Mark, and Luke. Could it be that Thomas' doubt about the resurrection before he touched the wounds of Jesus frightened the early church? What is going on here? Who had the political power to accept or reject certain gospels?

The political battles of early Christianity, the divisions between Orthodox and Roman Catholics one thousand years later, and the debates during the Reformation and counter-Reformation all shaped Christianity as we know it today. This is very important for all people to study—believers and non-believers, Christians and non-Christians—because people suffer in our society when someone proclaims "the Bible says" and then use this rhetoric to enact laws that limit freedom and democracy based on their interpretation of religious scriptures. As an aside, I believe that an informed citizenry in a democracy must do the same historical investigation of the Koran, the Hindu scriptures, and all religious texts. If there is no authoritative bible, then an argument cannot be made to do something because it is in the scriptures. I want to deconstruct the notion of a unified metanarrative called *the* bible with my students to help eradicate prejudice and unjust social structures. I am not interested in trying to prove who was right or wrong. Rather, I am interested in teaching my students that there has never been a universally agreed upon list of books to include in the Christian Bible. The beliefs and rituals that evolved over two centuries reflect this diversity. Thus, to argue that "the Bible says" is illogical. There are different books and different translations, and in 1945 the problem became more complex with the discovery in Egypt of a library of 52 books that had been previously suppressed. Some might contend that

Pagels is trying to discredit Christianity. I strongly disagree. She is presenting historical information that makes some religious leaders uncomfortable, but for many others this information inspires a deeper faith. Scholar Frank Kermode (2003) explains:

> If one already possessed an incontestable version of truth, all these deviations could be seen as deplorable—comparable, perhaps, to "wild analysis" in the Freudian tradition. But Pagels looks about the Christian world today and rejoices at the proliferation of "new forms" Christianity is taking in Africa, North and South America, Korea, and China. She cannot be reconciled to churches that claim sole access to the truth of doctrine and discipline. Nag Hammadi seemed to show her that one must shed all such prejudices. The reward, she believes, may be a truer knowledge not only of Christianity, in whatever institutional form, but also of the other great religions. (p. 10)

This, in a nutshell, is my postmodern theological proposal in this chapter: diversity, eclecticism, and ecumenism bring us closer to wisdom and justice. One must give everything away to become rich, let go in order to live, experience suffering in order to understand joy.

As a quick aside, the immensely popular novel and film *The Da Vinci Code* uses some of these ideas to explore secret dimensions of Christian sects like Opus Dei. *The Da Vinci Code* is a thrilling mystery novel, but it is a work of fiction that happens to use historical figures and works of art by Leonardo Da Vinci in order to frame a murder investigation at the Louvre in Paris. This novel has enraged some conservative religions critics and fascinated others. Elaine Pagel's book, on the other hand, is a theological and historical study. I recommend both books, but I urge readers to distinguish between the different genres in these volumes.

We return now to our investigation of scriptural interpretation. Despite the warnings in the various scriptural texts examined above, we must remember that prophecy begins with a sense of revelation and that mysticism is ignited by an encounter with wisdom, beauty, or the holy. The postmodern curriculum as theological text is rooted in such an experience. Paul Ricoeur (1981) locates the birth of the text in the oral tradition and spoken word:

> The difference between the act of reading and the act of dialogue confirms our hypothesis that writing is a realization comparable and parallel to speech, a realization which takes the place of it and, as it were, intercepts it. Hence we could say that what comes to writing is discourse as intention-to-say and that writing is a direct inscription of this intention, even if, historically and psychologically, writing began with the graphic transcription of the signs of speech. This emancipation of writing, which places the latter at the site of speech, is the birth of the text. (p. 147)

The rebirth of theology in contemporary curriculum research is embedded in the spirituality, religious myth, and oral rituals—the *ruach ephphatha* (spoken breath)—of communities and cultures that experience divine revelation, cosmological harmony, and the journey toward wisdom. Exegetes have used the principles of hermeneutics, the process of interpretation, to uncover the layers of religious experience in these theological texts. The hermeneutical process produces what Ricoeur (1981) calls "a double eclipse of the reader and writer" (p. 147). It replaces the relation of dialogue, which directly connects the voice of one to the hearing of another. (We will examine this in detail in the next chapter.)

Unfortunately, the theological texts have been used by religious fundamentalists, cult leaders, gurus, extremist pastors and imams, and other preservers of unexamined truth to further eliminate this dialogue. The theological text has been converted into the rigid curriculum that we have been warned about: a voiceless, breathless prescription for a code of behavior to reach nirvana, perfection, salvation, and eschatological bliss by those who would propose their religion as *the* curriculum in an appeal to premodern worldviews. Joseph Campbell complained about this problem in an interview with Bill Moyers in *The Power of Myth* (1988, pp. 91–121).

The model of the theological text as a religious curriculum must be inverted if it is to be appropriate for the postmodern era. This paradigm has forced our society into a perverse and untenable choice: eliminate religion from the public schools—as if students and teachers could remove their metaphysical souls as one would remove one's hat before entering the classroom—or impose a state-sanctioned orthodoxy on the schools—as if religious education could be reduced to a melting-pot formula for universal salvation. There is an alternative in postmodern curriculum scholarship. However, the alternative becomes recognizable only once the premodern paradigm of the theological text as curriculum is critiqued for having led the global community into a tragic stalemate characterized by contemporary versions of inquisitions, crusades, witch hunts, and assassination contracts. The call of the Iranian Ayatollah Khomeini for the murder of Salman Rushdie, the author of *The Satanic Verses* (1989), is an obvious example. The dogmatism of the model of the theological text as curriculum will lead only to further ideological conflagration.

Likewise, the modern technological approach to curriculum development will continue to avoid the questions of morality, spirituality, and theology as essential elements of schooling because these issues are considered outside the modern scientific parameters of the schools. This stalemate requires that we invert the syllogism and reexplore the theological dialogue. Thus, revisionary postmodern scholars propose a model of curriculum as theological text where the educational enterprise will include the metaphysical dialogue. In this proposal, self-reflection, intuition, nonrational discourse, nonlinear teaching methodologies, meditation, and wisdom are all encouraged and nurtured in the curriculum. Only in this context will T. S. Eliot's probing question to modernity, "Where is the Wisdom we have lost in knowledge?," become intelligible.

Andrew Greeley's (1992) proposal for the reform of Catholic schools is an example of the frustration of some with the closing of parochial schools. Greeley's proposal appeals to many reform-weary lay leaders who have struggled to resolve the dilemmas facing parochial schools, only to be thwarted by a premodern authoritarian clerical bureaucracy. It also appeals to many reform-weary bishops and pastors who have struggled to provide funding to improve or expand parochial education, only to be blackmailed by self-serving lay contributors committed to modern public and private school models. Greeley's solution is the laicization of Catholic education. Some educational leaders who are frustrated with the status quo will defend this proposal as an opportunity to break with authoritarian structures of the past. Others who value strong pastoral leadership in a premodern spirit will be horrified by the prospect of secularization of the schools.

Laicization of parochial schools has already been implemented in some parts of the United States where consolidation, declining revenues, dwindling enrollments, and the loss of religious teachers reached a peak a decade ago. The experiment with laicization was viewed by some as a miserable failure. Only time will tell if postmodern structures emerge or if a reactionary return to premodern visions of parochial education evolves. Andrew Greely's proposal offers several insights into the dilemmas of the model of curriculum as theological text for the postmodern era for both parochial schools and public schools.

First, there has been a loss of identity in parochial schools brought on by the ravages of modernity. Having moved out of the cultural ghettos of the 1800s and into mainstream American culture by the 1960s, many religious minorities in contemporary society have become immersed in the ideology of modernity. While the messages of materialistic self-gratification, militaristic competitiveness, rampant overconsumption, and pandering paternalism pervade the media and the marketplace in an orgy of technological splendor, the subtler influences of modernity on the religious psyche have been ignored. The language of popular culture in modern society says as much about the human spirit as it does about material objects: "terminate," "slash and burn," "random acts of senseless violence," "leveraged buyout," "hostile takeover," "nuke," and so forth.

Greeley's assertion that there can be laicization of parochial schools without further secularization assumes that society has somehow transcended these ravages of modernity. However, the problem remains that there is a numbness that pervades our entire culture. William Faulkner ([1950] 1965) identified this phenomenon when he wrote in his speech of acceptance upon the award of the Nobel Prize for Literature that the tragedy of modern society is a general and universal physical fear so long sustained that we can even bear it. Walker Percy (1961) has also addressed this issue through his characters, who struggle against the cultural numbness of modern society and seek to emancipate the alienated self. Binx Bolling, in Percy's novel *The Moviegoer*, typifies the malaise that has overtaken the spirit of the individual and deadened the desire to search for meaning and wisdom. Binx is, in effect, hypnotized by the ideology of modernity.

Søren Kierkegaard (1849), in *The Sickness unto Death*, spoke to this hypnotic state when he wrote that the specific character of despair is the fact that it is unaware of being despair. Postmodern education no longer suppresses the despair. The impact of hopelessness on society, which also permeates the educational milieu in the schools, is integral to postmodern curricular revisions. As long as educators continue to dicker over bureaucratic issues like clericalism versus laicization and centralization versus site-based management, parochial, public, and private schools will all remain moribund.

All educational institutions must address the despair, the malaise, and the fear that has overtaken the human community as the result of oppressive and destructive modern bureaucratic and technological structures. Contemporary curriculum scholars probe the question of what good it will do for any school system to survive if spiritual disintegration and despair continue unabated. Like Percy's Binx Bolling, curriculum development in the postmodern era undertakes the search for something more important; and this search includes the attempt to envision an appropriate theological education for postmodern schooling that will help society to transcend this fear and malaise.

Second, the impact of modernity discourages support for theological self-reflection by deemphasizing, for example, autobiography, ethnography, phenomenology, spirituality, mystical traditions, ecumenism, and narrative research. This is coupled with zealous preference for theological foundations through emphasis on, for example, systematics, textual criticism, canonicity, and formal catechesis. This preference actually emerges from cultural and individual isolationism. Modernity has encouraged the isolation of the individual, frozen in quantifiable time and space, unable to establish personal relationships, unable to remember past experiences, and incapable of affecting the future course of global events. A modern intelligentsia that disparages self-understanding is no better than premodern fundamentalists who denigrate rigorous intellectual investigation. A constructive postmodern curriculum, however, integrates both theology and self-reflection. While the intelligentsia and the fundamentalists battle for religious superiority, like the scribes and pharisees described above, society wallows in cultural malaise—the kind of malaise that Jim Wallis (2005) is concerned about. In commenting on the unresolvable conflict between individual conscience and state-sanctioned orthodoxy, Stephen Arons calls for the complete separation of school and state:

> Without a complete separation of school and state, the governing process of American schooling has been increasingly undermined by unresolvable value conflict, and individual freedom of belief, expression, and political participation have been hobbled. Schooling has become a major means of transmitting culture. When government imposes the content of schooling it becomes the same deadening agent of repression from which the framers of the Constitution sought to free themselves. (1983, p. 189)

Critics characterize Arons' position as an adventure in monopolis, because the realm of freedom is confined to a private sector threatened by a monopolistic, totalizing public sphere. Both Stephen Arons and Andrew Greeley are theoretically blinded by a crude social Darwinism that promotes individual freedom in lieu of a genuine sociopolitical theory or a postmodern educational theology. Arons' critics refuse to concede the public educational struggle for emancipatory education to a premodern denominational religious culture (Whitson, 1988a). Likewise, postmodern scholars refuse to concede the theological curriculum struggle for spiritually emancipatory education to those entrenched in modernity and dependent upon oppressive cultural structures. They also refuse to concede the debate to premodern reactionaries who ignore ecumenical developments. Arons and Greeley remind us of the untenable alternative facing educators today: a premodern, insensitive autocracy (which they abhor) or a modern, ineffective bureaucracy (which they unconsciously perpetuate). A curriculum development theory rooted in theological self-reflection is the only viable alternative to this stalemate.

An example of such an alternative is found in the work of many contemporary educational scholars. Professor Michael O'Malley (2003, 2005, 2007) is perhaps typical. His ethnographic research recognizes that an ethic of exclusion, which separates a discourse of the soul from educational practice, is debilitating, untenable, and dangerous. The conscious absence of soul from education limits the efficacy of the pedagogical project and actually creates conditions in which social ills—anxiety, racism, poverty, exclusion—flourish. O'Malley (2003) writes:

> Emaciated in spirit, a people cannot effectively pursue the demanding challenges of dialoging across cultures, economies, races, and other borders— locally and worldwide. A postmodern thick description of soul constructed through my phenomenological inquiry identifies transcendent, relational, and ethical dimensions of the human person that interrogate experience for meaning, intimacy, and healing agency. A critical pedagogy of human soul actively interrupts processes of isolation and dehumanization such as adolescent experiences of sexual abuse, depression, self-mutilation, parental and peer judgment, and creates possibilities for meaning, relationship, and ethical action. I propose ... ways of experiencing, knowing, and acting: Imagining a new creation; Meaning as transcendent encounter—receiving communion; Testimony to the transformative beauty of intimacy; Agency for the life of the world: An ethic of hopeful possibility.

The postmodern schooling debates are moving away from bureaucratic solutions and shifting to a new vision rooted in spiritual liberation, as seen in the work of O'Malley and many others. (For some of the most recent reflections on this topic by leading scholars Svi Shapiro, Kathleen Kesson, Howard Zinn, Nel Noddings, and many others, see the *Journal of Curriculum and Pedagogy*, Winter 2005.) Reorganizing responsibility and authority does not address the theological issue of how to confront cultural malaise, despair, and fear in modern American society. In order to appropriately address these important issues, a reconceptualization of religious education that includes a synthesis of community models of education is emerging. For some parochial schools, this would reflect the best features of community-based models such as *To Teach as Jesus Did* (NCCB, 1972). For public schools, this would reflect the empowerment models found in programs such as the Dade County Florida Public Schools (Dreyfuss, Cistone, & Divita, 1992) or the Windham Southeast District in Vermont (James, Heller, & Ellis, 1992). Postmodern schooling will reject the negative features of bureaucratic reform structures of any school system and promote the spirit of postmodernism found in emerging models of education globally. The goal is to move the parochial school debate beyond the structural issues such as vouchers, laicization, and funding and move the public school debate beyond the legal issues related to separation of church and state and site-based management. My postmodern vision for curriculum and schooling includes, but is not limited to, the following three elements.

First, community cooperation rather than corporate competition will characterize the postmodern school. The corporate business model that school boards impose on public, parochial, and private schools will perpetuate the destructive competitive atmosphere that exists in our contemporary American society. This is certainly true of boards in public education, where bureaucratic gridlock is often overwhelming. The postmodern school is a place where relations between people are viewed primarily in cooperative terms and not in coercive business terms. Peter Sola (1989) contends that the growing alliance between business and education is embedded in the free enterprise philosophy of corporate capitalist institutions. He argues that, during the era of local control of schools in the early 1800s, school boards reflected the community. However, since the mid-1800s there has been a radical change in the social composition of school boards. Sola (1989) writes:

> By the end of the progressive era, school boards consisted mainly of business persons and professionals and seldom of teachers, blue collar workers, or women. If ... school boards represent largely business and professional classes, and if the school administrative staff largely keeps their collective eye on "the bottom line," who is ensuring that schools are performing their primary tasks? (p. 78)

Postmodern curriculum research challenges the structures of modernity that are reflected in the composition and ideology of school boards.

Additionally, postmodern curriculum research promotes other important elements of schooling, including the search for wisdom through theological experiences, the creation of cooperative and ecologically sustainable learning environments, and the commitment to reverent, democratic, and just community models of schooling. Schooling should not serve the interests of economic competition and corporate greed. The postmodern educational community is moving beyond this modern phenomenon identified by Sola (1989) when he writes: "The business of America is developing educational policy for business. The business of American education has really become inseparable from American business" (p. 81).

The reconceptualization in curriculum theory challenges educators to no longer view the world as being at the service of the competitive, mechanistic, and materialistic self-interests of corporation and wealthy elites. Schools are viewed as dynamic communities committed to critical thinking, discovery learning, theological inquiry, autobiographical analysis, ecological sustainability, aesthetic wide-awakeness, social justice, compassion, and ecumenism. Of course, this is demonstrated not by simply promulgating a district mission statement that reflects these values but rather by enhancing the quality of cooperative relationships embedded in the local community.

Second, a holistic process perspective rather than reductionism will permeate the postmodern curriculum and the theological milieu. Theologians such as Karl Rahner, Carl Peter, and Jürgen Moltmann have established a foundation for a renewed understanding of the future. This theology, called proleptic eschatology, because the future is viewed as that which brings to completion what has already been set in motion, replaces the modern concept of time that denies the future and promotes immediate self-gratification. It also replaces the fundamentalist's futuristic view, in which salvation is disconnected from the present and experienced only after death. These are the two predominant visions of the future that the American public brings to schools from popular culture, but neither informs contemporary curriculum development models.

Curriculum development in the postmodern era understands that the past and the future are integral to a self-reflective spirituality. As we discussed in chapter 2, history is not taught as a series of events on a linear time line to be memorized. Rather, it is an unfolding story in which each student is an active participant in shaping the meaning of events and in constructing the future course of global communities. This anticipatory view of history, which many scholars contend is urgently needed to address global crises in a just manner, is accessible through postmodern theology. This concept will be explored further at the end of the book.

Third, postmodern schooling provides a multilayered, interdisciplinary curriculum that integrates spirituality and theology into every dimension of the educational process. Today it is no longer assumed by curriculum scholars that the best way to study a problem, especially with an eye toward coming up with a solution, is to do so in terms of one of the traditional disciplines, subdisciplines, or courses. A new understanding of knowledge in conjunction with a vision of interdependence, spirituality, and wisdom rather than the values of the modern engineer, scientist, and economist is emerging. The curriculum as a theological text provides expanded opportunities for students and teachers to explore alternative solutions to the ecological, health, and economic problems of the world today. In short, I believe that there are alternative approaches to energy consumption, transportation, and housing that can protect the earth by using renewable resources and sustainable practices. Powerful economic and political interests consistently block these alternatives and convince a fearful and uninformed public to support the modern status quo socio-political and economic arrangements that are so destructive of life. There are also alternatives to war and violence. A lack of a vision of postmodern alternatives allowed the US government to rush into a "war of choice" in Iraq in 2003 based on faulty intelligence and historical amnesia— and without proper planning and forethought. This is repeated across the globe to the point that life on the planet is threatened. The absurdity of this situation makes an exploration of the postmodern alternatives imperative.

The traditional behavioral-technical curriculum of the public school system, which many private school boards and administrators are so apt to imitate, is seen as outmoded and inappropriate for all school systems. It is thus considered foolhardy to emulate this model in the development of postmodern curriculum. Many religious schools, for example, are evolving into clones of public and private institutions that happen to teach a few religion courses. Likewise, many public schools and universities smugly believe that the addition of a course in "the Bible as literature," a degree program in comparative religion, or a moment of silence at graduation ceremonies will fully address the theological question in the curriculum. These views are severely problematic. A vision of a new model that integrates spirituality and theology throughout the school curriculum and community is the alternative that is now being proposed to address the crises of the postmodern world.

Because the very nature of postmodern schooling is eclectic, ecumenical, and inclusive, the first and most important lesson to be derived from this chapter on theology and education is that postmodern schooling will *not* simply add a new course in theology to the curriculum in order to pacify religious interest groups. Rather, the nature of schooling will change to reflect postmodern values. Although there is not a monolithic master plan for including religious education in postmodern schools, the discussion of curriculum as theological text has presented insights into the evolving milieu proposed for postmodern schooling today, which is understood as reverent, reflective, inclusive, cooperative, just, holistic, and caring.

Creating a reflective environment in schools is not dependent upon Supreme Court decisions. It flows out of school architecture, school schedules, teacher attitudes, and classroom environments that encourage flexibility, critical literacy, agency, diversity, autobiography, ecumenism, global interdependence, ecological sustainability, narrative inquiry, and other postmodern values. Beginning in the earliest years of schooling, and continuing throughout the educational process, students should be given time and space during the day, within academic organizations and throughout academic experiences, to question, reflect, investigate, meditate, and ponder. Leisurely and thought-provoking visits to museums, nature trails, and local historical sights will be integral to the curriculum. Reflective dialogue with grandparents, younger students, multicultural professionals, community activists, politicians, and religious leaders will be regular occurrences. Active community involvement in environmental projects, health and social services, and ethnic preservation will become a priority. The borders between the school and the community in the postmodern curriculum will be dissolved, and thus the *quality* of reverent relationships will replace the quantity of correct answers on tests as the focus of education.

Curriculum theorists contend that, in this environment, prayer does not need to be mandated or prohibited, for it will flow from within the individual's experiences of life. This is one postmodern response to the dilemma of prayer and religion in the curriculum. In *Exiles from Eden: Religion and the Academic Vocation in America*, Mark R. Schwehn (1992) writes that achieving community at the end of modernity and the beginning of postmodernity means connecting to virtues and experiences that have traditionally been thought to be spiritual. In a review of his book, Yvonna Lincoln (1994), following Schwehn, points out that these spiritual values are equally essential to "the process of genuine learning (and therefore meaningful teaching). Those virtues—faith, humility (piety), charity, self-denial, and friendship—tend to be both social virtues and those that sustain genuine communities" (p. 36). Schwehn argues that education must be attentive to these virtues, or all attempts at internal reform will prove ultimately useless. He also contends that Max Weber and several of his contemporaries led higher education astray by stressing research—the making and transmitting of knowledge—at the expense of shaping moral character. Schwehn sees an urgent need for a change in orientation and calls for a "spiritually grounded education in and for thoughtfulness" to replace individualistic behavior and the "doing my own work" syndrome derived from the Enlightenment, with a communitarian ethic grounded in spirituality.

Creating a cooperative learning environment in schools is not dependent upon classroom lesson plans. Cooperation will evolve only after a dramatic change takes place in the concept of schooling itself. Empowering teachers to cooperate in the development of an interdisciplinary curriculum that is not limited to compartmentalized blocks of time is one important first step. Encouraging student cooperation in the development of seminar-style classes where circles and centers replace rows of desks is another step.

Discovery laboratories, multisensory projects, autobiographical narratives, oral history projects, engaging seminars, aesthetic awareness, and provocative field experiences involving groups of students, teachers, and other community members will become the norm rather than the exception. Socratic dialogue that seeks understanding, respect, and synthesis rather than predetermined answers will be the hallmark of the postmodern theological curriculum.

Creating stimulating learning environments is not dependent on the latest technology. Teachers do not need to be actors, barkers, magicians, or technicians to interest young people in education. Teachers and parents are encouraged to become mentors and guides who will inspire students to seek wisdom and understanding as part of a community of learners. In postmodern schooling, teachers, administrators, and parents will recognize that they are not experts with all the answers but fellow travelers on the lifelong journey of learning. T. S. Eliot (1971) answered his question "Where is the wisdom we have lost in knowledge?" in his poem "Little Gidding":

We shall not cease from exploration.

And the end of all our exploring

Will be to arrive where we started

And know the place for the first time.

Through the unknown, remembered gate

When the last of earth left to discover

Is that which was the beginning;

At the source of the longest river

The voice of the hidden waterfall

And the children in the apple-tree

Not known, because not looked for

But heard, half-heard, in the stillness

Between two waves of the sea.

Quick now, here, now, always—

A condition of complete simplicity

(Costing not less than everything)

And all shall be well and

All manner of thing shall be well

When the tongues of flame are in-folded

Into the crowned knot of fire

And the fire and the rose are one. (p. 145)

If the theological curriculum is the active process of seeking, running, and ruminating, then the evolution of postmodern schooling will provide the milieu where spirituality, mystery, intuition, poetry, ethics, and religious sensibilities can flourish. Contemporary scholars conclude that the time of the usefulness of the modern bureaucratic model of curriculum development has ended. Public, private, parochial, apprenticeship, and home schooling are all challenged to transcend this model by contemporary curriculum scholars. As we envision curriculum development in the postmodern era, it is time to return to that place where we started and know the place for the very first time.

This now brings us to the end of part I. We have explored curriculum development as a field of study with particular emphasis on the meaning of postmodernism, historical analysis, the reconceptualization, and theology. Of course, there are many other ways of framing curriculum development in the postmodern era, and part II will introduce the scholarship of various postmodern curriculum discourses that are emerging today. The chapters there will each provide a short introduction to these discourses in order to acquaint students and curriculum specialists with the scope of the postmodern curriculum. However, it must be remembered that the eclectic, aesthetic, ironic, playful, linguistic, social, theological, and political dimensions of postmodernism will necessitate that the short vignettes in part II serve as an introductory guide to postmodern curriculum and not a definitive normative outline. The theological process challenges educators to explore curriculum in a way that gives possibility to the living word, in all its mystery, ambiguity, and complexity. The theological curriculum leads us directly into this exploration, sometimes called hermeneutics, which begins our focus on contemporary curriculum development paradigms in the next chapter.

Part II
Complicated Conversations in Contemporary Curriculum Development

five
The Hermeneutic Circle and the Interpretive Process

Curriculum development in the postmodern era foregrounds an approach to understanding the meaning of texts, laws, language, historical artifacts, and pedagogy called hermeneutics. Many scholars, for example Roy J. Howard (1982), describe hermeneutics as the art of interpretation. Others explain it as intersubjective communication and answerability (Slattery, Krasny, & O'Malley, 2006). Several forms of interpretive inquiry in educational research explore such understanding: phenomenology, critical literacy, semiotics, poststructuralism, heuristics, autobiography, aesthetics, and ethnography. Edmund C. Short (1991) has edited an excellent collection of essays that explore these forms of curriculum inquiry. William G. Tierney and Yvonna S. Lincoln (1997) provide concrete examples in *Representation and the Text: Re-Framing the Narrative Voice*. William Pinar and William Reynolds (1992) have written about hermeneutics in curriculum as a phenomenological and deconstructed text. The attention to hermeneutics has expanded dramatically in recent years, and the complexity of the interpretive process is perhaps best explicated by Norman Denzin and Yvonna Lincoln (2005) in the popular and comprehensive *Handbook of Qualitative Research*. Without denying the uniqueness and importance of various approaches to understanding curriculum development, this chapter will explicate interpretive inquiry from the perspective of hermeneutics. Later chapters will return to the other forms of curriculum inquiry.

David Jardine (1992) writes: "The returning of life to its original difficulty is a returning of the possibility of the living Word. It is a return to the essential generativity of human life, a sense of life in which there is always something left to say, with all the difficulty, risk, and ambiguity that such generativity entails. Hermeneutic inquiry is thus concerned with the ambiguous nature of life itself" (p. 119). Curriculum inquiry is also concerned with the ambiguous and ironic dimensions of education: an unexpected question triggers an exciting and provocative tangent; the changing moods and emotions of individuals create a unique and often perplexing life-world in classrooms; the same methodology is not always successful with every group of students; atmospheric changes in the weather alter the atmosphere of the school; past experiences, cultural norms, and family dynamics influence values and behaviors; religious experiences and denominational regulations govern mental processes and shade interpretations of religious texts. Teachers cannot predict the ambiguous and ironic nature of life itself, especially in the classroom, and postmodern understandings of hermeneutics as an investigation into the ambiguous nature of being and knowledge now inform and enrich contemporary curriculum paradigms. Thus, along with David G. Smith (1991), I argue that all discourses about postmodernism are interpretive and hermeneutic endeavors (Slattery et al., 2006). Two important scholars, Hans-Georg Gadamer and Jacques Derrida (1989), have debated this point in the book *Dialogue and Deconstructionism*, and some of their concerns will be part of our discussion in this chapter.

The art and science of interpretation is the central enterprise of school curriculum. The selection of textbooks and educational media reflects a prejudice in favor of particular styles, methodologies, politics, or worldviews. Reading programs in elementary schools vary from district to district and classroom to classroom, with some emphasizing basal texts, others emphasizing literature. Some curriculum materials foreground linear progression through discrete skills, others deemphasize these practices in favor of meaning-centered approaches. Some control rigidly for a singular methodology, others support eclectic combinations of a variety of materials and approaches that integrate all of the language arts. Historical interpretation is particularly volatile in school districts. Texts are regularly castigated and occasionally banned. Historical analysis varies from text to text, nation to nation. Should Columbus be presented as a saint and hero or a villain and marauder? Was the bombing of Hiroshima and Nagasaki necessary to end World War II and save American lives, an act of murder of innocent civilians as the Japanese government was preparing to surrender, a warning to the Soviet Union and others with global ambitions, a military necessity, or human insanity? What caused the collapse of the Soviet Union—internal economic collapse, external pressure from the United States, ethnic conflicts and ambitions of the people of the Soviet Union, or a combination of these factors? The mere mention of alternative interpretations of history from official government propaganda can result, at best, in charges of historical revisionism or, at worst, in loss of job, imprisonment, and death. This occurs in all countries of the world, including democracies. Consider the case of Martin Harwit, the director of the Smithsonian Air and Space Museum, who was fired in 1995 by the US Congress amid controversies about historical interpretation in his World War II exhibit.

A dramatic example of the dangerous conflicts that arise from hermeneutic analysis can be found in the various memorial events surrounding the fiftieth anniversary in 1995 of the destruction of Hiroshima and Nagasaki by the United States' atomic bombs at the end of World War II. I joined my colleagues John Weaver of Georgia Southern University and Toby Daspit of Western Michigan University in an investigation of hermeneutics and the politics of memory construction at the Bradbury Science Museum in Los Alamos, New Mexico, where the bomb was developed, and at the National Air and Space Museum in Washington, DC, where an historical display was being prepared by Martin Harwit, along with his staff, university historians Edward Linenthal, Stanley Goldberg, and Martin Sherwin, and military historians Richard Kohn, Herman Wolk, and Richard Hallion (Weaver, Slattery, & Daspit, 1998). Harwit believed that these historians would represent the various stakeholders and veteran organizations in the installation of the exhibit (Harwit, 1996). An attempt was made to examine the historical evidence related to the bombing of Hiroshima and the various archival records that inform historians who research these events—not all of whom agree with the official US position that the bombing was necessary to save American lives (Zezima, 2001). Instead, the proposed exhibit triggered an intense political backlash that resulted in the cancellation of the exhibition. Harwit's analysis of the cancellation is summarized at the beginning of his book *An Exhibit Denied: Lobbying the History of the Enola Gay*:

> *An Exhibit Denied* describes the planning and ultimate cancellation of an exhibition that nobody ever saw, but that nonetheless precipitated the most violent dispute ever witnessed by a museum. A national frenzy, fanned by lobbyists and the media, thwarted the Smithsonian Air and Space Museum's attempt to mount an exhibition featuring the *Enola Gay*, the B-29 bomber that had dropped the atomic bomb on Hiroshima. [This book examines] the decade long effort to restore the *Enola Gay*, the largest restoration project ever undertaken by the museum; recalls the help and support initially provided by General Tibbets and a small band of men he had commanded on the atomic missions to Hiroshima and Nagasaki; shows how a handful of World War II veterans became disillusioned and began to oppose the museum's display of the aircraft; and describes how these men succeeded in calling on powerful veterans' organizations, aerospace lobbyists, and congressmen for help in their cause. All the while, a separate drama was unfolding in Japan, where the prospects of an exhibition of the *Enola Gay* in a national museum in the heart of Washington raised an entirely different set of concerns. The book reminds us that James Smithson had founded the Smithsonian Institution for the "increase and diffusion of knowledge." In a democracy, predicated on an informed citizenry, the function of a national museum is to inform the public. In exhibiting the *Enola Gay*, the National Air and Space Museum sought to depict the aircraft's pivotal role in twentieth century history—in all but ending World War II, but also ushering in a nuclear age that remains problematic to this day. This attempt was thwarted when congressional pressure forced the exhibit's cancellation. (1996, pp. i–ii)

What was so controversial about this exhibit that it was attacked by Speaker of the House Newt Gingrich and removed by the United States Congress? As noted above, it discussed not only the end of World War II, but also the lingering problems associated with the development of nuclear weapons and the impact on civilians when the bombs were dropped. The ethical fallout from nuclear proliferation must cause us to ponder and reflect on these issues. Unfortunately, powerful lobbyists and congressmen did not allow the public the opportunity to ask penetrating questions and examine the historical record in all of its complexity. Earl Lee (2001) reminds us:

> When the Smithsonian Institution tried to put on the *Enola Gay* exhibit, the project came under considerable criticism from Veterans' groups which objected to graphic photographs of the human casualties of the atomic bombing of

Hiroshima. Interestingly enough, an earlier exhibit on the use of the V2 bombs by the Nazis, including graphic photographs of the human devastation in London, did not provoke a reaction. The Enola Gay exhibit was ... replaced by more politically expedient exhibit. (pp. 77–78)

Museums are complex places of learning that can be used either to advance critical thinking or to support the status quo political and cultural agenda. Museums, like curriculum texts, can open up spaces for reflection, create epistemological curriculum spaces, or limit access to ideas and possibilities (Ellsworth, 2005; Cary, 2006).

When the news of the controversy about the *Enola Gay* exhibit became public, my colleagues and I decided to travel to Washington, DC, and to another exhibit at the Bradbury Science Museum in Los Alamos, New Mexico, in August of 1995 to interview participants, investigate the exhibits, and analyze the controversy. Our research attempted to frame a wider discussion about negotiation and contestation in museums and the ways in which counter-hegemonic, non-linear, and postmodern spaces may be created so that multiple hermeneutic understandings and dangerous knowledge may be constructed and deconstructed. We argued that museums should present multiple perspectives and various interpretations of historical, cultural, religious, and political phenomena—even if it is painful to investigate and discuss dangerous memories.

The hermeneutic dimension of this research exposes the fact that the contents and the use of museums are contested and often co-opted for political purposes. They are also used spatially to project certain messages disguised as truth. Modernist notions of linear time, from past to present to future, are infused into museums when curators and boards view the museum as a repository of the past or as vaults for preservation of high culture. I propose that the ways in which memories are created and constructed in museums can either advance knowledge, agency, and democracy or support narrow partisan perspectives. Despite memory manipulation by many directors, educators, and curators, museums can be recovered as progressive sites for transcending hegemonic manipulation, for developing counter-hegemonic responses, and for creating fresh understandings beyond both the hegemonic and the counter-hegemonic, as happened in the Bradbury Museum.

The initial debate over the *Enola Gay* exhibit in Washington began when some veterans became outraged because they did not want the dropping of the atomic bomb remembered as controversial but rather as heroic. They believed revisionist historians were suffering from collective amnesia, forgetting facts and the context surrounding the actual event. The idea of collective amnesia, couched in the derogatory language *revisionist*, permitted these veterans to disguise their assumptions and beliefs as *truth* without problematizing their notions about important historical events. Moreover, it allowed them the opportunity to exercise their power to proclaim a crisis of knowing and learning and, eventually, to construct a solution to this crisis that fit their worldview. Memory creation implies that collective amnesia exists only as a rhetorical construct used to disguise one's power and justify one's social position and to determine who or what will be remembered or valued. It is part of the responsibility of educators and museum directors to challenge hegemonic urges that attempt to silence historical analysis. Martin Harwit stood firm in his conviction to provide the public with an opportunity to investigate Hiroshima and the *Enola Gay* with an eye toward the continuing struggle with nuclear proliferation and the dangers it presents to the global community. Unfortunately, the Smithsonian exhibit was denied by Congress, and Harwit lost his job. Nonetheless, Martin Harwit provides a striking example of an ethical prophetic voice working for hermeneutic understanding through education.

The Bradbury Science Museum in Los Alamos was also embroiled in controversy when we visited in August of 1995. This museum had decided not to address the problems associated with nuclear weapons and the complexity of the historical record at Hiroshima. Activists in Santa Fe pressured the museum to include these topics, and they eventually received approval to display several large panels depicting the effects of the nuclear bombs on the civilians in Hiroshima, along with some of the historical text that had been denied in Washington. Some veteran groups protested this decision, claiming that it was insensitive to those who gave their lives for America and freedom to be subjected to *revisionist* history and images of dead and dying Japanese. The fact that many historians have questioned the *official* interpretation of the bombing infuriated some veterans. Not all historians agree that it was necessary to bomb civilian targets—or even use nuclear weapons—to end World War II. Other historians have reviewed the records carefully in the intervening years to discover many other connections to the Soviet Union and postwar US intentions. My goal here is not to settle the historical debate, but rather to report on the struggle to allow a discussion of the various historical accounts in museums, classrooms, and school curriculum.

The activists argued that the American public deserves to know the complex historical record and various hermeneutic interpretations. As mentioned above, hermeneutics threatens powerful people because it may not confirm the interpretations that keep them in wealth or power. In the end, the small cramped corridor that was provided for the activists to display several floor-to-ceiling displays was divided in two, and the veterans were given half of the space for a military display with a traditional interpretation of the bombing of Hiroshima—despite the fact that this information was readily available and prominently displayed in several other venues. Nonetheless, the activists and veterans were required to share the small space, which ironically created additional opportunities for media coverage and dialogue.

I arrived in Los Alamos on a sunny afternoon on August 6, 1995, with my mother, step-father, and children. We entered the museum and toured the permanent science exhibits first. We eventually made our way to the small corridor where the peace activists and the veterans had won the right to display their historical records and photographs. It was the fiftieth anniversary of the bombing, and American veterans had gathered at Los Alamos along with several Japanese educators and some survivors of the explosion in Hiroshima. It was a profound moment. Dozens of elderly American and Japanese men and women were engaged in long pensive discussion about their experiences. My family and I were welcomed into the circle in the cramped hallway with both groups of survivors. Everyone was respectful, even in their disagreements about the historical record. I will never forget the moment when fifty years of history merged in human empathy as the elderly American military men and the frail Japanese bombing survivors extended peace signs and agreed that they wanted no more bombs.

I am so grateful that my children were a part of this experience. Katie was eleven years old. My mother was also eleven years old in 1941 when she heard the news that the Japanese had bombed Pearl Harbor. In 1995, after our family experience in Los Alamos, my mother wrote the following poem describing her life as a young girl in Louisiana during World War II and how those memories were rekindled fifty years later at the Bradbury Science Museum. As arts-based researchers contend, writing poetry is perhaps an excellent response to questions of hermeneutic interpretation.

Seek the Realm of Peace

1941
Lazy Louisiana sunshine
shivers through December woods
a family drive on a Sunday afternoon
crackling car radio
always out of tune
bombs are blasting war
so peacefully.
How could this be *a day of infamy?*
Age 11 doesn't know the word
11 understands the deed.

12 draws the shades for blackouts
flips off lights
so she can scan her battlefield
for fireflies disobeying curfew
then dreams them into marching men
a million miles away.

13 memorizes patriotic posters
Use less sugar and stir like hell
Lucky Strike green has gone to war
green dye—men die
black blood
prints their names each day.

14 snuggles against the console
for Roosevelt's fireside chats

this voice that comforts her

will die—no resurrection

Truman tries

But she forgets to listen.

15 dreams of bright canteens

too young—she still can dream

of all the men who'd dance with her

kiss her lips

forget this war and all its slogans

all save one: *Give 'em hell Harry.*

Hell fell twice

as atoms split the generations

1995

50 years of faded dreams awake

as a postmodern pilgrimage to Los Alamos

conjures my ghosts

hidden in a half century of distractions.

We enter

through a gift shop

overstocked with toy men dressed for war

"Little Boy" and "Fat Man" bombs

with all their deadly plastic playthings.

We see

beyond that room

not quite out of sight

a wall—one lousy little wall

to regurgitate it all

HIROSHIMA AND NAGASAKI

landscapes of nothingness

populated by skin

of melting bodies, faces fused.

BATAAN DEATH MARCH

tortured American
faces buried in the mud
of their inferno.

We memorize
with solemn eyes
compelled to digest the aged rot
of hideous past.

We hear
Japanese teachers with symbolic paper cranes and
American veterans with weight of all their wounds
resting on canes
politely exchange passionate discourse.

We stand
behind a blood red rope
and wait
as others mark on pages of a book
for all who look to see
ink bled from the heart.

My granddaughter 11
takes her turn with words
"We shouldn't have dropped the bomb."
11 understands the deed
perhaps that's all she needs
to understand.

I recall
my perception of war
at age 11
and my apprehension of wars that followed
and of the wars to come
I touch my son.

A Japanese grandmother bows

"Ah, BIG son."

Rising sun

proud

flaming red ball

beneath the mushroom cloud

that vaporizes infamy.

"Please, no more bombs."

Japanese words in broken English.

She presses a ceramic crane

no larger than a distant star

into my palm.

No more bombs

no more infamy

I touch her hand as we walk away

two grandmothers yearning for peace

our eyes shielded

against the harsh sunlight

of Los Alamos.

(Burke, 1995; 2009, pp. 35–38)

Modernity has been characterized by a search for an underlying and unifying truth and certainty that can render the self, the cosmos, subjective experiences, and historical events as coherent and meaningful. In the midst of war, terrorism, violence, and environmental degradation, these modern urges are understandable because many citizens are living in fear and despair. We want to live without fear, but we are constantly afraid of *the terrorists*, our food supply, and wrinkles that show our age. We get Botox shots for our wrinkles, eat organic vegetables from Whole Foods, and bomb Iraq and Afghanistan into oblivion. But somehow this is not enough to quell our fears. So, we choose not to live our desperate and fearful lives. We want to live free of fear, but we are afraid to live because to live might mean that we will die. So, we clutch our fear and lie awake in our beds waiting for the next terrorist to attack. Michael Fisher (2010) is one of the most insightful authors on this topic today. In his book *The World's Fearlessness Teachings: A Critical Integral Approach to Fear management/Education for the 21st Century* we learn to deconstruct fear and develop holistic and integral attitudes and practices.

Some of my college students bring this modern desire for absolute truth and certainty to the classroom, and they are confused by my critique of unifying truth and unquestioned metanarratives about historical events—like the one discussed above—or other discussion of literature, religion, sexuality, gender, or culture. However, most of my students eventually come to appreciate the postmodern perspective that the human condition and the cosmos are irreducible and irrevocably pluralistic, existing in a multitude of sovereign units and sites of authority, with no horizontal or vertical order either in actuality or in potency. In this environment, knowledge and truth are contested, constructed, tentative, and emerging. This is not a denial of truth or historical facts; rather, postmodernism contends that *truth* with a small "t" rather than a capital "T" is a more appropriate understanding in the postmodern world. Absolute "Truth" has no room for humility, complexity, multiplicity, eclecticism, ecumenism, and doubt. I thoroughly enjoyed the way that the author John Patrick Shanley, winner of the 2005 Pulitzer Prize for Drama and Tony Award for Best Play on Broadway, addressed this concept in his play *Doubt*. Cherry Jones portrays a Catholic nun forced to confront her notions of certainty and truth about her colleague, a Catholic priest played by Bryan F. O'Byrne, whom she suspects of illegal and immoral conduct. The audience is left to navigate through the complex world of truth and doubt without definitive answers.

Literature in the school curriculum presents another example of hermeneutic controversy. What authors and texts should be included in the syllabus? Which novels and poems should be canonical and which are to be ignored? Walt Whitman's "O Captain! My Captain!" and "When Lilacs Last in the Dooryard Bloom'd" are found in most high school anthologies. However, Whitman's poem "I Saw in Louisiana a Live-Oak Growing," with its comparison of the oak tree to manly love, is seldom included. Whitman's praise of Abraham Lincoln is enshrined in the curriculum; his praise of same-gender love is often ignored in the curriculum. This decision is a hermeneutic one. This is also the case when literature and poetry are explicated in the classroom. What is the psychology of Hamlet, for example, in the Shakespearean tragedy? Was he vengeful, suicidal, confused, depressed? All of these? None of these? I have read *Hamlet* many times, and each reading reveals a more complex and robust character. This is the genius of Shakespeare and not a fault. Can a student read *Hamlet* from her or his autobiographical experience and conclude something different? Which interpretations are allowed and validated in classroom discussions and essays? This, too, is a hermeneutic decision. I believe that educators must understand the multiple approaches to hermeneutics that influence their curricular decisions—whether conscious or unconscious—and reflect deeply on the social, political, historical, and global implications of their interpretive acts in order to provide an appropriate, engaging, and just curriculum for students.

Hermeneutics was also at the forefront of political discussions in the US in 2005 as citizens carefully examined President George W. Bush's nominations of John Roberts as Chief Justice of the United States and Harriet E. Miers and Samuel Alito, Jr., as justices of the Supreme Court, and again in 2009 when President Barack Obama nominated Sonia Sotomayor and Elena Kagan as justices. The way that the new justices and their colleagues interpret the US Constitution and legal statutes will have a dramatic impact on all citizens for many years to come. Commentators have noted that retired Justice Sandra Day O'Connor was often the swing vote in many 5 to 4 decisions on crucial issues facing the US. These close votes remind us that the interpretation of constitutions and laws is not universal. If it were, then the votes of our legal scholars on the Supreme Court would always be unanimous. If nine preeminent scholars cannot agree on the meaning of the Constitution, then something else must also be at work in the interpretive process.

What is at work are assumptions about the meaning of the language of the Constitution, the unique political philosophy and religious beliefs of each justice, the conflicting interpretations of the historical legal record of previous cases, and personality idiosyncrasies of each judge. Timing and historical circumstances also influence decisions by justices. In other words, hermeneutic interpretation of laws and constitutions is a complex and ambiguous human endeavor and not simply a scientific application of universally agreed upon guidelines. This is also true in many contexts: school boards interpreting the rules in handbooks; imams, shamans, chiefs, rabbis, and pastors interpreting the Koran, the Bhagavad Gita, the Torah, the Hindu scriptures, the Book of Mormon, or the King James Bible; teachers grading student essays; docents commenting on the meaning of a work of art in a museum; and referees making a call at a ball game. Instant reply of controversial calls in sports does not always settle a dispute. No two people interpret a handbook, a work of art, a legal text, an athletic play, or a religious book in the exact same way. There are many things at work in each of us: vantage point, cultural heritage, religious experience, tastes, values, prejudices, exposure to ideas, physical capacity of eyesight or brain synapses, level of tolerance, education, philosophy. And, even if two people do share virtually identical philosophies, theologies, and political ideologies, they will often diverge in the way that they believe the rules should be implemented or understood in various circumstances.

Think about it. Consider any world religion. Schisms and divisions are commonplace. The role of women in society or in church leadership varies from country to country and from denomination to denomination. The Episcopal Church, with a majority vote, ordained Rev. Gene V. Robinson, an openly gay man with a partner, as a bishop. Other Christian denominations, and even some Episcopalians and Anglicans, vehemently protested this action. The Koran is interpreted differently with respect to social and religious practices, women's dress, and worship in Saudi Arabia, Iran, France, Indonesia, India, or Mexico. The socio-political and cultural context matters. Wars and political battles related to the interpretation of sacred texts and religious practices have been waged between Shiite and Sunni Muslims, Protestant and Catholic Christians, Zionist and Reform Jews, Tibetan and Chinese Buddhists, and Hindus of various castes in India. Hermeneutic interpretation is not only controversial, but it can be violent and deadly at times.

Consider debates within Islam. Fatwas, the legal opinions promulgated by Islamic scholars, have proliferated in the Muslim world in recent decades. This can be attributed to many factors, including access to the Internet. Fatwas sometimes contradict each other, and faithful Muslims must choose which authority to believe. This has led to a debate over who can legitimately issue a fatwa. Since the decrees sometimes challenge state-sanctioned interpretations of the Koran and Islamic practices, many governments have become alarmed. Geoff Porter has written: "Yet criticizing fatwas about divisive issues like the propriety of killing civilians and Shiites can be dangerous for officials. The Saudi government is trying another tactic, zeroing in on what it considers frivolous fatwas in order to rally support for tougher measures on who can and who cannot issue fatwas" (2005, p. 13). Within every religion there is a growing concern about legitimate interpretations of texts and the legitimacy of those authorities who interpret. Who can legitimately issue a fatwa? Which fatwas are frivolous? Who decides?

Consider debates in the US about reproductive rights and abortion. As Supreme Court nominees are examined by senators, some are looking for candidates to uphold the precedent in *Roe* v. *Wade*, others are seeking to confirm judges who will overturn *Roe* v. *Wade*. Some believe that the 1973 decision was mistaken because it removed the decision-making authority on abortion from the individual states. Others believe that *Roe* was a victory for the individual freedom of all women in the US to consult privately with their family and physician to make reproductive decisions. Another volatile dimension of the debate is religious interpretation. For those who use Hebrew and Christian scriptures to *prove* their case, they must turn to hermeneutics for guidance. Michael Luo (2006) writes that the word "abortion" appears neither in Christian scriptures nor in a concordance—the list of specific words mentioned in the Bible. Thus supporters and critics of abortion who use religion to justify their position must turn to interpretations of conflicting passages to support their stance. For example, in Luke's gospel, when the baby "leaps in the womb of Elizabeth," does it mean that the baby had consciousness—as anti-abortion forces believe—or does it mean that the fetus had typical reaction of sensory awareness appropriate for that stage of pregnancy—as pro-choice advocates believe? This is one of three passages used by opponents of abortion to argue for overturning *Roe* v. *Wade*. Assuming that it is even appropriate to use religious scriptures to argue a Supreme Court case, there is not one passage that directly mentions the word "abortion." Thus, hermeneutics must be used to construct an interpretation of the meaning of each passage that is considered relevant in the debate. And, as we have seen above, denominations and individuals rarely agree on the same interpretation of scriptures in Christianity, Islam, Judaism, or Hinduism. This is true even when the scripture mentions the word in question, say, "divorce," "slavery," or "prayer." These words are interpreted differently because of changing cultural contexts, ambiguity of language, and variations in translation. Now imagine trying to find the precise admonishments on stem-cell research, nuclear energy, or feeding tubes in an ancient book of faith. In 2011, ballot measures in Colorado and Mississippi asked voters to define a zygote as a person. Is a fertilized egg that has not attached to the uterus a person? When exactly does a human life begin? If a unique and legal person exists at conception, should birth-control devices be outlawed and miscarriages be investigated as murders? These are not just scientific questions; they are philosophical questions that demand a hermeneutical method should be employed.

Why is hermeneutics so controversial? For one thing, the stakes are very high when courts, churches, mosques, and councils declare the one *true* meaning of a text. National ideologies, religious practices, financial arrangements, and personal freedoms, among other things, may be challenged or restricted.

A second problem is the nature of the interpretive process itself. Consider the confirmation process for US Supreme Court nominees or the equivalent judicial nomination process in other nations. Some politicians and citizens are deeply committed to selecting judges who are *strict constructionists*. Others demand justices who are *textualists* or *intentionalists* or *originalists*. Some cringe at the thought of a *judicial activist*, while others believe that strong activist judges must redress civil injustices like slavery or segregation. Professor Stanley Fish has thought deeply about this issue and explains the complexity of legal hermeneutics:

> If interpreting the Constitution—as opposed to rewriting it—is what you want to do, you are necessarily an *intentionalist*, someone who is trying to figure out what the framers had in mind. Intentionalism is not a style of interpretation, it is another name for interpretation itself. Think about it: if interpreting a document is to be a rational act, if its exercise is to have a goal and a way of assessing progress toward that goal, then it must have an object to aim at, and the only candidate for that object is the author's intention. What other candidate could there be?
>
> One answer to this question has been given by justice Antonin Scalia and others under the rubric of *textualism*. Textualists insist that what an interpreter seeks to establish is the meaning of the text as it exists apart from anyone's intention. According to Scalia, it is what is *said*, not what is *meant*, that is the *object of our inquiry*.
>
> The problem is that there is no such object. Suppose that you are looking at a rock formation and see in it what seems to be the word *help*. You look more closely and decide that, no, what you are seeing is the effect of erosion, random marks that just happen to resemble the English word. The moment you decide that nature caused the effect, you have lost all interest in interpreting the formation, because you no longer believe that it has been produced intentionally, and therefore you no longer believe that it is a word, a bearer of meaning.
>
> It may look like a word ... but in the absence of the assumption that what you're looking at is a vehicle of an intention, you will not regard it as language. It is not until you change your mind and become convinced that the formation was, in fact, designed, that the marks will become language and it will be appropriate to interpret them. (Fish, 2005, p. A25)

Fish continues by explaining that, once you decide that the word "help" was intentionally written, you still have to decide what it means. It could be a message from a person in distress. It could be a direction like "Need help? Look here." Maybe it is a petition to God? Or maybe it is a reference to a song title by the Beatles? Scrutinizing the word itself will not tell you which of these things it means. Thus, for Fish, intention is not something that is added to language; it is what must already be assumed. Intention comes first, and meaningful language follows. Is it possible, then, for any hermeneut to be a textualist if a text cannot be created without purpose and intention? Or can a meaningful text be created without intention? This is a significant dilemma.

On the issue of judicial activism, which can be defined as substituting one's preferred meaning of a text for a clearly encoded meaning, Fish contends that one cannot override a meaning that isn't there:

> Indeed, because texts do not declare their own meanings, activism, at least of a certain kind, is inevitable. You must actively try to figure out what the author or authors had in mind .... And while the text as written can be a piece of evidence, it cannot—just as the rock formation cannot—be self-sufficient and conclusive evidence. It follows that any conclusion you reach about the intention behind a text can always be challenged by someone else who marshals different evidence for an alternative intention. Thus, interpretations of the Constitution, no matter how well established or long settled, are inherently susceptible to correction and can always (but not inevitably) be upset by new arguments persuasively made in the right venues by skilled advocates. (Fish, 2005, p. A25)

Is hermeneutics, then, simply a language game, an oratorical contest, or a political battle? Or are there constraints on the activist or interpretivist projects? Must we forsake hermeneutic interpretation in favor of textualism? Some would argue *no*! If we are attuned to the nature of the text and constrained by the knowledge of what the object is and its authorial intention, then we do not have to reduce hermeneutics to textualism. Judicial activism that abandons constraint and simply works a text over until it yields a meaning chosen in advance is not a form of hermeneutic interpretation, but simply a form for rewriting the text. Fish (2005) continues, "The answer is that with that constraint handed down by the past, law and predictability disappear and are replaced by irresponsibility and the exercise of power. If you can just make it up when interpreting the Constitution, you can also make it up when deciding whether or not to honor your contractual obligations, and so can everyone around you" (p. A25).

In summary, the argument presented here is that we cannot rely simply on what the text communicates, and we cannot arbitrarily impose contemporary understandings on the text. As we saw in the introduction, all texts are complex and must be deconstructed on multiple levels. Thus, unless one rejects the belief that historical texts and contracts have some meaning for the present, everyone is an intentionalist to some degree.

The complexity of the hermeneutic interpretive process is at work on a daily basis in courts, school board chambers, religious tribunals, history and science classrooms, museums, galleries, publishing companies, legislative political bodies, literary analysis classes, and a plethora of other institutions. This hermeneutic context may leave individual teachers, believers, or citizens feeling frustrated because interpretation seems to be hopelessly devoid of clarity and normative guidelines. Some people prefer to ignore hermeneutic discussions altogether and simply accept without question the interpretations of rules, laws, bibles, and handbooks by the courts, civil authorities, religious leaders, or educational administrators. "Never question your pope, president, principal, pastor, or parent" might be their mantra. In other words, understanding the meaning of texts is so difficult that only an absolute authority can be trusted to explain the truth. This is not an unusual position. Religious institutions, governments, and corporations often demand unquestioning loyalty from their members.

An English, mathematics, history, or science teacher with this philosophy will never allow a student to evaluate or question the interpretation of a work of literature, an historical analysis, or the application of formula or scientific theory in the textbook because there is only one correct way to explicate a poem, understand an historical event, or conduct a scientific experiment. The proper authority always knows the correct answer or procedure. Some people become dogmatic or even violent as they seek to impose their interpretation of laws, scientific theories, literature, and religious texts on other people.

One of the glaring problems with this approach to hermeneutics is that various authorities, including supreme courts or church conclaves, seldom agree with one another. To whom do you turn for guidance if your spiritual leader, political representative, legal guardian, philosophical system, and religious text are all in disagreement on the correct interpretation of an issue? Who has the final authority? What is the *truth* or *Truth*? Can every person trust his or her own conscience, or must every personal belief be subject to affirmation by a higher authority? And who decides which higher authority is legitimate when various factions are in conflict? There is no universal agreement on the absolute authority of the Pope, Jesus, the Dali Lama, Confucius, Devi, the Koran, the Kabala, Vodun spirits, the US Constitution, the Torah, the Humanist Manifesto, the Hindu scriptures, or any other text for that matter. In fact, as we saw in the introduction, eclecticism and diversity dominate in the postmodern world. But does this mean that we are doomed to relativism and nihilism, as critics of postmodern thought contend? I do not think so. Let's continue to explore other hermeneutic possibilities.

Every discipline is replete with examples of geniuses who defied the norms and beliefs of their field and broke free to create fresh understandings and dramatic new inventions. Albert Einstein dropped out of school. He understood the world in ways that were very different from the Newtonian worldview that dominated science in the 19th century. Newton, of course, was correct. For every action there is an opposite and equal reaction. What goes up must come down. However, Einstein recognized that these principles of physics were not absolutely true in all circumstances, and with $E = MC^2$ Einstein ushered in a scientific revolution in the 20th century that was responsible for the technological inventions that changed our lives. Newton was correct, but not absolutely correct.

The genius, inventor, or prophet is often castigated. Consider the Impressionist painters in Paris in the 19th century. The French academic painter William Bouguereau was considered the master teacher at the time. He rejected the Impressionist paintings from art shows at the Salon because they lacked the precision and color of the traditional style. While both the academic and the Impressionist painters are prominently displayed in all important museums today, the Impressionist art of Monet, Manet, and Renoir is certainly more popular and recognizable to the general public than Bouguereau's paintings.

In a similar example from the history of music and dance, the elite orchestral and ballet audience in Paris in 1913 disrupted the opening performance of Igor Stravinsky's *Le Sacre du printemps* (*The Rite of Spring*) with the ballet directed by Sergei Diaghilev of the Ballets Russes and performed by Vaslav Nijinsky, the dancer known at the time as the Eighth Wonder of the World and the God of Dance (Ostwald, 1991). Why did the audience revolt? The performance offended the sensibilities of the music and dance connoisseurs of Paris. Peter Ostwald (1991) describes the scene this way:

> The "old guard" of wealthy patrons, critics, and overdressed snobs in one section felt violated by the extreme modernity of *Sacre* and took sides against the younger, poorer, and more radical "avant garde" of artists, musicians, and writers in another section. Fistfights broke out. Dowagers were mauled. Gentlemen stood on their chairs screaming and pummeling their neighbors. The savagery of the dancers on stage was nothing compared to the rioting of the public evoked by Stravinsky's score and Nijinsky's choreography. (pp. 70–71)

Today the works of Stravinsky and Nijinsky are considered brilliant achievements in the arts that established new music and dance sensibilities. In fact, Stravinsky's *The Rite of Spring* remains familiar to the general public because the score was used in the popular Disney cartoon *Fantasia*. Consider any art, dance, or music legend—Elvis Presley, Miles Davis, Mark Morris, The Beatles, jazz innovators, rappers—and you will find controversy and rejection by religious zealots, political gatekeepers, and aesthetic elites.

The same is true in athletics and sports. A personal example from the late 1960s comes to mind. I was a high jumper at my school, and we all wanted to imitate Dick Fosbury, the American track and field athlete who won the gold medal in the high jump event at the 1968 Olympic Games in Mexico City. At the 1968 games Fosbury revolutionized high jumping with a new technique, which became known as the Fosbury Flop. Instead of leaping over the bar in the traditional forward scissor motion—the dominant method of the time—Fosbury turned as he leapt, flinging his body backward over the bar with his back arched, following with his legs and landing on his shoulders. The Fosbury Flop was banned by our coaches and prohibited before the 1968 Olympics. It was considered unorthodox and dangerous. Today the Fosbury Flop is the standard technique. This is just another example of what some might say is the "stone rejected by the builder that became the cornerstone."

What is the role of hermeneutics in such a complex and contested terrain? Is interpretation doomed forever to be a function of power, privilege, and politics? Is our only choice either authoritarianism or relativism? There is, of course, another alternative to this dilemma. We can engage in the hermeneutic process knowing that universal agreement or even broad consensus is impossible—and maybe not even desirable. We can be mindful at every turn to deconstruct the sedimented perceptors that prevent us from recognizing the great artist, musician, athlete, film maker, scholar, dancer, or scientist who can move individuals beyond the status quo and enhance the human condition. We can take the position that greater clarification, deeper understanding, and ecumenical acceptance are reasonable expectations of human beings and also the only remedy to the violence and dysfunction that characterizes the modern world. I hold this belief. Hermeneutics is the art and process of interpretation that can lead not only to understanding but also to personal growth and social progress. This chapter explores hermeneutics with an openness to this possibility.

Before addressing postmodern hermeneutics, let's review the historical understandings of hermeneutics and the contemporary philosophical discourses on hermeneutics.

This overview will seem complex and esoteric to those unfamiliar with the topic. Additionally, the meaning of knowledge and interpretation itself is disputed by various scholars, making the discourse about hermeneutics appear contradictory at times. However, this introduction is necessary in order to make the proposals later in this chapter for understanding curriculum development as a "hermeneutic circle" more comprehensible. Let's explore hermeneutics in more depth.

Hermeneutics has a history of serious scholarship in biblical interpretation and 19th-century philosophical attempts to deal with the problem of how we understand the complex actions of human beings. Contemporary hermeneutics, as derived from the phenomenological philosophers Martin Heidegger and Edmund Husserl, acknowledges that discourse is an essential constituent element of textual understanding. Understanding, as we noted above, sets free what is hidden from view by layers of tradition, prejudice, and even conscious evasion. While these prejudices must be acknowledged, for Hans-Georg Gadamer, as a starting point for hermeneutic inquiry, hermeneutic interpretation, for Heidegger, was moving toward understanding as emancipation from tradition, prejudice, and evasion.

Hermeneutics, in its broadest formulation, is the theory of interpreting oral traditions, verbal communications, and aesthetic products. Aristotle used hermeneutics in the title of one of his works (*Peri hermenia*), and there was a school of interpretation in ancient Alexandria. In early Christian communities hermeneutics referred to the criteria for textual interpretation in order to establish normative religious and legal community practices. The Greek *hermeneuenin* (to interpret) referred to Hermes, the winged messenger of the Greek gods, who explained the decisions of the gods to other gods and to mortal humans. Hermes conveyed messages of both clarity and ambiguity. Hilly Bernard (1994) explains:

> Perhaps this [clarity and ambiguity] was a deliberate contrivance on the part of the heavenly rulers, an act attempting a representation of the complexity of language, in order to keep their subordinates in a state of humble submission. The hermeneutic tradition confronts the issue of complexity, ambiguity, interpretation, intentionality, and meaning, and asserts the inescapable subjective in human inquiry. As such, it serves as a rejection of the scientific philosophy and its premise of an objective reality "out there" to be discovered using a prescribed methodology. This mono-methodological approach of science stresses causal relationships, while the quest of the hermeneuticist is the development of theories of understanding through the interpretation of language. (p. 10)

Bernard's concise summary of hermeneutic inquiry is consistent with the approach to postmodern interpretation in many contemporary curriculum discourses.

Hermes, in addition to explaining and interpreting the messages of the gods, was a trickster. Postmodernists revel in the irony that the official messenger of the gods was also a cunning deceiver! Popes, pastors, principals, and presidents have often lied to us. This reminds us that layers of meaning, prejudice, and intention surround all curricular artifacts, thus necessitating a hermeneutical study to expose not only the irony of deception but also the implications of historical analysis. Historical, textual, artistic, and autobiographical interpretation in the postmodern era all acknowledge this double-edged dimension of clarity and ambiguity in hermeneutics. However, unlike modern empiricists who demand unbiased certainty and scientific proof, postmodern scholars celebrate the irony of interpretation by recognizing that ambiguity is integral to the human condition and the natural world. Postmodern hermeneutics affirms the importance of subjective understanding and conceives of understanding as an ontological (study of being) problem rather than an epistemological (study of knowledge) problem. Therefore, Hermes the messenger and deceiver becomes the model par excellence of interpretation in the postmodern era.

There are at least six ways that I describe hermeneutics with my colleagues Karen Krasny and Michael O'Malley (Slattery et al., 2006):

1. Contemporary scholars contend that *traditional theological hermeneutics* is the empirical science of interpretation of canonical religious texts within their historical context by a magisterium intent on defining the meaning of the text. Exegetes, with a concern for linguistic and grammatical accuracy, are considered experts who establish the criteria for authoritative textual interpretation;

2. Scholars argue that *conservative philosophical hermeneutics* is grounded in the tradition of Protestant theologian Friedrich Schleiermacher and philosopher Wilhelm Dilthey. It has inspired educational reformers such as E. D. Hirsch. These theorists would maintain that, through correct methodology and hard work, the interpreter should be able (a) to break out of her historical epoch in order to understand the author as the author intended and/or (b) to transcend historical limitations altogether in order to reach universal, or at least objective, truth. The intention of hermeneutics is to reproduce the meaning or intention of the text. Well-defined methodologies guide the anthropological and historical search for objectivity;

3. *Contextual hermeneutics* recognizes social and historical conditions as essential in the interpretive process. Interpreters are now understood to move within a hermeneutical circle that requires the specification of historical conditions in textual interpretation. Hans-Georg Gadamer calls attention to preunderstandings which underpin interpretation. He terms the condition and the perspectives of interpreters their "horizons" and the act of understanding the sense of a text "the fusion of horizons." Through this fusion of horizons the interpreter enters the tradition of the text, and thus shares in the text's particular representation of truth. Gadamer writes about relationships in the hermeneutic circle that transcend the technical sign-systems of the modern age;

4. *Reflective hermeneutics* is seen in Paul Ricoeur, who takes a different approach when he argues that the first understanding of the sense of the text must be validated through some explanatory procedures. Ricoeur contends that the movement from a structuralist science to a structuralist philosophy is bound to fail. Structuralism, insofar as it precludes the possibility of self-reflection, can never establish itself as a philosophy;

5. *Poststructural hermeneutics* is inspired by Nietzsche and Heidegger and practiced by deconstructionists like Kristeva, Baudrillard, Derrida, and Foucault. Here,

interpreting, like reading, is more a case of playing or dancing or ruminating, in the etymological sense of the Latin *ruminare*, rather than application of methods. Shaun Gallagher contends that poststructural interpretation requires playing with the words of the text rather than using them to find truth in or beyond the text. Additionally, poststructural hermeneutics will play an interpretation of a text against itself. This becomes an endless process of critique and deconstruction—a language game, some will say, in order to demonstrate that all interpretations are contingent, emerging, and relative; and

6. *Critical hermeneutics* developed in the tradition of critical theorists and finds inspiration in Marx, Freud, Habermas, Marcuse, Gramsci, and the Frankfurt School of social criticism. On the one hand, it is similar to poststructural hermeneutics to the extent that its social and political objectives are to deconstruct hegemonic power arrangements and create individual liberation from oppressive class structures. Critical hermeneutics deconstructs economic systems and social metanarratives by challenging false consciousness in order to uncover the ideological nature of beliefs and values. The goal is to promote distortion-free communication and a liberating consensus. Gallagher contends that critical hermeneutics is like conservative philosophical hermeneutics to the extent that it promises objectivity in the eradication of false consciousness. Critical hermeneutics expects to accomplish in politics, religion, aesthetics, education, and psychology a consensus beyond ideology. Thus, an absolutely objective perspective can be attained if the right methods can be employed to escape our historical constraints. Deconstructionists would contend that critical hermeneutics shares the naive optimism of theological and conservative hermeneutics that language, through ideal communication, will deliver truth and engender significant non-linguistic emancipation and liberation.

These six approaches sometimes overlap and inform each other. I use them as explanatory narratives rather than as cohesive systems of thought. As we continue to investigate hermeneutics, these narratives will help us to organize the various proposals for interpretation in curriculum.

Hermeneutic inquiry was almost exclusively empirical before the 19th century. As a science of interpretation, traditional hermeneutics was concerned originally with understanding religious texts, canonical scriptures, and non-canonical writings within their own historical, cultural, and social milieu. The difficulty of such interpretive tasks is immense—postmodernists would contend impossible—because the worldview of contemporary societies cannot replicate ancient cosmologies and subjectivities in which the original text was produced. Thus, while the search for the original meaning or intentions of an author of a text is an important project, a final understanding of exactly what the text means or of the singular intentions of an author is not possible. In the example discussed above of the word "help" scrawled on a rock, we might be able to discern whether or not it was produced by erosion or human action. With methods of discovery and investigation, we might even come closer to understanding possible meanings or motives if a human actor wrote the word. But even the human author is not aware of all the implications of an action or a word. As we saw in the introduction, postmodern philosophers like Foucault and Derrida remind us that there is no original author. All persons are influenced—consciously and unconsciously—by social, cultural, and psychological factors. All of our thoughts and texts have been formed in relation to previous texts. Prior to this postmodern understanding, hermeneutics represented a concern for the process of defining the meaning of the text, especially normative religious texts, and the development of the criteria for authoritative text interpretation. Early hermeneutics investigated the text with the belief that absolute meaning could be uncovered.

Early Greek and Jewish thinkers were concerned with appropriate interpretation of the Torah, the prophets, and the wisdom literature of the Hebrew scriptures. The allegorical method was employed to understand linguistic and grammatical components of scriptural texts to appropriate this meaning within the wider spiritual framework of the time. Werner Jeanrond (1988) explains: "Philo of Alexandria united the Jewish and Greek hermeneutical traditions and developed the thesis that an interpretation should disclose the text's spiritual sense on the basis of an explanation of the text's literal sense" (p. 462). This concept of hermeneutics expanded with the influence of Christian interpreters who sought to confirm their belief in salvation in Jesus Christ. Hebrew scriptures were interpreted in the light of the Christian faith in Jesus, arguing that the promises to Israel were fulfilled. The Christian hermeneut Origen emphasized the need for text interpretation in both the historical-grammatical (literal) sense and the spiritual sense, so as to provide access and understanding for every interpreter of sacred writings. Following Origen, Augustine developed his philosophy of language, where the "sign" points to the "thing," a concept that is understood differently, as we have seen, by postmodern semioticians.

Semiotics, the study of the meaning of language and the relationship between signs, symbols, and historical representation, critiques hidden assumptions, uncovers excluded meanings, and deconstructs linguistic interpretations. Texts and contexts, agents and objects of meaning, social structures and forces, and their complex interrelationships together constitute the irreducible object of semiotic analysis. Robert Hodge and Gunter Kress (1988) explain:

> The term "semiotics" is relatively new for many people, and a number of conceptual difficulties continue to attach to its use. Semiotics has been defined as "the science of the life of signs in society" .... So defined it has a scope which is breathtaking in its simplicity and in its comprehensiveness. ... Semiotics offers the promise of a systematic, comprehensive and coherent study of communications phenomena as a whole, not just instances of it. ... "Mainstream semiotics" emphasizes structures and codes, at the expense of functions of social uses of semiotic systems. ... It stresses system and product, rather than speakers and writers or other participants in semiotic activity as connected and inter*acting* in a variety of ways in concrete social contexts. It [traditional semiotics] attributes power to meaning, instead of meaning to power. It dissolves boundaries within the field of semiotics, but tacitly accepts an impenetrable wall cutting off semiosis from society, and semiotics from social and political thought. Many ... have rejected semiotics because of such objections. (pp. 1–2)

Hodge and Kress do not reject semiotics but offer an approach to interpretation that addresses the problem of social meaning as well as ways that meaning is constituted. Bowers and Flinders (1990) call this *critical semiotics,* "where attention is given to cultural conventions or codes, that in turn generate the signs that serve as the basic unit of communication" (p. 22). Bowers and Flinders draw on a number of areas of inquiry concerned with different aspects of the culture–language–thought connection that are related to the judgments that teachers face as they attempt to direct and orchestrate communication in the classroom. They conclude: "In one sense, these processes, which constitute the symbolic medium of the classroom that teachers and students must continually interpret and give meaning to, are interrelated" (p. 23).

In this sense, semiotics, like hermeneutics, is concerned with interpretation of texts, contexts, or artifacts. It provides the possibility of analysis of contemporary social problems and of explaining the processes and structures through which meaning is constituted. This emerging understanding of critical semiotics challenges Augustine's literal meaning of signs. In postmodern semiotics the "sign" may point to nothing or to many "things" simultaneously, and in every case the culture–language–thought interrelationship must be interpreted. Additionally, the meaning of power and the processes through which meaning is constructed are becoming the focus of semiotic as well as hermeneutic analysis in the postmodern era. Let us now return to our investigation of the development of hermeneutics.

Like Augustine, Thomas Aquinas, author of the *Summa theologiae,* emphasized the literal sense of language. Aquinas became the definitive authority on textual interpretation, and since the 13th century has been presumed to support the literal interpretation as the accurate bearer of *Truth.* Jeanrond (1988), echoing centuries of Thomistic theology, writes:

> According to Aquinas, appropriate interpretation is the task of dogmatic theology while exegesis concentrates on the purely philological task of preparing the text for theological understanding. Since the Council of Trent (1545–1563), the ultimate decision on the criteria and the validity of results of biblical interpretation remained the prerogative of the teaching office (Magisterium) of the Roman Catholic Church. (p. 463)

A major controversy concerning the status of Thomistic hermeneutics occurred in the 1990s. Matthew Fox, (until his removal in 1993) a Dominican priest, as was Aquinas, published in 1992 a new interpretation of the latter's works entitled *Sheer Joy: Conversations with Thomas Aquinas on Creation Spirituality.* Fox had already been silenced for one year by Cardinal Joseph Ratzinger and the Vatican prior to the publication of this book, primarily as the result of an ongoing debate over the doctrinal purity of Fox's "creation spirituality" and "original blessings." Cardinal Ratzinger, now Pope Benedict XVI, was the watchdog for correct interpretation, which remains a major preoccupation not only of the Roman Catholic Church but of many other global religions as well. Doctrinal authorities seek to control interpretation of texts so that contradictions to religious beliefs will not challenge their authority. In his work Fox emphasizes a cosmological vision of creation with the ontological goodness of human beings, rather than their sinfulness, as primary. Charles Jencks (1992) comments:

> The lesson Fox draws from many such recent discoveries is that the universe is a fairly benign place, with a countless set of "gifts." These show Christians have had some priorities wrong: they should acknowledge not just original sin, which has been bearing down and repressing consciousness for sixteen centuries, but "original blessing." Although there are indeed accidents, suffering, real evil and constant warfare (creativity can be as much negative as positive) we can clarify from our existence here the answer to a perennially important question. It is one that Einstein posed: is the universe a fundamentally good place, should we be optimistic? The answer, of course, hangs in the balance and depends on how we treat the earth and ourselves, as well as the other endangered species. (p. 36)

In developing his postmodern vision, Fox (1992) relies heavily on the hermeneutic interpretation of Hebrew and Christian scriptures. And now, with the publication of *Sheer Joy*, he has produced a hermeneutical narrative study that reevaluates, and possibly replaces, seven centuries of Christian hermeneutics in the Thomistic tradition. You can understand why Pope Benedict XVI attempted to silence him!

Fox begins by claiming that Thomas Aquinas was not a Thomist. He asserts: "I descholasticize Aquinas by interviewing him. I … ask him our questions and allow him access to our pressing issues in spirituality. This is important because the questions that preoccupied his thirteenth-century contemporaries are of course not always the issues that concern us" (1992, p. 2). Fox explains that his interview method is designed to uncover the "person behind the analytic mind" so as to interpret for contemporary society the meaning of philosophical categories such as "evil" or" morality." He offers new interpretations of Aquinas' biblical commentaries to move beyond the scholastic methodology that typified the latter's other works: "Following the inner logic of the biblical text, he [Aquinas] is free to make connections, let his creative genius work, and allow his heart as well as his head to speak. Here his passion often comes tumbling out—especially when he is speaking of his favorite love, wisdom" (p. 3). This historical perspective of the dual role of hermeneutic interpretation as both analytic and intuitive confounds scholastic theologians, and by way of extrapolation it also confounds those committed to modern curriculum development methods and materials. The irony of the double-coded discourse of multiple understandings challenges the binary logic of modernity and the absolute metanarratives of the Enlightenment project. Contemporary approaches to curriculum development embrace this dual role of hermeneutics and investigate the irony of apparent contradictions in interpretation, as we saw in our discussion of Hermes, because the complexity of meanings provides a more robust understanding of the text. This provides access to fresh insights that can break free of historical prejudice, religious dogmatism, and unjust social structures.

Fox is working to move beyond the modern era's fix on hermeneutical interpretation as mechanistic and literalistic. "Enlightenment prejudices have often been employed in interpreting Aquinas over the centuries" (1992, p. 7). He terms his creation spirituality "postmodern" (p. 7) in a more constructive rather than deconstructive sense, and he employs hermeneutics to recover premodern wisdom embedded in the biblical treatises written by Aquinas in the 13th century in order to bring those insights to a contemporary, postmodern cosmology. Fox concludes that some Thomists, while frequently rejecting much of Descartes and modern philosophy in argumentation, in fact have often succumbed to rationalist tendencies in vigorous attempts to prove Aquinas was scientific and respectably rational. This has often limited them to the scholastic texts of Aquinas and the linear thinking of scholasticism. "I believe Aquinas deserves—and we today require from Aquinas—a nonlinear celebration of his amazingly mystical *and* intellectual thought" (Fox, 1992, p. 12). As students of curriculum, we can see in Fox's interpretation of Aquinas' biblical commentaries a hermeneutical process that seeks to reevaluate scholastic theology. This is the hermeneutics of a double-edged sword that offers fresh insights for some but anxiety for others. Regardless of the ways that the work of Matthew Fox will be judged by scholars in years to come, he has "raised the ante" in the debate over hermeneutical interpretation. For students of curriculum, his work offers suggestive parallels to issues of text interpretation in all curriculum subjects and in particular underlines the religious origins and present uses of hermeneutics. The theological debates over its meaning will illuminate the contemporary discussions of hermeneutics in philosophical and educational scholarship.

While the literalistic practice of biblical interpretation in the Thomistic scholastic tradition continued to dominate through the Protestant Reformation, the emphasis on the scriptures during that time promoted reading and understanding biblical texts by individual believers rather than papal officials. Thus, the Reformation had the effect of deemphasizing the interpretation of scripture by the Roman Magisterium. Following the Enlightenment, hermeneutics was reevaluated by Friedrich Schleiermacher (1768–1834), who rejected all formal, extratextual authorities as illegitimate imposition on individual acts of understanding. Schleiermacher's work discredited special theological or legal hermeneutics: "Rather, *every* written text must be understood both in terms of its individual sense (psychological understanding) and in terms of the linguistic procedures through which this sense is achieved (grammatical understanding). Hermeneutics is now understood as the art of understanding the sense of the text. Allegorical interpretation is ruled out, the text must be allowed to speak for itself" (quoted in Jeanrond, 1988, p. 463). Schleiermacher's work paved the way for contemporary developments in hermeneutical understanding.

Paul Ricoeur (1981) has contended that a movement of deregionalization began with the attempt to extract a general problem from the activity of interpretation that is each time engaged in different texts, and "the discernment of this central and unitary problematic is the achievement of Schleiermacher" (p. 45). Before Schleiermacher, a philology (historical linguistic study) of classical texts and a literalistic exegesis (critical analysis) of sacred texts predominated. After Schleiermacher, it became clear that the hermeneutical process required that the individual interpreter should discern the operations that are common to these two traditional branches of hermeneutics, philology and exegesis. The possibility of the value of the individual subjective interpreter began to gain ascendancy in philosophical hermeneutics. This also paved the way for curriculum theories that foregrounded autobiography, autoethnography, and respect for the professional judgment of teachers and subjective interpretation of students in classrooms.

Awareness of historical conditions came to dominate hermeneutical understanding during the 19th century. Interpreters were now understood to move within a hermeneutical circle that required the specification of historical conditions in textual interpretation. As mentioned previously, Hans-Georg Gadamer (1975) calls attention to preunderstandings that underpinned interpretation, terming the condition and the perspectives of interpreters their "horizons" and the act of understanding the sense of a text "the fusion of horizons." Through this fusion of horizons the interpreter enters the tradition of the text and thus shares in the text's particular representation of truth. Gadamer (1976) writes about relationships in the hermeneutic circle that transcend the "technical sign-systems" of the modern age:

> Each [person] is at first a kind of linguistic circle, and these linguistic circles come in contact with each other, merging more and more. Language occurs once again, in vocabulary and grammar as always, and never without the inner infinity of the dialogue that is in process between every speaker and his [or her] partner. That is the fundamental dimension of hermeneutics. (p. 17)

Gadamer concludes by stating that genuine speaking, which has something to say and therefore is not based on prearranged signals but rather seeks words that reach the other human person, is the universal human task. This is the hermeneutic circle that educators must enter in the postmodern era.

Although Gadamer's hermeneutics has been criticized by some for his refusal to allow for methodological controls of the act of interpretation, many education scholars rely on him to support their critique of narrow instrumental views of schooling. Truth, they contend, cannot be collapsed into methods, the mainstay of the traditional approach to modern curriculum development, especially in "methods" courses in colleges of education. Rather, we must approach texts with our preunderstandings, suspend our prejudices, and engage in dialogue. David Blacker (1993), for example, argues that Gadamer's effort involves a reconstruction of the humanist sense of education as *Bildung*, which emphasizes what is done *to* individuals rather than what individual persons actually *do*. Blacker (1993) writes:

> To make the notion of *Bildung* more concrete, then, Gadamer recasts it as a dialogue between interpreter and tradition in which the latter is experienced as a Thou. This point must be stressed: he is not saying that individuals like teachers and students in every case ought to engage in an intersubjective give-and-take. … Accordingly, sharing in this historically-constituted conversation does not mean that I experience tradition as the opinion of some person or other, but that I am able to enter into it as into a game made up of myself and other persons but not reducible to any one of us. In this edifying tradition-forming, revising and conversing dialogue taking place in language—Hegelian Spirit conversing with itself—arises *Bildung*, which I see as the normative dimension of philosophical hermeneutics. (p. 7)

Traditional theological hermeneutics, as we have seen above, will insist on a normative methodology. However, this normative methodology is not Blacker's conversing dialogue. The traditional normative methodology is determined by an external authority. In contrast, postmodern philosophical hermeneutics will validate text interpretation that arises from the dialogue of individuals working within the context of a community circle where the other, whether human person, tradition, or artifact, is experienced as a "Thou" and not an "It" (Buber, 1965). For Gadamer, the hermeneutic circle is used to facilitate understanding and to open up "possibilities," while the traditional technical approach to hermeneutics is seen as dehumanizing. This is the same deadening effect of technical authoritarian approaches to curriculum development that have emerged from the application of accountability and scientific management models in schools.

Paul Ricoeur (1981) takes a different approach. In *Hermeneutics and the Human Sciences*, he argues that the first understanding of the sense of the text must be validated through some explanatory procedures and that the movement from a structuralist science to a structuralist philosophy is bound to fail. Ricoeur's translator, John Thompson, explains that structuralism, insofar as it precludes the possibility of self-reflection, can never establish itself as a philosophy:

> An order posited as unconscious can never, to my mind, be more than a stage abstractly separated from an understanding of the self by itself; order in itself is thought located outside itself. A genuinely reflective philosophy must nevertheless be receptive to the structuralist method, specifying its validity as an abstract and objective moment in the understanding of self and being. This imperative forms one of the principal guidelines for Ricoeur's recent work on the theory of language and interpretation. (Cited in Ricoeur, 1981, p. 10)

Ricoeur's interest evolved, in part, from his initial efforts in the 1930s at the Sorbonne, as a graduate student with Gabriel Marcel, to formulate a concrete ontology infused with the themes of freedom, finitude, and hope. However, he became intent on discovering a more rigorous and systematic method than he found in Marcel. The phenomenology of Edmund Husserl provided this method, and in turn led to the development of a reflective philosophy disclosing authentic subjectivity for understanding human existence. At the same time, Ricoeur was convinced that necessity and freedom were integral aspects of that existence. Finally, he turned to the problem of language, and here he engaged hermeneutics:

> I propose to organize this problematic [the historicity] of human experience and communication in and through distance around five themes: (1) the realization of language as a discourse; (2) the realization of discourse as a structured work; (3) the relation of speaking to writing in discourse and in the works of discourse; (4) the work of discourse as the projection of a world; (5) discourse and the work of discourse as the mediation of self-understanding. Taken together, these features constitute the criteria of textuality. (1981, p. 132)

Ricoeur thus moves the hermeneutical process beyond theological understanding to a more general level of human understanding. His work has influenced a number of contemporary curriculum scholars, including William Reynolds. In *Reading Curriculum Theory: The Development of a New Hermeneutic*, Reynolds (1989) presents an analysis of conservative and critical traditions in curriculum theory, employing the method developed by Ricoeur for reading literary texts. In keeping with the Ricoeurian project, Reynolds' study is also a documentary of the growth of self-understanding emerging from a fusion of horizons with the texts.

Ricoeur's theory of hermeneutical understanding was judged as politically naive by contemporary German philosopher Jürgen Habermas (1970). Habermas insisted that "only a critical and self-critical attitude toward interpretation could reveal possible systematic distortions in human communication and their impact on our interpretive activity" (quoted in Jeanrond, 1988, p. 463). Thus, in its contemporary form, hermeneutics is faced with three interrelated concerns: understanding, explanation, and critical assessment. The last implies that a community of interpreters must work to unmask ideological distortions, limited "objective" interpretations, and analysis of the meaning of the text. This community of interpreters opens hermeneutics to the postmodern discussion. Interpretation in postmodern philosophy must include a relational dimension that is mutually critical.

These developments in hermeneutics in the 19th and 20th centuries from Schleiermacher and Dilthey to Heidegger and Husserl, to Gadamer and Ricoeur, and most recently to Habermas, have confronted traditional scholars with a difficult dilemma: either engage philosophers in debates over the nature of hermeneutics in a mutually critical correlation or remain committed to a formalist, extratextual hermeneutics as provided by direct divine inspiration and/or ecclesiastical and bureaucratic authority. Some propose dialogue with philosophers to make use of the philosophical developments in hermeneutics to enhance textual interpretation, and thus identify and correct possible ideological distortions in understanding, especially if the process includes a wide spectrum of contributors to the development of a renewal in education.

Just as theology and philosophy are being challenged to enter the "hermeneutic circle" and be open to new understandings, so, too, the curriculum field faces similar challenges. There remain curriculum specialists at work today who would seek to return to the security of a traditional authority, the curricular magisterium that has provided legitimation for the modern paradigm of curriculum development in the spirit of Frederick Taylor's scientific management or Ralph Tyler's curriculum rationale. However, hermeneutics has also influenced those who seek to understand curriculum phenomenologically, as well as others who seek political and autobiographical understanding. Originally confined to scriptural interpretation, hermeneutics now engages all those involved in the project of understanding and critical assessment of any text. This tradition is discussed in a book on curriculum inquiry entitled *Informing Education Policy and Practice Through Interpretive Inquiry*, by Nelson Haggerson and Andrea Bowman (1992). In this text the authors seek to recover mythopoetic, cosmological, and narrative dimensions of theological hermeneutics while engaging the philosophical hermeneutics of Ricoeur, Gadamer, and Heidegger. Haggerson and Bowman's scholarship demonstrates the importance of qualitative and interpretive research, an approach that permeated research by the 1990s and became firmly established in the mainstream of the university with the First Annual Congress on Qualitative Research at the University of Illinois at Urbana-Champaign in 2005.

Haggerson and Bowman bring to contemporary curriculum debates what Hans Kung, David Tracy, and other contemporary theologians have brought to theology: a mutually critical correlation between hermeneutics as understanding, explanation through multiple qualitative paradigms, and critical assessment from the multiple viewpoints of theology, philosophy, and the human sciences. The affirmation of these multiple viewpoints is the essence of the hermeneutic circle for curriculum development in the postmodern era. From this perspective knowledge combines the infinite with the finite; knowledge is provisional, contextual, and temporal. There is no terminal point of knowing, only continual movement through the hermeneutic circle.

Haggerson and Bowman use the metaphor of a running stream from four perspectives to explain the multiple viewpoints of hermeneutic inquiry. In their first perspective, called the "rational/ theoretical" paradigm, the researcher is on the edge of the stream assuming the role of the objective observer who makes generalizations and predictions about the flow of the water. This parallels traditional social science experimental research. Second, in the "mythological/practical" paradigm, the researcher gets in a boat, experiences the stream, and becomes a participant observer. Here the researcher is interested in the mutual impact of the stream and the researcher on each other. Haggerson and Bowman (1992) write: "She doesn't want to predict what the stream will do or be in the long run, but how it will respond to her probing at the present and how she will respond to it. That is the 'mythological' aspect of the paradigm" (p. 12). They see traditional ethnography with its distance between the observer and the observed, as well as traditional anthropology and oral history research, as representative here. The third paradigm is called the "evolutionary/transformational" because the researcher becomes the stream as a total participant. This parallels Gestalt therapy, dream analysis, and autobiographical methods of inquiry. Bowman comments, "I came to understand this phenomenon when I started to write a personal journal. As I wrote, I was able to get in touch with myself, as well as with my teaching practice. The more I reflected through my writing, the more my teaching and knowledge of myself evolved or was transformed. I realized I was the stream. My practice had been informed in a very subtle way, actually through my intuitions" (Haggerson & Bowman, 1992, p. 13). In this paradigm there is only a very subtle difference between therapy, teaching, and inquiring. These first three stages prepare the researcher for the fourth paradigm, which leads to hermeneutics. The researcher actually crosses the stream to the other bank, bringing all the previous experiences along. Haggerson and Bowman (1992) explain:

> Having had all of those other experiences, the researcher now climbs out of the stream on the other side and dries off. When she looks back at the stream she is confident of the forces that direct the stream and she takes on the responsibility of helping all concerned with the stream become aware of the forces so they can be emancipated from those that are detrimental to human well-being. In other words, she demystifies the stream. Furthermore, the researcher takes appropriate

action to help remove the coercive forces as well as to reveal them. ... The stream, of course, can be the curriculum, the school, the administration, or the teachers' organization, all of which have manifest and hidden agendas. (p. 14)

This fourth paradigm is called the "normative/critical" because, through critical analysis, the researchers, in the spirit of Habermas, attempt to identify all the manifest and hidden factors and emancipate themselves and others from them. The forces are the norms by which society functions, and the critical research informs both educational policy and practice in relation to these norms, rules, myths, and traditions. Critical analysis and action research are the examples of methodologies of this paradigm.

In the metaphor of the stream, Haggerson and Bowman provide one concrete example of the way that curriculum theorists work to explore interpretive inquiry. This, they claim, is the basis of a postmodern hermeneutics in curriculum studies. No longer will objective, experimental projects that attempt to verify hypotheses for the purpose of articulating generalizations, predictions, and causal probabilities dominate educational research. Other research paradigms will also be legitimated and encouraged. As a result, understanding, awareness, emancipation, demystification, and transformation will all become possible, thus forming the basis of hermeneutic interpretation in curriculum studies.

In this postmodern milieu, curriculum development will focus on the community of interpreters working together in mutually corrective and mutually collaborative efforts. The entire curricular experience is now open to reflection because everything requires recursive interpretation. Without this postmodern perspective, Hermes the trickster would continue to have the opportunity to deceive educators. Curriculum development in the postmodern era no longer turns to bureaucratic authorities to dictate the official methodologies of instruction and the official interpretation of texts. Educators will not be seen as passive receptors of a "teacher-proof curriculum" who simply implement standardized goals and objectives and administer state-mandated tests for bureaucrats. Rather, a postmodern community of interpreters and teachers will enter the hermeneutic circle and engage each other in the process of understanding the text, the lived experience, and the self in relation to the other. This will support the three fundamental elements of inquiry that comprise the hermeneutic circle at work in all human understanding as originally defined by Schleiermacher (1978): the inherent creativity of interpretation; the pivotal role of language in human understanding; and the interplay of part and whole in the process of interpretation. Thus, hermeneutic inquiry is a creative act and not just a technical function.

Curriculum development in the postmodern era supports efforts to include this community circle of creative interpretation that respects the interplay of individuals and the groups to which they belong into the fabric of the schooling experience. By doing so, postmodern curriculum incorporates the position of James B. Macdonald (1988), who insisted, "The fundamental human quest is the search for meaning and the basic human capacity for this search is experienced in the hermeneutic process, the process of interpretation of the text (whether artifact, natural world, or human action). This is the search (or research) for greater understanding that motivates and satisfies us" (p. 105).

As a final caveat, curriculum scholars must be cautioned that hermeneutic inquiry has the potential to infuriate and incite those committed to traditional authoritative and bureaucratic structures. David G. Smith (1991) has written an eloquent and accessible summary of hermeneutic inquiry in which he offers the following insights into Hermes and the hermeneutic tradition as a warning for postmodern curriculum studies:

> Hermes, as well as being the deliverer of messages between the gods and from gods to mortals on earth, was known for a number of other qualities as well, such as eternal youthfulness, friendliness, prophetic power, and fertility. In a sense, all of these features are at work in the hermeneutic endeavor to this day, as the practice of interpretation attempts to show what is at work in different disciplines and, in the service of human generativity and good faith, is engaged in the mediation of meaning. There is one further aspect of Hermes that may be worth noting, namely, his imprudence. ... Students of hermeneutics should be mindful that their interpretations could lead them into trouble with "authorities." (p. 187)

Postmodern hermeneutics can be dangerous, for it uncovers, interprets, clarifies, deconstructs, and challenges all fields of study, including curriculum development models and methods that have been enshrined in the sacred canon of curriculum texts for decades. It is troubling to the traditional curriculum magisterium and *No Child Left Behind* and *Race to the Top* bureaucrats, but refreshing and empowering to educators and researchers who employ it in their interpretive inquiry. As we explore the discourses on race, gender, sexuality, economics, ethnicity, philosophy, ecology, politics, aesthetics, autobiography, and science in the coming chapters, the hermeneutic circle will continue to inform our discussion of curriculum development in the postmodern era.

six

Gender, Sexuality, Race, and Ethnicity in a Multicultural and Diverse Milieu

I am angered by the irrational prejudice and violent hatred that I have seen in my life-time. Far too many people have been maimed, annihilated, deprived, and demoralized in the name of religion, truth, vengeance, greed, and nationalism. This violence not only destroys the lives of individual human persons but also endangers our entire global community. A consuming hatred prevents us from moving forward to address urgent ecological, economic, health, energy, and water issues. The horrific results of prejudice and hatred are clear today: ethnic cleansing and rape in Rwanda, Bosnia, and Sudan; government and military slaughter of civilian protestors in Syria, Egypt, and so many other countries; hate crimes against minority persons; suicide bombings; and indiscriminate killing of innocent civilians in wars. The history of the 20th century is filled with other tragedies: "comfort women" during World War II, the Holocaust, apartheid, Jim Crow laws, trafficking of children for prostitution and abuse, lack of aggressive prevention and treatment of pandemic diseases like HIV/AIDS, lynchings, civil wars, and depletion of resources.

Where is our humanity? If we could honestly address racism, sexism, homophobia, ethnic bias, and religious hatred, then we would have so much more energy to expend on the terrible problems of this planet. Today we are faced with theft and economic manipulation by wealthy elites in government and corporations that leaves the vast majority of citizens unemployed, underemployed, or left out of meaningful work and sustenance. Energy companies and manufacturers routinely poison the land, water, and oceans and ignore health and safety of citizens and wildlife. We must address these issues. Our survival as a species depends upon uniting in our common humanity. If we could ameliorate ethnic divisions, how much more energy would be available to com-bat poverty, pollution, unemployment, and resources? Why do we fail to comprehend this simple concept? Why have we not been able to make significant progress on these issues in my lifetime? I am proud to work with curriculum scholars who are committed to issues of justice and compassion. We are determined to work for multicultural understanding and social action in schools and society, but we are not necessarily hopeful that we can succeed at this critical juncture in human history.

The evidence is abundantly clear that the human community is incredibly diverse, and our multicultural diversity is one of our greatest strengths to be celebrated and not a liability to be eradicated. Understanding our common humanity demands respect and appreciation for the diversity that enriches us all. I had hoped that by the new millennium humanity would have advanced beyond the sexism, racism, heterosexism, ethnic bias, and religious violence that plagued civilization in the 20th century. Did we not learn anything from Rosa Parks, Martin Luther King, Jr., and the civil rights movement in the US, Nelson Mandela and Desmond Tutu and the end of apartheid in South Africa, the movements for women's suffrage, gay rights, and fair labor laws in the US, Oscar Romero's work for the fundamental rights of the poor in El Salvador, and Gandhi's nonviolent revolution that gave birth to democracy in India?

Why do we remain mired in irrational bigotry, segregation, fear, and judgment? I wish that I did not need to write this chapter, but it is as necessary today as it was in the 1950s when I was a child. I want to be clear: curriculum development in the postmodern era must aggressively and consistently include lessons and experiences that will ameliorate the divisions and hatred we face in the world today. We must address the continuing ignorance, greed, and bigotry that perpetuate sexism, racism, heterosexism, and ethnic divisions; everything we teach is incomplete if we do not constantly foreground issues of prejudice and violence in our schools and society.

I was a first-grade student in New Orleans in 1960, the year that another first-grade student, Ruby Bridges, became nationally known as the first African-American student to integrate our public schools. Boycotts and demonstrations engulfed New Orleans in 1960. I show two excellent films about school segregation and the civil rights movement in my classes to inform my students who are too young to remember these difficult events: *The Ruby Bridges Story* and *Mighty Times: The Life of Rosa Parks*. These films, and many others like them, are an integral part of curriculum in the postmodern era.

As a White boy growing up in a very diverse yet segregated southern city, I had little contact with African Americans or other multicultural communities. The one exception over the years was the African-American women, named Eunice, Florida, and Lucille, who worked in our home as maids and the African-American family that lived in a small dilapidated building on my great-grandfather's farm and worked his fields. The father was named Pouncy, and his son Henry cleaned my grandparents' home. These people were intimately connected to my family, but we did not relate to them in their cultural context. The boundaries were clearly established. I also have memories of constantly hearing racist jokes and derogatory comments about people of color in my community. It was ingrained in my mind as a young child that African Americans were inferior, dangerous, and dirty. I vividly remember one occasion as a child when I was in the Sears department store near my grandparents' home with several cousins. I was thirsty and accidentally drank from the wrong water fountain—the one marked "colored only." One of my cousins teased me and said that I was now a "nigger." I was afraid that I had caught a terrible germ or affliction. Everything in my cultural context was designed to teach me that African Americans were inferior. Servitude was justified based on religion; I often heard the statement "The Bible says slaves be obedient to your masters." Segregation and subjugation were justified based on religious scriptures, irrational fears, and racial bigotry.

As I reflect on these memories, it is disturbing to me that my community and nation were so irrational and ignorant. It is also incredible that we remain entrenched in racism and prejudice today. The legal restrictions of segregation and Jim Crow began to be dismantled after the 1954 *Brown* v. *Board of Education Supreme Court* decision and the 1962 Voting Rights Act, but the messages of prejudice and hatred remain deeply ingrained in our psyche—sedimented perceptors in postmodern language. We have much work to do to examine our unconscious prejudices and deconstruct the vestiges of racism and other forms of bias.

During the school boycott by White families following Ruby Bridges' enrollment in William Franz Public School, I recall an incident that caused a huge shift in my consciousness. Three White women rang our doorbell and asked my mother to sign a petition to "keep the Negroes out of our schools." White families were under tremendous pressure to sign the boycott, and resistance often carried severe consequences. It took tremendous courage for progressive-thinking Whites to resist segregation and racism. But many did. My mother was a thirty-year-old with two young boys in 1960, and as she looked carefully at the petition the women pressured her: "Mrs. Slattery, you do not want your boys sitting on the *turlit* [toilet] in the restrooms with the Negro children, do you?" My mother did not sign the petition. Years later she told me that the arrogance of these women jolted her. Their inflection of the word "turlit," their haughty superiority, and their fear of people who were not like them caused my mother to realize that she did not share their way of thinking. Her small act of resistance had a huge impact on my consciousness.

Arrogance and ignorance about race, gender, sexuality, and ethnicity are the root causes of senseless suffering: bullying in schools, segregation in society, workplace discrimination, salary inequities, identity confusion and repression, hate crimes, and much more. In addition to arrogance and ignorance, another emotion that needs to be examined is disgust, for this too influences how we respond to people who are different. Susan Edgerton (2001) has examined this emotion in an educational context and writes:

> In educational studies that focus on classroom relationships around such categories as race, gender, sexual orientation, and ethnicity, one almost invariably finds reference to basic human emotions such as love (as, for example, with Nel Noddings' work on the ethic of caring), hatred, anger, and fear. I explore the emotion of disgust as an important factor in both educational theory and practice around human and other natural relationships. While a great deal has been written about the workings of disgust …, there is little written about the specific relationship of disgust to educational theory and classroom practice. I believe this relationship is a significant one. (pp. 1–2)

Edgerton reminds us that the causes of disgust can result from a number of factors: taste preferences, unconscious repressed desires, or cultural taboos. Martha Nussbaum (2001) writes at length about disgust in a paper entitled "Secret Sewers of Vice: Disgust, Bodies, and the Law":

> Disgust is a powerful emotion in the lives of most human beings. It shapes our intimacies and provides much of the structure of our daily routine, as we wash our bodies, seek privacy for urination and defecation, cleanse ourselves of offending odors with toothbrush and mouthwash, sniff our armpits when nobody is looking, check in the mirror to make sure that no conspicuous snot is caught in our nose-hairs. In many ways our social relations, too, are structured by the disgusting and our multifarious attempts to ward it off. Ways of dealing with repulsive animal substances such as feces, corpses, and spoiled food are pervasive sources of social custom. And most societies teach the avoidance of certain groups of people as physically disgusting, bearers of a contamination that the healthy element of society must keep at bay. (pp. 2–3)

Nussbaum recognizes the possible underlying evolutionary basis of disgust, but argues that this emotion becomes an irrational and often damaging psychological implant through acculturation and association—as with my experience at the "colored only" water fountain. We must carefully explore the cultural history of those things and people we find disgusting, because disgust is often a matter of long-term acculturation that no longer makes sense in a postmodern context. Edgerton (2001) continues:

> Our disgust reactions often either provide a rationalization for violence or for removing ourselves from disagreeable situations in cynical, a-social non-action. As such, Nussbaum warns that the appearance of disgust should signal a warning to one so afflicted to reflect deeply on its source, and that disgust-ingness should never be a player in the consideration of law or policy-making. Clearly, this topic has implications for educational thought around issues of diversity and difference, imperialism in the curriculum, and our relations to the non-human natural world. It is not, however, my goal to either praise or condemn the human emotion called disgust, but simply to try to locate some of its operation in our schools and curriculum, and to point toward the consequences that it might bring about. Our emotions have cognitive content, thus the curriculum must surely educate our disgust. (p. 3)

We must educate ourselves and our students about these issues. At the heart of curriculum development is a commitment to a robust investigation of cultural, ethnic, gender, and identity issues. If we are going to ameliorate prejudice and violence, then we must understand the often irrational and harmful basis of our disgust and hatred—both as individuals and as a culture. We must explore conscious and unconscious emotions such as fear, visceral loathing, and disgust (Fisher, 2010).

I will now move to a complicated investigation of gender and sexuality—both of which have many complex cultural norms and taboos associated with them that produce disgust—from five perspectives: biological sex, gender identity, gender role, sexual behavior, and sexual orientation. All five are interrelated, of course, but none is automatically determined by the others. Recall the example in chapter 5 of the frustrated father of a seventh-grade boy who wanted to create works of art rather than play football. The father believed that taking art lessons would make his son gay. The expected gender norms in families and society do not equate with sexual orientation. There are gay football players and heterosexual artists. Sexual orientation does not mandate specific sexual behavior either, as in the case of gay men and lesbians who enter heterosexual marriages—and may even have children—in order to please family or adhere to a social or religious norm. Sometimes straight men and women perform homosexual acts as a part of a team initiation or fraternity ritual—but this does not make them "turn gay" or change their sexual orientation. Sometimes straight people perform in same-sex erotica films in a practice known as "gay for pay." Lesbian women, too, can perform for straight men without changing their sexual orientation. Both heterosexual and homosexual people can choose to be celibate or monogamous, or to have multiple sexual partners of the same or different genders over the course of their lifetime. Clothing, body piercing, hairstyle, and lifestyles vary among people of all genders and identities. People sometimes behave sexually in ways that do not match their orientation, gender identity, or cultural norms. But the behavior itself does not change their orientation or identity. In another example, there is not a correspondence between biological genitalia and gender identity for transgender and transsexual persons because the psychology of gender does not always match the biology of genitalia, hormones, or chromosomes. Likewise, gender roles in occupations and relationships are not correlated with or conditioned by biology and identity. But we are ahead of the discussion. Let's examine the first of our five topics: biological sex.

There are three important texts that frame my investigation of gender and sexuality in this chapter: *Sexuality and the Curriculum*, by James T. Sears (1992); *Sexing the Body: Gender Politics and the Construction of Sexuality*, by Anne Fausto-Sterling (2000); and *The End of Gender: A Psychological Autopsy*, by Shari L. Thurer (2005). My approach to understanding gender and sexuality in the curriculum is very similar to James Sears' lucid explanation in "Centering Culture: Teaching for Critical Sexual Literacy Using the Sexual Diversity Wheel," in the *Journal of Moral Education*, in which he proposes a model of critical sexual literacy. He offers four curricular models for multicultural sexuality education: tolerance, diversity, difference, and *différance*. Sears (1997) writes:

> There has been considerable debate regarding sex education in both the United States and Great Britain. The debate, however, has been conceptually limited as advocates of a sex-free curriculum have stressed abstinence and "secondary virginity" with their battle against proponents of a sex-based curriculum who emphasize protection and "responsible sexual behaviour." Whether their source be biblical or biological, both groups share a common conception of sexuality as unidimensional, universal, and unmoving. These essentialist notions often are coupled with a lack of appreciation for the pervasive influence of culture on understandings of our sexual selves and these behaviours which follow. (p. 273)

Postmodern theory deconstructs essentialist notions and provides a different way to look at the debates about sexuality in society and sex education in the school curriculum. I think that these fresh insights can help us to break free from the current stalemate in the discussions about sex education and other related issues. Let's explore how this might be accomplished.

I begin the process of deconstructing essentialist notions of gender and sexuality in all of my lectures by watching the short documentary *XXXY,* produced by the Intersex Society of North America, and the film *Sex Games: Questions of Gender at the Olympics*, about the history of gender regulations in the Olympics. This may seem like a strange place to begin, but I find that ignorance about biological diversity is almost universal among my students—both graduate and undergraduate. Most students claim that they have never heard the word "intersex," and they are shocked to learn that, by some estimates, one out of every 200 births worldwide are children born intersex (Fausto-Sterling, 2000). This can range from the very rare hermaphroditism to the occasional chromosomal anomalies such as Congenital Adrenal Hyperplasia (CAH), Androgen Insensitivity Syndrome (AIS), Turner Syndrome, and Klinefelter Syndrome. In other words, many children are not born with the assumed XY chromosome pattern for males and XX chromosomes for females. Additionally, some people are born with ambiguous genitalia, an extra Y chromosome, an additional X chromosome, inner testes, an ovo-testis, or a number of other intersex differences. I must emphasize that I am only discussing biology at this point and not gender identity or sexuality. Most of my students immediately want to make inferences about gender roles, sexual orientation, or sexual function as soon as I show these films and begin discussing intersexuality. These issues will come later. For now, we are only investigating biological diversity in human beings.

This is what the Intersex Society of North America says about these issues:

> The Intersex Society of North America (ISNA) is devoted to systemic change to end shame, secrecy, and unwanted genital surgeries for people born with an anatomy that someone decided is not standard for male or female.

We have learned from listening to individuals and families dealing with intersex people that:

- Intersexuality is primarily a problem of stigma and trauma, not gender.
- Parents' distress must not be treated by surgery on the child.
- Professional mental health care is essential.
- Honest, complete disclosure is good medicine.
- All children should be assigned as boy or girl, without early surgery. (http://www.isna.org/)

Medical professionals and health-care providers are gradually becoming more aware of the need to carefully examine issues related to intersexuality and in many cases to refrain from performing surgery on infants. The lives of many individuals have been harmed by our ignorance and insensitivity—as well as our insecurity about masculinity, femininity, and sexuality. I tell my students that, if for no other reason, they must become familiar with intersexuality because they will certainly have intersex children in their schools and in their family who deserve love and understanding just like any other child.

The second issue that I will explore is diversity in gender identity. All people identify psychologically and emotionally as a man, a woman, transgender, or androgynous—and this identity is not contingent upon biology. It is often assumed that an individual with male genitalia, XY chromosomes, and testosterone will automatically identify as a man. This is usually the case, but not always. Transgender persons understand themselves on a deeply personal and psychological level as a gender that does not parallel the biological characteristics of a traditional male or female. And some androgynous people identify and dress as either male or female. Gender identity is very complex and fluid. Some transgender persons assume a name and clothing to match their gender identity; others will choose to have surgery to align their physical and psychological selves and refer to themselves as transsexual. Here is one description:

> Transsexuality, also termed "Gender Dysphoria" is now reaching the point of being reasonably well understood, though many myths and general foolishness about the subject still abound. This document concerns the classic definition of transsexuality .... Intersexuality and transgenderism will not be addressed other than obliquely. ...
>
> Gender and Sex are very separate things, though the terms are often considered interchangeable by the less aware. Sex is physical form and function while Gender is a component of identity. There can be considered to be some legitimate overlap in that the brain is structured in many sex-differentiated ways, and the brain is the seat of identity. However, with regard to the dilemma of the transsexual, the difference between sex and gender are at the very core of the issue.
>
> A transsexual person, born to all appearance within a given physical sex, is aware of being of a gender opposite to that physical sex. This conflict, between gender identity and physical sex, is almost always manifest from earliest awareness, and is the cause of enormous suffering. It is common for transsexuals to be aware of their condition at preschool ages.
>
> This agony can and does lead to self destruction unless treated. The incredible difficulties that surround achieving treatment are themselves often agonizing, the sum total of which can play havoc with the lives of the gender dysphoric. Indeed, it is apparent that some fifty percent of transsexuals die by age 30, usually by their own hand. This morbidity is known as the 50% Rule.
>
> Being a transsexual is not something that can be ignored or suppressed forever. Unlike the fascinations of the crossdresser or the partially altered transgenderist, the absolute compulsion of classical transsexualism is a matter of life and death. Social oppression, culturally indoctrinated shame, self loathing, and

bigotry slaughter transsexuals. With treatment and support, comes survival and a successful life. The success rate for the treatment of transsexuals is among the highest in medicine.

Transsexuality occurs roughly equally in both physical males and physical females, and is caused by factors (such as a critically timed hormonal release caused by stress in the mother, or by the presence of hormone mimicking chemicals present during critical development) which interfere with fetal development. Transsexuality occurs independently of sexual orientation [most transsexuals are also heterosexual], and occurs in humans and in other animals, such as apes, monkeys, dogs, cats, rats, and mice, among those studied. (http://trans sexual.org/what.html)

The third issue I will explore is gender role. People who deviate from gender norms in schools and society often experience ridicule, ostracization, and even physical violence. Educators must be at the forefront of addressing these problems. As anthropologists and sociologists have noted for decades, cultural norms for gender behavior vary from community to community, nation to nation. Norms also vary over time within the same community. The roles of males and females are almost always socially constructed and not biologically determined. The significant influence of the media in shaping notions of masculinity and femininity cannot be overstated. From *Glamour* to *Playboy* and *GQ* to *Playgirl*, on the Internet and in advertising, seductive images of women and men shape our understanding not only of what it means to be male or female, but also of our body image and relational expectations. Advertisers, of course, want to sell magazines and products, but they also want to create self-image and lifestyle patterns to insure product loyalty and maximum consumption. We are all seduced and deceived by advertising and media on some level, and for many people the propaganda extracts a heavy price—anorexia, steroids, battering, violence, and dysfunction (Jhally, 1999, 2002, 2003, 2004). However, it is not only media images that shape our understanding of gender. Child-rearing practices, preparation of meals, occupations, hobbies, mating rituals, and social customs are established formally by laws and informally by family customs for men and women in many societies—but there are exceptions to gender-role norms in all societies as well. For example, women are expected to do the cooking in many societies, but in my home state of Louisiana, in the Cajun culture, it is often the men who cook. We can all think of many examples of gender roles and expectations from our own cultures.

We will now examine several specific issues related to gender roles, and the first is courtship and marriage. Courtship in many Western societies involves engagements, diamond rings, white dresses, and elaborate church ceremonies. These practices seem strange and excessive in other societies—as well as to some people in the US! Marriages in some Eastern cultures are arranged by parents and require dowries, long-term financial responsibilities, and specified housing arrangements. This seems absurd to many people in Western cultures. However, even in the US, marriage was an obligation and not a choice for personal intimacy before the 20th century. The work of sociologist Stephanie Coontz (2000, 2005) is instructive here. She has studied marriage, family, and child-rearing practices in the US from the 1850s to the present, and she clearly documents that there is not a unified history of marriage and certainly not a golden age of marital bliss. The 1950s TV shows like *Leave it to Beaver* were a myth. Coontz also documents how marriage has evolved in the US over time, and thus that further changes should be expected. Her titles are *The Way We Never Were: American Families and the Nostalgia Trap* and *Marriage: A History from Obedience to Intimacy, or How Love Conquered Marriage*. I do not believe that anyone can conduct a thorough and honest discussion about gender and marriage in the US without first reading these two books.

Another important source for understanding marriage in the US is *Advertising and the End of the World*, by Sut Jhally (2004). In this film, Jhally takes us into the world of advertising and shows the pervasive influence of media and material consumption in our lives. He links the looming global ecological disaster to our greed and consumption and addresses the paradox of affluence in the US: material goods promise us happiness, but they fail to deliver. Greed and selfishness trump generosity and sharing, and collective issues such as the environment and health care are pushed to the margin. *Government* and *community* become "dirty words" that interfere with individual autonomy and blissful consumption. Jhally quotes Margaret Thatcher, British Prime Minister in the 1980s, who often said that there is no such thing as society, only individuals and their families. President Ronald Reagan often repeated this mantra of right-wing conservativism. I heard Tucker Carlson on MSNBC in 2005 say something very similar after the Katrina disaster hit New Orleans: the biggest mistake that the people in New Orleans made, he advised, was expecting the government to come to their rescue. Government, in his opinion, should not be in the business of rescuing people. We each must take care of ourselves and our family because, as Thatcher–Reagan conservatives believe, there is no such thing as society. Of course, the people who were trapped and suffering in New Orleans were mostly elderly, poor, and African American. Most did not have transportation, and many had never left the city in their lives. But this information does not matter to the corporate elites in the US, who continue to receive tax cuts, military protection from enlisted servicemen and servicewomen who are often poor, unrestricted use of non-renewable natural resources, transportation infrastructure, and corporate welfare for their businesses—and all from the very same government they despise. There is no such thing as society in their minds, anyway. We will talk more about issues related to corporations, racism, the environment, and Katrina in chapter 8.

But what does this have to do with marriage and gender roles, you may be thinking? A lot. Jhally (2004) contends that corporate advertising is a cultural system of stories and values that promotes a profound propaganda—especially in relation to gender and sexuality. In the case of our marriage rituals, the history of the De Beers diamond empire is essential reading in order to connect the dots between diamond mines in South Africa, apartheid, racism, advertising campaigns ("A diamond is forever"), cultural myths of happiness, economic greed, and destruction of the planet—and all for a lousy rock that is not even a scarce resource! De Beers actually manipulated the market to create an artificial scarcity of diamonds—remember Enron?—and initiated the emotional necessity of a diamond engagement ring through intense advertising in the early and mid-20th century. In order to create new customers and even larger profits, we have an advertising campaign today aimed at couples to promote the 25-year anniversary diamond necklace as a requirement for true love and lasting happiness. Watch the commercials carefully, and listen to the corporate propaganda. Then read the sordid and racist history of diamonds in *The Last Empire: De Beers, Diamonds, and the World*, by Stefan Kanfer (1995). The next time you hear the phrase "A diamond is forever," you may want to remember the history of the De Beers diamond empire and its later absorption under the Oppenheimers by the Anglo-American Corporation. From the opening depiction of the grim diamond fields, Kanfer's book is the story of cutthroat capitalists, the economic and racial development of South Africa, and a multinational corporation that controls virtually the world's entire diamond and gold trade. The diamond ritual began with a corporate advertising campaign and has now become accepted as tradition and truth and a part of our cultural gender expectations in society. Those who wear diamonds should think about racism, apartheid, economic exploitation of workers, and ecological destruction every time they look at their diamond rings. Those who work in schools must also examine the ways that advertising and corporations shape not only attitudes about gender and sexuality but all dimensions of a child's life (Molnar, 1996).

As you can see from the previous discussion, the interconnection of race, gender, and sexuality with courtship rituals, ecology, and media advertising is a complex web. Here are some more issues related to gender roles in society: divorce is prohibited in some nations but permitted in others; gay civil unions are gaining social acceptance in countries like Great Britain but strictly prohibited in others; gay marriage is legal in Spain, Canada, South Africa, the Netherlands, Belgium, and some US states; interracial marriage is socially accepted in most cities and is no longer legally prohibited in the US, but it remains a taboo in some cultures. Some school sports are co-ed, others are gender specific. The Olympics announced in 2004 that transgender athletes will be allowed to participate. Gradually women have been accepted in traditional all-male sports, including football, wrestling, and baseball in some US states. Women cannot drive or vote in Muslim countries like Saudi Arabia, but they can in Turkey. Occupations are clearly segregated by gender in some societies, but open to men and women in others. As the US became more open in the 1960s to occupational diversity of men and women in the workforce, society still remained uncomfortable. For example, when men first entered nursing they were called "male nurses" to protect them from stigma and taunting. Of course, the first women doctors were not called "women surgeons." Again, this is a reflection of gender-role perceptions in society. Gender roles in the postmodern world are slowly changing to become more inclusive and eclectic, but the backlash against women who cross gender boundaries, young couples who forgo traditional marriage rituals, gays who marry, and men who do not conform to masculine stereotypes remains a significant—and sometimes deadly—problem.

Despite the acceptance of gender-role diversity in the postmodern era, there remains intense pressure on people to conform to traditional norms. First, the ease of navigating social structures is appealing to those who do not want to challenge the status quo. Some find it easier just to go along with the expectations rather than fight for alternative preferences or desires. Second, power and money accrue to those who work within the hegemonic gender norms of society. Acceptable behavior is rewarded; unacceptable behavior is punished. Third, it can be very dangerous to step outside of an expected gender role. This may take the form of family pressure or bullying and can even escalate to violence. Fourth, and I suspect most prevalent, is the fear that deviations from cultural gender roles would indicate or lead to sexual behavior that is taboo. The powerful emotion of disgust clouds our judgments—as with the father above who was very concerned that his son might become homosexual if he did art instead of football. Again, I must repeat that biological sex, gender identity, and gender role are neither the cause nor the effect of specific sexual behaviors, orientations, or lifestyles.

I remember the story of one young man in a graduate class years ago. He shared a narrative about his first day of kindergarten. He was the youngest of five children, and he had heard so much about school from his four older sisters. He could not wait for his turn to go to school. In the evening before his first day at kindergarten, his father came into this young man's bedroom with a trash can and took a few of his toys from the shelf. The boy had toys that had been passed down to him from his sisters and cousins, including some Barbie dolls that he played with. The father vigorously ripped the heads and arms off of the dolls, threw the pieces into the trash can, and said to the young man, "It is time for you to grow up and not be a sissy. You are going to school tomorrow, and men do not play with dolls." As my student recalled this story, he trembled. He said that he could still feel the anger and confusion of that traumatic moment in his life. I would contend that the father's behavior and comments are literally and metaphorically a form a child abuse. You see, if young men are not allowed to express compassion and care as children for fear of being a "sissy"—and if they are taught to rip the limbs off of dolls—then it is not a stretch to assume that they will have a difficult time nurturing their own children as adults. Psychologists warn us that it is a clear sign of future violent behavior when children torture and mistreat animals. Ripping the heads off of the Barbie dolls is also a step in that direction. The father's behavior is rooted in gender-role normativity and fear of femininity in his son. Was the father disgusted by deviation from gender-role expectations he had learned in his youth? Was he afraid of homosexuality? Was he encultured into gender expectations? No matter what the reasons, the father's response is probably quite typical. If so, all the more reason that curriculum scholars must study gender carefully and include gender diversity in the schools—especially since ignorance, fear, and disgust contribute to sexism, occupational limitations, and the tragedy of child abuse in society.

Another tragedy is bullying and violence based on gender and identity difference. John Aston has studied gay bashings and murders and reports that the typical high school student hears anti-gay slurs 22.5 times a day, that 69% of youths perceived to be either gay or lesbian experience some form of harassment or violence in school, with over half of these experiencing it daily, and that over one-third of youth reported hearing homophobic remarks from faculty or school staff (Aston, 2001b). Additionally, Aston cited a 1993 Massachusetts Governor's Commission on Gay and Lesbian Youth study which reported that 85% of teachers oppose integrating gay/lesbian/bisexual studies within their curriculum (Aston, 2001a). Psychologist Karen Franklin's landmark study found that thrill-seeking, peer dynamics, and societal permission and encouragement were the primary reasons for anti-gay assailant motivations (Franklin, 1997).

This attitude of permission to kill not only gays and lesbians, but Jews, Blacks, Muslims, immigrants, and other minorities, is promoted in several political groups, churches, and websites today. Just glance at the website for the American Nazi Party to get a chilling glimpse of the hate rhetoric. I show several films to my students to impress upon them the seriousness of this ethical nightmare: the dramatic fictional account of teenagers in Los Angeles in the film titled *American History X*—a must see for all educators concerned about hate crimes—and *Licensed to Kill*—a documentary that interviews men in prison who killed gays and lesbians. One of the frightening aspects of both the fictional and the documentary film that must give pause to critical educators is that the permission to murder is rooted in scriptural passages, church sermons, and hate-filled rhetoric learned in educational settings. Our teaching convictions must direct us to counter hate speech in all of its manifestations. Ignorance of the pervasiveness of this problem and silence in the face of hate crimes or hate speech constitute a moral failure of educators and citizens that amounts to complicity in the crime.

John Aston followed up on Karen Franklin's research with a case study of one gay assailant in Houston, Texas, titled "Deconstructing Heterosexism and Homophobia in Schools":

> This investigation focuses on the internal and external factors that led to Jon Buice's murderous assault along with nine of his adolescent peers on a gay man, Paul Broussard, in Houston on the night of July 4, 1991. The study examines the societal sense of permission to harass and assault those who violate gender norms, with a particular focus on the role of schools as passively and sometimes actively contributing to a sense of permission. ... This case study shows that Jon was more typical than atypical of young male adolescents in our highly gendered and patriarchal society. He was driven by thrill seeking and peer dynamics to attack societally-permitted targets rather than by any knowingly anti-gay ideology. The members of Jon's school and community may make convenient scapegoats of Jon and his companions, but this study indicates that we are all implicit in such acts, and ends with suggestions about ways to end our school's complicity in such grim oppression. (2001b, pp. iii–iv)

As we study gender and sexuality issues, we must examine our own complicity and silence on bullying, teasing, and violence against minorities and those perceived as different in schools and society. We will read more about other dimensions of gender research later in this chapter.

The fourth category that I will explore is sexual behavior. People choose to engage in a variety of intimate and emotional sexual expressions that are sometimes with a person of the same gender, sometimes with a person of the opposite gender, and sometimes with themselves alone, as in the case of masturbation. Some people are asexual—they have no desire or interest in any sexual experiences. Some people choose to be celibate—a requirement, for example, of Catholic clergy, Buddhist monks, and some other religions, but also practiced by individuals for periods of time for various other reasons. Additionally, people are not static in their sexual behaviors; they may move in and out of various expressions of their sexuality throughout their lifetime. But these expressions of sexuality are not determined by the gender of the individual or restricted by gender identity, nor are they automatically indicative of sexual identity, as we will see in category five below. Expressions of sexual behavior by straight, gay, or bisexual persons may be connected to emotional, psychological, and physiological desires and attractions, but behaviors are also conditioned by experimentation, incarceration, drunkenness, peer pressure, curiosity, or financial incentive.

What is the purpose and function of sexual behavior? Some assume that sexual behavior in humans and animals is exclusively for the purpose of procreation. It is seen as a function of natural laws of reproduction. Others believe that sexual behavior primarily provides mutual support and pleasure for adults in a relationship. Some societies and religions insist that procreation and sexual relationships must occur only in a heterosexual and monogamous marriage. Some cultures and societies are less restrictive on the nature of relationships. Procreation today is more diffuse with the availability of sperm and egg donors, artificial insemination, surrogate mothers, and the like. Historically, polygamy is prevalent and even expected in many cultures in Africa, the Middle East, and even occasionally in the US. It was not shocking to the people in France when in 1996 the wife, children, mistress, and child of the mistress all attended the funeral of their former president François Mitterrand. When Saudi King Fahd died in 2005, all three of his wives attended the funeral, much to the surprise of some in the US. In January of 2010, South Africa gained its third first lady when President Jacob Zuma married Tobeka Madiba, his fifth marriage and third concurrent spouse. With another fiancee in the wings and rumors about a possible future engagement, there was speculation that South Africa may in the future have five or more first ladies. Additionally, with the long history of rape of Black women and the children conceived by Black mistresses of White men on US plantations—from Thomas Jefferson to Strom Thurmond—feigned surprise seems quite naive and misplaced. There are tremendous gender equity problems and social justice issues related to the way that women are treated as property and sex objects. The sex trade that enslaves women and young girls in the US and internationally is an appalling and ongoing tragedy. I will discuss this topic of rape and abuse in more detail at the end of chapter 10. However, for now, I want to make a clear distinction between sexual abuse, which must be prosecuted and deplored, and intimate sexual behaviors between consenting adults.

What is the natural form of sexual behavior? When the film *March of the Penguins* was released in 2005, many "family values" conservative commentators praised it for using penguins to demonstrate the natural principle in the animal kingdom of monogamous relationships and parental love for offspring. The film did present an inspiring testimony to family life, but ironically these commentators were caught off guard when scientists and zookeepers pointed out that, in some species of penguin, couples rarely mate for life and occasionally penguins form gay relationships. It is impossible to argue for a singular natural form of sexual behavior based on the animal kingdom because of the incredible diversity of reproductive and mating patterns. So, can we turn to human history as a guide for a metanarrative of natural human sexual behavior? That will not work either. Anthropologists have documented much diversity across cultures throughout human history (Coontz, 2005). Papua New Guinea presents a very interesting case in point, as reported in the *National Study of Sexual and Reproductive*

Knowledge and Behaviour in Papua New Guinea (Jenkins, 1994). The norms for sexual and reproductive behaviors vary dramatically from society to society. And Coontz (2005) has documented how marriage itself has evolved in the US. Can we turn to religions to help us? Yes, of course. But we will not find unanimity among Hinduism, Islam, African spiritualities, Judaism, Voodoo, and Christianity—nor within these religions either. The natural form of sexual behavior is postmodern—eclectic and poly-morphous—and there is no authoritative metanarrative to which we can turn to give us a natural or religious norm. Reproduction, mating, and sexual behavior in humans and animals have always been eclectic and diverse.

It is also important to note, as we saw above, that expressions of intimacy and sexuality by consenting adults are not in any way equated with pedophilia, pederasty, or bestiality. As explained by psychologists and researchers, the abuse, sex trafficking, and rape of children, teenagers, and animals have nothing to do with intimate sexual expressions and partnerships between consenting adults. In an attempt to confuse the public and call into question sexual diversity, those who are uncomfortable with same-gender relationships, bisexual intimacy, non-genital-to-genital sexual expressions like oral or anal sex, and non-marital heterosexual partnerships will often compare these diverse expressions of sexuality to the despicable and illegal rape of children. This comparison—and others like bestiality—is a category mistake and a logical fallacy. While there are sexual predators and pedophiles among transsexuals, heterosexuals, bisexuals, and homosexuals, the vast majority of pedophiles are statistically, in fact, heterosexual male relatives and neighbors with prominent community visibility, who most often rape and abuse young girls. But from listening to news reports the general public might think that Catholic priests, coaches, boy scout leaders, and gay men are all pedophiles and child abusers. This is not true, yet the stigma persists. Yes, a very small percentage of all of these people abuse children. But sociological research does not support the stereotypes. These sedimented perceptors and category mistakes hap-pen, in part, when we attempt to define an entire group of people by a particular sexual behavior (e.g., all Catholic priests are pedophiles, all college coaches rape young boys in the locker rooms, all single females behave like the characters in *Sex in the City*, all French women are bisexual, all gay men are promiscuous and have AIDS, all straight men cheat on their wives, all televangelists cavort with prostitutes, all female athletes are lesbians, all Christians are heterosexual, all single men over 35 are gay, all transsexuals are homosexual, all Black men are rapists, all straight men get turned on by wearing woman's underwear, all male politicians cheat on their spouses). Can you see the absurdity and danger in such gross generalizations and blatant errors of fact, even if there is statistical evidence of some truth in each of these scenarios? Sensationalism of a few prominent cases in the media may give the appearance of gen-eralizations. But why do they persist?

Returning to our discussion of sexual abuse, remember that this is a crime committed by an individual person and not a category of persons. Just because most child sexual abuse is committed by a step-father, an uncle, or a male relative against a young girl does not mean that all heterosexual males are rapists and pedophiles. Likewise, just because a few clergy, coaches, and scout leaders molest teenage boys, this does not mean that all clergy and coaches are pederasts. Finally, sexual orientation does not correlate with any form of sexual abuse for heterosexuals, homosexuals, or bisexuals. I will have more to say about this topic in chapter 10.

There is one more significant point to be made as we conclude this section: sexual behavior does not define a human being. In fact, for most people, intimate sexual activity with a partner or lover is only one among many components—albeit a beautiful and important one—in their lives. Sexual behavior in a loving partnership—whether gay, straight, or bi—is only one dimension of a person's life. The modern obsession with categorizing people exclusively by this one dimension is illogical and damaging. People of all genders and orientations have diverse sexual behaviors. As we noted above, some are monogamous for life, some are serially monogamous, some are polygamous, some are promiscuous, some are celibate, some engage in oral and anal sex, and some are masturbators. However, all are human beings with full and rich lives that are not defined or limited by their sexuality. Yes, some people have sexual addictions and a few commit criminal sexual behavior. These individuals must be treated appropriately within the law and within the best practices of medicine and psychiatry. However, it is important that we stop stereotyping people by ethnicity, gender, and orientation based on sedimented assumptions and prejudices about sexual behavior. In order to nurture children in schools—and protect them from abuse—educators must be very well versed in the sociology and psychology of gender roles and sexual behaviors. An appropriate curriculum on these topics is essential—especially in an age of HIV/AIDS and other life-threatening sexually transmitted diseases and Internet predators.

Sexual orientation, the fifth and final category, is not determined by or directed toward any specific sexual behavior that we discussed above. Sexual orientation is the fundamental attraction and emotional comfort that a person feels for another human being. It is about companionship, relationships, and attractions. This may be with someone of the same gender, the opposite gender, or both male and female. Straight people have sexual orientation! When does a person become aware of their sexual orientation as gay, straight, or bisexual? Most people report that they began to feel their attractions early in life, and psychologists report that, based on recent scientific studies of the brain and other qualitative studies of human genetics and psychology, sexual orientation appears innate at birth as a part of a person's identity. Are people born gay or straight or bisexual? My experiences with counseling college students and with scientific research lead me to believe absolutely yes. However, I also know that awareness evolves over time in different individuals. Questions and confusion about sexuality are normal for all young people, no matter what their sexual orientation, especially in environments where there is a lack of information or support. Pressure from parents, peers, and pastors about expected gender identity or sexual identity creates an environment where many young people are tormented and sometimes even commit suicide. This is a tragic situation that educators must understand and address. An excellent film that I use in my classes is titled *Jim in Bold*—the story of a Pennsylvania high school student named Jim Wheeler (see www.jiminbold.com). Go online and watch the excellent trailer for this film.

The debate about "nature versus nurture"—the source by birth or by socialization for sexual orientation, athletic ability, musical talent, intelligence, or personality traits—is very complex and ultimately unresolvable. This is not something that can be proven once and for all. So, rather than becoming mired in this debate, I prefer to acknowledge the "nature versus nurture" discussion, learn what we can from scientists and anthropologists, and then move on to allow individual people to serve as the expert on their own sexual identity. We all have traits and talents that are a unique and mysterious combination of genetics, psychology, family heritage, education, and socialization. Endless debates about "nature versus nurture" will not help us to move forward to address the larger context.

Another complex dimension of sexual identity is the influence of religion. On the one hand, individual religions should be free to make rules regarding a range of issues—within, of course, the parameters and legal restrictions of a democratic society. For example, religions cannot practice cannibalism or child sacrifice; nor can they withhold basic human rights of education, nutrition, and health care from members. But religions can impose celibacy, regulate rituals for marriage, prohibit divorce or contraception, and restrict sexual behaviors of their members. However, the rituals and morals of any one religion cannot become the norm for all citizens in a democracy. As we read in chapter 4, religions have historically had tremendous influence in shaping culture—sometimes for the good of society, and sometimes not. Today we are engaged in difficult debates about gay marriage, stem-cell research, the role of women in society, the availability of contraceptives and abortion, transsexual gender identity, and many other issues. For example, a ballot issue in 2011 seeking to define life as beginning at conception was rejected by voters in Colorado and Mississippi. This "personhood" amendment had the support of many pro-life and anti-abortion activists, but the implications for birth control, in vitro fertilization, criminal investigations of miscarriages, and the like caused many voters to pause and recognize the complexity of these issues even within a religious context. Some religions want to impose their moral code on all citizens; others do not. In chapter 4 we examined the appropriate and inappropriate connections between religion and government. Now, in chapter 6, we must explore the connection between religion and issues of gender and sexuality.

Let's consider religious debates about homosexuality in Christianity—noting, of course, that similar debates are occurring in Judaism, Hinduism, and Islam as well. I am struck by the fact that various official interpretations of the exact same passage in various Christian bibles—remember from chapter 4 that there are many bibles and different contradictory translations—do not include the word "homosexual." As we saw in chapter 5, all hermeneutic translations of texts reflect cultural, linguistic, psychological, and political motivations. For example, the New American Bible (Roman Catholic) uses this litany: "No fornicators, idolaters, adulterers, sodomites, thieves, misers, drunkards, slanderers, or robbers will inherit God's kingdom." (Does that list include everyone?) We also pointed out in chapter 5 the problems associated with various linguistic interpretations of words. Consider as an example the word "sodomite." From Foucault (1990a, 1990b), in *The History of Sexuality*, we learn about the creation of "homosexuality" as a discursive and social concept for surveillance and regulation in the 19th century. Thus, to infer homosexuality from the word "sodomite" is linguistically and historically inaccurate. We cannot undertake a complete historical exegesis in this chapter, so I would recommend, in addition to Foucault's books, the texts *The New Testament and Homosexuality* (Scroggs, 1983) and *What the Bible Really Says About Homosexuality* (Helminiak, 2000) as a good overview of the problem of interpretation on this topic. I seek to problematize, deconstruct, and reevaluate decontextualized and uncritical socio-political positions based on literal proof-texting of any kind. This is the postmodern project of deconstruction presented in the introduction of this book.

Scroggs divides theologians into two camps: those who believe that the Christian Bible opposes homosexuality and those who believe that it does not oppose homosexuality. In the first group there are five different positions taken by theologians, congregations, and denominations:

1. The Bible opposes homosexuality and is definitive for what the Church should think and do about it. Thus, ordination of homosexuals and same-sex marriages are prohibited.
2. The Bible opposes homosexuality, but it is just one sin among many (e.g., the list in 1 Corinthians 6). There is no justification for singling homosexuality out as more serious than other sins castigated in the Bible. Thus, ordination (and, in some cases, same-sex civil unions) for homosexuals may permitted.
3. The Bible opposes homosexuality, but the specific injunctions must be placed in the larger biblical context of the theology of creation, sin, judgment, and grace. This position is divided into two sub-groups: those who argue from the position of creation and see homosexuality as a deviation from the male and female sexual union, and those who argue from the principle of love and support wholesome and edifying human relationships of any kind. Thus, the believer is free and called to responsibility to make *independent* judgments about what counts as "human relationships which affirm life and love."
4. The Bible opposes homosexuality but is so time- and culture-bound that its injunctions may and should be discarded if other considerations suggest better alternatives. If Leviticus and Paul are addressing situations so foreign to our own times, there is no reason to apply those judgments—which is already the case for dietary restrictions, clothing, and other issues—and thus ordination and same-sex marriages are possible.
5. The Bible does not oppose homosexuality, only homosexual acts. This is the position of the Roman Catholic Church and some other denominations. Thus, heterosexuals and homosexuals may be ordained as long as they pledge celibacy to the local bishop. This may change for future seminarians under Pope Benedict XVI. Some people are born homosexual and some are born heterosexual, and their sexual identity and orientation are not the issue. Rather, celibacy is the virtue required for all priests and all homosexuals as well, since they are not allowed to marry.

Scroggs then discusses the how these five interpretations affect church law and community practices in many denominations. Obviously, there have been many changes in church discipline and congregational practices since the publication of this book in 1983—with some pastors and Christian churches becoming more affirming to homosexual members, same-sex unions or marriages, and the ordination of openly gay and lesbian pastors—and even a bishop in the Episcopalian Church. There are obviously widespread differences in church practices and theological positions—from the open and affirming stance of the United Church of Christ at one end of the spectrum to the condemnation and exclusion of the Church of Christ at the other end. The most important thing to note is that there is not universal agreement within or among Christian denominations on a wide array of gender and sexuality issues—including divorce, serial monogamy, women as pastors, lesbian clergy, gay civil unions and marriage, celibacy, stem-cell research, transsexual gender identity, abortion, and contraception.

The second category is those theologians and congregations who do not believe that the Bible opposes homosexuality: 1) the Bible does not oppose homosexuality because it does not speak of true or innate homosexuality but rather only of same-gender sexual behavior by people who are not homosexual (which we discussed above); and 2) the Bible does not oppose homosexuality because the texts cited to prohibit gay and lesbian relationships do not deal with homosexuality. The texts are being misrepresented. For example, as noted above, the word "sodomite" has no contemporary scholarly translation and must be judged a mistranslation. The actual prohibition was prostitution and not homosexuality. In both of these cases, these theologians and pastors argue that it does not make sense to prohibit gays and lesbians from marrying and serving as ministers. Scroggs presents the multiplicity of interpretations and practices in Christian denominations and theological seminaries. While legal prohibitions may exist in the wider society, the practices within Christian churches—and other religions—vary dramatically. It is this variety of understandings that must be allowed to enter the hermeneutic circle and inform those who are unaware of such various interpretations and church practices.

Applying the hermeneutic process and textual analysis to contemporary issues is enlightening for some and disturbing for others. Some students and scholars embrace the invitation to enter the hermeneutic circle; others retreat baffled or angry. It is amazing that, more than any other issue, a careful hermeneutical study that deconstructs notions of gender, sexual orientation, and identity constructions, as we have done in this chapter, generates such hostile responses. Without intending to elide the continuing tragedy of racism and classism to which we will turn shortly, and without blurring the boundaries of race, class, ability, orientation, ethnicity, and gender, I am convinced that the civil rights issues exposed by queer theory and identity politics must continue to be foregrounded in our teaching, curriculum research, and social activism. This is one of the very important ethical and civil rights issues of our time, and, if we can overcome prejudice based on gender identity and sexual orientation, many more doors will be open for human rights in multiple other areas. Let's explore some of these as we continue our analysis of critical ethical issues related to gender, sexuality, and race. For now, we should ask ourselves why gender, sexual orientation, and identity issues are so controversial and divisive in schools and society.

The complexity of these issues is reflected in the impossibility of crafting legal language to cover all possibilities of gender and sexual identity. In the gay marriage debates in the US, one interesting case in Texas presages future dilemmas for those trying to craft legislation limiting marriage to one man and one woman. In 2000 a lesbian couple in Texas was legally married with the official approval of the Fourth

Court of Appeals. How could these two women legally marry, since Texas law defines marriage as between one man and one woman? The event was reported this way: "On a lovely late summer evening of September 16, 2000, a lesbian couple from Houston was married—complete with a marriage license. This historic event marked the first time a same sex couple has been legally wed in the United States" (Texas Triangle, 2000). For those who thought that gay marriage was not legal until 2004, in Massachusetts, this case may seem a bit odd. Here is how Chief Justice Phil Hardberger ruled in this case: "Male chromosomes do not change with either hormonal treatment or sex reassignment surgery. Biologically, a post-operative female transsexual is still a male" (Texas Triangle, 2000, p. 3). In other words, one of the women was considered a man in the eyes of Texas law because she has a Y chromosome. A similar situation occurred in the 1988 Olympics. Anne Fausto-Sterling (2000) describes the incident:

> In the rush and excitement of leaving for the 1988 Olympics, Maria Patino, Spain's top woman hurdler, forgot the requisite doctor's certificate stating, for the benefit of the Olympic officials, what seemed patently obvious to anyone who looked at her: she was a female. But the International Olympic Committee (IOC) had anticipated the possibility that some competitors would forget their certificates of femininity. Patino had only to report to the "femininity control head office," scrape some cells off the side of her cheek, and all would be in order—or so she thought. (p. 1)

For those too young to remember, some countries in the 1950s had been caught sneaking men disguised as women into the Olympics in order, they believed, to give them an advantage and win more gold medals in women's competitions. This was at the height of the Cold War, and athletic competition mimicked battlefield combat. Additionally, the Olympics policed gender in an effort to mollify those who feared that women's participation in sports threatened to turn them into manly creatures. In 1912, Pierre de Coubertin, founder of the modern Olympics (from which women were originally banned), argued that women's sports were against the laws of nature. The Olympics employed femininity control because of sedimented perceptors that the very act of competing meant that female athletes could not be true women. In the context of gender politics, policing for identity and sex made sense at the time. But of course, in a policy of blatant gender discrimination, men were not required to submit to a "masculinity control head office." But that is another story. Returning to Maria Patino:

> A few hours after the cheek scraping she got a call. Something was wrong. She went in for a second examination, but the doctors were mum. Then, as she rode to the Olympic stadium to start her first race, track officials broke the news: she had failed the sex test. She may have looked like a woman, had a woman's strength, and never had reason to suspect that she was not a woman, but her examination revealed that Patino's cells spotted a Y chromosome, and that her labia hid testes within .... According to the IOC's definition, Patino

was not a woman. She was barred from competing on Spain's Olympic team. Down and out, Patino spent thousands of dollars consulting with doctors about her situation. They explained that she had been born with a condition called *androgen insensitivity*. (Fausto-Sterling, 2000, p. 2)

Maria Patino had a Y chromosome and hidden testes that produced testosterone, but her cells could not detect this minuscule hormone. Thus, her body did not develop male characteristics and, because of her body's inability to respond to the testosterone at puberty, she developed breasts and female characteristics. Despite the inner testes and the extra Y chromosome—the pattern is XXY—she had grown up as a female, developed a female form, and had a boyfriend. She knew she was a woman, no matter what the IOC ruled. After years of medical examinations and legal battles, Patino was declared a woman and reinstated on the Spanish Olympic squad in 1992.

When should the presence of a Y chromosome determine gender? Who should make this decision? Does it make any difference if a person had genital surgery—as a trans-sexual adult or an intersex infant? What if a woman has a hidden testis and trace presence of testosterone in her cells? How much testosterone determines gender?

As people become more comfortable identifying as transsexual, intersexual, and transgender, how will the law define their gender? Some conservative critics of Judge Hardberger were horrified that he opened the door to chromosomal tests as the basis for determining gender. What if a biological woman with an extra Y chromosome—like Maria Patino—was lesbian and wanted to marry another woman? The critics wanted the definition of male and female to be based on the genitalia at birth and not chromosomes or hormones. But what happens to the many children who, according to Brown University biologist Anne Fausto-Sterling, are born intersex and with chromosomal anomalies and/or ambiguous genitalia? How will these people be classified—male or female? And now that many families and doctors are choosing not to perform gender assignment surgery on infants, what happens as intersex people grow up and simply identify as intersex and not male or female? We cannot make laws to cover all complex combinations of biological sex, gender identity, sexual behavior, and sexual orientation. The world is not as simple as modern dualism pretended. The *New York Times* described our contemporary postmodern society in an article titled: "Polymorphous Normal: Has Sexual Identity—Gay, Straight, or Bi—Outlived Its Usefulness?" (D'Erasmo, 2001) as follows:

> While it would be going too far to say that we have reached the end of sexual identity—reports of the end of anything, like history, or money, or Cher, tend to be highly exaggerated—it seems that something different is emerging on the street these days, a new music coming out of the cultural radio. It is composed of, and heard by, ordinary women and men of all varieties who sleep with, fall in love with, live with and break up with both women and men over the courses of their lives, the current of desire flowing easily over the gender divide and leading them where it may. At this moment these people tend to be artists, students, and other cultural explorers, but they probably won't be lonely for long. This is not a move-ment, certainly not an identity; it is unnamed, unbannered—more like a space

without a sign, filled with little lights. If pushed, some of these people, sighing, will call themselves bisexual or queer, but only as a political convenience, short-hand for "not straight." A gay-liberation movement that began with a riot [Stonewall, 1969], followed by ferocious battles over what one may or may not do in one's bedroom, AIDS, a young man beaten and left for dead against a fence [Matthew Shepard in Laramie, Wyoming], lesbian mothers losing custody of their children, the relentless policing of every gradation of sexual difference—over the past 20 or 30 years; sexual identity has often seemed like both a war zone and a weapon. Amid this sometimes deadly balkanization, it is as though some citizens have begun slipping way from the fray to meet in the side streets, not in uniform. (p. 106)

One prominent researcher who agrees with D'Erasmo's analysis and answers in the affirmative to the title question in the article is Shari Thurer (Thurer, 2005), who explains that queer theory in academic parlance seeks to subvert the entire concept of identity, but she cautions that this has immense anti-liberal political consequences. How can there be a women's liberation movement is there is no such identity as "woman"? How can you have gay liberation if there is no category "gay"? Thurer contends that "the average gay on the street, or anyone on the street, views 'queer' as another label, albeit a hip, less restrictive one than 'homosexual' or 'lesbian.' In popular culture it means an identity that is sexier, more transgressive, that signals a deliberate show of difference, that doesn't want to be assimilated or tolerated" (2005, p. 99). Whether we understand queer theory as a deconstructive subversion of identity categories or a deliberate transgressive identity, it is important to remember that the explosion of understandings of gender and sexuality in the entire global community renders modern normative categories obsolete. I believe that queer theory is a cultural and academic phenomenon that will expand in complex and interesting ways in the years ahead—and no amount of legislation or religious proselytizing will convert queer subjects into normalized automatons. The cats are out of the bag, so to speak, and we all know that it is impossible to herd cats. My fear is that traditionalists and bigots will spew more vicious inflammatory rhetoric in an attempt simply to kill the "runaway cats." We must be vigilant not only to protect people from harassment, especially students who appear different from the gender and sexual identity norms in schools, but also to advance a postmodern democratic society with genuine compassion, identity freedom, and liberty and justice for all.

One tragic example of the results of ignorance and fear about queer identities in the postmodern eclectic world is the brutal murder in 1999 of Private Barry Winchell, a member of the 101st Airborne Infantry, the "Screaming Eagles," stationed at Fort Campbell, Kentucky. An army private named Calvin Glover bludgeoned Winchell—whom he thought was gay—to death. Glover was goaded into battering Winchell by Justin Fisher, Winchell's roommate, who taunted Glover for losing a fight with Winchell, whom he referred to as "a faggot." Thurer (2005) describes the incident:

The harassment against Winchell started when Fisher found out that Winchell was in love with Calpernia Addams, a pre-operative transsexual nightclub performer to whom Fisher had introduced him. Fisher then instigated a four-month gay-bashing campaign against Winchell, which culminated in his brutal murder by Glover. At one point, the victim Winchell and his sergeant had gone to the inspector general's office to complain about the ceaseless hostilities directed against him, but to no avail. At the trial for Winchell's murder, a forensic psychiatrist revealed that the Iago-like Fisher suffered from "transvestic fetishism," meaning that Fisher had turned to wearing women's underwear for sexual arousal since the age of 14. Fisher was known to be attracted to one of Addams' drag queen entertainer colleagues, Kim Mayfield. The murderer, Glover, was sentenced to life imprisonment, and in a plea bargain got 12 years. (pp. 95–96)

There are several important lessons to learn from this tragic story—an event that is not as unusual or isolated as readers may think. According to Thurer (2005), these events can be interpreted in four possible ways: first, Winchell died in a common fight, or what the base command called a "physical altercation" among young soldiers; second, Winchell died of a horrific gay-bashing incident, and not simply an ordinary fight on the base, as some gay rights activists contend; third, Winchell died as a result of Fisher's homosexual jealousy, and not as the result of a homophobic hate crime, as some right-wing commentators contend; fourth, Winchell's death was the result of category mistakes because it had nothing to do with "real" sexuality at all, as queer theorists contend. Although he was the victim of an anti-gay hate crime, Winchell was not homosexual. Prior to Calpernia Addams, he dated only females and identified as straight. He considered Addams his girlfriend and not as a boyfriend. Likewise, Addams regarded herself as a heterosexual woman trapped in a male body and was taking hormonal treatments and preparing for gender reassignment surgery. The instigator, Fisher, did not consider himself gay either, and the vast majority of males who cross-dress privately for sexual arousal and have interest in erotic lesbian sex scenes and fetishes about transgender persons are heterosexual. Straight men are as complex as gay men, as most women know very well. Every element of the Winchell tragedy falls into the gray in-between area of sex and gender.

Utimately, it mattered little whether Winchell was "really" gay or not. What mattered was that he was perceived to be gay. In schools and society—and even at Fort Campbell—most people fall into a gray area in gender and sexuality. In fact, maybe everyone is really queer to some degree. Consider the fact that no one fits perfectly into all five of the categories of biological sex, gender role, gender identity, sexual behavior, and sexual identity discussed above. Does one same-sex encounter for curiosity in middle school make someone gay for life? Ten experimental encounters over three years? Twenty? Does making art rather than playing football make a student less than a true man? How do we categorize heterosexual cross-dressers, a lesbian married to a man, a biological female with a Y chromosome or an inner testis, a heterosexual army private with a transsexual girlfriend, or two women in Texas with female genitalia (one constructed surgically) with XX and XY chromosomes who want to get married? Undoubtedly, some readers are shaking their heads and saying that these are isolated extreme examples. I have been collecting data and reading research on this topic for fifteen years. Like postmodern theorists and queer theorists, I am convinced that there is no such thing as a fixed category of normal. The possibilities for gender and sexual identity are too diverse and individual persons too complex and fluid to create rigid categories.

So what should we do in schools and societies? First, educate ourselves so that we do not continue to make category mistakes that harm students and citizens. Second, recognize that the stable categories of the modern era were a distortion, and we cannot return to a perceived golden era of gender and identity dualities. All of the issues presented above are a part of the rich fabric of human history. In fact, in some native cultures the intersex child was considered blessed by the gods with a unity of opposites, and not as a deformed anomaly to be killed or hidden in shame. Third, learn to love and appreciate all of the people with unique genders and identities that come into our schools and families. They have tremendous insights and creative imagination to share with all of us. Fourth, put an end to the taunting and bullying that perpetuates violence. Ignorance and exclusion can sometimes lead to murder and suicide. Fifth, show films and read challenging literature that expose students to gender and identity diversity in all of its forms. We are not only educating the broader society, we are actually helping ourselves, because the diversity exists in our immediate community whether we choose to recognize it or not. We are stronger when we unite in our common humanity with a respect for our diversity. Sixth, reach out to the marginalized and remember that most world religions demand a preferential option for those in need. Seventh, examine our own autobiography and sedimented perceptors for the ways in which gender and sexuality bias has deformed each of us, and work vigorously to excavate the unconscious and liberate repressed wounds that not only cause internal torment but also provoke us to rip the heads off of dolls and force kids to play sports against their will.

A study of queer theory can help us to evaluate the complexity of the competing notions of identity politics and enlarge the hermeneutic circle, hopefully to advance a more compassionate, ecumenical, and authentic society. We will develop a more active social conscience in the process. There is a growing body of scholarly literature in curriculum studies that helps us to do this by deconstructing gender and identity issues (Britzman, 1995; Sears, 1992; Sears and Epstein, 1999; Letts and Sears, 1999; Pinar, 1994, 1998; Kumashiro, 2001, 2004; Macgillivray, 2002; Talburt, 2000). We now turn our attention to race and ethnicity, and then we will return to an integrated perspective on race and gender at the end of the chapter.

To introduce the themes in the next section, consider this passage by bell hooks in *Killing Rage, Ending Racism*:

> A vision of cultural homogeneity that seeks to deflect attention away from or even excuse the oppressive, dehumanizing impact of white supremacy on the lives of black people by suggesting black people are racist too indicates that the culture remains ignorant of what racism really is and how it works. It shows that people are in denial. Why is it so difficult for many white folks to understand that racism is oppressive not because white folks have prejudicial feelings about blacks (they could have such feelings and leave us alone) but because it is a system that promotes domination and subjugation? The prejudicial feelings

some blacks may express about whites are in no way linked to a system of domination that affords us any power to coercively control the lives and well-being of white folks. That needs to be understood. (hooks, 1995, pp. 154–155)

Along with bell hooks, I see racism as a system of domination and power. Along with Joe Feagin (2000, 2006), I understand racism to be systemic and deeply rooted in the American character. As a White male, I accrue privileges that are not accessible to people of color. The long history of slavery, Jim Crow, and voting discrimination systematically excluded African Americans and other minorities. Richard Rodriguez (2002) documents the parallel struggles of Hispanic people in America and their contribution as the largest minority population to the legacy of the US. The legacy of such discrimination reverberates today, and the privileges of the plantation still benefit me. For clarification, I believe that all people of any race or ethnicity can be prejudiced and biased. White people experience the pain of hatred, exclusion, and insults. But this is not the racism of domination and privilege as bell hooks describes it above. The most important first step in addressing and ameliorating the legacy of racism in the US is for White people to acknowledge this fact. White people hold an important key to solving the problems of racism, but they too often whine about some perceived *reverse discrimination*—a linguistic smokescreen and manipulation that is a logical fallacy and category mistake. Peggy McIntosh ([1988] 1992) explains:

I have come to see White privilege as an invisible package of unearned assets that I can count on cashing in each day, but about which I was "meant" to remain oblivious. White privilege is like an invisible weightless knapsack of special provisions, assurances, tools, maps, guides, codebooks, passports, visas, clothes, compass, emergency gear, and blank checks. Since I have trouble facing White privilege and describing its results in my life, I saw parallels here with men's reluctance to acknowledge male privilege. Only rarely will a man go beyond acknowledging that women are disadvantaged to acknowledging that men have unearned advantage, or that unearned privilege has not been good for men's development as human beings, or for society's development, or that privilege systems might ever be challenged and *changed*. (p. 71, emphasis in original)

Another introductory thought that must be mentioned as we begin exploring race and ethnicity is the importance of recognizing that the dominant group is an equal player in the discussion of any minority issue. McIntosh points out that race is not just about people of color—it is about White people too. Gender is not just about women—men have gender and gender issues as well. Sexual orientation exists for all people—including straight people. In fact, the failure of the dominant group to see themselves as a part of the solution—or even a part of the discussion—is one of the most intractable problems we face as we explore cultural and ethnic issues. I challenge readers to reconsider their privilege or positionality, whatever it may be. White people could begin by reading the work of Michelle Fine and her colleagues on this topic (Fine et al., 1997; Fine & Weis, 2003).

As a final introductory comment, my discussion of race in this chapter emphasizes White and Black dynamics. This is not to deny the many complex dimensions of race and discrimination. Angela Valenzuela (1999), for example, has written the award-winning book *Subtractive Schooling: U.S.-Mexican Youth and the Politics of Caring*, which addresses the concerns of Hispanics in US schools. Her study is based on a three-year qualitative and quantitative case study of achievement and schooling orientations among immigrant Mexican and US-born Mexican-American youth in an urban, predominantly Latino, Houston high school. Like another important activist for children and appropriate curriculum in schools, Susan Ohanian (www.susanohanian.org/), Valenzuela documents the ways that children are left behind in US schools despite the rhetoric of *No Child Left Behind*. The research of Valenzuela and Ohanian is some of the most important curriculum work being done in education today. However, as Joe Feagin points out, White and Black is the foundational and archetypal racism in the US, and our ability to address all issues of justice in schools and society must examine this perspective issue first and foremost. Feagin (2000) writes:

> The great scholar of the African diaspora, C. L. R. James, once argued strongly that the oppressive situation of African Americans is the number one problem of racism in the modern world. If the problem of racism cannot be solved in the United States, it cannot be solved anywhere. I focus on this critical case of white-on-black oppression in the United States. One reason for this is practical: given limited space, this focus means that I can dig deeper into the development, structure, processes, and likely future of one major case of racism. My decision is also theoretically motivated. I will show that white-on-black oppression is in several important respects the archetype of racial oppression in North America. For example, African Americans were the only racial group specifically singled out several times in the U.S. Constitution for subordination within the new nation. The leading theorist of the U.S. Constitution, James Madison, noted that from a white man's point of view "the case of the black race within our bosom … is the problem most baffling to the policy of our country." A few decades later, white-on-black oppression would be central to the bloodiest war in U.S. history, the Civil War. Within American society, African Americans have been dominated and exploited in much larger numbers than has any other group. Over nearly four centuries, tens of millions of African Americans have had their labor and wealth regularly taken from them. In contrast to other groups, their original languages, cultures, and family ties were substantially obliterated by their being torn from Africa, and the oppression faced under slavery and segregation was extremely dehumanized, racialized, and systematic. No other racially oppressed group has been so central to the internal economic, political, and cultural structure and evolution of American society—or to the often obsessively racist ideology developed by white America over many generations. Thus, it is time to put white-on-black oppression fully at the center of a comprehensive study of the development, meaning, and reality of this nation. (p. 3)

The scholarship on race and ethnicity in postmodern curriculum studies is more than a review of the legal issues related to segregation, integration, and affirmative action in schools, debates about the validity of assessment for minority students, the development of programs to reduce ethnic tension on school campuses, or the inclusion of multicultural literary selections in language arts classrooms. It is more than the accountability debates about raising test scores for minority students that we reviewed at the beginning of this book (Skrla & Scheurich, 2004). While these topics are important, racial issues in the postmodern curriculum emphasize investigations of the self and conceptions of the self in relation to the other. Toni Morrison (1989) has written that "the trauma of racism is, for the racist and the victim, the severe fragmentation of the self" (p. 16). She includes this additional caveat that reflects the thinking of many postmodern curriculum theorists as well: "We are not, in fact, 'other'" (p. 9). James Baldwin (1971) expands on Morrison's position:

> If ... one managed to change the curriculum in all the schools so that [African Americans] learned more about themselves and their real contributions to this culture, you would be liberating not only [African Americans], you'd be liberating white people who know nothing about their own history. And the reason is that if you are compelled to lie about one aspect of anybody's history, you must lie about it all. If you have to lie about my real role here, if you have to pretend that I hoed all that cotton just because I loved you, then you have done something to yourself. You are mad. (p. 8)

African-American authors and poets, particularly Toni Morrison, Langston Hughes, James Baldwin, Maya Angelou, Alice Walker, and Ernest Gaines, as well as Latin American authors and other ethnic writers, have become moral voices in the wasteland of modernity where race has been reduced to a social problem in need of a quick-fix solution or a token ethnic event for "cultural awareness week" or "Black History Month." Ronald Wilhelm (1994) discusses some of the problems associated with the latter:

> When historian Carter G. Woodson initiated Negro History Week celebrations in 1926, he ... sought to establish the legitimacy of [African-American] presence in past and present U.S. society as well as to strengthen contemporary African-American culture and values. ... Almost 70 years later, the official curriculum of many U.S. public schools sanctions only selected elements of African-American history and culture. Fragmentary evidence suggests a discrepancy between the rhetoric of official school district policy and the actual classroom practices regarding Black History Month. (p. 217)

Maya Angelou, along with other poets and spokespersons for ethnic and gender issues, has often commented that it is preferable to integrate African-American, Asian-American, Native American, and Latin American history openly and comprehensively throughout the curriculum rather than limiting Black history or women's history to a single month. However, until such time as multicultural studies are widely accepted and incorporated into the curriculum, ethnic celebrations such as "Black History Month" will remain necessary in the schools. Others are not as conciliatory. Khallid Muhammad (1994), outspoken follower of Nation of Islam leader Louis Farrakhan and controversial for his anti-Semitic rhetoric, denounces the concept of Black History Month:

> For Black history celebrations, White people give us one month out of the year—the shortest one they could find—to celebrate our greatness, our glory, our honor and to celebrate our infinite history. With 12 months out of the year we must study their moment in time. We can no longer accept a Black History Day, a Black History Week, or a Black History Month, knowing that we are father and mother of all who walk on this earth. (p. 1)

It is clear from these varied voices that racial, multicultural, gendered, and ethnic issues will remain at the forefront of heated campus debates and curricular investigations in the postmodern era.

Ernest Gaines' novel *A Lesson Before Dying* (1993) is perhaps typical of the literary works that can inform our understanding of curriculum in the postmodern era and support efforts to move beyond the discrepancies reported by Wilhelm. Gaines' text is particularly appropriate for students of curriculum because the protagonist, Grant Wiggins, is a teacher struggling to understand his career and the meaning of education in a racist society. In the excerpt below Wiggins is speaking to Jefferson, a young Black man who has been falsely accused of murder and is awaiting execution. In his trial, Jefferson had been called a hog. Jefferson, it was argued by his court-appointed defense attorney, was not responsible for his actions because he was less than human and not intelligent. Wiggins, who had left home to earn a college degree, has returned to teach at the African-American plantation school. He has been coerced by an aunt to meet with Jefferson daily in the final thirty days before the execution and to teach him to read and thereby appreciate his own self-worth.

I use this novel as a reading in many of my graduate curriculum courses not only because it passionately conveys important contemporary curricular themes, but also because it demonstrates that postmodern curriculum development must include aesthetic, autobiographical, political, and literary dimensions. Additionally, the excerpts from Jefferson's journal in chapter 29 are a powerful indictment of modern approaches to language that have dominated English classes and suppressed the important autobiographical dimension of the writing process. Jefferson's journal also provides support for the whole language philosophy in many curriculum programs. Gaines' novel is perhaps the clearest literary example of this postmodern understanding of the interrelationship of race, culture, and teaching in curriculum studies. The character Grant Wiggins begins:

> "Jefferson," I said. We had started walking. "Do you know what a hero is, Jefferson? A hero is someone who does something for other people. He does something that other men don't and can't do. He is different from other men. He is above other men. No matter who those other men are, the hero, no matter who he is, is above them." I lowered my voice again until we had

passed the table. I could never be a hero. I teach, but I don't like teaching. I teach because it is the only thing that an educated black man can do in the South today. I don't like it; I hate it. I don't even like living here. I want to run away. I want to live for myself and for my woman and for nobody else. (Gaines, 1993, p. 191)

Gaines introduces the dilemma facing Grant Wiggins as a teacher. Wiggins is the reluctant emerging hero, trying to understand himself and the social context of the South that shapes his life. Soon Wiggins turns his attention to Jefferson and continues:

The White people out there are saying that you don't have it—that you're a hog, not a man. But I know they are wrong. You have the potentials. We all have, no matter who we are. Those out there are no better than we are, Jefferson. They are worse. That's why they are always looking for a scape-goat, someone else to blame. I want you to show them the difference between what they think you are and what you can be. To them you're nothing but a nigger—no dignity, no heart, no love for your people. You can prove them wrong. You can do more than I can ever do. I have always done what they wanted me to do, teach reading, writing, and arithmetic. Nothing else—nothing about dignity, nothing about identity, nothing about loving and caring. (1993, pp. 191–192)

Postmodern curriculum scholars understand the frustration of Gaines' protagonist. Race and gender studies ultimately allow educators to see that dignity, identity, and caring are central to understanding curriculum. Feminist scholar Nel Noddings (1984, 1992) is recognized for bringing these issues—particularly the concept of caring—to the forefront of contemporary curriculum discourses in her popular books *Caring: A Feminine Approach to Ethics and Moral Education* and *The Challenge to Care in Schools: An Alternative Approach to Education*. Noddings (1984) writes:

The one-caring, male or female, does not seek security in abstractions cast either as principles or entities. She remains responsible here and now for this cared-for and this situation and for the foreseeable futures projected by herself and the cared-for. ... Today we are asked to believe that a woman's "lack of experience in the world" keeps them at an inferior stage in moral development. I am suggesting, to the contrary, that a powerful and coherent ethic and, indeed, a different sort of world may be built on the natural caring so familiar to women. (pp. 43–46)

This natural caring is also seen in Gaines' novel when Wiggins laments the fact that White society never thought that Blacks were capable of learning about caring and identity. Just as Noddings rejects the belief that women are inferior because of their perceived lack of experience, Gaines rejects the belief that African Americans are infe-rior because of their perceived lack of common humanity and ability to care. Gaines' protagonist continues:

"[They would say] 'Teach those niggers how to print their names and how to figure on their fingers.' And I went along, but hating myself all of the time for doing so. ... Do you know what a myth is, Jefferson?" I asked him. "A myth is an old lie that people still believe in. White people believe that they are better than anyone else on earth—that's a myth. The last thing they ever want to see is a Black man stand, and think, and show that common humanity that is in all of us. It would destroy their myth." (1993, p. 192)

Race, gender, and cultural studies in the postmodern curriculum are about shattering myths, especially those that perpetuate repression of the dignity and identity of the self and those that perpetuate racism, sexism, violence, homophobia, genocide, religious bigotry, political repression, and cultural elitism. In support of the dignity of the individual, as well as an indictment of racism, Gaines concludes this scene with Wiggins imploring Jefferson to stand tall and not crawl to his death like a hog to be butchered:

As long as none of us stand, they're safe. ... I want you to chip away at that myth by standing. I want you—yes you—to call them liars. I want you to show them that you are as much a man—more a man than they can ever be. That jury? You call them men? That judge? Is he a man? The governor is no better. They play by the rules their forefathers created hundreds of years ago. Their forefathers said that we're only three-fifths human—and they believe it to this day. ... When I showed him the notebook and pencil I brought you, he grinned. Do you know why? He believes it was just a waste of time and money. What can a hog do with pencil and paper? (1993, p. 192)

In order to understand postmodern curriculum as a racial, gendered, and multicultural experience, students of curriculum must listen carefully to voices such as those of Grant Wiggins and Jefferson in Ernest Gaines' novel. Postmodern scholars, like Wiggins, insist that, if we continue to play by rules created by our ancestors that no longer make sense in the postmodern world and that repress the dignity and identity of students, curriculum will continue to be a meaningless technocratic endeavor removed from human experience. Also tragic is the fact that not only will schools suffer the debilitating effects of malaise and hopelessness, but society will continue to experience the justified indignation and vocal resistance of those who have experienced a loss of dignity and identity. In a controversial book written from prison entitled *Makes Me Wanna Holler*, Nathan McCall (1993) reflects on his angry youth and shows why young Black men who feel that they have no options in a society that devalues them try to gain self-respect by adopting a code of hyper-masculinity and violence, as documented in the film *Touch Guise: Violence, Media, and the Crisis of Masculinity* (Jhally, 2002). Commentator Jackson Katz describes the "tough guise" as a *pose of defiance* that is meant both to frighten and to reject oppressors, but the pose also has the effect of alienating young men and escalating violence. The postmodern curriculum must address these issues of self-identity and dignity, not only to help young men understand the cultural context of racism and sexism that has infected them but also to promote justice and compassion in society.

It is instructive to consider the story of Stanley Tookie Williams (2004), author of *Blue Rage, Black Redemption*, if we want to understand how to help angry "tough guise" youth move from a life of gangs and violence to peaceful and nonviolent agents for self-respect and activists for justice. Williams wrote about how this can be done from his prison cell in California, where he was on death row for gang violence and murder in Los Angeles. Williams was a peacemaker on death row. He was nominated five times for the Nobel Peace Prize for his work in helping to prevent gang violence and four times for the Nobel Literature Prize for his children's books, which warn young people about the pitfalls of joining a gang and expose them to alternatives. He maintained innocence of the crimes of which he was accused, and he faced racist discrimination throughout his trial. How did Stanley Tookie Williams move from gang life and co-founder of the notorious and violent Crips in Los Angeles to anti-gang peace activist? We must read his book and understand the context of desperation, deception, and poverty that contributes to the gang violence we seek to eradicate. This is not to excuse violence, only to understand it so that we can make appropriate changes in our schools and society. Schools and curriculum that vigorously address these issues are a part of the solution. Building more prisons and larger schools structured like prisons are a part of the problem. Just as the US war and occupation in Iraq actually inflamed more violence, created more terrorists, and did nothing to make the US safer, the continued emphasis on surveillance, accountability tests, scientific management, fortress-like school buildings, and prison mentality in classrooms will produce more alienation, school drop-outs, deprofessionalized and demoralized teachers, and disaffected students joining gangs in society. The very thing that we think will make us safer actually exacerbates the problem. Read Tookie Williams' book to find out more.

I would be remiss if I did not conclude this section on prisons and gangs with some comments about capital punishment and racism. I have been an opponent of the death penalty for my entire life. This does not mean I am soft on crime. I absolutely endorse firm punishment for crime and life in prison without parole for first degree murder— possibly a much harsher punishment than death. We will not stop cycles of killing with more killing. I recently had the opportunity to participate in a forum for the film *An American Life: The Journey from Violence to Hope* (www.qofj.com). This film follows the lives of four men. David Kaczynski turned in his brother, the Unabomber, to the authorities; Gary Wright, the eleventh target of the Unabomber, survived to face his perpetrator in the courtroom; Bill Babbitt sacrificed his younger brother's life for the greater good; and Bud Welch claimed his daughter's body from the rubble of the Oklahoma City bombing. What brings these men together is a story about overcoming tremendous personal pain and loss and embracing compassion and healing. I participate in a vigil at the governor's mansion in Austin on the evening of every execution in Texas. It always amazes me that the strongest voices to end capital punishment are family members who have lost a relative to murder. What leads some people to this position?

As a young high school teacher in south Louisiana in the 1970s, I often spoke out forcefully against state-sanctioned killing. I cited statistics on the expense of implementing the death penalty, the unbalanced application of the death penalty on racial minorities and the poor, the ability of the wealthy to buy their way out of sentencing, and the hundreds of well-documented cases of innocent people being put to death—a phenomenon that even led the Republican governor of Illinois in the late 1990s to place a moratorium on capital punishment in his state. The fact that the United States is one of the only industrialized democracies that imposes capital punishment should cause us to ponder our politics. However, support for the death penalty remains strong, though it is declining steadily as people begin to understand the barbarism of the practice. Why are vengeance, retribution, and hatred so deeply rooted in some societies?

On November 5, 1977, I was decorating the Rice Festival Building in New Iberia, Louisiana, with a group of my students in preparation for the Homecoming Dance. I was a young teacher at Catholic High School, and I very much enjoyed the extracurricular activities. One of my favorite students was David LeBlanc, a strapping young man with an infectious smile. David was in my English class, and he volunteered to help me with projects after school on numerous occasions. I had not noticed that David and his girlfriend Loretta Bourque were missing at the dance, but it was not until early the next morning that the terrible news of David and Loretta's murder was confirmed when a sheriff's deputy brought a senior ring to the school, where the principal and several teachers had gathered. This was the only identifying artifact at the crime scene, and we were asked to confirm the initials "DAL" on the ring. David Augustin LeBlanc, December 21, 1960–November 5, 1977. The senior class offered the following tribute to David in the class yearbook: "David pursued a very active life. He enjoyed his friends and loved his school. His memory lightens up our lives with the thought that we too can live as fully and purely as he did." Whenever I discuss capital punishment, I always begin by recalling the memory of David LeBlanc and Loretta Bourque and the terrible tragedy inflicted upon them, their families, and their friends by their ruthless murderers—brothers Elmo and Patrick Sonnier.

Many people will recognize the story of David and Loretta because their murder was made famous in a book, film, and opera titled *Dead Man Walking*. Susan Sarandon won the Academy Award for Best Actress in 1996 for her portrayal of Sister Helen Prejean, a Catholic nun and author of the book, who worked in Hope House for the poor in New Orleans and was inspired to visit the Sonnier brothers in Angola prison in Louisiana. I was reluctant to see this film when it came out because of my lingering pain over David and Loretta's violent murder, but I eventually took one of my classes to view it and discuss capital punishment over coffee afterwards. I was surprised by this film, for it accurately portrayed the multiplicity of complex emotions surrounding the events in Louisiana in the late 1970s. *Dead Man Walking* forces viewers to recognize the layers of emotions that contribute to our reactions to the death penalty today.

Immediately after it was known in the community that David and Loretta had been murdered, talk of retribution and violent retaliation became rampant. The White community quickly concluded that David and Loretta must have been killed by Black men, and a few began discussing a vigilante response against the Black community. I remember seeing cars of Black youth circling the funeral home in St. Martinville, Louisiana, at David's wake, apparently aware that they were being targeted. Emotions escalated as Whites accused Blacks and Blacks taunted Whites. The pastor tried to calm the tension, even orchestrating an emotional rendition of "Let There be Peace on Earth and Let it Begin With Me" at the funeral Mass. Tears flowed in a steady stream of despair.

It was not long before the murderers were apprehended, and much to the shock of the White community—but not a surprise in the Black community—Elmo and Patrick Sonnier were young White oil-field workers high on drugs. If vigilante justice had been applied, innocent Black men would have been killed—as so often happened with lynchings in the South in previous times and as so often happens in capital punishment cases today when death is erroneously applied to innocent people. I witnessed first-hand the wave of emotions that led irrational and racist citizens to strike out in revenge. Capital punishment must end because innocent people are regularly caught up in the cycles of fear, vengeance, and racism.

The opening scene of the film *A Lesson Before Dying* should convince anyone of the unjust power structures that routinely convict innocent poor and minority people and condemn them to death. The closing scene of the play and film *The Laramie Project* should also give us pause. In this play Matthew Shepard's father asks the court to spare his son's killer in order to stop the cycles of violence. Capital punishment is one of the most important ethical issues of our time, and all educators must view these films and plays—as well as read many historical and legal texts—so that they will be prepared to lead our students and citizens to deeper understandings of appropriate justice that avoids retribution, revenge, and error. We are all diminished when we get trapped in cycles of violence and killing.

Sisiter Helen Prejean continues to speak out against capital punishment, but always with a deep compassion for victims of crime. She reminds us to reject a barbaric practice that does not deter crime, reduce violence, save money, or impart justice—but this most certainly does not equate with insensitivity for victims of crime. There are many high-profile cases of parents who insist that the death penalty not be applied to the murderers of their children, and the parents of Matthew Shepard in Wyoming are one example. These parents know that capital punishment only perpetuates cycles of violence. Rather, they argue for life sentences without the option of parole. This certainly reflects my understandings as well. Removing violent criminals and murderers from society with life sentences is an alternative available to us, and many religious leaders, such as Pope John Paul II, consistently used this argument in an attempt to persuade those countries that still use the death penalty to change their practices. We are not safer or more secure in a society that sponsors murder in any form. Bob Hebert (2002) provides the most recent studies that clarify this ethical issue:

> In the spring of 2000 a team of lawyers and criminologists at Columbia University released the first phase of the most far-reaching study of the death penalty in the United States. It showed that the system of capital punishment was riddled with unfairness and incompetence, with serious errors erupting with alarming frequency at every stage of the process. The study showed that of every three capital sentences reviewed, two were overturned on appeal. Those were cases in which at least some of the mistakes were caught. No one knows what percentage of the remaining cases were tainted. Today [February 11, 2002] the team is releasing a massive second phase of the study, which focuses on why there are so many mistakes in death penalty cases, and what can be done about them. The study [directed by law professor James S. Liebman] describes the capital punishment system as "broken." (2002, p. A29)

Read this chilling report and ask yourself how a civilized democracy can continue to allow such a barbaric practice and why the United States is willing to accept a high level of error that routinely executes innocent people. Then listen to the supporters of the death penalty, and we think that you will agree that they are driven by retribution, fear, and hatred.

If you have not read Mark Twain's *War Prayer*, please do so. It is a stunning rejection of both warmongering and the ushering off to war of young men to massacre the enemy in the name of a compassionate God. Twain was outraged that the US government—particularly Theodore Roosevelt—would be willing to sacrifice the lives hundreds of thousands of Muslim men, women, and children in the Philippines in order to protect US business interests. He condemned the many ministers who used their pulpits to blindly support a war against the "evildoers" of the time. Although Twain was labeled unpatriotic in 1906 by legislators, ministers, and citizens for his anti-war *War Prayer*, I suggest that he was honoring a prophetic responsibility for justice.

Following thematically from this discussion of race and retribution, the scholarship on gender in curriculum studies in the postmodern era is more than an analysis of the role of schoolmarms in the 19th century, the impact of the women's suffrage and gay rights movements on schooling, sex-role differentiation in classrooms, gender bias in textbooks, sex education programs, and health clinics on campuses. While these issues are very important and worthy of continued study, gender issues in the curriculum, like racial issues introduced above, are primarily about ways of knowing, the embodiment of social and textual relationships, male and female identity, empowerment, and conceptions of the self. Madeleine Grumet, as we discussed in chapter 4, addresses these issues in *Bitter Milk: Women and Teaching*. Grumet (1988b) introduces her book as follows:

> In Sri Lanka, young women sometimes experience psychotic responses to adolescence as they struggle with the ambivalence provoked by the separation from families. In *Medusa's Hair* the anthropologist Gananath Obeyesekere tells us that these periods of distress are called "dark night of the soul" experiences. He describes a ritual tonic that the afflicted girls drink to release them from their trouble. It is called bitter milk and is a mixture of milk and crushed margosa leaves, the same bitter portion that mothers apply to their nipples when they wish to wean their babies. Bitter milk, fluid of contradictions: love and rejection, sustenance and abstinence, nurturance and denial. ... I have written this book to explore these contradictions. ... I am attempting to understand what teaching means to women. Women constitute the majority of all public school instructional personnel; nevertheless, our experience of this work is hidden. ... It is hidden from our students, our colleagues, and even from ourselves. Its absence is not a mere oversight. Nor is it that we have been so busy doing it that we haven't taken the time to think about it. There is something about the task itself, the way it wedges itself into our lives, the way we place it somewhere between our work and our labor, our friendships and our families, our ambition and our self-abnegation, that has prohibited our speaking of it. Sometimes it seems to me that it is everything that could possibly matter to us, ... the fundamental argument of this text is that knowledge evolves in human relationships. (pp. xi–xix)

The conception of the self as student, teacher, parent, or scholar emerges, for Grumet, from the knowledge that evolves, especially for women educators, in "bitter wisdom of this sweet work" (p. xx). Curriculum development in the postmodern era engages women, men, Hispanics, African Americans, European Americans, North American First Nations, gays, lesbians, heterosexuals, transsexuals, and every person of diverse heritage, religion, identity, and culture in the dialogue about knowledge, relationships, and the self. And, with Grumet, this knowledge is seen as evolving within human relationships.

Particular emphasis is given to different ways of knowing and learning by scholars concerned about race and gender issues. Even legal and bureaucratic structures are acknowledging the diversity of ways of learning with recent enforcement of Section 504 laws, bilingual programs, and educational inclusion regulations. Many curriculum scholars have also explored ways of knowing and learning, and a text that articulates this theme especially well is *Women's Ways of Knowing: The Development of Self, Voice, and Mind*, by Mary Belenky, Blythe Clinchy, Nancy Goldberger, and Jill Tarule. Case studies, narratives, and interviews are described throughout the book, and chapter 9, entitled "Toward an Education for Women," begins with two poignant stories about women who were in their first year of undergraduate studies. The first story is about a woman in an introductory science class:

> The professor marched into the lecture hall, and placed upon his desk a large jar filled with dried beans, and invited the students to guess how many beans the jar contained. After listening to an enthusiastic chorus of wildly inaccurate estimates, the professor smiled a thin, dry smile, revealed the correct answer, and announced, "You have just learned an important lesson about science. Never trust the evidence of your own senses." (Belenky et al., 1986, p. 191)

The authors report that this student's sense of herself as a knower was shaky, and it was based on the belief that she could use her own firsthand experience as a source of truth. However, this professor took away her only tool for knowing. The woman dropped the course immediately.

The second story is about a woman in an introductory philosophy course where the professor came into the class carrying a large cardboard cube and asked the class what it was. The students said a cube. The professor then asked the class to describe a cube, and they said that a cube had six equal square sides. Finally, the professor asked how they knew the object had six equal square sides when they could not see all sides of the cube, and then responded:

> We can't look at all six sides of a cube at once, can we? So we can't exactly see a cube. And yet, you're right. You know it's a cube. But you know it not just because you have eyes but because you have intelligence. You invent the sides you cannot see. You use your intelligence to create the "truth" about cubes. (p. 192)

The student then explained her reaction to this classroom encounter:

> It blew my mind. You'll think I'm nuts, but I ran back to the dorm and I called my boyfriend and I said, "Listen, this is just incredible," and I told him all about it. I'm not sure he could see why I was so excited. I'm not sure I understand it myself. But I really felt, for the first time, like I was really in college, like I was sort of *grown up*. (p. 192, emphasis in original)

The authors contend that both stories are about the limitations of firsthand experience as a source of knowledge—the truth about either the jar of beans or the cube:

> The lesson the science professor wanted to teach is that experience is a source of error. Taught in isolation, this lesson diminishes the student, rendering her dumb and dependent. The philosophy teacher's lesson was that although raw experience is insufficient, by reflecting on it the students could arrive at truth. It was a lesson that made the students feel more powerful ("sort of grown up"). (p. 193)

Belenky, Clinchy, Goldberger, and Tarule use these and similar stories to confirm the self as knower and thus empower students, especially women, whose intuitive and perceptive sense of the truth has been ignored in schooling, to develop their voice, their mind, and their affirmation of self. This is the same philosophy advanced by many scholars studying not only women but also students of color (Scheurich & Young, 1997; Bernal, 2002; Sleeter & Bernal, 2004).

As Belenky, Noddings, and other feminist scholars remind us, the postmodern curriculum is moving beyond inane attempts to cast racial, gendered, and cultural issues simply in terms of tolerance and representation of minorities and historically excluded groups. Cultural literacy programs designed to assimilate all students into a great American melting-pot culture are being challenged for their innate biases, which perpetuate explosive structures of dominance and control. Curriculum is about empowerment and liberation. In this sense, racial, gender, and cultural dimensions of the postmodern curriculum are also concerned with the politics of power (Apple, 1982, 1985, 2004; Roman & Apple, 1990; Aronowitz, 1992; Giroux, 1992; Sleeter & Bernal, 2004), which we will explore in more detail in chapter 9. Patricia Hill Collins (1990) recognizes that race, gender, and class are interlocking categories that must be reconceptualized and transcended to create new categories of connection. She describes Black feminist thought as a process of self-conscious struggle to empower women and men to create a humanist community vision. Curriculum theorists such as Peter McLaren (1993, 1997), Louis Castenell and William Pinar (1993), Madeleine Grumet (1988c), and Camron McCarthy (1990, 1993; McCarthy & Apple, 1988) (among others) have cautioned, however, that these issues, particularly race, must not be subsumed under political scholarship.

Grumet adamantly resists limiting her curriculum scholarship to the domain of gender analysis. She insists that it is also phenomenological, autobiographical, aesthetic, and much more. The tendency to divide curriculum development into various competing discourses vying for ascendancy is counterproductive and the antithesis of postmodern thinking. Grumet (1988c) writes: "Feminist scholars work to bring together domains of experience and understanding that history and culture have kept apart. For what it means to teach and learn is related to what it means to be male or female and to our experience of reproduction and nurturance, domesticity, sexuality, nature, knowledge and politics" (p. 538). Although I share her sentiment, the arbitrary categorization of the postmodern discourses in this book could be challenged by feminist and race scholars as a contradiction of Grumet's premise. However, I hope that the fluidity of curriculum discourses is evident throughout all of the chapters in part II, thus minimizing rigid categorization of individual authors or texts.

Another contemporary feminist curriculum theorist is Janet L. Miller. Miller began to make links between feminist theory and those curricularists who privileged autobiography and the study of the individual's educational experience in the 1970s. Following a feminist critique of patriarchal modes dominant at that time in the curriculum field, she argued for an integration of emotion and intellect as well as an examination of the curricular forms that distort and deny women's educational experience. Miller (1992) writes that equity is not enough. Feminist theory requires that one change the very character of educational institutions, the academic disciplines, and the curricular representations of academe. In her work, Miller (1980, 1987, 2005) excavated the unconscious ways she and other female teachers internalized patriarchal assumptions about who they were as women and teachers, and she established a linkage between women curriculum theorists and philosophers of education such as Maxine Greene.

Following from the example of Janet Miller's feminist autobiographical scholarship, the diversity of race, gender, sexuality, culture, and ethnicity in the schools today is seen by postmodern scholars as an opportunity for all students to learn from each other not only about differences but also about the self. Camron McCarthy (1990) utilizes the concept of *nonsynchrony* in curriculum development to highlight this point, arguing that the strength of the curriculum comes from its inclusiveness and diversity rather than from its uniformity and cultural homogeneity. McCarthy and Apple (1988) write: "The issues of culture and identity must be seriously incorporated into a nonsynchronous approach to racial domination in schooling" (p. 276). McCarthy (1993) identifies three approaches for dealing with racial inequality in schooling:

> Proponents of cultural understanding advocate sensitivity and appreciation of cultural differences—a model for racial harmony. Cultural competence proponents insist on the preservation of minority ethnic identity and language and "the building of bridges" between minority and mainstream culture. Finally, models of cultural emancipation go somewhat further than the previous two approaches in suggesting that a reformist multicultural curriculum can boost the school success and economic futures of minority youth. (p. 242)

While McCarthy investigates race from the perspective of the curriculum, philosopher Cornel West (1988, 1990, 2001) perhaps best summarizes the postmodern questions of race and society when he writes: "Black cultural workers must constitute and sustain discursive formations and institutional networks that deconstruct earlier Black strategies for identity formation, demystify power relations that incorporate class, patriarchal, and homophobic biases, and construct more multivalent and multidimensional responses that articulate the complexity and diversity of Black practices in the modern and postmodern world" (1990, p. 105). West and McCarthy represent those scholars who are leading the discussion of race in the postmodern era to another level of understanding that includes identity, complexity, and diversity.

Curriculum development programs in the past have tended to ignore issues of race, gender, and ethnicity because curriculum was seen as something that reflected an objectively knowable structure that existed "out there," independent of race and gender, and simply waiting to be discovered and memorized by students. Anthony Whitson challenges this assumption with his concept of "heteroglossia" in the curriculum, the inclusion of multifaceted and conflicting voices. Whitson (1988b) explains:

> Partial discourses [that deny the political reality of diverse policies and practices in the curriculum] operate by representing education as a monological process, [thus] denying the educational importance of the principle Bakhtin refers to as "heteroglossia": the principal of dialogical otherness intrinsic in all social language use, including effective pedagogical communication. One implication of heteroglossia is that a political struggle among social dialects and voices is to be found at the heart of any single utterance, animating the contextualized meaning of that utterance, and supporting the linguistic competence that speakers must command in order to participate in social life. From this perspective, it is absolutely essential that the public school curriculum *must* include the mutually discordant voices and accents of diverse race, class, and gender elements of our society. (p. 281)

Whitson (1991) also seeks to break free from the reproduction of the status quo to a more open and free society in which students learn to navigate through more than one discourse in an effort to communicate and make decisions. He argues that students must investigate confrontational ideas outside their prior knowledge and experience—especially in the realm of race and gender—in order to develop social competence. Through this confrontation, students alter conceptions of the self and society. Whitson advocates entering "otherness" to establish authentic dialogue and new understanding. He takes the cultural literacy debates beyond the mainstream inculcation models represented by E. D. Hirsch, Jr. (1987).

The postmodern aversion to master narratives, cultural literacy programs, disembodied learning, homogenized curriculum guides, and disconnected objective goals is evident in the curriculum discourses surrounding race, gender, and ethnicity. Additionally, multicultural issues have often been ignored in modern schooling practices because they are controversial and contentious. Any serious examination of race, gender, and ethnicity causes bureaucrats and technocrats to be fearful of what turmoil might erupt if these issues are addressed openly. There is a pervasive distrust of the capacity of individuals to engage in dialogue in a democratic milieu for the purpose of achieving greater understanding. Therefore, schooling has reflected the societal preference of suppressing what seems to be either irrelevant or controversial in the curriculum. Curriculum development in the postmodern era is exposing the disastrous consequences on the human psyche of this modern notion of curriculum as racially, gender, and culturally neutral, and it is bringing these discourses to the forefront of conscious reflection in scholarship and schooling.

In chapter 5 we introduced the concept of postmodern hermeneutics as a community circle of interpretation and understanding for the purpose of affirming a meaningful lived experience. In this chapter, we now see that curriculum scholarship insists that the hermeneutic circle is impossible outside the context of race, gender, sexual identity, culture, and ethnicity. The opposition to multicultural voices in modern society is pervasive. This has led some to conclude that radical separatist movements are the only viable alternative. Others continue to work within existing structures to expose the bankruptcy of modern hierarchical bureaucracies that have traditionally excluded women, gays, lesbians, Hispanics and Latinos, Native Americans, Asians, African Americans, people of color, the hearing impaired, the physically challenged, religious sects, and any number of other individuals from the dominant power positions in American society. Peter Maas Taubman (1993b), following Michel Foucault (1990a, 1990b) and foreshadowing queer theory, which we reviewed above (Thurer, 2005), suggests three strategic possibilities for bringing about the transformation of the dominant sexual grid: a detotalization and deconstruction of sexuality, a temporary reclaiming of the fixtures of "women," "lesbian," and "homosexual" for political purposes, and a radical nominalism that views sexual categories as abstract concepts with no objective reference or universal meaning. Taubman's work initiated poststructural investigations of gender issues in curriculum studies.

No matter what method of critique or investigation is selected by gender-focused and multicultural scholars, one thing is abundantly clear in their writing: the postmodern curriculum will no longer ignore race and gender and no longer accept minimal gratuitous tolerance and tokenism as a solution. The deconstruction of traditional master narratives related to race, gender, identity, and ethnicity and the emergence of autobiographical, phenomenological, and poststructural analyses are integral to postmodern curriculum scholarship. Chapter 7 will explore the philosophical foundations for such a move.

Multicultural debates recognize that people look at the world through different lenses (Scheurich & Young, 1997). Our metaphysics, coupled with the social milieu in which we live, influences the creation of our worldview and our sense of self. We are also influenced by cultural norms and social constructions of others, both consciously and unconsciously. The story of a recent cross-country move by friends who were relocating to Louisiana from Arizona provides an example of this social construction. The couple asked me to secure a rental house for them prior to their summer arrival. A house on my street was available, so I made the deposit and necessary arrangements. The family arrived in Louisiana exhausted, U-Haul trailer in tow. I gave them a tour of their new house, and then we began to unload the trailer. The couple noted the extreme difference in climate between the dry desert landscape of Arizona and the tropical humidity and lush vegetation of south Louisiana. Particularly, they noted that the yard was in need of immediate attention. Not having a lawnmower and lawn-care equipment, my friend (who is White) walked to the house next door, where a bare-chested Black man, sweating profusely, was cutting the grass. Before I could make introductions, my friend asked the gentleman how much he charged for cutting the grass. The man mowing the lawn smiled and said, "Nothing, I live here."

Prior to their arrival in Louisiana, I had failed to mention to my friends the ethnic composition of the neighborhood. Not having had much contact with African Americans in his previous Arizona community, my friend unconsciously projected a culturally conditioned bias in this new context and assumed that this Black man must be a hired laborer. My friend is a teacher who openly professes a strong commitment to social justice and religious values. However, even his personal commitment to egalitarian values was not sufficient to help him deconstruct and understand the social context of his new neighborhood and recognize his sedimented perceptors. This scenario is repeated in classrooms and other social institutions all the time, and it demonstrates the urgency of addressing the complexity of race, gender, and sexual identity issues in curriculum studies, especially from the perspective of the social construction of reality and the politics of identity formation. As we have noted throughout this chapter, there is an abundance of excellent literature emerging in this sector of the curriculum field.

Ground-breaking research is being done in schools and classrooms that examines the impact of race and racialized dynamics of curriculum on teachers' perceptions and practices and students' well-being and achievement (Lewis, 2004; Pollock 2004; Parrott, 2006). Scholars have really just begun to seriously question and explicitly probe what seems to be our public schools' consistent inability to serve poor, minority students, resulting in striking inequities in all measures of achievement, access to quality schools, highly qualified teachers, and access to opportunity after graduation. Research that probes the impact of race on teachers and students and uncovers how our public school system is actively contributing to the privileging of some and the marginalization of others (through policy, curriculum, and daily classroom interaction) is critical if we are ever to realize our claims of providing a quality public education for all children. Skrla and Scheurich (2004) write: "The apparent inability of our public school system to be as successful with children of color, particularly with those from low income families, as it is with middle class White children is a direct threat to our claims to be a truly democratic society" (p.14).

If the curriculum ignores sedimented perceptors, identity formation, and social construction, and if it suppresses individual visions and dreams in the content and context of education, and if individuals are constantly required to conform to someone else's worldview, then dreams will be repressed, hope will be suppressed, people will incorporate the other's vision of themselves into their own self-understanding, and/or they will lash out in anger against those systems that exclude their voice. The latter things are occurring today as splinter groups vie for dominance and control. Riotous gangs, manipulative cults, separatist organizations, fascist political movements, conservative retrenchment, fundamentalism, subversive violent activism, and reactionary ideology all share one thing in common: fear and anger. As we have examined throughout this chapter, the postmodern curriculum attempts to deconstruct modern society in order to expose the futility of this fear and anger. It is important to note that postmodern deconstructionism is intent not on destruction but rather on the explication of the internal contradictions of the metanarratives that have led to racial, ethnic, identity, and gender bias and the accompanying global conflagration and degradation that have threatened to annihilate humanity.

The absurdities of modernity, especially in the 20th century, are regularly incorporated into the curriculum scholarship of the postmodern era, not in order to perpetuate paralysis and hatred but to constantly remind us of the consequences of racism, sexism, homophobia, and cultural elitism. This list of places must shake our conscience: we must remember Auschwitz, My Lai, Salem, Sarajevo, Rwanda, Sudan, East Timor, Cambodia, Little Rock, Hiroshima, Laramie, Birmingham, New York, Baghdad, Abu Ghraib, Bhopal, Bosnia, Jasper, Greenwich Village, and Los Angeles. It is important to read this litany and reflect on the enormity of the problem.

Racial and gender studies are not intent on further reducing human persons into the shell of the "minimal self," a term popularized by Christopher Lasch (1984). Lasch exposes the bankruptcy of modernity and the effect of devastation of modern concepts of the self on the human psyche. Rather, race and gender studies are the vehicles for exposing the impotence of traditional curriculum development in the face of the tragedies of contemporary global society. No serious curriculum scholar in the postmodern era can ignore these issues, despite efforts by many to do so.

Of course, before scholars explore the issues surrounding race, gender, and ethnicity in curriculum scholarship, it is important to note that there is not consensus on the approach that should be taken to address these issues in postmodern schooling. For example, Canadians H. Ed Thompson and Ken Baldson (1993) have written that they are feminists by virtue of the fact that they support feminine values in educational scholarship and androgynous relationships for both men and women. The feminine is not limited by genitalia, but rather androgyny is an integral dimension of the human person. Others will disagree, arguing that the feminine, while incorporating a diversity of values and perspectives available to both men and women, can be fully experienced and understood only by women. Some feminist separatists demand such gender stratification.

An analogy that I often use for my graduate students may be instructive. The analogy centers on the idea of black and white from two different perspectives: physics and pigment. In physics, black is the absence of all light and the absence of all color, as in the void of total darkness. On the other hand, white light is the fullness of the entire spectrum of color, as in the refraction of white light entering a prism to form a rainbow. In pigment, black and white take on the opposite values. Black is the fullness of all colors mixed together, while white is the absence of all color. Thus, depending on the context, black and white may represent similar or opposite perspectives. Especially it is important to note that black and white are dependent on each other for their very definition and existence—another example of the problematic nature of dualisms and bifurcations.

I use this analogy to suggest that objectifying and condemning persons based on color is not only immoral but also illogical. The objectification of *blackness* or *redness* or *yellowness* or *whiteness*, and by extrapolation *masculinity* and *femininity*, as we saw above, results from socially constructed norms. There are numerous historical examples of the absurdity of our socially constructed racial and gender values. In the state of Louisiana a birth certificate was required to list a child as "Negro" if he or she had as little as one thirty-second non-Caucasian, African ancestry. This practice was not challenged until the 1970s (Diamond & Cottrol, 1983). Another law—called *commorientes*—which was not repealed until 1985, established inheritance procedures which assumed that, if both a husband and a wife were killed in an accident simultaneously, the female would have expired first and the stronger male would have survived longer. Inheritance disputes were settled based on this assumption. Another example involving race was widely reported in March of 1994, when a high school principal in Alabama threatened to cancel the prom when he heard that a Black student and a White student planned to attend the dance as a couple. The principal's ban on interracial dating caused an avalanche of both protest and support. Pertinent here is the comment of one student, who asked, "Who am I to date, since I am biracial, with a White mother and a Black father?" The principal, she reported, chastised her parents for making a mistake, noting that she was evidence of the damaging result of tolerance of interracial dating. The principal has a history of controversial positions, and this case continues to draw national attention. There is some opposition to interracial dating from African-American leaders as well. Khallid Muhammad (1994) warns Black men: "You want to wear your X hat, but you want to have a white girl on your arm. ... Now don't get me wrong. A White girl is alright for a White boy, but I'm talking about rebuilding the Black family" (p. 2). Racial purity has proponents among extremists and bigots in all ethnic groups.

Historically, European Americans and African Americans are two sides of the same cultural coin, two interrelated narratives in the American story, two interrelated elements of the American identity. Projected as "other" and repressed, African Americans' presence in the American self has been explored by Frantz Fanon (1967, 1970). Like James Baldwin (1971) and others, Fanon understood that *white* is a fabrication made possible by the construction of the concept *black*. For Fanon, there can be no *black* without *white*, and vice versa. One cannot understand the identity of one without the other. The sequestered suburban white student is thus uninformed without understanding that he or she is also—in the historical, cultural, and psychological sense—African American. Because *white* does not exist apart from *black*, the two coexist and intermingle, and the repression of this knowledge deforms us all. All Americans can be understood as racialized beings; knowledge of who we have been, who we are, and who we will become. In this sense, the postmodern curriculum—our construction and reconstruction of this knowledge for conversation with the young—is a racial experience (Castenell & Pinar, 1993; Gallager, 2000). Gallager (2000) contends that, while attitudes about racialized others should be part of our understanding of White racial identity, it is overly constricting to construct an identity based solely on those external attitudes. Unfortunately, traditional White racial identity models do not allow Whiteness to be understood in ways other than being in opposition to non-Whites. Put another way, "neglecting the experiences of African-American [and others] people in our curriculum is not only detrimental to African-American children, it is also a great source of the miseducation of other children who continue to be poorly prepared for a multicultural world" (Boateng, 1990, p. 77).

An examination of the ways that cultures deal with contradiction is illustrative. In Western philosophy there is a history of difficulty with oppositional aspects of reality: male and female, body and soul, thinking and feeling, light and dark, good and evil, machine and living organism, Black and White. Oliver and Gershman (1989) contend that we employ two intellectual and practical techniques for dealing with these contradictions. The first is domination and/or destruction. We attempt to control or eliminate the oppositional pole of the bifurcation. The second strategy is dialectic. We attempt to transform both poles of a contradictory set of metaphors into a higher level of under-standing. Thesis and antithesis are debated until a higher level of synthesis emerges as the departure point of a further dialectic seeking the perfect society or ultimate truth. Eastern philosophies, especially as seen in the yin and the yang, offer another alterna-tive, where opposites are seen as complementary sets within a single entity. Oliver and Gershman (1989) explain: "There is maleness within femaleness and vice versa; males and females also comprise an organic unity; in essence all being is both mystical unity (or 'in' a unity) as well as differentiated form" (p. 148). Unfortunately, the result is that those who view the world as a multiplicity of antagonistic and dangerous dualisms and opposites see domination, destruction, and endless dialectic as the only solution.

This dualistic mentality sent the US government headstrong into Iraq in 2003 with-out carefully considering legitimate alternatives to a war of choice that, according to most informed scholars and analysts in 2006, was promoted with misleading, inac-curate, and possibly falsified intelligence; initiated with poor planning, too few troops, and inadequate supplies; and executed in a manner that inflamed Muslims and caused unexpected insurgency. The US leaders should have paused and listened to the largest global protest in history in March of 2003, but President George W. Bush insisted on defining the world in his terms of neatly compartmentalized competing forces of good and evil. This is not to deny or minimize the horrific crimes of Saddam Hussein. Rather, scholars now know the mistakes that were made in the process of seeking to remove an evil dictator. And one of those mistakes, in my view, was relying on an inappropriate philosophy of dualisms that pervades modern thinking.

I believe that, in the context of our discussion of racism, we also need to ask why the US refused to intervene to stop ethnic cleansing and the slaughter of millions of people in Bosnia (under the watch of George H. W. Bush), Rwanda (under the watch of Bill Clinton), and Sudan (under the watch of George W. Bush), and why the US, from Ronald Reagan's presidency to the present, has allowed HIV/AIDS to ravage African nations without aggressive intervention. Comments about concern for atroci-ties in Iraq ring hollow when Africa is ignored in our foreign policy. What are the racist implications of US foreign policy? Postmodern curriculum studies investigate these issues carefully and ask difficult questions. As noted above, we view the world as complementary and organic, and thus the destructive nature of modernity must be overcome if we are going to appropriately address ethnic cleansing, pandemic disease, and ruthless dictators in the postmodern era. We must learn from our mistakes in Iraq, Bosnia, Rwanda, and Sudan—and in justice we must continue to rebuild and restore these nations.

The examples presented above demonstrate that we must be attentive to political policy in the curriculum, which we will examine more closely in chapter 9. We must also be alert to the socially constructed norms and values that must be deconstructed, a practice integral to postmodern philosophy. Shifting back to our discussion of race—although the comments above are integrally related to gender and ethnicity as well—southern literature, especially in the novels of William Faulkner, reminds us that the blood of many races—especially Native American, Black, and White—courses through the veins of all southerners. While the mixed bloodlines of the South may be denied and repressed in order to support the myth of an elite aristocracy and perpetuate unequal power relations and economic slavery, the presence of the "other" in the bloodlines of southerners is indisputable.

Another similar analogy is used by Carl Sagan, who has often written that there are a finite number of hydrogen and oxygen atoms in our ecosphere. These same atoms have formed and re-formed water molecules throughout history. Since the human body is composed primarily of water molecules, all of which are continuously recycled to create new rivers, oceans, plants, animals, and human beings, we are literally created from the same atoms of "the other." While this analogy may be helpful, postmodernists caution that race, gender, and sexual identity must not be reduced to biological or genetic analysis because these categories are socially constructed. In the worst-case scenario, parents or government could identify a "gay gene" so that homosexual babies could be aborted, or a "corrective gene" to make Black babies light skinned or women more submissive—or whatever normative behavior or look is desired. Designer children may be just a test tube away. Hitler's racial science with cranial measurement is an obvious example of the abuses that can result from hereditarian ideologies (Goldhagen, 1996). There continue to be debates about race and heredity in educational literature. Ornstein and Levine (1993, p. 380) present a concise summary of this research. The publication of *The Bell Curve*, by Richard Herrnstein and Charles Murray (1994), should remind us that biological determinism continues to influence many people.

An additional example from a poststructural perspective will expand on this concept. (Poststructuralism as a postmodern philosophy is introduced here and will be discussed in more detail in the next chapter.) The assumption of modern rationalism is often that *black* and *white* refer to antecedent biological or genetic conditions and express essential qualities. They derive meaning from an invariant transhistorical system that is glued together by the binary opposition of *black* and *white* (Pinar et al., 1995). Postmodernists reject the transhistorical assumptions of black and white, and poststructuralists expand the critique to argue that the meaning of black or white is discursively created. Poststructuralism seeks understanding of how "blackness" and other racialized categories are constructed in particular discourses and how those discourses are selected, organized, and inscribed in a particular society.

William Pinar et al. (1995) explain the poststructural reaction to these appeals to unities, totalities, origins, and metanarratives as a discursive strategy used to legitimate and disguise the exercise of power:

> At its most general level, poststructuralism attacks not only essentialism, universalism, transcendentalism, and humanism, but the very idea of a Western logos as well. It mounts this attack at the level of discourse where it works to reveal and resist the oppression of specific discursive practices, such as discourses on sexuality and race. Dispersion and multiplicity replace unity and totality. Or, to put the matter another way, the assumed truth of constructions is deconstructed. One does not ask, for instance, what is the Good, the True, the Beautiful, or, what is "woman," the "self," or what is "homosexual"? Instead, one investigates the various discourses which create each of these by articulating them as somehow essential and universal truths. We can see emerging in this attack an "enemy" whose identity becomes explicit [in] the work of

deconstruction, associated with the name Jacques Derrida. That "enemy" is Western thought itself, and the primacy given to "reason" as a way of grasping reality and truth. (p. 370)

Pinar and his colleagues succinctly explain the poststructural objections to reason, totality, and metanarratives. They continue by showing how Derrida would challenge the privileged position of reason itself. Poststructuralism, then, attempts to map discursively how the idea of truth as a grasp on things must necessarily have a nonmetaphorical sense and how the "nonmetaphorical" and the "other" are constructed by the intersection of discursive and nondiscursive practices. Ultimately, postmodern curriculum discourses, particularly those rooted in poststructuralism, seek to deconstruct modern constructions of race, gender, identity, and ethnicity based on Enlightenment notions of reason and to expose the ways that this construction perpetuates unjust power relations and violence against minority people.

I have found over the years that these poststructural insights, as well as the analogies presented above, infuriate many students. These analogies shatter the stereotype of the self as genetically pure, biologically unadulterated, culturally unified, and totally separated from the "other," especially the racially, sexually, gendered, or culturally different and dangerous other. In my analogies, however, I also present the position of postmodern scholars, especially David Ray Griffin, that, although we all share in a common humanity with common molecular heritage, the uniqueness of the individual cannot be minimized. Constructive postmodernism, as we saw in chapter 1, recognizes that the strength of the whole is derived from a respect for the contribution of each individual, a contribution that is preserved only if the entire edifice of life is understood as an integrated and interdependent whole. In this sense, curriculum development in the postmodern era from both the poststructural and the constructive perspective insists that racism, patriarchal structures, sexism, heterosexism, and cultural elitism must be exposed and challenged. Additionally, it is recognized that Cartesian dualisms and the denial of the interconnectedness of experiences actually undermine personal and global survival.

The effort to include cultural theory and multiculturalism in the curriculum has often been understood as a postmodernist project. In this regard, Bridges (1991) writes, "What troubles us [conservatives] about multiculturalism is its inevitable association with the agenda of postmodernism" (p. 3). For Bridges, postmodernism represents a threat to cultural values and norms enshrined in the modernist canon. He discusses the rhetorical tradition in Western thought that there are at least two sides to every question, and that any question is best understood by one who can argue both sides with equal effectiveness. The goal then of inquiry, understood rhetorically, is not objective truth but reasonable belief, the state of being persuaded. This led in the 17th century to an embrace of the logic of Cartesian dualism, giving rise to the natural sciences. Bridges writes that the Enlightenment project started a rejection of rhetorical conceptions of reason and knowledge. Thus, it should not be surprising that multiculturalism, queer theory, critical race theory, and cultural studies have created controversy, especially among radical conservatives, who see their task as defense of the Enlightenment project of reason and order or rhetorical conceptions of knowledge.

The emerging curricular concerns about gender equity, human sexuality education, racial and ethnic bias in hiring practices and classroom instruction, sexual orientation, minority representation, multicultural literature, cultural and civic literacy, and a litany of other volatile issues remind us of the importance of integrating race, gender, identity, and ethnicity into the fabric of our understanding of curriculum development. As this chapter has reminded us, all these issues must ultimately focus on the autobiographical expression of the self-in-relation and the cultural context of the postmodern society.

In summary, curriculum development in the postmodern era respects and celebrates the uniqueness of each individual person, text, event, culture, and educative moment, but all within the context of an interdependent cosmological view. All occasions are important and dynamic parts of the fabric of the whole. By ignoring race, gender, sexual identity, and ethnicity as integral to education, modern curriculum development models have actually contributed to the frustration, anger, and violence that threaten to destroy civilization. The analogies and poststructural insights above should help to reinforce the critical importance of racial, gendered, and cultural curriculum discourses in the postmodern era. My frustration about the slow pace of change mentioned in the opening lines of this chapter is tempered when I read the work of scholars, poets, activists, theologians, film makers, and teachers who are making a difference on these issues every day. Students of curriculum development must explore education from these perspectives in order to understand the complexities of our postmodern world. There is a growing body of curriculum research emerging from scholars sensitive to the postmodern understandings of race, gender, sexual identity, and ethnicity as introduced in this chapter, and this literature will continue to be central to efforts to understand curriculum development. This has been a long and challenging chapter to write, and I believe that I have only scratched the surface of these issues. There is so much more to say and do.

seven
Postmodern Philosophies in Curriculum Studies

All educators at one time or another in their pre-service training or graduate degree program have studied philosophy of education. Many teachers dread taking these philosophy courses, often for good reasons. In some cases, philosophy of education is presented as a sacred depository of incontestable ideas and relics of some distant and golden age of human thinking. These timeless truths and values may be understood as latent in a student's mind, waiting to be brought to consciousness, as idealists believe. On the other hand, truth may be uncovered by studying objects in the natural world using the scientific method, as realists believe. However, in both cases, since perennial truths and values are beyond reproach, they often become inert ideas or scientific facts to be memorized rather than tentative and contextualized discourses to be evaluated critically, as postmodernists believe. Additionally, the individual thinkers and writers who articulate perennial philosophies are either enshrined as icons of humanity or castigated as subversive villains intent on destroying the truth, depending on the prejudice of the professor.

Philosophy of education is all too often presented in a way that is inaccessible to students. The specialized language and jargon of many philosophical discourses are dense and obtuse. Some professors of philosophy of education are dense and obtuse as well, lacking passion, wisdom, praxis—reflection and action beyond verbalism and activism (Freire, 1970)—and *phronesis*—a personal practical knowledge that engenders social competence (Henderson and Kesson, 2004). Some pedagogical styles and methodologies are contrived and impersonal. As a result, education students often feel that philosophy is removed from their lived experience and their classroom practice. Henderson and Kesson (2004) seek to counteract these trends in *Curriculum Wisdom: Educational Decisions in Democratic Societies* by exploring seven alternatives rooted in Greek thought: *techne*, or craft reflection; *poesis*, or soulful attunement to the creative process; *praxis*, or critical inquiry; *dialogos*, or multiperspectival inquiry; *phronesis*, or practical and deliberative wisdom; *polis*, or public moral inquiry; and *theoria*, or contemplative wisdom. Taken together, these seven processes provide a lived experience for philosophy in education.

School districts often promulgate philosophy and mission statements that many teachers, parents, students, and school personnel find irrelevant or inadequate. Committees are sometimes formed to revise the philosophy of the university or school district, only to discover that their real concerns and problems are never clearly articulated and seldom addressed in practice. As a result, many educational philosophies collect dust until it is time to bring them off the shelf, almost like a religious ritual, to be presented for accreditation or evaluation. Somehow the philosophy statement magically justifies the existence and value of the curriculum and instruction programs in the institution.

As we have already seen throughout this book, many disturbing practices are justified in the name of philosophy and ideology, and we need only explore the education system in Hitler's Germany, Stalin's Russia, and Mao's China to find some obvious examples (Pinar et al., 1995). However, philosophy and ideology have also supported abuses in American education: segregation and tracking (Oakes, 1985; McNeil, 1986; Weis, 1988; Page, 1991; Anyon, 2005); racism (Stannard, 1992; Gay, 2000; Castenell & Pinar, 1993; West, 2001; Watkins, 2001); corporate manipulation (Shea et al., 1989; Spring, 1993, 2004); gender research bias (Gilligan, 1982); patriarchal structures (Lerner, 1986; Grumet, 1988b); savage economic inequalities and injustices (Daly & Cobb, 1989; Kozol, 1991, 2005); religious proselytization (Provenzo, 1990; Lugg, 2004); social control (Franklin, 1986, 1988; McLaren, 2005); and political conflict of interest and indoctrination (Apple, 2000, 2004; Giroux & McLaren, 1989; Apple & Christian-Smith, 1991; Wexler, 1992; Spring, 2004). Philosophy of education obviously cannot be a neutral bystander in the schooling debates and cultural controversies of contemporary American society.

The research cited above has created an atmosphere where the field of philosophy of education is being forced to consider new understandings of itself. While philosophy of education has enjoyed periods of respect and notoriety, particularly during the time of John Dewey in the early 20th century (Schubert, 1986), the field has been marked in recent decades by controversy and a concern for leadership (Maxcy, 1991, 1993). Part of the responsibility for the turmoil in the field of philosophy of education clearly rests on the shoulders of professors in the 1950s and 1960s, a time when the field sought legitimacy by aligning itself with departments of philosophy rather than education. In the 1950s there was a move to create separate departments of philosophy of education, history of education, and sociology of education. Professors with degrees in the "parent" disciplines of philosophy, history, and sociology were preferred to lead these programs in many universities. John Dewey and Boyd Bode, both of whom received degrees in philosophy rather than education, were models for those who sought legitimacy for the ascendancy of "pure philosophy" in philosophy of education studies.

John Dewey (1859–1952) was both philosopher and educator. His synthesis of Darwinian evolutionary theory, the scientific method, democracy, aesthetics, and the philosophy of pragmatism was the basis of his work as an educational reformer. He viewed education as a process of experience and social activity, and the school was intimately related to this process in the society it served. Dewey actually taught philosophy at several universities after receiving his doctoral degree in philosophy from Johns Hopkins University in 1884. However, it was his work as the director of the

University of Chicago Laboratory School from 1896 to 1904 and his leadership of the combined departments of philosophy, psychology, and pedagogy there that integrated his philosophical and educational interests. Dewey's pragmatic educational philosophy became the basis of learning activities at the laboratory school. By the time of his death in 1952 other philosophers of education considered Dewey's movement from philosophy to education to be the preferred model for all university departments of philosophy of education.

By the early 1960s, some philosophers of education argued against the notion of analytic philosophy as the primary discipline that directs the field. Philip G. Smith (1965), in *Philosophy of Education*, argued that the issues and problems in the educational field are unique, thus making it problematic to do analytic philosophy "on top of" education. Reading the journal of the Philosophy of Education Society, *Educational Theory*, and the yearbooks of the National Society of the Study of Education reveals a constant tension over this issue for the past several decades. Whereas one editor may emphasize analytic philosophy and alienate scholars closely aligned with pedagogical practice, a new editor may emphasize the application of pragmatism in schooling and offend analytic philosophers. However, this trend to promote philosophy or education was not universal. For example, the rise of a foundations of education program at the University of Illinois in the 1950s underlines the growing interest in an eclectic approach to anthropology, history, sociology, and philosophy within the field of education. The American Educational Studies Association (AESA) and its publication *Educational Studies* provide leadership for the scholarly discipline of educational foundations.

Once the theoretical split between philosophy and education occurred in many universities, it created much tension and suspicion within both departments. Philosophers of education often were not accepted in either the philosophy or the education departments, and when some professors attempted to shift allegiances back to education departments in the 1980s the division was too intense for easy reconciliation. Spencer Maxcy (1993), in *Postmodern School Leadership*, chronicles these contemporary crises, especially in educational administration, and concludes that philosophy, education, and leadership cannot be separated in postmodern schooling. He recognizes that the central issue for philosophy of education today is how to conduct research and theoretical investigations that will be viable from the perspective of the social sciences and humanities, while remaining firmly rooted in the particular concerns for postmodern leadership in schools. Maxcy acknowledges that the contentious battles over the meaning of philosophy of education in the past have had a profound impact on the field, especially as reflected in its inability to engender leadership in education. If dynamic and respected leadership is to emerge, a postmodern philosophy of education must move beyond the modern bifurcation of philosophy and education to an eclectic integration that incorporates and celebrates both.

I have attended the conferences of the PES (Philosophy of Education Society), APA (American Philosophical Association), and APPE (Association for Process Philosophy of Education). I presented formal papers at some of these conferences and attended many sessions with other professors of philosophy of education. Theoretical tension and methodological debates in the field still exist. Analytic methodologies, the logic of rationalism, decontextualized discourses, dialectical analysis, and/or the mainstream social science emphasis of empiricism still dominate the scholarship of many philosophers. Richard Rorty (1979), in *Philosophy and the Mirror of Nature*, exposes philosophy's difficulty in shifting from this analytic mode. Along with Rorty, Stephen Toulmin (1982) recognizes multiple ways of knowing and has rejected the aspiration to achieve *episteme*—true and certain knowledge. Belief, says Toulmin, is about as close as we can ever get.

One of the articulate philosophers of education on the topic of justified true belief and its implications for education is Professor Mark Ortwein of the University of Mississippi. Ortwein believes traditional approaches to epistemology in the 20th century failed to do justice to the complexities of knowledge and related cognitive states. He argues that standard theories of knowledge have focused exclusively on the properties of beliefs (e.g., the nature of a justified belief) while entirely neglecting the subjective role of persons in the act of knowing. According to Ortwein, such belief-based epistemology bears little consequence for the actual intellectual activity of persons. He argues, instead, that epistemology ought to redirect its focus on to persons. To this end, he draws upon virtue epistemology, a relatively new theoretical approach in epistemology that investigates the intellectual dispositions or virtues that dispose persons to excellent doxastic (belief-related) practices. These intellectual virtues include, among others, open-mindedness, intellectual honesty, and conscientiousness. Persons possessing such attributes, argues Ortwein, are better positioned to acquire justified belief. For this reason, he believes that schools serve an important epistemic function. He writes: "education is both an important social institution and a central player in the formation of students' epistemic practices. Virtue epistemology can (and does on some accounts) operate as a form of regulative epistemology—that is, an epistemological framework providing noetic [thinking] guidance" (Ortwein, 2012, p. 1).

In this milieu of emerging epistemological understandings, and as a result of the reconceptualization of curriculum studies, the field of curriculum theory rather than the field of philosophy of education has often taken the lead in promoting the postmodern philosophical discourses that integrate education and philosophy. Curriculum theorists deconstruct and often reject the search for *episteme* and the dominant methodologies of empiricism, the Hegelian dialectic, rationalism, and analytic philosophy. They generally draw eclectically and combinationally from one or more of the following theoretical approaches in their pedagogy and research: phenomenology, autobiography, existentialism, arts-based research, pragmatism, deconstruction, queer theory, critical race theory, poststructuralism, feminism, hermeneutics, complexity theory, and critical theory. Thus, fundamental differences have emerged between some educational philosophers and curriculum theorists.

One of the primary reasons for the ostracization of philosophers of education by philosophy departments at some universities is that education professors are generally shunned and ignored on college campuses. Consider the following comments by philosopher Bruce Wilshire (1990) of Rutgers University, in his provocative book *The Moral Collapse of the University: Professionalism, Purity, and Alienation*:

> Educators in universities seldom talk about education. Administrators talk
> about administrative problems, professors talk about problems in their special

fields of study, and those who do talk about education, professors in education departments, are generally despised and shunned. Besides, even if one does listen to this latter group, one usually hears education talked about as if it were just another special field of study, not as something that vitally concerns us all just because we are human. (p. 21)

Wilshire's indictment of education professors should be taken as a challenge rather than an insult. Many curriculum theorists have accepted this challenge to move the field of education beyond the rigid parochialism and instrumentalism Wilshire condemns. They also address another problem identified by Elliot Eisner, who contends that philosophy is often regarded as an academic distraction in programs preparing researchers in the social sciences. Eisner (1991) writes: "Philosophy is nagging, it cajoles students into asking questions about basic assumptions, it generates doubts and uncertainties, and, it is said, it keeps people from getting their work done" (p. 4). Eisner proposes that the central concepts in the social sciences— validity, truth, fact, theory, objectivity, structure—are themselves philosophical in nature. Curriculum theory incorporates the scholarship of many disciplines, especially contemporary philosophies, in order to address Wilshire's critique and Eisner's concerns and to revive the vital issues of the meaning of human life, knowledge, schooling, justice, democracy, compassion, and ecology in the postmodern era. William Pinar (2004a), in *What is Curriculum Theory?*, suggests that it may be time for colleges of education to give up the fight to continue teacher training and certification. State legislatures have gradually eliminated education as a major, except for early childhood and elementary degrees, and politicians continue to cut funding and support for colleges of education. Some universities are responding by adding programs in human development or other related fields in order to attract funding or support. However, Pinar suggests that we may have to downsize and refocus our efforts on education as a scholarly study, as Wiltshire suggests. In response to former secretary of education Rod Paige, who said that schools of education would lose their exclusive franchise over teacher preparation but would emerge stronger in the long run, Pinar (2004a) writes:

Given the anti-intellectual political condition in which we work—including the betrayal of our professional organizations—Paige might be right. If teacher certification were decoupled from coursework in education, if the "troubled marriage" between teachers and education was ended, then those who study education would do so out of intellectual interest. The field would suffer a cataclysmic contraction—education schools would become small, perhaps reorganized as small departments of education in Colleges of Arts and Sciences—but the field that survived (if one survived at all) would be an academic, intellectual field, one worthy of the name. (p. 220)

Philosophy of education in the first half of the 20th century was an important and independent genre in the study of the foundations of education. However, as its importance began to diminish by the 1960s, departments of philosophy of education were consolidated or dismantled. Philosophy of education was subsumed in many universities under departments of educational leadership, administration, or policy studies. This association has been, as we have seen above, an uneasy alliance. Especially insulting to some is the fact that philosophy of education has become either an elective or a short unit of study in foundations courses in most undergraduate and many graduate degree programs. Since the reconceptualization of curriculum studies in the 1970s, the field of curriculum theory has begun to incorporate philosophical discourses into the very fabric of the study of curriculum and instruction. It may be that curriculum theorists will provide the leadership that will help to return philosophy of education to prominence in the postmodern field of education.

The renewal of philosophical understandings of curriculum studies might offer the best hope for finally transcending the drudgery and disconnectedness of the curriculum methods courses that continue to be driven by objective lesson planning. Too many pre-service programs continue to focus exclusively on systematic planning and objective codification; the concerns of postmodern society militate against the continuance of trivial pursuit in education. Yet this is what classroom practice has been reduced to in the modern age. Postmodern philosophical understandings insist that we must deconstruct and/or transcend modernity because it has reached the apex of absurdity in schooling practices that prioritize rote memorization, reward mastery of trivial facts, and proclaim the winners of a game show like *Wheel of Fortune* or *Jeopardy* as the most intelligent.

This postmodern vision proposes that curriculum development courses that have traditionally been taught as methods for practical application or systematic implementation of the Tylerian model in the schools must be replaced by courses that emphasize curriculum theory. This is exemplified by the explosion of interest theoretical positions, including what Nicholas Burbules (1993a) calls "dialogue in teaching," Cleo Cherryholmes (1988b) and Nicholas Burbules (1993b) call "critical pragmatism," Spencer Maxcy (1993) calls "postmodern leadership," Donald Schon (1983, 1991) calls "reflection-in-action," Paulo Freire (1970, 1985, 2001) calls "praxis," William Stanley (1992) calls "curriculum for utopia," Maxine Greene (1978) calls "wide awakeness," Paulo Freire and Donaldo Macedo (1987) call "critical literacy," Jürgen Habermas (1970) calls "emancipatory knowledge," Hans-Georg Gadamer (1976) calls "fusion of horizons," William Doll (1993) calls "a transformative vision," Hannah Arendt (1958) calls "emancipatory interests," James Anthony Whitson (1991) and James Henderson and Kathleen Kesson (2004) call *"phronesis,"* Henry Giroux (1992) calls "border pedagogy," Geneva Gay (2000) calls "culturally responsive teaching," and William Schubert and William Ayers (1992) call "teacher lore," and many other approaches to incorporating philosophical dialogue into pedagogy that parallel the themes of qualitative humanistic inquiry. Courses such as curriculum development, elementary and secondary curriculum, supervision of instruction, and curriculum evaluation are now exploring the meaning and context of education from these various philosophical and theoretical perspectives. Curriculum development in the postmodern era emphasizes discourses that promote understanding of the cultural, historical, political, ecological, aesthetic, theological, and autobiographical impact of the curriculum on the human condition, social structures, and the ecosphere rather than the planning, design, implementation, and evaluation of context-free and value-neutral schooling events and inert information.

The growth of curriculum theory as a field of study in the past decade has presented a formidable challenge to philosophers of education: either engage curriculum theorists in philosophical dialogue or retreat into the security of a moribund field. The field of curriculum development itself has been called moribund in the past. Before the reconceptualization, Joseph Schwab (1970) identified the field's "flight from the practical." Six years later Dwayne Huebner (1976) declared it dead because of a lack of focus and unity. By the end of the 1970s William Pinar (1978) declared the field "arrested" and suggested that Jürgen Habermas' notion of emancipatory knowledge might stimulate movement. While there will always be a few philosophy of education courses offered in departments of educational foundations and leadership, curriculum theorists and philosophers of education are joining together to move the philosophic dialogue beyond the moribund and arrested field of the past to a new vision. In some cases the fields naturally merge because philosophers of education teach curriculum theory courses and/or curriculum theorists teach philosophy of education courses in foundations departments. There is even a slowly emerging cooperation at a few universities between philosophy and education departments. These encouraging practices indicate that a postmodern perspective, albeit controversial, is beginning to blur the distinctions between curriculum theory and philosophy of education.

It is also important to note that the field of curriculum theory, as pointed out in the introduction to this book, has many hostile and competitive factions at odds with one another: political theorists, feminists, pragmatists, queer theorists, critical race theorists, neo-Marxists, phenomenologists, multiculturalists, poststructuralists, deconstructionists, and constructive postmodernists. Critics are sometimes justified in their caution in such a climate about engaging curriculum theorists in scholarly dialogue. Additionally, curriculum theorists remain in conflict with traditionalists, perennialists, and essentialists, who have dominated much of the school reform proposals. The contentious nature of these debates also raises concerns for those seeking to incorporate curriculum theory into their curriculum development programs. However, despite efforts to silence curriculum theorists using ad hominem labels such as "politically correct" or "feminazi," there is no hope of eliminating the postmodern philosophical discourses that are integral to curriculum development in the postmodern era.

This introduction to the climate of philosophy of education is important because it will help to locate the discussion of postmodern curriculum development in the context of the contemporary field. Philosophic understanding is a central dimension of contemporary curriculum discourses, and exploring this milieu and its ever changing nature is essential for those navigating the waters of the curriculum field in these turbulent times. Curriculum development courses today that do not include these philosophic understandings of education as the foundation of their investigations deny students access to contemporary educational studies. It is irresponsible to ignore the philosophical dimension of postmodern curriculum studies today.

For example, I teach two graduate courses at Texas A&M: Curriculum Development and Philosophy of Education, both required core courses. These courses inform and complement each other.

I observe four rather distinct perspectives in conflict over the philosophical agenda of curriculum development: essentialists, who are committed to the perennial truths of

Platonic idealism or scientific realism as it is applied to the school curriculum; traditionalists, typically associated with educational foundations departments, who are committed to synoptic reviews and dispassionate analyses of philosophy of education as a field of study; curriculum theorists, typically associated with departments of curriculum and instruction, who utilize phenomenology, feminism, poststructuralism, deconstructionism, neo-Marxism, or neopragmatism to support revisionist understandings of the post-Tylerian curriculum; and, finally, those philosophers and theorists who have been able to contemplate the parochial philosophical debates, weigh the arguments, and articulate a broader vision of an emerging postmodern curriculum. The challenge is to begin the process of uncovering the layers of possibilities that exist in the study of curriculum theory that will inform and enrich our understanding of education and our experience of schooling in the postmodern era.

Two of the philosophies that are most challenging to understand, but also widely influential in curriculum studies, are poststructuralism and deconstructionism. Understanding curriculum theory from the poststructural and deconstructed perspective involves enlarging our modes of cognition (Pinar & Reynolds, 1992), engaging in methods of critique and analysis (Cherryholmes, 1988b), and analyzing contemporary culture and history (Jameson, 1991) in order to challenge and subvert the central values, organizing metaphors, and discursive strategies of modernism. In this sense, poststructuralism and deconstructionism share a common purpose with postmodernism: exposing the contradictions and fallacies embedded within the themes of Western thought and Enlightenment rationality. However, the purpose, as we saw in the introduction, is not destruction. Jacques Derrida explains:

> I was quite explicit about the fact that nothing of what I said had a destructive meaning. Here and there I have used the word deconstruction, which has nothing to do with destruction. ... It is simply a question of being alert to the implications, to the historical sedimentation of the language we use—and that is not destruction. (1972, p. 271).

What is this "historical sedimentation" that Derrida deconstructs? First, it is the dualism of Cartesian philosophy (following from 17th-century French philosopher René Descartes), with its separation of ego from the external world and its consequent emphasis on control and manipulation, which anticipated the bureaucratic and technological society of the 20th century. Second, it is Enlightenment philosophy and rational humanitarianism that anticipated the French Revolution and the rise of the political ideologies of the 19th century: liberalism, socialism, and radicalism. Allan Megill (1985) concludes: "It is clear, I think, that modern intellectual history has up to now been mainly defined by the thought of the Enlightenment" (p. 340). Megill predicts that, despite the importance of the Enlightenment in defining the terms of contemporary discourse, social problems, and institutions, it will not continue much longer. This is evident because of the decline of the old Kantian, Cartesian, and Hegelian certainties, as well as the malaise and dysfunction within politics and institutions—including schooling—which are products of Enlightenment moral, social, and political theory. Megill explains: "Following Rorty, I have characterized Nietzsche, Heidegger, Foucault, and Derrida as 'reactive' thinkers. Clearly, it is against the Enlightenment project, and against the elaboration and modification of that project in Romanticism and historicism that these thinkers react" (p. 340).

I agree that poststructuralism and deconstructionism are reactions to modern philosophies rooted in Enlightenment notions that have given rise to liberalism, socialism, and radicalism. Many scholars argue that analytic Enlightenment philosophies have pushed society to the limits of absurdity in the 20th century: in the economic realm, laissez-faire liberalism has led to unrestrained materialistic capitalism and ecologically destructive consumerism and corporate globalization; in the political realm, militant and tyrannical communism has led to oppressive centralized authority and debilitating community malaise; and, in the social realm, fascist dictatorships have engendered bigotry, genocide, and violence. Scholars like Allan Megill emphasize that Derrida, Foucault, and other deconstructive and poststructural thinkers challenge the basic assumptions of these economic, political, and social theories in order to support postmodern philosophical perspectives that will expose the contradictions embedded within Enlightenment rationality and hopefully overcome the detrimental and debilitating effects of structuralism and modernity.

Although poststructuralism, deconstructionism, and postmodernism are often used interchangeably to describe the critique of modernity described above (Sarup, 1989), there are important distinctions. Poststructuralism refers to those theoretical movements emerging in France that had grown out of and then opposed structuralism (Descombes, 1980). It is a response to those theories that purport to discover invariant structures in society, the human psyche, history, consciousness, and culture. Poststructuralism is thus an assault on structuralism as well as an outgrowth of it. It includes an attack on humanism, as well as on existentialism and phenomenology. While structuralism has many definitions, Cleo Cherryholmes (1988b) presents a general overview of structuralism as an analysis and philosophical orientation that privileges structures, systems, or sets of relations over the specific phenomena that emerge in, are constituted by, and derive their identity from those structures and sets of relations.

Structuralism has sought to identify the systems that create meaning; poststructuralism has sought to dismantle the system in order to expose the variable and contingent nature of systems. Deborah Britzman writes about poststructural views of identity in which the notion of a unitary, cohesive self is deconstructed. Britzman (1992) challenges the idea that individuals have an authentic core or essence that has been repressed by society:

> Rather than appeal to a timeless and transcendent human nature, poststructural thought traces "the constitution of the subject within a historical framework" (Foucault, 1980, p. 117). There is concern with how subjectivities become configured as an effect of history and how they are then produced. ... In poststructural analysis, meaning is never fixed or stable. Nor is reality, in any sense, understood as objectively "out there" or simply apprehended through language. Instead, meaning becomes the site of departure, a place where reality is constructed, truth is produced, and power is effected. Poststructuralist approaches are concerned with the inherited and constructed meanings that position our understanding of social life. (p. 25)

I support this concept of the self and subjectivity in poststructuralism and seek to extend this analysis of structuralist views of subjectivity. In general, however, structuralists attempt to stop the hemorrhaging of subjectivity in to the world. Not only would reality and meaning be found in and established by invariant structures, but the subject itself, and human consciousness generally, would be construed as products of invariant structures. What distinguishes the structuralist move is not only the more technical definition of structure but, more important, the turn to language as the medium through which structures will reveal themselves. Language becomes for structuralism the field of investigation.

This turn to language is credited to the linguistic theory of Ferdinand de Saussure, who had a broad influence on structuralism. He argued that language should be studied not in terms of its history but in terms of its extant structures, that languages are systems of signs that consist of signifier and signified, that meaning is generated not by correspondence between words and things (signifier and signified) but by the sign's and signifier's relationships and differences from other signs and signifiers, and, finally, that relationships are dualisms or binary opposites (such as light/dark, male/female) which constitute foundational structures that help determine difference or meaning. Saussure also distinguished between *langue* (language and the collectivity of signs) and *parole* (speech and the empirical reality of the embodiment of language). Saussure (1959) explains:

> The signifier, though to all appearance freely chosen with respect to the idea that it represents, is fixed, not free with respect to the linguistic community that uses it. The masses have no voice in the matter, and the signifier chosen by language could be replaced by no other. The fact, which seems to embody a contradiction, might be called colloquially "the stacked deck." (p. 71)

As a result of the influence of Saussure's linguistic theory, language became a field of study, semiotic structures and systems of signs became gateways to meaning, and traditional ways of articulating knowledge, history, and culture were exploded to reveal deep structures that called into question the taken for granted distinctions between dualisms such as fact and fiction, rational and irrational, or myth and reason.

The attack on the subjective, on humanism, and on the Enlightenment project were utilized by the more radical structuralists and became the basis for the emergence of poststructuralism. The more conservative elements of structuralism, such as linguistic idealism, ahistoricism, and language analysis, were attacked. If, as structuralism maintained, underlying structures constitute reality and meaning, what is the relationship between the human mind and these systems of meaning? The structuralist answer is that the human mind itself is structured in a way that corresponds to the structures "out there." This is where poststructuralists such as Michel Foucault, Jacques Lacan, Gilles Deleuze, and Julia Kristeva accused structuralism of neo-Kantianism and only a partial break with humanism, for it reproduced the humanist notion of an unchanging human nature. Foucault (1972b) argued that structuralism's attempt to "establish a system of homogeneous relations: a network of causality that makes it possible to derive each of them, relations of analogy that show how they symbolize one another, or how they all express one and the same central [structure]" (pp. 9–10) did not take into account the social and political construction of such systems. The attack also included a critique of structuralism's blindness to its own involvement in the articulation of systems using language. This brings us back to Rorty's claim, at the beginning of this chapter, that traditional philosophy of education is unable to see its own complicity in the analytic paralysis that exists in contemporary philosophy of education scholarship.

As we examine the language critique of poststructuralists, particularly by Foucault, it is important to read their work not literally but ironically. In this sense poststructuralism shares with postmodernism a sense of the irony, but perhaps with a more playful intent. Therefore, poststructuralists are not so much guides as opponents. Poststructuralism is not a system, but opposition to the structure of understanding as a unified system. Megill (1985) explains:

> We ought to view their writings, as we view the work of the artist, as existing in a state of tension with the given. Foucault, for example, is clearly the double of conventional historians, who challenge, and who ought to be challenged by, his work. ... Derrida's deconstruction—his brilliant self-parody—helps bring to light the latent absurdity residing on both sides of this opposition, and thus helps us to see the limitations of each. In short, we ought to approach aestheticism in a spirit of sympathetic skepticism. (p. 345)

This "sympathetic skepticism" and ironic "latent absurdity" described by Megill form an integral part of postmodern visions, especially as expressed in poststructuralism and deconstructionism. This very brief introduction to poststructural and deconstructive perspectives on postmodernism demonstrates their complexity. Simple definitions are impossible—even a contradiction of the premise of deconstructionism—because every linguistic explanation must be exposed for its internal contradictions. In this sense, deconstructionism is not a method but a critique. Additionally, some would argue for a greater distinction between poststructuralism, deconstructionism, and postmodernism than I have introduced here. However, for those beginning the investigation of contemporary curriculum development discourses, the unifying themes of social, linguistic, and aesthetic critique of modernity and Enlightenment notions of reason, totality, knowledge, and institutions weave a common thread through poststructuralism, deconstructionism, and postmodernism.

While this chapter has attempted to make the contemporary discussions of philosophies in curriculum theory accessible to readers in a brief introductory overview, the attempt to do this is risky. For to simplify complex ideas such as poststructuralism and deconstructionism, which continue to evolve over the lifetime of many writers, and to summarize multiperspectival philosophies whose meanings are constantly debated by scholars is impossible. Therefore, readers are urged to explore these philosophies in much greater detail in primary texts, critical reviews, and secondary analyses. In doing so, it will be clear that philosophy is not an exact science but rather an ongoing exploration by those who are truly passionate about wisdom, *sophia*, *currere*, *praxis*, and *phronesis*.

Curriculum theorists utilize contemporary philosophies to expand our understanding of curriculum and instruction, whether it be from phenomenological, poststructural, deconstructive, feminist, process, or critical perspectives. These philosophical perspectives were never a concern in the traditional Tylerian Rationale, for the systematic design of goals and objectives superseded the autobiographical, historical, political, theological, ecological, and social context of the learning experience. Contemporary philosophies in curriculum studies remain foreign and irrelevant to many traditionalists in the curriculum field. However, the explosion of their incorporation makes them impossible to ignore any longer. Curriculum development no longer excludes the essential dimension of philosophical investigations in education, for philosophy provides access to reflective understanding, heightened sensitivity, historical grounding, contextual meaning, and a liberating praxis. In this sense philosophy is not simply a study of perennial truths but rather a vehicle for engendering justice, compassion, self-exploration, empowerment, critical thinking, and, as we will explore in the next chapter, ecological sustainability in a threatened global environment. Quite possibly the emerging discourses shared by curriculum theorists and philosophers of education may signal the beginning of a new respect for education professors in the universities and a return to prominence of philosophical understandings of curriculum in the postmodern era.

eight
Curriculum for Interdependence and Ecological Sustainability

Jacques-Yves Cousteau (1910–1997) was an internationally recognized spokesperson for the Earth and seas. Even in his eighties, the explorer who once reveled in the mystery of marine life and brought the splendor of underwater adventure alive accepted a new mission. Marlise Simons (1994) reported on Cousteau's campaign against environmental degradation later in his life:

> These days, the captain of the Calypso ... is talking less about nature's beauty and railing more against humans who use dynamite or drift nets to fish, who drain marshes and lagoons, who cut passages through atolls, who change the course of rivers, who wipe out all species, who pollute everywhere. Above all, he has set himself tasks more portentous than his past calls for conservation: he lobbies policy makers to redefine progress, complains of the hypocrisy and cruelty of the free-market system and warns of the self-destructive course taken by humanity. "I'm now fighting for my own species," Cousteau said. "I finally understood that we ourselves are in danger, not only fish." (p. A-6)

Cousteau was intimately familiar with the Earth and seas, and his passionate warning about the self-destructive course of humanity is one among a chorus of voices that have put ecological sustainability at the forefront of policy debates. Among those voices are educators who recognize the dual role of the school curriculum as an opening to inform students about the dangers of environmental pollution, global climate change, unrestrained population growth, the destruction of rainforests and wetlands, and the depletion of the protective ozone layer and as an opportunity for initiating them into holistic practices that will contribute to a postmodern global consciousness essential for ecological sustainability. Educators have an incredible opportunity to be at the forefront of social change on the issues of sustainability and survivability.

In just the past century the human population has increased by a factor of four, and it continues to grow exponentially. During this same time water use has increased by a factor of nine, while limited water resources grow significantly more toxic. Carbon dioxide emissions have grown by a factor of 17, marine-fish catch by 35, and industrial output by 40 (Montenegro & Glavin, 2011). The warnings are abundant, but the political and individual will to address ecological crises is tepid.

The emerging field of biocultural diversity examines important connections between language, culture, and ecology. Maywa Montenegro and Terry Glavin (2011) contend that, even before we have been able to take stock of the enormous diversity that exists today (from undescribed microbes to undocumented languages), a destructive epidemic carries away an entire human language every two weeks, destroys a domesticated food-crop variety every six hours, and kills off an entire species every few minutes. The fallout from the biocultural destruction is not merely an assault on our aesthetic or even ethical values. As cultures and languages vanish, along with them go vast and ancient storehouses of accumulated knowledge. And, as species disappear, along with them go not just valuable genetic resources but critical links in complex ecological webs. Montenegro and Glavin (2011) write:

> Resilience theory, and the nascent field of resilience science associated with it, begins with the basic premise that human and natural systems act as strongly coupled, integrated systems. These so-called "social-ecological" systems are understood to be in constant flux and highly unpredictable. And unlike standard ecological theory, which holds that nature responds to gradual changes in a correspondingly steady fashion, resilience thinking holds that systems often respond to stochastic events—things like storms or fires—with dramatic shifts into completely different states from which it is difficult, if not impossible, to recover. Numerous studies of rangelands, coral reefs, forests, lakes, and even human political systems show this to be true: A clear lake, for instance, seems hardly affected by fertilizer runoff until a critical threshold is passed, at which point the pond abruptly turns murky. A reef dominated by hard coral can, in the aftermath of a hurricane, flip into a state dominated by algae. A democratic nation stricken by drought, disease, or stock market crashes can descend into political chaos. (p. 2)

The work of biocultural scholars like Montenegro and Glavin addresses important connections between language, ecology, and culture that are familiar to most educators who understand the significance of interdisciplinary curriculum and holistic models of human interaction in classrooms that both inform and transform.

Scholars committed to the dual role of the curriculum as informative and transformative have sounded an urgent warning to educators: ecological sustainability and holistic models of teaching should be the primary focus of the postmodern curriculum. Mary Evelyn Tucker (1993), speaking from the perspective of the 1990s, cautioned that "the reality of a global environmental crisis, the focus of the Earth Summit in Rio de Janeiro in June of 1992, together with the demise of communism, has suddenly created an urgent agenda in this transitional decade that must be met with novel educational, social, and political programs" (p. 1). I am not sure that we rose to the occasion in the 1990s. In the new millennium the voices became more urgent as glaciers began to melt and catastrophic weather changes and hurricanes forced us to pay closer attention. In 2005, even conservative Fox News ran a global warming special alert titled "The Heat is On," and a few evangelical Christians began to write about the duty of religious people to protect the Earth. The stakes are so high and the evidence of impending disaster so clear that alliances are being formed across political and religious divides—both in the US and internationally. I have been an activist for environmental issues since my undergraduate college days. Initially, I was most interested in mercury poisoning in fish. Then I became aware of deforestation in Haiti and Brazil and the connection between "slash and burn" practices and beef consumption. Later I adopted a vegetarian diet, primarily as an expression of a spiritual communion with life on the planet, but also as a way to express my protest of destructive environmental policies, the cruel treatment of animals, and the depletion of resources.

As an aside, my vegetarianism was not initially inspired by a concern for health issues when I was 22, but now at age 58 I see the significant connection between my diet and my good health. Our diets are very personal, and I do not believe that a vegetarian diet or vegan lifestyle is the only way to protect the Earth or an individual's health. I am the only vegetarian in my family, and I am also an excellent Cajun and Creole chef. I often cook meals for my family and friends such as chicken and Andouille sausage gumbo or shrimp creole. It is important for me to remind readers again of the passage from the introduction of this book: "I can teach you my steps, but you will have to hear your own music." Each person has to figure out for themselves how they will apply the information in this chapter on environmental issues to their lives. In the postmodern era there is no single method or practice that works for all people. As I read new books and study current research, I sometimes change my diet, behaviors, and perspectives.

As I mentioned above, my first memory of environmental issues was in high school in 1969, when I studied the impact of mercury poisoning in fish as part of a research project. For over forty years I have advocated for action to reduce mercury poisoning. Finally, in 2011, new Environmental Protection Agency standards on mercury and air toxins for power plants were implemented. The new rules will potentially deliver huge benefits at a modest cost. Those who are predisposed to protest EPA regulations have already begun to complain and seek to overturn the rules. This is amazing, since even opponents of environmental regulation understand that mercury is an extremely dangerous and potent neurotoxicant. Paul Krugman (2011) writes:

> the expression "mad as a hatter" emerged in the 19th century because hat makers of the time treated fur with mercury compounds, and often suffered nerve and mental damage as a result. Hat makers no longer use mercury, but a lot of mercury gets into the atmosphere from old coal-burning power plants that lack modern pollution controls. From there it gets into the water, where microbes turn it into methylmercury, which builds up in fish. (p. 3)

The EPA warns that methylmercury exposure is a particular concern for women of childbearing age, unborn babies, and young children, because studies have linked high levels of this toxicant to damage to the developing nervous system, which can impair children's ability to think and learn. Certainly, as educators, we cannot simply teach language, mathematics, and science without understanding that we teach children in context. If mercury poisoning—or lead poisoning or other toxic nerve damage— impairs children's ability to learn, then no amount of curriculum planning and program development can improve learning or even increase test scores. Sometimes I wonder if we really care about children and education when we regularly ignore environmental and social issues that are so destructive of the well-being of students.

It is worth reflecting on the rest of Paul Krugman's essay on the EPA regulations on mercury:

> The new rules would also have the effect of reducing fine particle pollution, which is a known source of many health problems, from asthma to heart attacks. In fact, the benefits of reduced fine particle pollution account for most of the quantifiable gains from the new rules. The key word here is "quantifiable": E.P.A.'s cost–benefit analysis only considers one benefit of mercury regulation, the reduced loss in future wages for children whose I.Q.'s are damaged by eating fish caught by freshwater anglers. There are without doubt many other benefits to cutting mercury emissions, but at this point the agency doesn't know how to put a dollar figure on those benefits. Even so, the payoff to the new rules is huge: up to $90 billion a year in benefits compared with around $10 billion a year of costs in the form of slightly higher electricity prices. This is, as David Roberts of Grist says, a very big deal. With everything else that has been going on in U.S. politics recently, the G.O.P.'s radical anti-environmental turn hasn't gotten the attention it deserves. But something remarkable has happened on this front. Only a few years ago, it seemed possible to be both a Republican in good standing and a serious environmentalist; during the 2008 campaign John McCain warned of the dangers of global warming and proposed a cap-and-trade system for carbon emissions. Today, however, the party line is that we must not only avoid any new environmental regulations but roll back the protection we already have. And I'm not exaggerating: during the fight over the debt ceiling, Republicans tried to attach riders that, as Time magazine put it, would essentially have blocked the E.P.A. and the Interior Department from doing their jobs. … More generally, whenever you hear dire predictions about the [negative] effects of pollution regulation, you should know that special interests always make such predictions, and are always wrong. For example, power companies claimed that rules on acid rain would disrupt electricity supply and lead to soaring rates; none of that happened, and the acid rain program has become a shining example of how environmentalism and economic growth can go hand in hand. (Krugman, 2011, p. 3)

Douglas Sloan, professor of history and education at Teachers College, Columbia University, insists that the present ecological crisis includes not only the destruction of the environment and its natural beauty but the virulence of spreading racism and narrow nationalisms, the indiscriminate extension of science and technology into every sphere of life, and the worldwide destruction of cultural richness and sources of meaning. The world is, Sloan warns, "collapsing under the impact of the homogenizing influences of the modern mindset and its attendant institutions [where] educational systems … force children at an ever-earlier age into an adult culture already shot through with futility, greed, and banality" (1993, p. 1). Ecological and holistic visions of curriculum recognize that all these dimensions are interwoven with the others, and all must be grasped together as symptoms of a deeper crisis of the whole human being.

Along with Jacques Cousteau, Mary Evelyn Tucker, Maywa Montenegro, Terry Glavin, and Douglas Sloan, curriculum theorists understand that human life hangs in the balance. In this chapter I explore curriculum from a globally interdependent ecological perspective that begins by examining the crisis of survivability. Postmodern educators understand that destruction of the ecosphere and the human psyche are interrelated. Nonviolence will emerge only when the scientific bifurcations that have been ingrained in the modern consciousness since the Enlightenment are replaced by a postmodern holistic philosophy. Coretta Scott King (1993) writes about this change in consciousness:

> Nonviolence is not just about one person, one family, or one community, it is a holistic philosophy. All life is interrelated; we are all tied together. Problems that affect people in Beijing, China, also affect people in Harlem, U.S.A., and everywhere else in the world. We must be concerned about others as well as ourselves; we cannot just focus on our own problems. We must study the cultures and languages of the whole world. We need to study the history of people who are different from ourselves, those who are outside our borders as well as those who are inside. Martin [Luther King, Jr.] used to say that we are all tied together in an inescapable network of mutuality. What affects one directly affects all indirectly. (pp. xii–xiii)

Coretta Scott King echoes the postmodern philosophy of curriculum development introduced in this chapter. A holistic perspective is essential for the emergence of compassion, optimal learning environments, nonviolent conflict resolution, just relationships, and ecological sustainability.

Our investigation of curriculum development for ecological sustainability opens with a personal issue that is very painful but also very instructive for our purposes in this chapter—the devastation of my hometown of New Orleans by Hurricane Katrina in 2005. I will begin by repeating exactly what appeared in the first edition of this book in 1995, along with some excerpts written in 1999 that appeared in print in 2003 (Slattery & Rapp, 2003) and further reflections in 2006 in the third edition. Immediately after Katrina hit, I was shocked and angry to hear some politicians say, "We had no idea that this would happen." Numerous government reports, scholarly books, and newspaper investigations outlined the environmental, political, and infrastructure problems in south Louisiana. It is clearly reported in John M. Barry's (1997) important book *Rising Tide: The Great Mississippi Flood of 1927 and How it Changed America.* Information about levees, wetlands, and floods in south Louisiana has been available for decades, but too many people at the state and federal levels were not reading or listening.

The National Wetlands Research Center was established at the University of Louisiana at Lafayette to investigate and ameliorate coastline erosion and habitat destruction. The Army Corp of Engineers—also investigated for deficient construction engineering—clearly stated in many reports in the 1990s that the levees were sufficient to protect New Orleans only from a category 3 hurricane. The politicians did know what would happen in New Orleans, and they chose not to act. Will we begin to act on the other urgent ecological issues we face today, or will we decide not to read and listen again? The floods in New Orleans are a warning about other pressing issues in our environment. On the companion website you will find my analysis from the 1990s through 2006 as it appeared in previous editions of this text. Here I will discuss my current analysis in 2012.

Seven years after Katrina, parts of New Orleans are flourishing. The remodeled and newly renamed Mercedes Benz Superdome is hosting dozens of major cultural and sporting events, among them playoff and championship games in football, including LSU and the Saints in 2012. The French Quarter and Garden District are alive with elite social parties and gaudy tourist attractions. Jazz Fest and Mardi Gras are better than ever. Private and parochial schools that enroll about a third of the student population are flourishing, and graduates continue to attend the most prestigious universities in the nation. There is a slow trickle of working-class residents returning to newly constructed housing in a few neighborhoods. Some of these houses, built by television celebrities, religious organizations, and generous volunteers, are models of energy efficiency and sustainability. The Hispanic population has grown dramatically, but not without conflict and immigration debates among some long-time residents. However, large sections of the residential neighborhoods for middle-class and working-class people still lie abandoned and in ruins. National reports claim that the new charter school system in New Orleans is a model of efficiency and academic success for the entire nation. Of course, as we saw in chapter 2, the local retired superintendent challenged the glowing reports of charter school success. Many of the broken levees have been replaced with sturdy drainage pumps and stronger levees. The lack of attention to the wetlands and levees in other parts of the city continues to worry engineers and residents. The Mississippi River Gulf Outlet ("Mr. Go," as it was nicknamed) that contributed to so much of the flooding has been closed. However, pipeline drilling and oil canal transportation continue unabated in the wetlands. (Disclosure: like many landowners in Louisiana, I personally benefit from oil and gas production, natural gas hydraulic fracturing, and drilling pipelines. We are all embedded in the economic structures of the energy industry, either directly in our investment portfolios, land ownership, or capital gains, or indirectly in favorable pricing structures or secondary service industries. An investigation of the web of connectivity reveals just how dependent and economically integrated we all are to the energy industry!) The massive BP oil spill of 2010 did tremendous damage, but television commercials in 2011 made things seem like the tourism and seafood industries are back to normal. Many would disagree with those commercials, especially displaced workers and devastated businesses that have not been compensated. Environmentalists warn that the long-term impact on the Gulf of Mexico will certainly be serious, but precise information will only come with long-term research and funding. Critics argue that both funding and research are woefully inadequate, thus hiding the true impact. However, the BP spill has already been devastating in some of the dead zones in the gulf and localized wetlands. Deep-water drilling is back, and those who benefit from the economics of oil and gas are thriving. Safety plans and curtailment for future disasters are still inadequate. In short, we have seen infrastructure improvements, the resumption of energy production, economic enhancement for some, revitalized tourism, and limited rebuilding in the neighborhoods. A large charter school system has been created. The cultural life is dynamic, albeit changing in positive and perhaps some not so positive ways. Sporting and entertainment activities are thriving. Volunteer cooperatives and neighborhood activism are dynamic and exemplar, but the working poor, uninsured, homeless, and mentally ill are as desperate now as before Katrina. Educational renewal is a distant dream; racial and socio-economic divisions remain deeply entrenched. Fortunately, New Orleans has not been tested by another major hurricane yet, but it will certainly happen again, since this is an integral part of the ecosystem.

In 2009, I decided to be a part of the rebuilding process. Along with my colleague James Jupp of Georgia Southern University, I wrote a proposal to open a charter school in New Orleans (Slattery, 2011). This may seem like a contradiction based on what you have read in this book. However, in the postmodern spirit, there is no single metanarrative or method to address these complex problems. Since charter schools form the major vehicle for educational change in public schools, I decided to attempt to work within the system to open a charter school that is faithful to the philosophy you are reading in this text. Unfortunately, we were rejected in the finalist phase of the competition in 2009. But we will try again soon. Let's read the proposal first, and I will comment further at the end. What Dr. Jupp and I were attempting to do is to create an International Baccalaureate school with a focus on the arts, music, and local history. We believe that such a curriculum is essential to counteract globalization in favor of sustainable community. Additionally, we had hoped to bring together the various religious, racial, and ethnic communities of New Orleans. Here is how we described our project:

> We intend to start an exemplary International Baccalaureate school in the context of the rich history of the city of New Orleans. This charter school has the potential to contribute positively to the rebuilding of the educational system and social structures of New Orleans if it is attentive to the physical, psychological, and cultural context of the city. Obviously, the citizens of New Orleans have been traumatized by the devastation of Hurricane Katrina in 2005. However, prior to Katrina, New Orleans was a city steeped in contradictions: the *joi de vivre* of the Mardi Gras, Jazz Fest, and international tourism contrasted with the poverty, crime, and desperation of the majority of citizens; the glitz and glamour of casinos, Bourbon Street, championship sporting

events, and political conventions contrasted with the rotting infrastructure of the neighborhoods, schools, and levees; the abundance of decadent foods for tourists and socialites contrasted with the malnourishment and poverty of children; pristine Catholic and private schools with advanced curriculum and stately facilities for the middle class and wealthy (mostly white) contrasted with totally dysfunctional, dangerous, and neglected public schools for the poor (mostly black) citizens; abundant commerce, ports, industry, and tourism but high unemployment and abject poverty among the people. New Orleans is known as "The Big Easy" to outsiders, but is called "Little Haiti" and "The City That Care Forgot" among locals. There has been little opportunity for a quality education for the majority of children in New Orleans. This charter school will provide excellence in the midst of depression and desperation.

We are interested in locating the school in the 7th Ward of New Orleans, a section of town that was particularly hard hit by the floods in 2005. This neighborhood in New Orleans is near the intersection of St. Bernard Avenue and Interstate 10. It is in close proximity to the French Quarter and easily accessible from all parts of the city. The school will stand symbolically in the heart of the New Orleans and bring diverse students together from all parts of the city in order to contribute, in some small way, to a new social order in the community as the city is rebuilt.

Why do we chose this location? We are participating in the fund raising project of the New Orleans Public Library system, and we have a particular connection to the rebuilding of the libraries. On August 29, 2007, President Bush and Laura Bush visited New Orleans on the second anniversary of Katrina. During this visit, Laura Bush met with leaders of the public library rebuilding committee and was named honorary chairperson. One of the branch libraries that was totally devastated in Katrina was the Nora Navra Library on St. Bernard Avenue in the 7th Ward. We are committed to the expansion and rebuilding of this branch library.

Nora Navra was my great-aunt. [Recall the story of her sister Dora Narva in chapter 3.] Aunt Nora lived in a magnificent home on St. Charles Avenue from the 1880s to the 1940s. She inherited a large estate from her father, the founder of the Jacob Candy Company in New Orleans. Aunt Nora was Jewish and a member of Touro Synagogue. She never married. She used her wealth to support social causes in New Orleans. Her philanthropy was much appreciated by many. She had a particular concern and compassion for the poor black children of the 7th and 9th Wards of New Orleans, and she bequeathed a sizable estate to the New Orleans Public Library system for the construction of a branch library. The Nora Navra Library opened in 1954 and served the educational needs of many poor children and citizens until it was destroyed by Katrina. We are committed to the effort to expand and rebuild the Nora Navra Library. (The history of Aunt Nora's philanthropy is tied into the history of the quadroon ball room in New Orleans and other political, economic, religious and racial dimensions of the city.)

Because this library is well known and much appreciated in the community, we want to connect this charter school to the historical significance of Nora Navra's wisdom and compassion. She knew the importance of education, reading, and libraries. But she also knew the importance of bringing together the diverse people of a racially, culturally, religiously, and economically divided city. We intend to locate the International Baccalaureate school physically, historically, and psychologically in this rich cultural context of New Orleans. We intend to extend Nora Navra's legacy, and possibly even name the school "The Nora Navra IB Academy." Such a designation will provide legitimacy and cultural context for the school. It will also attract donors and supporters who share the original vision of the Nora Navra Library. Finally, we believe that this IB school will contribute to educational excellence and cultural diversity for a city that so desperately needs beacons of hope.

Dr. Jupp and I believe that the best way through the "Nightmare that is the Present" (Pinar, 2004a, 2011) is to engage the process fully with deep understanding of the economic systems at work. This project was an attempt to bring together process philosophy and economic policy in a devastated community with local history and the cultural commons and autobiographical connections at the heart of the project. This, we believe, is the most effective way of dismantling the management and accountability structures that we deconstruct in our scholarship. We believe that this can be accomplished by similar projects. While we will continue to work on this project, we will also look for ways to intersect process and economic policy for the greater good. Ultimately, we are cautiously optimistic that we can deconstruct the negative aspects of accountability and standards by working tirelessly within the current system in New Orleans. We may not see the fruits of our labor in our lifetime, but our example might, perhaps, help to shift the conversation about education in New Orleans, in the US, and in the world in some small ways. This is the holistic approach I advance in this chapter and which is also evident in recent curriculum studies scholarship (Flinders, 2009; Pinar, 2007). Let's explore the holistic philosophy further.

I begin this holistic investigation with Fritjof Capra, who, in addition to his technical research in the field of high-energy physics, has written a number of theoretical works on modern science. The methods and theories of modern science, Capra contends in *The Turning Point: Science, Society, and the Rising Culture*, are leading to the self-destruction of humanity. This is exactly what we just explored in relation to the environment and post-Katrina in New Orleans. It is only through a vision of a new postmodern reality with a reconciliation of science and the human spirit that a future will be accessible for the global community. Capra (1982) writes:

> We have high inflation and unemployment, we have an energy crisis, a crisis in health care, pollution and other environmental disasters, a rising wave of violence and crime, and so on. The basic thesis of this book is that these are

all different facets of one and the same crisis, and that this crisis is essentially a crisis of perception. Like the crisis in physics in the 1920s, it derives from the fact that we are trying to apply the concepts of an outdated world view—the mechanistic world view of Cartesian–Newtonian science—to a reality that can no longer be understood in terms of these concepts. We live today in a globally interconnected world, in which biological, psychological, social, and environmental phenomena are all interdependent. To describe this world appropriately we need an ecological perspective which the Cartesian world view does not offer. (pp. 15–16)

Capra succinctly summarizes not only the theme of this chapter but also the postmodern curriculum development paradigm that is being investigated throughout this book.

Modern visions of education, as characterized by the Tylerian Rationale, behavioral lesson plans, context-free objectives, competitive and external evaluation, accountability politics, dualistic models that separate teacher and student, meaning and context, subjective persons and objective knowledge, body and spirit, learning and environment, and models of linear progress through value-neutral information transmission, are no longer acceptable in the postmodern era. In fact, according to David Orr (1992), they are at the root of our ecological crisis. David Bohm (1988) warns that "a postmodern science should not separate matter and consciousness and should therefore not separate facts, meaning, and value" (p. 60). Science would then be inseparable from a form of intrinsic morality. This separation is part of the reason for our present desperate situation (Bohm, 1988).

The technical and independent ideology of modernity not only is destructive of the human psyche but also threatens the very survival of the human species. If this sounds alarmist to some, the scholarship of curriculum theorists with an ecological focus does not apologize for this sense of urgency. At the end of Capra's earlier book, *The Tao of Physics*, he tied the conceptual shift of modern physics to these social implications, warning:

I believe that the world view implied by modern physics is inconsistent with our present society, which does not reflect the harmonious interrelatedness we observe in nature. To achieve such a state of dynamic balance, a radically different social and economic structure will be needed: a cultural revolution in the true sense of the word. The survival of our whole civilization may depend on whether we can bring about such a change. (1975, p. x)

Curriculum theorists and related scholars have joined in the revolution proposed by Capra and suggested a vision of "sacred interconnections" (David Ray Griffin, 1990), "responsive teaching" (Chet Bowers & David Flinders, 1990), "ecological literacy" (David Orr, 1992), "holistic curriculum" (John P. Miller, 1988), "curriculum as place" (Patrick Slattery & Kevin Daigle, 1994), "the sacred circle" (Robert Regnier, 1992), "a post-liberal theory of education" (Chet Bowers, 1987), "insight-imagination" (Douglas Sloan, 1983), "a critical process curriculum" (Kathleen Kesson, 1993, 2005), "an inspiring holistic vision" (Ron Miller, 1993), "transformative critical praxis"

(Donna Houston & Peter McLaren, 2005), and "the unity of related plurality" (Donald Oliver & Kathleen Gershman, 1989). The vast amount of curriculum scholarship with a holistic and ecological emphasis by these and other widely respected educators is indicative of the centrality of such issues in the postmodern era. How will these ecological and holistic theories of curriculum and instruction be incorporated into postmodern schooling?

The first important change taking place in the postmodern curriculum is in the relationships that exist in classrooms. These changing relationships in turn foster ecological and global sensibilities. For example, in classrooms, even in lecture halls with fifty students, professors learn the names and interests of all students and let them know that their opinions and questions will not only be respected but encouraged. Reflective dialogue, autobiographical journals, nonconfrontational debate, cooperative investigations, and probing questions are the focus of the classroom experience. I begin with the assumption that we all bring to the course important perspectives that need to be explored. I also assume that students, on an intuitive level, are anxious to read, think, write, and engage in the learning experience. While the level of commitment may vary from person to person—and my own intensity may fluctuate depending on personal, family, or university commitments—I have yet to be disappointed by this classroom milieu. In fact, my experience is that, when students are trusted and empowered in a holistic environment, the quantity and quality of their scholarly work improve exponentially. Students become far more demanding of themselves, especially when learning and self-discovery replace grades and course credits as the focus of the curriculum.

The traditional modern classroom has not allowed for a holistic and ecological atmosphere, especially because of the power arrangement of rows of desks with a podium and chalkboard in the front of the room. This structure reinforces the role of the teacher as the authority and information dispenser separate from the passive students, who need to be controlled and measured for optimal productivity. Rows of desks in classrooms evolved for two reasons: the need to control and organize larger numbers of students entering schools in the nineteenth century and the expectation that schools would prepare students for the linear social structures of the modern world. In the early part of the 20th century the majority of students leaving public schools pursued careers in factories, farming, or the military, where assembly lines, planting columns ("a long row to hoe"), and rank-and-file marching formations not only dictated the physical structure of the workplace but also reflected the ideology of modern society. Students, it was understood, needed to be inculcated into a milieu of social control so that they would be prepared to fall in line, obey commands without thinking, and repeat functions mechanically without hesitation. This was considered to be especially important for the immigrant population, who needed to be immersed in the American melting-pot culture in order to ensure cultural cohesion. Social control as a function of schooling was seldom questioned—except by some social reconstructionists and progressive educators. This factory model of curriculum was being challenged in the scholarly literature in 2006, and significant changes have been proposed for middle grades education for over twenty years. Secondary schools are now experimenting with smaller "schools within schools" in order to reshape curriculum and instruction from a factory model to a holistic community model.

Barry Franklin (1986, 1988) in *Building the American Community: The School Curriculum and the Search for Social Control* and "Whatever Happened to Social Control? The Muting of Coercive Authority in Curriculum Discourse," explores this issue of social control. He locates social control in the service of the reproduction of cultural structures of the status quo. Mass immigration mobilized sentiment in this country for cultural standardization, a concern that remained in the 1990s and is at the root of conservative educational reform movements. Franklin contends that earlier forms of explicit coercion in schooling (such as the repression of languages, dress, and customs of immigrant children) have been replaced by persuasion, economic entice-ment, and other "democratic" forms of social control. He argues that social control has not disappeared from curriculum development. Rather, it has been muted and disguised so that its coercive agenda is less detectable. Additionally, social control that once served as inculturation into middle-class values and privileges now functions to legitimize and preserve corporate capitalism. Curriculum theorists from a variety of perspectives utilize Franklin's research to contest modern curriculum development models. Those whose research includes an ecological and holistic interest especially see the danger of the deceptive social control that exists in education and society today. The challenge to raise our consciousness concerning the ecological, psychological, and spiritual destruction that had resulted from social control in education is becoming ever more difficult, especially since educational institutions, according to Franklin, are complicit in this process. The preservation of the educational bureaucracy depends on the continuation of modernity and social control. Thus, some curriculum theorists worry that the rhetoric of smaller schools and holistic middle schools and high schools will not result in any significant changes. In fact, the opposite may actually be the case as administrators and teachers conform to the standardization of the *No Child Left Behind* accountability philosophy.

While the development of social control in order to build a cohesive US community continues to have many proponents today, especially among those who believe that schools must repair the social disintegration that has resulted from rampant individu-alism, relativism, and a lack of common values, postmodern philosophies insist that schooling must transcend linear structures rather than return to social and psycho-logical models of control that have dominated curriculum development in the past. The conservative reaction begun in the 1980s reform movements in education insists on a different agenda: cultural literacy, laissez-faire capitalism, traditional values, Western culture, nationalism, and unquestioning patriotism (Shea et al., 1989).

The emerging postmodern holistic and ecological models of curriculum dissolve the artificial boundary between the outside community and the classroom. Postmodern teaching celebrates the interconnectedness of knowledge, learning experiences, interna-tional communities, the natural world, and life itself. However, like John Dewey (1934b, 1938), who warned that not all experiences produce growth, values, and social consequence, it is also important for teachers to orchestrate holistic learning experiences thoughtfully and carefully. Field trips, guest speakers, nature studies, and visits to museums are encouraged, and not just for the sake of alleviating boredom or for indoctrinating students with a narrow political or cultural perspective. Additionally, if a video presentation, lab project, or field trip is simply used as a reward for good behavior or as a filler in a hectic school schedule, the postmodern perspective of the interconnectedness of experiences is lost. Understanding the difference between these two perspectives is essential for appropriate ecological models of education. Dewey (1938) clarifies the distinction:

> Traditional education did not have to face this problem [of utilizing a wide variety of experiences in the curriculum]; it could systematically dodge this responsibility. The school environment of desks, blackboards, a small school year, was supposed to suffice. There was no demand that the teacher should become intimately acquainted with the conditions of the local community, physical, historical, economic, occupations, etc., in order to utilize them as educational resources. A system of education based upon ... experience must ... take these things constantly into account. The tax upon the educator is another reason why progressive education is more difficult to carry on than was ever the traditional system. (p. 40)

Dewey's concerns echo the concerns of postmodern educators. The classroom environment and interconnectedness of experiences remain a central priority in holistic and ecological curriculum scholarship.

Holistic and ecological models of education have encouraged me to arrange my classrooms in seminar circles rather than rows of desks and to leave the classroom for outdoor classes. As simple as this change in architecture may seem, it has been one of the most significant and liberating events in the evolution of my pedagogy over the past twenty years. Manly Hall (1988) discusses the importance of architectural arrangements:

> The Greeks taught that buildings and dwellings profoundly influenced human conduct. The soul receiving into itself the impression of shapes is offended by deformity and strengthened and inspired by noble proportions. ... Buildings are thoughts and emotions in stone, concrete, steel, and other materials. All structures have their karmic consequences. ... All genuine mandalas are intended to picture forth some aspect of universal harmony. The inward experience of the infinite scheme usually results in a refinement of the various expressions of human activity. (p. 167)

Education is one human activity that is profoundly affected by attention to environment and inner experience. Landscape, says David Orr (1992), shapes mindscapes. In seminar circles and outdoor settings we can see faces and body language, listen with empathy, and become aware of our interconnectedness. The linear patterns of modernity were designed to eliminate the possibility of human contact, reflection, and thinking. Paul Shepard (1977) explains that the stability of communities is a consequence of the interplay between the psyche and the physical environment: "Terrain structure is the model for the patterns of cognition. ... Cognition, personality, creativity, and maturity—all are in some way tied to particular gestalts of space" (p. 22). Thus, knowledge of a place, of where you are and where you come from, is intertwined with knowledge of self. David Orr contends that, since it diminishes the potential for maturation and inhabitance, the destruction of places is psychologically ravaging as well. Orr (1992) writes, "If Shepard is right, and I believe that he is, we are paying a high price for the massive rearrangement of the North American landscape of the past fifty years" (p. 130). Hall (1988) also warns about the consequences of modern architecture for the human soul:

> Progress, according to modern prevailing standards, must be essentially soulless. A building should exist only for utility, art for ingenuity, music for emotional excitation, laws for the advancement of material economic expansion, and recreational activities strictly for sensory enjoyment. As a result of constant association with mediocrity, human conduct is no longer influenced by overtones of beauty and integrity. This has contributed to the disintegration of modern society [and the environment]. ... When the human being no longer pauses to read what Paracelsus called the "living book of nature," he loses contact with those basic values which alone can reveal ... origin and destiny. ... Those seeking genuine mystical enlightenment must release a power of soul awareness in themselves and allow their own intuition to indicate the direction they must travel in their earthly pilgrimage. (pp. 167–168, emphasis added)

In order to understand the ecological interconnectedness and holistic curriculum theories of the scholars identified above—Bowers, Flinders, Orr, Regnier, Ron Miller, John P. Miller, Tucker, Griffin, Houston, McLaren, Kesson, Douglas Sloan, and Pinar—attention must be directed to architecture, classroom milieu, the natural environment, and the inner environment of students and teachers.

The circle as an important structure for developing postmodern theories of education is proposed by Robert Regnier of the University of Saskatchewan. Regnier (1992) suggests a process pedagogy based on an aboriginal approach to healing using the Sacred Circle teachings of Canadian Plains Indians at Joe Duquette High School in Saskatoon. Healing, as well as teaching, is seen as integral to the transition toward meaning, wholeness, connectedness, and balance:

> The Sacred Circle is a "traditional symbolic circle" which incorporates the spiritual beliefs of many Indian tribes of North America. ... It symbolises harmony and the belief that life occurs within a series of circular movements that govern their relationship with the environment. ... The Sacred Circle drawn into four quadrants differentiates physical, emotional, spiritual, and intellectual dimensions of personal development. Through this model, students are encouraged to view themselves as a whole person who can become self-determining. This self-determination requires envisioning ideals in each area and examining the connections within each area. (1992, pp. 1, 13)

Regnier uses the philosophy of Alfred North Whitehead to demonstrate that human development, learning, teaching, and curriculum development are all manifestations of process. By recognizing human growth and learning as genesis and process, it is possible to construct a pedagogy that reflects the dynamic, interdependent, and cyclical character of reality. Regnier continues by criticizing Western metaphysics, which abstracts, categorizes, and isolates individuals rather than seeing reality as a unitary continuous process.

An interesting thing happened in one of my classroom seminar circles during a summer session. A woman unexpectedly brought her ten-year-old son to class one day. She was taking three courses and expected that her child would sit quietly and remain attentive in her science lab and physical education activity course. She worried, however, that he might become bored during our history of American education class. She arrived with the boy without time for introductions, and he sat quietly in the room. The next day the woman reported that her son enjoyed his day at the university, and, to her surprise, he particularly enjoyed our education class. He told his mother that it was fun because he spent the entire time listening to everyone discuss ideas in the circle while he tried to figure out which one was the teacher. In postmodern classrooms teachers are guides and mentors who orchestrate self-reflective learning experiences, joining in the sacred circle described by Regnier but not dominating and manipulating in the process.

Donald Oliver and Kathleen Gershman (1989) propose that Eastern thinking will help us to understand the importance of the circle in educational experience. They use the *I Ching* from ancient China (see Figure 8.1) to propose that the world, like the classroom, is a unity of related plurality rather than a series of adversarial fragments that compete with one another for domination or privilege.

Mary Aswell Doll (1991) expands on Oliver and Gershman's idea of circles as an image for understanding the local and global interrelationship of postmodern thought in an address entitled "Dancing the Circle":

> Once upon a time the world went to sleep and dreamed that God was the center of the universe. The philosopher Nietzsche woke up, proclaiming the dream a nightmare and God dead. Later, the poet Yeats agreed, saying, "Things fall apart, the center cannot hold." Both the philosopher and the poet were startled, however, when Heraclitus, dreaming from a deeper dream many centuries earlier, said, "The center is everywhere," implying "the gods are all around and the goddesses are within." I would like to talk about circles and inner gods and goddesses. The circle's round shape is soft, recursive; it curves back upon itself. It is in constant motion; therefore, it is dynamic, using its own inner energy to spiral movement inward, toward reflection. The circle also spirals outward toward what the new science of chaos calls fractal patterns, which loop and loop again, forming harmonic swirls. The loopings, either inward or outward, are, we could say, geysers for the imagination. (p. 1)

Doll's literary and philosophic reflections on the circle move next to the symbolic circle of the yin and yang of Eastern mysticism, where masculine and feminine principles of dark and light blend together in a permanent dance inside the circle. The masculine principle of reason, logic, and order—the light—is tucked within the feminine principle of intuition, magic, and imagination—the dark. No one principle dominates; the two are enfolded together.

This same principle applies to theories of learning that reject the bifurcation of left brain and right brain in favor of complementary and integrated whole brain philosophies (Caine & Caine, 1991). Additionally, there is an emerging ecological view of cognitive science and situated learning that sees learning processes as including external as well as inside-the-head events (Bereiter & Scardamalia, 1992; St. Julien, 1992, 1994). Lev Vygotsky (1978), for example, writes about externalization—the creation of artifacts and changes in the environment that support and thus become part of cognitive processes. James J. Gibson (1979), in *The Ecological Approach to Visual Perception*, contends that our cognitive systems have evolved in such a way that critical elements of the environment and their pragmatic implications are directly perceived without the need for mediating symbolic processes, interpretations, and concepts. Bereiter and Scardamalia (1992) report: "One group of researchers is explicitly concerned with educational implications of what they term 'situated cognition.' [They] are undertaking an ambitious program of research that ranges from studies of learning in work settings to developing an environmentally situated approach to artificial intelligence" (p. 536).

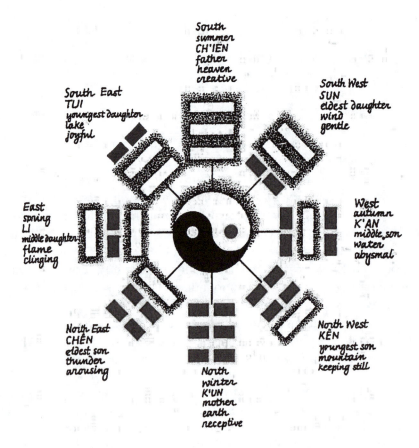

Figure 8.1

Figure 8.1 represents the complementary rather than the contradictory nature of diverse elements in the cosmos as presented in the 4,000-year-old *Book of Changes*, or *I Ching*, from ancient China. The cosmology is based on the dynamic unity of the dark (*yin*—represented by the broken line) and the light (*yang*—represented by the solid line) principles. We would note the balanced statement of abstractions (the trigrams) in relationship to the grounded concrete aspects of nature (e.g., lakes, mountains) as well as the facts of human community (kin and temperament designations). The world is thus presented as a unity of related plurality, rather than as a series of adversarial fragments which compete with each other for domination or privilege. We are thus not forced to ask which is superior, the abstract or the concrete? Nature or humans? Earth or heaven? The son or the daughter? Plurality/diversity complements unit.

John St. Julien (1992) explores situated cognition, which he describes as a response to particular projects that are centrally concerned with the contrast between schooling and "real world" experience as they relate to competence. He develops a conception of the person thinking (in-the-head-thought) which is at once compatible with the findings of situated cognition that the person is not radically separate and that offers a principled way to understand how successful transfer might occur across practices and situations. St. Julien (1992) writes:

> The field of understanding needs to span the distance from biologically constrained understandings of learning and thinking to socially situated theories of knowledge and cognition to be useful in the design of instruction. The person needs to be understood as neither discontinuous nor unproblematically integrated with the situation in which they find themselves acting. (p. 8).

Connectionism, he continues, is a perspective that blurs the distinction between the mind and the brain in the same way that situated cognition blurs the distinction between the self and the world.

St. Julien's scholarship on the confluence of the perspectives of connectionism and situated cognition contributes to the postmodern efforts to transcend bifurcation, Cartesianism, and the modern habit of thinking of the mind as operating logically. He views the way out of this logical mode as a "new analytic" based on networks of relations and interactive representations such as chaos, nonlinear dynamics, and ecology. St. Julien hopes that a material theory of learning may emerge to displace the descriptive theorizing that currently characterizes modern approaches to knowledge acquisition of facts that are separated from the learning context and the learner's situation. This modem approach to knowledge acquisition dominates schooling and must be replaced in postmodern education with a new analytic of learning. Such theories are emerging in postmodern and poststructural discussions. St. Julien (1992) comments on this emerging theory: "A solid theory of the material constitution of learning spanning the range from structured external symbols which are materially present in the world to a connectionist approach to the learning of these socially organized categories should prove to be invaluable to our hopes of building a pedagogy that enhances our students' competence" (p. 13). He echoes the hermeneutic search of James Macdonald as he concludes, "It is this hope that finally, I submit, motivates all of us" (p. 13).

Following from this discussion of situated cognition, connectionism, whole brain learning, and Eastern mysticism, Mary Aswell Doll (1991) offers the following expanded insights:

> This dynamic blending of opposites suggests, to me, what our Western culture needs to hear from Eastern culture. Instead of our Western fascination with moving forward, stepping up, going on—and stepping on—we need to reflect. Progress has polluted our waters both in the environment and in our selves. Progress has endangered our species both in the wilderness and in the wild places of our selves. Chemicals have been abused both against the bugs and against what bugs our selves. We have extended our notion of progress so that we have forgotten our selves, rooted in a collective past. (p. 5)

To be rooted is to be soiled, circled down into nature's roots. However, the words "soil" and "dirt" have taken on a derogatory meaning. Common parlance suggests that soil and dirt no longer nourish our roots. However, this is not so with the symbolic circle of the yin and yang—dark and light dance together in continuous improvisation. The circle is a dance.

Susan W. Stinson is a dancer and curriculum theorist. In her essay "Dance as Curriculum, Curriculum as Dance," from the excellent collection of essays on curriculum and the arts entitled *Reflections from the Heart of Educational Inquiry*, edited by George Willis and William Schubert (1991), she snares many of her ecological interests: sensory experience, metaphors, improvisation. Stinson (1991) writes, "Dance gives me a center, a place to start from: curriculum is the continuing journey" (p. 190). She uses the metaphor of personal knowledge—of knowing something in our bones—which allows us to extend our boundaries and make important connections to the world. Her early dance career was marked by efforts to control and perfect her body, which was an adversary to overcome. She explains: "Control is as much an issue in curriculum as it is in dance: we fear that institutions, as well as bodies, will not work without control" (p. 190). Stinson's curriculum theory, like the other holistic and ecological proposals seen throughout this chapter, provides an alternative to control and manipulation by emphasizing cooperative relationships.

Curriculum scholars in the postmodern era have taken the metaphor of ecological and psychological destruction and thoughtfully applied it to the schooling process in many books, including *Responsive Teaching: An Ecological Approach to Classroom Patterns of Language, Culture, and Thought* (Bowers & Flinders, 1990); *The Holistic Curriculum* (John P. Miller, 1988); *The Renewal of Meaning in Education: Responses to the Ecological Crisis of Our Time* (Ron Miller, 1993); and *Ecological Literacy: Education and the Transition to a Postmodern World* (Orr, 1992); David Orr (1992, 2002) is perhaps representative of those who believe that education must transcend current practices and address ecological sustainability:

The modern world arose as a volcanic eruption so suddenly and massively that it buried or transformed all that had preceded it, including landscapes and mindscapes. It is difficult to know how much we have lost, but I believe that for all of the increases in conveniences and speed, we have lost a great deal of the richness and experience of a life that once existed. The losses are not all visible. The most serious have to do with the way we think and what we think about. For all of our gross national product, most live increasingly barren lives in an increasingly impoverished land. ... Until we confront what modernity has done to us as a people and resolve to do otherwise, we can only put Band-Aids on a terminal problem. (1992, p. 181)

The solution to the ecological and psychological devastation of modernity for Orr and other scholars is the development of a postmodern paradigm. Orr calls it ecological literacy. This will involve recovering older notions of virtue found in antiquity as well as developing a sense that the self is inseparable from a larger community that is part of a cosmological vision. It will also involve regaining a moral and historical consciousness that will foster interconnectedness within a larger perspective. "The modern world has destroyed the sense of belonging to a larger order which must be restored as the foundation of a postmodern world" (Orr, 1992, p. 182). Specifically, Orr proposes the reintroduction of moral philosophy throughout the curriculum, community settings on school campuses, and experiences in education that foster virtue. He concludes: "The transition to the kind of postmodern society envisioned in this ... book cannot be done cheaply. It will cost something, perhaps a great deal. But there is a far higher price waiting to be paid" (p. 183). I feel the same way about the post-Katrina reconstruction efforts along the gulf coast, discussed above.

To avoid ecological disaster, education must point the way toward "deep cultural changes," according to Chet Bowers. This will not be accomplished through government attempts to engineer social changes or through a politicized system of signs. Bowers (1993) observes:

Nor have modern totalitarian regimes been able to deal with the basic problem of our era: human rights and the ecological crisis. The political process has a dismal record. ... The development of spiritual languages may have the best potential for helping us avoid the political process moving beyond excessive regulation to the friend–enemy conflicts that now seem to be on the increase. (p. 216)

The challenge for educators, according to Bowers, will be to find suitable analogues for songs, stories, dance, and art, either from the histories of the many cultural groups in society or from current cultural artifacts. Ultimately, educators must be receptive to including in the curriculum the contributions of various cultural groups and relate this to living in a sustainable balance within the larger web of life. This receptivity by educators "will require escaping from many of the prejudices that are now the basis of our modern hubris" (p. 216). Bowers, like Orr, recognizes that global change begins with local community efforts and classroom practices by individual educators. Neither Bowers nor Orr proposes a new modern master plan but rather a postmodern receptivity to a vision of education for ecological sustainability. Chet Bowers, like Jacques Cousteau, worries about what we are doing to the physical environment. However, he advances the dialogue by asserting that modern liberalism and Enlightenment rationality have produced an emphasis on individualism and reasoning that prevents ecological sensibilities and cooperative community efforts.

The higher price described by Orr and the modern hubris described by Bowers ultimately refer to the ecological destruction that follows the demise of learning and the collapse of self in the modern world. The meaning of the turmoil in the inner life of a person's actions can be understood only in terms of the latent and unconscious content that moves the individual. Thus, postmodern education that is attentive to ecological concerns must begin with attention to the unconscious as well as the physical, emotional, and psychological places of education. Successful interpretations that lead to understanding and healing can be formulated only by uncovering the salient unconscious factors. This uncovering of the unconscious occurs in a realm of the place where the individual experiences his or her temporal reality. The subjectivity of place can free persons from the obsession of modernity to objectify and quantify human experience and from the pseudo-objectivity of positivism. Along with Henry Giroux, Kathleen Kesson, and William Pinar, I propose that a language of possibility can emerge to help transform both schooling and public life. Schools are one of the few places where students can experience a language of community and democratic life, and therefore emancipatory education can emerge from the chaos in the educational milieu (Giroux, 1991, 2005). It is thus significant that curriculum scholars promote analyses that explore the external and internal chaos in order to create healing and compassionate environments in classrooms, which in turn will move outward to local communities and ultimately effect global ecological transformations.

Resistance to such transformations, for example, were evident when Rachel Carson (1962) published her scathing commentary of the pesticide industry. Foremost, it became obvious to all activists that "very powerful pressure groups would not only vote against necessary changes in the direction of responsible ecological policies, but they also had the power and influence to monopolize the mass media with counter information" (Naess, 1995). Carson ushered in a wave of activism on behalf of the environment and our relationship to it. It was clear that an ethics of dualisms and ego was no longer adequate to deal with some of the major ethical problems of the day. With the possibilities and uncertainties today of nuclear proliferation, racism, global warming, psychic alienation, terrorism, and war at even greater levels, an ethics of inclusiveness, rootedness, care, connection, and unity through difference is essential. My vision and convictions in this chapter are born out of movements such as the Norwegian Green Party and their attempts to root sustainability, ecological justice, and human and nonhuman rights with realities of economic growth and technological advances:

> Social development can proceed only at the cost of the quality of life, which after all, is a basic value; social and global solidarity implies reversing the trend

towards the growing differences between rich and poor; the material standards in the rich countries must be reversed; and bureaucracy and the power of capital must also be reduced. [This program] includes a technology adapted to nature and humans, cultural diversity, viable local communities, and a respect for nature and life. Other key issues included an increase in the minimum wage; redistribution of wealth; decentralization and the support of small organizations; the participation of children and the young in productive work; ecological architecture that gives children access to free nature, not just parks; transfer of military resources to environmental tasks; global cooperation and security; and the support of groups who work for alternative kinds of societies. (Sessions, 1995, p. 252)

I believe that modern progress can only be justified if it prevents the massive destruction of indigenous cultures and the Earth's natural and ecosystems. Otherwise, modern progress destroys the very people it is attempting to advance. Profit is acceptable if it does not come at the cost of the spiritual, environmental, gendered, cultural, or racial dislocation and its symptoms. Simply, our profit, products, and modern progress, as well as our spirits, must be balanced and rooted "with" and "for" the quality of life deserved by all human and nonhuman life forms.

I approach the current ecological crises with fear and despair, but also with profound determination. Studies of deep ecology, ecofeminism, environmental racism, and postmodern ethics are inspirational points of departure because they are more politically lively, courageous, aesthetic, probing, personal, and risky than conventional wisdom. Each "offers an alternative vision of the world in which race, class, gender, and age barriers have been eliminated and basic human needs have been fulfilled" (Merchant, 1992, p. 236). I see educators as healers and caretakers of the Earth in all of its complexity, spirituality, chaos, primal urges, and difference in this "self-educating universe" (Sessions, 1995). Much of the inspiration derives from the possibility that teachers will extend an awareness of the human experience to what George Sessions describes as "those profound communications made by the universe about us, by the sun and moon and stars, the clouds and rain, the contours of the earth and all its living forms ... [that draw] us back into itself to experience the deepest of all mysteries" (1995, p. 15).

As we come to the end of this chapter, let us reflect on *Radical Ecology* by Carolyn Merchant (1992, 2005), *Earthcare: Women and the Environment and Ecology*, also by Carolyn Merchant (1996, 2008), and Arne Naess' *Deepness of Questions and the Deep Ecology Movement* (1995). The following are just a few of the suggestions that these visionary women share with us for action in the postmodern era. Can you find ways to incorporate these concerns into your curriculum?

- The dangers of radioactive, toxic, and hazardous wastes to human health and reproduction have been exposed by citizen activists, and regulations concerning disposal have been tightened.
- The rapid clear-cutting of tropical rainforests and northern hemisphere old growth forests by corporations on both public and private lands and the associated decimation

of rare and endangered species have been brought to public awareness, and cutting in some areas has been curtailed.

- The dangers of pesticides and herbicides on foods and in water supplies and the availability of alternative systems of agriculture have been made visible.
- Direct, nonviolent action has become an acceptable and highly visible means of political protest.
- Alternative, nonpatriarchal forms of spirituality and alternative pathways within mainstream religions that view people as caretakers and/or equal parts of nature rather than dominators are being adopted by more and more people.
- The need for ecological education and individual commitment to alternative life-styles that reduce conspicuous consumption and recycle resources has begun in many schools and communities.
- Resources should be replenished, environments restored, and biodiversity maintained by all industries and businesses, especially transnational corporations.
- Reproductive health care and family planning should be available to all women.
- Unnecessarily complicated means to reach a goal or end should be avoided and simple means used.
- There should be endeavors to maintain and increase the sensitivity and appreciation of goods of which there is enough for all to enjoy.
- There needs to be an appreciation of ethnic and cultural difference among people.
- There should be a concern about the situation of the Third and Fourth Worlds and the attempt to avoid a material standard of living that is too much higher than that of the needy.
- People should appreciate and choose meaningful work rather than work to make a living.
- People should attempt to satisfy vital needs rather than desires and to reduce the number of possessions.
- People should try to act resolutely and without cowardice in conflicts, but to remain nonviolent in word and deeds.
- There should be a move toward vegetarianism and veganism, total or partial.

We have come full circle in this chapter, so to speak. We have moved from environmental concerns to classroom arrangements, to post-Katrina rebuilding, to an ecological metaphor, to psychological investigations, to steps for activism. In every case we have seen a concern for interrelationships, deep ecological, holistic models, and natural processes. This understanding of curriculum development challenges educators to prioritize global interdependence and ecological sustainability in their postmodern paradigms. Chapter 9 will explore another approach to postmodern curriculum studies by scholars who take this message seriously, especially as it may inform the political arrangements in postmodern society.

nine
Utopian Visions, Democracy, and the Egalitarian Ideal

In the discussion of the reconceptualization of curriculum studies in chapter 3, we saw that feminist theory and political theory gained ascendancy in the curriculum field in the 1980s. One of the leading scholars in the political sector by 1980 was Michael Apple. At that time, Apple was interested in understanding the relationship between education and economic structure and the linkages between knowledge and power. In *Ideology and Curriculum*, Apple (1979, 2004) summarizes his position:

> In essence, the problem has become more and more a *structural* issue for me. I have increasingly sought to ground it [education and economics, knowledge and power] in a set of critical questions that are generated out of a tradition of neo-Marxist argumentation, a tradition which seems to me to offer the most cogent framework for organizing one's thinking and action about education. (p. 1)

He then outlines an approach to curriculum studies that emphasizes modes of material production, ideological values, and class relations, as well as racial, sexual, and politico-economic structures of social power and the impact of these issues on the consciousness of people in their historical and socio-economic situations. Apple (1979) concludes that his curriculum theory "seeks to portray the concrete ways that prevalent (and ... alienating) structural arrangements—the basic ways institutions, people, and modes of production, distribution, and consumption are organized and controlled—dominate cultural life. This includes such day-to-day practices as schools and the teaching and curricula found within them" (p. 2).

In the postmodern field in the 1990s, feminist and political scholarship became two among many eclectic approaches to curriculum studies. This chapter will introduce political scholarship, often called critical theory, which has emerged since the early work of Michael Apple, and will explore its implications for curriculum development in the postmodern era. Particularly, the vision of utopia, democracy, and egalitarianism, so integral to the American political and educational psyche, will inform our discussion. Democracy is an ideal that is filled with possibilities but also that is part of the ongoing struggle for equality, freedom, and human dignity. In a sense, this egalitarian vision reflects the human quest for an educational system that upholds and promotes the highest aspirations, dreams, and values of individual persons, not only in the United States but also throughout the global community. At the same time we must understand and deconstruct the political practices that deny equality and justice to some persons and advantage and privilege others—usually the wealthy and corporate power brokers and their allies. In fact, in 2010, the US Supreme Court even defined corporations as persons with legal standing. The logic of corporate power, money, and domination reached an even higher level.

What should be the focus of curriculum in the postmodern era if egalitarian ideals, democratic citizenship, and utopian visions are to be integral to education? How can education in the postmodern era transcend the polarization that exists between those who promote equality, justice, and agency for all human persons, especially the impoverished and politically repressed, and those who staunchly defend individual liberty because they believe that egalitarianism has led to socialist practices that destroy the rights of the entrepreneur, the capitalist, the genius, or the investor? In short, can we really have both *liberty* and *justice* for all? A postmodernist would answer affirmatively because the two are inextricably bound up in each other.

Following the Renaissance and the rise of the political theories of the Enlightenment, it was widely believed that liberty and justice could be engineered in societies. As we saw in chapter 7, some characterize these movements as liberalism, socialism, and radicalism. Postmodern political perspectives seek to reconceptualize, deconstruct, and/or replace these modern political theories and the resultant devastation that occurred in the 20th century because of the materialism, communism, fascism, corporatism, globalization, and isolationist individualism that has grown out of them. Postmodernism recognizes that modern political theories have reached a level of absurdity that threatens to destroy life and democracy, and even some of the very concepts that have oriented critical educational theories, such as emancipation, hegemony, and social transformation, have been exposed for problematic applications (Cherryholmes, 1988b; Stanley, 1992; Bowers, 2006). While such analysis is important, postmodernists adamantly uphold the vision of justice, equality, liberation, freedom, and compassion that underlines critical theory.

As we reviewed in the introduction, some critics such as Chet Bowers question whether political curriculum theorists today are simply ultramodernist revolutionaries recycling neo-Marxist ideology; others will contend that critical curriculum theory offers a fresh alternative for education in the postmodern era that will engender social justice. The answer to this debate is not clear, and, depending on the individual research being promulgated, both perspectives may have validity at times. Critical theory, while certainly not a unified system of thought, contains some general assumptions: all thought and power relations are inexorably linked; these power relations form oppressive social arrangements; facts and values are inseparable and inscribed by ideology; language is a key element in the formation of subjectivities, and thus critical literacy—the ability to negotiate passages through social systems and structures—is more important than functional literacy—the ability to decode and compute; oppression is based in the reproduction of privileged knowledge codes and practices. These assumptions of critical theory challenge educators to look carefully at their classroom practices. For example, in literacy education, how much time is devoted to functional activities and how much effort is directed toward cultural literacy, social systems, and critical literacy? How does our approach to literacy deny agency to students? What is the impact on democracy when citizens are not given access to ideas and are disempowered in society?

This chapter does not attempt to categorize various scholars or draw any definitive conclusions about the validity of critical theories. However, the contribution of political scholars to contemporary curriculum discourses is not only enormous but also responsible for focusing attention on the plight of those who are disempowered in society. Samuel Bowles and Herbert Gintis (1976), for example, in their classic work write about correspondence theories that draw parallels between economic and educational stratification. Schools, they contend, contribute to the cultural reproduction of class relations and economic order, which allows for very little social mobility. Beverly Gordon echoes this theory when she writes that the "bootstrap ideology" as part of the American dream has been very difficult for African Americans and other people of color as a group to realize:

> What we are witnessing is not simply racism—the picture is far more complex. It is a picture of an evolved culture that combines racism with elitism, an inherited, empirically bounded Spencerian rationale, and capitalism. What does this say about fairness, equity, and justice in society? … Students must know about power and the uses of power, that is, political and economic forces. … Students must develop the will to be active participants in the society all of their lives— so that the society, in fact, lives up to its democratic ideals. … True democracy will be achieved only when all citizens have the knowledge and the motivation to live up to society's highest values and when economic and political opportunities are made equally available to all its constituents. (1989, pp. 99–101)

It is abundantly clear that critical theory exercises an extremely important role in the curriculum field, as we have seen above in the research of Apple, Bowles, Gintis, and Gordon. Other political scholars include Philip Wexler (1992); Theodore Brameld (1956, 1971); William Stanley (1992); Paulo Freire (1970, 1985, 2001); Peter McLaren (1989, 1997, 2005); Jonathan Kozol (1975, 1991, 2005); Stanley Aronowitz (1992, 2006, 2008); Paul Willis (1977); Dennis Carlson (1992; Carlson & Gause, 2007); Lois Weis (1983, 1988); and Henry Giroux (1988, 1992, 1993, 2005), who is perhaps the most recognized figure in this sector of the field. Giroux (1988) summarizes the egalitarian vision of critical theorists:

> We must develop a social vision and commitment to make the liberal arts supportive of a democratic public sphere in which despair will become unconvincing and hope a practice for students and teachers alike, regardless of race, class, religion, gender, or age. (p. 261)

Creating a democratic educational vision that provides hope for all teachers and students is central to critical theory. Some of the specific questions and concerns that are raised in the process of developing this vision include the following: How do students acquire knowledge in schools? Is knowledge reproduced in schools to support the status quo systems of inequity? How do students and teachers resist the structures and knowledge that are conveyed not only in classroom instruction but also in the lived experience of the school environment? How do schools shape visions, values, and outlooks on life? Whose interests are being served by the perpetuation of these outlooks? Do these visions, values, and outlooks promote equality, justice, agency, and empowerment, or do they reinforce bigotry, inequality, and repression? How can schooling be an instrument to promote social justice? And, as Elizabeth Ellsworth (1989) asked, how can teachers and scholars foster democracy and agency without becoming oppressive themselves?

In the construction of an emancipatory view of education, philosophers and theorists as diverse as John Dewey ([1916] 1985), George S. Counts (1932), and Hannah Arendt (1958) have contended that schools should challenge the social order. Crises in education and society are reflected in the debate about the role of schools in advancing social issues, democratic themes, and utopian values. Should education, as Dewey (1899) asked, be a function of society or should society be a function of education? In other words, should schools participate in the process of reproducing the knowledge, interests, and values of the dominant society, or should they advance democracy while promoting an emancipatory approach to knowledge and learning so as to re-create a just and compassionate society? Dewey believed the latter, and so do the critical theorists. So did the social reconstructionists of the early 20th century.

The social reconstructionists were concerned with two major premises. First, society is in need of constant reform and change and, second, such change must involve both structural changes in education and the use of education in reconstructing society. George S. Counts is perhaps one of the most well known of the social reconstructionists. In his important essay *Dare the Schools Build a New Social Order?*, the themes of this movement are clear. Counts (1932) summarizes the feeling of many:

> [Education] ... must ... face squarely and courageously every social issue, come to grips with life in all of its stark reality, establish an organic relation with the community, develop a realistic and comprehensive theory of welfare, fashion a compelling and challenging vision of human destiny, and become less frightened than it is today at the bogies of *imposition* and *indoctrination*. (Cited in Ozmon & Craver, 1990, p. 189)

Counts points out that the concept of indoctrination in education is horrifying to most citizens, who would reject such imposition. However, schooling is complicit in forms of social control and indoctrination that result in social injustices. What should be done about this? Counts (1932) continues:

> There is the fallacy that the school should be impartial in its emphases, that no bias should be given in instruction. We have already observed how the individual is inevitably molded by the culture into which he (sic) is born. In the

school a similar process operates ... [and] some selection must be made of teachers, curricula, architecture, methods of teaching .... Teachers, if they increase their stock of courage, intelligence, and vision, might become a social force of some magnitude. ... That the teachers should deliberately reach for power and then make the most of their conquest is my firm conviction. (Cited in Ozmon & Craver, 1990, p. 190)

Teachers, Counts contends, must accept their role in reconstructing society because of the problems of the social situation of the modern era. This reminds me of the arguments made by Orestes Brownson against the common school movement of Horace Mann, which we reviewed in chapter 4. Counts (1932), reflecting many sentiments of postmodern political thinkers who will follow him years later, warns:

We live in troubled times; we live in an age of profound change. In order to match our epoch we would probably have to go back to the fall of the ancient empires. ... Consider the present condition of the nation. ... Here is a society that manifests the most extraordinary contradictions: a mastery over the forces of nature is accompanied by extreme material insecurity; dire poverty walks hand in hand with the most extravagant living the world has ever known; an abundance of goods of all kinds is coupled with privation, misery, and even starvation; great captains of industry close factories without warning and dismiss the workmen by whose labors they have amassed huge fortunes through the years; consumption is subordinated to production and a philosophy of deliberate waste is widely proclaimed as the highest economic wisdom. ... [We] stand confused and irresolute before the future [and] seem to lack the moral quality necessary to quicken, discipline, and give direction. In a recent paper professor Dewey has, in my judgment, diagnosed our troubles: "The schools, like the nation, are in need of a central purpose which will create new enthusiasm and devotion, and which will unify and guide all intellectual plans." (Cited in Ozmon & Craver, 1990, pp. 191–192)

The search for a central purpose of education, as introduced by George Counts, John Dewey, and social reconstructionists, that will provide new enthusiasm to address the economic and moral decay of modern society remains a concern of political theorists in the postmodern era.

Critical theorists like Henry Giroux (1988) also question "whether schools [should] uncritically serve and reproduce the existing society or challenge the social order in order to develop and advance its democratic imperatives" (p. 243). Giroux, as we noted above, has concluded that the development of a social vision and commitment to make the liberal arts supportive of a democratic public sphere must be a priority in postmodern education. Hope must replace despair as the central practice for students and teachers, regardless of race, class, religion, gender, sexuality, language, ability, ethnicity, or age.

In addition to critical theorists like Giroux, liberation theologians propose the development of a social vision and a commitment to an emancipatory view that would promote hope for all people, especially the poor, regardless of race, class, religion, gender, or age (Gutiérrez, 1973). Liberation theologians reevaluate historical realities and advocate changes that are contrary to dominant social trends but nevertheless linked to a deep current of desire for liberation of the poor. Like the postmodern proposals that insist on the elimination of dualisms in favor of integrated wholeness (Jencks, 1986; Griffin, 1988a, 1988b; Slattery & Rapp, 2003) and the proposals of process philosophy that reject bifurcations of space and time (Whitehead, [1929] 1978), liberation movements and political theories seek unity and integration of human life and the social, political, and economic realms. Political scholarship rejects the tendency to separate curriculum from human response in the social order. This gives rise to social action, especially for those excluded and disempowered. This process parallels in many ways John Dewey's concept of ideals and imagination giving rise to social consequences and values (Dewey, 1934a). This understanding of the purpose of curriculum in educational institutions by critical theorists is explained by Giroux (1988):

> All too often [tradition in the liberal arts] translates into an instrumentalism more appropriate to producing disciplinary specialists than to providing forms of moral leadership necessary for advancing the interests of a democratic society. In its most expressive form, this tradition views that the purpose of liberal arts is to initiate students into a unitary [Western] cultural tradition. In this view, excellence is acquiring an already established tradition, not about struggling to create new forms of civic practice and participation. Culture is viewed as an artifact to be taken out of the historical warehouse of dominant tradition and uncritically transmitted to students. (p. 245)

Just as Giroux resists viewing culture as an artifact and the school as an instrument of uncritical transmission of the artifact, so too does the postmodern curriculum resist the concept of knowledge as simply an artifact to be transmitted uncritically by educational institutions. These postmodern theories unite politics and social ethics in such a way that the concept of deferred justice must be challenged.

Critical theory derives from the work of post-Marxist theorists of the Frankfurt School, who study socio-economic class structures and the ways that school curriculum and curricularists unwittingly perpetuate such structures. These structures, critical theorists argue, enslave subjected classes. Critical theorists contend that these people require a liberating pedagogy. An important early example of critical theory in practice is presented by Paulo Freire in *Pedagogy of the Oppressed*. Freire (1970) demonstrates how the "banking" concept of education is an instrument of oppression:

> Oppression—overwhelming control—is necrophilic; it is nourished by love of death, not life. The banking concept of education [is] an act of depositing in which students are the depositories and the teacher is the depositor. ... Instead of communicating, the teacher issues communiques and makes deposits which the students patiently receive, memorize, and repeat. [This] serves the interests of oppression and is also necrophilic. Based on a mechanistic, static, naturalistic, spatialized view of consciousness, it transforms students into receiving objects. It attempts to control thinking and action, leads men to adjust to the world, and inhibits their creative power. (pp. 64–66)

Freire (1970) contends that those committed to empowerment and liberation must reject the banking concept in its entirety and adopt instead a problem-posing concept where people are viewed as conscious beings in relation to the world: "Problem-posing education, responding to the essence of consciousness (intentionality), rejects communiques and embodies communication. Liberating education consists in acts of cognition, not transferals of information" (p. 66). When the illiterate peasants of Freire's Third World classrooms, as well as uncritical students of First World schools, begin to participate in a problem-posing and problem-solving educational experience, they begin to develop a new awareness of self, a new sense of dignity, and ultimately an experience of hope. Freire (1970, 2001), speaking for all critical theorists, contends that "no pedagogy that is truly liberating can remain distant from the oppressed by treating them as unfortunates and by presenting for their emulation models from among the oppressors" (cited in Schubert, 1986, p. 313). Paulo Freire is a major figure in political educational discourses, and students of curriculum development should study his works as well as secondary sources such as the important collection of essays by Peter McLaren and Peter Leonard (1993) entitled *Paulo Freire: A Critical Encounter* and Peter McLaren's (2000) *Che Guevara, Paulo Freire, and the Pedagogy of Revolution*. The definitive biography of Freire, by James Kirylo (2011), is titled *Paulo Freire: The Man From Recife*.

The self-conscious critique is an essential element of critical theory. Giroux characterizes the pedagogical goals of critical theory as a means "to assess the newly emerging forms of capitalism along with the changing forms of domination that accompanied them, to rethink and radically reconstruct the meaning of human emancipation, and [to engage in] self-conscious critique" (1988, pp. 7–8). This critique of the contradictions in culture allows theorists to distinguish what should be from what is. As the conditions of suffering are recognized and articulated, models for change will emerge.

The utopian, democratic, and egalitarian visions of many critical theorists emerge from their own self-conscious critique of their autobiographical schooling experiences. Jonathan Kozol (1967) was inspired to publish his first book, *Death at an Early Age*, as a result of his experiences as a young White man teaching English to disadvantaged African-American children in Boston's public schools. Kozol relates the story of his frustration with dilapidated facilities, overcrowded classrooms, and outdated textbooks. While browsing through a bookstore in Boston, he caught sight of a collection of poems with a picture of a new African-American poet on the cover. He purchased the book for his class. He not only wanted to show the students what a new book looked like but also that there were black poets, since none was represented in the school textbooks. Kozol (1967) explains how he was fired for "curricular deviation" because he read from Langston Hughes' poem that asked, "What happens to a dream deferred? Does it dry up like a raisin in the sun? ... Or does it explode?" He relates how one particularly angry young woman who had resisted him throughout the course was enthralled by the poem and asked to borrow the book. She went home and memorized the poem. The poetry of Langston Hughes transformed the students and the curriculum, but this particular poem also alarmed the school authorities, who were afraid of what might happen if poor black children were exposed to "radical" poetry. Since it was not included in the curriculum guide or district syllabus, Kozol was fired. Kozol has gone on to write many inspiring books about such topics as the lack of education for the children of the homeless and migrant workers, the politics of literacy in America, the savage economic inequalities of schooling in the US, and his 2005 book about racial injustice titled *The Shame of the Nation: The Restoration of Apartheid Schooling in America*. Reading the works of Jonathan Kozol would be a good place to start the investigation of educational political commentaries for beginning students of curriculum development.

Curriculum students might also want to explore the work of another critical theorist who was originally inspired by autobiographical experiences, Peter McLaren. McLaren (1989, 2005) has written a comprehensive and accessible introduction to critical pedagogy that includes excerpts from his journal while teaching at an elementary school in one of Toronto's inner-city suburbs, known as the Jane-Finch Corridor. McLaren (1989) writes in *Life in Schools: An Introduction to Critical Pedagogy in the Foundations of Education* the following summary:

> In my attempt to understand how schooling "really" works, I was soon struck by the range of sociological theories that explain how schools can and do disempower delegitimate, and disconfirm the lives of disadvantaged children. I discovered as well that schools operate through a "hidden curriculum" which incarcerates students in the "semiotics of power" and works against the success of racial minorities, women, and the poor. Yet I was also made aware of how schools could work in emancipatory ways to empower students to accomplish, in the words of Paulo Freire, "reading the word and reading the world." (p. x)

In this book McLaren addressed two important questions: first, Why is critical pedagogy so important for schooling today?; and second, a question that traditional curriculum theory and mainstream educational theories have avoided, What is the relationship between what we do in classrooms and our efforts to build a just society?

McLaren's book provides an excellent outline of the central elements of critical pedagogy. As we saw above, one of these elements is the concept of the "hidden curriculum," which refers to the unintended outcomes of the schooling process. The hidden curriculum contrasts with the overt curriculum, which is the official curriculum of the syllabus, lesson plan, or scope and sequence guide. The null curriculum refers to those elements of the overt curriculum that are omitted due to time constraints, omissions, or prejudice of the teacher. Critical theorists contend that the hidden curriculum and the null curriculum have a much more profound impact on students than the overt curriculum. For example, if a United States history teacher skips the Civil War and the civil rights movement, a message about the importance of issues related to racism in American history is indelibly implanted in the psyche of the students. Also, if the same American history teacher presents the structure of democracy in a classroom environment that is repressive and undemocratic, students learn more about democracy from the classroom environment than from the course material.

Another important element of critical theory includes the study of forms of knowledge. Critical theory follows a threefold distinction regarding forms of knowledge posited by the German social theorist Jürgen Habermas: technical knowledge, which can be measured and quantified; practical knowledge, which is geared toward helping individuals understand social events that are ongoing and situational; and emancipatory knowledge, which attempts to reconcile and transcend the opposition between technical and practical knowledge. Emancipatory knowledge helps us to understand how social relationships are distorted and manipulated by relations of power and privilege (see Table 9.1).

Another important issue that Peter McLaren addresses is the dialectical nature of critical pedagogy, which allows the educational scholar to see the school not simply as an arena of indoctrination or social control or a site for instruction but also as a cultural terrain that promotes student empowerment. This dialectical perspective allows critical theorists to see the school as a site for both domination and liberation, thus incorporating Habermas' notion of emancipatory interests.

Ultimately, critical theory is directed in the interest of emancipation, change, and liberation. William Schubert (1986) summarizes:

> Emancipation refers to freeing one's self to enable growth and development from the taken-for-granted ideology of social conventions, beliefs, and modes of operation. It strives to renew the ideology so that it serves as a basis for

Type of Science or Inquiry	Empirical/Analytical	Hermeneutic	Critical
Interest Served	Technical	Practical	Emancipatory
Social Organization	Work	Interaction	Power
	Mode of Rationality		
	Posits principles of control and certainty	Emphasizes understanding and communicative interaction	Assumes the necessity of ideological critique and action
	Operates in the interests of law-like propositions that are empirically testable	Sees human beings as active creators of knowledge	Seeks to expose that which is oppressive and dominating
	Assumes knowledge to be value free	Looks for assumptions and meanings beneath texture of everyday life	Requires sensitivity to false conciousness
	Assumes knowledge to be objectified	Views reality as intersubjectively constituted and shared within a historical, political, and social context	Makes distorted conceptions and unjust values problematic
	Accepts unquestioningly, social reality as it is	Focuses sensitively to meaning through language use	Examines and explicates value system and concepts of justice upon which inquiry is based

TABLE 9.1 Overview of Empirical, Hermeneutic, and Critical Inquiry Derived from the Work of Jurgen Habermas

reflection and action. This requires modes of organization that emphasize power. It is perceived necessary to empower people, whatever their situation in institutionalized education, to question the value of such forces as the governance structures that direct their political life, the systems by which goods and services are generated and delivered that govern their economic life, the rules and conventions that define their social life, and the beliefs and ideals that contribute to their psychological life. (p. 318)

In critical theory, as individuals become aware of these political, economic, social, and psychological dimensions articulated above by Giroux, McLaren, Gordon, Kozol, and Schubert, and as students experience a problem-posing education as proposed by Freire, they will be stirred by a new hope. People will no longer be willing to be mere objects responding to changes occurring around them. Rather they will be more likely to take upon themselves the struggle to change the structures of society that have until the present served only to oppress. In order for the experience of hope to inspire active participation in social change and social justice, there must be a clear understanding of the meaning and implications of a liberating ideology, egalitarian ideals, and utopian visions.

In education, it is teachers, often women, who work to empower students despite the institutional burdens that plague them. Madeleine Grumet (1988b) documents this concept in her classic text *Bitter Milk: Women and Teaching*, as she explores the passage women teachers make daily between their public and private worlds and the contradictions they confront when they bring their commitments to children into the politics and knowledge systems of institutional education. Grumet offers a view of teachers divided by opposing forces. She writes: "The task when viewed in the structural complexity of our social, political, economic situation appears herculean" (1988b, p. 29). However, she offers advice consistent with critical theories, challenging women teachers with the following insight:

Only when we suspend the despair that isolates us from our history and our future can our reproductive capacity reclaim the promise of our species, not merely to conceive but to reconceive another generation. We, the women who teach, must claim our reproductive labor as a process of civilization as well as procreation. The task is daunting. (1988b, p. 29)

The task is also intimidating; but it is not impossible. Empowering teachers, peasants, students, and laborers to become leaders of emancipatory education and liberating community is the task before curriculum development scholars from the postmodern critical perspective.

What is unique about postmodern critical theory that differentiates it from earlier reconstructionism and neo-Marxism? William Stanley, in *Curriculum for Utopia*, contends that critical theory today presents a more complex and useful critique of educational theory and practice by way of having incorporated the insights of the new sociology, feminism, cultural studies, neopragmatism, and poststructuralism with social reconstructionism, neo-Marxism, and postmodernism. He contends that, on occasion, reconstructionism has verged on social engineering because the reconstructionists were preoccupied with what they perceived as relativist dangers inherent in pragmatism. Social reconstructionists tended to overemphasize the power of rationality, science, and the possibility of objective knowledge (Stanley, 1992). Stanley continues by arguing that neither despair nor a flight from ethics is appropriate:

> The insights of postmodern and poststructural theory have made clear that we can no longer apply totalizing critiques, metanarratives, or any other appeals to objective knowledge or transcendental values. Nevertheless, while radical hermeneutics and poststructuralism have revealed our knowledge to be more contingent and problematic, it does not follow that projects aimed at human betterment are either irrational or impossible. (1992, p. 220)

Stanley listens to the voices and vision of many curriculum theorists from the past as he projects a postmodern understanding of a reconceptualized reconstructionism and proposes a curriculum for utopia. His vision of curriculum for utopia insists upon the following: competence for practical judgment (*phronesis*); an ongoing critique so that empowerment and social transformation are not rendered impotent and problematic in themselves (Cherryholmes, 1988b); the meeting of minimal socio-cultural conditions in order to enable the realization of human interests; the absence of certain forms of domination, such as sexism, homophobia, racism, censorship, political oppression, and monological approaches to curriculum, that distort and limit human interests; and an affirmation that human suffering should inspire compassion for otherness, so that "we try to extend our sense of 'we' to people whom we have previously thought of as 'they'" (Rorty, 1989, p. 192). Stanley concludes that this is a "critical pedagogy of neither/nor, oriented by a poststructuralist rejection of false dichotomies, awareness of the unknowable, understanding of the limits of rationality, and an awareness of the dangers posed by both, and the terrorism of closure or monologue" (1992, p. 222).

Along with William Stanley and Madeleine Grumet, I believe that postmodern pedagogy and curriculum development face tremendous barriers due to injustice, economic inequality, sexism, homophobia, racism, despair, and other terrors of the modern world that are rampant in our global society. The postmodern utopia offered here is not the perfect world of apocalyptic and idealistic dreams; rather it is a vision of hope, justice, compassion, *phronesis*, community, inclusiveness, and dialogue. This emerging concept of utopia as an ethical vision, as distinct from earlier neo-Marxist critical theories, is apparent in the postmodern literature of many disciplines. If critical scholarship is to move beyond Enlightenment notions of politics and the individual in order to create a postmodern dialogue, this vision of utopia and ethics must be included. Perhaps typical is the conclusion of Libby Falk Jones and Sarah Webster Goodwin (1990), in *Feminism, Utopia, and Narrative*, that utopian discourse, as a complex mode of being rather than a naive program, incorporates values that build just, compassionate, and sustainable communities. In this same sense curriculum development in the postmodern era is not a naive program of studies, but rather a complex integration of values that concretize hope in school communities and engender determination to act for the good of the global community.

As introduced at the beginning of this chapter, the systematic effort to understand curriculum politically began in earnest in the 1970s. The traditional notion that curriculum could be developed, conducted, and evaluated in a politically neutral manner was dismantled. Likewise, the traditional assumption that schools function as avenues of upward social and economic mobility was discredited. The rejection of these ideas by political curriculum theorists has been accompanied by the construction of a political understanding of schooling that includes an analysis of reproduction of status quo values and power arrangements, resistance to dominant structures, ideology as inscribed in cultural and social arrangements, and the predominant influence of these cultural, social, and power arrangements called hegemony. Recent political theory has also incorporated into its domain of analysis notions of critical literacy, critical race theory, eco-feminism, queer theory, postmodernism, and poststructuralism. For example, Henry Giroux has attempted to revive resistance theory by incorporating poststructuralism and African-American feminism. Others, such as Michael Apple, continue to emphasize neo-Marxist class struggle.

In another recent example, Karen Krasny of York University writes about the emphasis on social efficiency and rising neoliberalism in education:

> America's historic preoccupation with social efficiency has given rise to a sweeping neoliberalism. Fixated on regulating human conduct in the service of profitable outcomes, education appears increasingly less concerned about the ability of students and teachers to take in the *sense of things* in ways that would provide them with imaginative tools to remake their world. (2006, p. 28, emphasis in the original)

Here Krasny reminds us that the impact of social efficiency and accountability in the schools actually strips us of the possibility of conducting the critical work necessary to create agency and justice. She continues:

> Education throughout the Western world has adopted a corporate rhetoric where terms like outcomes-based, targeted groups, tracking systems, performance scales, quality assessment, executive summaries, efficiency studies, standards, performance analysis, cost benefits, ratings-focused, and bottom-line define the work of curriculum and pedagogy. Education took on an even greater "exchange value" in the nineties as free market economists like Milton Friedman entered the US educational arena to argue in favor of school vouchers and schools of choice as a response to the perceived failings of schools to meet the grade. Such initiatives modeled on trickle-down economics merely fueled competition and furthered the project of elitism robbing much needed funding from overburdened public schools. In true top-down management style, individual ethical and historical agency are readily subsumed in a hierarchical arrangement in which provinces and states track district performance, districts track school performance, schools track teacher performance, teachers track student performance, and everyone has someone to blame. (2006, p. 32)

There have been many critics of political theories in curriculum studies who have attempted to address the concerns raised by Krasny and others using a different political analysis. Philip Wexler, for example, charges that this work is reactionary and that reproduction and resistance theories are simply recycling 1960s activist movements without regard for movements in history and society since that time. Wexler (1992) uses social and historical analysis traceable to the Frankfurt School but also employs poststructuralism as a discursive basis of a social psychology of the schooling experience. Chet Bowers (1987, 1993, 2005), as we have seen, has formulated a postliberal theory of curriculum that incorporates communicative competence and ecological models that challenge liberal political theories.

As we have explored in this chapter, there are emerging forms of critical theory which offer the possibility of advancing social, cultural, and ideological arrangements that have an impact on schooling today. However, there appears to be conflict as to whether political curriculum theory should remain rooted in Marxism and the Frankfurt School or engage poststructural, racial, ecological, queer, and gendered perspectives in the curriculum field. The debates over these issues certainly will intensify in the coming years as the dangers of global conflict force us to reevaluate our understanding of the world.

ten
Aesthetic Inquiry, Arts-Based Research, and the Proleptic Moment

"The meaning of a word to me is not as exact as the meaning of a color. Colors and shapes make a more definite statement than words. I am often amazed at the spoken and written word telling me what I have painted. Where I was born and where and how I have lived is unimportant. It is what I have done with where I have been that should be of interest. Color is one of the great things in the world that makes life worth living to me, and I have come to think of painting as my effort to create an equivalent of the world in color—life as I see it." (Georgia O'Keefe)

There are at least eight ways to explore curriculum development from a postmodern aesthetic perspective:

1. a review of postmodern art and architectural movements and their impact on society and culture, along with their political implications—for example, in Charles Jencks' (1986, 2002) *What is Post-Modernism?* and *The New Paradigm in Architecture*, Dennis Earl Fehr's (1993) *Dogs Playing Cards*, or Landon Beyer's (1988) *Art and Society: Toward New Directions in Aesthetic Education*;

2. a study of the interrelationship between postmodern philosophies and art—for example, Michel Foucault's (1973) poststructural analysis of René Magritte's painting in *This is Not a Pipe*, Elizabeth Ellsworth's (2005) *Places of Learning: Media, Architecture, Pedagogy*, or Maxine Greene's (1978, 1995, 2001) social justice and phenomenological investigations of education in *Landscapes of Learning*, *Releasing the Imagination*, and *Variations on a Blue Guitar*;

3. an analysis of texts that have provided a transition from the dominant quantitative paradigms of evaluation in schooling toward an aesthetic and qualitative understanding of curriculum and instruction—for example, in George Willis and William Schubert's (1991) *Reflections from the Heart of Educational Inquiry:*

Understanding Curriculum and Teaching through the Arts, William Tierney and Yvonna Lincoln's (1997) *Representation and the Text: Re-Framing the Narrative Voice*, or Elliot Eisner's (1997, 2001) *The Enlightened Eye* and *The Educational Imagination*;

4. a study of the correspondences between aesthetic experiences and curriculum—for example, in John Dewey's (1934b) *Art as Experience* or Ronald Padgham's (1988) "Correspondences: Contemporary Curriculum Theory and Twentieth-Century Art";

5. a review of the phenomenological literature that understands knowledge as a human construction and social life as an enacted, meaning-embedded experience, inseparable from human beliefs, values, and creativity—for example, in Ted Aoki's (1988) "Toward a Dialectic Between the Conceptual World and the Lived World" or Max van Manen's (1993) *The Tact of Teaching: The Meaning of Pedagogical Thoughtfulness*;

6. an exploration of notions of knowledge acquisition and of thinking that are distinct from mainstream social and behavioral science—for example, in Thomas Barone's (1993) "Breaking the Mold: The New American Student as Strong Poet" or Denise Palmer Wolf's (1992) "Becoming Knowledge: The Evolution of Art Education Curriculum";

7. understanding curriculum through arts-based educational research—for example, "The Educational Researcher as Artist Working Within" (Slattery, 2001);

8. aesthetic work that is co-relational, collaborative, and co-poietic, as in the work of Rita Irwin and Alex de Cosson (2004) and Barbara Bickel's (2011) "A/r/tographic Collaboration as Radical Relatedness." The A/r/tographic research is explored comprehensively in *Being with A/r/tography*, edited by Stephanie Springgay, Rita Irwin, Carl Leggo and Peter Gouzouasis (2008).

In all eight of these approaches to qualitative, aesthetic, humanistic, and arts-based inquiry in curriculum studies there is an interest in exploring ways of knowing and learning that create what William Pinar and Madeleine Grumet (1976) call "synthetical moments." In the synthesizing moment there is a reconstruction of the self and an experience of solidarity of the intellect, the body, the spirit, and the cosmos, as well as an intrinsic coherence of time, place, and meaning. Michel Serres (1982) writes about a sense of contemporaneousness. He uses provoking metaphors and analogies to explain that there is convergence in particular events where many things come together and similar forms provide a passage for making connections on the journey of life. While Serres insists on keeping things separate, his analogies help to make connections through which we experience contemporaneousness. Both Pinar and Grumet and Serres provide options for rethinking modern obsessions with establishing causal links in space over time. Linear explanations are replaced by concepts of contemporaneousness, convergence, and synthesis. Such meaning-full and awe-full moments are integral to the postmodern curriculum and not peripheral. Herbert Kliebard (1992a) warns:

> [Humanism] has come to be associated with a set of subjects, a segment of the school curriculum, believed to have the power to stir the imagination, enhance the appreciation of beauty, and disclose motives that actuate human behavior. ...

The arts—music, painting, sculpture, poetry—[are] the highest forms of expression by which human beings convey their experience and their aspirations. These, it turns out, are the very subjects that have suffered the steepest decline in the American school curriculum during the course of the twentieth century, a decline which, if continued, will at best make artistic expression and appreciation the province of a handful of sensitive souls. (p. 3)

Curriculum studies in the postmodern era take Kliebard's warning to heart and prioritize artistic and aesthetic experiences, humanistic values, synthetical self-understanding, and a sense of contemporaneousness in the schooling process. The arts are no longer understood to be at the periphery of the curriculum; rather, they are the heart and soul of teaching, pedagogy, and human growth. We are all aware that the arts are often marginalized or absent from the school curriculum. However, we must remember that the arts, particularly music, were considered the pinnacle of education for the ancient Greeks and the heart of the curriculum for many cultures throughout the ages.

A postmodern aesthetic curriculum includes the integration of eclectic, ironic, and kaleidoscopic experiences that affirm the uniqueness of individual creativity and the contemporaneousness of time and place, as well as global solidarity. Modern curriculum development paradigms, with their emphasis on rational discourse, time on task, lesson implementation, and objective evaluation, discourage aesthetic experiences while elevating mathematical computation, scientific methods, and reading comprehension in the core of the curriculum. Music, fine arts, drama, dance, poetry, speech, band, painting, and the like have been relegated to the fringe, often the first casualties of budget cuts or scheduling conflicts. Postmodernism prioritizes the dramatic, the artistic, the nonrational, and the intuitive dimensions of the human person in the learning process. Rather than cutting art from the heart of the curriculum, postmodern education encourages aesthetic reflections from the heart in educational inquiry.

Perhaps John Dewey provides the most cogent analysis of aesthetics in education in his book *Art as Experience*. Dewey (1934b) considers the significance of the arts, and concludes, "In the end, works of art are the only media of complete and unhindered communication between man and man [*sic*] that can occur in a world full of gulfs and walls that limit community of experience" (p. 105). Cleo Cherryholmes (1994) extends Dewey's position: "I choose to highlight Dewey's emphasis on experience because it is less restrictive than transactional realism. To illustrate the possibilities that 'experience' opens up, I extend my comments to aesthetics. Aesthetics ... is a central but almost universally overlooked aspect of research" (p. 16). Cherryholmes is one of many scholars today who recognize the potential of aesthetics to inform our curriculum research and schooling practices. Richard Rorty (1982) provides philosophical support for this position:

The burden of my argument so far has been that if we get rid of notions of "objectivity" and "scientific method" we shall be able to see the social sciences as continuous with literature—as interpreting other people to us, and thus enlarging and deepening our sense of community. ... One can emphasize, as

Dewey did, the moral importance of the social sciences—their role in widening and deepening our sense of community. Or one can emphasize, as Michel Foucault does, the way in which the social sciences have served as instruments of the "disciplinary society," the connection between knowledge and power rather than between knowledge and human solidarity. (pp. 203–204)

In either case, both Dewey and Foucault point the way to a consideration of human solidarity. Following Rorty, Cherryholmes (1988b, 1999) contends that this human solidarity, which is informed by his critical pragmatism, involves making episte- mological, ethical, and aesthetic choices and translating them into discourse practices.

The experience of curriculum introduced above is orchestrated in such a way that improvisation and spontaneity enhance the educational experience. Like improvisa- tional jazz, zydeco, or cajun music, one sound or beat leads to another, forming an eclectic mixture of instruments and rhythms. Success in improvisational music and curriculum has one fundamental requirement, according to David Smith (1991): "The group members must be committed to staying 'with' each other, constantly listening to subtle nuances of tempo and melody, with one person never stealing the show for the entire session" (p. 198). In education, this community solidarity requires the giving of oneself over to conversation with young people and building a common shared reality in a spirit of self-forgetfulness in order to discover oneself in relation to the entire com- munity experience. This is true not only in music, but, for Smith and others who explore qualitative inquiry, it is especially true in curriculum studies in the postmodern era (Smith, 1991).

Qualitative inquiry and research cannot be planned using modern concepts of posi- tivism, nor can it be imposed uniformly upon students with statistical certainty. Phenomenologists at the forefront of much qualitative curriculum inquiry insist that the subjective encounter creates authentic understanding—and it may happen unex- pectedly. Just as daydreams and nightmares may surprise the imagination, so does the aesthetic encounter. A sunset, a storm, a song, a passionate relationship, a word of praise, or even a dramatic tragedy may spark understanding and engender a synthetical experience. In order to understand aesthetic inquiry, educators must remove the blind- ers of modernity and look at curriculum through different lenses. Curriculum leaders must begin by replacing inspectional and clinical models with experiential, autobio- graphical, and metaphorical reflection that utilizes multi- and extrasensory phenomena and perceptions simultaneously to expand our understanding of the whole educative moment contemporaneously. Only in this way will we move toward the postmodern aesthetic curriculum.

Orchestration requires that teachers and students enter a new zone of cognition and self-reflection where the whole experience is greater than the sum of discrete individual activities. An art critic, for example, does not measure percentages of colors mixed on the painter's palate. Rather, the critic as connoisseur evaluates the impact of the unique balance of color in the entire context of the painting as used by the artist to achieve a synthetical and empathetic relationship with the viewer. A wine connoisseur may sniff the cork, swirl the wine in a glass, and take a sample taste. However, the connoisseur does not "grade" a wine on texture, smell, taste, and visual quality in isolation. The final product, whether a painting or a fine wine, is a masterpiece if all the sense experiences cohere and engender a synthetical experience. Elliot Eisner has advanced this concept in his research in educational evaluation:

> [Connoisseurship] is a matter of noticing, and noticing requires perceptivity. *Perceptivity* is the ability to differentiate and to experience the relationships between, say, one gustatory quality in the wine and others. Like the interplay of sounds in a symphonic score, to experience wine is to experience an interplay of qualitative relationships. Wine connoisseurship requires an awareness of not only qualities of taste but also qualities of appearance and smell. The color at the edge of a red wine when the glass is tipped is indicative of its age, the browner it is, the older. The ways in which its "legs" hang on the inside of the glass says something about its body. The perfume or nose of a wine is another quality that counts. ... Our connoisseurship of wine is influenced by more than our ability to differentiate the subtle qualities of wine we taste and to compare them in our sensory memory with other wines tasted. It is also influenced by our understanding of the conditions that give rise to these qualities. ... Enologists now are highly trained in the chemistry and the science of winemaking, yet in the end, the making of wine is an art. (1997, pp. 64–65)

The art of winemaking, like the art of teaching, requires that we experience qualitative nuances of wines and classrooms. It also requires judgments about the qualities experienced. Ultimately, the aesthetic experience, and not a formula or lesson plan, is the true measure of quality. Eisner concludes that educational inquiry will be more complete and informative when we increase the range of ways we describe, interpret, and evaluate curriculum and instruction. The inclusion of aesthetic and qualitative approaches to inquiry, along with the development of connoisseurship as a teacher competency, will "contribute to the improvement of educational practice by giving us a fuller, more complex understanding of what makes schools and classrooms tick" (Eisner, 1997, p. 8).

Eisner's connoisseurship moves curriculum and evaluation away from modern notions of prescriptive behaviorism where teachers and students simply enact or implement preconceived notions of teaching and knowledge—such as the accountability evaluation instruments for teachers and promotion exams for students. However, Eisner is really a transitional figure in the emerging aesthetic curriculum field. Postmodernism will deconstruct the concept of connoisseurship, with its notion of expertise or masterpiece, and shift the aesthetic judgment to a multiplicity of voices and subcultures.

The complexity of understanding aesthetic experiences is difficult for those of us living in a modern mechanistic society where connoisseurship and qualitative evaluation, much less postmodern multiplicity and eclecticism, do not conform to the logic of positivism, behaviorism, rationalism, and structural analysis. However, postmodernism provides an aesthetic vision where multiplicity replaces binary hierarchies and subjectivity replaces pastiche. Here synthetical experiences can be understood like Gadamer's "fusion of horizons," where the individual is not subsumed or imitated but integrated with the hermeneutic circle, as we discussed in chapter 5.

An investigation of the interrelationship of hermeneutics and subjectivity in the educational context could move the discussion of schooling practices beyond methodological rules and principles of interpretation toward an understanding of interpretation committed to *community conversation* and the *hermeneutic circle*, as proposed by Richard Rorty and Georg Wilhelm Friedrich Hegel. This understanding of the hermeneutic experience resembles the sequencing of events that befall a traveler; the details of the journey are utterly unknown in advance, as the process unfolds in a unique and unrepeatable sequence. This is the concept of experience that guides Hegel's *Phenomenology*, philosophies of *Bildung*, and the understanding of reading and interpretation in the work of Hans-Georg Gadamer, which we will explore below. This understanding is distinct from empirical accounts of experience because it allows for self-consciousness and self-formation, not in the sense of invariant constructs of human consciousness, but in a poststructural sense of emergent, ambiguous, tentative, and eclectic identities. This is similar to our discussion of multiple identities in chapter 6, where I argued that there is no singular invariant human identity but rather ambiguous, emerging, and eclectic identities. It is here that the discussion of hermeneutics and subjectivity finds common ground.

Postmodern hermeneutic interpretation—an apparent oxymoron—is possible if grounded in aesthetic experience and subjectivity and if attentive to the Aristotelian sense of *applicato*—that is, grounding interpretation in experience. An educational experience which incorporates lived experiences called *Bildung*—without separating learning from its application to oneself, as happens in technical, managerial, and behavioral models—encourages interpretation within our subjective contexts. It is here that forms of self-encounter emerge where teachers and students are aesthetically present to the subject matter they study in schools rather than assuming they possess all knowledge and can control it. Possessing subject matter reduces learning to the accumulation of inert information in preparation for meaningless standardized tests—a concept that Whitehead vigorously critiqued. I believe that schooling practices that emphasize the inculcation of inert ideas will continue unabated until the emergence of a hermeneutic conversation based on engaged experience and community action with a commitment to the arts and aesthetics.

The following classroom example may be helpful in understanding this concept. In the constant drumbeat of testing, accountability, and reform movements in the schools, the voices of human persons are often drowned out, stamped out, and extinguished. A reverent silence, empathetic listening, democratic conversing, and hermeneutic understanding become the first casualties of the accountability tidal wave in education. In our schools, classrooms, religious institutions, and civic spaces, we find that lived experience, active imagining, and social activism are too often replaced with inert information, empty rituals, self-promotion, and oppressive drudgery. I am reminded of an event that occurred in my son's middle school classroom 15 years ago. We were living in Cleveland at the time, and Josh played hockey year round in the local leagues. Hockey consumed his time and attention, and schoolwork was often a chore. Politicians and education bureaucrats in Ohio were demanding an ever increasing commitment to proficiency testing called OPT and accountability by principals, teachers, and students.

Josh's middle school was experimenting with a prototype test in art history. Many of my graduate students at the time reported that some Ohio art teachers were demanding that art be added to the battery of proficiency tests required in elementary and middle schools. Proponents of the art proficiency exam claimed that they wanted to elevate their subject matter to the level of math, reading, social studies, and science. However, I suspect that they were also very interested in protecting their jobs. It is much more difficult for a school board to justify a reduction in the budget for the art curriculum or an RIF (Reduction in Force) of art teachers if all students are required to pass an art history proficiency exam. In any case, there was a concerted effort by some educators to get the middle school students ready for the art test. On the one hand, I was pleased to see the renewed interest in the arts. On the other hand, I was horrified that the art curriculum was being manipulated for political and accountability purposes.

For better or for worse, my son became a pawn in this art history pilot project. One art teacher serviced each grade level for the entire middle school with an "art on the cart" program. For one semester the students would rotate schedules to view a series of slides and films and take notes on the life of an artist or sculptor, the date of birth and death of the artist, titles of specific works of art, artistic styles, and historical periods. Some time was also devoted to hands-on arts and crafts. The good news is that Josh still has a creative self-portrait that he completed in that class hanging in his room amid six NHL hockey posters, a Cleveland Indians flag, and other baseball and hockey memorabilia.

Josh's art teacher was enthusiastic about her program and committed to the art curriculum. She was also exhausted from the demands of teaching hundreds of students each semester throughout the school building. The lack of supplies in this predominantly low-income district made matters even worse. A few half-hour lectures each week in preparation for an accountability art test did not provide the time or space needed for releasing the imagination and synthetical experiences. I suspect that the rigorous demands of the art curriculum took an exacting toll on this teacher's aesthetic sensibilities.

Josh came home one day and announced that his teacher showed a film in class about Georgia O'Keeffe and her painting *Cliffs Beyond Abiquiu: Dry Waterfall*. He was unusually animated as he discussed this film. I was thrilled. Josh did not often actively participate in art class at school and, like most kids his age, he seldom commented on school activities at home. In fact, he had been known to occasionally participate in silly middle school mischief. However, Josh had never been punished at school, for he is generally mild mannered and polite.

When Josh was telling me about the O'Keeffe film, he also mentioned that the teacher had punished him for talking it. I was surprised and queried further. Apparently, while watching the film, Josh impulsively blurted out "I saw that painting in the Cleveland Museum of Art." The teacher did not appreciate the disruption. Further, she insisted that there were only paintings of calla lilies and morning glories by O'Keeffe in the Cleveland Museum of Art. She had been there numerous times, and she knew with certainty that O'Keeffe's *Cliffs Beyond Abiquiu: Dry Waterfall* was not on display in the museum. She tried to continue with the lesson, but Josh interrupted again and insisted that he did see it in the Cleveland Museum of Art. "I saw it in a private room on the roof with some person who runs the museum. You know, the lady with all the money who buys the paintings. I think they call her the *creator.*" At this point the teacher was frustrated by the interruptions and delays in the lesson plan. The class was howling in uproarious laughter. Josh's remark was passed off as silly middle school mischief. When he came home from school that day, Josh was baffled that his teacher and the other students did not believe him. It was no big deal to him. He professed little interest in art (except the design of hockey logos), but he was surprised that the art teacher did not know that this special O'Keeffe painting was owned by the Cleveland Museum of Art.

In the hectic schedule of the art curriculum, the art teacher had little time for life experiences, listening, and conversing. She missed a wonderful teachable moment—like Aristotle's *applicato* above—and one of those special opportunities to extend the lesson and enhance the learning experience for the entire class—like Gadamer's *Bildung.* You see, Josh was very familiar with Georgia O'Keeffe and her paintings. I am a volunteer museum docent, and my children have tagged along with me (often reluctantly) to museums all over the United States and Canada. Having lived in New Mexico in my youth, and having seen Georgia O'Keeffe when I lived at a monastery in Abiquiu, I often talk to my children about this special time in my life. When I take my children to museums, I speak passionately about my experiences in New Mexico and my love for O'Keeffe's paintings.

One of the most influential O'Keeffe paintings in my life is *Cliffs Beyond Abiquiu: Dry Waterfall.* The chief curator of the Cleveland Museum of Art at the time, Dr. Diane DeGrazia, also loves this painting, and she displayed it in her private office on the top floor of the museum. When I lived in Cleveland I made special arrangements to visit Dr. DeGrazia's office with my children and my mother. It was an emotional visit, especially when my mother shared with the children that when she dies she wants her ashes scattered in the desert of Abiquiu along the Chama River that runs through the monastery and Ghost Ranch near O'Keeffe's home. It is here that my mother also painted in the desert. We have several of her oil canvases—including one of the Abiquiu desert—hanging in our home. We also have framed reproductions of the *Cliffs Beyond Abiquiu* by O'Keeffe on prominent display. Josh and his sisters Michelle and Katie have been immersed in the artwork of Georgia O'Keeffe since childhood. While visiting the museum, my mother shared with the family this moving poem that she had written by creating the persona of Georgia O'Keeffe:

Georgia O'Keeffe at Ghost Ranch

Far from Manhattan skies

scraped with girders,

pristine calla lilies and crimson

poppies cultivated on canvas,

I have found my place

with craggy cathedrals

beyond human influence.

Before these mountains were, I am

and I shall leave with them.

Our painting time together

disappears, then stays

frozen into ice I lay upon

waiting for the morning light to reveal

what came before, and is now

compelling me, create what is to be.

Even the death of bones

demands delivery of their pregnant past,

as the moon rises above the pelvis void

alive with cerulean blues

precisely planned,

as though my hand

defines reincarnation.

Now I stand like a moth

pinned by walking stick

to this sacred ground

in which I am eternally encased.

If you dare look with painter's eyes

you will see my wrinkles

forming the ash grey hills of Abiquiu,

ascending through pinks and ochers

of mountain strata.

I am bones building nature's skyscrapers. (Burke, 2009, p. 95)

In addition to his grandmother's poem, another connection to the landscape for Josh was our family trip to New Mexico the previous summer to visit the place where O'Keeffe painted, where his dad once lived, and where his grandmother's ashes may one day be scattered. During the visit, each kid was given time to explore the desert alone and to walk along the river barefooted and in silence, imagining that they were an artist, explorer, native American Pueblo teenager, or native child being initiated into the mystery of the desert landscape. These experiences were not reflected in the short video presented in Josh's art history classroom. Any video that ignores the lived experience of the artist, the particularity of the culture and the place of her art, and an invitation for the viewer to enter into this aesthetic space misunderstands the significance of *Bildung*, art as experience (Dewey, 1934a), and the importance of application in the interpretive process. The middle school art history curriculum did not capture the depth of understanding Josh possesses about Georgia O'Keeffe and her desert landscape. His contribution was overlooked in the rush to complete the lesson and prepare students for the Ohio proficiency test. In fact, the art history proficiency movement is at times an obscene curriculum that stifles teachable moments, life experiences, listening, conversing, and hermeneutic understanding. Even the teacher appears to be disconnected from the art she loves and teaches. The curriculum has become what Whitehead accurately portrayed as inert ideas lacking enchantment and romance (Whitehead, 1929).

Current educational philosophies and structures often militate against teachers and students becoming actively engaged in releasing the imagination, critically analyzing ideas, experiencing romance or passion in the curriculum, and understanding our culture and society. The hermeneutic circle that seeks conversation and understanding is perceived as dangerous, for teachers and students might become engaged and empowered. They might actually bring the fullness of their life experiences into the curriculum. They might even begin to create Dewey's social consequences and value. The possibilities are endless; the resistance is immense.

While some students in Josh's art history class may have memorized the information necessary to pass the experimental proficiency exam, all students lost an opportunity to listen and converse about Georgia O'Keeffe and Joshua Slattery in that middle school classroom. Such life stories create a context whereby the information will be internalized and remembered for a lifetime and not simply used for short-term recall on a test that is limited to names, dates, places, and titles. I believe that it is a moral failure of educators when we do not actively resist data transmission and inert curriculum in schools and insist that experience and application be foregrounded in the classroom. A hermeneutic conversation and an affirmation of experience as *Bildung* then become not only possible but also transformative.

The beginning of my personal journey to understand this postmodern aesthetic perspective occurred unexpectedly in the Metropolitan Museum of Art in New York City during a high school trip. Our teacher took us to the museum to view a retrospective exhibit of the history of art through the eyes of several painters from medieval times through abstract expressionism. I walked hurriedly through the art of the ages with my high school friends, anxious to get to the end so that we could move on to our pizza lunch. As we made our way into the final gallery, a huge canvas covering an entire wall startled us. The canvas was filled with swirls of color, particles of glass and dirt, random drippings from paint brushes, and splashes from buckets of paint. We all laughed at this mess, and we mused aloud why it would be included in a major art exhibit. We rushed to the exit to meet our chaperon for lunch. As I reached the exit, a magnetic pull from the painting caused me to freeze. I realized that I had to go back into the gallery and investigate this strange painting, so I asked my teacher to let me stay in the museum. He agreed, but my friends urged me to come out. The tug-of-war ended as I sent them ahead and returned to the painting.

I walked alone and stood face to face with myself before Jackson Pollock's *Autumn Rhythm*. The intensity of the emotions of this artist touched a nerve in my adolescent confusion. I sensed the pain of his struggles and suffering, which seemed to parallel my own inner turmoil. Pollock's frustration with social structures reverberated with my own indignation about the Vietnam War, racism, and social injustice. Pollock's battle with alcoholism leaped from the canvas and caused me to reflect on my own family's struggle with this disease. I did not "know" Jackson Pollock at the time, but I came to experience his emotions as I encountered *Autumn Rhythm*. Just as "knowing" in biblical literature refers to intercourse, there was a bond of intimacy that intensified as I stood with Pollock's painting.

Hundreds of people must have come and gone while I spent an hour or more in the room. However, time stood still for me. I was not a painter; I had never formally studied art. I had never heard of Jackson Pollock, but I became the artist through his painting as his journey and my journey were united in a synthetical moment. When I reluctantly left the museum and caught up with my friends, I could not explain the mysterious events that occurred as I stood before *Autumn Rhythm*.

Jackson Pollock continues to influence my life and my education, and you will find examples of my own paintings inspired by my encounter with Pollock on the companion website to this text. I experienced a phenomenological moment of revelation and personal understanding that, like the beauty and intensity of nature in autumn, defines my life. Studying the technical details of the abstract expressionist style of painting or the biography of Jackson Pollock could never have replaced that synthetical moment in the Metropolitan Museum of Art. However, following my encounter with *Autumn Rhythm* I have devoured every book available on these topics. This demonstrates a central dimension of qualitative aesthetic inquiry in the postmodern curriculum: the experience of disturbance, perturbation, contemporaneousness, or synthetical moments will inspire students to read, to research, to explore, to learn, to meditate, and to expand their understanding of the initial experience. It can also ignite a passion for justice and compassion.

The aesthetic dimension of the postmodern curriculum is clearly reflected in this story about *Autumn Rhythm* and Jackson Pollock. Knowledge is not logically ordered and waiting to be discovered; rather it is constructed in experiences of the whole body and being.

> The intellect may raise all kinds of questions—and it is perfectly right for it to do so—but to expect a final answer from the intellect is asking too much of it, for this is not in the nature of intellection. The answer lies deeply buried under the bedrock of our being. (Suzuki, Fromm, & DeMartino, 1960, pp. 48–49)

Autumn Rhythm did not provide answers to my intellect; rather, it touched the bedrock of my being and initiated a search for meaning and understanding, not only about art history, abstract expressionism, and Jackson Pollock, but most significantly about the purpose of life, the reason for suffering, the tragedy of alcoholism, and the relationship between inner confusion and external turmoil. My visit to the Metropolitan Museum of Art, it turns out, was not simply a retrospective art lesson, it was a border crossing, a seminal moment, a synthetical event—a postmodern curricular experience—that initiated a lifelong journey into the realm of contemporary art and postmodern living. This experience created a context within which the future study of art has been appealing, satisfying, lifegiving, and educational.

This experiential basis for understanding art and curriculum has been important in my life ever since my encounter with Jackson Pollock's *Autumn Rhythm*. Installation art has the same aesthetic impact on me today. Edward and Nancy Kienholz are especially inspiring and provocative.

When Edward Kienholz began his work in the 1950s, his style was likened to that of the Beat poets, who "raged against a nation that by all outward appearances was content with itself and ostensibly relieved of the burden of self-reflection" (Raskin, 1996, p. 38). During this time, Americans were reacting to the launch of the Soviet spaceship Sputnik and its implications for education and national defense interests. McCarthy-era anti-communist sentiment at an apex, our national attention turned to an external enemy as we sought to rid the world of communism. Deep personal reflection, however, led some visionary people to examine the apparent contradictions between our overt national policies and the actions undertaken by our newly developed military-industrial economy. Were we really concerned about the liberation of human beings or had we come to understand ourselves in the context of the economic advantage of the business of war? Unfortunately, in the US this same question dominates today. Edward Kienholz exposed such contradictions ingrained in the US consciousness of the 1950s and 1960s, and his prophetic art inspires ethical reflection in our current global crisis.

Edward and Nancy Kienholz began to work collaboratively in 1972. Inspired by their shared vision of the prophetic nature of their work, they created assemblages to express their outrage at child abuse, war, poverty, religious hypocrisy, sexism, and violence against Native Americans and other indigenous and minority cultures. They also probed the decay of the human spirit in the modern age. Their sculptures were created with common household objects and discarded industrial materials—as if to say that injustice is everywhere in our day-to-day lives. This highlighted the irony of their themes as seen in the major retrospective of their work in 1996 at the Whitney Museum in New York City. The museum presented a collection of striking images designed both to reflect and to deconstruct the human condition (Hopps, 1996).

One of Edward Kienholz's earliest creations, completed in 1959, reflects the condition of the archetypal American male. This sculpture, titled *John Doe*, was constructed with a store display mannequin cut in half at the waist. The two halves were placed back to back on a baby stroller base. The penis was severed and stored in drawer below the stroller. A carved section of the man's chest forms a hole that contains a wooden cross instead of a heart; a stovepipe connects both sections of the body leading to the cross. The sculpture portrays the American male as a bifurcated hero; he is depicted as limbless, powerless, heartless, and impotent. The emptiness of his existence—void of emotional, sexual, or spiritual passion—shocks the viewer and forces a reevaluation of macho male media images. When I view slides of this artwork with my students, the males initially react defensively. They argue that this is an outdated stereotype. They contend that men are no longer macho, spiritually empty, and vacuous. Then the women begin to speak, affirming the macho image and—yes—even the sexual immaturity and repression of men! The male students are shocked that the women affirm Kienholz's critique of men. The artwork opens a dynamic space for communication and reflection about the nature of gender, sexuality, spirituality, and passion.

Jane Doe, the sculpture's counterpart, fares no better, and the women are afforded an opportunity for self-reflection. She is constructed with the head of a child's female doll attached to a small chest of drawers covered by the lace-laden skirt of a bridal gown (Hopps, 1996). The absence of arms adds to her defenseless and passive stance. As the body takes on the appearance of a table, the relationship between the feminine nature and the act of service is dramatic. The three drawers—representing three stages of womanhood—are covered with the lace wedding gown, requiring the viewer to lift the skirt of the woman-turned-servicetable in order to reveal her inner humanity. Such imposition and exploitation of women is all too common. The viewer becomes voyeur and must now confront her or his own complicity in exploitation and subjugation. Unlike our male students who react with anger toward *John Doe*, the women initially react with shock and sadness as they view *Jane Doe*. The intensity of the image forces a self-analysis that is often painfully true.

The images created by both Edward and Nancy Kienholz enabled them to assume the role of the prophet and challenge those who view their art to consider important social issues such as gender roles, violence, and subjugation. The use of common materials to construct images of exaggeration effectively communicated the struggle inherent in various critical causes. Because the images are sometimes disturbing—particularly their child abuse series—the artists are able to engage the imagination and evoke the emotional connection and response necessary for lasting impact. Adding to this response is the three-dimensional nature of the work, which allows the observer to interact with the piece and step away from what Suzi Gablik calls the subject–object separation found in much contemporary art. Not only does the observer become a participant, but the dimensionality of the work allows movement into the space of the tableau, thereby evoking, in the postmodern sense, an intense and ironic juxtaposition (Gablik, 1991; McElfresh-Spehler & Slattery, 1999).

Another artist that inspires my postmodern sensibilities is Anselm Kiefer, a German citizen born at the end of World War II who now works in the US, who addresses political and social issues in his large canvases and installations. He challenges his German contemporaries—indeed, all modern women and men—to ponder and deconstruct those aspects of 20th-century German history that many would like to forget. Kiefer is attentive to the complexity of memory construction and anti-memory deconstruction that we discussed in chapters 2, 3, and 5 (Weaver, Slattery, & Daspit, 1998). Gilmour (1990) explains the purpose behind Kiefer's artistic approach to memory:

> Kiefer moves beyond modernism by violating its taboos against representation, narrative, and historical allusion and by the decisive ways in which he employs art to confront reality. At the same time, he raises fundamental doubts about the received world view of modernity. Although the avant-garde were radical in their criticism of the art world, Kiefer's challenge extends further toward the

roots of modern humanity's outlook. He does so by turning the canvas into a theater of interacting forces that exposes tragic conflicts engendered by modern life. By synthesizing the traditional and the modern, the mythological and the rational, the simulated and the real, Kiefer achieves a puzzling and provocative mixture of elements that inspire us to reconsider our assumptions and formulate our visions anew. (p. 5)

For example, Kiefer's *Lot's Frau* (Lot's Wife), completed in 1989 and found in the collection at the Cleveland Museum of Art, depicts a barren and scorched landscape with two sets of converging railroad tracks at the horizon. Constructed with a substructure of lead mounted on wood and overlaid with canvas, the work evokes images of abandonment, suffering, and deep loneliness. Above the horizon explode huge white puffs of what might be seen as smoke or clouds or human ashes.

This painting challenges us to look back at tragedies of the 20th century such as the Holocaust and environmental disasters. The viewer becomes like Lot's wife, who looked back on the cities of Sodom and Gomorrah as they were being destroyed in the biblical story. Traditional religious authorities have assumed that she was cast into a pillar of salt for her disobedience to a vengeful God who had commanded that Lot and his family move away without turning around. Yet Lot's wife ignored the patriarchy to look back in compassion and love at the friends and family she had left behind. In the agony of her exodus, she would not erase the memory of her loved ones. In the looking back, she is transformed and becomes the salt of the Earth, not as a punishment as the traditional patriarchal theology has assumed, but rather as a model of the prophetic vision—for salt is the substance of wisdom in alchemy and in biblical literature. Kiefer has even been known to mix salt, ash, and semen in the paint, assuring us that there is life, healing, and preservation in the backward glance and in uncovering the unrecognizable. It is the attempt to erase the memory, to walk forward without looking back and becoming salt, that is most dangerous. Without healing salt, Lot's semen produces a dysfunctional progeny that eventually self-destructs at the end of the biblical story—the part of the narrative that most preachers ignore.

Kiefer has called us to become the pillar of salt for an Earth where global communities have repeatedly burned and bombed their cities, scorched the earth, and obliterated innocent people for centuries. Gilmour (1990) concludes:

Kiefer's palpable grasp of the powers of imagination enables him to fulfill one pedagogical task of postmodern art: teaching us the importance of the habitat of the earth. His refusal to forget the consequences of war, the threat of nuclear destruction, and the negative outcomes of technology keeps being projected, in his Theater of Cruelty staging, against the symbol of the earth. But even more than that, this artist brings fire to the earth, which purifies our vision of the abstract images of nature and history that stand at the root of so many of these consequences. His visionary sketch of the habitat for postmodern humans recalls us to the elemental relationship we have to the earth, to its place within the cosmos, and to previous human cultures who have understood so well the limits of human powers. (p. 175)

Kiefer allows us to enter the landscape of ecological concern in the broadest sense. He challenges our most intuitive and rational assumptions about our relationship to the Earth and to one another. As our imaginations are engaged through our interaction with his art, the voice of imagination and change may emerge. The call is compelling; the response is vital.

Kiefer offers the opportunity not only to deconstruct memories of violence and destruction but especially to elicit fresh understandings of the positionality of the self in relation to memories. We will now take a circuitous route back to Kiefer through the work of bell hooks, Jean-Michel Basquiat, Friedrich Nietzsche, and Michel Foucault.

bell hooks has written about the 1992 retrospective of the work of Jean-Michel Basquiat at the Whitney Museum of Art in New York City. Following the release of Julian Schnabel's film *Basquiat* (1996), there has been a renewed interest in the life of this widely misunderstood artist. bell hooks (1993) writes:

> It is much too simplistic a reading to see works like *Jack Johnson*, 1982, *Untitled (Sugar Ray Robinson)*, 1982, and the like, as solely celebrating black culture. Appearing always in these paintings as half-formed or somewhat mutilated, the black male body becomes, iconographically, a sign of lack and absence. ... In Basquiat's work, flesh on the black body is almost always falling away. Like skeletal figures in the Australian aboriginal bark painting, ... these figures have been worked down to the bone. To do justice to this work, then, our gaze must do more than reflect on surface appearances. Daring us to probe the heart of darkness, to move our eyes beyond the colonizing gaze, the paintings ask that we hold in our memory the bones of the dead while we consider the world of the black immediate, the familiar. To see and understand these paintings, one must be willing to accept the tragic dimension of black life. ... Basquiat's work gives that private anguish artistic expression. (pp. 71–72)

This anguish described by hooks also permeates Kiefer's paintings. As Basquiat confronts us with the naked black image, Kiefer confronts us with the naked ravages of postwar terrain. The body is diminished in Basquiat; the landscape is barren in Kiefer. As we noted above, *Lot's Frau* depicts two abandoned and bombed out railroad tracks vanishing into a desolate plateau on the horizon at the center of the canvas and an allusion to the backward glance of Lot's wife in the biblical story.

The backward glance transforms our lives. With Nietzsche, this takes us to the point of becoming more of what we are not so as to free ourselves from the limits of what we live. We do this in order to illuminate that which has remained unrecognizable. Nietzsche (1968) writes about "dangerous books" and concludes:

> Somebody remarked: "I can tell by my own reaction to it that this book is harmful." But let him only wait and perhaps one day he will admit to himself [sic] that this same book has done him a great service by bringing out the hidden sickness of his heart and making it visible. Altered opinions do not alter a man's character (or do so very little); but they do illuminate individual aspects

of the constellation of his personality which with a different constellation of opinions had hitherto remained dark and unrecognizable. (p. 15)

Nietzsche's "dangerous books" are parallel to the "dangerous looks" described above. It is our challenge in museums and classrooms to create spaces where the dangerous can prod us to construct and re-construct memories that can illuminate aspects of our autobiography and our culture that have remained hidden or unrecognizable.

bell hooks (1993) contends that Basquiat's work delineates the violence that results when the culture and traditions of a people are erased. Sodom and Gomorrah have been the scapegoats for colonization and hegemonic domination for too long. We must look back with the heroine of the biblical narrative, Lot's wife, and become the pillar of life-giving salt for the Earth. hooks (1993) concludes, "The erasure is rendered all the more problematic when artifacts of that vanishing culture are commodified to enhance the aesthetics of those perpetuating the erasure" (p. 72). Thus, the memory of Lot's wife is commodified for a conservative religious hermeneutic, and Sodom and Gomorrah remain fixed in the collective memory as evil and decadent. That image has been perpetuated to support violence of all sorts, including most often an illogical condemnation of homosexuals with the term "sodomite." This reading of the text undermines such injustice. Kiefer, Basquiat, and hooks refute the vanquishing and challenge such destructive interpretations.

It is in this spirit that, when I was a professor in Ohio, I took my students to view *Lot's Frau* in the Cleveland Museum of Art. Typical of the reaction of my students who are willing to deconstruct linear notions of time and space and look back, look within, and look forward in a single glance is the response of David, an 18-year-old freshman. After meditating before this painting for almost an hour, David insisted that he felt the very real presence of the Holocaust. He told me that, for the first time in his life, he truly understood the Holocaust, and he was haunted by the intensity of Kiefer's desolate landscape. Why, he asked, was the memory so haunting? Why did he feel so present in this desolate landscape?

Early in the next semester David contacted me to say that over the winter break he had discussed his experience at the museum with his devoutly Christian parents. David's glance had uncovered a purposeful erasure of a family memory, the death of Jewish ancestors in the Holocaust. His parents for the first time revealed to him that their parents were themselves children of Jewish parents killed in the Holocaust. David, like Lot's wife, found himself in the imagery of smoke, clouds, salt, and ashes on Kiefer's canvas. David is not unlike many of us who discover ourselves within the phenomenological lived experience of the arts. This is one reason why the arts are so essential in the postmodern curriculum. This story reflects my vision of aesthetics and curriculum. We must re-member our bodies and re-connect our lives if the colonization and erasure that has been inflicted upon us is to be resisted, overcome, and transformed. Literally, we are holistically a part of the global landscape and the historical event; the aesthetic experience allows us to enter the process of healing and understanding.

Like Foucault's notion of "simulated surveillance" and "governmentality," which engenders the kind of blind obedience that regulated Lot and persuaded him not to look back, the refusal of museums and classrooms to challenge sedimented perceptors and explode colonizing structures of power also regulates our bodies and imprisons our minds. Most tragically, it stifles the aesthetic imagination and silences the creative urge. The artwork of Anselm Kiefer deconstructs educational, political, and social structures that have created such surveillance and sought to extinguish the passion for justice. This is why qualitative arts-based research is so central to curriculum development in the postmodern era.

These curriculum landscapes and experiences of transformative pedagogy seen in the works of art discussed above challenge the educational community to reevaluate the traditional understanding of the learning environment. Even a traditionalist like Mortimer Adler (1982) writes: "Our concern with education must go beyond schooling. … Education is a lifelong process of which schooling is only a small part. Schooling should open the doors to the world of learning" (pp. 9–11). The postmodern world demands awareness of the environment and openness to the deep ecology of learning:

> The forests speak out, the oceans beckon, the sky calls us forth, the plants want to share their story, the mind of the universe is open to all of us, the planet wants to instruct. Educators, through their methods and their content, can either open wide the doors to this wonder or narrow the doorways to offer only a partial view which they can then control. (LePage, 1987, p. 180)

Andy LePage argues that participation in the environment is far more educational than passive observation. Participation in new environments and expanded horizons provides students and teachers with insights into alternative strategies for living, and therefore expanded possibilities for the future. These possibilities, in turn, offer a vision of hope to people who otherwise would be unaware of alternatives. In this sense, aesthetic theories also inform social and political theories of education, as Landon Beyer proposes.

Attention to the alternatives that provide hope is called "wide-awakeness" by the philosopher of education Maxine Greene. She argues for a strong emphasis on arts and humanities in education to promote this wide-awakeness and self-understanding that emerge from synthetical moments. Greene turns to the poet Henry David Thoreau for inspiration. According to Greene (1978), "Thoreau writes passionately about throwing off sleep. He talks about how few people are awake enough for a poetic or divine life. He asserts that to be awake is to be alive" (p. 162). David Orr (1992) also turns to Thoreau for understanding: "Thoreau did not research Walden Pond, rather, he went to live 'deliberately'" (p. 125). Thus, for Thoreau, *Walden* becomes a mosaic of philosophy, poetry, natural history, geology, folklore, archeology, economics, politics, and education, and in this sense aesthetics leads to wholeness. Orr (1992) explains: "Thoreau's subject matter was Thoreau; his goal, wholeness; his tool, Walden Pond; and his methodology, simplification" (p. 125). This is the antithesis of the modern curriculum that artificially separates subject matter, isolates and analyzes discrete parts, and obfuscates simple beauty. Orr (1992) concludes:

> Aside from its merits as literature or philosophy, *Walden* is an antidote to the idea that education is a passive, indoor activity occurring between the ages of

six and twenty-one. In contrast to the tendencies to segregate disciplines, and to segregate intellect from its surroundings, *Walden* is a model of the possible unity between personhood, pedagogy, and place. For Thoreau, Walden was more than his location. It was a laboratory for observation and experimentation; a library of data about geology, history, flora, fauna; a source of inspiration and renewal; and a testing ground for the man. *Walden* is no monologue, it is a dialogue between a man and a place. In a sense, *Walden* wrote Thoreau. His genius, I think, was to allow himself to be shaped by his place, to allow it to speak with his voice. (pp. 125–126)

This, too, is the postmodern curriculum: the inspiration of nature and poetry; the unity of self, pedagogy, and place; becoming through encounters with place; and uncovering the voice of self-expression. Aesthetic inquiry engenders this postmodern curriculum.

While the technological influences of modern society on the curriculum are increasing feelings of hopelessness and powerlessness, qualitative inquiry has the potential to create what Greene calls a "different kind of breathing" and a sense of "wide-awakeness." This is essential for postmodern transformation. The debilitating modern alternatives to wideawakeness are characterized by Paulo Freire (1970) as a "culture of silence" that allows for the uncritical absorption of only official (i.e., state, school, expert) renderings of life; by Susanne Langer (1957) as a "society of formless emotion" that has neglected the education of feeling; and by Donald Schon (1983) and Donald Oliver and Kathleen Gershman (1989) as "technical rationality" that depends on instrumental problem-solving by the application of scientific theory and techniques devoid of reflection-in-action and deep personal knowing with the whole body. Education must explore new landscapes of learning if transformation, liberation, and hope are to replace the decadence, inertia, and decay of modernity. Freire, Langer, Barone, Schon, Oliver, Gershman, Beyer, LePage, Greene, Orr, and Eisner, among others, warn of the harmful consequences of our continued attachment to modern models of rationality that avoid artistic, intuitive, and nonrational ways of knowing. Eisner (1997) writes:

> Knowledge is considered by most in our culture as something that one discovers, not something that one makes. Knowledge is out there waiting to be found, and the most useful tool for finding it is science. If there were greater appreciation for the extent to which knowledge is constructed—something made—there might be a greater likelihood that its aesthetic dimension would be appreciated. (p. 32)

David Ray Griffin documents the ecological and social disasters that lurk ahead if our worldview does not shift from a modern to this postmodern aesthetic vision. Griffin (1988a) warns: "A great deal is at stake. We must collectively move from mechanistic and dualistic worldviews and positivist and other antiworldviews to an ecological worldview" (p. 102).

Art is one of the primary places where an ecological mode of learning with emphasis on knowledge construction occurs. An adequate aesthetic pedagogy might enable contemporary learners to break with assimilative power and reconstitute certain works of art as occasions for convergence, synthetical moments, understanding of the self, and social critique. The individual's encounter with art can be an occasion for transformation, transcendence, and praxis, and thus a critical dimension of the postmodern curriculum.

The artistic landscape as an occasion for learning is actually a revolutionary development in the philosophical understanding of art. It is a kind of theory that focuses upon the response to a work of art in order to account for it and to account for the importance of the aesthetic mode in human life. It is important to distinguish how these phenomenological assumptions contrast with the traditional ontological philosophy of art, which deals with beings as they are in themselves regardless of the way they are apprehended or of the fact that they are apprehended at all.

Phenomenology, on the other hand, is based on the assumption that we cannot speculate about what beings are in themselves. Rather, the emphasis should be placed on *possibility* and *becoming* as a goal of the curriculum, for human consciousness can never be static. Jean-Paul Sartre argues that human consciousness (being-for-itself) can never become a substance or an objective thing (being-in-itself), and this is why possibility must be the focus of educational inquiry. Hence, each new experience adds to the accumulated meaning of experience for each individual and sets the stage for present and future possibilities. While the present is conditioned by the past, every moment is also pregnant with future possibilities for change and new directions. The aesthetic experience can inspire new personal realizations, as John Dewey (1934b), in *Art as Experience*, explains:

> A work of art, no matter how old or classic, is actually not just potentially a work of art only when it lives in some individual experience. A piece of parchment, of marble, of canvas, it remains self-identical throughout the ages. But as a work of art it is re-created every time it is aesthetically experienced. ... The Parthenon, or whatever, is universal because it can continue to inspire new personal realizations in experience. (pp. 108—109)

Pablo Picasso (1971) has described artistic creation in a similar way:

> A picture is not thought out and settled beforehand. While it is being done it changes as one's thoughts change. And when it is finished it still goes on changing according to the state of mind of whoever is looking at it. A picture lives a life like a living creature, undergoing the changes imposed on us by our life from day to day. This is natural enough, as the picture lives only through the man who is looking at it. (p. 268)

Picasso and Dewey reflect one of the important phenomenological dimensions of postmodern aesthetics: events find their meaning in subjective encounters where knowledge is constructed and reconstructed in every new situation. In this sense, a work of art truly exists only in the encounter. If locked in a darkened vault, a painting is simply an aggregate of materials. Art, like the curriculum, is the process of becoming and re-creating in each new situation. Phenomenology seeks description of how the world is experienced by persons, or, for Martin Heidegger, a method or science of the phenomenon of consciousness. The purpose is not just description of phenomena, but the understanding of what lies behind them, their *being* or ontology. Phenomenological understanding of curriculum replaces the modern obsession with standardized interpretation of literature and fine arts (especially in humanities departments, ironically), predetermined methodologies and styles for writing, painting, and researching, and universal master narratives that can be applied to knowledge acquisition. For Maurice Merleau-Ponty (1962) perception is primary, as in the actual feelings of an amputated limb perceived by amputees—called the phantom limb. Ozmon and Craver (1990) explain: "Abstract truth is not self-evident in perception, but perception has with it the potential for arriving at the truth in a more subtle fashion as it is sensed or experienced rather than as it is filtered through the philosophical dogmatisms and assumptions of the past" (pp. 246–247).

Yvonna Lincoln (1992), in an essay on curriculum inquiry and the humanistic tradition, expands on this concept of phenomenological perception and relates it to lived experience:

> Phenomenology enjoys a status today as a soundly conceived philosophical school, the bent of which is to return experience to the lived rather than the instrumental or conceptual world and to view the conceptual world as one given meaning and mediated by the lived, present being and temporal experience. ... Phenomenologists are themselves increasingly concerned with the abstractions represented by the scientific, technological, and instrumental approaches to curriculum that prevailed during the first half of this century. The notion of the curriculum as a set of concepts, ideas, and facts to be mastered; students as empty vessels to be filled with those concepts; and pedagogy as a set of techniques to be acquired by teachers is often rejected by contemporary curricularists. (p. 91)

Max van Manen and other contemporary phenomenologists support this rejection of traditional techniques. There is a growing body of evidence and a set of moral suasions that students themselves are capable of rich inner lives, that their experience is worth eliciting and building on, and that pedagogy is a form of interactive relationship rather than a bag of tricks to be assembled in the teaching process (van Manen, 1988).

The development of phenomenology as applied to artistic-aesthetic expression has roots in cubism and flourishes with abstract expressionism of the 20th century. These movements are in contrast to the High Renaissance, and they are foreign to painters such as Raphael. The traditional understanding of art in the Renaissance held that content is predetermined and that the artist must focus on the form through which content is conveyed. Raphael utilized art apprentices to help paint his canvas or mural from the cartoon. This would be considered anathema to phenomenologists, who comprehend form and content as congruent. Ronald Padgham (1988) writes: "The content in the new theory is the individual in the process of becoming; becoming that which he [or she] has not yet been, but that which he [or she] is capable of becoming" (p. 377).

Maxine Greene applies this understanding of form and content to education and contends that involvement with the arts and humanities has the potential to provoke reflectiveness. She challenges educators to devise ways of integrating arts into what is taught at all levels of the educational enterprise. This has direct implications for social and moral issues in postmodern curriculum and in art education. Greene (1978) explains the implications as follows:

> I would like to believe that the concerns of art educators are akin to those I have described: to enhance qualitative awareness, to release imagination, and to free people to see, shape, and transform. I would hope for the kinds of curricula that permit an easy and articulated transaction between making and attending. (p. 74)

The congruence of form and content is revealed in such works as *Nude Descending a Staircase* (1912), by Duchamp. The illusion of movement is created in the cubist painting exactly as a camera would capture it in frames many years later. Picasso's sculptures likewise reveal a vision of what had never been seen before, for no one before Picasso, in *Guernica*, had seen the now obvious similitude between the pointed saddle and handlebars of a bicycle and the visage of a bull (Greene, 1978). Furthermore, abstract expressionists like Pollock reveal the intensity of their emotional responses in paintings such as *Autumn Rhythm*, where the experience of the observer becomes a communion with the artist. Twentieth-century artists have frequently discussed the existential and phenomenological nature of their methodology. Ronald Padgham contends that there is no right or wrong way to teach, just as there is no right or wrong way to paint. There is only one's natural way. Padgham (1988) states: "To discover one's natural way necessitates self-discovery or consciousness of self" (p. 367). Jackson Pollock (1971) explains how this process evolves:

> When I am in my painting, I am not aware of what I am doing. It is only after a short get acquainted period that I see what I have been about. I have no fears about making changes, destroying the image, etc. Because the painting has a life of its own, I try to let it come through. It is only when I lose contact with the painting that the result is a mess. Otherwise there is pure harmony, an easy give and take, and the painting comes out well. (p. 548)

This experience in turn leads to new expressive qualities in the observer's world.

The phenomenological understanding of experience and wide-awakeness that leads to transformation is found in many diverse works, such as Stravinsky's *The Rite of Spring*, Picasso's *Guernica*, Faulkner's *The Bear*, and Joyce's *Portrait of the Artist as a Young Man*. Greene (1978) continues:

> Lacking wide-awakeness, I want to argue that individuals are likely to drift, to act on impulses of expediency. They are unlikely to identify situations as moral ones or set such cases; it seems to me, it is meaningless to talk of obligation: it may be futile to speak of consequential choice. (p. 43)

The result of this postmodern paradigm shift in education and art can create a renewed sense of hope. Social change becomes possible because individual transformation is a process that can be experienced in the community of artists and aesthetic educators. Social progress occurs as individuals change, not when institutions change. Postmodern curriculum scholars contend that attentiveness to the moral dimension of existence should permeate classrooms, and that teachers should be clear about how to ground their own values. We are no longer in a situation where character training, values clarification, and systems of rewards and punishment will make children virtuous, just, and compliant. "We recognize the futility of teaching rules, of preaching pieties, or presenting conceptions of the good. Moral education, rather, must be as specifically concerned with self-identification in a community as it is with judgments persons are equipped to make at different ages" (Greene, 1978, p. 47).

Form and content should no longer be seen as separate; in the postmodern curriculum they are congruent. For the educator, inquiry and reflection merge with lecturing. Thus, a pedagogical, an aesthetic, or a theological dualism is no longer sufficient or viable. The content of the curriculum is the individual in the process of becoming that which he or she has not yet been but which he or she is capable of becoming. The various disciplines become part of the form and content, and a congruence is achieved.

The congruence of form and content is not only a phenomenological experience, it also has eschatological implications. Once the congruence is understood, then the limitations of time and space begin to diminish. They melt into the landscape like the watches in Salvador Dali's painting *The Persistence of Memory*. Experiences are no longer frozen in time. Learning elicits new experiences that encourage a futuring—a going beyond the present state of malaise. Teachers who themselves are submerged, who feel in some sense "finished," like the chairs or blackboards in their rooms, lack the moral persuasion to inspire students to critical questioning, to nurture aesthetic experiences, or to connect learning to creative thinking. Unfortunately, there is often nothing occurring in many classrooms; no talking, no questioning, no thinking, no exploring, and thus no convergence or synthesis. Teachers must be in touch with their own inner landscapes—their own aesthetic experiences—in order for education to become a process of discovery, learning, and self-understanding.

Qualitative aesthetic experiences involve critical reflection. It is a kind of knowing called praxis: a knowing that becomes an opening to possibilities and empowerment. Greene (1978) calls it "a poem about one human being's self-formation, recaptured through a return (in inner time) to an original landscape, the place where it all began" (p. 15). This experience of returning is not only necessary for wide-awakeness, but also for autobiographical wholeness and self-reflection. It even goes beyond the aesthetic encounters discussed above. The emphasis has shifted from the external to the internal and artists seek an inner experience that creates an interconnectedness. Otherwise, enthusiasm and hope will be lost. Without that awareness and that hope, teachers find it unimaginably difficult to cope with the demands of children in the schools today. Like Horace Smith in Theodore Sizer's (1984) classic book *Horace's Compromise: The Dilemma of the American High School*, teachers will "neither have the time nor energy, nor inclination to urge their students to critical reflection: they themselves have suppressed the questions, and avoided backward looks" (p. 38).

This, then, is the implication of aesthetics for the postmodern curriculum: transformation and learning are stimulated by a sense of future possibilities and sense of what might be. Building community and enabling personal awakeness are crucial in this process. Maxine Greene (1978) moves toward the postmodern curriculum as she advises:

> I would lay stress upon talking together, upon the mutual exchange that expresses lives actually lived together, that forges commonalities. I would work for the kind of critical reflection that can be carried on by persons who are situated in the concreteness of the world, by persons equipped for interrogation, for problematization, and for hermeneutic interpretation of the culture—of the present and the past. (p. 107)

This can be accomplished: schooling flourishes in some places because of emphasis on this type of community building. Once engaged in the journey, the traveler no longer remains isolated and separated from the dreams and visions that give sustenance for exploration and praxis. A postmodern transformative pedagogy is most clearly seen as the engagement of this journey by students and teachers who are confident that the consummation of education is liberation and synthesis.

An awareness and sensitivity toward many environments—physical, psychological, spiritual, and social—is an integral part of the proposals that inform the postmodern curriculum. Participation in aesthetic environments provides the educational community with alternative strategies for living and expanded possibilities for the future. Because postmodern curriculum understands the future as that which brings to completion what has already been set in motion, the alternative possibilities offer a vision of hope for schools and society. This vision would remain idealized and romanticized were it not for the dimension of aesthetic understanding and hope called "wide-awakeness" by Maxine Greene, "fusion of horizons" by Hans-Georg Gadamer, "praxis" by Paulo Freire, "reflection-in-action" by Donald Schon, "connoisseurship" by Elliot Eisner, "becoming" by Ronald Padgham, "experience" by John Dewey, "rich inner lives" by Max van Manen, "synthetical moments" by William Pinar and Madeleine Grumet, and "contemporaneousness" by Michel Serres.

Although characterized in many unique, ironic, and even contradictory ways, the aesthetic dimensions of learning in postmodern curriculum emphasize the primacy of experience, the merging of form and content, the recursion and convergence of time, the celebration of the self-conscious individual, and the understanding of phenomenological experience. This perspective on curriculum offers the individual a process for growing and becoming. It also offers schools an opportunity for critical reflection that is open to what has not yet been but what is also absolutely possible. Without this vision, teachers and students will have neither the time nor the energy, neither the hope nor the endurance, to move beyond the modern technological models and toward the emerging postmodern curriculum. Aesthetics, the fine arts, and qualitative inquiry are integral to the creation of landscapes of learning and synthetical moments of self-understanding for curriculum development in the postmodern era. In fact, aesthetic phenomena may ultimately be the only justification for our curriculum theorizing, even for our very existence, according to Friedrich Nietzsche (1968), when he writes in *The Birth of Tragedy*: "We have our highest dignity in our significance as works of art—for it is only as an aesthetic phenomenon that existence and the world are eternally justified" (p. 52).

Contemporary curriculum theorists seek to recover this dignity and advance aesthetic sensibilities in schools and society. At the beginning of this chapter it was noted that there are various ways of investigating arts and aesthetics in education. The companion website to this text includes a space for artists and educators to submit images and artist statements that extend the understanding of curriculum as aesthetic text and arts-based research. I urge readers to look at these statements and images and I encourage arts-based educational scholars to submit examples for inclusion on the website. Barbara Bickel, of the University of Southern Illinois at Carbondale, is the president of the Arts-Based Educational Research Association (ABER). Her artist statement is a thoughtful and inspiring example of the extensive scholarship in ABER, and her statement appears first on the website. This is followed by an extensive discussion of my arts-based research and images of some of my installations, where this discussion of arts and aesthetics can continue.

Part III
Curriculum Development in the Postmodern Era

eleven
Time and Complexity

We do not conceive of sudden, radical, irrational change as built into the very fabric of existence. Yet it is. And chaos theory teaches us, Malcolm said, that straight linearity, which we have come to take for granted in everything from physics to fiction, simply does not exist. Linearity is an artificial way of viewing the world. Real life isn't a series of interconnected events occurring one after another like beads strung on a necklace. Life is actually a series of encounters in which one event may change those that follow in a wholly unpredictable, even devastating way. That's a deep truth about the structure of our universe. But, for some reason, we insist on behaving as if it were not true.

Michael Crichton (1990) *Jurassic Park*, p. 171

I once was asked to conduct a one-hour seminar for school principals on the topic of "time management." I did not have any particular interest in this topic, and I was reluctant to accept the invitation. However, the seminar director was a friend, and he convinced me that I could say something interesting to a group of school leaders, especially since I had been a principal for many years. For the next several weeks I was preoccupied and anxious about this presentation. I felt certain that the principals would be expecting a practical program with suggestions for improving organizational skills in order to reduce the pressure of their demanding schedules, and I was not sure of the best method of conducting the seminar in order to address their very real day-to-day concerns.

Frustrated and uncertain, I immersed myself in time-management literature for several days. I read *The 7 Habits of Highly Successful People*, by Stephen Covey (1989), *The One Minute Manager*, by Kenneth Blanchard and Spencer Johnson (1981), *Organize Yourself!*, by Ronni Eisenberg (1986), and the classic ethnography used in many leadership courses, *The Man in the Principal's Office*, by Harry Wolcott (1973). I reviewed the time-management methods that I had used myself as a principal, such as organizational flow charts, five-year plans, delegation to department heads, computerized appointment schedules, comprehensive and detailed handbooks, a binder filing system, informative newsletters, and master calendars. As I prepared for this seminar, all the exhaustion of my career as a principal came rushing back to my mind. I remembered that, no matter how well a school was organized, the unexpected and unpredictable were the daily norm: bomb threats on exam days; board members bursting into my office with a new idea or a complaint; malfunctioning telephones, heaters, air conditioners, and toilets; emergency discipline meetings; crying secretaries, crying teachers, crying students; head-lice outbreaks in first grade; early dismissals for inclement weather on football playoff games days; outstanding teachers who were transferred in the middle of the year; food fights in the lunchroom. Donald Schon called this "managing messes." I was exhausted remembering these incidents and the last-minute planning that was a constant part of school leadership. I also remembered the barrage of complaints, especially from teachers, whenever the school schedule was disrupted. Time was viewed as a precious commodity to be allocated judiciously.

School principals know that randomness and chaos more accurately define their lives than predictability and stability, and yet modern bureaucrats continue to frustrate educators by organizing schools around the modern conception of time as controllable and manageable. As I was preparing for this time-management seminar, I also happened to be reading an article from the journal *New Scientist* and several books on chaos theory and the new sciences, including *The Tao of Physics*, by Fritjof Capra (1975), *The Reenchantment of Science: Postmodern Proposals*, edited by David Ray Griffin (1988), *Order Out of Chaos: Man's New Dialogue with Nature*, by Ilya Prigogine and Isabelle Stengers (1984), *Chaos: Making a New Science*, by James Gleick (1987), *A Brief History of Time: From the Big Bang to the Black Holes*, by Stephen Hawking (1988), *The Cosmic Blueprint: New Discoveries in Nature's Creative Ability to Order the Universe*, by Paul Davies (1988), and, most significantly, *The Structure of Scientific Revolutions*, by Thomas Kuhn (1970). The contrast between the two sets of readings was dramatic and disturbing.

Thomas Kuhn reminded me that one of the tasks of the historian of science is to "describe and explain the congeries of error, myth, and superstition that have inhabited the more rapid accumulation of the constituents of the modern science text" (1970, p. 2). The more I reflected on chaos theory, and the more I recognized the problematic nature of organization in modern schooling, the clearer it was that I would have to change the focus of my preparation for the time-management seminar. Reading the following conclusion in Kuhn's book confirmed my conviction: "In both political and scientific development the sense of malfunction that can lead to crisis is a prerequisite to revolution" (p. 92). The sense of malfunction and crisis in education was abundantly clear, and thus Kuhn's hypothesis raised the possibility of a paradigm shift in the organization and curriculum of the schools in my mind. Chaos theory, complexity theory, and the new sciences provided metaphors as well as a scientific basis for a different understanding of time and education, and this became the focus of my presentation with the administrators. It was a seminar that those present will certainly remember—for better or for worse!

Chaos theory, popularly referred to as the butterfly effect, studies the behavior of dynamical systems that are highly sensitive to initial conditions. Small differences in initial conditions, such as those due to rounding errors in numerical computation, yield widely diverging outcomes for chaotic systems, rendering long-term prediction impossible in general. Weather conditions and human behavior can be observed and understood within context and within a range of possibilities, but cannot be determined with certainty. This is true even though any future behavior is fully determined by their initial conditions if no random elements are involved. In other words, the deterministic nature of these systems does not make them predictable. This behavior is known as deterministic chaos, or simply chaos. Complexity theory is the study of such complex systems. In curriculum theory, teaching and learning is understood as such a complex dynamical system

Chaos and complexity theory, according to William Doll, gives meaning and substance to the language of disequilibrium, reflective intuition, surprise, puzzlement, confusion, zones of uncertainty, nonrationality, and metaphoric analysis. Doll writes: "Metaphoric analysis is hardly possible within a model structured around behavioral objectives, competency based performance, accountability, mastery learning, and effective teaching" (cited in Caine & Caine, 1991, p. 19). It is the disequilibrium itself that provides opportunities for creative tension and self-reflection. The term "chaos" was first coined by physicist Jim Yorke. As Yorke says, "We tend to think science has explained how the moon goes around the earth. But this idea of a clocklike universe has nothing to do with the real world" (cited in Briggs, 1992, p. 12). John Briggs describes chaos as a natural state of the universe, and he uses weather as an example: "With its variability, general dependability, and moment to moment unpredictability, weather infiltrates our schedules, sets or undermines our plans, affects our moods, and unites us with the environment and each other. Weather is also an example of a mysterious order in chaos" (1992, p. 13). In 1961, at MIT, Edward Lorenz discovered a disturbing fact. He realized that the mere accumulation of more information about variables related to the weather, such as wind speed, humidity, temperature, lunar cycles, and even sunspots, does not help to increase the accuracy of long-range weather forecasts. Dynamic and complex systems like weather, he found, are composed of many interacting elements, and the slightest perturbation has a significant impact on future patterns. Following Lorenz, researchers have examined all dynamic systems, from the human brain to electrical circuits, for evidence of chaos. Our interest here is the curriculum and the classroom, where chaos theory and complexity can help us to understand the postmodern vision that challenges the static and controllable universe of classical physics.

Chaos theory provides support for the aesthetic, political, gendered, racial, queer, cultural, theological, and ecological postmodern proposals that we discussed in part II of this book. We now explore the new sciences and their relationship to curriculum development, perhaps the most revolutionary research to support the postmodern paradigm shift.

Prigogine and Stengers have challenged the traditional social science approach to research in part because the mechanistic view of reality is being called into question in almost every field of scientific endeavor. New discoveries are unfolding in the universe that contradict the absolute principles of the classical sciences and the scientific method. Complexity replaces certainty. Prigogine and Stengers (1984) have demonstrated that systems in equilibrium and disequilibrium behave differently, and that order can emerge out of chaos. James Gleick (1987, 2008) and Paul Davies (1988, 1995, 2008) contend that there is an emerging science of complexity that is built in part on the fact that hidden in apparent chaos are complex types of order. The postmodern curriculum encourages chaos, nonrationality, and zones of uncertainty because the complex order existing here is the place where critical thinking, reflective intuition, and global problem-solving will flourish. The standardization of rote memorization, conformity, control, and time management, following from the faculty psychology movement of the 19th century and the scientific management movement of the 20th century (see glossary), restrict learning to a one-dimensional level imposed uniformly upon students and teachers alike. In order to move away from standardization into complexity and this new zone of cognition, educators must adopt a new postmodern vision.

How is this postmodern vision possible within a bureaucratic paradigm committed to the principles of modernity? James Lovelock (1979), in his popular Gaia hypothesis, provides an example based on the image of the Earth from the moon:

> The new understanding has come from going forth and looking back to the Earth from space. The vision of that splendid white flecked blue sphere stirred us all. It even opened the mind's eye, just as a voyage away from home enlarges the perspective of our love for those who remain there. ... We now see the air, the ocean and the soil are much more than mere environment for life; they are a part of life itself. ... There is nothing unusual in the idea of life on Earth interacting with the air, sea and rocks, but it took a view from outside to glimpse the possibility that this combination might constitute a single giant living system. (Cited in Tucker, 1993, p. 11)

Lovelock contends that the vision of the Earth from the moon began a paradigmatic change in the relationship between human persons and the environment. In the same sense, a vision of curriculum development from the perspective of the new sciences can create a paradigm shift in our educational practices that will replace the linear, objective, and time-management models that have dominated our thinking. If this seems to be an exaggeration, consider the emphasis we place on managed time in schools: class schedules and bells to differentiate time blocks; researchers who measure time on task, wait time between questions, and the relationship between the transition time and the academic performance of students; structured practice times, feeding times, and dismissal times; discipline plans that take away time in time-out rooms; timed tests and examinations; and duty times, planning times, and meeting times for teachers. Time is understood to exist as an independent metaphysical reality capable of being managed and organized for maximum efficiency.

Newtonian models and mechanistic systems on which modern educational paradigms are constructed ignore the developments in the sciences which indicate that social systems are interactive and open ended, and that time is an integral part of the reality. Both space and time are entities that are interwoven into matter. Paul Davies (1990) observes:

Space and time are a part of the plan of the physical universe; they are not just the stage on which the great drama is acted out, but are a part of the cast. We have to talk about the creation of space and time as well as matter and energy. ... The world was made with time and not in time. (p. 11)

Einstein set the stage for understanding space–time with his theory of relativity and his writings on electromagnetic radiation of atomic phenomena in quantum theory, both published in 1905 (Davies, 1995). Einstein strongly believed in nature's inherent harmony, and he sought to find a unified foundation of physics by constructing a common framework for electrodynamics and mechanics, the two separate theories of classical physics. This is known as the special theory of relativity.

Relativity unified and completed the structure of classical physics, and it also drastically changed traditional concepts of space and time. The foundation of the Newtonian worldview is now suspect. In Einstein's theory of relativity, space is not three dimensional and time is not a separate entity. Both are intimately connected in a four-dimensional continuum called space–time. It is now impossible to understand time outside the context of space, and vice versa. Capra (1975) explains:

There is no universal flow of time, as in the Newtonian model. Different observers will order events differently in time if they move with different velocities relative to the observed events. In such a case, two events which are seen as occurring simultaneously by one observer may occur in different temporal sequences for other observers. All measurements involving space and time thus lose their absolute significance. In relativity theory, the Newtonian concept of an absolute space as the stage of physical phenomena is abandoned, and so is the concept of an absolute time. Both space and time become merely elements of the language a particular observer uses for describing the observed phenomenon. (pp. 50–51)

Einstein expanded on the special theory of relativity to include gravity in 1915, with the publication of his proposal of the general theory of relativity. While the special theory of relativity has been demonstrated by innumerable experiments, the general theory remains the object of investigation. However, it is widely accepted in the study of astrophysics and cosmology. In the general theory the force of gravity has the effect of "curving" space and time, and thus abolishes the concept of absolute time and space. Capra (1975) concludes: "Not only are all measurements involving space and time relative; the whole structure of space–time depends on the distribution of matter in the universe, and the concept of 'empty space' loses its meaning" (p. 52). Einstein set the stage for the emergence of the new physics and new ways of understanding the universe. Chaos theory and complexity in the postmodern era are informing all disciplines, including curriculum development and educational leadership.

Complex systems can improve in the midst of turmoil. Curriculum models based on modern visions of Newtonian physics have attempted, like a clockwork universe, to impose uniformity. Every lesson, every goal and objective, must conform to predetermined principles, cultural forms, social structures, or curricular guides. Curriculum development in the postmodern era, on the other hand, is based on a new science: a complex, multidimensional, eclectic, relational, interdisciplinary, and metaphoric system. These complex systems in science and education challenge the second law of thermodynamics, which sees the universe as running down as entropy increases. Paul Davies contends that there is no claim that the second law of thermodynamics is invalid, only that it is inadequate because it applies only to closed systems that are isolated from their environments. Davies (1990) writes: "When a system is open to its environment and there can be an exchange of matter, energy, and entropy across its boundaries, then it is possible to simultaneously satisfy the insatiable desire of nature to generate more entropy and yet have an increase in complexity and organization at the same time" (p. 10). Thus, the universe as a whole can be seen as a closed system while subsystems of the universe remain open to their environments. This is a crucial element of postmodernism: radical eclecticism necessitates an openness to diverse subcultures and environments that can increase in complexity. In the same sense, the curriculum is now seen as an open system that exists in complexity. After observing open and closed systems and their environments, the French Jesuit paleontologist Pierre Teilhard de Chardin (1959a) wrote: "We are now inclined to admit that at each further degree of combination something which is irreducible to isolated elements emerges in a new order. ... Something in the cosmos escapes from entropy, and does so more and more" (cited in Davies, 1990, p. 10).

Something in the classroom and in the curriculum must also escape from entropy. William Doll, in *A Post-Modern Perspective on Curriculum*, contends that, just as the physical sciences in the 17th century led society into modernity, the new physics is ushering in postmodernity. Doll (1993) turns to Werner Heisenberg's uncertainty principle to support his claim. In traditional modern physics scientists believe that, if they can improve their measurements and calculate with infinite precision, absolute understanding of the universe and its physical properties would follow. Heisenberg disagreed, and he demonstrated that it does not matter how accurate the instrument or measurement because the act of measuring changes the outcome of the measurement process itself. Teachers have always instinctively known this to be true. The presence of an observer in the classroom measuring effective teaching changes the dynamics of the lesson and alters the class being observed.

The Heisenberg uncertainty principle examines the subatomic world and contends that, if we choose to measure one quantity (e.g., the position of the electron), we inevitably alter the system itself. Therefore, we cannot be certain about other quantities (e.g., how fast the electron is moving). Since an interaction is involved in every measurement, and since measurements are involved in observations in modem science and education, some physicists argue that the act of observation changes the system. While this applies to the interaction of particles in quantum physics, a few scientists are beginning to extend this principle to the realm of consciousness as well. Further, because some particles exist so briefly, they are not considered to be real, but "virtual." Thus, the universe as we know it is ultimately based on chance and randomness at the subatomic level. Can quantum physics inform postmodern curriculum? Let us explore further.

In classical physics, everything is known and can be measured. In quantum physics, uncertainty is built into the metaphysical reality. Position and velocity of an electron cannot be measured simultaneously, not because the observer is not looking carefully but because there is no such thing as an electron with a definite position. Electrons are "known" only in their relationship to other electrons. Electrons do not orbit the neutron like a planet, as most physics books reported until recent years. Rather, an electron exists in a cloud like a twin. Neither a particle nor a wave, the electron is described more by its relationship and potentiality than by its actuality. Each electron, in a sense, enfolds in itself the universe as a whole and hence all its other parts, emphasizing internal relatedness. In the postmodern curriculum it does not make sense to evaluate lessons, students, and classrooms based on predetermined plans, outcomes, or standards, for, like the elusive electron, relationships and potentialities explain their existence—and not predetermined structure. Fritjof Capra (1975) explains:

> The exploration of the subatomic world in the twentieth century has revealed the intrinsically dynamic nature of matter. It has shown that the constituents of the atom, the sub-atomic particles, are dynamic patterns which do not exist as isolated entities but as integral parts of an inseparable network of interactions. These interactions involve a ceaseless flow of energy manifesting itself as the exchange of particles; a dynamic interplay in which particles are created and destroyed without end in a continual variation of energy patterns. The particle interactions give rise to the stable structures which build up the material world, which again do not remain static, but oscillate in rhythmic movements. The whole universe is thus engaged in endless motion and activity; in a continual cosmic dance of energy. (p. 211)

Reading this passage reminds me of the motion and energy of classrooms and schools. If the universe on the quantum level and on the cosmic level is not rigid and fixed, why does our vision of curriculum, schooling, and research remain fixated on the metaphor of classical modern physics? William Doll (1993) contends that our current school curricula are not merely based on a scientific-efficiency model (Kliebard, 1986), "but have their foundations in seventeenth- to nineteenth-century modernist thought" (p. 158). The "naturalness" of this thought needs to be questioned, for what is self-evident in one paradigm becomes absurd in another. "In an intellectual time frame, Copernicus and Einstein represent the extreme boundaries of the modern paradigm, with Descartes and Newton as the medians. But, of course, as with any extremes, Copernicus and Einstein also represent the bridges between paradigms, one with the pre-modern the other with the postmodern" (Doll, 1993, pp. 21–22).

What is this postmodern paradigm in the sciences that is revolutionizing curriculum theory and other disciplines? David Ray Griffin believes that it is a reenchantment. At the root of modernity and its discontents is a disenchanted and mechanistic worldview that denies to nature the qualities of subjectivity, experience, and feeling. Griffin (1988a) writes: "Because of this denial, nature is disqualified—it is denied all qualities that are not thinkable apart from experience" (p. 2). A postmodern organic understanding of life provides the basis for a reenchantment of science that will support a new vision of the cosmos. Stephen Toulmin, in his important book *The Return to Cosmology: Postmodern Science and the Theology of Nature* (1982), contends that we must think about the cosmos as a single integrated system where all things in the world—human, natural, and divine—are related in an orderly fashion. This cosmic interrelationship—quantum interconnectedness—is central to the postmodern curriculum. David Bohm (1988) explains:

> Because we are enfolded inseparably in the world, with no ultimate division between matter and consciousness, meaning and value are as much integral aspects of the world as they are of us. If science is carried out with an amoral attitude, the world will ultimately respond to science in a destructive way. Postmodern science must therefore overcome the separation between truth and virtue, values and fact, ethics and practical necessity. To call for this non-separation is, of course, to ask for a tremendous revolution in our whole attitude to knowledge. But such a change is necessary, and indeed long overdue. Can humanity meet in time the challenge of what is required? (pp. 67–68)

Likewise, can curriculum development meet the challenge of what is required? Why is it so difficult to move beyond the modern paradigm in curriculum development to this postmodern vision?

One of the reasons for our difficulty with moving to a postmodern vision is our modern attachment to practical solutions to resolve immediate problems. Classical physics provides the structures for addressing these types of concern. In our daily experience we can function in what has been called the "zone of middle dimension," where classical physics can still be useful. On a daily basis we can deliberately remain oblivious to the quantum and cosmic phenomena. We are like the character Neo in the film *The Matrix* before he makes the decision to enter the Matrix to discover the inner workings of the social context. Unaware of this dimension of "space–time," we can convince ourselves that classical physics, traditional management practices, and modern curriculum development paradigms, if perfected, can solve the ecological, sociological, and educational crises of our time. We fail to recognize complexity and the interrelatedness of actions. Postmodernism challenges us to enter a new zone of cognition. Although the "zone of middle dimension" may have been useful in the modern era, the negative consequences of ignoring the quantum and cosmic dimensions of the physical universe threaten the survivability and viability of life. Postmodern visions of space–time must be infused into our management and curriculum development paradigms. A Kuhnian revolution is truly underway, and educators cannot afford to ignore these postmodern developments.

What is this paradigm and new conception of curriculum as chaos? First, it is not destructive and purposeless. William Doll (1993) explains chaos concisely in reference to a phase space diagram of a nonlinear system, commonly called a Lorenz attractor—after Edward Lorenz, who first used this type of graph to show a systems view of weather patterns:

> First, chaos is not a wild, random abandon. Far from it; the pattern is quite orderly but complex. Chaos refers to this complex ordering. It is not possible

to predict with complete accuracy where the next point on the trajectory will be (no two trajectories repeat exactly), but neither do the points fly beyond the bounds of the diagram. Two, the trajectories have both "bounds" and a center "attractor" area. Neither of these are precisely defined, but as the trajectories fly out from the center area they are attracted back, only to fly out again. The system, in its dynamic tension between moving out and back, has an overall coherence. Three, on occasion, any given point on the trajectory will "flip over" from one "owl's eye" or "butterfly wing" to the other. These "flip over" events are certain to happen over time but unpredictable for any given moment. One cannot say when such a flipping will occur, only that it will. The pattern is random, but it is a pattern. (p. 93)

Reread this passage from Doll's text again, substituting the classroom for the phase space diagram. Think of student experience when reading about flip-over events. Replace chaos in your mind with a dynamic interchange in the classroom during which many students are eager to contribute. Chaos in the classroom is such an event. First, there is a central attractor—a thematic unit, an experiment, or a short story. Second, the discussion will move back and forth from one point to another without predictability—but all the questions and comments are contained within the framework of the lesson theme. Third, flip-over events in the classroom are unpredictable and may lead to a dynamic integration of new ideas into the curriculum.

This approach to complexity in curriculum also includes an interdisciplinary understanding of cognition and learning. Professor Sherrie Reynolds of Texas Christian University, chair of the Complexity and Chaos group of the American Educational Research Association, draws on the work of Gregory Bateson and explains:

Most of the newer theories study cognition from a scientific point of view. Varela, Thompson and Rosch propose that the phenomenological approaches of Merleau-Ponty, Husserl and the Buddhist traditions are as essential and important as the scientific view. They believe that we must honor both the lived human experience and the scientific understanding before the two become irreconcilable. They say that when it is cognition or mind that is being examined, the dismissal of experience becomes untenable, even paradoxical. In this belief, they echo Ulric Neisser, who said that if psychology doesn't explain everyday human inner experience it is not useful. While each model is different, taken together they point to new and promising directions in cognition. These new directions include:

Cognition is constrained but not determined by the characteristics of the sensory end organs and other biological structures.

Cognition is autopoetic and, thus, can be triggered but not caused.

Cognition and consciousness are emergent.

The dynamics of Cognition are non-linear.

Cognition occurs at points of instability, far from equilibrium.

Cognition co-evolves and is co-constructed.

Cognition is best studied at the interface of several perspectives, including at least neurological, phenomenological, cultural, social.

We did not, until recently, have the cognitive tools to explore cognition as an emergent, dynamic co-determined phenomenon. These tools have come from the "New Sciences" and were foreshadowed by Gregory Bateson's understanding of cybernetics. Gregory Bateson was a scholar and a seeker. He studied and worked across disciplines searching for "patterns that connect." He built worlds of ideas in which unity became visible and descriptions of human cognition more closely approximated experience. Contemporary theorists sometimes disagree with Bateson and with each other, however there is a pattern that connects them. Traditional models of cognition assume that organisms learn to survive by constructing an internal representation of their environment. The more isomorphic the relationship between environment and representation, the more "true" the representation, and the more useful it is to the survival of the organism. This is one of the important points of divergence in newer cognitive theories. (Reynolds, 2004b, pp. 126–128)

In summary, Reynolds, Doll, and other contemporary curriculum scholars challenge the clockwork universe of classical physics, which was developed before thermodynamics. They challenge static notions of cognition and propose isomorphic relationships. In the spirit of the new sciences, they also challenge the picture of the cosmos as nothing but a random collection of particles acted upon by blind forces and capable of being controlled by artificial structures. Newton gave us a picture of a uniform universe in which every particle moved according to strictly defined laws of motion, where all events were the result of the unwinding of a gigantic mechanism. Time had no real significance because the state of the universe at all times and in all places is precisely determined. This is a sterile cosmology in which time is just a parameter and does not offer any opportunity for change, flux, unfolding, or chaos. It creates an ideology of false security. In the postmodern sense, time management is impossible, because the universe is not created *in* time and space but *with* time and space.

The date for my seminar on time management arrived. I was assigned the last session in the afternoon. The back of the room was filled with exhausted administrators who had been required to give up a Saturday for "leadership points." No one sat in the front. We did not even begin on time! I started the seminar by relating a story of my experience attending a rural Black church over the past several years. Musicians and choir members come to the sanctuary one at a time, robe, and prepare their instruments and materials. Parishioners arrive and greet each other and talk about community activities. Slowly, steadily, yet unnoticeably, a level of energy begins to fill the church. The volume of interchange rises as the piano begins to be played louder. The choir members gradually gather and softly clap their hands. And then suddenly the celebration begins! All the music and clapping come together in a thunderous explosion of energy. Unlike most other churches, no one comes to a microphone to call for attention, or to announce the page number of the first hymn, or even to offer greetings. These things happen spontaneously in this African-American church, for everyone is present and open to the complexity of the moment in the midst of apparent confusion. There is no need to ask people to rise and open books to sing, for the congregation is intuitively immersed in the music of the moment. Here, the service takes on a life of its own. No one looks to watches to determine the starting time of the service. As one gentleman told me, "It starts when everyone is ready." Sometimes the preacher speaks for minutes, sometimes for hours, but he knows when to fall silent and when to raise his voice. The congregation speaks with him in a double-voiced chorus of "Amens" and "Alleluias!" The pastor and the people are not separate; they operate in a dynamic harmony.

This is an example of the interrelationships that must also pervade curriculum development in the postmodern era—like improvisational jazz, which we discussed in chapter 10. The curriculum must build to a crescendo in an environment of unified space–time. Random and improvisational events build on each other and create a symphonic community experience (see Wheatley, 1992). There is order in the chaos of contemporary paradigms of curriculum development. Some administrators left my seminar disappointed; they did not receive a list of new time-saving practices to organize their professional lives. Others left the seminar refreshed; they experienced an understanding of life-saving insights that would change their conception of space–time. Curriculum development in the postmodern era is a cosmic vision accessible to those educators willing to see order emerging from the complexity and chaos of life.

twelve
A Vision of Curriculum in the Postmodern Era

The postmodern reply to the modern consists of recognizing that the past, since it cannot really be destroyed, because its destruction leads to silence, must be revisited: but with irony not innocently. ... Irony, metalinguistic play, enunciation squared. Thus, with the modern, anyone who does not understand the game can only reject it, but with the postmodern, it is possible not to understand the game and yet to take it seriously. Which is, after all, the quality (the risk) of irony. There is always someone who takes ironic discourse seriously. ... I believe that postmodernism is not a trend to be chronologically defined, but rather an ideal category or, better still, a *kunstwollen*, a way of operating.

Umberto Eco (1984),
from *Postscript to The Name of the Rose*

In the scriptorium of Umberto Eco's novel *The Name of the Rose*, a group of 14th-century Franciscan monks is busily work at translating and illuminating texts under the strict—albeit unlikely—supervision of an elderly blind brother. The elderly monk acting as the communicative agent for the magisterial authority of the Church harries the monks along if he hears them chatting among themselves. In this way, he curtails any discussion about the texts being worked on. Acting as guardian and gatekeeper, he declares that the library alone is testimony to truth and error and that, once a text has been transcribed, it assumes its place in the library in the locked room on the floor above, to which only he has access. Maintaining the authority of interpretation depends on preventing the monks from engaging aesthetically with the texts. In Eco's medieval mystery, defiance has the ultimate consequences, as the library is ultimately destroyed. Eco's novel provides us with an illustrative example of the authoritative notion of Truth and metanarrative interpretation that renders the possibility of engaging a text impossible. The dialogic becomes monologic. According to Martin Buber's dialogic principle "I and Thou," the necessary conditions for dialogue can occur only when one is aesthetically present to the other. Curriculum in the postmodern era becomes an aesthetic engagement and a search for deeper understanding that will lead to justice, compassion, and ecological sustainability where the boundaries between the center and the margin are blurred. Curriculum must create spaces (Cary, 2006; Miller, 1990) where all students have access to texts and interpretations. Communities of scholars, teachers, and students must engage in the hermeneutic process together. Educators and students do not transcribe texts in silent isolation under the unquestioned direction of a magisterial authority, as described in Eco's *The Name of the Rose*. Rather we all enter the hermeneutic circle that I discussed in chapter 5. This is the antithesis of modern obsessions with linear authority, governmentality (Foucault, 1979, 1980; see also glossary).

One important principle underlying my proposal for reconceptualizing curriculum development and the interpretive process of texts in schools and classrooms is that aesthetic awareness is tantamount to the ethical responsibility of a dialogic consciousness. As Buber insisted, the instinct for communion is the longing for the world to become present to us as a person. Mikhail Bakhtin (1990) asserts that aesthetics emerges as the consummation of what is built through the productive collaboration among interlocutors. In other words, our subjective mental consciousness is structured intersubjectively through sensory perception. In Deweyan terms, aesthetics provides us with the interpretive stuff that allows us to envision alternate scenarios and possibilities to morally problematic situations. This capacity for imaginative projection is also found in Bakhtin's notion of answerability. In this case, engaging in the curriculum in aesthetic and imaginative ways becomes a moral responsibility for all educators. We cannot govern or lead, like the blind monk in Eco's novel, in an attempt to prevent students from engaging the text and each other.

Interpretation should emphasize possibility and becoming, for human consciousness can never be static. Sartre, too, argues that human consciousness (being-for-itself) can never become a substance or an objective thing (being-in-itself), and this is why dialogic ambivalence and indeterminacy rather than a static ontology must be the focus of curriculum inquiry. Hence, each new experience adds to the accumulated meaning of experience for each individual and sets the stage for present and future possibilities. Throughout this book I have described this as the *proleptic experience* or the *synthetical moment*. Some might call it a gestalt or heightened consciousness. However, no matter what name we give to this experience, we must recognize that, while the present is conditioned by the past, every moment is also full of future possibilities for change and new directions. Reconceptualizing the interpretive process in curriculum in the postmodern era, therefore, must include forms of inquiry open to the shifting vantage points among various stakeholders and the intersections of competing voices. Refusing to succumb to the synthesis in the Hegelian dialectic in which difference is subsumed, a dialogic hermeneutics functions differently in different contexts and invites participation from a wide range of disciplines and persons. Curriculum development now becomes more inclusive, interdisciplinary (perhaps even non-disciplinary), and interspersed. Within the curriculum field, possible frameworks include but are not limited to the many theories that we have studied in this book: theology, hermeneutics, queer theory, postcolonial theory, gender studies, ecological sustainability, constructivism, critical race theory, cultural studies, aesthetics, and critical pedagogy.

The preceding philosophical reflections on postmodern thought attempt to create an image of time and space that is very different from the irreversible linear arrow and progressive sequence of modernity. Time is not an irreversible line on a trajectory where new and modern understandings are better than the outdated past. Postmodernism reconceptualizes time as duration, poststructuralism as eternal recurrence. On the one hand, time is a duration where the past is embedded in the present, as Henri Bergson contends. On the other hand, for Nietzsche, nothing abides, but all returns to be destroyed again and again. The *process* of becoming endures, but nothing in that process endures, except as repeated enduring states. Modern notions of being, Nietzsche argues, have arisen from discontent with becoming. Eternal recurrence is more than "mere" becoming; it reveals the eternal value of every moment. In both duration and eternal return, Bergson and Nietzsche reject modern notions of linear time in favor of the process of becoming that is so integral to postmodernism.

The kaleidoscope is distinct from the telescope, which uses lenses and mirrors to gather the light emanating from distant objects in order to observe them more precisely. It is also different from the microscope, which renders minute objects distinctly visible. The kaleidoscope, in contrast, produces a succession of symmetrical designs using mirrors to reflect the constantly changing patterns made by bits of colored glass at the end of a tube. The kaleidoscope creates constantly changing images and yet is always symmetrical within its own context. The telescope condenses what is fixed and charts a perceived unchanging universe. The microscope enlarges and isolates in order to categorize. Postmodernism is like the kaleidoscope; this book has been an attempt to create kaleidoscopic sensibilities. The designs were constantly changing and becoming something new, and yet all of them remained interrelated. Unlike telescopic attempts to condense and microscopic attempts to enlarge, kaleidoscopic postmodernism celebrates the diverse and complex understandings within each unique context.

The complexity of the postmodern vision cannot be reduced to a single definition or a new master narrative. It must be experienced within its own context. The nature of postmodernism requires what we described in chapter 11 as chaos. John Briggs (1992) presents an appropriate metaphor for curriculum development:

> Complex natural phenomena such as weather can't be stripped down, cleaned off, and studied under glass in a laboratory. An individual tree is the result of a vast, shifting set of unique circumstances, a kaleidoscope of influences such as gravity, magnetic fields, soil composition, wind, sun angles, insect hordes, human harvesting, other trees, [and] continuously active forces, far too numerous to determine in detail. (p. 14)

And so it is with curriculum development in the postmodern era—a kaleidoscopic and eclectic phenomenon that is the result of a vast, interrelated web of ideas, texts, personalities, architectural structures, literary narratives, and much more.

In this final chapter I will begin to connect the web of ideas discussed in the preceding chapters with the milieu that teachers face in the traditional school setting, especially in light of the dominance of restructuring reform movements and accountability movements in recent years. We will explore the ways that schools can create the kind of aesthetic sensibilities described above as they experience curriculum in the postmodern era. John Dewey's question as to whether *schools are a function of society or society is a function of schools* undergirds our discussion, with an emphasis on the latter. This chapter will point the way for educators to engage postmodern thought without succumbing to the malaise, fraud, and rigidity that paralyzed school reform movements and curriculum development programs in the modern era.

As we have seen throughout this book, the transition from the structures of modernity to a postmodern global society is in process. Donald Oliver and Kathleen Gershman (1989) assert: "We are at the end of an age, so that its metaphors and symbols no longer explain where we have been nor inform us about what next to do" (p. 7). Economic, ecological, environmental, ethical, and educational equilibrium are all being called into question. As we have seen, chaos and complexity are evident (Gleick, 1987; Davies, 1988; Doll, 1993; Reynolds, 2004a, 2004b). This is distressing to many educators and confusing to others. Is the complexity to be celebrated as an indication of a postmodern self-reorganization of the open-system cosmology of the new physics (Prigogine and Stengers, 1984)? William Doll (1993) writes: "A process whereby chaos and order are enfolded within each other, uniting to form a more complex, comprehensive, and sometimes 'strange' new order [is] the new vision ... of a post-modern view" (p. 88). Katherine Hayles (1984) writes about the concept of chaos bound inextricably to order, as in the yin and the yang in Eastern thought.

In contrast to this view, some ask if chaos is evidence of social decline and moral decay in contemporary men and women who refuse to accept the perennial truths of the closed-system universe of modernity. Allan Bloom (1987) warns: "The crisis of liberal education is a reflection of a crisis at the peaks of learning, an incoherence and incompatibility among the first principles with which we interpret the world, which constitutes the crisis of our civilization" (p. 346). Turmoil is pervasive; however, its long-term impact is still unfolding. Will renewal emerge from our malaise and anguish or is hope finally and irrevocably irrelevant? How can we remain determined to act for justice? However, if hope is not terminal, then perhaps the process of writing the modern postmortem on hope is itself the genesis of the resurrection of a new paradigm of curriculum development for the postmodern era. Along with Gramsci, possibly we can have "pessimism of the spirit, but optimism of the will." As we have seen throughout part II, philosophy, theology, social theory, gender studies, political theory, and literature offer many rich sources of reflection on this concept, thus providing insights for a curriculum that will be instructive for the postmodern global society.

The modern educational structures created in the spirit of Frederick Taylor's scientific management, Ralph Tyler's curriculum rationale, Abraham Maslow's hierarchy of needs, Benjamin Bloom's domains of learning, B. F. Skinner's behaviorism, Jerome Braner's early work in cognitive structures, and the systems of other patriarchs of contemporary curriculum development still dominate our rhetoric and practice on all levels of schooling. In fact, all teachers have certainly been exposed to these theories throughout their formal teacher training. However, the demoralization of educators, the disenfranchisement of students, and the dissatisfaction of stakeholders in educational systems are all indications that something is terribly wrong. These theories, despite their contributions to previous generations, have proved to be impotent in the face of growing turmoil in the modern world. Schools are too often characterized by departmental isolation, deadening accountability, lifeless conformity and standards, racial and gender divisiveness, political maneuvering, violent crime, professional jealousy, decaying and environmentally hazardous infrastructures, and savage economic inequalities. There are efforts to develop cooperative research and interdisciplinary scholarship on some campuses, but unfortunately these minimal efforts are discouraged by the very structure of the education bureaucracy and the competitive nature of schooling in general. The threat of budgetary cutbacks, bureaucratic reorganization, explosive and confrontational structures, suffocating accountability programs, and performance evaluations looms ominously on the horizon for educators. Many tenured teachers and professors publicly criticize the bureaucracy while languishing in their own malaise. Curriculum committees spend their time reviewing course proposals, clarifying goals and objectives, and debating changes in the state curriculum guides or university catalogues, oblivious to the contemporary curriculum discourses that have been introduced throughout this book. Creative energies are most often directed toward income-producing research and activities, competitive athletics, and social events, while important but fiscally unproductive and/or politically controversial projects languish for lack of interest or support. Discipline, violence, deprofessionalization, and drug abuse are most often cited as the critical issues facing teachers and students in the schools. How can curriculum renewal, particularly the call for transcending the structure of the disciplines and creating an interdisciplinary/multidisciplinary curriculum for the postmodern era, proceed under these conditions?

The first important step is for educators to reflect on the global perspective that is influencing crises in education in the US and elsewhere. Global transformations have brought the promise—but not necessarily the reality—of freedom from military dictatorships and totalitarian regimes to some societies (e.g., Chile and South Africa in the 1990s; Egypt, Tunisia, Libya, and the Middle East in the 2000s), repression of democratic movements in others (e.g., China's Tiananmen Square, Syria, and Iran), renewal of ethnic brutality in many countries (e.g., Bosnia-Herzegovina and Rwanda), and massive starvation, rape, impoverishment, and genocide as the result of political instability in still others (e.g., Somalia, North Korea, and Sudan). Some countries have simultaneously experienced both the exhilaration of liberation and reunification and the anguish of emergent racism (e.g., Germany) and ethnic conflict and regional economic decline (e.g., Russia). France exploded in violence in 2005. The US and Britain invaded and occupied Iraq in 2003. Economic crises in 2011 brought citizens to the streets in Greece, Italy, and the Occupy Wall Street movement. Some traditional democracies have witnessed an explosion of violent crime and racial unrest. Kidnapping in Colombia and Nicaragua have put judges and politicians at risk and threatened the functioning of the judicial process. Brutal drug wars and murders in Mexico are at a crisis level. Global terrorism, environmental degradation, economic recession, religious intolerance, institutional racism and sexism, psychological paralysis, and chemical addiction have reached epidemic proportions. Natural disasters from tsunamis, hurricanes, droughts, and earthquakes have exposed the inability of governments to protect citizens. We can no longer pretend that these issues are outside the domain of curriculum development. They are at the heart of curriculum inquiry. As I stated in the preface to this book, analysis and investigation of these global issues are at the heart of curriculum development.

I believe that it is particularly important to understand and address the complexities of global economic systems and competing economic philosophies, otherwise we are all at risk of manipulation by sleek advertising and corporate greed that confuses the uninformed and inflicts unjust economic hardship on workers, the middle class, and the poor. Occupy Wall Street was successful in explaining that the latter comprise the 99% of the population. The top 1% of the population controls the wealth and squeezes the majority of the working population.

There are two texts that I regularly use to investigate economic issues. The first is titled *For the Common Good: Redirecting the Economy Toward Community, the Environment, and a Sustainable Future*. The authors are Herman E. Daly, professor at the University of Maryland and formerly, in the 1980s, a professor of economics at LSU, where he was a popular elective course professor for graduate students in education, and John B. Cobb, who is a world-renowned theologian and member of the Greening of Higher Education project that I noted in the preface. Their main goal is to deconstruct neoclassical economic theory and set forth a more holistic model that more fully accounts for the individual, the community, and the natural world. Daly and Cobb (1989) discuss the implicit assumptions and theoretical fallacies governing contemporary economic scholarship. According to them, contemporary economic theory holds to a crude, mechanistic worldview of *homo economicus* as an autonomous individual driven solely by self-interest and of society as an aggregate of such individuals. This view tends to equate gains in society as a whole with the increases in goods and services acquired by its individual members, but it says nothing about the changes in the quality of the relationships that constitute that society. The authors therefore propose a "paradigm shift" from economics conceived as "crematistics" (maximization of short-term monetary gain) to the sort of economics Aristotle called "*oikonomia*" (management of a household aimed at increasing its use value over the long run for the community). In "economics for community," their term for the latter alternative, there is no aim for unlimited accumulation or "growthmania." Instead, "true wealth is limited by the satisfaction of the concrete need." Such a conversion entails a departure from radical individualism to the notion of a "person-in-community," as well as a fundamental shift away "from cosmopolitanism to communities of communities." Daly and Cobb claim that the emerging global society must develop democratically controlled institutions at all levels: international, national, and local. It also needs to create a decentralizing context for economic activities that returns institutional control to people, roots economic interests in local soil, and reestablishes some sense of human community. Of course, Daly and Cobb are a minority voice in the hyper-corporate structures ruled by the US Supreme Court to be legal persons. Corporate personhood is the status conferred upon corporations under the law, which allows them to have rights and responsibilities similar to those of a natural person (see *Citizens United* v. *Federal Election Commission*,

2010). There is also the long history in politically conservative rhetoric from Margaret Thatcher and Ronald Reagan that there is no such thing as community, only individuals. Libertarian individualism, as espoused most recently by US presidential candidate Ron Paul, presents another barrier to Daly and Cobb's vision. The conservative economic bible *The Road to Serfdom* (Hayek, 1947) presents another challenge to Daly and Cobb's economics for community and common good. I require my students to read Hayek and study the economic policies of Reagan and Thatcher in the 1980s as part of their research. We also compare and contrast major figures on the left and right, such as Milton Friedman and John Maynard Keynes, as well as investigations of Marxism, critical theory, and critiques in poststructuralism. Students and citizens are better equipped to challenge injustices when they understand the philosophical foundations of contemporary economic debates.

The second book I use extensively is *The Shock Doctrine: The Rise of Disaster Capitalism*, by Naomi Klein (2007). This text provides details on how corporate and international trade interests manipulate and eventually control the community wealth of nations through privatization while inflicting tremendous suffering and death on the population. I was reading this book in 2009, on a long flight to Cape Town to attend the International Association for the Advancement of Curriculum Studies convention. What I found on my four-week adventure throughout South Africa was a confirmation of all that Naomi Klein writes. The shock of the end of apartheid brought not only political change but also economic solidification of privatization. While visiting the Apartheid Museum in Soweto, I listened to many interviews with Nelson Mandela's political assistants, who said that they assumed that political power would translate into economic power. They were wrong; and the devastating consequences are evident throughout South Africa. I also spend a lot of time in South America, particularly lecturing at the Universidad Alberto Hurtada in Santiago de Chile. Klein's insights about dictatorships—particularly Augusto Pinochet in Chile from 1973 to the early 1990s—that impose economic privatization through brutal dictatorships undermine arguments for the benevolence of Friedman's privatization economics. Naomi Klein begins and ends her book with an analysis of post-Katrina New Orleans. This adds weight to the arguments against current school structures in the city. She sets the stage for exactly what is happening: the dismantling of the public school system for charter schools and privatization of public education, which we reviewed in chapter 8.

Schooling, from primary classrooms to graduate schools, has experienced parallel turmoil. Teachers are demoralized and administrators are immobilized, leading many to retreat to the comfort zone of self-righteous ideological certainty. Students and teachers at risk of physical harm divert their energy from learning to survival. In this environment, tangible evidence of structural and curricular transformation is rare, despite rhetoric about accountability, academic freedom, cultural literacy, political correctness, interdisciplinary studies, site-based management, national assessment, professional standards, mastery teaching and learning, cognitive learning, charter schools of excellence, and the like. It appears as though the educational accountability reforms proposed are totally unrelated to the problems facing the global community. Has humanity anesthetized ethical visions and repressed social justice? Is this absurd phenomenon further evidence of the end of hope?

Recent scholarship indicates a movement toward global standardization in curriculum, suggesting that a single concept of contemporary society may be moving toward global dominance. This phenomenon of curricular similarity is not restricted to developed countries, where one might expect to find some degree of standardization. Curricular differences between developing and developed countries are not as great as one might expect (Raymond, 1991). This should not be surprising. Franchises, subdivisions, strip malls, international commerce, global trade agreements, information cyberspace, satellite media, mass culture, tourism, and interstate commerce have depersonalized communities and made cities and schools indistinguishable from one another. In an ironic twist, the congestion at prominent natural and historical landmarks is so overwhelming and threatening to the preservation of the monuments themselves that governments have closed some original landmarks and created simulated versions nearby for tourist consumption. Thus, tourists in London from India may take their picture with wax figures of Gandhi, the royal family, or the Beatles at Madame Tussauds. Japanese tourists may experience a taste of the old American Wild West at EuroDisney in France. Virtual sex is available on the Internet, and cybersex cam connections, with people creating online identities for consumption worldwide, are available 24 hours a day. The authentic is repressed while the imitation becomes the new reality, and modern men and women are oblivious to the difference. Postmodernism refers to this as "hyperreality," contending that reality has collapsed exclusively into images, illusion, and simulations. The model is more real than the reality it supposedly represents. Jean Baudrillard (1983) writes: "Hyperreality is that which is already produced" (p. 146). Our dreams, Carl Jung reminds us, are closer representations of the self because they are unencumbered by the suppression and denial that dominate our waking hours in modern society. Modern life is really an imitation. Modern curriculum development is an illusion. I believe that we should attend to our dreams and awaken aesthetic sensibilities.

Contemporary society, like education, has reached the apex of modernity, an absurd psychodrama of self-destruction. Startled and frightened by the modern experience, people retreat from global consensus to the protection of a "minimal self" (Lasch, 1984) impervious to the interconnectedness of human communities and the interdependence of all phenomena (Bergson, 1950). Modernity does not offer a vision of order in chaos, a whole to part relationship, or a global experience in the local context. It should not be surprising, then, that teachers and students in such a climate would also find security in a "minimal curriculum" that isolates disciplines and departments, separates knowledge from the learner, seeks meaning apart from context, judges learning on memorization, suppresses and annihilates differences, and immortalizes the competitive victor. The commitment of modernity to Cartesian dualism and bifurcated structures is pervasive. However, a postmodern vision will thrive only once there is a clear understanding of the negative impact of the modern milieu on the human spirit that has been rent asunder.

Reflecting the prevailing social trends, educators appear to be blinded to the epochal nature of global transformations as they employ modern strategies to alleviate the pain of the byproducts of social upheaval. Perhaps the natural disasters of recent years, such as the South Asian tsunami, the Japanese earthquake, and Hurricane Katrina, have awakened a new sense of urgency—but perhaps not. Modern technology does not address the educational problems we face, despite the fact that modern technology has provided us with some important achievements. The spiritual, aesthetic, historical, socio-political, ethical, racial, gendered, sexual, and cultural dimensions of the human community, as we discussed throughout part II of this book, must be incorporated into our understanding of curriculum. Understanding curriculum, from this point of view, must take precedence over traditional curriculum development and program planning. As we saw in chapters 3 and 4, the process of running the race, *currere*, rather than the racecourse itself, should be the focus of the curriculum.

A clear articulation of a postmodern process vision of curriculum development that includes the concept of *currere* is urgently needed, and this vision could be a prophetic statement for a world in turmoil and denial. The fragmentation of society and individual persons, as also reflected in the fragmentation of disciplines and departments in schools, is a central concern of the emerging postmodern era. The disciplinary structure of the curriculum is comfortable to students, faculty, and administrators not only because it is familiar but also because many have not experienced, or even considered, a postmodern alternative. Interdisciplinary, aesthetic, and multidimensional alternatives must be incorporated into schooling. This book has been an attempt to expose more educators to the postmodern possibilities. Postmodern voices are abundant in the arts, sciences, and humanities.

A credible curriculum for the postmodern world must keep an eye toward the trends and issues discussed above. We must rigorously investigate global understandings of curricular programs, policies, practices, and philosophies, but not for the purpose of reforming and refining them. The postmodern vision must transcend and transform the traditional bureaucratic approach to curriculum development. However, the primary focus must remain keenly centered on the particular context of local educational communities and specific cultural concerns, as well as on individual autobiographies, as noted throughout this book. Both the global and the local are important, and they must not be bifurcated. An integrated understanding of the individual and society is of critical importance. George S. Counts made the following important observation:

> The historical record shows that education is always a function of time, place, and circumstance. In its basic philosophy, its social objective, and its program of instruction, it inevitably reflects in varying proportion the experiences, the conditions, and the hopes, fears, and aspirations of a particular people or cultural group at a particular point in history. (Cited in Gutek, 1993, p. 88)

The long-standing and almost perennial philosophical debate between those, like Mortimer Adler and Robert Hutchins, who argue that education is a universal process that reflects a monolithic conception of human nature, and those, like Counts, who insist that education must be culturally relevant to particular situations and societies can be instructive to our discussion of the transformation of curriculum development in the postmodern era. We must be careful not to become polarized at either end of this debate. The more appropriate position recognizes the interdependence of the global condition and the local context. Perhaps Alfred North Whitehead (1929, 1933),

in *Aims of Education* and *Adventures of Ideas*, best explained this concept of interdependence. As education moves from the individual story in Whitehead's initial stage of
romance, through the process of finding commonalities and differences in his second
stage of *precision*, to his final stage of *generalization*, Whitehead (1933) understands
that the commonalities and connections signify that a "harmony of the whole is
bound up with the preservation of the individual significance of detail" (p. 264). Thus
individual pluralism in specific contexts gives strength to the whole edifice of education. We might call this kaleidoscopic community sensibility; Charles Jencks calls it
radical eclecticism. Jencks (1992) succinctly explains why postmodernism must be
radically eclectic:

> We must be aware ... that a complete sublation, or Hegelian dialectic which
> resolves contraries, is not always the result or goal of post-modernism: parts,
> sub-assemblies, sub-cultures often keep their unassimilated identity within the
> new whole. Hence, the conflicted nature of the pluralism, the radical eclecti-
> cism of the postmodern style. (pp. 14–15)

In the spirit of Whitehead's analysis and Jencks' radical eclecticism, some initial guiding principles for an integrated global and local vision for curriculum development in
the postmodern era will be discussed below.

First, a process approach to education is capable of engendering a significant reconceptualization of the nature of schooling globally, as well as the experience of education locally, because it respects the unique development of the individual and recognizes
the interrelationship of all experiences. The emergent nature of this reconceptualization rejects hierarchical, authoritarian, patriarchal, and hegemonic ideologies, as well
as models of curriculum committed exclusively to educational outcomes outside process and context. We must begin with the autobiographical (Pinar and Grumet, 1976)
and the "intuition of duration" (Bergson, 1950, p. 27) and then support and encourage
individuals to make connections to broader concepts. Dewey (1938) and Whitehead
(1929) demonstrated that this process can be rigorous and scientific without sacrificing
the experience of the individual. For example, one of my graduate students teaches an
oral history project at a local high school. Students volunteer for this experiential
social studies class. Two meetings per week are held at a local antebellum plantation
museum and two meetings on the high school campus, while one day is used for community research. The goal of the class is to allow students to construct an oral history
in the community that can be used at the museum. A particular concern of the project
organizers is that the names of the plantation owners are noted throughout the
museum, but the enslaved Africans are mentioned only on one plaque as having
resided in the "slave quarters." The names of the enslaved people are known in the
community, and the students are trying to reconstruct and reinterpret the history of the
plantation through interviews and artifacts. This is an example of a curriculum that
incorporates the historical, aesthetic, racial, autobiographical, and philosophical issues
presented throughout part II. It is uniquely local in character but global and historical
in its impact.

Second, the modern behavioristic emphasis in schooling, as exemplified in the unre-lenting commitment to behavioral objectives, learning hierarchies, "value-neutral" empirical-analytical methodologies, goals and objectives, rote memorization, and com-petitive learning environments, is not only outmoded but also detrimental to the emer-gence of an appropriate global postmodern educational experience. Whitehead (1929) protested against this modern perpetuation of "inert ideas." He wrote in *Aims of Education*: "Students are alive, and the purpose of education is to stimulate and guide their self-development. ... Teachers should also be alive with living thoughts. The whole book is a protest against dead knowledge, that is, against inert ideas" (p. v). In order for classrooms to reflect Whitehead's vision, teachers must be lifelong learners and students must be leaders of instruction. A hermeneutic circle must be formed in classrooms where the discourse is shared, empowering, emerging, and tentative. This is a dramatic break with modern bureaucratic curriculum paradigms. Is there a method for implementing a new postmodern paradigm? Yes: one teacher, one student, and one classroom at a time. Postmodernism cannot be imposed uniformly, but it can provide the philosophical support for a change in consciousness that will necessarily lead to new practices. This is called evoking, a postmodern alternative to re-presenting or represen-tation. Evoking—as we discussed in the introduction—is assumed to free one's analysis of objects, facts, descriptions, generalizations, experiments, and truth claims from abso-lute master narratives. Educators must evoke rather than impose representations.

Third, a constructive postmodernism as understood by David Ray Griffin (1988a), William Doll (1993), and Donald Oliver and Kathleen Gershman (1989), among many others, as distinct from deconstructive or critical postmodernisms, offers an important emerging approach to understanding curriculum. Poststructural and deconstructive philosophies are also making an important contribution to our understanding of lan-guage, especially as language reflects and influences worldviews. Educators in the postmodern era are not reticent to engage both poststructuralists and constructivists, males and females, and a diversity of all people of all colors, races, sexualities, and spiritualities in dialogue and to incorporate language analysis and process philosophy into our curriculum proposals. For example, Patti Lather (1994) distinguishes between "close reading which constructs a realist tale; a structural reading which constructs a critical tale; a situated reading which constructs a reflective tale; and a poststructural reading which constructs a deconstructive tale" in order to help educators move beyond empirical-analytical reading methodologies to a more empowering poststruc-turalism. Madeleine Grumet (1988b) offers a phenomenological approach to reading and language that "celebrates the presence of an absence" in the educational experi-ence. Grumet (1988b) writes: "Meaning is something we make out of what we find when we look at texts. It is not the text" (p. 142). Lather and Grumet demonstrate that postmodernism is eclectic and kaleidoscopic, and that it should move beyond the oppressive structures of modernity. The postmodern curriculum challenges us to get on with the business of providing concrete options and inspiring determination to act in the midst of global social and educational crises.

Fourth, the curriculum itself must be viewed primarily as *currere* (Pinar & Grumet, 1976) and support the context necessary to move from romance through precision to generalization (Whitehead, 1929). Our educational proposals must also attend to the problem of alienation, destruction, decadence, and evil (Griffin, 1976; Noddings, 1989; Jencks, 1992; Kozol, 2005) so as to avoid the pitfalls of facile utopianisms prevalent in some political analyses, while at the same time being careful not to succumb to a nihilistic existentialism devoid of spirituality and aesthetic values as found in some philosophies (Stanley, 1992). Administrators and teachers must be attentive to language, especially as it is politically, socially, and historically embedded. Our language must be inclusive at all levels of communication.

Recent scholarship would argue that communication in classrooms must be embodied. Karen Krasny (2004), for example, adopts an embodied perspective to explore the complex relationship between the aesthetic and moral value of literature. Drawing on recent advances in neuroscience and the emerging field of consciousness studies, Krasny explains how sensory imagery and emotional responses associated with the phenomenal experience of the reader are mapped by the body and stored in the reader's autobiographical memory. The human capacity to recombine and reconfigure existing images and to form new ones allows readers to achieve empathetic identification with characters and to try out solutions to morally problematic situations within the safe confines of the text. Krasny argues that the richness of the literary experience is realized as it brings us face to face with the fundamental ambiguity of our existence—the chance to explore the human potential for good and evil.

Fifth, and finally, as we have seen in part II, there is important curriculum scholarship that incorporates hermeneutics (Haggerson & Bowman, 1992), phenomenology (Greene, 1978, 2001; Grumet, 1988b; van Manen, 1990, 1993), social psychoanalysis and liberation theology (Slattery & Rapp, 2003), process theology (Griffin, 1988b; Griffin, Beardslee, & Holland, 1989), spiritualities (Hammerschlag, 1988, 1993; Purpel, 1989, 2005), race (McCarthy, 1990; Castenell & Pinar, 1993), feminism (Noddings, 1989, 1992; Miller, 1990, 2005), and specific cultural issues that will support efforts to understand curriculum for global transformation and expose postmodern proposals to a wider audience. The transformation of curriculum will be most fruitful if cooperative research includes a variety of these contemporary voices.

In presenting these five short summary comments, I am reminded that curriculum scholars must avoid the temptation to construct a traditional metaphysics and epistemology to justify a postmodern view of curriculum development. Bergson (1950) writes that "metaphysics is the science which claims to dispense with symbols" (p. 24). Oliver and Gershman (1989) expand on this thought:

> It is obvious to us that we have come to confuse those issues which require the deepest kind of ontological knowing with issues that might be clarified and resolved through technical knowing. This confusion permeates education. We come to see problems of curriculum selection (what is worthwhile knowing and how to learn it) as translatable into a technical field of study through which one can identify the appropriateness of bits of explicit information, or the value of a certain skill. This confusion in the selection of modalities of knowing we would call the technical fallacy. (p. 15)

While the nature of the human person, knowledge construction, spirituality, and ethics should be included in our postmodern proposals, this must be accomplished by utilizing a process approach within the context of democratic community experience. In other words, we must arrive at a vision of curriculum for the postmodern era using the very process proposed for global curriculum educational transformation, described throughout part II, and not resort to the technical fallacy as described by Oliver and Gershman. If postmodern curriculum truly offers an alternative for schooling today, it must emerge in a context employing the very principles proposed. If not, then post-modernism degenerates into another ultramodern project. Oliver and Gershman's ontological knowing, which is expressed through mystical experience, reflection, metaphor, poetry, drama, liturgy, dreams, and music rather than the analytic and linear language of technical knowing, is perhaps the preferable model to ensure faithfulness to the postmodern context.

These general concepts offer a glimpse into the thinking that underlines the perspective of contemporary curriculum scholars. These are not absolute principles, nor do they attempt to form a coherent philosophical paradigm. They are simply pivotal ideas in the schema of an approach to curriculum that could contribute to the transformation of education in the postmodern era.

Curriculum studies in the postmodern era remind us that debates about the canon, goals, and objectives of the curriculum, while certainly important to the process of clarifying the content and structure of the educative events planned by school districts and universities, are of limited value in our efforts to improve education and society. In fact, the competitive nature of these debates engenders futility because it often results in polarization and protracted confrontation. If curricular concerns are limited to dialogue about the canon, the content of course descriptions, methods of quantitative evaluation, and the sequence of course offerings, we have effectively eliminated the discussion of postmodern approaches to understanding curriculum that move beyond disciplinary structures as proposed throughout this book.

Curriculum debates must be redirected to the understanding of curriculum, the construction of the individual in relation to educative moments, the development of autobiographical, aesthetic, intuitive, and proleptic experience, and the socio-cultural and socio-political relations emerging from an understanding of the individual in relation to knowledge, other learners, the world, and ultimately the self. In short, we must move from the modern paradigm of curriculum development in the disciplines to the postmodern paradigm of understanding curriculum in various contexts in order to move toward justice, compassion, and ecological sustainability. In this sense, curriculum development is always shifting perspectives and constantly reflecting new and liberating visions of learning and living. This is the postmodern hermeneutic process of uncovering layers of meaning, deconstructing master narratives, affirming women's ways of knowing, creating ecological sustainability, uncovering the wide-awakeness of the aesthetic vision, engendering poststructural sensitivities, affirming curriculum spaces and queer sensibilities, and ultimately experiencing a determination to act in our educational journey. The postmodern curriculum, in all its eclectic perspectives, offers an opportunity for education to move beyond moribund modes of analysis to a new understanding of curriculum development in the postmodern era.

The crisis of modernity arises precisely because history and time are conceived of as linear and thus capable of being broken. If the present can be broken, it can also be conceived of as degraded and meaningless. Then the modern pathos is projected backward and forward, projecting this vision on every present—past, present, and future. Postmodernism reconnects space–time with individuals and society in order to transcend this modern embedded pathos. James Macdonald (1988) writes: "The impetus for choosing and becoming in us is not something that need be externally imposed; but it is rather a process of helping others see possibilities and helping them free themselves from going beyond this present state of embedded existence" (p. 163). Postmodern schooling must reconnect students and teachers, space and time, meaning and context, the knower and the known, humanities and sciences, and, especially, past, present, and future. What modernity has rent asunder, postmodernity reevaluates as radically eclectic by embracing the fragmented ambiguity. Postmodernism celebrates the process of becoming and the interdependence of eternal becoming.

Humanity desperately needs an alternative to dominant philosophies and eschatologies that have blurred, and ultimately destroyed, the vision of the eternal recurrence and the interconnectedness of past, present, and future. A postmodern understanding of curriculum offers a potential vision of justice, complexity, compassion, ecological sustainability, spirituality, and internal relatedness. A proleptic understanding of the integration of time, place, and self is one of the essential elements of curriculum development for the postmodern era (Slattery, 1989).

What is this proleptic vision for curriculum development in the postmodern era? While definitions and master narratives of this emerging paradigm are to be resisted, this book has presented a vision of the postmodern curriculum that is radically eclectic, determined in the context of relatedness, recursive in its complexity, autobiographically intuitive, aesthetically dialogic, embodied, phenomenological, experiential, simultaneously quantum and cosmic, hopeful in its constructive dimension, radical in its deconstructive movement, liberating in its poststructural intents, empowering in its spirituality, ironic in its kaleidoscopic sensibilities, and, ultimately, a hermeneutic search for greater understanding that motivates and satisfies us on the journey. With T. S. Eliot,

We shall not cease from exploration,

And the end of all our exploring

Will be to arrive where we started

And know the place for the first time.

Glossary

A detailed version of this glossary can be found on the Companion Website to this book:

www.routledge.com/cw/slattery

Aesthetics is the philosophy of art. Aesthetics investigates ways of seeing and perceiving the world. In curriculum studies, aesthetics is integral to various concepts related to imagination, experience, creativity, culture, and public pedagogy. Together, aesthetics and ethics form a branch of philosophy called axiology. Ethics examines morality, justice, and human behavior; aesthetics examines notions of beauty, goodness, and perception. Together, aesthetics and ethics examine beauty, goodness, justice, and judgment. Some define aesthetics as a critical reflection on art, culture, and nature. Aesthetics commonly is known as the study of sensory and emotional values called judgments of sentiments and tastes. Aesthetics creates a mutual and reciprocal interaction between the world and an individual, and our lived experience requires aesthetics. Properly understood and executed, teaching and learning is an aesthetic experience.

Autobiography can be understood as a partial narrative or a comprehensive life history of the self, psychoanalytic investigations of the self, analysis of identity constructions, investigations of past, present, and future dimensions of the self by an individual, a written text describing one's life journey and future goals, or possibly even distortions, delusions, and embellishments about one's life history. Autobiography is integral to contemporary understandings of curriculum, and autobiographical connection to academic subject matter is essential for learning.

Bifurcation and related notions of dualism indicate the splitting or separating of things into two parts. I use the concept of bifurcation to highlight divisions and ruptures in schools and society, as well as dualism of mind and body, left brain and right brain, arts and sciences, administrators and staff, students and teachers, gifted and remedial, male and female, gay and straight, Black and White, and an endless series of divisions that are complicated and interrupted in the postmodern era. The language of bifurcation, dualism, and "Balkanization" contributes to ways of thinking about schools and society that reinforces and reinscribes competition, domination, and, ultimately, the tragedies of the modern era.

Bildung. From the German *Bildungsroman,* education is seen as a self-striving to become fully developed and directed toward justice, goodness, and virtue in life. *Bildung* as growth and development is a broader concept of learning beyond formal schooling, and it is directed toward self-conscious life formation. Curriculum development is thus understood more broadly to include all aspects of the life journey.

Chaos Theory and Complexity Theory. Chaos theory, popularly referred to as the butterfly effect, studies the behavior of dynamical systems that are highly sensitive to initial conditions. Small differences in initial conditions, such as those due to rounding errors in numerical computation, yield widely diverging outcomes for chaotic systems, rendering long-term prediction impossible in general. Weather conditions and human behavior can be observed and understood within context and within a range of possibilities, but cannot be determined with certainty. This is true even though the future behavior of these systems is fully determined by their initial conditions if no random elements are involved. In other words, their deterministic nature does not make them predictable. This behavior is known as deterministic chaos, or simply chaos. Complexity theory is the study of these complex systems. In curriculum theory, teaching and learning is understood as such a complex dynamical system.

Chthonian. Of or pertaining to the underworld; beneath the surface. I use the word "chthonian" in connection with depth psychology and Jungian dream analysis to elucidate the role of the unconscious in curriculum and education. I also use it in relation to ecology and floods to understand the complexity of natural processes in nature, human consciousness, and the learning process.

Conscientization is described in the writing of Brazilian educator Paulo Freire as a process of critical reflection through which people gain insight into the socio-political structures of their world as well as the capacity to act to transform oppressive dimensions of those structures. Freire's work provides a major contribution to understanding political dimensions of education as it assumes that education is a political act. Freire's understanding of conscientization emerges from literacy campaigns conducted in Brazil under the liberal government of João Goulart. Literacy campaigns directed by Freire focused on the formation of a critical consciousness of students and teachers in a process of mutual collaboration and engagement with the world. Central to this mutual process of conscientization is an understanding of political history as always in development and growth. Thus, it becomes the job of teachers and students to engage in and create historical conditions that advance justice and compassion.

Constructivism is a theory of knowledge often associated with Jerome Bruner, John Dewey, Maria Montessori, Jean Piaget, and Lev Vygotsky. Constructivism assumes that humans generate knowledge and meaning from experiences and describes the process of learning. It is not a prescriptive pedagogy, even though it is often associated with various pedagogic approaches such as active learning, place-based learning, project learning, and experiential learning. Constructivist theories of knowledge (epistemologies) can advance positive social change and school renewal. However, curriculum development in the postmodern era cannot be reduced simply to implementing constructivist practices.

Critical Theory. There are two meanings of critical theory which derive from two different intellectual traditions associated with analysis and critique: critical social theory and literary criticism. (1) Critical social theory emerges, in a broad sense, from European traditions of Marxist scholarship. Critical theory, historically speaking, is a continual reckoning of the Marxist tradition in the historical present. The two major rewrites of the Marxist tradition are the Frankfurt School of Social Science and the Birmingham School of Cultural Studies. The Frankfurt School sees critical theory as a form of self-reflective knowledge about our entrapment in systems of domination or dependence, and, therefore, critical social theory seeks to reduce the scope of oppression and injustice in the world. The term "critical theory" was defined by Max Horkheimer of the Frankfurt School as a social theory oriented toward critiquing and changing society as a whole, in contrast to traditional literary theory oriented only to understanding or explaining it. In the sociological and non-literary sense, critical theory is the critique of domination in order to advance justice and emancipation. This is done by politicizing social problems and situating them in historical and cultural contexts. The Birmingham School embraces Antonio Gramsci's understanding of hegemony (see below) as a lens for analyzing cultural production. Birmingham School scholars like Stuart Hall and Paul Willis couple strong readings of Gramsci's hegemony with analyses of cultural phenomena, including school cultures. Specifically, Birmingham School scholars work with hegemony as a lens for understanding working-class lives and speech, resistances in youth culture, meanings of alternative cultural styles, and dominant (yet invisible) White, heterosexual, Christian, and masculine cultural representations.

(2) Literary criticism is a form of hermeneutic interpretation (see below) used to understand the meaning of human texts and symbolic expressions. This version of critical theory seeks to establish and enhance the understanding of literature in the search for truth and meaning. Some contend that this form of critical theory is not oriented toward radical social change or even toward the analysis of society, but instead seeks understanding of novels, short stories, and other writings. Some consider literary criticism merely an aesthetic process devoid of critical social concerns. In curriculum studies, most scholars believe that literary criticism and aesthetics do contribute significantly to critical social analysis as well as individual and social transformation. Both versions of critical theory have focused on the processes of synthesis, production, or construction by which the phenomena and objects of human communication, culture, and political consciousness come about.

Cultural Commons. We might understand the commons, in general, as those material and cultural spaces that belong to everyone, upon which our survival depends, and which are not, or should not be, abandoned to the logic of private economic interests or corporate ownership.

Currere is a Latin word that translates "to run the racecourse." The word "curriculum" derives from *currere*, and its etymological history is fundamental for understanding the meaning of curriculum development. Professors William Pinar and Madeleine Grumet developed a four-step process for *currere* that is explained in chapter 2. The most important thing to note about *currere* is that it defines curriculum as a *process* rather than simply as an *object*.

Curriculum is often defined as the lesson plans, textbooks, instructional materials, evaluation strategies, media, and technology generated by teachers, administrators, school boards, and publishers for student consumption and classroom instruction. In short, curriculum artifacts contain the things that the community or state expects the students to learn. Some scholars expand this definition to include formal co-curricular activities such as music and agriculture programs and/or school-sponsored extracurricular activities in the arts and athletics. Others will expand the definition of curriculum further to take in all formal and informal learning experiences related to homework assignments, socialization activities, health and nutrition, field trips, popular culture, community festivals, and youth culture. Finally, some scholars will challenge all of these definitions of curriculum and expand the definition to encompass all formal and informal life experiences that contribute to student growth, social consequence, and values. Curriculum development in the postmodern era embraces the broadest definitions of curriculum.

Curriculum theory is the interdisciplinary study of educational experience (see Pinar, 2004a; Kliebard, 2004). It is an established academic field of study that emerged in the 1970s following the reconceptualization movement in curriculum studies.

Deconstruction is a sophisticated method of critical analysis of human artifacts such as written documents, textbooks, artwork, musical compositions, films, media, and the like. Deconstruction can include contextualizing, evoking, troubling, historicizing, challenging, analyzing, and interrupting. In schools we need to deconstruct handbooks, textbooks, curriculum guides, administrative memos, letters to parents, essays written by students, test questions, visual images, student performances in sports and the arts, and any other human artifact that is a part of the teaching and learning process or school context.

Dualism and the Cartesian–Newtonian Science. The modernist science emerging in the 1600s rested on the separation of the knower and the known, a cardinal tenet of the Cartesian–Newtonian (referring to René Descartes and Sir Isaac Newton) way of organizing the world. Descartes' analytical method of reasoning, often termed reductionism, asserted that one can appreciate complex phenomena best by reducing them to their constituent parts and then piecing these elements back together according to causal laws. This analysis took place within Descartes' separation of the mind and matter. Cartesian dualism divided human experience into two distinct realms: an internal world of sensation and an objective world composed of natural phenomena. Drawing on this dualism, scientists subsequently asserted that one could uncover the laws of physical and social systems objectively; meanwhile, the systems operated apart from human perception, with no connection to the act of perceiving. In schools and classrooms today we often continue to devalue intuition, insight, autobiographical reflection, and inner experience and emphasize instead objective lessons, measurable outcomes, and test scores. This is the continuing legacy of Cartesian dualism.

Ecofeminism is committed to interrogating and transforming domination that has historically been linked to sexism, racism, classism, heterosexism, ageism, and religious intolerance and extends the commitment to justice to the domination and ecological devastation of nature. Ecofeminism has roots in critical feminism, liberal feminism, radical and socialist feminisms, and Black and third world feminisms.

Ecumenism typically refers to dialogue and cooperation among Christian denominations aimed at unity among diverse churches but not unification of all sects into a single church. Sometimes ecumenism is understood more narrowly to indicate relations in a strictly orthodox sense. In this orthodox definition, Catholic–Islamic or Catholic–Hindu dialogue is not ecumenical because Muslims and Hindus do not share a common spiritual baptism with Christians. The Roman, Orthodox, and Anglican churches describe this kind of spiritual communication with non-Christian religions as "interfaith dialogue" rather than "ecumenism." Etymologically, ecumenism refers to the inhabited world or global in extent or influence. Any cooperative activity that encompasses the world or involves the inhabitants of the world can be described as ecumenical. I use ecumenism in this broader sense by advocating for dialogue and cooperation across differences of any kind in a global context.

Environmental Racism. Poor, migrant, undocumented, and homeless people, along with abandoned children, AIDS orphans, and working-class adults at the lower end of the economic ladder—who are most often people of color, indigenous people, and other racial minorities—live on the most environmentally polluted lands in the most neglected and dangerous neighborhoods, with rotting infrastructure and festering poison from lead pipes and paint, toxic emissions, contaminated soil and groundwater, and poisonous landfills.

Epistemology is the study of knowledge and knowing. It is concerned with finding the truth or the meaning of the idea of the truth. Epistemologists want to understand the answer to the question "What is true?" Is truth the same in every circumstance? Is knowledge and truth preordained by a God, or gods, or nature? Is knowledge inert or is it constructed?

Essentialism is a theory of education which holds that foundational concepts and basic skills are critically important to a culture and should be taught to all students. The best techniques for teaching these essential skills are by time-tested and historically validated methods. Essentialism is also a philosophical theory ascribing ultimate reality to *essence* embodied in a thing and perceptible to the senses (in contrast to the philosophy of nominalism). Essentialism emerged primarily as a reaction against progressivist approaches.

Faculty Psychology. In the early 19th century an influential movement called faculty psychology (or mental discipline) emerged from the findings of many scholarly reports—including, in 1828, *The Yale Report on the Defense of the Classics*, which is sometimes considered the beginning of the US curriculum field. *The Yale Report* expressed two key concepts in faculty psychology: discipline and furniture. The aim of the curriculum, it said, was to expand the capacity of the mind and store it with knowledge. This curriculum philosophy sought to arrange the information the memory gathers as one would arrange furniture in a room. Additionally, it proposed that one exercise the muscles of the brain routinely like those in the rest of the body.

Gnosticism is a philosophical and religious movement which started in pre-Christian times. The movement and its literature were essentially wiped out at the end of the 5th century CE (Common Era) by Catholic heresy hunters and the Roman Army. The name is derived from the Greek word *gnosis*, which translates literally as knowledge. The English words "insight" and "enlightenment" also capture the meaning of *gnosis*. Gnosticism is not factual, intellectual, rational knowledge. Rather, it involves the relational or experiential knowledge of the divine or spiritual nature within us.

Governmentality is a term developed by the French philosopher Michel Foucault in the late 1970s to investigate the notion of power. Foucault argues that power is not only a top-down hierarchical structure of the state, but also any form of social control in disciplinary institutions such as schools, hospitals, prisons, and psychiatric wards. Power can also manifest itself positively by producing internalized knowledge within individuals that can guide behavior. Governmentality applies to a variety of historical periods and to specific power regimes. However, Foucault often used it in reference to neoliberal practices of advanced liberal democracies. In this case, the notion of governmentality refers to societies where power is de-centered and its members play an active role in their own self-government. This necessitates an active role by individuals for self-regulation. Neoliberal governmentality is based on the predominance of market mechanisms and restrictions on the action of the state.

Hegemony is a word used to describe domination through the creation of consensual social practices and cultural norms. Powerful elites use institutions—especially schools, churches, and the media—to win consent from the masses of people who are dominated and oppressed. Hegemony is a word that describes the social, cultural, ideological, theological, and economic influence exerted by a dominant group over a population. The powerful ruling group, or "hegemon," acquires some degree of consent from the subordinates, as opposed to dominance purely by force. The leaders of a religious sect can gain emotional and financial consent from members using fear, guilt, and threats of excommunication and/or eternal damnation.

Hermeneutics is the art and science of interpretation. Judges and lawyers interpret constitutions and legal documents. Museum docents interpret works of art. Religious authorities and individual believers interpret the meaning of the Koran, Bible, Hindu Scriptures, Gita, Torah, and other sacred texts. Literature teachers and students interpret the themes, metaphors, and character traits in short stories and novels. Math and science teachers interpret formulas, symbols, and directions for experiments. Athletes interpret the game plan, signals from the coach, field conditions, and the formations of opponents as they call a play or prepare a winning strategy for the game. School leaders interpret the school handbook and assign consequences and punishments when rules are broken. Teachers interpret the quality of an essay and assign a grade based on a rubric, a comparison to other essays, or a subjective judgment. Romantic partners interpret the moods, facial expressions, words, and touches of their lover to ascertain arousal and make judgments about sincerity, commitment, or fidelity. Parents interpret the seriousness of a child's cry. Interpretation is an art and a science that is critically important in education.

Heterosexism and Homophobia. Heterosexism is the assumption that all persons are heterosexual. Heterosexism (or hetero-normativity) is a privileging of economic systems (i.e., insurance, tax codes, inheritance laws), cultural institutions (i.e., marriage, adoption), and social organizations (i.e., clubs, religions, schools) for the benefit of heterosexual persons and heterosexual relationships, as well as those persons who are perceived to be heterosexual. Heterosexism can also refer to negative attitudes, bias, and discrimination against gay men, lesbians, and bisexuals (as well as transgender, transsexual, and intersex persons who are assumed to be homosexual) in favor of opposite-sex sexuality and relationships. It can include the presumption that everyone is heterosexual and/or the presumption that opposite-sex attractions and relationships are the norm and therefore superior. Homophobia refers to antipathy toward homosexuality and/or fear of gay men and lesbians that stems from the essentialist cultural notion that maleness–masculinity and femaleness–femininity are complementary and normative. Homophobia as a fear of homosexuality can be internalized in gay men and lesbians as well as heterosexuals and bisexuals and persons of any gender or sexual identity. Thus, it can be a deeply entrenched assumption that influences the psychology and behavior or all persons and cultural institutions.

Hidden Curriculum. Many scholars in recent years have challenged the idea that the explicit curriculum published by the school as the official curriculum is the only important dimension of the schooling process. Scholars find a "hidden curriculum" behind the explicit, stated, and published curriculum. For example, Michael Apple (2004) suggests that schools and classrooms socialize students to the values that are a part of the culture of the school and society. The hidden curriculum often works like a subliminal message. Schools and classrooms can be places where certain behaviors are normalized and subliminally suggested through the expectations, rewards, and culture of the school.

Historicize. To historicize is to locate a text in historical, cultural, etymological, sociopolitical, and theological contexts. This is a method of deconstruction that attempts to understand and evaluate a text within its historical context. This historical context exerts tremendous influence over current practices.

Identity politics refers to actions by members of a specific identity group to unite together in solidarity in order to advance political, economic, or social change. Oppressed or marginalized persons in these groups seek to articulate their oppression, raise awareness of the oppressive structures and institutions against which they struggle, and advance their self-interest. Largely an outgrowth of the civil rights and women's rights movements of the 1960s, identity politics has expanded beyond racial or gender divisions and extends today into sexual orientation, ethnicity, citizenship, gender identity, and other identities. In the 1960s, marginalized and oppressed groups sought recognition *for* their differences, not in spite of them. By focusing so much energy on a specific political agenda, critics argue, practitioners of identity politics can become just as closed minded or exclusionary as those they claim are oppressing or marginalizing their group. Other critics point out the complexity, for example, of a bisexual woman with African American and Hispanic biological heritage who has unique and complicated intersections of various identities. For critics of identity politics, the idea that an individual must choose a single identity category is considered problematic, unjust, and illogical.

Interdisciplinary curriculum is applied within education and pedagogies to describe teaching practices and curriculum development models that use methods and insights of several established disciplines or traditional fields of study. Interdisciplinarity engages researchers, students, and teachers in the goals of connecting and integrating knowledge and understanding from several academic schools of thought, professions, or technologies—along with their specific perspectives—in the pursuit of a common task, a cross-disciplinary understanding, or a more robust and meaningful understanding of a theme. I contend that, in order to accomplish an interdisciplinary curriculum, a teacher or student must first become an interdisciplinary person. However, the entire interdisciplinary project is problematized and deconstructed by postmodern scholars who contend that modern disciplines are actually metanarratives that maintain binary oppositions and intellectual regulation.

Intersex. A person whose chromosomes, genitalia, and/or hormones do not align with a medical dictionary definition of a "standard" male or "standard" female form is described as intersex. Some children are not born with the "standard" XY chromosome pattern for males or XX chromosome pattern for females. Classifying persons as male or female thus becomes more complicated than assumed.

Liberation theology has a long history in Latin American theological and resistance movements that drew on various traditions of Catholic humanism in the aftermath of the Spanish Conquest. Contemporary expressions of liberation theology emerged in Latin America in the 1960s as a critical, theological response to overwhelming conditions of poverty and oppression. Liberation theology has both informed and been informed by the critical pedagogical work of the Brazilian educator Paulo Freire (see Conscientization above), with liberation theologians evidencing particular reliance on Freire's understanding of conscientization as critical participation in emancipatory, transformative action within history. Curriculum scholars have explored parallels between liberation theology and the method of *currere* and identified a language of possibility and transformation within the former that can inform a practice of critical pedagogy.

Metanarrative. A narrative is a story, and the prefix "meta" means beyond or about. Therefore, a metanarrative is a story *about* a story, encompassing and explaining other smaller or local stories within totalizing narrative schemes. In critical theory and postmodernism, a metanarrative (sometimes also called a master narrative or grand narrative) is an abstract idea that claims to be a comprehensive explanation of all historical experience or knowledge. Some philosophers contend that a metanarrative is a global or totalizing cultural narrative schema which orders and explains all knowledge. Many postmodern authors criticize metanarrative with increasing skepticism toward the totalizing attempt to organize all knowledge into some form of transcendent and universal truth.

Metaphysics addresses questions of reality. Metaphysicians study the condition of being and existing in the world (ontology) as well as the structure of the universe itself (cosmology). They also investigate the nature of first principles and ultimate forces in the universe in order to answer the question "What is real?" Metaphysics is one of the three branches of philosophy: metaphysics, epistemology, and axiology (see Aesthetics above).

Modernism can refer to the time period after the Enlightenment and up to the 20th century, including industrialization and the technological age. Modernism is also a cultural movement in the arts that encourages self-consciousness. In addition, the term can refer to a way of thinking about the world that is scientific and rational and advances human progress and development. In philosophy, modernism follows from René Descartes, whose writings provided support for notions of dualism and rationalism in the modern era.

Null curriculum refers to what is omitted or left out of the curriculum—that is to say, those authors, ideas, topics, chapters of texts, and controversial issues that go undiscussed in schools.

Perennialism is the belief that the aim of education is to ensure that students acquire understandings about the great ideas of Western civilization. These ideas have the potential for solving problems in any era. The focus is on teaching ideas that are everlasting, on seeking enduring truths which are constant, not changing. Perennialists believe that the natural and human worlds at their most essential level do not change. Teaching these unchanging principles is critical.

Phenomenology is a philosophy of consciousness that seeks description of how the world is experienced by persons. The purpose of phenomenology is not just the description of phenomena, but the understanding of what lies behind them. Phenomenological understanding of curriculum replaces the modern obsession with standardized interpretation, predetermined methodologies and styles for writing and researching, and universal metanarratives that can be applied to knowledge acquisition. For Maurice Merleau-Ponty, perception is primary. Phenomenologists are increasingly alarmed by the abstractions represented by the scientific, technological, and instrumental approaches to curriculum. The notion of the curriculum as a set of concepts, ideas, and facts to be mastered, of students as empty vessels to be filled with those concepts, and of pedagogy as a set of techniques to be acquired by teachers is often rejected by contemporary curricularists.

Positivism. The 19th-century French philosopher August Comte popularized the word "positivism." He argued that human thought had evolved through three stages: the theological stage, where truth rested on God's revelation; the metaphysical stage, where truth derived from abstract reasoning and argument; and the positivistic stage, where truth arises out of scientifically produced knowledge. Comte sought to discredit the legitimacy of nonscientific thinking that failed to take into account "sense knowledge" (knowledge obtained through the senses and empirically verifiable).

Postmodernism. There are many ways to describe postmodernism, but there is no single definition. For some, postmodernism is our contemporary time period—as in "the postmodern era"—but not "after the modern era" or "anti-modernism," because postmodernism incorporates the best features and overcomes the worst features of the modern era. Others understand postmodernism to be a mood, an attitude, and a way of experiencing the world in the time period since 1950. The roots of postmodernism are most evident in art, architecture, and various aesthetic sensibilities.

Poststructuralism and Structuralism. It might be helpful to know that poststructuralism, deconstruction, and postmodernism are often used interchangeably to describe the critique of modernity. Poststructuralism refers to those theoretical movements emerging in France that had grown out of and then opposed the philosophies of structuralism, which purported to discover invariant structures in society, the human psyche, history, consciousness, and culture. Poststructuralism is thus an assault on structuralism as well as an outgrowth of it. Structuralism might be best understood as an analysis that privileges structures, systems, or sets of relations over the specific phenomena that emerge in, are constituted by, and derive their identity from those structures and sets of relations. Structuralism has sought to identify the systems that create meaning; poststructuralism has sought to dismantle the system in order to expose the variable and contingent nature of systems. Deborah Britzman writes about poststructural views of identity in which the notion of a unitary, cohesive self is deconstructed. She challenges the idea that individuals have an authentic core or essence that has been repressed by society. Rather than appeal to a timeless and transcendent human nature, poststructural thought traces the constitution of the subject within a historical framework. There is concern with how subjectivities become configured as an effect of history and how they are then produced. In poststructural analysis, meaning is never fixed or stable. Nor is reality, in any sense, understood as objectively "out there" or simply apprehended through language. Instead, meaning becomes the site of departure, a place where reality is constructed, truth is produced, and power is effected.

Process philosophy teaches that reality is conceived as a *process* of creative advance in which many past events are integrated in the events of the present, and in turn are taken up by future events. With a foundation in the metaphysical system of Alfred North Whitehead, and a methodology that integrates both speculation and empirical verification, process thought seeks to integrate and reconcile the diverse facets of human experience (i.e., ethical, religious, aesthetic, and scientific intuitions) into one coherent explanatory scheme. The most common applications of process thought are in the fields of philosophy and theology. However, process has also found a meaningful foothold in many other discussions, including ecology, economics, physics, biology, education, psychology, feminism, and cultural studies. Process thinking, in general, seeks to elucidate the developmental nature of reality, emphasizing becoming rather than static existence or being. It also stresses the interrelatedness of all entities. Process describes reality as ultimately made up of experiential events rather than enduring inert substances. The particular character of every event, and consequently the world, is the result of a selective process where the relevant past is creatively brought together to become that new event. The universe proceeds as "the many become one, and are increased by one" in a sequence of integrations at every level and moment of existence. Process thought thus replaces the traditional Western "substance metaphysic" with an "event metaphysic."

Progressivism. Progressive education is a pedagogical movement that began in the 19th century and has persisted in various forms to the present. John Dewey was its foremost proponent in the early 20th century. One of his tenets was that education should improve the way of life of citizens through their experiencing freedom and democracy in schools. It is an alternative to the accountability movement reflected in *Race to the Top* and *No Child Left Behind*. The term "progressive" is used to distinguish this pedagogical movement from the traditional curriculum, which was rooted in classical preparation for the university and strongly differentiated by socio-economic level. Progressive education values present experience and employs place-based learning projects, experiential learning, integrated curriculum focused on thematic units, problem solving and critical thinking, development of social skills, collaborative and cooperative learning projects, social responsibility for democracy, and integration of community service and service learning projects into the curriculum.

Prolepsis. A proleptic moment is any experience that transcends linear segmentation of time and creates a holistic understanding of the past, present, and future simultaneously. It is the moment in a novel when all of the events of the narrative coalesce. Christian theologians have used the word "proleptic" to describe the fullness of time—past, present, and future—in the person of Jesus Christ. William Pinar employs the term "synthetical moment" to describe the prolepsis. In psychology, proleptic is parallel to the notion of gestalt. I use this important word to indicate the fullness of time and experience—past, present, and future—in a single instant.

Proleptic eschatology. Eschatology is a theological term that is used to refer to the "end times" of the earth and the hope for future things unseen. It is different because it understands that future events are already unfolding and embedded in the present moment and past events. There are at least three possible approaches to eschatology: realized eschatology, futuristic eschatology, and proleptic eschatology.

Public pedagogy is a theoretical construct focusing on various forms and sites of education and learning occurring beyond formal schooling practices; in institutions other than schools, such as museums, zoos, libraries, and public parks; in informal educational sites such as popular culture, media, commercial spaces, and the Internet; and in/through figures and sites of activism, including public intellectuals, grassroots social activism, and various social movements (see Sandlin, O'Malley, & Burdick, 2011).

Reconceptualization. In the early 1970s, a movement in the field of curriculum studies began to shift the focus of curriculum from scientific management and the Tylerian Rationale to a process of understanding curriculum as an interdisciplinary study of educational experience. Curriculum theorists in the 1970s relied upon critical theory, gender and sexuality studies, feminist theories, critical race theory, literary criticism, aesthetics, political theories, theology, phenomenology, psychoanalytic theory, autobiography, and cultural studies as the foundation of the movement.

Relativism is the philosophical doctrine that all criteria of judgment are relative to the individuals and situations involved. Truth, moral judgment, and aesthetic values are not universal or absolute but may differ between individuals or cultures. This should not be confused with relativity in physics and astronomy.

Schools of Philosophy. Throughout the text I refer to several schools of philosophy and educational theories.

(a) **Idealism.** Idealism proposes a metaphysics that sees the world of ideas of the mind as reality. To exist, something must be perceived by the mind. Reality thus appears in the realm of the spiritual or ideas. A person can find true knowledge (epistemology) by "seeing with the mind's eye" and seeing the consistency of ideas.

(b) **Realism.** Realism shares much in common with idealism, particularly the belief that truth is unchanging. Realists, however, look outward to the physical world using their senses to discover and affirm truth. Natural Law—a belief that absolute laws of nature exist and should govern human behavior—forms the ethics of realism. Beautiful art, therefore, must replicate nature. The educational philosophy of essentialism (not to be confused with existentialism) reflects realism. Essentialism mandates lessons that teach basic factual knowledge in reading, writing and mathematics—the so-called three R's—and science, history, and foreign languages. It emphasizes the scientific method of hypothesis, testing, and generalization, but it tends to encourage structured learning environments designed to achieve mastery of basic information and skills (see Essentialism above).

(c) **Thomism.** Thomist philosophy posits that rational acts determine what is good and that creative intuition about what is reasonable determines what is beautiful.

Logical reason and revelation guide people to the truth and to God. Thomism dates back to the Dominican Catholic priest Thomas Aquinas in 13th-century France. Aquinas combined his philosophical study of Plato and Aristotle with his religious training to help explain Christian faith and the notion of an immortal soul. His followers expanded Aquinas' philosophy and developed a Thomistic metaphysics that sees the world as the realm of reason and of God. Teachers are encouraged to include subject matter of both the intellect and the spirit in the curriculum, and particularly religious doctrines. Disciplining the mind and controlling behavior to conform with natural law is the proper goal of education.

(d) **Pragmatism.** Pragmatism is a uniquely American philosophy associated with William James, Charles Sanders Peirce, and John Dewey. It differs markedly from the first three philosophies in that it emphasizes a need for change and adaptation. It pictures a world of experience in which one must test hypotheses to see what works. Truth is based on this experience; morality is determined by society rather than natural law; and beauty changes according to the public taste. Two educational theories are associated with the philosophy of pragmatism: progressivism and reconstructionism. Progressive educators base their subject matter on social experiences. Thus, they value a social studies curriculum highly. They ask students to solve practical problems using groups and projects, and everyone's participation is critical. The reconstructionists take this participation one step further by proposing that education reconstruct society by addressing current events and social problems. Believing that education extends beyond the information in books to include outside involvement in the community, reconstructionists promote social activism for change. Ultimately, reconstructionists and many progressive educators believe that the teacher should guide students in projects and activities that will improve society rather than simply teach lessons that conform to the status quo social arrangements that are unjust in so many ways.

(e) **Existentialism.** There are many varieties of existentialism, from that of Christian existentialists, who find hope in the examination of the present, to that of nihilists, who find that the present world is absurd. There are philosophers like Jean-Paul Sartre and Albert Camus who protest traditional formulations of philosophy and emphasize the tragic, sometimes absurd nature of life; other philosophers, like Simone de Beauvior and Maxine Greene, emphasize the importance of social action to combat the tragedies of the modern world. Literature and the arts become central to this process of understanding and acting. Existentialists believe that existence precedes essence; phenomenologists believe that immediate subjective understandings of events are the source of reality. In other words, we find truth when we examine our present existence rather than some preconceived notion of the essential characteristics of the world and human beings. Existentialists promote human freedom and the need for people to take responsibility for creating goodness and beauty in the world. Since existentialists reject any absolute public norm, existentialism as an educational philosophy promotes alternative approaches to teaching and learning. Students have lots of choices and electives, especially in art, moral philosophy, literature, and other studies that encourage them to become inner directed. Students should discover for themselves the best methods for learning, and ultimately develop personal responses.

(f) Marxism. Like existentialism, Marxism is a difficult philosophical position to describe briefly because there are so many "Marxisms" with conflicting interpretations. Often in Western societies the mere mention of the name Karl Marx evokes intense negative reaction and precludes productive discussion of Marxist educational philosophies. Marxist analysis is not equivalent to describing the social and political system of China or the former Soviet Union. It involves primarily the protest against the bourgeois—having to do with the conventional, selfish materialistic capitalist class—society produced by the advent of industrialization. In this context, Marx argued that social and political phenomena have their genesis in the material (economic) aspects of everyday life. His notion of dialectical materialism asserted that institutions must be studied in their historical context to trace the ways that economic production has shaped them. This material base determines the class structure of a society, which, in turn, affects all aspects of everyday life, especially the division of classes into those who own the factories and businesses (the means of production) and those who have only their labor to offer (the workers). When workers become politically conscious of their exploitation, they will transform into revolutionaries who will work to change the unfair socio-economic reality. Schooling and education within the class-divided society, Marx argued, is a farce because schools and educational funding structures serve only to further the interests of the dominant class. Pedagogical activity in such a climate is an act of terror against the workers and their children, he reasoned. Once the revolution had succeeded, then schooling could begin to raise consciousness and serve the needs of the working class. Such schools would combine productive labor with academic learning and physical education for the purpose of producing well-rounded and fully developed human beings.

(g) Behaviorism. Behaviorists believe that behavior is fundamental to understanding mental phenomena, and thus behaviorism might best be described as a psychological theory rather than a philosophy. Scientific behaviorism is associated with J. B. Watson and B. F. Skinner, who searched for independent variables (stimuli) of which behavior (reactions) were a function. Thus, environmental conditions play an important role in determining mental activities and physical responses. Schools can teach students by reinforcing positive stimuli and modify student behavior by withholding the reinforcing stimuli. To demonstrate how all human behavior, including cognition and intelligence, can be shaped by the process of selective reinforcement and extinction of responses by prolonged disassociation from an old stimuli was the ultimate goal of behaviorism. It has an immense influence on educational theories, testing and assessment practices, classroom management, and organizational practices in schools. However, cognitive theories and constructivism have replaced theories of behaviorism as the dominant ways of thinking about teaching and learning.

(h) Feminism. Feminists challenge traditional philosophies because they fail both to seriously examine women's interests, issues, and identities and to recognize women's ways of being, knowing, and acting. Following the lead of the early feminist Mary Wollstonecraft and 20th-century philosopher Simone de Beauvoir in her important book *The Second Sex*, many feminists argue against essentialism—the belief that women are essentially and naturally docile, subservient, vain, frivolous, and less intelligent than men. Wollstonecraft argued that education and socialization had made women dependent and docile, but that, given the chance, women could prove themselves just as morally and intellectually capable as men. While some feminists prefer to emphasize the problems associated with gender stereotyping and bias, others focus on the subjugation and oppression of women and the ways that exterior social forces shape women's consciousness. The literature describes three waves of feminism. First-wave feminism refers to an extended period of feminist activity during the 19th century and early 20th century in the United Kingdom and the United States. Originally it focused on the promotion of equal contract and property rights for women and the opposition to chattel marriage and ownership of married women (and their children) by their husbands. However, by the end of the 19th century, activism concentrated primarily on gaining political power, particularly women's suffrage. Second-wave feminism refers to the period of activity in the early 1960s and lasting through the late 1980s and often marked with the publication in 1963 of *The Feminine Mystique*, by Betty Friedan. Friedan co-founded in 1966 the National Organization for Women, which aimed to bring women into the mainstream of American society as fully equal partners with men. Second-wave feminism has continued since that time and coexists with what is termed third-wave feminism. The scholar Estelle Freedman compares first- and second-wave feminism, saying that the first wave focused on rights such as suffrage, whereas the second wave was concerned largely with other issues of equality, such as ending discrimination. The feminist activist and author Carol Hanisch coined the slogan "The Personal is Political," which became synonymous with the second wave. Second-wave feminists saw women's cultural and political inequalities as inextricably linked and encouraged women to understand aspects of their personal lives as deeply politicized and as reflecting sexist power structures. Third-wave feminism began in the early 1990s, arising as a response both to perceived failures and to the backlash against initiatives and movements created by the second wave. It seeks to challenge or avoid what it deems the second wave's essentialist definitions of feminine, which they contend overemphasized the experiences of upper-middle-class White women. A poststructuralist interpretation of gender and sexuality is central to much of the third wave's ideology. Third-wave feminists often focus on "micro-politics" and challenge the second wave's paradigm as to what is, or is not, good for females.

(i) **Eastern Philosophies.** Many prominent Eastern philosophies are traced to China, Japan, India, and the Middle East. While each of these cultures contributes unique perspectives, it is common in Eastern philosophy to focus on the inner life rather than outer experience. In fact, philosophy in the Eastern tradition is more of a way of life than a subject to be studied. Intuition, inner peace, tranquility, attitudinal development, and, in some cases, mysticism are all emphasized, with religion and philosophy being more intimately intertwined than in Western philosophy. It is important to note that Eastern philosophies have also influenced Western social, political, and religious ideas, and vice versa. One important dimension of the Eastern philosophical tradition is the emphasis not only upon knowing but also upon teaching others. Buddha, Confucius, Jesus, and Muhammad were all teachers. The Sumerian goddess Inanna, the Hindu goddess Saraswathi, and the Vedic goddess Maya–Shakti–Devi all inspire teaching and learning. Inanna is a goddess who undergoes death and resurrection and teaches ways of being that necessitate sacrifice, humility, and reunification. Saraswathi is the goddess of wisdom who is always shown with a book in one of her hands; Hindu children are taught to pray to her for the gift of education and success in school. Devi (the Indian name for woman) is the teacher of the Vedic gods themselves concerning the ultimate ground and source of their own powers and being. Since these prophets, teachers, gods, and goddesses from Eastern cultures inspire the religious and social mythology of many cultures, teachers should be inspired to examine Eastern philosophy more closely. For example, Taoism (which means "way" or "path") is an influential philosophy in China that reflects on the movement of the universe and the way of harmony. Lao-Tzu set down such teachings in the *Tao Te Ching* in the 5th century BCE at the same time as Socrates, Aristotle, Plato, and the pinnacle of Greek philosophy. The Tao guides individuals in the development of their inner life so that they can meet the challenge of any difficulty.

(j) **Humanism.** The roots of humanism are found in the thinking of Erasmus (1466–1536), who attacked the religious teaching and thought prevalent in his time to focus on free inquiry and rediscovery of the classical Greek and Roman traditions. Erasmus believed in the essential goodness of children. He contended that humans have free will, moral conscience, the ability to reason, aesthetic sensibilities, and religious instinct. He advocated that the young should be treated with respect and that learning should not be forced or rushed because it proceeds in stages. Humanism was developed as an educational philosophy by Jean-Jacques Rousseau (1712–1778) and Johann Pestalozzi (1746–1827), who emphasized the basic goodness of humans, understanding through the senses, and education as a gradual and unhurried process in the natural development of human character. Humanists believe that the learner should be in control of his or her own destiny. Since the learner should become a fully autonomous person, personal freedom, choice, and responsibility are the focus. The learner is self-motivated to achieve, and the desire to learn is intrinsic. Recent applications of humanist philosophy in education focus on the social and emotional well-being of the child, as well as cognitive development. Teachers emphasize freedom from threat, emotional well-being, and self-fulfillment as espoused in the theories of Abraham Maslow, Carl Rogers, and Alfred Adler.

Scientific management is associated with the theories of Frederick Taylor and Max Weber that analyzed and synthesized workflow to improve labor productivity. Taylor investigated ways for workers to increase their efficiency, and he believed that decisions based upon tradition and rules of thumb should be replaced by precise procedures developed after careful study of an individual at work. The application of scientific management is contingent on a high level of managerial control over employee work practices. The purpose is to increase efficiency, decrease waste, and base all decisions on empirical evidence. Some educational accountability programs model these management theories. Pushed to its logical extreme, scientific management deskills workers and students and dehumanizes classrooms and the workplace. Taylorism is often associated with Fordism because of the emphasis on mass production, with optimal task-oriented, repetitive, tedious, and menial labor practices. There is considerable debate in educational literature and research about the benefits and problems that may result from scientific management, efficiency, and/or accountability movements. The work of Franklin Bobbitt applies many of these efficiency principles to schools and curriculum. Bobbitt published "The Elimination of Waste in Education" in 1912 and *The Curriculum* and *How to Make a Curriculum* in 1918 and 1924, respectively. Some credit Bobbitt with the discursive shift from methods to curriculum and his 1918 text as a significant legitimizing of events in the history of the field of curriculum studies.

Scientific Realism. The European love affair with scientific realism emerged five centuries ago when philosophers and scientists began to understand that medieval ways of seeing the world no longer answered the complex problems of the time. When bubonic plague, the Black Death, swept across Europe in the 14th century, killing one in every four people, rulers found themselves powerless to control it. Every traditional medieval response—prayer, mysticism, scapegoating, and magic—failed. When a society cannot understand, let alone solve, a challenge to its existence, its conception of reality collapses or a new guiding vision rushes forward. Under the threat of the Black Death, Western society began to develop a new way of seeing the world that would lead directly to scientific realism. The Black Death ushered in what historians refer to as modernity, or the era of scientific revolution. Science helped Western society understand and control a bit better the exterior environment, the world of matter and energy.

Sedimented Perceptor. A sedimented perceptor is an entrenched bias or assumption that is deeply buried in a person's unconscious. Sedimented perceptors can result from cultural conditioning, religious upbringing, social taboos, academic indoctrination, informal schooling, peer pressure, psychological fear, and parental manipulation. People often act or react in situations based on these deeply held biases and assumptions, which are often irrational, bigoted, or unexamined. Sometimes people will profess a positive conscious belief but act upon a deeply held bias that they cannot consciously identify. Bullying in schools and prejudice in society are both the result of sedimented perceptors in action.

Semiotics might be understood as the study of signs and symbols that are used as means of language or communication and how literary forms and conventions affect the meaning of language. Semiotics can also be understood as the study of signs, symbols, and design elements of visual texts that work together to produce meaning. There are three branches of the study of semiotics: (1) semantics is the relation between signs and the things to which they refer; (2) syntactics is the relations among signs in formal structure; and (3) pragmatics is the relation between signs and their effects on those people who use them. Writers such as Umberto Eco propose that every cultural phenomenon can be studied as communication.

Simulacrum as the study of signs and symbols has always been of interest to philosophers and is fundamental to the work of educators. Plato speaks of image making either as a faithful reproduction of the original or as distorted intentionally to make the copy appear correct to viewers. Nietzsche suggests that most philosophers, by ignoring the reliable input of their senses and resorting to the constructs of language and reason, arrive at a distorted copy of reality. Modern French social theorists see four possibilities in an image: (1) a basic reflection of reality; (2) a perversion of reality; (3) a pretence of reality (where there is no model); and (4) a simulacrum, which "bears no relation to any reality whatsoever." In Jean Baudrillard's concept, like that of

Nietzsche, simulacra are perceived as negative, but Gilles Deleuze takes a different view, seeing simulacra as the avenue by which accepted ideals, or a "privileged position," could be "challenged and overturned." Deleuze defines simulacra as "those systems in which different relates to different by means of difference itself. What is essential is that we find in these systems no prior identity, no internal resemblance."

Social Reconstructionism. The social reconstructionists were concerned with two major premises. First, society is in need of constant reform and change, and, second, such reform must include both structural changes in education and the use of education in reconstructing society. George S. Counts (1889–1974) is perhaps one of the most well known of the social reconstructionists. He argued that education must face squarely and courageously every social issue and establish an organic relationship with the local community. Reconstructionist educators focus on a curriculum that highlights social reform. Theodore Brameld (1904–1987) is considered the founder of social reconstructionism. He recognized the potential either for human annihilation through technology and human cruelty or the capacity to create a beneficent society using technology for human compassion. Paulo Freire (1921–1997) was a Brazilian whose experiences living in poverty led him to champion education and literacy as the vehicle for social change. In his view, humans must learn to resist oppression and not become its victims, or oppress others. To do so requires dialog and critical consciousness, the development of awareness to overcome domination and oppression. Rather than "teaching as banking," in which the educator deposits information into students' heads, Freire saw teaching and learning as a process of inquiry in which the child must invent and reinvent the world. The curriculum focuses on student experience and taking social action on real problems, such as violence, hunger, international terrorism, inflation, and inequality.

Theology is the academic study of God, gods, or goddesses, as well as sacred texts, religious rituals, wisdom literature, eschatology, creation narratives, and topics related to religion and spirituality. The methods of deconstruction and hermeneutics are used by theologians to investigate rituals, sacred texts, and historical documents related to world religions. A theologian is an academic scholar who may or may not be a member of a religion or a person of faith.

Tylerian Rationale. Curriculum development has been concerned with Professor Ralph Tyler's four basic questions in his syllabus at the University of Chicago and published in 1949. These four questions have so dominated the study of curriculum for the past sixty years that they have, in effect, become a curriculum metanarrative called the Tylerian Rationale. The influence of Tyler on the history of curriculum development cannot be overemphasized. The reconceptualization of curriculum studies seeks to move beyond the Tylerian formulation.

Visual culture is the scholarly study of various forms of technology, advertising, film, and other media that have a visual image component and privilege seeing, vision, and visual technologies, both mechanical and critical. Visual culture is often an interdisciplinary academic field related to cultural studies, art history, critical theory, philosophy, and anthropology.

References

Adler, Mortimer J. (1982). *The paideia proposal: An educational manifesto*. New York: Macmillan.

Aikin, Wilford. (1942). *The story of the eight-year study: With conclusions and recommendations*. New York: Harper & Brothers.

Alexander, Jacqui. (2005). *Pedagogies of crossing: Meditations on feminism, sexual politics, memory, and the sacred*. Durham, NC: Duke University Press.

Allen, James, Als, Hilton, Lewis, John, & Litwack, Leon F. (2000). *Without sanctuary: Lynching photography in America*. New York: Twin Palm.

America 2000: An educational strategy. (1991). Washington, DC: U.S. Government Printing Office.

Anyon, Jean J. (2005). *Radical possibilities: Public policy, urban education, and a new social movement*. New York: Routledge.

Aoki, Ted Tetsuo. (1985). *Toward curriculum inquiry in a new key*. (Department of Secondary Education Occasional Papers Series, #2, rev. ed.). Edmonton: University of Alberta.

———. (1988). Toward a dialectic between the conceptual world and the lived world: Transcending instrumentalists in curriculum orientation. In William F. Pinar (Ed.), *Contemporary curriculum discourses* (pp. 402–416). Scottsdale, AZ: Gorsuch Scarisbrick.

———. (1992). Layered voices of teaching: The uncannily correct and the elusively true. In William F. Pinar & William M. Reynolds (Eds.), *Understanding curriculum as phenomenological and deconstructed text* (pp. 17–27). New York: Longman.

Aoki, Ted Tetsuo, Franks, D., & Jacknicke, K. (Eds.). (1987). *Understanding curriculum as lived: Curriculum Canada VII*. Vancouver: University of British Columbia.

Apple, Michael W. (1979). *Ideology and curriculum*. Boston: Routledge & Kegan Paul.

———. (1982). *Education and power*. Boston: Routledge & Kegan Paul.

———. (1985). *Teachers and texts: A political economy of class and gender relations in education*. New York: Routledge & Kegan Paul.

———. (2000). *Official knowledge* (2nd ed.). New York: Routledge & Kegan Paul.

———. (2004). *Ideology and curriculum* (3rd ed.). London: Routledge & Kegan Paul.

Apple, Michael W., & Christian-Smith, Linda (Eds.). (1991). *The politics of the textbook*. New York: Routledge & Kegan Paul.

Arendt, Hannah. (1958). *The human condition*. Chicago: University of Chicago Press.

Armstrong, V. I. (Ed.). (1971). *I have spoken*. Chicago: Swallow Press.

Aronowitz, Stanley. (1992). *The politics of identity: Class, culture, social movements*. New York: Routledge.

———. (2006). *Left turn: Forging a new political future*. New York: Paradigm.

———. (2008). *Against schooling: For an education that matters*. New York: Paradigm.

Arons, Stephen. (1983). *Compelling belief: The culture of American schooling*. New York: McGraw-Hill.

Aston, John. (2001a). Autopsy of hate: Ten years later. *Outsmart, 8*(6), 64–69.

——. (2001b). Deconstructing heterosexism and homophobia in schools: Case study of a hate crime by an adolescent offender. *Dissertation Abstracts International*, Vol. 62-04A (UMI No. 3011676). New York: McGraw-Hill.

Bahmueller, C. F. (Ed.). (1991). *Civitas*. Calabasas, CA: Center for Civic Education.

Bakhtin, Mikhail M. (1990). *Art and answerability: Early philosophical essays*. M. Holquist (Ed.). Austin: University of Texas Press.

Baldwin, James. (1971). Author's notes, *Blues for Mister Charlie*. In J. Glassner & C. Barnes (Eds.), *Best American plays*. New York: Crown.

——. (1988). A talk to teachers. In R. Simonson & S. Walker (Eds.), *Multicultural literature: Opening the American mind*. St. Paul, MN: Graywolf.

Barone, Thomas. (1993). Breaking the mold: The new American student as strong poet. *Theory into Practice, 32*(3), 5–18.

Barry, John M. (1997). *Rising tide: The great Mississippi flood of 1927 and how it changed America*. New York: Simon & Schuster.

Baudrillard, Jean. (1983). *Simulations*. New York: Semiotext(e).

Bauman, Zygmunt. (1993). *Postmodern ethics*. Oxford, England: Blackwell.

——. (2000). *Liquid modernity*. Cambridge, England: Polity.

——. (2003). *Liquid love: On the frailty of human bonds*. Malden, MA: Blackwell.

Beauvoir, Simone de. (1949). *The ethics of ambiguity*. (Bernard Frechtman, Trans.). New York: Philosophical Library.

Behar, R., & Gordon, D. A. (1995). *Women writing culture*. Berkeley: University of California Press.

Belenky, Mary Field, Clinchy, Blythe McVicker, Goldberger, Nancy Rule, & Tarule, Jill Mattuck. (1986). *Women's ways of knowing: The development of self, voice, and mind*. New York: Basic Books.

Bennett, William J. (1987). *James Madison High School: A curriculum for American students*. Washington, DC: U.S. Department of Education.

——. (1988). *James Madison Elementary: A curriculum for American students*. Washington, DC: U.S. Department of Education.

Bereiter, Carl, & Scardamalia, Marlene. (1992). Cognition and curriculum. In Philip W. Jackson (Ed.), *Handbook of research on curriculum* (pp. 517–542). New York: Macmillan.

Bergson, Henri. (1946). *The creative mind: An introduction to metaphysics*. (M. L. Andison, Trans.). New York: Philosophical Library.

——. (1950). *Time and free will*. (F. L. Pogson, Trans.). London: Allen & Unwin.

Berliner, David C., & Biddle, Bruce J. (1995). *The manufactured crisis: Myths, fraud, and the attack on America's public schools*. Reading, MA: Addison Wesley.

Bernal, D. D. (2002). Critical race theory, Latino critical theory, and critical raced-gendered epistemologies: Recognizing students of color as holders and creators of knowledge. *Qualitative Inquiry, 8*(1), 105–126.

Bernard, Hilly. (1994). *Hermeneutics and education: Discourse/practice*. Unpublished dissertation prospectus, University of New Orleans.

Bernard, Hilly, & Slattery, Patrick. (1992). Quantum curriculum. Paper presented at the *JCT* Bergamo Conference, Dayton, OH.

Beutow, H. A. (1988). *The Catholic school: Its roots, identity, and future*. New York: Crossroad.

Beyer, Landon E. (1988). Art and society: Toward new directions in aesthetic education. In William F. Pinar (Ed.), *Contemporary curriculum discourses* (pp. 380–397). Scottsdale, AZ: Gorsuch Scarisbrick.

Bickel, Barbara. (2011). A/r/tographic collaboration as radical relatedness. *International Journal of Qualitative Methods, 10*(1), 22–38.

Bissinger, H. G. (1991). *Friday night lights: A town, a team, and a dream*. New York: HarperCollins.

Blacker, David. (1993, March). Education as the normative dimension of philosophical hermeneutics. Paper presented at the annual meeting of the Philosophy of Education Society, New Orleans.

Blanchard, Kenneth, & Johnson, Spencer. (1981). *The one minute manager*. New York: Berkeley Books.

Bloch, Ernst. (1968). Man as possibility. In R. Capps (Ed.), *The future of hope* (pp. 3–27). New York: Herder & Herder.

——. (1970). *A philosophy of the future*. New York: Herder & Herder.

——. (1986). *The principle of hope*. Oxford, England: Blackwell.

Bloom, Allan. (1987). *The closing of the American mind*. New York: Simon & Schuster.

Boateng, F. (1990). Combatting deculturalization of the African-American child in the public school system: A multicultural approach. In K. Lomotey (Ed.), *Going to school: The African-American experience* (pp. 73–84). Albany: State University of New York Press.

Bobbitt, Franklin. (1918). *The curriculum*. Boston: Houghton Mifflin.

Bohm, David. (1988). Postmodern science and a postmodern world. In David Ray Griffin (Ed.), *The reenchantment of science* (pp. 57–68). Albany: State University of New York Press.

Bonhoeffer, Dietrich. (1942). From stations on the way to freedom. In *A testament to freedom* (G. Kelly & F. Nelson, Trans.). New York: Macmillan.

——. (1966). *The cost of discipleship*. New York: Macmillan.

——. (1971). *Letters and papers from prison*. New York: Macmillan.

——. (1997). *Creation and fall: A theological exposition of Genesis 1–3* (Douglas Bax, Trans.). Minneapolis: Fortress Press.

The Book of Mormon. (1961). (Joseph Smith, Trans.). Salt Lake City, UT: Church of Jesus Christ of Latter Day Saints.

Books, Sue. (1992). Literary journalism as educational criticism: A discourse of triage. *Holistic Education Review*, 5(3), 41–51.

——. (1998). *Invisible children in the society and its schools*. Mahwah, NJ: Lawrence Erlbaum.

Bourriaud, Nicolas. (2002). *Relational aesthetics*. (S. Pleasance & F. Woods, Trans.). Dijon, France: Presses du réel.

Bowers, Chet A. (1987). *Elements of a post-liberal theory of education*. New York: Teachers College Press.

——. (1993). *Education, cultural myths, and the ecological crisis*. Albany: State University of New York Press.

——. (2001). *Educating for eco-justice and community*. Athens: University of Georgia Press.

——. (2005). How Peter McLaren and Donna Houston and other "green" Marxists contribute to the globalization of the West's industrial culture. *Educational Studies*, 37(2), 185–195.

——. (2006). *Revitalizing the commons: Cultural and educational sites of resistance and affirmation*. New York: Lexington Books.

Bowers, Chet A., & Flinders, David J. (1990). *Responsive teaching: An ecological approach to classroom patterns of language, culture, and thought*. New York: Teachers College Press.

Bowles, S., & Gintis, H. (1976). *Schooling in capitalist America*. New York: Basic Books.

Brady, Jeanne. (1995). *Schooling young children: A feminist pedagogy for liberatory learning*. Albany: State University of New York Press.

——. (2006). Public pedagogy and educational leadership: Politically engaged scholarly communities and possibilities for critical engagement. *Journal of Curriculum and Pedagogy*, 3(1), 57–60.

Brameld, Theodore. (1956). *Toward a reconstructed philosophy of education*. New York: Holt, Rinehart, & Winston.

——. (1971). *Patterns of educational philosophy—Divergence and convergence in culturological perspective*. New York: Holt, Rinehart, & Winston.

Bridges, Thomas. (1991). Multiculturalism as a postmodernist project. *Inquiry: Critical Thinking across the Disciplines*, 7(4), 3–7.

Briggs, John. (1992). *Fractals: The pattern of chaos: Discovering a new aesthetic of art, science, and nature*. New York: Simon & Schuster.

Britzman, Deborah P. (1992). The terrible problem of knowing thyself: Toward a poststructural account of teacher identity. *CT: An Interdisciplinary Journal of Curriculum Studies*, 9(3), 23–50.

——. (1995). Is there a queer pedagogy? Or, stop reading straight. *Educational Theory*, 45(2), 151–165.

Brownson, Orestes. ([1839] 1971). The Boston Quarterly Review. In Michael B. Katz (Ed.), *School reform: Past and present*. Boston: Little, Brown.

Buber, Martin. (1965). *I and thou*. (R. G. Smith, Trans.) (2nd ed.). New York: Scribner.

Burbules, Nicholas C. (1993a) *Dialogue in teaching: Theory and practice*. New York: Teachers College Press.

——. (1993b). Process philosophy and critical pragmatism. Paper presented at the Appe Summer Institute, University of the South.

Burke, Pattie C. S. (1995). Collected poems. Scottsdale, AZ: Unpublished manuscript.

——. (2009). *Women and pedagogy: Education through autobiographical narrative*. Troy, NY: Educator's International Press.

Burns, J. F. (2002, January 27). Bin Laden stirs struggle on meaning of jihad. *New York Times*, p. 1.

Caine, Renate Nummela, & Caine, Geoffrey. (1991). *Making connections: Teaching and the human brain*. Alexandria, VA: ASCD Press.

Campbell, Joseph, & Moyers, Bill. (1988). *The power of myth*. New York: Doubleday.

Capra, Fritjof. (1975). *The tao of physics*. Berkeley, CA: Shambhala.

——. (1982). *The turning point: Science, society, and the rising culture*. New York: Bantam Books.

Carlson, Dennis L. (1992). *Teachers and crisis: Urban school reform and teachers' work culture*. New York: Routledge.

Carlson, Dennis L., and Gause, C. P. (Eds.). (2007). *Keeping the promise: Essays on leadership, democracy, and education*. New York: Peter Lang.

Carmody, Denise L. (1991). *The good alliance: Feminism, religion, and education*. New York: University Press of America.

Carpenter, B. Stephen. (2006). Why I am a Muslim. College Station, TX: Personal communication.

Carroll, James. (2004). *Crusade: Chronicles of an unjust war*. New York: Henry Holt.

Carson, Rachel. (1962). *Silent spring*. Greenwich, CT: Fawcett.

Carson, Terrance R. (1987). Understanding curriculum and implementation. In T. Aoki, D. Franks, & K. Jacknicke (Eds.), *Understanding curriculum as lived: Curriculum Canada VII*. Vancouver: University of British Columbia.

——. (1992). Remembering forward: Reflections on educating for peace. In William F. Pinar and William M. Reynolds (Eds.), *Understanding curriculum as phenomenological and deconstructed text* (pp. 102–115). New York: Longman.

Carter, Jimmy. (2006). *Our endangered values: America's moral crisis*. New York: Simon & Schuster.

Cary, L. J. (2006). *Curriculum spaces: Discourse, postmodern theory and educational research*. Mahwah, NJ: Peter Lang.

Castenell, Louis A., Jr., & Pinar, William F. (1993). *Understanding curriculum as racial text: Representations of identity and difference in education*. Albany: State University of New York Press.

Caswell, Hollis L., & Campbell, Doak S. (1935). *Curriculum development*. New York: American Book Company.

Center for a Postmodern World. (1990). *Position paper on postmodernism*. Claremont, CA: Claremont Graduate School of Theology.

Chapman, Tracy (1995). *The rape of the world*. [Song lyrics]. Elektra Entertainment Group.

Chazan, B. (1985). *Contemporary approaches to moral education: Analyzing alternative theories*. New York: Teachers College Press.

Cheney, Lynn V. (1994, October 20). The end of history. *Wall Street Journal*, p. A22.

Cherryholmes, Cleo. (1988a). An exploration of meaning and the dialogue between textbooks and teaching. *Journal of Curriculum Studies, 20*(1), 1–21.

——. (1988b). *Power and criticism: Poststructural investigations in education*. New York: Teachers College Press.

——. (1994). More notes on pragmatism. *Educational Researcher, 23*(1), 16–18.

——. (1999). *Reading pragmatism*. New York: Teachers College Press.

Chopra, Deepak. (2005). *Peace is the way: Bringing war and violence to an end*. New York: Harmony Books.

Christian-Smith, Linda. (1987). Gender, popular culture, and curriculum: Adolescence romance novels as gender text. *Curriculum Inquiry, 17*(4), 365–406.

Clinton, Hillary Rodham. (1996). *It takes a village*. New York: Touchstone.

Cobb, John B., Jr. (1988). Ecology, science, and religion: Toward a postmodern worldview. In David Ray Griffin (Ed.), *The reenchantment of science* (pp. 99–113). Albany: State University of New York Press.

Cohen, Robert. (1996). Moving beyond name games: The conservative attack on the U.S. history standards. *Social Education, 60*(1), 49–54.

Coleman, James S., & Hoffer, T. (1987). *Public and private high schools: The impact of communities*. New York: Basic Books.

Collins, Patricia Hill. (1990). *Black feminist thought*. London: HarperCollins Academic.

Coontz, Stephanie. (2000). *The way we never were: American families and the nostalgia trap*. New York: Basic Books.

——. (2005). *Marriage: A history from obedience to intimacy, or how love conquered marriage*. New York: Viking Press.

Costner, Kevin. (Producer/Director). (1990). *Dances with wolves*. [Film]. Los Angeles: Orion.

Counts, George S. (1932). *Dare the schools build a new social order?* New York: John Day.

Covey, Stephen R. (1989). *The 7 habits of highly effective people*. New York: Simon & Schuster.

Cox, Harvey. (1984). *Religion in the secular city: Toward a postmodern theology*. New York: Simon & Schuster.

Daly, Herman E., & Cobb, John B. (1989). *For the common good: Redirecting the economy toward community, the environment, and a sustainable future*. Boston: Beacon Press.

Davies, Paul. (1988). *The cosmic blueprint: New discoveries in nature's creative ability to order the universe*. New York: Simon & Schuster.

——. (1990). Cosmogenesis. *Creation Spirituality, 6*(3), 10–13.

——. (1995). *About time: Einstein's unfinished revolution*. New York: Simon & Schuster.

——. (2008). *Quantum aspects of life*. London: Imperial College Press.

Dawkins, Richard. (2006). *The God delusion*. New York: Houghton Mifflin.

Denzin, Norman K., & Lincoln, Yvonna S. (2005). *Handbook of qualitative research*. New York: Sage.

D'Erasmo, Stacey. (2001, October 14). Polymorphous normal: Has sexual identity—gay, straight, or bi—outlived its usefulness? *New York Times*, Sunday magazine, pp. 104–107.

Derrida, Jacques. (1972). Discussion: Structure, sign and play in the discourse of the human sciences. In R. Macksey & E. Donate (Eds.), *The structuralist controversy* (pp. 247–272). Baltimore: Johns Hopkins University Press.

——. ([1972] 1981). *Positions*. Chicago: University of Chicago Press.

Descombes, V. (1980). *Modern French philosophy*. New York: Cambridge University Press.

Dewey, John. (1897). My pedagogic creed. *The School Journal, 54*(3), 77–80.

——. (1899). *The school and society*. Chicago: University of Chicago Press.

——. (1922). *The public and its problems*. New York: Holt & Company.

——. (1934a). *A common faith*. New Haven, CT: Yale University Press.

——. (1934b). *Art as experience*. New York: Minton, Balch, & Company.

——. (1938). *Experience and education*. New York: Macmillan.

——. ([1916] 1985). *Democracy and education 1916*. Carbondale and Edwardsville: Southern Illinois University Press.

Diamond, C. T. Patrick. (1999). Editorial. *Curriculum Inquiry*, 29(3), 261–272.

Diamond, Raymond T., & Cottrol, Robert J. (1983). Codifying caste: Louisiana's racial classification scheme and the Fourteenth Amendment. *Loyola Law Review*, 29, 255.

Doll, Mary Aswell. (1991). Dancing the circle: Address to the Cambridge School of Weston, Cambridge, MA, June 8.

Doll, Ronald C. (1996). *Curriculum improvement: Decision making and process* (9th ed.). Boston: Allyn & Bacon.

Doll, William E., Jr. (1993). *A post-modern perspective on curriculum*. New York: Teachers College Press.

Dreyfuss, G. O., Cistone, P. J., & Divita, C., Jr. (1992). Restructuring in a large district: Dade County, Florida. In Carl D. Glickman (Ed.), *Supervision in transition* (pp. 43–51). Alexandria, VA: ASCD Press.

Edgerton, Susan. (1993). Love in the margins. In Louis Castenell & William F. Pinar (Eds.), *Understanding curriculum as racial text: Representation of identity and difference in education* (pp. 55–82). Albany: State University of New York Press.

——. (1996). *Translating the curriculum: Multiculturalism into cultural studies*. New York: Routledge.

——. (2001). Disgust and the production of violence. Paper presented at the Curriculum and Pedagogy Conference, University of Victoria, British Columbia, Canada, October 10–13.

Eisenberg, Ronni. (1986). *Organize yourself!* New York: Macmillan.

Eisner, Elliot W. (1991). *The educational imagination: On the design and evaluation of school programs*. Upper Saddle River, NJ: Prentice-Hall.

——. (1993). Invitational conference on the hidden consequences of a national curriculum. *Educational Researcher*, 22(7), 38–39.

——. (1997). *The enlightened eye: Qualitative inquiry and the enhancement of educational practice* (2nd ed.). New York: Macmillan.

——. (2001). *The educational imagination: On the design and evaluation of school programs* (3rd ed.). New York: Macmillan.

Eliot, T. S. (1971). *The collected poems and plays of T. S. Eliot: 1909–1950*. New York: Harcourt, Brace, & World.

Ellsworth, Elizabeth. (1989). Why doesn't this feel empowering? Working through the repressive myths of critical pedagogy. *Harvard Educational Review*, 59(3), 297–324.

——. (1997). *Teaching positions: Difference, pedagogy, and the power of address*. New York: Teachers College Press.

——. (2005). *Places of learning: Media, architecture, pedagogy*. New York: RoutledgeFalmer.

Elmore, Richard F., & Sykes, G. (1992). *Curriculum development*. New York: Macmillan.

Ettinger, Bracha L. (2005). Copoiesis. *Ephemera: Theory and Politics in Organization*, 5, 703–713.

Fadiman, James, & Frager, Robert. (1997). *Sufism*. New York: HarperCollins.

Fanon, Frantz. (1967). *Black skin, white masks*. New York: Grove Press.

——. (1970). *A dying colonialism*. Harmondsworth, England: Penguin.

Faulkner, William. ([1950] 1965). Speech of acceptance upon the award of the Nobel Prize for Literature, Stockholm, December 10. In James B. Meriwether (Ed.), *Essays, speeches, and public letters of William Faulkner* (p. 65). New York: Random House.

Fausto-Sterling, Anne. (2000). *Sexing the body: Gender politics and the construction of sexuality*. New York: Basic Books.

Feagin, Joseph R. (2000). *Racist America: Roots, current realities, & future reparations*. New York: Routledge.

———. (2006). *Systemic racism: A theory of oppression.* New York: Routledge.

Fehr, Dennis Earl. (1993). *Dogs playing cards: Powerbrokers of prejudice in education, art and culture.* New York: Peter Lang.

Fine, Michelle, & Weis, Lois. (2003). *Silenced voices and extraordinary conversations: Reimagining schools.* New York: Teachers College Press.

Fine, Michelle, Weis, Lois, Powell, Linda C., & Wong, L. Mun. (1997). *Off white: Readings on race, power, and society.* New York: Routledge.

Finn, Chester E., Jr. (1991). *We must take charge: Our schools and our future.* New York: Free Press.

Fish, Stanley. (2005, July 19). Editorial: Intentional neglect. *New York Times,* p. A25.

Fisher, R. Michael. (2010). *The world's fearlessness teachings: A critical integral approach to fear management/education for the 21st century.* Lanham, MD: University Press of America.

Fleener, Jayne, Doll, William, & St. Julien, John (Eds.). (2004). *Chaos, complexity, curriculum and culture.* New York: Peter Lang.

Flinders, David J. (2009). *The curriculum studies reader* (3rd ed.). New York: Routledge.

Foucault, Michel. (1972a). *Power/knowledge.* New York: Pantheon.

———. (1972b). *The archaeology of knowledge and the discourse on language.* (A. M. Sheridan Smith, Trans.). New York: Pantheon.

———. (1973). *This is not a pipe* (J. Harkness, Trans.). Berkeley: University of California Press.

———. (1977). *Language, counter-memory, practice.* Ithaca, NY: Cornell University Press.

———. (1979). *Discipline and punish: The birth of the prison.* New York: Vintage Books.

———. (1980). *Power/knowledge: Selected interviews and other writings, 1972–1977.* Colin Gordon (Ed.) (Colin Gordon et al., Trans.). New York: Pantheon.

———. (1990a). *The history of sexuality,* Vol. 1: *An introduction* (R. Hurley, Trans.). New York: Vintage Books.

———. (1990b). *The history of sexuality,* Vol. 2: *The use of pleasure* (R. Hurley, Trans.). New York: Vintage Books.

Fox, Matthew. (1992). *Sheer joy: Conversations with Thomas Aquinas on creation spirituality.* San Francisco: Harper.

Franklin, Barry M. (1986). *Building the American community: The school curriculum and the search for social control.* Philadelphia: Falmer Press.

———. (1988). Whatever happened to social control? The muting of coercive authority in curriculum discourse. In William F. Pinar (Ed.), *Contemporary curriculum discourses.* Scottsdale, AZ: Gorsuch Scarisbrick.

Franklin, Karen. (1997). Hate crimes or rites of passage? Assailant motivation in antigay violence. *Dissertation Abstracts International,* Vol. B57-12 (UMI No. 9715571).

Freire, Paulo. (1970). *Pedagogy of the oppressed.* New York: Herder & Herder.

———. (1971, March). Conscientizing as a way of liberating. *Contacto.* Also in *Liberation Theology.* A. T. Hennelly (Ed.). (1990). Maryknoll, NY: Orbis Books.

———. (1985). *The politics of education: Culture, power, and liberation.* South Hadley, MA: Bergin & Garvey.

———. (2001). *Pedagogy of freedom: Ethics, democracy, and civic courage.* New York: Rowman & Littlefield.

Freire, Paulo, & Macedo, Donaldo. (1987). *Literacy: Reading the word and reading the world.* South Hadley, MA: Bergin & Garvey.

Fuller, P. (1985). *Images of God: The consolations of lost illusions.* London: Chatto & Windus.

Gablik, Suzi. (1991). *The reenchantment of art.* New York: Thames & Hudson.

———. (1995). Connective aesthetics: Art after individualism. In S. Lacy (Ed.), *Mapping the terrain: New genre public art* (pp. 74–87). Seattle, WA: Bay Press.

Gadamer, Hans-Georg. (1975). *Truth and method.* G. Borden & J. Cumming (Ed. & Trans.). New York: Seabury.

———. (1976). *Philosophical hermeneutics.* David E. Linge (Ed. & Trans.). Berkeley: University of California Press.

Gadamer, Hans-Georg, & Derrida, Jacques. (1989). *Dialogue and deconstructionism: The Gadamer–Derrida encounter.* Albany: State University of New York Press.

Gaines, Ernest J. (1972). *The autobiography of Miss Jane Pittman.* New York: Bantam Books.

——. (1993). *A lesson before dying.* New York: Alfred A. Knopf.

Gallager, C. A. (2000). White like me? Methods, meaning, and manipulation in the field of White studies. In F. Winndance Twine & J. W. Warren (Eds.), *Racing research, researching race: Methodological dilemmas in critical race studies* (pp. 67–92). New York: New York University Press.

Gallagher, Shaun. (1992). *Hermeneutics and Education.* Albany: State University of New York Press.

Gay, Geneva. (1994). *At the essence of learning: Multicultural education.* New York: Teachers College Press.

——. (2000). *Culturally responsive teaching: Theory, research, and practice.* New York: Teachers College Press.

Gibson, James J. (1979). *The ecological approach to visual perception.* Boston: Houghton Mifflin.

Gilligan, Carol. (1982). *In a different voice.* Cambridge, MA: Harvard University Press.

Gilmour, J. C. (1990). *Fire on the earth: Anselm Kiefer and the postmodern world.* Philadelphia: Temple University Press.

Giroux, Henry A. (1981). *Ideology, culture, and the process of schooling.* Philadelphia: Temple University Press.

——. (1983). *Theory and resistance in education: A pedagogy for the opposition.* South Hadley, MA: Bergin & Garvey.

——. (1988). *Schooling and the struggle for public life: Critical pedagogy in the modern age.* Minneapolis: University of Minnesota Press.

——. (Ed.). (1991). *Postmodernism, feminism, and cultural politics: Redrawing educational boundaries.* Albany: State University of New York Press.

——. (1992). *Border crossings: Cultural workers and the politics of education.* New York: Routledge.

——. (1993). *Living dangerously: Multiculturalism and the politics of difference.* New York: Peter Lang.

——. (2005). *Against the new authoritarianism: Politics after Abu Ghraib.* New York: Arbeiter Ring.

Giroux, Henry A., & McLaren, Peter. (1989). *Critical pedagogy, the state, and cultural struggle.* Albany: State University of New York Press.

Giroux, Henry A., Penna, Anthony N., & Pinar, William F. (1981). *Curriculum and instruction.* Berkeley, CA: McCutchan.

Gleick, James. (1987). *Chaos: Making a new science.* New York: Viking Press.

——. (1999). *Faster: The acceleration of just about everything.* New York: Pantheon.

——. (2008). *Chaos: Making a new science* (3rd ed.) New York: Penguin.

Glickman, Carl. (1992). *Supervision in transition.* Alexandria, VA: ASCD Press.

Global Alliance for Transforming Education (GATE). (1991). Education 2000: A holistic perspective. *Holistic Education Review,* 4(4 [Supplement]), 1–18.

Glock, C., & Bellah, R. (1976). *The new religious consciousness.* Berkeley: University of California Press.

Goldhagen, Daniel J. (1996). *Hitler's willing executioners: Ordinary Germans and the Holocaust.* New York: Alfred A. Knopf.

Goodlad, John I., Soder, Roger, & Sirotnik, Kenneth A. (Eds.). (1990). *The moral dimensions of teaching.* San Francisco: Jossey-Bass.

Goodman, Jesse. (1987). Masculinity, feminism, and the male elementary school teacher. *Journal of Curriculum Theorizing,* 7(2), 30–60.

——. (1992). *Elementary schooling for critical democracy.* Albany: State University of New York Press.

Gordon, Beverly M. (1989). The bootstrap ideology of educational reform: What the recent reports say about the current and future status of Blacks in higher education. In Christine M. Shea, Ernest Kahane, & Peter Sola (Eds.), *The new servants of power: A critique of the 1980s school reform movement* (pp. 87–102). New York: Greenwood Press.

Graham, Robert J. (1991). *Reading and writing the self: Autobiography in education and the curriculum.* New York: Teachers College Press.

Greeley, Andrew M. (1982). *Catholic high schools and minority students.* New Brunswick, NJ: Transaction Books.

——. (1992). A modest proposal for the reform of Catholic schools. *America, 166*(10), 234–238.

Greene, Maxine. (1978). *Landscapes of learning.* New York: Teachers College Press.

——. (1995). *Releasing the imagination.* New York: Teachers College Press.

——. (2001). *Variations on a blue guitar: The Lincoln Center lectures on aesthetic education.* New York: Teachers College Press.

Griffin, David Ray. (1976). *God, power, and evil: A process theodicy.* Philadelphia: Westminster Press.

——. (Ed.). (1988a). *The reenchantment of science: Postmodern proposals.* Albany: State University of New York Press.

——. (Ed.). (1988b). *Spirituality and society: Postmodern visions.* Albany: State University of New York Press.

——. (Ed.). (1990). *Sacred interconnections: Postmodern spirituality, political economy, and art.* Albany: State University of New York Press.

Griffin, David Ray, Beardslee, W. A., & Holland, J. (1989). *Varieties of postmodern theology.* Albany: State University of New York Press.

Griffin, David Ray, Cobb, John B., Jr., Ford, Marcus P., Gunter, Pete A. Y., & Ochs, Peter. (1993). *Founders of constructive postmodern philosophy: Peirce, James, Bergson, Whitehead, and Hartshorne.* Albany: State University of New York Press.

Grumet, Madeleine R. (1988a). Bodyreading. In William F. Pinar (Ed.), *Contemporary curriculum discourses* (pp. 453–473). Scottsdale, AZ: Gorsuch Scarisbrick.

——. (1988b). *Bitter milk: Women and teaching.* Amherst: University of Massachusetts Press.

——. (1988c). Women and teaching: Homeless at home. In William F. Pinar (Ed.), *Contemporary curriculum discourses* (pp. 531–540). Scottsdale, AZ: Gorsuch Scarisbrick.

Gutek, G. L. (1993). *American education in a global society: Internationalizing teacher education.* White Plains, NY: Longman.

Gutiérrez, Gustavo. (1973). *A theology of liberation.* Maryknoll, NY: Orbis Books.

Gyatso, Tenzin. (2005, November 12). Our faith in science. *New York Times,* p. A27.

Habermas, Jürgen. (1970). *Knowledge and human interests.* Boston: Beacon Press.

Haggerson, Nelson, & Bowman, Andrea. (1992). *Informing educational policy and practice through interpretive inquiry.* Lancaster, PA: Technomic.

Hall, Manley P. (1988). *Meditation symbols in Eastern and Western mysticism: Mysteries of the mandala.* Los Angeles: Philosophical Research Society.

Hammerschlag, Carl A. (1988). *The dancing healers: A doctor's journey of healing with Native Americans.* San Francisco: Harper & Row.

——. (1993). *The theft of the spirit.* San Francisco: Harper & Row.

Harwit, M. (1996). *An exhibit denied: Lobbying the history of the Enola Gay.* New York: Springer.

Havel, Vaclav. (1992, March 1). The end of the modern era. *New York Times,* p. E15.

Hawking, Stephen W. (1988). *A brief history of time: From the big bang to black holes.* New York: Bantam Books.

Hayek, F. A. (1947). *The road to serfdom.* Chicago: University of Chicago Press.

Hayles, N. Katherine (1984). *The cosmic web.* Ithaca, NY: Cornell University Press.

Haynes, Charles. (1990). *Religion in American history: What to teach and how.* Alexandria, VA: ASCD Publications.

Hebert, B. (2002, February 11). The fatal flaws. *New York Times,* p. A29.

Heidegger, Martin. (1962). *Being and time.* (John Macquarrie & Edward Robinson, Trans.). New York: Harper & Row.

Helminiak, D. A. (2000). *What the Bible really says about homosexuality* (7th ed.). San Francisco: Alamo Square Press.

Henderson, James G., & Hawthorne, R. D. (1995). *Transformative curriculum leadership.* New York: Macmillan.

Henderson, James G., & Kesson, K. R. (2004). *Curriculum wisdom: Educational decisions in democratic societies.* Upper Saddle River, NJ: Merrill/Prentice-Hall.

Henderson, James G., & Slattery, Patrick (2004). Editors' introduction: The arts create synergy for curriculum and pedagogy. *Journal of Curriculum and Pedagogy, 1*(2), 1–7.

——. (2005). Editors' introduction: History of curriculum and pedagogy. *Journal of Curriculum and Pedagogy, 2*(1), 1–8.

Hennelly, A. T. (Ed.). (1990). *Liberation theology: A documentary history.* Maryknoll, NY: Orbis Books.

Herrnstein, Richard, & Murray, Charles. (1994) *The bell curve: Intelligence and class structure in American life.* New York: Free Press.

Hirsch, E. D., Jr. (1987). *Cultural literacy: What every American needs to know.* Boston: Houghton Mifflin.

Hitchens, Christopher. (2007). *God is not great: How religion poisons everything.* New York: Twelve Books.

Hlebowitsh, Peter W. (1993). *Radical curriculum theory revisited.* New York: Longman.

Hochschild, Adam. (1999). *King Leopold's ghost: A story of greed, terror, and heroism in colonial Africa.* Boston: Houghton Mifflin.

Hodge, Robert, & Kress, Gunter. (1988). *Social semiotics.* Ithaca, NY: Cornell University Press.

hooks, bell (1993). Altars of sacrifice: Re-membering Basquiat. *Art in America, 11*(3), 67–75.

——. (1995). *Killing rage: Ending racism.* New York: Henry Holt.

——. (2005). *The publications of bell hooks.* Retrieved from http://www.synaptic.bc.ca/ejournal/hooks.htm

Hopps, W. (Ed.). (1996). *Kienholz: A retrospective.* New York: Whitney Museum of Art.

Houston, Donna, & McLaren, Peter. (2005). The "nature" of political amnesia: A response to C. A. Bowers. *Educational Studies, 37*(2), 196–203.

Howard, Roy J. (1982). *Three faces of hermeneutics.* Berkeley: University of California Press.

Hudson CEE Explorer. (1996). Hudson school board rejects AP history text. *CEE Newsletter, 3*(2), 1–4.

Huebner, Dwayne E. (1975). Curriculum as concern for man's temporality. In William F. Pinar (Ed.), *Curriculum theorizing: The reconceptualists.* Berkeley, CA: McCutchan.

——. (1976). The moribund curriculum field: Its wake and our work. *Curriculum Inquiry, 6*(2), 2–11.

——. (1991). *Educational activity and prophetic criticism.* New Haven, CT: Yale University Divinity School.

——. (1996). Challenges bequeathed. Paper read to the faculty and students of Louisiana State University, Baton Rouge.

——. (1999). *The lure of the transcendent: Collected essays by Dwayne E. Huebner.* Vicki Hills (Ed.). Mahwah, NJ: Lawrence Erlbaum Associates.

Hughes, Langston. (1973). The negro speaks of rivers. In R. Ellmann & R. O'Clair (Eds.), *The Norton anthology of modern poetry* (pp. 634–635). New York: W. W. Norton.

Hunter, Madeline. (1982). *Mastery teaching.* El Segundo, CA: TIP.

Husserl, Edmund. (1964). *Phenomenology of internal time-consciousness.* Bloomington, IN: Midland.

Irwin, Rita L., & de Cosson, Alex (Eds.) (2004). *A/r/tography: Rendering self through arts-based living inquiry.* Vancouver, BC: Pacific Educational Press.

Jackson, Philip (Ed.). (1992). *Handbook of research on curriculum.* New York: Macmillan.

James, S., Heller, D., & Ellis, W. (1992). Peer assistance in a small district: Windham Southeast, Vermont. In Carl D. Glickman (Ed.), *Supervision in transition* (pp. 43–61). Alexandria, VA: ASCD Press.

James, William. (1958). *Talks to teachers: On psychology; and to students on some of life's ideals*. New York: W. W. Norton.

Jameson, Fredric. (1991). *Postmodernism and the cultural logic of late capitalism*. Durham, NC: Duke University Press.

Jardine, David W. (1992). Reflections on education, hermeneutics, and ambiguity: Hermeneutics as a restoring of life to its original difficulty. In William F. Pinar and William M. Reynolds (Eds.), *Understanding curriculum as phenomenological and deconstructed text* (pp. 116–130). New York: Longman.

Jeanrond, Werner. (1988). Hermeneutics. In J. Komonchak, M. Collins, & D. Lane (Eds.), *The new dictionary of theology* (pp. 462–464). Wilmington, DE: Michael Glazier.

Jencks, Charles. (1986). *What is post-modernism?* New York: St. Martin's Press.

——. (1988). *Architecture today*. New York: Harry N. Abrams.

——. (Ed.). (1992). *The post-modern reader*. New York: St. Martin's Press.

——. (2002). *The new paradigm in architecture*. New Haven, CT: Yale University Press.

Jenkins, Carol. (1994). *National study of sexual and reproductive knowledge and behaviour in Papua New Guinea*. Papua New Guinea: Institute of Medical Research.

The Jerusalem Bible (1966). Garden City, NY: Doubleday.

Jhally, Sut. (1999). *Killing us softly: Advertising's image of women*. Featuring Jean Kilbourne. [Film]. Northampton, MA: Media Education Foundation.

——. (2002). *Touch guise: Violence, media, and the crisis of masculinity*. Featuring Jackson Katz. [Film]. Northampton, MA: Media Education Foundation.

——. (2003). *Wrestling with manhood: Boys, bullying and battering*. [Film]. Northampton, MA: Media Education Foundation.

——. (2004). *Advertising and the end of the world*. [Film]. Northampton, MA: Media Education Foundation.

Jones, Libby Falk, & Goodwin, Sarah Webster (Eds.). (1990). *Feminism, utopia, and narrative*. Knoxville: University of Tennessee Press.

Jung, C. G. (1977). *Synchronicity: An acausal connecting principle*. (R. F. C. Hull, Trans.). Princeton, NJ: Princeton University Press.

Kanfer, Stefan. (1995). *The last empire: De Beers, diamonds, and the world*. New York: Farrar Straus Giroux.

Kelly, Geoffrey B., & Nelson, F. Burton. (2003). *The cost of moral leadership: The spirituality of Dietrich Bonhoeffer*. New York: Eerdmans.

Kermode, Frank. (2003, June 15). Another gospel of truth: A review of *Beyond belief* by Elaine Pagels. *New York Times*, Book Review, p. 10.

Kesson, Kathleen. (1993). Critical theory and holistic education: Carrying on the conversation. In Ron Miller (Ed.), *The renewal of meaning in education* (pp. 92–110). Brandon, VT: Holistic Education Press.

——. (2005). On bumblebees and pleiades: Schooling and the great journey of the soul. *Journal of Curriculum and Pedagogy*, 2(2), 28–32.

Kierkegaard, Søren. ([1849] 1980). *The sickness unto death: A Christian psychological exposition for upbuilding and awakening* (H. V. Hong & E. H. Hong, Trans.). Princeton, NJ: Princeton University Press.

Kimball, Charles. (2002). *When religion becomes evil*. San Francisco: HarperCollins.

King, Coretta Scott. (1993). *My life with Martin Luther King, Jr.* (rev. ed.). New York: Henry Holt.

Kirylo, James D. (2011). *Paulo Freire: The man from Recife*. New York: Peter Lang.

Klein, N. (2007). *The shock doctrine: The rise of disaster capitalism*. New York: Henry Holt.

Kliebard, Herbert M. (1986). *The struggle for the American curriculum: 1893–1958*. Boston: Routledge & Kegan Paul.

——. (1992a). *Forging the American curriculum: Essays in curriculum history and theory.* Boston: Routledge & Kegan Paul.

——. (1992b). Constructing a history of the American curriculum. In Philip W. Jackson (Ed.), *Handbook of research on curriculum* (pp. 157–184). New York: Macmillan.

——. (2004). *The struggle for the American curriculum: 1893–1958.* New York: RoutledgeFalmer.

Konikoff, Judy. (1993). An interview with Dr. Carl Brasseaux. Unpublished graduate research paper, Louisiana State University, Baton Rouge.

Kozol, Jonathan. (1967). *Death at an early age.* Boston: Houghton Mifflin.

——. (1975). *The night is dark and I am far from home: A political indictment of the United States public schools.* New York: Continuum.

——. (1991). *Savage inequalities: Children in America's schools.* New York: Crown.

——. (2005). *The shame of the nation: The restoration of apartheid schooling in America.* New York: Crown.

Krasny, Karen. (2004). *Imagery, affect, and the embodied mind: Implications for reading and responding to literature.* Unpublished doctoral dissertation, College Station: Texas A&M University.

——. (2006). Prophetic voices: Three books to encourage us to listen beyond historical silence. *Curriculum Inquiry, 36*(1), 27–36.

Kridel, Craig. (1998). The eight-year study revisited: Lessons from the past for the present. *Curriculum Studies, 9*(2), 7–26.

——. (Ed.). (2000). *Books of the century catalogue.* Columbia, SC: Museum of Education.

——. (Ed.). (2010). *Encyclopedia of curriculum studies.* New York: Sage.

Kristof, Nicholas D. (2005, April 6). The pope and hypocrisy. *New York Times*, p. A29.

Krugman, Paul. (2011, December 25). Springtime for toxics. *New York Times*, p. 3.

Kuhn, Thomas. (1970). *The structure of scientific revolutions.* Chicago: University of Chicago Press.

Kumashiro, Kevin K. (2001). *Troubling intersections of race and sexuality: Queer students of color and anti-oppressive education.* New York: Routledge.

——. (2004). *Against common sense: Teaching and learning toward social justice.* New York: Routledge.

Kung, Hans. (1988). *Theology for the third millennium: An ecumenical view.* New York: Doubleday.

Kushner, Harold S. ([1981] 2001). *When bad things happen to good people.* New York: Knopf.

Langer, Susanne K. (1957). *Problems of art.* New York: Charles Scribner.

Lasch, Christopher. (1984). *The minimal self: Psychic survival in troubled times.* New York: W. W. Norton.

Lather, Patti. (1989). Ideology and methodological attitude. *Journal of Curriculum Theorizing, 9*(2), 7–26.

——. (1991). *Getting smart: Feminist research and pedagogy with/in the postmodern.* New York: Routledge.

——. (1994). *Gender issues in methodology: Data analysis in the crisis of representation.* Brochure for conference held by AERA Winter Institute, Clearwater, FL.

Lee, Earl. (2001). School textbooks. In Russ Kick (Ed.), *You are being lied to: The disinformation guide to media distortion, historical whitewashes, and cultural myths* (pp. 73–78). New York: Disinformation Company.

Lemonick, M. D. (1992). Echoes of the big bang. *Time, 139*(18), 62–63.

LePage, Andy. (1987). *Transforming education: The new 3 r's.* Oakland, CA: Oakmore House Press.

Lerner, Gerda. (1986). *The creation of patriarchy.* New York: Oxford University Press.

Leroy, J. T. (2001). *The heart is deceitful above all things.* New York: Bloomsbury.

Letts, W. J., & Sears, J. T. (Eds.). (1999). *Queering elementary education: Advancing the dialogue about sexuality and schooling.* Lanham, MD: Rowman & Littlefield.

Lewis, A. E. (2004). *Race in the school yard: Negotiating the color line in classrooms and communities.* New Brunswick, NJ: Rutgers University Press.

Lincoln, Yvonna S. (1992). Curriculum studies and the traditions of inquiry: The humanistic tradition. In Philip W. Jackson (Ed.), *Handbook of research on curriculum* (pp. 79–98). New York: Macmillan.

——. (1994, March). Piety and purpose: Reclaiming élan for higher education. *Educational Researcher, 23*(2), 35–36.

Loewen, James W. (1995). *Lies my teacher told me: Everything your high school history textbook got wrong.* New York: Simon & Schuster.

——. (2000). *Lies across America: What our historic sites get wrong.* New York: Simon & Schuster.

Lovelock, James E. (1979) *Gaia: A new look at life on earth.* New York: Oxford University Press.

Lugg, Catherine A. (2004). One nation under God? Religion and the politics of education in a post-9/11 America. *Educational Policy, 18*(1), 169–187.

Lugg, Catherine A., & Tabbaa-Rida, Zeena. (2006). Social justice, religion, and public school leaders. In Catherine Marshall & Maricela Oliva (Eds.), *Leadership for social justice: Making revolutions in education.* Boston: Pearson/Allyn & Bacon.

Luo, Michael. (2006, November 13). On abortion, it's the bible of ambiguity. *New York Times,* Week in Review, pp. 1–3.

Lyotard, Jean-François. (1984). *The postmodern condition: A report on knowledge.* Minneapolis: University of Minnesota Press.

Macdonald, James B. (1988). Theory, practice, and the hermeneutic circle. In William F. Pinar (Ed.), *Contemporary curriculum discourses* (pp. 101–113). Scottsdale, AZ: Gorsuch Scarisbrick.

Macgillivray, I. K. (2002). *Sexual orientation and school policy: A practical guide for teachers, administrators, & community activists.* New York: Educator's International Press.

MacKeracher, Dorothy. (2004). *Making sense of adult learning.* Toronto, Ontario: University of Toronto Press.

Maguire, Daniel C., & Fargnoli, A. N. (1991). *On moral grounds: The art/science of ethics.* New York: Crossroad.

Malewski, Erik. (Ed.). (2009). *Curriculum studies handbook: The next moment.* New York: Routledge.

Mancuso, David. [Producer]. (1991). *Old man river* [Film]. New Orleans: Aquarium of the Americas.

Mann, Horace. ([1848] 1957). Twelfth annual report of the [Massachusetts] Board of Education. In Lawrence Cremin (Ed.), *The republic and the school: Horace Mann on the education of the free man.* New York: Teachers College Press.

Marsh, Colin J., & Willis, George. (1999). *Curriculum: Alternative approaches, ongoing issues* (2nd ed.). Upper Saddle River, NJ: Prentice-Hall.

Marshall, Catherine, and Oliva, Maricela. (Eds.). (2006). *Leadership for social justice: Making revolutions in education.* Boston: Pearson/Allyn & Bacon.

Marshall, J. D., Sears, J. T., & Schubert, W. H. (2000). *Turning points in curriculum: A contemporary American memoir.* Upper Saddle River, NJ: Merrill/Prentice-Hall.

Marty, M. E. (1984). *Pilgrims in their own land: 500 years of religion in America.* Boston: Little, Brown.

Maxcy, Spencer J. (1991). *Educational leadership: A critical pragmatic perspective.* New York: Bergin & Garvey.

——. (Ed.). (1993). *Postmodern school leadership: Meeting the crisis in educational administration.* Westport, CT: Praeger.

McCall, Nathan. (1993). *Makes me wanna holler.* New York: Random House.

McCarthy, Camron. (1990). *Race and curriculum.* London: Falmer Press.

——. (1993). Multicultural approaches to racial inequality in the United States. In Louis Castenell & William F. Pinar (Eds.), *Understanding curriculum as racial text: Representations of identity and difference in education* (pp. 225–246). Albany: State University of New York Press.

McCarthy, Camron, & Apple, Michael. (1988). Race, class, and gender in American education: Toward a nonsynchronous parallelist position. In Lois Weis (Ed.), *Class, race and gender in American education* (pp. 3–39). Albany: State University of New York Press.

McElfresh-Spehler, R., & Slattery, P. (1999). Voices of imagination: The artist as prophet in the process of social change. *International Journal of Leadership in Education*, 2(1), 1–12.

McIntosh, Peggy. ([1988] 1992). White privilege and male privilege: A personal account of coming to see correspondences through the work in women's studies. In M. Andersen and P. H. Collins (Eds.), *Race, class, and gender: An anthology*. Belmont, CA: Wadsworth.

McLaren, Peter. (1989). *Life in schools: An introduction to critical pedagogy in the foundations of education*. New York: Longman.

——. (1993, January). Multiculturalism and the postmodern critique: Towards a pedagogy of resistance and transformation. *Cultural Studies*, 7(1), 118–146.

——. (1997) *Revolutionary multiculturalism: Pedagogies of dissent for the new millennium*. Boulder, CO: Westview Press.

——. (1998). *Life in schools: An introduction to critical pedagogy in the foundations of education* (3rd ed.). New York: Longman.

——. (2000). *Che Guevara, Paulo Freire, and the pedagogy of revolution*. Lanham, MD: Rowman & Littlefield.

——. (2005). *Capitalists and conquerors: Critical pedagogy against empire*. New York: Rowman & Littlefield.

McLaren, Peter, & Dantley, Michael. (1990). Leadership and a critical pedagogy of race: Cornel West, Stuart Hall, and the prophetic tradition. *Journal of Negro Education*, 59(1), 29–44.

McLaren, Peter, & Leonard, Peter. (Eds.). (1993). *Paulo Freire: A critical encounter*. London and New York: Routledge.

McNeil, J. D. (1990). *Curriculum: A comprehensive introduction* (4th ed.). Boston: Little, Brown.

McNeil, Linda. (1986). *Contradictions of control: School structure and school knowledge*. New York: Routledge & Kegan Paul.

Megill, Allan. (1985). *Prophets of extremity*. Berkeley: University of California Press.

Menand, Louis. (2001). *The metaphysical club: A story of ideas in America*. New York: Farrar Straus Giroux.

Merchant, Carolyn. (1992). *Radical ecology: The search for a livable world*. New York: Routledge.

——. (1996). *Earthcare: Women and the Environment*. New York: Routledge.

——. (2005). *Radical ecology: The search for a livable world* (2nd ed.). New York: Routledge.

——. (2008). *Ecology: Key concepts in critical theory* (2nd ed.). New York: Humanity Books.

Merleau-Ponty, Maurice. (1962). *Phenomenology of perception*. London: Routledge & Kegan Paul.

Miller, Janet L. (1980). Women: The evolving educational consciousness. *Journal of Curriculum Theorizing*, 2(1), pp. 238–247.

——. (1987). Women as teacher/researchers: Gaining a sense of ourselves. *Teacher Education Quarterly*, 14(2), pp. 52–58.

——. (1990). *Creating spaces and finding voices*. Albany: State University of New York Press.

——. (1992). Women and education: In what ways does gender affect the educational process? In Joe L. Kincheloe and Shirley Steinberg (Eds.), *Thirteen questions* (pp. 151–158). New York: Peter Lang.

——. (2005). *Sounds of silence breaking: Women, autobiography, curriculum*. New York: Peter Lang.

Miller, John P. (1988). *The holistic curriculum*. Toronto: Ontario Institute for Studies in Education.

Miller, Page Putnam, & Thelen, David. (1993). Historians and archivists. *Chronicle of Higher Education*, 40(16), p. B3.

Miller, Ron. (Ed.). (1993). *The renewal of meaning in education: Responses to the ecological crisis of our time*. Brandon, VT: Holistic Education Press.

Miller, William Ian. (1998). *The anatomy of disgust*. Cambridge, MA: Harvard University Press.

Molnar, Alex. (1996). *Giving kids the business: The commercialization of America's schools*. New York: Westview/HarperCollins.

Moltmann, Jürgen. (1967). *The theology of hope*. London: SCM Press.

Montenegro, Maywa, & Glavin, Terry. (2011). *Scientists offer new insights into what to protect in the world's rapidly vanishing languages, cultures, and species*. Recovered from http:// seedmagazine.com/content/article/in_defense_of_difference/

Moore, Mary Elizabeth M. (1989, October 15). The art of teaching from the heart: The heart of the matter. Paper presented at the School of Theology, Claremont, CA.

Moran, Gabriel. (1981). *Interplay: A theory of religion and education*. Winona, MN: St. Mary's College Press.

Morrison, Toni. (1989). Unspeakable things unspoken: The Afro-American presence in American literature. *Michigan Quarterly*, Winter, pp. 1–34.

Muhammad, Khallid. (1994). Nation of Islam speaker urges Black students to "wake up." *The Vermilion*, 90(ix), 1–2 [University of Southwestern Louisiana Student Weekly].

Naess, A. (1995). Deepness of questions and the deep ecology movement. In G. Sessions (Ed.), *Deep ecology in the 21st century: Readings on the philosophy and practice of the new environmentalism* (pp. 213–21). Boston: Shambhala.

Nash, Gary. (2004). *The American people: Creating a nation and a society*. New York: Pearson/Allyn & Bacon.

NCCB (National Conference of Catholic Bishops). (1972). *To teach as Jesus did: A pastoral message on Catholic education*. Washington, DC: U.S. Catholic Conference Publications Office.

Needleman, J. (Ed.). (1989). *Tao te ching by Lao Tsu*. (Gia Fu Feng & Jane English, Trans.). New York: Vintage.

Newman, Joseph W. (1990). *America's teachers: An introduction to education*. New York: Longman.

——. (1997). *America's teachers: An introduction to education* (3rd ed.). New York: Longman.

Nhat Hanh, Thich. (1995). *Living Buddha, living Christ*. New York: Riverhead.

Nieto, Sonja. (2004). *Affirming diversity: The sociopolitical context of multicultural education*. New York: Allyn & Bacon.

Nietzsche, Friedrich. (1968). The birth of tragedy. In *Basic writings of Nietzsche*. Walter Kaufmann (Ed. & Trans.) (3rd ed.). New York: Modern Library.

Noddings, Nel. (1984). *Caring: A feminine approach to ethics and moral education*. Berkeley: University of California Press.

——. (1989). *Women and evil*. Berkeley: University of California Press.

——. (1992). *The challenge to care in schools: An alternative approach to education*. New York: Teachers College Press.

——. (1995). *Philosophy of education*. Boulder, CO: Westview Press.

——. (2005). Can spiritual/theological discourse guide curriculum and pedagogy? *Journal of Curriculum and Pedagogy*, 2(2), 10–15.

Nord, Warren A. (1995). *Religion and American education: Rethinking a national dilemma*. Chapel Hill: University of North Carolina Press.

Nord, Warren A., & Haynes, Charles. (1998). *Taking religion seriously across the curriculum*. Alexandria, VA: ASCD Press

Nussbaum, Martha C. (2001). Secret sewers of vice: Disgust, bodies, and the law. In Susan Bandes (Ed.), *The passions of law*. New York: New York University Press.

Oakes, Jeannie. (1985). *Keeping track: How schools structure inequality*. New Haven, CT: Yale University Press.

O'Gorman, R. T. (1987). *The church that was a school: Catholic identity and Catholic education in the United States since 1790.* Washington, DC: NCEA Catholic Education Futures Project.

Oliva, Peter F. (2001). *Developing the curriculum* (5th ed.). Boston: HarperCollins.

Oliver, Donald W., & Gershman, Kathleen W. (1989). *Education, modernity, and fractured meaning: Toward a process theory of teaching and learning.* Albany: State University of New York Press.

O'Malley, Michael P. (2003). *Construcing a critical pedagogy of the human soul through a postmodern analysis of Kairos.* Unpublished doctoral dissertation, St. Joseph's University, Philadelphia.

——. (2005). Constructing a critical pedagogy of human soul: An ethnography. Paper presented at the American Educational Research Association annual meeting, Montreal, Canada, April 12.

———. (2007). Conceptualizing a critical pedagogy of human soul: Ethnographic implications for curriculum studies. *Journal of Curriculum and Pedagogy,* 4(1), 84–112.

———. (2009). Reconstituting the imagined community in Chile: Ethnographic inquiry into a public pedagogy of the 2006 student protests and dictatorship era desaparecidos. Paper presented at the International Association for the Advancement of Curriculum Studies Triennial Conference, Cape Town, South Africa, September.

O'Malley, Michael P., Roseboro, Donyell. L., & Hunt, John. (2012). Accountability, fiscal management, and student achievement in East St. Louis, IL, 1994–2006: Implications for urban educational reform policy. *Urban Education,* 47(1), 117–143.

Ornstein, Allan C., & Levine, Daniel U. (1993). *Philosophical foundations of education* (5th ed.). Boston: Houghton Mifflin.

Ornstein, Allan C., Behar-Horenstein, Linda S., & Pajak, Edward F. (2003). *Contemporary issues in curriculum.* New York: Allyn & Bacon.

Ornstein, Allan C., Pajak, Edward F., and Ornstein, Stacey B. (2010). *Contemporary issues in curriculum* (5th ed.). New York: Prentice-Hall.

Orr, David W. (1992). *Ecological literacy: Education and the transition to a postmodern world.* Albany: State University of New York Press.

——. (2000, January 14). Green building at Oberlin in a new dream house for environmental science. *Chronicle of Higher Education,* p. A-14.

——. (2002). *The nature of design: Ecology, culture, and human intention.* Oxford, England: Oxford University Press.

Ortwein, Mark J. (2012). Virtue epistemology and education. Oxford, MS: Unpublished manuscript.

Osajima, Keith. (1992). Speaking silence. *Journal of Curriculum Theorizing,* 9(4), 89–96.

Ostwald, Peter. (1991). *Vaslav Nijinsky: A leap into madness.* New York: Carol Publishing Group.

Owens, Yvonne. (2007). Magical bodies: A collaborative vision. In Nané Jordan (Ed.), *Elicit bodies: Art exhibition and performance ritual / R. Michael Fisher and Barbara Bickel* (pp. 9–16). Vancouver, BC: In Search of Fearlessness Research Institute.

Ozmon, Howard, & Craver, Samuel. (1990). *Philosophical foundations of education* (4th ed.). Columbus, OH: Merrill.

Padgham, Ronald. (1988). Correspondences: Contemporary curriculum theory and twentieth-century art. In William F. Pinar (Ed.), *Contemporary curriculum discourses* (pp. 359–379). Scottsdale, AZ: Gorsuch Scarisbrick.

Pagano, Jo Anne. (1990). *Exiles and communities: Teaching in the patriarchal wilderness.* Albany: State University of New York Press.

Page, Reba. (1990). *Curriculum differentiation: Interpretive studies in the United States' secondary schools.* Albany: State University of New York Press.

——. (1991). *Lower-track classroom: A curricular and cultural perspective.* New York: Teachers College Press.

Pagels, Elaine. (2005). *Beyond belief: The secret gospel of Thomas*. New York: Random House.

Pajak, Edward. (1989). *The central office supervisor of curriculum and instruction: Setting the stage for success*. Boston: Allyn & Bacon.

Parrott, Jennifer L. (2006). *Understanding curriculum in context: Exploring the perceptions, attitudes, and practices of White teachers in classrooms with African American students*. Unpublished doctoral dissertation, Texas A&M University.

Percy, Walker. (1954). *The message in the bottle: How queer man is, how queer language is, and what one has to do with the other*. New York: Farrar Straus Giroux.

——. (1961). *The moviegoer*. New York: Ivy.

——. (1987). *The thanatos syndrome*. New York: Farrar Straus Giroux.

Peter, Carl. (1974). Metaphysical finalism in Christian eschatology. *The Thomist, 38* (January), 125–145.

Phenix, Phillip. (1975). Transcendence and the curriculum. In William F. Pinar (Ed.), *Curriculum theorizing: The reconceptualists* (pp. 323–337). Berkeley, CA: McCutchan.

Picasso, Pablo. (1971). Conversations. In H. B. Chipps (Ed.), *Theories of modern art: A source book of artists and critics* (p. 268). Berkeley: University of California Press.

Pinar, William F. (1975). *Curriculum theorizing: The reconceptualists*. Berkeley, CA: McCutchan.

——. (1978). Notes on the curriculum field 1978. *Educational Researcher, 7*(8), 5–12.

——. (Ed.). (1988a). *Contemporary curriculum discourses*. Scottsdale, AZ: Gorsuch Scarisbrick.

——. (1988b). Time, place, and voice: Curriculum theory and the historical moment. In William F. Pinar (Ed.), *Contemporary curriculum discourses* (pp. 264–278). Scottsdale, AZ: Gorsuch Scarisbrick.

——. (1994). *Autobiography, politics, and sexuality: Essays in curriculum theory, 1972–1992*. New York: Peter Lang.

—— (Ed.). (1998). *Queer theory in education*. Mahwah, NJ: Lawrence Erlbaum.

——. (1999). Response: Gracious submission. *Educational Researcher, 28*(1), 14–15.

——. (2001). *The gender of racial politics and violence in America: Lynching, prison rape & the crisis of masculinity*. New York: Peter Lang.

——. (Ed.). (2003). *International handbook of curriculum research*. Mahwah, NJ: Lawrence Erlbaum.

——. (2004a). *What is curriculum theory?* Mahwah, NJ: Lawrence Erlbaum.

——. (2004b). The synoptic text today. *Journal of Curriculum Theorizing, 20* (Spring), 7–22.

——. (2006). *The body of the father and the race of the son: Noah, Schreber, and the curse of the covenant*. New York: Palgrave Macmillan.

——. (2007). *Intellectual advancement through disciplinarity: Verticality and horizontality*. New York: Sense.

——. (2011). *What is curriculum theory?* (2nd ed.). Mahwah, NJ: Lawrence Erlbaum.

Pinar, William F., & Grumet, Madeleine R. (1976). *Toward a poor curriculum*. Dubuque, IA: Kendall/Hunt.

Pinar, William F., & Reynolds, William M. (Eds.) (1992). *Understanding curriculum as phenomenological and deconstructed text*. New York: Longman.

Pinar, William F., Reynolds, William M., Slattery, Patrick, & Taubman, Peter Maas. (1995). *Understanding curriculum: An introduction to the study of historical and contemporary curriculum discourses*. New York: Peter Lang.

Pollock, Jackson. (1971). My painting. In H. B. Chipps (Ed.), *Theories of modern art: A source book of artists and critics* (pp. 540–556). Berkeley: University of California Press.

Pollock, Mica. (2004). *Colormute: Race talk dilemmas in an American school*. Princeton, NJ: Princeton University Press.

Porter, Geoff D. (2005, October 16). Editorial: God is in the rules. *New York Times*, Week in Review, p. 13.

Posamentier, A. S. (2002, January 2). Madam, I'm 2002 – a numerically beautiful year. *New York Times*, p. A25.

Prigogine, Ilya, & Stengers, Isabelle. (1984). *Order out of chaos: Man's new dialogue with nature.* New York: Bantam Books.

Provenzo, Edward F., Jr. (1990). *Religious fundamentalism and American education.* New York: State University of New York Press.

Purpel, David E. (1989). *The moral and spiritual crisis in education: A curriculum for justice and compassion in education.* New York: Bergin & Garvey.

——. (2005). Educational discourse and spirituality. *Journal of Curriculum and Pedagogy,* 2(2), 16–21.

The Qur'an. (1990). (M. H. Shakir, Trans.). Elmhurst, NY: Tahrike Tarsile Qur'an.

Raskin, M. (1996). Ed Keinholtz and the burden of being an American. In Walter Hopps (Ed.), *Keinholtz: A retrospective* (pp. 38–43). New York: Distributed Art Publishers/Whitney Museum of Art.

Ravitch, Diane. (2011). Let your voice be heard. *Thought & Action: The NEA Higher Education Journal,* 27 (Fall), 111–118.

Raymond, C. (1991, March 6). New study finds convergence of school curricula worldwide. *Chronicle of Higher Education,* p. A8.

Regnier, Robert. (1992). The sacred circle: Foundation for a process pedagogy of healing. Paper presented at the Sixth Annual Meeting of the Association of Process Philosophy of Education, Louisville, KY, April 24–26.

Reynolds, Sherrie. (2004a). Gregory Bateson and theories of cognition. In M. Jane Fleener, William E. Doll, and John St. Julien (Eds.), *Chaos, complexity, curriculum and culture: A conversation.* New York: Peter Lang.

——. (2004b). Patterns that connect: A recursive epistemology. In M. Jane Fleener, William E. Doll, and John St. Julien (Eds.), *Chaos, complexity, curriculum and culture: A conversation.* New York: Peter Lang.

Reynolds, William. (1989). *Reading curriculum theory: The development of a new hermeneutic.* New York: Peter Lang.

Ricoeur, Paul. (1981). *Hermeneutics and the human sciences.* J. Thompson (Ed. & Trans.). Cambridge, England: Cambridge University Press.

Robinson, J. M. (Ed.). (1977). *The Nag Hammadi Library.* San Francisco: Harper & Row.

Rodriguez, Richard. (2002). *Brown: The last discovery of America.* New York: Viking Press.

Roman, Leslie, & Apple, Michael. (1990). Is naturalism a move away from positivism? In Eliot Eisner & Alan Peshkin (Eds.), *Qualitative inquiry in education* (pp. 38–73). New York: Teachers College Press.

Roman, Leslie, & Christian-Smith, Linda. (1987). *Feminism and the politics of popular culture.* London: Palmer.

Rorty, Richard. (1979). *Philosophy and the mirror of nature.* Princeton, NJ: Princeton University Press.

——. (1982). *Consequences of pragmatism.* Minneapolis: University of Minnesota Press.

——. (1989). *Contingency, irony and solidarity.* Cambridge, England: Cambridge University Press.

——. (1997, November 1). Lofty ideas that may be losing altitude. *New York Times,* p. A19.

Ruether, Rosemary R. (1983a). *Sexism and God-talk: Toward a feminist theology.* Boston: Beacon Press.

——. (1983b). *To change the world: Christianity and cultural criticism.* New York: Crossroad.

Rushdie, Salman. (1989). *The satanic verses.* New York: Penguin.

St. Julien, John. (1992). Explaining learning: The research trajectory of situated cognition and the implications of connectionism. Paper presented at AERA, San Francisco, April.

——. (1994). *Situated cognition.* Unpublished doctoral dissertation, Louisiana State University, Baton Rouge.

Sandlin, J. A., O'Malley, M. P., & Burdick, J. (2011). Mapping the complexities of public pedagogy scholarship: 1894–2010. *Review of Educational Research,* 81(3), 338–375.

Sarup, M. (1989). *An introductory guide to post-structuralism and postmodernism.* Athens: University of Georgia Press.

Saussure, Ferdinand de. (1959). *Course in general linguistics.* New York: McGraw-Hill.

——. (1974). *Course in general linguistics.* J. Culler (Ed.) (W. Baskin, Trans.). London: Falmer.

Saylor, J. G., Alexander, W. M., & Lewis, A. J. (1981). *Curriculum planning for better teaching and learning* (4th ed.). New York: Holt, Rinehart, & Winston.

Scheurich, James J., & Young, Michelle D. (1997). Coloring epistemologies: Are our research epistemologies racially biased? *Educational Researcher, 26*(4), 4–16.

Schilling, S. Paul. (1977). *God and human anguish.* New York: Abingdon Press.

Schleiermacher, Friedrich D. E. (1978). Outline of the 1819 lectures. *New Literacy History, 10*(1), pp. 1–16.

Schnabel, Julian. (1996). *Basquiat* [Film]. New York.

Schon, Donald A. (1983). *The reflective practitioner: How professionals think in action.* New York: Basic Books.

——. (1987). *Educating the reflective practitioner.* New York: Basic Books.

——. (1991). *The reflective turn.* New York: Teachers College Press.

Schubert, William H. (1986). *Curriculum: Perspective, paradigm, possibility.* New York: Macmillan.

Schubert, William, & Ayers, William. (Eds.). (1992). *Teacher lore: Learning from our own experience.* New York: Longman.

Schwab, J. J. (1969). The practical: A language for curriculum. *School Review, 78,* 1–23.

——. (1970). *The practical: A language for curriculum.* Washington, DC: National Education Association.

Schwehn, Mark R. (1992). *Exiles from Eden: Religion and the academic vocation in America.* Oxford, England: Oxford University Press.

Scroggs, R. (1983). *The New Testament and homosexuality: Contextual background for contemporary debate.* Philadelphia: Fortress Press.

Sears, James T. (1990). *Growing up gay in the South.* New York and London: Haworth Press.

——. (1992). *Sexuality and the curriculum: The politics and practices of sexuality education.* New York: Teachers College Press.

——. (1997). Centering culture: Teaching for critical sexual literacy using the sexual diversity wheel. *Journal of Moral Education, 26*(3), 273–283.

Sears, James T., & Epstein, Deborah. (1999). *Dangerous knowing: Sexual pedagogies and the "master narrative."* New York: Continuum.

Sears, James T., & Marshall J. Dan. (Eds.). (1990). *Teaching and thinking about curriculum: Critical inquiry.* New York: Teachers College Press.

Serres, Michel. (1982). *Hermes: Literature, science, philosophy.* Baltimore: Johns Hopkins University Press.

Sessions, G. (Ed.). (1995). *Deep ecology for the twenty-first century.* Boston: Shambhala.

Shea, Christine, Kahane, Ernst, & Sola, Peter. (1989). *The new servants of power: A critique of the 1980s school reform movement.* New York: Greenwood Press.

Shepard, Paul. (1977). Place in American culture. *North American Review* (Fall), pp. 22–32.

Short, Edmund C. (Ed.). (1991). *Forms of curriculum inquiry.* Albany: State University of New York Press.

Simons, Marlise. (1994, January 30). Cousteau says oceans vandalized. *Lafayette Sunday Advertiser, 128*(129), p. A6.

Sinclair, Upton. (1906). *The jungle.* New York: Doubleday, Page.

Sizer, Theodore. (1984). *Horace's compromise: The dilemma of the American high school.* Boston: Houghton Mifflin.

Skrla, Linda, & Scheurich, James Joseph. (Eds.). (2004). *Educational equity and accountability: Paradigms, policies, and politics.* New York: RoutledgeFalmer.

Slattery, Patrick. (1989). *Toward an eschatological curriculum theory.* Unpublished dissertation, Louisiana State University, Baton Rouge.

——. (1992a). Toward an eschatological curriculum theory. *Journal of Curriculum Theorizing*, 9(3), 7–21.

——. (1992b). Theological dimensions of the school curriculum. *Journal of Religion & Public Education*, 19(2–3), 173–184.

——. (1995). *Curriculum development in the postmodern era*. New York: Garland.

——. (2001). The educational researcher as artist working within. *Qualitative Inquiry*, 7(3), 370–398.

——. (2011). A process philosophy analysis of the intersection of economic policy, school reform, and cultural commons: Implications for curriculum studies. *Journal of the American Association for the Advancement of Curriculum Studies*, 7(1), 1–12.

Slattery, Patrick, & Daigle, Kevin. (1994). Curriculum as a place of turmoil: Deconstructing the anguish in Ernest Games' *Pointe coupee* and Walker Percy's *Feliciana*. *Curriculum Inquiry*, 24(4), 437–461.

Slattery, Patrick, & Morris, Marla. (1999). Simone de Beauvoir's ethics and postmodern ambiguity: The assertion of freedom in the face of the absurd. *Educational Theory*, 49(1), 21–36.

Slattery, Patrick, & Rapp, Dana. (2003). *Ethics and the foundations of education: Teaching convictions in a postmodern world*. Boston: Allyn & Bacon.

Slattery, Patrick, Krasny, Karen, & O'Malley, Michael. (2006). Hermeneutics, aesthetics, and the quest for answerability: A dialogic possibility for reconceptualizing the interpretive process in curriculum studies. *Journal of Curriculum Studies*, 32(6), 537–558.

Sleeter, Christine E., & Bernal, D. D. (2004). Critical pedagogy, critical race theory, and antiracist education: Implications for multicultural education. In J. A. Banks & C. A. McGee-Banks (Eds.), *Handbook of research on multicultural education* (2nd ed). New York: Macmillan.

Sloan, Douglas. (1983). *Insight-imagination: The recovery of thought in the modem world*. New York: Teachers College Press.

——. (1993). Forword. In Ron Miller (Ed.), *The renewal of meaning in education* (pp. 1–5). Brandon, VT: Holistic Education Press.

Smith, C. (2005). *Soul searching: The religious and spiritual lives of American teenagers*. Oxford, England: Oxford University Press.

Smith, David G. (1988). Experimental eidetics as a way of entering curriculum language from the ground up. In William R. Pinar (Ed.), *Contemporary curriculum discourses* (pp. 417–436). Scottsdale, AZ: Gorsuch Scarisbrick.

——. (1991). Hermeneutic inquiry: The hermeneutic imagination and the pedagogic text. In Edmund C. Short (Ed.), *Forms of curriculum inquiry* (pp. 187–210). Albany: State University of New York Press.

Smith, E., & Tyler, Ralph. (1942). *Adventures in American education III: Appraising and recording student progress*. New York: Harper & Brothers.

Smith, Philip G. (1965). *Philosophy of education*. New York: Harper & Row.

Smith, Roberta. (2011, December 27) Crystal Bridges, the art museum Walmart money built, opens. *New York Times*, Opinion, p. 1.

Sola, Peter. (1989). The corporate community on the ideal business-school alliance: A historical and ethical critique. In Christine M. Shea, Ernest Kahane, & Peter Sola (Eds.), *The new servants of power: A critique of the 1980s school reform movement* (pp. 75–83). New York: Greenwood Press.

Spring, Joel. (1993). *Conflict of interests: The politics of American education* (2nd ed.). New York: Longman.

——. (2004). *The American school: 1642–2004* (6th ed.). New York: Longman.

Springgay, Stephanie. (2004). Inside the visible: Arts-based educational research as excess. *Journal of Curriculum and Pedagogy*, 1(1), 8–18.

Springgay, Stephanie, Irwin, Rita L., Leggo, Carl, & Gouzouasis, Peter. (Eds.). (2008). *Being with A/r/tography*. Rotterdam, the Netherlands: Sense.

Stanley, William B. (1992). *Curriculum for Utopia: Social reconstructionism and critical peda-gogy in the postmodern era*. Albany: State University of New York Press.

Stannard, David E. (1992). *American Holocaust: Columbus and the conquest of the new world*. New York: Oxford University Press.

Stark, R., & Brainbridge, W. S. (1985). *The future of religions: Secularization, revival, and cult formation*. Berkeley: University of California Press.

Stinson, Susan W. (1991). Dance as curriculum, curriculum as dance. In George Willis & William H. Schubert (Eds.), *Reflections from the heart of educational inquiry* (pp. 190–196). Albany: State University of New York Press.

Suzuki, D. T., Fromm, Erich, & DeMartino, Richard. (1960). *Zen Buddhism and psychoanalysis*. New York: Grove.

Talburt, Susan. (2000). *Subject to identity: Knowledge, sexuality, and academic practices in higher education*. Albany: State University of New York Press.

Tanner, Daniel, & Tanner, Laurel, (2007). *Curriculum development: Theory into practice* (4th ed.). Upper Saddle River, NJ: Pearson Merrill/Prentice-Hall.

Taubman, Peter Maas. (1993a). Canonical sins. In Louis Castenell & William F. Pinar (Eds.), *Understanding curriculum as racial text: Representation of identity and difference in education* (pp. 35–52). Albany: State University of New York Press.

——. (1993b). Separate identity, separate lives: Diversity in the curriculum. In Louis Castenell & William F. Pinar (Eds.), *Understanding curriculum as racial text: Representation of identity and difference in education* (pp. 287–306). Albany: State University of New York Press.

——. (2009). *Teaching by numbers: Deconstructing the discourse of standards and accountability in education*. New York: Routledge.

Taylor, Mark C. (1984). *Erring: A post-modern a/theology*. Chicago: University of Chicago Press.

——. (2004, October 14). *New York Times*, p. A-28.

Teilhard de Chardin, Pierre. (1959a). *The divine milieu*. New York: William Collins & Sons.

——. (1959b). *The phenomenon of man*. New York: Harper.

Texas Triangle. (2000, September 22). Lesbians make it legal. *Texas Triangle Newspaper*, p. 3.

Thompson, H. Ed, III, & Baldson, Ken (Eds.). (1993). *Sex and knowledge*. Saskatoon, Alberta: Hemlock.

Thorson, Andy. (2011). Personal communication. Texas A&M University, College Station.

Thurer, Shari L. (2005). *The end of gender: A psychological autopsy*. New York: Routledge.

Tierney, William G., and Lincoln, Yvonna S. (1997). *Representation and the text: Re-framing the narrative voice*. Albany: State University of New York Press.

Toffler, Alvin. (1990). *Powershift: Knowledge, wealth, and violence at the edge of the 21st century*. New York: Bantam Books.

Toulmin, Stephen. (1982). The construal of reality: Criticism in modern and post modern science. In W. J. T. Mitchell (Ed.), *The politics of interpretation* (pp. 99–118). Chicago: University of Chicago Press.

Toynbee, Arnold. (1947). *A study of history*. New York: Oxford University Press.

Troyna, Barry, & Hatcher, Richard. (1992). *Racism in children's lives: A study of mainly-white primary schools*. London and New York: Routledge.

Tucker, Mary Evelyn. (1993). *Education and ecology: Earth literacy and the technological trance*. Chambersburg, PA: ANIMA Books.

Tyler, Ralph. (1949). *Basic principles of curriculum and instruction*. Chicago: University of Chicago Press.

Valencia, Richard R., Valenzuela, Angela, Sloan, Kris, & Foley, Douglas, E. (2004). Let's treat the cause, not the symptoms: Equity and accountability in Texas revisited. In L. Skrla and J. J. Scheurich (Eds.) *Educational equity and accountability: Paradigms, policies, and politics*. New York: RoutledgeFalmer.

Valenzuela, Angela. (1999). *Subtractive schooling: U.S.-Mexican youth and the politics of caring*. Albany: State University of New York Press.

van Manen, Max. (1982). Edifying theory: Serving the good. *Theory into Practice, 21*(1), 44–49.

——. (1984). *Action research as a theory of the unique*. (Department of Secondary Education Curriculum Praxis Occasional Papers Series, #31). Edmonton: University of Alberta.

——. (1986). *The tone of teaching*. Richmond Hill, Ontario: Scholastic-Tab.

——. (1988). The relationship between research and pedagogy. In William F. Pinar (Ed.), *Contemporary curriculum discourses* (pp. 427–452). Scottsdale, AZ: Gorsuch Scarisbrick.

——. (1990). *Researching lived experience: Human science for an action sensitive pedagogy*. London, Ontario: Althouse Press.

——. (1993). *The tact of teaching: The meaning of pedagogical thoughtfulness*. Albany: State University of New York Press.

Visweswaran, Kamala. (1994). *Fictions of feminist ethnography*. Minneapolis: University of Minnesota Press.

Vygotsky, Lev S. (1978). *Mind in society: The development of higher psychological processes*. Cambridge, MA: Harvard University Press.

Wald, K. D. (1987). *Religion and politics in the United States*. New York: St. Martin's Press.

Wallis, Jim. (2005). *God's politics: A new vision for faith and politics in America—Why the right is wrong and the left does not get it*. San Francisco: HarperCollins.

Watkins, William H. (1993). Black curriculum orientations: A preliminary inquiry. *Harvard Educational Review, 63*(3), 321–338.

——. (2001). *The White architects of Black education: Ideology and power in America, 1965–1954*. New York: Teachers College Press.

Watson, Rodney. (2011). Charter Schools in New Orleans. Personal communication.

Watts, Alan. (1957). *The way of Zen*. New York: Vintage.

Weaver, J., Slattery, P., & Daspit, T. (1998). Museums and memory: Toward a critical understanding of the politics of space and time. *Journal of Curriculum Theorizing, 14*(4), 18–26.

Weis, Lois. (1983). Schooling and cultural production: A comparison of Black and White lived culture. In Michael Apple & Lois Weis, *Ideology and practice in schooling* (pp. 235–261). Philadelphia: Temple University Press.

——. (Ed.). (1988). *Class, race, and gender in American education*. Albany: State University of New York Press.

West, Cornel. (1988). Postmodernism and Black America. *Zeta Magazine, 1*(6), 27–29.

——. (1990). The cultural politics of difference. *October, 53*, 93–109.

——. (2001). *Race matters*. New York: Vintage Books.

Wexler, Philip. (1992). *Becoming somebody: Toward a social psychology of school*. London: Falmer Press.

Wheatley, Margaret J. (1992). *Leadership and the new science: Learning about organization from an orderly universe*. San Francisco: Berrett-Koehler.

Whitehead, Alfred North. (1929). *Aims of education*. New York: Free Press.

——. (1933). *Adventures of ideas*. New York: Macmillan.

——. ([1929] 1978). *Process and reality* (corrected ed.). David Ray-Griffin and Donald W. Sherburne (Eds.). New York: Macmillan.

Whitson, Anthony J. (1988a). Adventures in monopolis: The wonderland of schooling in Arons' *Compelling belief. Journal of Curriculum Theorizing, 7*(3), 101–108.

——. (1988b). The politics of "non-political" curriculum: Heteroglossia and the discourse of "choice" and "effectiveness." In William F. Pinar (Ed.), *Contemporary curriculum discourses* (pp. 279–331). Scottsdale, AZ: Gorsuch Scarisbrick.

——. (1991). *Constitution and curriculum*. London: Falmer Press.

Wieman, Henry Nelson. ([1946] 1969a). *The source of human good*. Carbondale: Southern Illinois University Press.

———. (1969b). The revolution of our time. *Interchange* (March–April). Center for Creative Interchange.

Wiles, J., & Bondi, J. C. (2002). *Curriculum development: A guide to practice* (6th ed.). Columbus, OH: Merrill.

Wilhelm, Ronald. (1994). Exploring the practice–rhetoric gap: Current curriculum for African-American history month in some Texas elementary schools. *Journal of Curriculum and Supervision, 9*(2), 217–223.

Williams, Stanley Tookie. (2004). *Blue rage, Black redemption.* Los Angeles: Damamli.

Willis, George. (1998). The human problems and possibilities of curriculum evaluation. In L. E. Beyer & M. W. Apple (Eds.), *The curriculum: Problems, politics, and possibilities* (pp. 339–357) (2nd ed.). Albany: State University of New York Press.

Willis, George, & Schubert, William H. (Eds.) (1991). *Reflections from the heart of educational inquiry: Understanding curriculum and teaching through the arts.* New York: State University of New York Press.

Willis, George, Schubert, William H., Bullough, Robert V., Jr., Kridel, Craig, & Holton, John T. (1993). *The American curriculum: A documentary history.* Westport, CT: Greenwood Press.

Willis, Paul. (1977). *Learning to labour.* Farnborough, England: Saxon House.

Wilshire, Bruce. (1990). *The moral collapse of the university: Professionalism, purity, and alienation.* Albany: State University of New York Press.

Wise, Arthur E. (1979). *Legislated learning: The bureaucratization of the American classroom.* Berkeley: University of California Press.

Wolcott, Harry. (1973). *The man in the principal's office: An ethnography.* New York: Holt, Rinehart, & Winston.

Wolf, Denise Palmer. (1992). Becoming knowledge: The evolution of art education curriculum. In Philip W. Jackson (Ed.), *Handbook of curriculum research* (pp. 945–963). New York: Macmillan.

Wraga, William G. (1999). "Extracting sun-beams out of cucumbers": The retreat from practice in reconceptualized curriculum studies. *Educational Researcher, 28*(1), 4–13.

Wuthnow, R. (1998). *After heaven: Spirituality in America since the 1950s.* Berkeley: University of California Press.

Zais, R. S. (1976). *Curriculum: Principles and foundations.* New York: Thomas Y. Crowell.

Zezima, M. (2001). Saving private power. In Russ Kick (Ed.), *You are being lied to: The disinformation guide to media distortion, historical whitewashes, and cultural myths* (pp. 219–228). New York: Disinformation Company.

Zinn, Howard. (1995). *A people's history of the United States: 1492–present.* New York: HarperCollins.

Subject Index

abortion, 130
accountability and testing, xi–xii, 248–250
advertising, 157–158
aesthetics, 99, 243–266, 295; and literature, xxv; and painting, 248–250, 252–256; and postmodern art, xiii, xxvi
architecture, 23, 219–220
autobiography, xvi–xvii, 66–72, 290–291, 295; and autobiographical accounts, x–xviii, 248–250, 252–254, 255, 258–260, 270–272, 279; and identity, 258–260; and self, 235, 288; and self-destruction, 288

back to basics, xii–xiii
bifurcation *see* dualism
Bildung, 142–143, 252, 296
biocultural diversity, 208–209
Black History Month, 174–175
brain based learning, 56–58
breathing, 260
Brown v. *Board of Education*, 151–152
Buddhism, vxii–vxiii, xxii–xxiii

capital punishment, 179–181
Center for a Postmodern World, 20–21
chaos, 26–27, 270–279; and complexity, 271–275; and physics, 272–275

charter schools, 213–215
Chile and education, 22
circle and sacred circle, 217, 220–222, 224
classroom environment, xxiv–xxv, 32–33, 35–36, 217–218
cognition, 276–279
common schools, 78–80
connoisseurship, 247–248
constructive postmodernism, 28–29, 291–292
critical theory, 232–235, 238–239, 289; and critical pedagogy, 235–237, 297–298
cultural commons, 224–226, 297; and cultural change, 225
currere, 289, 291–292, 298
curriculum analogy to medical field, xix–xx
curriculum spaces, 34–36

dance, 1–2
deconstruction, 2–5, 201–203, 205, 298
democracy *see* egalitarian ideal
disgust, 151–154
dualism, bifurcation, and Cartesianism, 295, 298

East St. Louis School, 48–49
eco-feminism, 226–228, 299
ecology, 29–30, 207–228; and the arts,
    258–260; and ecological literacy,
    227–228; and ecological sustainability,
    xxiii–xxiv, 265–266, 211–228
economic issues, 286–288
*Education 2000: A Holistic
    Perspective*, 71
egalitarian ideal and democracy,
    229–240
emancipatory interests, 237–238
Enlightenment, 25, 203–205, 226, 230
Environmental Protection Agency,
    210–211
epistemology, 198–199, 299
eschatology, 85–87, 90–91; and prolepsis,
    87–88; and time, 88–89
essentialism, 154, 201–202
ethics, 4–6
evil, 87
existentialism, 307
experience, 244–246, 261–266

faculty psychology and mental discipline,
    300
fear, 82–83, 127
feminist theory, 27–28, 33–34, 238–239,
    307–309
football and curriculum, 39–42, 153

Gaia hypothesis, 272
gay bullying, 39–42, 159–160
gender and feminism, 238–239; and
    LGBTIQ issues, 128–129, 149–193
Gnosticism, 78–79, 84
governmentality, 259–260, 300

hegemony, 38–42, 300
Heisenberg's Uncertainty Principle,
    274–275
hermeneutics, 119–147, 224, 281–282,
    300–301; and the hermeneutic circle,
    135–147, 248; and Hermes, 135,
    146–147; and the US constitution,
    131–133
heteronormativity, 38–42, 301

hidden curriculum, 301
Hiroshima and WWII exhibits, 120–127
history and historical analysis, 43–45,
    53–55, 301
holistic education, xix, 219–220
homosexuality *see* gender, and LGBTIQ
    issues
hyperreality, 288
hypostatic union, 98–100

I Ching, 222–224
identity, 258–260; and identity
    politics, 301
imagination, 243
integral education and fearlessness,
    82–83, 127
intelligent design and creation debates,
    79–81
international issues, 19, 22, 120–123,
    196–198, 285–286
intersex, 154–156, 302

Judaism *see* theology

kaleidoscope, 283
knowledge, 236–238; and emancipatory
    interests, 237; and ontological
    knowing, 260–261

Lemon v. *Kurtzman*, 83–84
liberation theology, 234–236, 302–303
lifelong learning, xv–xvii
linguistic theory, 204–205
literacy, 231, 297

Marxism and Neo-Marxism, 229–241, 308
metanarratives, 303
metaphors, 221
Mississippi River and ecology, 211–214
modernism, 294–295, 303
multiculturalism *see* race and ethnicity
museum education, 122–124,
    252–256

Native Americans, 1–2; and art, 252; and
    spirituality, 220–221
New Orleans, 49–52, 87

No Child Left Behind and *Race to the Top*, xi–xiii, xviii, 13–14, 21–22, 25, 47–48, 50–52, 218
non violence, 211

phenomenology, 66, 262–264, 303–304
philosophy, 195–206; and philosophy of education, 197–199
phronesis, 195, 200, 205, 239
physics *see* chaos
poetry, 96–97, 102, 115, 124–126, 128, 221, 250–252, 259–260, 294
politics, 199–200, 229–241
positivism and empiricism, 304
postmodernism, 2–4, 6–8, 17–27; and aesthetics, xxvi–xxvii, 245–246; and classroom application, 32–33; and historical periods, 17–25; and philosophical discourses, 197–198; and science, 26–27, 275–276
poststructuralism, 200–205, 304
premodernity, 19–21
process philosophy, 269–279, 305
progressive education, 305
prolepsis, 282–283, 305–306

race and ethnicity, 149–193; and antiracist theory, 231; and multiculturalism, 186–187; and racism, 231
reading, 77–78, 161–168
reconceptualization, 9, 11–13, 61–74, 201, 229, 282, 306
resilience theory, 208–209
Rite of Spring and Igor Stravinsky, 133–134

scientific management, 284, 310–311
sedimented perceptors, 310; and historical sedimentation, 202–203
self *see* autobiography
semiotics, 138–139, 311
sexism and sexuality *see* gender
sexual orientation, 163–166
simulacrum, 285, 311
social reconstructionists, 232–233, 312
social studies curriculum, 32–33
structuralism, 203–204; *see also* poststructuralism
synoptic textbooks, 10–11, 13
synthetical moments, 244–245, 282

theology, 75–116, 129–130, 139–140, 144; and LGBTIQ issues, 164–166; and religion, 76; and religious conflict, 83–85; and US history, 78
time, 269–279, 283; and memory, 264–265; and time management, 270–271, 279
truth, 128–129, 133, 281–282
Tylerian Rationale, 8–9, 26, 55–56, 200–201, 206, 216, 312

utopianism *see* egalitarian ideal

vegetarianism, 209–210

White privilege, 172–173, 188

Yale Report on Defense of the Classics, 57–58, 70

Name Index

Addams, Jane, 78
Adler, Mortimer J., 64, 259
Allah, 5
Allende, Salvadore, 22
Angelou, Maya, 174
Anselm, 97
Aoki, Ted Tetsuo, 244
Appelbaum, Peter, 63
Apple, Michael W., 229–230, 240, 301
Aquinas, Thomas, 139–141, 307
Arendt, Hannah, 200, 232
Aristotle, 135
Arons, Stephen, 110
Aston, John, 159–160
Augustine, 138
Ayers, William, 200

Bahmueller, C. F., 45
Baldwin, James, 174, 189
Barone, Thomas, 244
Barth, Karl, 97
Basquiat, Jean-Michel, 257–258
Bateson, Gregory, 277–278
Baudrillard, Jean, 3, 288, 311
Bauman, Zygmunt, 4, 17
Beberman, Max, 14
Bahar-Horenstein, Linda S., 10
Belenky, Mary Field, 182
Bennett, William J., xv, 64–65, 104
Bergson, Henri, 283, 288, 292

Berliner, David, 22
Beyer, Landon E., 243
Bickel, Barbara, 244, 266
Biddle, Bruce, 22
Blacker, David, 142–143
Bloch, Ernst, 7
Block, Alan, 63
Bloom, Allan, 64, 284
Bobbitt, Franklin, 69–70
Bode, Boyd, 69, 196
Bohm, David, 276
Bondi, J. C., 10
Bonhoeffer, Deitrich, xxiii–xxiv
Bowers, Chet. A., 29, 139, 216, 225–226,
    230, 241
Bowles, Samuel, 231
Bowman, Andrea, 11, 144–146
Brasseaux, Carl, 53
Briggs, John, 271
Britzman, Deborah P., 203, 304
Brownson, Orestes, 78–79, 233
Bruner, Jerome, 26
Buber, Martin, 4, 143, 282
Buddha, 309
Burbules, Nicholas C., 200
Burdick, 8, 306
Burke, Pattie Cotter, 124–127,
    250–251
Bush, George H. W., 64, 190
Bush, George W., 13, 25, 77, 128, 190

Caine, Geoffrey, 56–58, 222
Caine, Renate Nummela, 56–58, 222
Campbell, Doak S., 10
Campbell, Joseph, 108
Canter, Lee, 64
Capra, Fritjof, 215–216, 270, 273
Carmody, Denise L., 94–95
Cary, Lisa J., 34–35, 282
Carpenter, B. Stephen II, 63
Carson, Rachel, 226–227
Carter, Donna Jean, 57
Caswell, Hollis L., 10
Chapin, Harry, 73
Charlesworth, Rosalyn, xviii
Charter, W. W., 69
Cherryholmes, Cleo, 200, 203, 245–246
Clinton, Hillary, 77
Clinton, William, 190
Cobb, John B., Jr., 286–287
Confucius, 309
Comte, August, 304
Coontz, Stephanie, 157–158, 161–162
Copernicus, Nicolaus, 19
Costner, Kevin, 1
Counts, George S., 69, 232–233,
    289, 312
Cousteau, Jacques-Yves, 207, 211
Covey, Stephen R., 269
Cox, Harvey, 92
Crichton, Michael, 269

Diagnault, Jacques, xviii
Dali, Salvador, 264
Daly, Herman E., 286
Daspit, Toby, 120, 255–256
Davies, Paul, 270, 272–274
Davis, Brent, 62
Dawkins, Richard, 6, 76
Day, Dorothy, xxi–xxii
de Beauvoir, Simone, 7, 307–308
de Cosson, Alex, 244
Deleuze, Gilles, 3, 312
Denzin, Norman, 11, 119
deMan, Paul, 3
de Onis, Federico, 23
Derrida, Jacques, 2–6, 28, 92, 120, 202
Descartes, Réne, 202, 298

Dewey, John, xxi, 7, 13–14, 26, 69, 87,
    97, 196–197, 218–219, 232, 234,
    244–245, 261, 284, 290, 296,
    305, 307
Diamond, Patrick, xxi–xxii
Dilthey, Wilhelm, 144
Doll, Mary Aswell, 221, 224
Doll, Ronald C., 10
Doll, William E. Jr., xviii, 7, 11, 26–27,
    94, 271, 274–277, 284
Dubois, W. E. B., xxii, 78

Eco, Umberto, 281–282
Edgerton, Susan, 10, 12, 151
Einstein, Albert, 46, 133, 273
Eisner, Elliot W., xix, 11, 199, 244,
    247, 260
Eliot, Charles W., 69–70
Eliot, T. S., 96, 98, 108, 115, 294
Ellsworth, Elizabeth, 33, 36, 232, 243
Elmore, Richard F., 11

Fanon, Frantz, 189
Faulkner, William, xvi–xvii, 7, 88,
    109, 190
Fausto-Sterling, Anne, 153
Fehr, Dennis, 243
Fine, Michelle, 172
Finn, Chester E., Jr., 47
Fish, Stanley, 131–132
Fisher, R. Michael, 82, 127, 152
Flinders, David J., 139
Foucault, Michel, 3, 28, 164, 186, 204,
    243, 246, 257–258, 300
Fosbury, Dick, 134
Fox, Matthew, 140–141
Francis of Assisi, 101
Franklin, Barry M., 218
Franklin, Benjamin, 78
Franklin, Karen, 159–160
Freire, Paulo, 92, 200, 234–235, 296, 312
Friedan, Betty, 309
Friedman, Milton, 287

Gablik, Suzi, 255
Gadamer, Hans-Georg, 120, 135, 142, 248
Gaines, Ernest J., xxv, 174–177

Galileo, Galilei, 19

Gandhi, Mohandas, xxii, 150

Gay, Geneva, 11, 13

Gershman, Kathleen W., 33, 97, 189–190, 221, 292–293

Gibson, James J., 222

Gingrich, Newt, 121

Gintis, Herbert, 231

Giroux, Henry A., 12, 29–30, 43, 200, 231–234, 240

Glavin, Terry, 208, 211

Gleick, James, 88–89, 270

Glickman, Carl, 11

Goldhagen, Daniel, 84–85

Goodwin, Sarah Webster, 239

Gouzouasis, Peter, 244

Graham, Robert J., 71

Gramsci, Antonio, xxii, 284, 297

Greeley, Andrew M., 108–110

Greene, Maxine, 7, 184, 200, 243, 259–260, 263–265, 292, 307

Griffin, David Ray, 20, 28, , 92, 94, 192, 260, 275

Grumet, Madeleine R., 66–68, 88, 97, 181–184, 238–239, 244, 290–291, 298

Guattari, Felix, 3

Gutierrez, Gustavo, xxii, 76

Habermas, Jurgen, xxii, 144, 201, 236–236

Haggerson, Nelson, 11, 95, 144–146

Hall, G. Stanley, 69

Hall, Manley P., 219–220

Hall, Stuart, 297

Hammerschlag, Carl A., 1–2

Hanh, Thich Nhat, xxii–xxiii, 75–76, 88

Harwit, Martin, 120–123

Hassan, Ihab, 24

Havel, Vaclav, 25

Hegel, Georg Wilhelm Friedrich, 43, 248

Heidegger, Martin, 4, 28, 135, 262

Heisenberg, Werner, 7, 274

Henderson, Jim, 8, 12–13, 63, 195

Hermes, 135, 147

Heshel, Abraham Joshua, xxii

Hirsch, E. D., Jr., 104, 185

Hitchens, Christopher, 6, 76

Hlebowitsh, Peter W., 68–69

Hodge, Robert, 138–139

hooks, bell, 33, 171–172, 258

Horton, Myles, 62

Houston, Donna, 30

Howard, Adam, 62

Howard, Roy J., 119

Huebner, Dwayne, xx–xxi, xxvi, 95, 201

Hughes, Langston, 174, 235

Hunter, Madeline, 64

Husserl, Edmond, 135, 143

Irwin, Rita, 244

Jackson, Philip, 11, 13

James, William, 307

Jameson, Fredric, 3

Jardine, David W., 119

Jeanrond, Werner, 138

Jencks, Charles, 6, 18, 23–24, 42, 140, 243, 290

Jesus Christ, 98, 100, 103, 305, 309

Jhally, Sut, 156–157

John Paul II, Pope, 19

Jones, Libby Falk, 239

Jung, Carl, xvi, 288

Jupp, James, 213–215

Kant, Immanuel, 5

Kellner, Douglas, 3

Kennedy, John F., 79

Kesson, Kathleen, 8, 111, 195 216, 226

Keynes, John Maynard, 287

Khomeini, Ayatollah, 108

Kieffer, Anselm, 255–259

Kienholz, Edward and Nancy, 254–255

Kierkegaard, Søren, 5, 109

Kilpatrick, William Heard, 69

King, Coretta Scott, 211

King, Martin Luther, Jr., xxii, xxvi, 62, 150

Klein, Naomi, 287

Kliebard, Herbert M., 42, 52, 244–245

Klohr, Paul, 61
Kozol, Jonathan, xxv, 22, 44, 48, 235–236
Krasny, Karen, 119, 136–137, 240–241, 292
Kress, Gunter, 138–139
Kridel, Craig, 10
Kristeva, Julia, 3
Krugman, Paul, 209–210
Kuhn, Thomas, 19, 270
Kung, Hans, 76, 91–92, 145

Lacan, Jacques, 3
Langer, Susanne K., 260
Lao Tzu, 102, 310
Laplace, Pierre Simon de, 95
Lasch, Christopher, 188, 288
Lather, Patti, 27–28, 33, 291, 254
Leggo, Carl, 244
LePage, Andy, 259
Lincoln, Yvonna S., 11, 114, 119, 244, 262
Loewen, James, xxvi
Lorenz, Edward, 271, 276
Lovelock, James, 272
Lyotard, Jean François, 3, 24, 43

Macdonald, James B., x, 146, 224, 294
Magritte, Réne, 243
Malewski, Erik, 9, 11, 63
Mandela, Nelson, 150
Mann, Horace, 78–79, 85, 233
Marcel, Gabriel, 143
Marx, Karl, 43, 308
Maxcy, Spencer J., xviii, 197, 200
McCarthy, Camron, xviii, 184–185
McIntosch, Peggy, 172
McLaren, Peter, 30, 38, 217, 236–237
McVeigh, Timothy, 86
Megill, Allan, 202–203, 205
Melville, Herman, xvi
Merchant, Carolyn, 227–228
Merleau-Ponty, Maurice, 262
Miller, Janet L., 7, 11, 13, 61–62, 184, 292
Minella, Mary, 76
Moltman, Jurgen, 7, 88, 97, 112

Montenegro, Maywa, 208, 211
Montessori, Maria, 296
Moore, Charles E., xxvi
Moore, Mary Elizabeth M., 95
Moran, Gabriel, 94
Morris, Marla, 62
Morrison, Toni, xvii, 174
Muhammad, 98, 308
Muhammad, Khallid, 175, 189

Naess, Arne, 227
Navra, Dora, 54–55
Navra, Nora, 214–215
Newlon, Jesse, 69–70
Newton, Isaac, 298
Nietzsche, Friedrich, 5,89, 257–258, 266, 283, 311–312
Nijinsky, Vaslav, 133–134
Noddings, Nel, 82–83, 111, 176, 183, 292
Nussbaum, Martha, 151–152

O'Keeffe, Georgia, 243, 249–252
Oliva, Peter F., 10
Oliver, Donald W., 33–35, 97, 189–190, 221, 292–293
O'Malley, Michael P., 8, 22, 48–49, 111, 119, 136–137, 306
Origen, 138
Ornstein, Allan C., 10
Orr, David W., xxiii–xxiv, 7, 219–220, 224–226, 259
Ortwein, Mark, 198

Padgham, Ronald, 262
Page, Reba, 11
Pagels, Elaine, 76, 106–107
Pajak, Edward, 10–11
Parks, Rosa, xxii, 62, 150
Patino, Maria, 167–168
Peirce, Charles Sanders, 307
Percy, Walker, 23, 109
Perry, Rick, 83
Peter, Carl, 112
Phenix, Phillip, 94
Piaget, Jean, 26, 296

Picasso, Pablo, 261
Pinar, William F., xiii, xvi–xviii, 2, 9–11, 13, 31, 62, 66–68, 88, 119, 191–192, 199, 226, 244, 290, 298, 305
Pinochet, Augusto, 22
Plato, 311
Pollock, Jackson, xvi, 253–254, 263
Pounder, Diana, xviii
Prejean, Helen, 180
Prigogine, Ilya, 26, 270–271
Proust, Marcel, xvii
Purpel, David E., 91

Rahner, Karl, 112
Rapp, Dana, 11, 25
Ravich, Diane, xi–xii
Reagan, Ronald, xv, 64, 190, 287
Regnier, Robert, 220–221
Reynolds, Sherrie, 7, 277–278
Reynolds, William, 62, 119, 144
Rickover, Admiral Hyman, 14
Ricouer, Paul, 107, 143–144
Romero, Oscar, xxii, 150
Rorty, Richard, 3, 6, 20, 46, 198, 205, 245–246, 248
Roseboro, Donyell, 48–49
Rosetta, Santiago, 1
Ruether, Rosemary R., 98
Rugg, Harold, 69
Rushdie, Salmon, 108
Russell, Bertrand, 76

Sagan, Carl, 191
St. Julien, John, 223–224
Sandlin, Jenny, 8, 306
Santayana, George, 46–47
Sartre, Jean-Paul, 261, 307
Saussure, Ferdinand de, 204
Saylor, J. G., 10
Scheurich, James, 47
Schleirrmacher, Frederich D. E., 141, 146
Schon, Donald A., xix–xx, 200, 270
Schubert, William H., 9, 12, 53, 67, 200, 224, 237–238, 243
Schwab, Joseph, 201
Schwehn, Mark R., 114

Scroggs, R. 164–166
Sears, James T., 153
Seattle, Chief, 100–101
Serres, Michel, 244
Shepard, Paul, 219–220
Short, Edmund D., 12, 119
Sizer, Theodore, 11, 264
Skinner, B. F., 308
Skrla, Linda, 47
Slattery, Joshua, xv, 248–250
Slattery, Katie, xv, 54–55, 58–59
Slattery, Michelle, xv
Slattery, Patrick, 12, 119, 136–137
Sloan, Douglas, 95, 210–211
Smith, Anna Deveare, xxvii
Smith, David G., 62, 94, 120, 147, 246
Smith, Roberta, xiii
Smoot, George, 95
Sola, Peter, 112
Solomon, 98
Sophia, 98, 103
Spring, Joel, 78
Springgay, Stephanie, 63, 72, 244
Stanley, William B., 238–239, 292
Stengers, Isabel, 270–271
Stinson, Susan W., 224
Stravinsky, Igor, 73, 133–134
Sumara, Dennis, 62

Tanner, Daniel, 10
Tanner, Laurel, 10
Taubman, Peter Maas, xi–xii, 186
Taylor, Frederick, 61, 63, 144, 284, 310
Taylor, Mark C., 3–6, 24, 92
Teilhard, Pierre de Chardin, 80, 274
Thoreau, Henry David, 7, 259–260
Thorson, Andy, 39–41
Thurer, Shari L., 153, 169–170
Tierney, William, 11, 119, 243
Toulmin, Stephen, 198, 276
Toynbee, Arnold, 23
Tracy, David, 145
Tucker, Mary Evelyn, 208–209, 211
Tutu, Desmond, 150
Tyler, Ralph, 8–9, 11, 55–56, 61, 63, 144, 284, 312

Valenzuela, Angela, 173
van Manen, Max, 244, 262
Vygotsky, Lev S., 222, 296

Walker, Alice, 174
Wallis, Jim, 6, 76, 110
Warhol, Andy, 24
Washington, Booker T., 78
Watkins, William H., 77
Watson, Rodney, 50–52
Watts, Alan, 103
Weaver, John, 120, 255–256
Weis, Lois, 173
West, Cornel, 184–185
Wexler, Philip, 241
Whitehead, Alfred North, xii, 8, 26, 80,
    88, 95–96, 220, 252, 289–292, 305
Whitman, Walt, 128
Whitson, Anthony J., xviii, 185, 200

Wilde, Oscar, xvii
Wiles, J., 10
Williams, Stanley Tookie, 178
Willis, George, 224, 243
Willis, Paul, 297
Wilshire, Bruce, 198–199
Wolcott, Harry, 269
Wolf, Denise Palmer, 244
Woodson, Carter G., 174
Woolf, Virginia,
    xvi–xvii, 90
Wraga, William, 30–32

Yahweh, 5, 103
Yorke, Jim, 271

Zais, R. S., 10
Zeus, 103
Zinn, Howard, 111